Microsoft®

Microsoft®
SQL Server™ 2000
Administrator's
Companion

Marci Frohock Garcia
Jamie Reding
Edward Whalen
Steve Adrien DeLuca

PUBLISHED BY
Microsoft Press
A Division of Microsoft Corporation
One Microsoft Way
Redmond, Washington 98052-6399

Library of Congress Cataloging-in-Publication Data
Microsoft SQL Server 2000 Administrator's Companion / Marcilina S. (Frohock) Garcia, Jamie Reding,
Edward Whalen, Steve Adrien DeLuca.
    p. cm.
Includes index.
ISBN 0-7356-1051-7
    1. Client/server computing. 2. SQL server. 3. Relational databases. I. Garcia,
Marcilina S.

QA76.9C55 M532 2000
005.75'85--dc21   00-059281

Printed and bound in the United States of America.

1 2 3 4 5 6 7 8 9   QWT   5 4 3 2 1 0

Distributed in Canada by Penguin Books Canada Limited.

A CIP catalogue record for this book is available from the British Library.

Microsoft Press books are available through booksellers and distributors worldwide. For further information about international editions, contact your local Microsoft Corporation office or contact Microsoft
Press International directly at fax (425) 936-7329. Visit our Web site at mspress.microsoft.com. Send
comments to *mspinput@microsoft.com*.

Acquisitions Editor: David Clark
Project Editors: Kathleen Atkins, Anne Taussig, and Alice Turner
Manuscript Editor: Elizabeth Cate
Technical Editors: Dail Magee Jr. and Marzena Makuta

Contents at a Glance

Part IV
Built-In Server Features

Part V
Management, Tuning, Maintenance, and Troubleshooting

Part VI
Appendixes

Table of Contents

Part II
Installation and Setup

Part III
Using Microsoft SQL Server

Part IV
Built-In Server Features

Part V
Management, Tuning, Maintenance, and Troubleshooting

Acknowledgments

There are a number of people who played important roles in making this book possible. First of all, we would each like to thank our co-authors. We hope that by pooling our experience and our knowledge, we have made the book stronger. Next, we would like to thank the editorial team at Microsoft Press for their dedication and skill: David Clark, Anne Taussig, Kathleen Atkins, Alice Turner, Elizabeth Cate, Dail Magee Jr., and Marzena Makuta. You did an excellent job of organizing, scheduling, providing necessary materials, offering feedback, and asking the right questions to make this book better—and you did it in a kind and professional manner. It was great working with you all!

We owe a special thank you to Mitchell Schreoter for contributing to this book by writing Chapter 23, "Accessing Microsoft SQL Server from the Internet." We appreciate his expertise and his willingness to participate in the book, and we look forward to collaborating with him on future projects.

The author Marcilina S. (Frohock) Garcia would also like to thank Ed Whalen for being the lead on this book and for being so great to work with. Thanks to Jamie Reding for always answering our picky SQL Server questions. And thanks to Steve DeLuca for his great contribution to the book. I would like to thank my husband, Luis Garcia, and my 8-year-old stepdaughter, Marilyn Nicole Garcia, for their encouragement in writing this book. Hayabusa Luis? I also would like to thank my dear parents, Ron and Twila Jean Frohock, for their continuing prayers and support. And a special thank you to my grandparents, Benjamin and Wilma Frohock, for always being so proud of me, and to Vernon and Twila Harris, who are looking down from heaven. And of course, I would like to thank God, who made all of this possible.

The author Jamie Reding would like to thank Ed Whalen and Marci Garcia. As always, it has been great working with you both. I would also like to thank Steve DeLuca for his insight and contributions to this book. I would like to extend my thanks to my parents, Jack and Karen Reding. Thank you for all your support throughout the years. Finally, a very special thank you to my wife, Sharon, and my sons, Alex and Jackson, for their patience and support during the long process of writing this book. Hey guys, you are the best!

The author Edward Whalen would like to extend many thanks to Marci Garcia, who has been great to collaborate with on books. I would also like to thank Jamie Reding for taking the time to contribute to this book. In addition I would like to thank Steve DeLuca for his contribution to this effort and for the previous books he has worked on with me. And I would especially like to thank Mitch Schroeter for his work on Chapter 23. I would also like to thank my parents, John and Lilly Whalen, for their continuing support, and to mention my brother Robert, his wife Annette, and my very special nieces: Michelle, Valerie, and Natalie. Finally, I would like to thank my wife, Felicia, for putting up with me during the time I wrote this book.

The author Steve Adrien DeLuca would like to first thank the people on the management staff at Microsoft and the great Distributed Management Division, which I am extremely glad to be part of: people like Brian Valentine, Deborah Black, and Casey Kiernan (thanks for the help on our latest patent). I always felt lucky to work in this environment because I get to work with the best engineers in the industry, and I am lucky enough to call some of these people my friends. I would like to extend my thanks to those very talented engineers and friends that I work with such as Kevin Hodge, Juhan Lee, Paul Darcy, Sally Martin (my co-inventors on many different patents that we have applied for, all sponsored by Microsoft), Chad Verbowski, Iain Frew, Vij Rajarajan, Kishnan Nedungadi, James Johnston, Sheela Word, Cary Rohwer, Lauren Gallagher, Jenny Lehman, and Edward Williams. I can never adequately express the feeling I have for close friends such as Ed Whalen, Marci Garcia, and Jamie Reding, whom I have worked with for many years and co-authored with in previous writings. I also would like to thank friends that have supported me through the years such as Pat Beadles, Kathryn B. Hodge, Chef Guido and Cheryl D'Ambrosio, and Tony and Kris Vanacore. And last, but first in my thoughts, thanks to my family, especially my wife, Jean; my daughter, Tina; my sister, Sue; my brother, Nick; and my mother, Esther. I would like to dedicate this writing to the memory of my constant companion of 17 years, and one of the sweetest beings ever to grace the earth, Asta. A special thanks to the editing and publishing teams at Microsoft Press for so often turning my writing into English, and making my English understandable.

Introduction

Those of you who are currently using Microsoft SQL Server 7 might not notice significant changes on the surface when you move to Microsoft SQL Server 2000. You will soon observe, however, that SQL Server 2000 includes many enhancements. One major enhancement is increased support for larger memory models. In fact, when you use SQL Server 2000 in conjunction with Microsoft Windows 2000 Datacenter Server, you can access up to 64 gigabytes (GB) of physical memory. You might also be able to take advantage of enhanced Extensible Markup Language (XML) support, indexed views, and user-defined functions. As you begin using SQL Server 2000, you will also discover improvements in the tools, such as Enterprise Manager, Query Analyzer, and Profiler. SQL Server 2000 improves on SQL Server 7 in almost every area.

To those of you who are already familiar with SQL Server 7, this book will serve as a guide to the enhancements included in SQL Server 2000. To those of you who are new database administrators (DBAs) but are not necessarily familiar with SQL Server, this book will serve as an introduction to SQL Server technology. This book will help the novice get started.

What This Book Is About

We'll begin with the fundamentals of SQL Server and then build on those basics as we look at more advanced topics. As we go, we'll work through many examples of performing particular tasks. This book is divided into five parts:

- **Part I: Introduction to Microsoft SQL Server** This part provides an overview of SQL Server 2000. The chapters in Part I cover topics such as new SQL Server features, the relationship between SQL Server and Windows 2000, and the duties performed by DBAs. This information might be a review for some of you, but it works as the foundation for the remainder of the book. Chapter 1 was authored by Marcilina S. (Frohock) Garcia, Chapter 2 was authored by Jamie Reding, and Chapter 3 was authored by Edward Whalen.

- **Part II: Installation and Setup**   This part covers topics related to the installation and setup of SQL Server, including planning your SQL Server installation, installing SQL Server, and using SQL Server Enterprise Manager. You'll also learn how to create databases and tables and how to use SQL Server networking and Microsoft Cluster Services (MSCS). Chapters 8, 9, and 10 were authored by Marcilina S. (Frohock) Garcia; Chapters 7, 11, and 12 were authored by Jamie Reding; Chapters 4 and 5 were authored by Edward Whalen; and Chapter 6 was authored by Steve Adrien DeLuca.

- **Part III: Using Microsoft SQL Server**   This part describes how to use SQL Server and includes topics such as retrieving data by using Transact-SQL (T-SQL) and creating and managing tables by using T-SQL. You'll also learn how to create and use rules, defaults, and constraints as well as indexes, views, and transactions. Later chapters cover using advanced T-SQL, creating and managing stored procedures and triggers, loading the database, and accessing SQL Server from the Internet. Chapters 14, 15, 18, 21, 22, and 24 were authored by Jamie Reding; Chapters 13, 16, 17, 19, and 20 were authored by Marcilina S. (Frohock) Garcia; and Chapter 23 was authored by Mitchell Schreoter.

- **Part IV: Built-In Server Features**   This part looks at server-side features, devoting three chapters to database replication. You'll learn what replication is, how to configure it, and how to use it. Part IV also includes a chapter about Microsoft Distributed Transaction Coordinator (MS DTC) and a chapter about SQL Server 2000 Analysis Services. Chapters 25, 26, 27, and 28 were authored by Edward Whalen; and Chapter 29 was authored by Jamie Reding.

- **Part V: Management, Tuning, Maintenance, and Troubleshooting**   This part consists of a series of chapters that explain how to manage, tune, maintain, and troubleshoot a SQL Server system. The chapters in Part V cover SQL Server administration, backing up and restoring SQL Server, and user and security management. You'll also learn about query optimization and how to identify and solve common performance problems. Chapters 30, 31, and 36 were authored by Marcilina S. (Frohock) Garcia; Chapters 32, 33, and 35 were authored by Edward Whalen; and Chapter 34 was authored by Jamie Reding.

The authors of this book truly hope that you enjoy it and that it is useful in your daily work. And now, let's get started learning how to use SQL Server 2000.

About the Companion CD

The companion CD contains the fully searchable electronic version of this book, and additional reading material you might find useful. To view the electronic book, you must have Microsoft Internet Explorer 4.01 or later installed on your system. If you don't have Internet Explorer 4.01 or later, the setup program will offer to install the minimum files necessary and will not change the user's current settings or associations.

System Requirements

To install and run an electronic book, your system must meet the following requirements:

- 486/66 or higher processor
- One of the following operating systems:
  - Microsoft Windows 95
  - Microsoft Windows 98
  - Microsoft Windows NT 4 with Service Pack 3 or later
  - Microsoft Windows 2000 (any edition)
- Disk space:
  - To install and run an electronic book from a network (network installation): 10 MB
  - To install an electronic book to the hard drive (local installation): 20–31 MB
  - To install Microsoft Internet Explorer to the hard drive (local installation) and install and run an electronic book from a network (network installation): 110 MB
  - To install Microsoft Internet Explorer to the hard drive (local installation) and install and run an electronic book from the hard drive (local installation): 120–131 MB

Part I
Introduction to Microsoft SQL Server

Chapter 1
Overview of Microsoft SQL Server 2000

Microsoft SQL Server 2000 is a relational database management system (RDBMS). A relational database provides a means of organizing data by storing it in database tables. Related data can be grouped into tables, and relationships can be defined between tables as well—thus the name, relational database. Users access the data on the server through an application. Administrators access the server directly to perform configuration, administrative, and database maintenance tasks. SQL Server is a scalable database, which means that it can store substantial amounts of data and can support many users accessing the data at the same time.

SQL Server came into existence in 1989 and has changed significantly since then. Great improvements have been made to the product's scalability, integrity, ease of administration, performance, and features. In this chapter, we'll look at the two types of environments in which you can use SQL Server. Then we'll look at the new features and enhancements available in SQL Server 2000.

SQL Server Systems

A SQL Server system can be implemented as a client/server system or as a stand-alone desktop system. The type of system you design will depend on the number of users that will be accessing the database simultaneously and on the kind of work they will be doing. We'll examine both types of systems in this section.

Client/Server System

The client/server system can have either a two-tier setup or a three-tier setup. Regardless of the setup, the SQL Server software and databases reside on a central computer called the *database server*. Users have separate computers called *clients*. Users access the database server through applications on their client computers (in a two-tier system) or through applications running on a separate computer known as the application server (in a three-tier system).

Specifically, in two-tier systems, the clients run an application that accesses the database server directly via the network. The client therefore runs the business logic code and the code for presenting the results to the user. This type of client is known as a *thick client* because it performs these two operations. Figure 1-1 shows an example of a two-tier system. A two-tier setup can be useful when there is a relatively small number of users because each user connection requires system resources such as memory and locks. As a larger number of users connect, the system performance will degrade because of resource contention, in which case you might want to consider a three-tier solution.

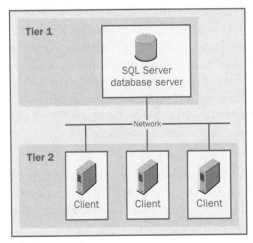

Figure 1-1. *A two-tier client/server system.*

As mentioned, a three-tier setup involves a third computer called the *application server*. In this type of system, the client computer's only tasks are running the code to request functions from the application server and then displaying the results. This type of client is called a *thin client*. The application server runs an application to perform the business logic; this application is *multithreaded,* meaning many users can access it simultaneously. The application server makes connections to the database server to access data and returns the results to the client. An example of this type of system is shown in Figure 1-2.

The advantage of a three-tier system is that you can allow the application server to organize all client connections to the database server, instead of letting each client make its own connection, which wastes resources on the database server. This concept is called *connection pooling*. Connection pooling means that client requests are put into a pool (literally, a queue) to wait for the next available connection. As a connection becomes free, it can be used for the next request in the queue. In a sense, connection pooling allows you to throttle the amount of work being done on the database server by configuring the number of connections that are in the pool and thus the number available to perform user work. (The number of connections is configurable through software.) It eliminates the need for a large number of user connections that can quickly use up resources and cause slow performance. You can implement connection pooling by using Microsoft Internet Information Server and connection-pooling software such as COM+, which is a component service provided with the Microsoft Windows 2000 operating system. We will not get into the details of how to use these products, because application programming is beyond the scope of this book.

Some enterprise systems and Web sites need more processing power than that provided by just one server. SQL Server 2000 provides the ability to partition tables across multiple servers, which share the data-processing load. See the section "Distributed Partitioned Views" later in this chapter for more information.

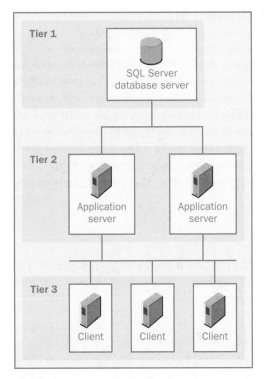

Figure 1-2. *A three-tier client/server system.*

Desktop System

SQL Server can also be used as a stand-alone database server that runs on a desktop computer or a laptop. This is referred to as a *desktop system*. The client applications run on the same computer that stores the SQL Server engine and the databases. Only one computer is involved in this system. Therefore, no network connection is made from client to server; the client makes a local connection to its local installation of SQL Server.

The desktop system is useful in cases in which a single user accesses the database or in which a few users who share a computer access the database at different times. For example, in a small store with one computer, several employees might access the store's database to insert customer and sales information, but they must take turns accessing the system. Also, as in this example, desktop systems are useful when the database or databases are small.

New Features and Enhancements of SQL Server 2000

SQL Server 2000 has so many new features and enhancements that we will not be able to tell you about all of them here, but we will look at several innovations. These features make SQL Server easier to use and manage, improve SQL Server's performance, and make SQL Server 2000 an excellent database platform not only for your small-scale online transaction processing (OLTP) applications but also for your large-scale OLTP, data warehousing, and e-commerce applications. This section describes some of the more interesting new features of SQL Server 2000, and it tells you about other improvements in SQL Server and where to find more information about them.

Server Enhancements

This section describes some of the new server-side features and enhancements of SQL Server 2000. Many of these will be described in more detail in later chapters.

Extended Memory Support

SQL Server 2000 Enterprise Edition can use the Windows 2000 Address Windowing Extensions (AWE) API to support large address spaces. SQL Server supports up to 8 gigabytes (GB) of memory on a server running Windows 2000 Advanced Server and close to 64 GB of memory on a server running Windows 2000 Datacenter. Only these two operating systems support AWE; neither Windows 2000

Professional nor Windows 2000 Server supports it. Also, a new SQL Server configuration parameter, *awe enabled*, enables SQL Server to use AWE.

More Info   See "awe enabled Option" in Books Online for more details.

Multiple Instances of SQL Server

With SQL Server 2000, you can run multiple instances of SQL Server on one computer. Each instance has its own system and user databases. Applications can connect to instances on a single computer in the same manner as they would connect to instances of SQL Server running on different computers. You create an instance by using the SQL Server installation CD. Also, one instance of either SQL Server 6.5 or 7 can run in conjunction with one or more instances of SQL Server 2000, but not both at the same time.

You can use instances to group common application tasks so that they will be served by a specific SQL Server instance. This can help reduce contention on the databases because each SQL Server instance will act independently of the others when performing tasks such as backing up data, carrying out jobs, creating indexes, updating statistics, and rebuilding indexes.

Distributed Partitioned Views

Distributed partitioned views is an exciting new feature in SQL Server 2000. This feature is valuable for database systems and Web sites that need the processing power of multiple servers to support a heavy transaction load. With this feature, you can horizontally partition a table across multiple computers running SQL Server and create a view across all member servers. The view makes it appear as if each server has a full copy of the table. Applications can reference the view and do not have to know which member server holds the data.

More Info   For details and guidelines on partitioned views, see "Creating a Partitioned View" in Books Online.

Failover Clustering

Failover-clustering administration features have been much improved for SQL Server 2000. Failover setup is no longer performed by running the Failover Cluster Wizard; rather, it is now part of the SQL Server setup process. Failover clustering is easier to install, configure, and administer in SQL Server 2000 than in previous versions. The list at the top of the following page includes some of the new administration tasks you can perform.

- Administer failover clustering from any node in the cluster
- Allow one failover cluster node to fail over to any other node in the cluster
- Reinstall or rebuild a virtual server in the cluster without affecting the other nodes in the virtual cluster
- Specify multiple IP addresses for a virtual server
- Add nodes to or remove nodes from the failover cluster by using the SQL Server setup
- Specify failover or failback to or from any node in the cluster

For more information about using Microsoft Cluster Services, see Chapter 12. In that chapter, you will learn what a cluster is, when it is useful, and how to configure SQL Server for clustering.

XML Support

Extensible Markup Language (XML) is a World Wide Web Consortium (W3C) standard for representing information in a structured document form, which can be used to transport data between heterogeneous systems. SQL Server 2000 has new features that support XML functionality. Basically, you can use XML to access SQL Server through HTTP via a URL. New features that support XML include the following:

- A FOR XML clause that you can use in SELECT statements to retrieve data as an XML document instead of in the standard rowset output
- New system stored procedures to help manage XML data
- XML update-grams that allow you to insert, update, and delete data in the database
- The ability to run queries and stored procedures directly through the URL using HTTP
- The ability to use templates and files in the URL to run multiple SQL statements
- The OLE DB Provider, which allows XML documents to be set as command text and to return a result set as a stream

See Chapter 23 for more information about using XML to access SQL Server. In that chapter, you will also learn some Internet-related programming concepts.

Database Maintenance Operations

SQL Server 2000 has been enhanced to improve the performance of and simplify some of the database maintenance operations that the administrator performs. These enhancements include faster differential backups, parallel database consistency checks (DBCC), and parallel scanning with DBCC. Differential backups now occur in an amount of time that is proportional to the amount of data that has been modified since the last full database backup. DBCC now takes advantage of systems that have multiple CPUs by running in parallel on the CPUs, thus increasing the performance (speed) of DBCC. It also now runs without taking a shared table lock when scanning a table, which allows updates to occur on the table simultaneously with the DBCC task.

Referential Integrity

Two new clauses allow you to specify the behavior of SQL Server when you modify a column in a table that is referenced by a foreign key in another table. These clauses are ON UPDATE and ON DELETE, and they can be used in the CREATE TABLE and ALTER TABLE statements. The options for these clauses are CASCADING and NO ACTION. CASCADING with ON DELETE means that if a row is deleted from the referenced (parent) table, that delete will cascade to the foreign key table so that the row will be deleted in the foreign key table as well. CASCADING with ON UPDATE is similar. It means that an update to the referenced column data in the parent table will be cascaded so that the foreign key table is updated in the same manner. If the NO ACTION option is used with ON DELETE or with ON UPDATE, SQL Server will return an error if a referenced row is deleted or a referenced column is updated, respectively, in the parent table, and the delete or update will be rolled back.

More Info   Look up "CREATE TABLE" or "ALTER TABLE" in Books Online for the syntax and for more details on these clauses.

Full-Text Searching

SQL Server 2000 includes two new features that provide greater functionality for full-text searching: change tracking and image filtering. Change tracking keeps a log of all the changes made to full-text indexed data so that the index can be updated with these changes. You can update the index manually by flushing the log on a periodic basis, or you can configure updates to occur to the index as they occur to the data by using the autopropagation option. Image filtering enables you to index and query documents that are stored in image columns by extracting textual information from the image data.

More Info For more information about full-text searching, see "Microsoft Search Service" in Books Online.

New Data Types

SQL Server 2000 includes three new data types to provide greater programming flexibility. The new data types are as follows:

- *bigint* An 8-byte integer type (This is the largest integer data type.)
- *sql_variant* A type that allows storage of values of different data types
- *table* A type that allows applications to temporarily store results for later use

Many other data types are available in SQL Server. For details about the new data types and all other SQL Server data types, see the section "System Data Types" in Chapter 10.

Index Enhancements

SQL Server 2000 features some new enhancements for indexing. They provide more flexibility with indexes by allowing you to do the following:

- Create indexes on computed columns
- Specify the order in which indexes are created, either ascending or descending
- Specify whether the index should be created by using parallel scanning and sorting

For information about these enhancements, see "Table Indexes" and "Parallel Operations Creating Indexes" in Books Online. For more information about indexes in general, see Chapter 17.

Administration Enhancements

Several enhancements in SQL Server 2000 are designed to help you administer SQL Server. These new features will make your job a little easier.

Log Shipping

Log shipping allows you to constantly dump and copy transaction log backups from a source server to a destination server or servers, and then load those logs onto the destination server or servers—automatically. You have, therefore, a warm standby of the database and a separate read-only system to perform queries, such as business reports, in order to remove this processing from the source server. You can configure the schedule for each step, which includes configuring delays between copies and loads of log backups.

More Info   See "Log Shipping" in Books Online for more information about this topic.

Performance Analyzer

Performance Analyzer is a new tool in Enterprise Manager. (It's found in the Management folder of each server.) You can use this tool to collect performance data on an individual database or on all databases. The trace data is stored in a table, and an OLAP cube is built from that data. Applications that can read OLAP cubes can be used to view and analyze the performance data.

More Info   For more details, see "Monitoring with Performance Analyzer" in Books Online.

SQL Server Profiler

SQL Server Profiler provides two new ways you can limit a trace: by time and by size of the trace file. You can also trace several new events. To find these, open Profiler and create or edit a trace file, go to the Events tab, and under Available Events, expand the new heading, Database. You will find these four new events: Data File Auto Growth, Data File Auto Shrink, Log File Auto Growth, and Log File Auto Shrink. Then expand the Performance heading and you will find these three new events: Show Plan Statistics, Show Plan All, and Show Plan Text. For more information about using Profiler, see Chapter 35.

SQL Server Query Analyzer

SQL Server Query Analyzer now includes an object browser that allows you to navigate and view database objects. To see this browser, open Query Analyzer, click Tools, and choose Object Browser. (The entire Tools menu is also new.) The browser appears on the left side of the Query Analyzer window. The other options on the Tools menu are Object Search, Manage Indexes, and Manage Statistics. Object Search allows you to search for specific objects in a database by object type, such as views, stored procedures, and user tables. The Manage Indexes and Manage Statistics options allow you to manage indexes and statistics using a graphical interface similar to the one in Enterprise Manager. In addition, the Query menu offers two new options: Show Server Trace and Show Client Statistics. For more details on using Query Analyzer, see Chapter 35.

Replication Enhancements

SQL Server 2000 enhances replication several ways. One of these is a new alternative to the immediate updating subscriber option. This new option is called queued updates. The queued updates option is specific to snapshot and transactional replication. By enabling queued updating, you allow a subscriber to modify published data locally (at the subscriber), even while the publisher is not connected to the subscriber. The transactions that perform the data modifications are queued up, sent to the publisher, and replayed asynchronously whenever the publisher does make a network connection with the subscriber. Loopback detection prevents the transactions from getting replicated back to the originating subscriber.

More Info   See "Queued Updating components" in Books Online.

Another enhancement, for all types of replication, is the support for replication schema changes. You can now add columns to or drop columns from publications and subscriptions without having to drop and re-create the publications and subscriptions. Also, you can now include the schemas for views, procedures, and user-defined functions as articles in a publication.

Merge replication has new enhancements specific to it as well, listed here:

- New conflict resolvers
- An option to resolve conflicts interactively
- Vertical filtering of merge publications
- The ability to add user-defined functions to dynamic filters
- Automated management of identity ranges at the subscriber
- The ability to have alternate publishers when synchronizing data

See Chapter 28 for more information about merge replication.

Additional Enhancements

This chapter has by no means provided an exhaustive list of the new features in SQL Server 2000. There are also many improvements in the areas of Data Transformation Services, OLAP Services, Meta Data Services, and English Query. These are highly specific and thus will not be described in detail here. To find information about these topics, see the following topics in Books Online:

- Data Transformation Service Enhancements
- What's New in Analysis Services
- What's New in Meta Data Services
- What's New in English Query

Summary

SQL Server 2000 is a relational database management system with many features that allow you to configure your system to meet your business needs, whether your company is a small business, an enterprise business, or an e-commerce business. In this chapter, we described the environments in which you can run SQL Server. We then covered some of the many new enhancements and features for SQL Server 2000. These provide easier administration, more flexibility, more useful functionality, and better performance. The rest of this book will teach you how to install and configure SQL Server, how to create databases and objects, how to manipulate data, how to administer and use SQL Server, and much more. So let's get going to Chapter 2 and learn about the operating systems on which SQL Server 2000 can run: Microsoft Windows NT and Windows 2000.

Chapter 2
The Microsoft Windows 2000 Platform

In February of 2000, Microsoft released the Microsoft Windows 2000 operating system family to the public. This collection of products provides a reliable, easy-to-use, and secure platform for Microsoft SQL Server 2000. Though Microsoft Windows NT 4 supports SQL Server 2000, Windows 2000 provides a more robust environment for SQL Server 2000 systems. In fact, SQL Server 2000 was developed on systems that were running Windows 2000.

The Windows 2000 Family

Windows 2000 is available in four editions: Windows 2000 Professional, Windows 2000 Server, Windows 2000 Advanced Server, and Windows 2000 Datacenter Server. In this chapter, you will learn about some of the features of the Windows 2000 product family and about some of the differences among the four products. This chapter is meant to provide only an overview, not an in-depth description, of the Windows 2000 products.

More Info For more detailed information about Windows 2000, visit Microsoft's Web site at *http://www.microsoft.com/windows2000*.

Windows 2000 Professional

Windows 2000 Professional is the new Microsoft operating system for corporate desktop and notebook systems. Windows 2000 Professional combines the best features of Windows 98, such as power management and Plug and Play device recognition, with the strengths of Windows NT 4, such as reliability and security. Windows 2000 Professional delivers increased computing power to desktop and notebook systems while lowering the total cost of ownership.

Windows 2000 Server

Windows 2000 Server builds on the Windows NT 4 Server product base. Windows 2000 Server integrates Web access, application support, networking, communications, and infrastructure services into one product. It also provides the base functions of file and print sharing. Windows 2000 Server features Active Directory directory services, which aids in managing a diverse and distributed network. We will examine Active Directory later in this chapter.

Windows 2000 Advanced Server

Windows 2000 Advanced Server includes all the features found in Windows 2000 Server and adds components to support mission-critical applications. Advanced Server includes features such as network load balancing, clustering, and greater support for symmetric multiprocessing.

Windows 2000 Datacenter Server

Windows 2000 Datacenter Server is a specialized product in the Windows 2000 Server family. Datacenter Server is designed to provide customers with integrated hardware and software support. Datacenter Server is jointly marketed, sold, and delivered by Microsoft and authorized vendors who integrate Datacenter Server with their hardware. Each hardware system incorporating Datacenter Server must go through a rigorous testing and certification process. This certification focuses on the entire system, not just individual components. Once the system is installed, it is supported by a new organization called the Microsoft Certified Support Center (MCSC) for Datacenter Server. Hardware and software experts from both Microsoft and the hardware vendors make up the staff of the MCSC, which means it can provide a single point of contact for all support issues. The MCSC provides the following services to Datacenter Server customers:

- An uptime guarantee of 99.9 percent or better
- Installation and configuration services
- System availability assessments
- 24-by-7 hardware and software support
- On-site hardware and software service

Datacenter Server is designed to meet the high availability and scalability needs of a company's data center. It supports up to 32 processors and 64 gigabytes (GB) of physical memory. This scalability enables all kinds of applications, from simple data warehousing to complex engineering simulations.

Windows 2000 Operating System Family Differences

The following table summarizes the differences between the Windows 2000 products.

Table 2-1. Windows 2000 products

	Windows 2000 Professional	Windows 2000 Server	Windows 2000 Advanced Server	Windows 2000 Datacenter Server
Function	Client OS for business desktop and notebook computers	Server OS providing file, print, intranet, and networking	Server OS providing support for applications and e-commerce services	Server OS providing line-of-business support for large, mission-critical applications
CPUs supported	2	4	8	32
Memory supported	4 GB	4 GB	8 GB	64 GB
Clustering	None	None	Two-node failover; 32-node Network Load Balancing	Four-node failover; 32-node Network Load Balancing
Minimum system requirements	133-MHz, Pentium-compatible CPU; 64 MB RAM; 1 GB disk space	133-MHz, Pentium-compatible CPU; 256 MB RAM; 1 GB disk space	133-MHz, Pentium-compatible CPU; 256 MB RAM; 1 GB disk space	133-MHz, Pentium-compatible CPU; 256 MB RAM; 1 GB disk space

Windows 2000 Components and Features

Now that we have covered the basics of the Windows 2000 family, let's focus on Windows 2000 features. These features can be divided into several categories: reliability, security, ease of use, system administration, mobile computing, performance and scalability, Internet access, and, finally, Active Directory.

Reliability

Windows 2000 incorporates many new features to increase the reliability of your system. Let's look at a few of these key features:

- **Windows file protection**   This feature protects the core Windows 2000 system files from being accidentally deleted or altered by either a user or an application. Windows file protection automatically verifies the source and the version of a system file before it is installed.

- **Driver certification** Each member of the Windows 2000 family implements certification of drivers and other system-level files. This certification ensures that the device drivers on your system have not been tampered with and that the device driver you are using is the one intended by the manufacturer of the hardware or software component.

- **Microsoft Installer** This tool works with Windows Installer Service and helps users install, configure, track, upgrade, and remove software programs correctly. This interface provides users with an intuitive and easy-to-use method for installing and removing diverse applications. In addition to providing interface support, Microsoft Installer can repair damaged applications. Microsoft Installer examines a large collection of components—such as the registry, files, and external resources—and monitors all component modification tasks. If a user accidentally deletes a critical component of an application, Microsoft Installer detects the missing component when the application is started again and restores the missing files. This feature protects only applications that are labeled "Certified for Windows 2000" or that have been installed with Microsoft Installer.

- **Kernel-mode write protection** This feature puts up a "fence" between applications and the critical kernel of the operating system. It protects the kernel from rogue device drivers that might cause a Windows NT 4 system to crash.

- **Fewer reboot requests** Previous versions of Windows frequently required you to reboot the system when you added or removed device drivers, applications, and so forth. With Windows 2000, these reboot requests have been dramatically reduced—to the point that many software installations do not require you to reboot.

- **Microsoft Internet Information Server (IIS) application protection** This feature isolates Web-based applications from the actual Web server code, ensuring that an application cannot crash the Web server. This feature does not apply to Windows 2000 Professional.

- **Windows 2000 logo program** Microsoft has developed a comprehensive set of standards for Windows 2000 applications. An application that carries the Windows 2000 logo is guaranteed to meet these standards and has therefore been certified for use with Windows 2000. The standards were developed with the cooperation of customers and third-party developers.

Security

Today's computing environments have differing security requirements. Windows 2000 allows you to customize the level of security to meet your needs. The following features assist you in securing both your computer and network access:

- **Windows NT file system (NTFS)**   The Windows NT file system is the core security technology in Windows 2000. NTFS provides file security at a group or user level.

- **Windows NT security model**   This feature permits only authorized users to access system resources. This model controls which user or users can access objects, such as files and printers, as well as which actions individuals can take on an object. In addition, you can enable auditing to track and monitor actions taken, as well as to track actions that a user attempted that would have violated a security policy.

- **Encrypting file system (EFS)**   This feature encrypts files with a randomly generated key. The encryption and decryption processes are transparent to the user. EFS requires your disks to be formatted with NTFS.

- **IP Security (IPSec) support**   IP Security helps protect data transmitted across a network. This is an integral component for providing security for virtual private networks (VPNs), which allow organizations to transmit data securely across the Internet. Figure 2-1 displays the IP Security configuration dialog box.

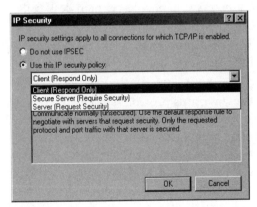

Figure 2-1. *The IP Security dialog box.*

- **Kerberos support**   This feature provides an industry-standard, highly secure authentication method for single-logon support for Windows 2000–based networks. The Kerberos protocol is an Internet standard and is highly effective when you are integrating Windows 2000 systems into an environment with a different operating system, such as UNIX.

Ease of Use

Some of the most important features of Windows 2000 are its ease-of-use features. Without these features, Windows 2000's myriad and complex functions would be extremely difficult to use. The operating system incorporates many new features that make it one of the most easy-to-use operating systems. Some of these features are listed here:

- **Plug and Play** This feature allows you to install hardware components with only minimal configuration. More than 12,000 devices support the Plug and Play standard.

- **Multilingual support** Windows 2000 allows complete flexibility in language selection to match a user's requirements.

- **Peer-to-peer support** Your Windows 2000 system can operate seamlessly with earlier versions of Windows on a peer-to-peer level. You can share all resources, including folders, printers, and other peripherals.

- **Personalized menus** Windows 2000 dynamically adapts the Start menu options to the way you work on your system. Your most-used applications stand out on the menu because infrequently accessed items are not immediately displayed.

- **Troubleshooters** These wizards are similar to the other wizards you might have seen, and they help you configure, optimize, and troubleshoot your system. Using troubleshooters results in fewer help desk calls, which increases productivity.

- **Windows Multimedia Previewer** This feature allows you to view a snapshot of a multimedia file while browsing in Windows Explorer before you actually open the file.

- **More and enhanced wizards** These wizards provide step-by-step prompts for performing both routine and challenging tasks on your system. Figure 2-2 shows a Windows 2000 wizard that can assist you in the backup and restore process.

- **IntelliMirror** The IntelliMirror feature enhances users' access to their information and software. This technology greatly benefits mobile users by allowing their computer resources to "follow" them regardless of the point from which they log on to the network. One example of IntelliMirror's benefits is the use of Offline Folders. These folders allow a user to keep working on key documents even if the network connection fails. One note: this feature requires folders to be on a server running Windows 2000 Server.

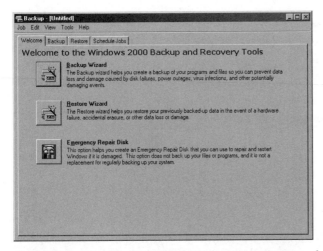

Figure 2-2. *The Windows 2000 Backup/Restore Wizard.*

- **Support for universal serial bus (USB)**   Windows 2000 provides native support for USB components. This allows you to connect USB devices to your system without configuring or rebooting it.

- **Graphical user interface (GUI)**   Windows 2000 builds on the user interface of Windows 98. This interface provides users with consistent and intuitive access to even complex operations. The Windows 2000 GUI is illustrated in Figure 2-3.

Figure 2-3. *The Windows 2000 graphical desktop.*

- **Network printer access** Any user can easily access printers across a network with Windows 2000. After a printer has been "published" in Active Directory, users can search for it based on criteria such as location, ability to print color, speed, or type. Figure 2-4 shows a dialog box from the Add Printer Wizard.

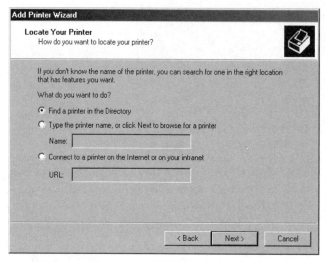

Figure 2-4. *A dialog box from the Add Printer Wizard.*

System Administration and Deployment

The Windows 2000 operating system family offers several features that enhance administration and deployment. These features aid in large-scale rollouts of the operating systems as well as in ongoing administration and maintenance. These features include the following:

- **System Preparation tool** This tool allows a system administrator to easily clone computer configurations, systems, and applications. SysPrep provides simpler, faster, and cost-effective deployment of Windows 2000 systems.

- **Setup Manager** This tool is a graphical wizard that guides system administrators through the process of designing and testing installation scripts for system deployment.

- **Remote operating system installation** This tool allows system administrators to standardize a desktop environment and rapidly deploy it across a network.

- **Microsoft Management Console (MMC)**   This tool provides a consistent environment for each administrative and management tool from Microsoft as well as from third-party providers. An example of an MMC environment is shown in Figure 2-5.

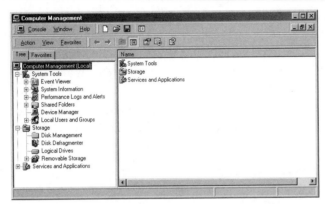

Figure 2-5. *The Microsoft Management Console environment.*

- **Windows Management Instrumentation (WMI)**   WMI provides a standard infrastructure for monitoring and managing all system resources. This allows third-party providers to develop consistent applications to monitor and control systems.
- **Group Policy Editor**   Group Policy Editor allows system administrators to define customized rules for virtually every facet of a user's computer environment. These policies cover areas such as security, user rights, desktop settings, and applications. The Group Policy editor window is shown in Figure 2-6.

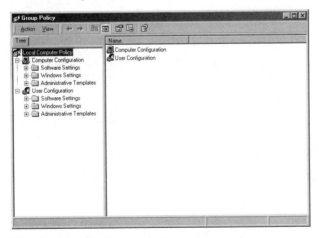

Figure 2-6. *The Group Policy editor window.*

- **Internet Explorer Administration Kit (IEAK)** IEAK enables system administrators to quickly deploy a customized version of Microsoft Internet Explorer 5.01 across multiple platforms. Administrators can install only the components and custom applications they need.

- **Microsoft distributed file system (Dfs)** Dfs enables the administrator to build a single, hierarchical view of multiple file servers and their resources on a network. Dfs makes it easy for users to locate services and resources. In addition, it can increase resource availability by maintaining multiple file copies across distributed servers.

- **Disk quotas** System administrators can set quotas on disk space usage per user and per volume. The Quota tab of the Local Disk Properties screen is shown in Figure 2-7.

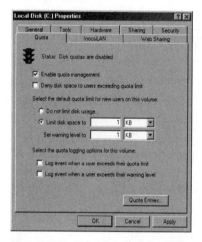

Figure 2-7. *The Quota tab of the Local Disk Properties screen.*

- **Hierarchical storage management** This feature automatically migrates data that has not been recently accessed to less expensive storage media. This maximizes high-speed, high-cost media usage for those applications and data that are the most heavily accessed.

- **Dynamic volume management** Windows 2000 Storage Manager allows administrators to add volumes, extend volumes, modify mirrors, or repair RAID 5 arrays while the server is on line and servicing requests, all without affecting the end user.

- **Automatic restart**   Services such as IIS can be set to restart automatically in the event of a failure, thereby minimizing downtime and administrator intervention.

- **Kill process tree**   If a system administrator identifies a rogue or errant application, he or she can easily kill the process and all related processes without rebooting the system.

- **Windows 2000 Configure Your Server Wizard**   This wizard provides a one-stop location for configuring the server system. See Figure 2-8 for an illustration of the Windows 2000 Configure Your Server Wizard.

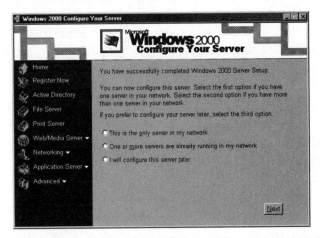

Figure 2-8. *The Windows 2000 Configure Your Server Wizard.*

- **Active Directory**   This component enables system administrators to manage Windows-based clients and servers through a consistent interface. See the section "Active Directory" later in this chapter for more information.

- **Delegated administration**   System administrators can delegate sets of administrator privileges to individuals, or to groups of users, without making them administrators of the system.

- **Remote management**   The Terminal Services component allows system administrators up to two concurrent sessions to perform remote administration on a server.

The Mobile Experience

Windows 2000 Professional was designed from the beginning to assist the note-book computer user and encourage notebook computing. Although the other Windows 2000 family members will run on a notebook system, they do not include the power management and offline features of Windows 2000 Professional. Several features were incorporated into Windows 2000 Professional that make it the desired mobile computing operating system.

- **Hibernate mode** This is a customizable feature that turns off the computer and monitor after a predetermined amount of time. When the system turns itself off, your desktop settings are maintained on the system hard disk drive. When you reactivate the system, the hibernate feature restores your programs and settings exactly as you left them.

- **Offline Folders and Files** You can disconnect from the network and work as though you were still connected. This feature allows you to create a mirror image of your documents that are stored on the network.

- **Offline viewing** You can make entire Web pages, including the graphics, available for offline viewing. You can later view the Web pages on your system, at your leisure, without being connected to a network.

- **Synchronization Manager** This tool allows you to compare and update your offline files and folders with those on the network servers.

- **Smart battery** Windows 2000 Professional provides a more accurate view of battery life. You can easily set options to maximize battery life without sacrificing performance. The Power Options Properties window is shown in Figure 2-9.

- **Hot docking** This feature allows you to dock or undock your notebook computer without changing your hardware configuration or rebooting your system.

- **Infrared Data Association (IrDA) support** This feature lets you share data in a secure, wireless environment between two Windows 2000–based computers using a standard infrared protocol.

- **Digital device support** Windows 2000 Professional supports removable storage devices such as digital video disk (DVD) and Device Bay peripherals.

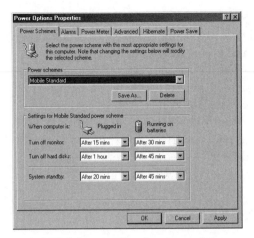

Figure 2-9. *The Power Options Properties window.*

Performance

Operating system performance is a critical plank in the Windows 2000 platform. Extensive performance testing was done at both the operating system level and the SQL Server level. Several features are included in Windows 2000 to address performance:

- **Overall faster performance**   Windows 2000 increases the performance of most systems. Smaller and more efficient memory footprints enable a Windows 2000 system to run up to 25 percent faster than a comparable Windows NT 4 system.

- **Faster multitasking**   The underlying architecture of Windows 2000 is full 32-bit. This architecture allows you to better use and manage the computing resources of your computer, so you can run more programs and perform more tasks simultaneously.

- **Scalability of memory and processors**   The Windows 2000 operating system family supports up to 64 GB of memory and up to 32 processors.

- **Cluster Services**   Available in Windows 2000 Advanced Server and Datacenter Server, Cluster Services allows the linking of multiple systems to provide increased availability and performance. In its simplest form, Cluster Services enables two servers to be clustered to provide an automatic backup if one system fails. Cluster Services can also be configured in a "scale-out" mode, where up to 32 servers running Windows 2000 Server are linked to provide processing power.

- **Network Load Balancing** Windows 2000 Advanced Server and Datacenter Server support Network Load Balancing (NLB). NLB allows the operating system to dynamically and evenly distribute incoming requests across a cluster of servers running Windows 2000 Server. Administrators can add capacity to their systems by simply adding NLB-configured servers as workloads demand it. Figure 2-10 illustrates a system configuration with NLB. In this example, four servers running Windows 2000 Advanced Server are configured as a virtual server group running Internet Information Server 5 and NLB. As requests from the Internet arrive, they are apportioned to the four servers to maximize performance and utilization.

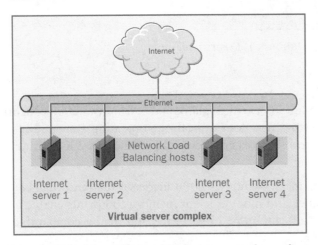

Figure 2-10. *Network Load Balancing sample configuration.*

- **Enhanced Active Server Pages (ASP) performance** IIS 5, included with Windows 2000 Server, Advanced Server, and Datacenter Server, includes many enhancements that streamline ASP processing. The flow of an ASP Web page through the system has been improved and Fast Path was added for those ASPs that do not require any script processing.

- **IIS CPU throttling** For configurations that combine Web-serving applications with other applications, system administrators can limit the amount of CPU time the Web application or applications can consume. This ensures that all concurrent applications can acquire processor time when required.

Internet Access

Internet support is another key component of the Windows 2000 operating system family. Internet technologies were designed as core components of the operating system to ensure high levels of integration and performance. Some of the Internet features of Windows 2000 are listed here:

- **Integrated Internet Explorer 5.01**   The latest incarnation of Internet Explorer is included on all editions of Windows 2000.

- **Internet Information Services 5**   The Server, Advanced Server, and Datacenter Server editions of Windows 2000 all include IIS 5. The integration of this component allows users to easily host and manage Web sites. IIS 5 includes Internet Information Services Manager, a graphical environment for configuring and managing one or more Web sites. Figure 2-11 illustrates the Internet Information Services manager console.

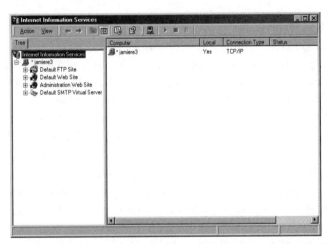

Figure 2-11. *Internet Information Services 5 Internet Information Services Manager.*

- **Strong development platform**   Internet Explorer supports a wide range of Internet programming languages, including Dynamic HTML, ASP, Java, and XML.

- **Automated proxy**   Internet Explorer 5.01 will automatically locate your proxy server and configure itself for Internet connection.

- **AutoComplete**   The browser remembers previously accessed sites and will complete a URL as you begin to type the first characters.
- **Web Folders**   Also called Web Document Authoring and Versioning (WebDAV), the Web Folders feature allows an Internet content creator to easily use drag-and-drop operations to publish Web pages on IIS 5.
- **Internet printing support**   Windows 2000 allows system administrators to share printer resources across the Internet so users can print to those printers via a URL.

Active Directory

Active Directory, a new feature in Windows 2000 Server, is the core management component for data and resources on a Windows 2000 network. This section provides an overview of Active Directory technology.

Active Directory Architecture

Active Directory is a place to store information about all network-based entities, such as applications, files, printers, and people. Active Directory provides a consistent method to describe any entity on a network, no matter how diverse the entities are. You can think of Active Directory as the main switchboard. It is a central authority that manages all the relationships among the distributed resources of a network. Active Directory contains management tools as well as security tools to maintain complete integrity and privacy of a network.

Active Directory is both a management tool and a user tool. Active Directory provides consistent user interaction with and access to the diverse and widespread resources of a network. The user no longer has to be concerned with determining a network resource location or name. With Active Directory, resources are "advertised" to those users who have been granted access. This advertisement is done via the Add/Remove Programs Wizard or the Add/Remove Printers Wizard.

Active Directory provides system administrators with a consistent set of components and controls to manage network resources. Active Directory simplifies management issues that characterize large, diverse networks; strengthens overall system security; and extends the interoperability of a network.

Active Directory provides a single point of management for all Windows-based user accounts, client systems, server systems, and applications. It also aids in organizing and integrating non-Windows systems. Active Directory allows organizations to further extend their systems to the Internet in a highly secure manner.

Active Directory is based on a hierarchical structure, which Figure 2-12 illustrates. Objects are used to represent users, groups of users, systems, devices, applications, and other network entities. Objects are kept in containers, which represent organizations, such as the legal department, or collections of related objects, such as printers.

Active Directory also manages the relationships among the various objects and containers. This allows system administrators to view the entire network as a comprehensive entity rather than looking in one place for resources and in another for resource relationships.

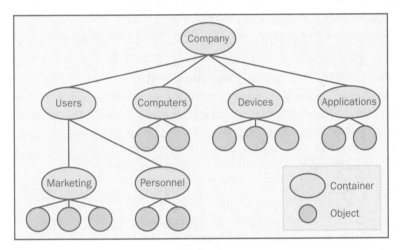

Figure 2-12. *Active Directory hierarchy.*

Each object in the Active Directory structure contains attributes that can describe a wide variety of characteristics. These attributes are secured so that potentially sensitive information can be hidden from everyone except those users or administrators who have a need to know. Each attribute attached to an object can have access rights assigned to it. In addition, a global access setting can be set for an object.

To maintain performance, availability, and flexibility, Active Directory uses multi-master replication. Administrators can create multiple copies of the directory, known as directory replicas, and locate them throughout their network. When a change is made anywhere on the network to any replica of the directory, the change is automatically replicated throughout the network.

Why Use Active Directory

We learned earlier that Active Directory simplifies management, strengthens network security, and eases interoperability. Let's look at each of these benefits in a little more detail.

Simplifies Management   Today's networks are often distributed across a large geographical area. Managing these diverse and widespread networks can become a time-consuming process. In addition, as the network becomes geographically larger, administrative functions are often replicated in several locations, leading to redundancy and coordination issues. Active Directory provides a single point of control for managing the diverse resources of a network.

Active Directory also aids in the deployment of applications and other software to user systems. In the past, a technician had to visit each user workstation that required a piece of software. This process was costly and slow. Later, tools were developed to allow application deployment from a central server. Though this technique was better, it lacked the integration into the overall network management process. Active Directory allows system administrators to deploy software within the existing security and management framework, thereby easing the burden of using separate tools for deployment and management.

Active Directory also allows administrators to delegate some administrative functions to a user or an organization, where appropriate. This is a secure delegation process and can allow those "power users" to provide IT skills at a departmental level, thus freeing the IT staff for other duties.

Strengthens Security   A critical component of Active Directory is the security services. Active Directory centralizes user authentication and management and enforces a role-based security model. Users and organizations are given roles that have predefined, yet editable, security aspects and rules. Administrators can choose to enable strict security on certain users and resources or to lessen it when appropriate. The security model of Active Directory supports security protocols such as the Kerberos protocol, X.509 certificates, and smart card technology. The security model also provides consistent security whether a user is locally connected to the network or dialed-in via a remote connection.

Extends Interoperability   As networks evolved, a diverse collection of resources and technologies evolved along with them. These technologies must work together to maximize the investment in their development and deployment. The current environment of most networks includes a collection of disparate directories for e-mail, applications, network devices, Internet/intranet firewalls, and e-commerce applications. Active Directory addresses this diversity by providing a set of standard interfaces for integrating applications and a set of open synchronization mechanisms to ensure that the Windows operating system components can actively interoperate with a wide variety of non–Windows operating system devices and applications.

Summary

This chapter has briefly introduced the family of Windows 2000 operating systems. Each family member—Windows 2000 Professional, Windows 2000 Server, Windows 2000 Advanced Server, and Windows 2000 Datacenter Server—provides specialized features to fit a variety of user needs. With Windows 2000, you can utilize the same operating environment from the notebook system to the high-performance, 32-processor systems of corporate data centers. With this information, you should be able to readily select the appropriate Windows 2000 platform for your SQL Server 2000 installation. In the next chapter, we will shift back into SQL Server mode and cover some of the responsibilities of the database administrator.

Chapter 3
Roles and Responsibilities of the Microsoft SQL Server DBA

There is no one set of duties for a Microsoft SQL Server database administrator (DBA). Each organization has a different database staff in terms of size and skill set. Some companies have one DBA who is responsible for the entire system, from development through maintenance. Other companies have hundreds of DBAs, and a single DBA has the responsibility for only a small portion of the operation of the system. No particular way is better; each company must do what best meets its needs.

Today database administration is one of the most sought-after and elite occupations in high technology. Good DBAs are always needed, and there never seems to be enough of them. By doing your best and continuing to learn, you will become more and more valuable.

In this chapter, you will see some tips on how to become the best DBA that you can. You will also learn about the basic duties of the SQL Server DBA, as well as more advanced duties. This is by no means an exhaustive list; there might be many more duties that you will be called on to perform. In any case, the DBA must be versatile and must have an even temper. This chapter explores the duties of the DBA and how to best perform those duties.

Basic and Optional Duties of the SQL Server DBA

The DBA might have a variety of duties, depending on his or her company. There is, however, a set of basic duties that most DBAs are charged with performing. If these duties don't match your job, don't worry; every DBA has different responsibilities. This chapter is designed to introduce you to the duties that you might not be familiar with and to offer the novice a window into the world of the DBA. The following responsibilities and jobs of the SQL Server DBA are divided into categories. These categories are not ordered by importance or by the amount of work that these responsibilities entail.

Installation and Configuration

The SQL Server DBA is often called upon to install new software on the system, to configure hardware and software, or at least to participate in the project. Sometimes the DBA is required only to create the specifications for the installation and configuration. In any case, the DBA should be involved in this process in order to guarantee that the system and the database are configured properly. Part of the DBA's job is to make sure that the system is configured to perform optimally with SQL Server.

Software Installation

The DBA must be involved not only with the installation of SQL Server but also with the installation of Microsoft Windows 2000 and other software components. Make sure that the proper options are set and that unnecessary components are *not* installed and configured. With the Windows 2000 installation, it is easy for unwanted components to be added unintentionally. Components such as Internet Information Server (IIS), Dynamic Host Configuration Protocol (DHCP) server, Message Queuing, and file and print services add a lot of overhead to the system, even though these services might not even be used or desired.

It is a good idea to create a document for the installation of Windows 2000 that includes a list of the components that you want installed on the system . This document can be used over and over again for installing Windows 2000. This provides a great deal of reproducibility and consistency in your Windows 2000 installation.

In addition to installing or assisting with the installation of Windows 2000, DBAs are responsible for the proper installation of SQL Server 2000. It is important to install SQL Server correctly because certain choices you make at that time are difficult to change without reinstalling the software. These choices include the location of SQL Server binaries and data files.

If it is your first SQL Server 2000 installation, it is a good idea to install the software on a test system before performing the installation on the production system. This allows you to try several options and become familiar with the installation process. As with the Windows 2000 installation, it is a good idea to document the installation process for SQL Server.

Hardware and Software Configuration

The DBA doesn't usually configure server hardware, but in some cases, you might have to perform this function. As with the installation process, if you do not actually configure the hardware and software yourself, you must be involved enough to guarantee that configuration is done to your specifications. As the SQL Server DBA, you must be able to specify the number of disk drives and controllers as well as provide the specification of any RAID controllers. Because you are ultimately responsible for the performance and the stability of the system, you must use your experience and knowledge to optimally configure the SQL Server system for capacity, performance, scalability, and growth.

As with the software installation, it is important to document your configuration. It sometimes helps to also document the reasoning behind your decisions. This will allow you to remember why you made the decisions you did. Remembering why these components were configured as they were will help with future modifications and upgrades. Be sure to document details such as which PCI buses were used and how RAID controllers were configured. Some configuration details require a reboot into diagnostics mode in order for you to find out the parameters, so documenting them as you set up the hardware might save some later time and effort.

Remember, the configuration of the system is ultimately your responsibility because the performance and the stability of the SQL Server database is your responsibility. So make sure that the system is configured properly for SQL Server. By documenting why your configuration choices have been made, you will help others understand and validate your decisions.

Security

Another responsibility of the SQL Server DBA is to monitor the security of the system and to report any problems. Often there are security experts, either at your company or with an outside firm, whom you can call if necessary. The scope of access to your system determines the type and the amount of security that your database needs. A system that is accessed by only a few trusted employees and is not connected to the Internet obviously requires less security than a database that is accessed from the Internet.

The security of the system is important because if someone were to break into your system and destroy or steal data, the expense to your company could be high. The security of the system begins with user management, which is described in the next section. In addition to managing users, you might be involved with designing and implementing the security plan for your network. This task is typically assigned to someone who has extensive experience in network security. If that description fits you, you might be a network security administrator as well as a DBA.

Network Security

Network security includes the purchase, configuration, and deployment of network proxy servers and security gateways. Many companies sell this kind of hardware/software solution. The person in charge of network security for a company is responsible for investigating and choosing the right solution for that company. The subject of network security could be a book by itself, so we won't address it here. Within SQL Server, auditing and user management are the main security tasks that you will be involved in.

System Auditing

System auditing involves monitoring both the SQL Server error log and the Windows 2000 event log, as well as using SQL Server Profiler to monitor activity within SQL Server. The SQL Server log and the event log contain valuable information about SQL Server, Windows 2000, and security. You should monitor these logs closely for any signs of trouble.

As mentioned, you can audit your system using SQL Server Profiler. Profiles can be created that log events such as failed login attempts. In addition, you can profile events such as data definition language (DDL) statements and INSERT, UPDATE, and DELETE operations. By using SQL Server Profiler, you can monitor specific events, as well as log times, user names, and activities.

Operations

The most time-consuming activities of the SQL Server DBA are probably the day-to-day operational jobs. These thankless jobs will probably bore you at times, but remember that these tasks are probably the most important activities that must be done. The DBA is responsible for the uptime of the system, and tasks such as backup and restore are critical to that uptime.

Backup and Restore

Many consider the backup and restore operations to be the most crucial tasks that the DBA is charged with. These operations ensure that the database will survive a massive hardware failure. If such a failure occurs, you must depend on the backup to return the database to service. The backup operation is consistent and straightforward, but you must frequently repeat it. To guarantee that the backups are good, you must also test and validate them regularly. By paying full attention to this activity, you can avoid mistakes and guarantee the safety of your system.

User Management

Another day-to-day task is user management. This consists of managing SQL Server logins and database roles. This is an important duty of the DBA because everyone who wants to use the database must have authorized access. This access is granted by the DBA, usually after a human resources department approves the change. Be sure to get approval before you grant access to each object within the database, and grant only as much access as the user needs. Avoid the temptation to grant blanket access to the database; the use of database roles is useful for granting specific access based on the needs of each department.

Other Routine Maintenance

Other routine maintenance might include tasks such as monitoring database space usage, rebuilding indexes, checking the validity of database objects, and monitoring the overall health of the system. Monitoring the system for changes is important. Any change, no matter how small, might be an indication of problems that are emerging. Many routine tasks are important enough that you should monitor them carefully. You can automate tasks such as rebuilding indexes and running consistency checks, but you should still check them occasionally.

Service Levels

Ensuring that the system provides a particular level of service is an important task. The service level that your system must provide might be specified in a contractual service level agreement (SLA). Even if it isn't, enabling the highest level of service possible is a responsibility and duty of the DBA. This task is accomplished by working for maximum uptime and by working for maximum performance via performance tuning, sizing, and capacity planning.

Performance Tuning and Monitoring

You should constantly monitor the performance of the system and take notes of any changes. If the system suddenly experiences higher response times, higher CPU usage, more context switches, and so forth, you might be seeing signs of an emerging problem. You need to monitor each system differently, and how you interpret the results of that monitoring will differ as well. You must determine, based on your system, how to judge whether it is running well or not. If performance problems are indicated, you must troubleshoot those problems and develop solutions.

You must periodically monitor the system's resource usage and performance. By monitoring the system, you can expand the system before performance degrades.

Once the system capacity has been reached, expansion might be much more expensive in terms of both money and downtime. SQL Server offers several tools for monitoring the system, which are described here along with other monitoring tools:

- **System Monitor**   Used to monitor SQL Server and Windows 2000 resource usage. System Monitor is a Windows 2000 feature that is accessible through the Start menu.
- **SQL Server Enterprise Manager**   Provides both resource usage information and some limited performance information.
- **Third-party RDBMS monitors**   Provide a combination of monitoring and alerting capabilities for relational database management systems (RDBMSs).
- **Network monitors**   Used for occasional network monitoring; they include Microsoft Systems Management Server (SMS) and third-party utilities.
- **User surveys**   Used to gather information about how users feel about the performance of the system. It is important to stay in touch with the user community and determine whether users are satisfied. Too often the only interaction between DBA and user is when there's a problem.
- **Tools for monitoring disk space usage**   Include Microsoft Windows Explorer and third-party monitoring tools. Some tools can monitor Windows 2000 as well as SQL Server.

The system might require tuning as the workload increases.

Sizing and Capacity Planning

In addition to tuning and monitoring the system, you will be called upon to determine whether it can handle the anticipated workload. By regularly performing sizing and capacity-planning tasks, you will be able to schedule capacity increases well in advance of any potential problems. Sizing and capacity planning are not easy jobs. You should call in outside help if you are concerned that the system might soon be reaching its capacity and you are not sure how to address that issue.

System Uptime

As mentioned before in this chapter, the uptime of the system is the responsibility of the DBA. If the system is not functioning optimally, your customers (the user community) will suffer. Any downtime can be costly to your company as well as to your users. Therefore, keeping the system up as much as possible is one of your main duties.

Planning and Scheduling of System Downtime

One way to reduce downtime is to carefully plan scheduled downtime. By scheduling downtime in advance, you can sufficiently warn the user community and staff so they can make other arrangements. The downtime should be scheduled so that there is sufficient time to perform all of the tasks that the downtime was planned for. In addition, you must make sure that all of the people that are affected by the outage are sufficiently notified. Of course, if your database serves the Internet, other arrangements might need to be made.

You might find it more convenient to schedule the downtime to occur on a regular basis, such as the first Sunday of every month. This arrangement will allow the user community to always be prepared for the downtime. Usually, this downtime is scheduled for off hours, in order to inconvenience as few people as possible.

Disaster Recovery

Another way of reducing downtime is to be prepared to recover in the event of a system failure. You must be prepared to recover in the event that the system is down for an extended time. Disasters take several forms. The system might crash because of a hardware failure. Replacing the failed component and rebooting the system usually solves this kind of problem. If the problem is a disk drive, a RAID array might save you from loss of service. If the entire array has failed, the database might require a restore from backup. In any case, this type of failure is usually solved in a matter of hours.

Rebooting the system might solve failures caused by a software problem, or the problem might require a database restore if the database has become corrupt. It is rare for software to fail in this way. However, database corruption can frequently be devastating.

A more severe problem would be the destruction of your data center. This can occur because of a natural disaster such as an earthquake, a flood, or a hurricane. This could result in the loss of computer systems and possibly power for days or even weeks. Another critical problem resulting from a natural disaster could be the loss of communications. So even though the data center might be back up and running, your system might not be back on the Internet for days or even weeks.

Creating a standby data center solves some of these problems. In the event that a disaster disables your main data center, the standby systems can easily be enabled in order to get your company back in business. This standby center might not be able to recover all of the transactions that had been submitted to the primary data center at the point of failure, but it might still be able to keep your business running until such time that you can recover the primary database. The DBA should be involved in planning and implementing the standby data center.

Documentation

The DBA is responsible for documenting every aspect of the database system, including hardware and software configuration, installation procedures, maintenance tasks, software updates, and any changes to the applications. This record can be used to help rebuild the system if necessary.

Documenting the system isn't exciting and requires a lot of discipline, but recording system facts and plans is really worth it in the long run. It is important for everyone involved with the development, deployment, and administration of a production system to document the work that is done. This policy allows others to determine what the current configuration of the system is, as well as what changes have been made in the past. You can use documentation when you clone systems or perform sizing and capacity planning. You can also use documentation as a construction manual if the system needs to be rebuilt. Many types of documentation can benefit from DBA involvement, as will be shown in this section.

The documentation can be maintained in either paper or electronic format, and exactly how it's done at your company is really up to you as the DBA. There are several methods you might use:

- A single document can be kept for the entire company. This document contains sections about each system in the company. System administrators, DBAs, and system operators should be able to access and modify this document.

- A single document can be kept for each system in the company. Again, everyone involved with the system must be able to make log entries in this document.

- System administrators, DBAs, and system operators can keep separate files. Only one segment of the administration community would be able to modify each type of log, but everybody must be able to view each type.

In the event of a system failure or data loss, having the complete history of the system can help pinpoint where the original failure might have occurred as well as help you reconstruct the system. After all, the reason for tracking failures is to avoid future failures. But if the documentation is to be effective, it must be complete. Never delete any documentation; only add to it.

The following lists are a guide to help you organize your documentation in a way that is effective for you. Most documentation should be divided into two major categories: configuration documentation and the system log.

Configuration Documentation

Configuration documentation should give you all the information you need to rebuild your system in the event of a major breakdown. That information should include the following:

- **Hardware configuration**   A detailed record of what hardware you have, how the hardware was configured, and any equipment that was added, such as additional disk drives or memory.
- **Software components**   A detailed record of which software components were added to the system and how each component was configured. Details such as which subcomponents were installed and what options were chosen are vital.
- **Database configuration**   Should include the database layout and schema, the names and locations of all data files, which filegroups each file belongs to, and how the groups were created. This information gives you a reference by which to identify what data files have been lost in the event of a disk array failure.
- **Software tuning**   Should include all system and database configuration parameters. When tuning changes are made, the new settings should be logged.

System Log

The *system log* is critical in the event of a system failure or performance degradation. You can use the following information to determine the sequence of events leading up to the failure and to aid recovery:

- **Observations**   An important part of the DBA's job is to notice changes in the system and to anticipate problems. Observations of unusual activity should be noted. Even a note as simple as "The system seems sluggish" might hold valuable clues in the event of a subsequent system failure.
- **System changes**   The DBA should record all changes made to the hardware, the operating system, and the database system. Entries should be in chronological order and should be complete but without unnecessary details.

- **System failures**   Anytime a disk drive or other component fails, the event should be documented in the system log. This information can be valuable in determining trends of component failures.

- **Backup and restore operations**   It is not necessary to update the log every time the system is backed up. However, requests for data to be restored should be logged to show patterns in user behavior as well as trouble spots in an application or a database schema.

- **Scheduled maintenance**   When scheduled maintenance is performed, the DBA should make a note of what was done to the system. This information can be the starting point of investigating a system failure that occurs soon after a scheduled maintenance.

By keeping track of critical events as well as of configuration information, you can determine where a problem has occurred and know how to get the system back to where it should be.

Design Documentation

Depending on how your company's information-technology department is organized, you might be required to participate in the original design of the system. In any case, you should become familiar with the design documentation because it will be your guide to the hows, whats, and whys of your system.

Operational Maintenance Plans

The general operational procedures should be carefully documented so that other DBAs or system operators can easily perform them. In many companies, the DBAs perform the day-to-day operational procedures, such as backups, restores, and user account maintenance. At other companies, system operators are charged with this task. The instructions should explain each step clearly enough for a novice to understand. Backup operations are usually done in off hours. As the DBA, you don't want to be bothered in the middle of the night in order to answer questions about the backup procedures, so it is to your benefit to make these instructions as complete as possible. Include information about areas that can be problems and how to solve them. The more complete the document, the more it will help you avoid having to answer questions and debug minor problems yourself.

Disaster Recovery Plans

The disaster recovery plan is used as a guideline for recovering from a loss of the production server. This document is critical if you need to quickly restore a failed system. Whenever the primary system fails, it is the responsibility of the DBA to get the system back on line as soon as possible. The primary system can fail at any time on any day. If the system fails on a weekend or an evening when you are not available, the disaster recovery plan will be a resource for the other DBAs or operators to recover the system as soon as possible.

In order to create the disaster recovery plan, you must analyze the system uptime requirements and risks to the system. With small installations that do not require near 100 percent uptime and that can tolerate some downtime caused by a major disaster, it might be sufficient to simply back up the system and rely on the backup tapes for recovery. Systems that require more uptime will require a solution with a higher degree of fault tolerance, such as running Microsoft Cluster Services (MSCS). For systems whose downtime costs millions of dollars per day, you must implement a more comprehensive approach. This solution usually involves creating a failover site in another area of the country so operations can continue even after a natural disaster. Failover sites can maintain system uptime even if the primary data center is off line for days or weeks. This type of plan must be documented carefully so that any member of the technical staff can begin implementing the failover.

Design and Development

Some companies utilize their DBAs for system development in addition to the more traditional database responsibilities. The DBA is familiar with the needs and operational loads of the current system and thus can provide valuable insight into the design of a new system. Design and development responsibilities might include any of those described in the following sections.

Data Modeling and Analysis

Data modeling is an important part of design. It involves planning the logical design of the database, including specifying data relationships and referential integrity constraints. To make this difficult process easier, you can graphically display the structure of the database schema to see how individual components are related. The data model shows the logical view of the database, which can then be abstracted to the physical database design. By properly modeling the database—that is, by creating an efficient logical and physical database layout—you can greatly enhance performance.

Database Design

Database design is usually carried out by database designers, but they often incorporate feedback from the DBA. Sometimes the DBA plays the role of database designer. Day-to-day interaction with the database gives the DBA a unique perspective that can help improve future designs.

Stored Procedure Development

From time to time, the DBA might be required to design or even develop stored procedures. Being so familiar with the database and the data, the DBA is uniquely suited for these tasks. Stored procedures might be simple, or they might require a great deal of effort to create, depending on the application and your company's needs.

Application Development

In some companies, the DBA participates in the development of the application that will access the company's database. This application, like the stored procedures, will benefit from your familiarity with your database. By helping to develop your company's application, you will enhance the application and facilitate data access.

Information Sharing

The DBA might be called upon to act as a consultant to developers, designers, and end users. This consulting might include the following tasks:

- Assisting end users individually with specific problems, developing a training curriculum, or even teaching that curriculum. In many cases, ad hoc SQL is used as well as packaged queries for decision support systems (DSSs).

- Providing developers with information about how the system has been used in the past and how new development can benefit users. This discussion might precede informing users about new tables and indexes available to them as well as any other new features users might find handy.

- Providing designers with input about how different design features can benefit users. The application that designers have developed might lack some features that the users want or need. Passing this information to developers can help future development. You are the most likely person for the users to come to with questions about how to use certain features, which makes you a good source of feedback to developers.

- Analyzing the data in the database and how that data is accessed. This information can help you with the capacity-planning and tuning process. It might also help you improve the database schema.

Miscellaneous

There are several miscellaneous responsibilities that the DBA might have to perform. These duties are explained in the following sections.

Cluster Administration

If you're running MSCS in conjunction with SQL Server, you might need to perform cluster maintenance and cluster administration tasks. Typically, the cluster will run on its own, but some administration tasks might be required as hardware is added and the cluster changes. Clustering is currently used for server failover, but in future versions of Microsoft Windows and SQL Server, scalable clustering will be available. This capability will increase the complexity of both the setup and the administration of the cluster. Until then, cluster administration is fairly straightforward.

Replication Administration

If you are using SQL Server replication, you might have to perform periodic maintenance tasks as the cluster evolves. These tasks include modifying the cluster attributes and upgrading software on the systems. Other maintenance tasks might involve adding memory or disk capacity to the system. Any changes to the cluster should be made only as a coordinated effort between the system administrator and the DBA.

Help Desk

In addition to the responsibilities mentioned above, the DBA has some miscellaneous duties such as participating in the help desk. Support specialists usually staff the help desk; however, you might be asked to help on occasion. The DBA might be a consultant to the help desk on occasion, or the DBA might be requested to train the support specialists in the use of new applications as well as database functions.

Purchasing Input

Often the DBA will be involved in hardware and software evaluation. This process might require reviewing specifications or creating and administering benchmarks. In many cases, you are called on to get copies of the software, install them on test systems, and evaluate the product on its usefulness to a particular user community. In other cases, you might be asked to review specification sheets on hardware and software and to make an evaluation based on these specifications alone.

Capacity Monitoring

The DBA must monitor the system regularly and plan for growth. In some cases, you can bring in specialists to size the system and to conduct capacity-planning exercises. Normally, however, the DBA is responsible for determining whether the capacity of the system is being reached and when performance will be degraded or when resources will be depleted. The DBA then recommends what additional resources are needed to achieve the desired system performance.

If you don't plan carefully, the system could run out of memory or disk space, or it could even overburden the processor. In any of these situations, performance would suffer. If the system's storage capacity is completely filled, transaction processing might even be halted. Diligent monitoring by the DBA can avert such problems.

Web Site Administration

In smaller companies, it isn't unusual for the DBA to be charged with running the company's Web site. Bigger companies often have large staffs that do nothing but Web site maintenance and development. This duty might be far removed from your DBA duties or closely related, depending on what database access your Web site requires. SQL Server is ideal for providing data to Web sites, and many tools and APIs are available within SQL Server and Windows 2000 for distributing information in that way.

DBA Tips and Techniques

As you have seen in this chapter, the DBA can have a variety of duties and responsibilities. How you perform these duties and live up to these responsibilities will contribute to how the user community feels about your company's DBAs and its Information Systems (IS) department in general. This section is advice concerning how to present yourself to the user community and how to handle delicate situations. These tips and techniques might not directly apply to your specific situations, so you should use your own judgment.

Dealing with the User Community

Depending on your specific duties, you might not deal directly with the user community. More likely than not, however, you will deal with users at least on occasion. The following sections present a few ways to make dealing with end users go a little more smoothly.

The Customer Is Always Right

Be diplomatic. Even if the customer (the user community) is giving you incorrect information, don't be controversial. The end user might not understand the problem completely or might not be able to describe the situation correctly. In any case, don't contradict the customer. Instead, be sympathetic and learn whatever you can about the problem from that person. After all, the reactions of people who use the system every day might be your best indication that a problem exists.

Listen

Listen to the user community. Become familiar with who the users are and what they do. At least on occasion, visit with end users and ask them how they think the system is performing. The user community is often the first to recognize that system performance is degrading.

Follow the Golden Rule

As you know, the Golden Rule is "Do unto others as you would have them do unto you." Don't degrade or contradict others in public, even if you are right. It is much nicer and more effective to educate users rather than contradict them. It will help you in the long run to gather allies rather than cause resentment. Taking this tack will help you become a DBA whom others respect.

System Tuning

System tuning is an important duty of the DBA. This section offers a couple of tips that can help you more effectively tune and maintain the system. One important tip to remember is that it is always a good idea to change only one thing at a time when tuning a system. By following this practice, you can easily determine which changes have improved system performance and which changes might have degraded system performance. Keeping good records also makes it much easier to tune the system.

The former suggestion is often difficult to follow if performance has degraded to the point that the situation is considered an emergency. In these cases, it is often necessary to use a "shotgun approach," in which multiple components are upgraded simultaneously. By upgrading several components at a time, you have a better chance of improving performance, but you might not learn anything about the cause of the problem. This tactic might also combine two or more changes that cancel each other out, thus providing no performance improvement at all.

Dealing with a Crisis

Every DBA has to deal with the occasional crisis. Here are a few tips to help you through those times.

Don't Panic

Problems that appear to be emergencies often turn out not to be urgent after some investigation. But it is easy for performance problems to escalate and become emergencies. By remaining calm, you can avoid costly mistakes. Sometimes it is better to walk away from the problem for a few hours and get some rest than to make a mistake that might add to the problem. Don't be afraid to solicit help if you need it. Taking on a problem that you are not prepared to handle might lead to more problems. Take it easy and don't panic.

Don't Jump to Conclusions

Verify the problem yourself. Don't just jump in based on what others have told you. It is not uncommon for a problem to be exaggerated or misinterpreted by the time the news gets to you. It is to your benefit to not take reports at face value; investigate the facts yourself.

Use Caution

Many mistakes are caused by someone's rushing to solve a problem. Some mistaken repairs are even worse than the original problem. Take your time. You can make a problem worse by working too fast and not being careful enough. Your first goal should be "Don't make the problem worse."

Get Some Rest

Don't work on little or no sleep. This is a disaster waiting to happen. It is better to fix problems when you are alert and coherent. The result of pushing yourself too hard might be to create a problem that is harder to fix. Take care of yourself. Don't make yourself sick.

Call for Help

If a problem gets too big for you to handle, don't worry about calling in some extra help. Plenty of specialists have the expertise to help you through your crisis. There is no shame in calling in help. In fact, calling in the right expert can enhance your reputation.

Summary

This chapter has given you an idea of the duties and the responsibilities of the SQL Server DBA. Of course, this book can't tell you exactly what your responsibilities will be. Companies might have hundreds of DBAs running their databases or only one or two. Just as the number of DBAs varies from company to company, the responsibilities of the DBA vary as well.

Some DBAs have responsibilities in addition to day-to-day database management, such as system design and application development. The duties of the DBA depend on both the needs of the company and the skills of the DBA. The more skills and experience that you acquire, the more valuable you become to your company.

Part II
Installation and Setup

Chapter 4
Designing a Microsoft SQL Server System

Before you even begin loading the operating system and Microsoft SQL Server, you should have a good idea how you want to design your SQL Server system. By carefully designing your SQL Server system, you can avoid costly downtime caused by having to either rebuild the system or reinstall SQL Server with different options. In this chapter, you will learn how to design a SQL Server system. In this book, the *SQL Server system* is the hardware and software that make up the computer that is actually running the SQL Server database. By comparison, when we talk in general about *a system,* we mean all of the hardware and software that make up all of the computers working on behalf of the user in order to access data from one or more SQL Server databases.

This chapter also gives you a brief introduction to the versions of Microsoft Windows 2000 and SQL Server that you might choose to install. Finally you will learn about the types of front-end applications that your company might purchase or create in order to access SQL Server and about how the application architecture can affect the future scalability and performance of your system.

System Requirements

To determine the requirements for an entire system, you must look at the function of the system. Once you have an idea of the purpose of a system, you can start looking at ways of using one or more computers to serve these requirements. You might find that one computer is sufficient or that you need many computers to achieve your goals. This chapter looks at those goals in general. Chapters 5 and 6 will more specifically describe how to design and configure the hardware.

In this chapter, we will look at system functionality and at what configuration decisions can be made based on that functionality. We will begin by looking at the types of applications that a system might be serving before looking at how the service level requirements can be defined.

System Application

What good is the SQL Server database without an application? Well, unless everyone in your company is an expert in SQL and enjoys putting together complex queries and viewing data in tabular form, it is not of much use. The application facilitates the use of SQL Server. Some applications make it clear that you are accessing a database, and other applications completely hide the fact that there is a database at all. In any case, it is important to design the application to easily provide users the service they desire, in a timely manner. In many cases, a slow, inefficient application causes frustration for end users. Eventually, if an application doesn't meet the customer's needs, the customer might find another company to deal with that provides better service.

Application types vary based on the function that they are serving. In general, there are three main functions: online transaction processing (OLTP) systems, decision support systems (DSSs), and batch processing systems. These functions have different requirements and might use drastically different types of applications.

OLTP

OLTP systems are characterized by many users accessing online data simultaneously. In addition, and probably of more importance, these users are waiting for a response from the system. OLTP systems take a variety of forms, such as the following:

- **Online purchasing**   These applications are widely used because Internet commerce is growing rapidly. When purchasing products over the Internet, users often experience a delay while data is transmitted, as well as while it is retrieved and processed. By minimizing the database access time, you improve the entire transaction time.

- **In-store purchasing**   When the cashier at a store swipes your credit card, that transaction is accessing a database. This transaction might pass through many systems before it accesses a database.

- **Business systems**   Every company has some sort of application that is accessing databases. It might be your accounts payable system, your purchasing system, your human resources system, your inventory control system, or a variety of other systems. These might be written as intranet applications, in a language such as C++ or Microsoft Visual Basic, or using a fourth-generation language (4GL) tool. In any case, the data eventually comes from a database.

All OLTP systems have one thing in common. The user is waiting on a response from them. It is your job to design a system that can adequately service user requests in the specified response time.

DSS

Decision support systems assist the user in making important business decisions by providing a specific result based on a business question. Here are a few examples of business questions that might be answered by a decision support system:

- Who are the top salespeople in each district; what are their best-selling products?
- What time of year does each product sell best?
- What was the result of lowering the price of an item?
- What is the average commission for salespeople by district?

Decision support systems are different from OLTP in that the user of a decision support system expects the result of a complex query to take a significant amount of time to be returned. Decision support queries can take anywhere from seconds to minutes to hours to complete. This does not mean that response time is not important, but some compromises can be made between throughput (performance for all users) and response time (performance for each user).

Batch Processing Systems

Batch processing systems process offline jobs that do not have any end-user component. The following tasks are typical jobs for this kind of system:

- **Daily refresh of data**   Some decision support systems require data to be reloaded every night, and batch processing systems often automate this task.
- **Data transformation**   This task is similar to data refresh, but the data is transformed.
- **Data cleansing**   This task accomplishes things like removing duplicate accounts from the database.
- **Offline billing**   This task could consist of performing nightly billing of customers.

Batch processing systems typically have no users waiting for their jobs to finish, but they also typically have a certain time frame in which they must conclude the tasks. For example, overnight loads of data cannot overlap morning logins.

Requirements

As you can see, it is important to get an idea of the types of applications that the system will need to support before you design the database server. Without knowing the requirements, you can't effectively design the system. As you will see later in this chapter and throughout the book, each system has its own requirements and properties. These requirements will prompt certain design decisions such as how many computers to use and whether you need distributed transaction processing.

Service Level Requirements

Among the most important factors going into the design of your system are the service level requirements. The service level requirements are usually specified in a *service level agreement* (SLA). The SLA is made between the supplier (the CIO) and the customer (the users). Whether a formal SLA is created really depends on who the customer is and how the services are provided.

For example, if you are contracting with an outside firm for database services, you will almost certainly have an SLA. In fact, this SLA is most likely a legally binding contract. If you are providing services to other in-house departments, you might not have a legally binding agreement. In any case, an SLA will spell out the level of service that is guaranteed to the customer. It might also include penalties if these service levels are not met. SLAs are described in more detail in Chapter 6.

When a level of service is guaranteed, you must design your system to handle that level of performance. A few areas that influence that design are discussed here: performance, capacity, and uptime.

Performance

One of the most important aspects of an SLA is the specification of the minimum acceptable system performance. A typical SLA will include a chart of various transactions that an application supports, a minimal service time for 100 percent of the transactions, and an optional, more stringent minimal service time for 95 or 90 percent of the transactions. For example, the SLA might specify that 90 percent of "add new customer" transactions must finish within 2 seconds and that all of them must finish within 3 seconds.

The provider of the services must maintain this level of performance, or a penalty might be involved. As a DBA, you are responsible for administering the system so that these service levels are maintained. In addition, you must anticipate when problems might begin to occur and add capacity to the system as necessary. You meet these responsibilities by constantly monitoring the system and periodically performing capacity-planning exercises.

Capacity

In addition to containing performance requirements, the SLA might also contain capacity requirements. Capacity of the system falls into several categories, such as disk space capacity, user capacity, network connection capacity, and so forth. It is your job to maintain the system so that it does not run out of capacity.

You maintain the capacity of the system by continually monitoring the system and taking action if it appears to be nearing a threshold. As you will see in Chapter 6, a certain amount of disk space should remain available at all times for workload spikes. If this buffer begins to be used frequently, additional resources should be added to the system. This is also true of CPU usage.

Uptime

In addition to specifications for performance and capacity, specifications for system uptime are usually included in an SLA. Requirements for system uptime demand that the system be available for users during specified time intervals. The SLA might specify 99.9 percent uptime seven days a week, 52 weeks a year, or it might specify uptime for eight hours a day, five days a week, depending on your company's needs. You are responsible for developing a plan for routine backup and recovery, as well as a disaster recovery plan, in order to maintain the required uptime.

System Components and Options

Now that you have had a brief introduction to the types of applications available and service level requirements, you are ready to decide which software to install on your system. You can choose from four versions of Windows 2000 and three versions of SQL Server 2000. In this section, you will learn the differences between these versions and why you might select one over another.

Windows 2000 Versions

The four versions of Windows 2000 are designed to provide the right software for the right application. The capabilities of Windows 2000 grow as you move from Windows 2000 Professional to Windows 2000 Server to Windows 2000 Advanced Server and finally to Windows 2000 Datacenter. The following sections describe the capabilities of each version. You should choose the version of Windows 2000 that provides the capabilities that you need, rather than just purchase the most expensive version with the most capabilities.

Windows 2000 Professional

Windows 2000 Professional is essentially the desktop version of Windows 2000. Typically, a system running Windows 2000 Professional will take advantage of only the SQL Server 2000 client components. However, if you need to run SQL Server on your computer, you can install the Personal Edition of SQL Server 2000. The Personal Edition permits only local access to the database. Access from other systems is not permitted.

Note Only the Personal Edition of SQL Server (and the client components) can be installed on Windows 2000 Professional.

Windows 2000 Server

Windows 2000 Server is designed as a server operating system, which means that installing Windows 2000 Server on a computer allows other systems to access resources on that computer. Windows 2000 Server supports SQL Server 2000 Standard Edition. Windows 2000 Server doesn't support systems with more than four CPUs and more than 4 gigabytes (GB) of memory. SQL Server 2000 allows remote clients to access the database as well.

Note Only SQL Server Standard Edition, SQL Server Personal Edition, and the SQL Server client components can be installed on computers that are running Windows 2000 Server.

Windows 2000 Advanced Server

Windows 2000 Advanced Server is also a server operating system. As with systems that run Windows 2000 Server, systems that run Windows 2000 Advanced Server allow other systems to access their system resources as well as SQL Server. In addition to having the capabilities of Windows 2000 Server, Windows 2000 Advanced Server supports up to eight CPUs and 8 GB of memory. In order to use Microsoft Cluster Services (MSCS) for failover support, you must be using Windows 2000 Advanced Server. In addition to supporting MSCS, Windows 2000 Advanced Server with SQL Server 2000 supports the new SQL Server clustering technology, updatable distributed views.

Note To utilize eight CPUs and 8 GB of memory within SQL Server 2000, you must run the Enterprise Edition of SQL Server. In addition, SQL Server Standard Edition, SQL Server Personal Edition, and SQL Server client components can be installed on Windows 2000 Advanced Server.

Windows 2000 Datacenter

The flagship version of Windows 2000 is the Datacenter Edition. This version supports all of the components that the other editions of Windows 2000 do, as well as up to 64 CPUs and 64 GB of memory. Windows 2000 Datacenter is available only from hardware vendors. In addition to integrating Windows 2000 Datacenter with their hardware, these vendors offer the highest level of support available for Windows 2000. This integration provides a single point of contact for Windows 2000 support and hardware support.

> **Note**   To utilize 64 CPUs and 64 GB of memory within SQL Server 2000, you must run the Enterprise Edition of SQL Server. In addition, SQL Server Standard Edition, SQL Server Personal Edition, and SQL Server client components can be installed on Windows 2000 Datacenter.

SQL Server Versions

In addition to the versions of Windows 2000 that you have to choose from, there are several editions of SQL Server. It is fairly easy to choose, based on the amount of memory and number of CPUs that you need to use. The editions of SQL Server are described here.

Client Software

The SQL Server 2000 client components consist of the network libraries and utilities needed to access a remote or local SQL Server system. These components are necessary for any system to access SQL Server, and they are identical regardless of which edition of SQL Server is installed.

Personal Edition

The Personal Edition of SQL Server is designed for small databases that are accessed locally on a client system. SQL Server 2000 Personal Edition does not allow other computers to gain access to the database.

Standard Edition

SQL Server 2000 Standard Edition is one of the two server editions of SQL Server 2000. The Standard Edition functions the same way the Enterprise Edition does except that a maximum of four CPUs and 4 GB of memory can be accessed from the Standard Edition.

Enterprise Edition

The Enterprise Edition of SQL Server supports all the features and functionality of all versions of Windows 2000. SQL Server 2000 Enterprise Edition requires Windows 2000 Advanced Server or Windows 2000 Datacenter. In addition, SQL Server 2000 Enterprise Edition supports 2-node failover clustering and updatable distributed views.

Version Comparison

This table shows the versions and capabilities of Windows 2000 and SQL Server 2000.

Table 4-1.   Version comparison

	SQL Server 2000 Personal Edition	SQL Server 2000 Standard Edition	SQL Server 2000 Enterprise Edition
Windows 2000 Professional	Limited capabilities No client access	N/A	N/A
Windows 2000 Server	Limited capabilities No client access	Server capabilities Up to 4 CPUs and 2 GB of memory	Server capabilities Up to 4 CPUs and 4 GB of memory
Windows 2000 Advanced Server	Limited capabilities No client access	Server capabilities Up to 4 CPUs and 2 GB of memory	Server capabilities MSCS Up to 8 CPUs and 8 GB of memory
Windows 2000 Datacenter	Limited capabilities No client access	Server capabilities Up to 4 CPUs and 2 GB of memory	Server capabilities MSCS Up to 64 CPUs and 64 GB of memory

As you can see, you have several choices. You should carefully consider your decision on what to purchase. Once you have installed the system, you will have to start from scratch if change your mind.

System Options

In addition to selecting an edition of SQL Server 2000 and a version of Windows 2000, you can take advantage of several other options. These options are described in the following section, and they include MSCS, SQL Server 2000 replication options, and updatable distributed views (new in SQL Server 2000

Enterprise Edition). Each of these options has specific capabilities and require-ments and therefore may or may not be useful with your configuration, as you will see in the next few paragraphs.

MSCS

MSCS stands for Microsoft Cluster Services and is a Windows 2000 option that works in conjunction with SQL Server 2000. MSCS provides the ability for one computer to act as a standby, or failover, server for another computer. This capability allows the recovery process to begin almost immediately in the event of a hardware or even a software failure.

MSCS requires a shared disk subsystem to be connected to both systems in the cluster. The SQL Server transaction log and data files, as well as executable files, must reside on this shared disk subsystem. In the event of a failure, indicated by the loss of a heartbeat signal, the standby system takes over the SQL Server func-tions. Because the standby system captures the IP address and system name, it appears to the outside world as though the primary database server has simply rebooted.

> **Note**   A cluster failover requires the same database recovery as any system that has rebooted suddenly. MSCS does not provide fault tolerance—merely quick recovery.

SQL Server Replication

SQL Server replication allows data from one SQL Server database to be replicated to another database system. There are several varieties of replication—snapshot, transactional, and merge—which are described in the following paragraphs. Which one would work best for you depends on your preferences and needs. SQL Server replication works on a publish-and-subscribe model, in which the publisher publishes the data and one or more subscribers receive copies of that data.

Snapshot Replication   Snapshot replication periodically takes a picture, or snapshot, of the data and provides that data for other systems to use. Snapshot replication operates only when the snapshot is being created and applied; thus, no overhead is incurred during normal operations. The downside to snapshot replication is that the data is only as current as the last snapshot, which could be quite old.

Transactional Replication Transactional replication starts with a snapshot, but from that point on, the transaction log on the publisher is continually read, and transactions that have been applied to the publisher are then applied to the subscriber or subscribers. This allows the subscriber or subscribers to be kept somewhat up-to-date. Of course, there is some delay between when a transaction is committed on the publisher and when it is applied to the subscriber or subscribers.

Merge Replication Merge replication is different from snapshot and transactional varieties in that updates take place on both the publisher and subscriber systems. SQL Server uses triggers and timestamps to coordinate the changes between the various systems involved in the replication. Merge is useful if multidirectional replication is required, but it has much higher overhead than snapshot or transactional replication.

Updatable Distributed Views

SQL Server 2000 introduces updatable distributed views. This option allows SQL Server systems to share a logical database, thus increasing scalability. The logical database can become large, and you can spread it across many computers to increase its capacity. Updatable distributed views are described in detail in Chapter 18.

Database Layout

An important part of designing the SQL Server system is laying out the database. This process involves the physical placement of transaction logs, data files, and so forth. This is one of the most important tasks involved in designing a SQL Server system because placement decisions are so difficult to reverse. Chapters 5 and 6 include tips on the physical placement of the transaction log and data files.

Transaction Log

The transaction log is critical to the operation, the stability, and the performance of the database server. Each database has its own transaction log; thus, each transaction log should be properly placed. The transaction log is used to record changes to the database, thus allowing the system to recover in the event of a failure. Because recovery relies on the transaction log, it is important that you use a RAID I/O device to protect this component of the database from possible faults. In the event of the loss of a disk drive, the transaction log should still be available.

In addition to protecting the transaction log from disk failure, you should ensure that the transaction log is on a high-performance device. If the transaction log is too slow, transactions must wait, which drastically affects the performance of the system. The transaction log should also be configured as fault tolerant. These requirements are covered in more detail in the next chapter.

Finally there must be sufficient space within the transaction log so that the system can run uninterrupted for a long period of time. If the transaction log fills up, all transaction processing ceases until space is freed up. Space is freed up by backing up the transaction log. However, backing up the transaction log can affect performance. Some DBAs prefer to create a sufficiently large transaction log so that it is necessary to back it up only once per hour or once per day. The transaction log should be sized to run for at least eight hours without having to be backed up. As you will learn later in this book, this is a simplification of the transaction log process.

Data Files

Data file placement is an entirely different process from transaction log placement. Depending on how the data files are accessed, you should place all of them on as many disks as possible, distributing the I/O load among all of the disk drives. This process is covered in more detail in the next chapter.

You should size data files so that there is enough capacity to handle system growth. You will sometimes be surprised by how fast your database grows. As data grows, so do indexes. Periodically you should check your system and perform a sizing and capacity-planning exercise.

So that you can plan the proper layout for the data files, the space should be calculated, performance needs should be assessed, and the proper number of disk drives should be created using a RAID subsystem. Whether or not fault tolerance is used will depend on your specific needs. Once the I/O subsystem has been determined, the data files should be evenly spread across controllers and disk drives.

Application

A major part of your system is the application, which should be designed to perform well now and in the future. In this section, you will learn how to design an application with performance, scalability, and growth in mind.

Architecture

The basic architecture of an application can take one of many forms. The major differences between application architectures have to do with the number of systems involved in the application. This distinction is known as the number of tiers. Many of the most popular applications are advertised based on the number of tiers they comprise.

Architecture Comparison

Each database application is divided into three distinct components. These components are as follows:

- **Database services**   This is the back-end database server and the data that resides in the database.

- **Application services**   This is the application or business logic that manipulates the data that is retrieved from the database.

- **Presentation services**   This is the user interface. The presentation services must be able to manipulate the data into an understandable form.

The differences between one-tier, two-tier, and three-tier architectures are in how these components are divided up. In a one-tier architecture, they are all part of one program. In a two-tier architecture, these components are split into two distinct parts. In a three-tier architecture, these components are divided into three distinct parts. This is shown in Figure 4-1 and described in more detail in the sections that follow it.

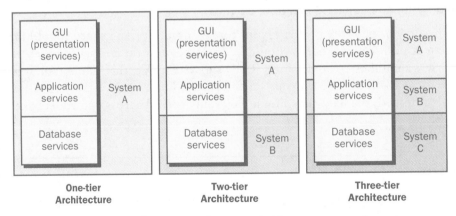

Figure 4-1. *Differences between architectures with one, two, or three tiers.*

One-Tier Architecture

The one-tier, or single-tier, architecture is a system in which the database, application, and presentation services (the user interface) all reside on one system. This type of system does no processing external to the platform on which it is running. An example of single-tier architecture is a Microsoft Access database with local presentation services.

It is rare nowadays to find a substantial single-tier application, especially on a Windows 2000 platform. However, many smaller, single-user applications are single tier. Examples of this are Microsoft Money, Quicken, and TurboTax. These applications typically reside on the same system on which they are running. It is much harder to find an example that uses SQL Server. In fact, even though you can run Enterprise Manager on the same system that the database resides on, it isn't really a single-tier application because the application uses SQL Server networking components. The fact that you happen to be running them on the same system is irrelevant.

Two-Tier Architecture

A two-tier application is one in which the presentation services and the database reside on different systems. The presentation services (user interface) layer usually includes application logic. A good example of a two-tier application is one that uses SQL Server Enterprise Manager. For this type of application, the user interface and the application logic reside in Enterprise Manager, but all of the data that the application uses to function resides in a SQL Server database on a different system.

Two-tier applications are common. You might have worked with many of these applications already. These applications are typically created in languages that support the Windows programming APIs, such as Microsoft Visual C++ or Visual Basic. With a two-tier application, each user must have one or more connections into the SQL Server database. This architecture can be inefficient because most of those connections will be idle for most of the time.

Three-Tier Architecture

Three-tier applications separate the database layer, the application layer, and the presentation services layer into three distinct components. Typical three-tier applications use the middle layer to multiplex connections from the presentation services layer, which reduces the number of connections into SQL Server. In addition, the middle layer can perform a great deal of the business logic, leaving the database free to do what it does best: deliver data.

There is some debate over whether Web-based applications are two-tier or three-tier applications. You can use this simple test: if the data presented in the presentation services layer could just as easily use a terminal or a Web browser, the application probably has two tiers.

As you can see, the separation of the components allows you to use multiple systems. In fact, typical systems start with one database server connected to several application servers that, in turn, serve many PC clients. How you design your system depends on the number of users and the type of application you choose.

Performance and Scalability

When you develop an application and a database schema, you should keep performance and scalability in mind. You make many choices during the application design phase that can eventually affect the performance and the scalability of the system. These choices include the following:

- **The use of temporary worktables**   Often these tables are effective when the database is small, but as the amount of data becomes larger and larger, they cease to function properly.

- **The use of aggregate functions**   The use of aggregate functions such as MIN(), MAX(), and AVG() scales with the amount of data used. So be careful that your data set does not eventually become unwieldy.

- **The use of indexes**   As the amount of data grows, the use of indexes becomes much more important, as you will see in Chapter 17.

- **The use of transactions**   The use of explicit transactions is great for assuring that operations are atomic. However, as the number of concurrent users grows, it is important to reduce locking as much as possible.

As you can see, you should keep several factors in mind if you want to design a system that performs well as the workload grows. By incorporating performance optimization techniques from the design stage, you should be able to create a scalable system.

Summary

As you have seen in this chapter, you must keep in mind many things when designing a SQL Server system. Unfortunately, it is not possible for anyone to simply tell you how to design your system. Even if you design systems for many companies, you will seldom end up with similar results because each company has its own needs and requirements.

This chapter covered several key points. You must assess the uptime requirements of your company and develop a design that will meet those requirements. This might mean multiple data centers, clustering, RAID I/O subsystems, or replication. In addition, the scalability and performance requirements of your system will influence its overall design. As you have seen in this chapter, you have a variety of options. Finally you should design the application with performance in mind. This foresight will result in a system that does not slow down as the data set grows and the number of users increases.

In the next chapter, many of the topics introduced in this chapter will be expanded. Chapter 5 will also teach you how the I/O subsystem works, what performance and fault tolerance issues you should consider, and how to plan and configure an optimal I/O subsystem.

Chapter 5
I/O Subsystem Configuration and Planning

When configuring your system, you must take special care to properly design and configure the I/O subsystem. The configuration of the I/O subsystem can either enhance or degrade the performance of your system. By understanding the limitations of the I/O subsystem and configuring your server to function optimally within those limitations, you will help ensure that it will provide the level of performance that you need.

In this chapter, we explore the I/O subsystem. We start with how a hard disk drive works and why it has fundamental performance limits. After learning about disk drives, you will learn about the various RAID solutions that are available to you and their performance characteristics. In addition, you will learn how to identify an I/O performance problem and how to solve that problem. This chapter also presents a number of I/O subsystem tips and recommendations. Finally you will learn how to properly configure Microsoft SQL Server 2000 in order to take advantage of the performance characteristics of your I/O subsystem.

Disk Drive Performance Characteristics

The disk drive (a.k.a. the hard disk) is one of the fundamental components of the computer system. Amazingly enough, the mechanics of disk drives have not changed much in the last 20 years. Disk drives are much more reliable and faster than they originally were, but fundamentally, they are the same. From a performance standpoint, disk drives are still one of the most important hardware components to tune. Properly speaking, you can't really tune a disk drive; however, by knowing its performance characteristics and limitations and configuring your system with those limitations in mind, you are, in effect, tuning the I/O subsystem.

Disk Drive Construction

The data storage component of a disk drive is made up of a number of disk platters. These platters are coated with a material that stores data magnetically. Data is stored in tracks, which are similar to the tracks of a record (or CD, for those of you who don't remember records). Each track, in turn, is made up of a number of sectors. As you get farther from the center of the disk drive, each track contains more sectors. Figure 5-1 shows a typical disk platter.

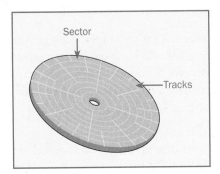

Figure 5-1. *Disk platter.*

Instead of having just one platter, a disk drive is often made up of many disk platters stacked on top of each other, as shown in Figure 5-2. The data is read by means of a magnetic head. This head is used both to read data from and write data to the disk. Because there are many platters, there are also many disk heads. These heads are attached to an armature that moves in and out of the disk stack, much like the arm that holds the needle on a record player. The heads and armatures are all connected; as a result, all heads are over the same point on all platters at the same time. Because disks operate in this manner, it makes sense for all heads to read and write at the same time; thus, data is written to and read from all platters simultaneously. Because the set of tracks covered by the heads at any one time resembles a cylinder, we say that data is stored in cylinders, as shown in Figure 5-2.

Disk drives can be made up of as few as one disk platter or more than six platters. The density of the data on the platters and the number of platters determine the maximum storage capacity of a disk drive. Some lines of disk drives are almost identical, with the exception of the number of disk platters. A popular line of disk drives has a 9-gigabyte (GB) disk drive with three disk platters and an otherwise identical 18-GB disk drive with six disk platters.

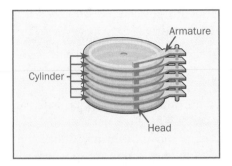

Figure 5-2. *Disk cylinders.*

Disk Drive Characteristics

Now that you have an idea of what makes up a disk drive, let's see how it works. First you will learn about the rotational characteristics of the disk drive, and then you will learn how disk seeks fit into the performance characteristics of disk drives.

Rotational Latency

Many high-performance disk drives spin at 10,000 revolutions per minute (rpm). If a request for data caused the disk to have to rotate completely before it was able to read the data, this spin would take approximately 6 milliseconds (ms), or 0.006 seconds. A rotational speed of 10,000 rpm equates to 166.7 rotations per second. This, in turn, translates to 1/166.7 of a second, or 6 ms, per rotation.

For the disk heads to read a sector of data, that sector must be underneath the head. Because the disk drive is always rotating, the head simply waits for that sector to rotate to the position underneath it. The time it takes for the disk to rotate to where the data is under the head is called the *rotational latency*. The rotational latency can be as long as 6 ms (if the disk has to rotate completely), but on average, it is around 3 ms.

The rotational latency is added to the response time of a disk access. So, when you are choosing disk drives for your system, it is extremely important from a performance standpoint that you take into consideration the length of the disks' rotational latency. As you have just seen, for a 10,000-rpm disk drive, the rotational latency is around 3 ms. Older generation disk drives spin at 7,200 rpm. With this type of disk drive, one rotation takes 8.3 ms, and the average rotational latency is about 4.15 ms. This length of time might not seem like a lot, but it is 38 percent longer than that of the 10,000-rpm disk drive. As you will see later in this chapter, this amount of response time can add a lot to your I/O times.

Disk Seeks

When retrieving data, not only must the disk rotate under the heads that will read the data, but also the head must move to the track where the data resides. The disk armature moves in and out of the disk stack to move the heads to the cylinder that holds the desired data. The time it takes the head to move to where the requested data resides is called the *seek time*. Seek time and rotational latency are represented in Figure 5-3.

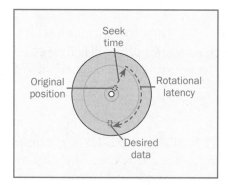

Figure 5-3. *Rotational latency and seek time.*

The time it takes for a seek to occur depends mainly on how far the disk heads need to move. When the disk drives are accessing data sequentially, the heads need to move only a small distance, which can occur quickly. When disk accesses are occurring all over the disk drive, the seek times can get quite long. In either case, by minimizing the seek time, you improve your system's performance.

Seek time and rotational latency both add to the time it takes for an I/O operation to occur, and thus they worsen the performance of a disk drive. Rotational latency is usually around 3 ms for 10,000-rpm disks. The seek time of the disk varies depending on the size and speed of the disk drive and the type of seek being performed.

Track-to-Track Seeks   Track-to-track seek time is the time the heads take to move between adjacent tracks. This type of seek is used when performing sequential I/O operations. A typical 10,000-rpm, 9-GB disk drive has a track-to-track seek time of around 0.8 ms. As you can see, for disks with a track-to-track seek time of only 0.8 ms, the rotational latency of approximately 3 ms is the larger factor in the disk drive performance. If the I/O operations are submitted to the disk drive fast enough, the disk drive will be able to access adjacent tracks or even read or write an entire track at a time. However, this is not always the case. In some cases, the I/O operations are not requested fast enough, and a disk rotation occurs between each sequential access. Whether this happens typically depends on the design and the speed of the disk controller.

Average Seek Time   The average seek time is the time the heads take on average to seek between random tracks on the disk. According to the specification sheet of an average 10,000-rpm disk drive, the seek time for such a disk is around 6 ms. Because almost all of the I/O operations that SQL Server generates are random, your disk drives will be performing a lot of random I/O.

The maximum seek time of this type of disk can be as long as 13 ms. The maximum seek occurs from the innermost track of the platter to the outermost track, or vice-versa. This is referred to as a *full-disk seek*. But normally, the seeks will not be full-disk seeks, especially if the disk drive is not full.

Disk Drive Specifications

In this section, you will see how fast a disk drive can perform various types of I/O operations. To make these calculations, you must have some information about the disk drive. Much of this information can be found by looking at the specifications of the disk drive that the disk drive manufacturer provides. The sample specifications in this chapter are for a 10,000-rpm, 9.1-GB disk drive. Other specifications for this typical type of disk drive are shown in Table 5-1.

Table 5-1.   Disk drive specifications

Specification	Value	Description
Disk capacity	9.1 GB	The unformatted disk capacity
Rotational speed	10,000 rpm	How fast the disk is spinning
Transfer rate	40 MBps	The speed of the SCSI bus
Average seek time	5.2 ms (read) 6 ms (write)	How long (on average) it takes to seek between tracks during random I/O operations
Track-to-track seek time	0.6 ms (read) 0.9 ms (write)	How long it takes to seek between tracks during sequential I/O operations
Full-disk seek time	12 ms (read) 13 ms (write)	How long it takes to seek from the innermost sector to the outermost sector of the disk, or vice versa
Average latency	2.99 ms	The average rotational latency
Mean time between failures	1,000,000 hours	On average, how long the disk lasts

As you will see, these types of specifications can help you determine the performance of the disk drive.

Disk Drive Performance

Several factors determine the amount of time it takes for an I/O operation to occur. These factors are as follows:

- The seek time required (for the heads to move to the track that holds the data)
- The rotational latency required (for the data to rotate under the heads)
- The time required to electronically transfer the data from the disk drive to the disk controller

So the time it takes for an I/O operation to occur is the sum of the times needed to complete the steps described here plus the time added by the overhead incurred in the device driver and in the operating system. Remember, the total time for an I/O operation depends mainly on whether the operation in question is sequential or random. Sequential I/O performance depends on track-to-track seeks. Random I/O performance depends on the average seek time.

Sequential I/O

Sequential I/O consists of accessing adjacent data in disk drives. Because track-to-track seeks are much faster than random seeks, it is possible to achieve much higher throughput from a disk when performing sequential I/O. To get an idea of how fast sequential I/O can occur, let's look at an example.

It takes approximately 0.8 ms to seek between tracks on a typical disk drive, as mentioned earlier. If you add the seek time to the rotational latency of 2.99 ms, you can conclude that each I/O operation will take approximately 3.79 ms. This would theoretically allow us to perform 264 sequential I/O operations per second (because each second contains 264 intervals of 3.79 ms). But with sequential I/O, other factors come into play, such as the SCSI bus bandwidth's limit of 40 megabytes per second (MBps) and operating system components such as the file system and the device driver. That overhead factors into the maximum rate of sequential I/O that a drive can sustain, which is around 250 operations per second (depending on how big the operations are). As you will see in Chapter 6, if you run a disk drive at more than 85 percent of its I/O capacity, queuing will occur; thus, the maximum recommended I/O rate is 225 operations per second.

Random I/O

Random I/O occurs when the disk heads must read data from various parts of the disk. This random head movement results in reduced performance. Again, let's look at the sample disk we covered earlier. Now instead of taking approximately 0.8 ms to seek between adjacent tracks on the disk, the heads must seek random tracks on the disk. This random seeking takes approximately 6 ms (on average) to complete, which is 7.5 times longer than the track-to-track seeks. A typical random I/O operation requires approximately 6 ms (on average) for the heads to move to the track where the data is held and 2.99 ms in rotational latency, for a total of 8.99 ms, giving a theoretical maximum of 111 I/O operations per second (because each second contains 111 intervals of 8.99 ms). Thus, using the same rule that you saw earlier, if you run a disk drive at more than 85 percent of its capacity, queuing will occur. Therefore, the maximum recommended I/O rate is 94 I/O operations per second. If you follow a rule of thumb that takes into account overhead in the controller, you would want to drive these disk drives at no more than 85 I/O operations per second.

When a disk drive performs random I/O, a normal latency (the time it takes to perform individual I/O operations) is 8.99 ms. When a drive is accessed faster than it can handle, queuing will occur, and the latency will increase. This is shown in Figure 5-4. As you can see, the closer the number of operations per second gets to the disk's recommended maximum rate, the longer the latencies get.

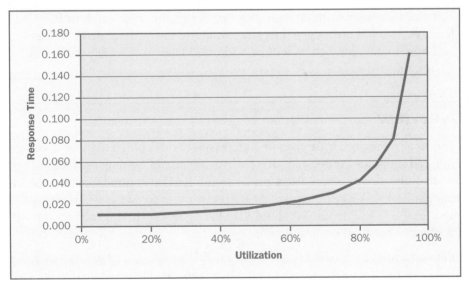

Figure 5-4. *I/O operations per second as a function of latency.*

In fact, if you get to 100 percent, queuing will certainly occur and performance will degrade dramatically. As you will learn later in this book, SQL Server (like all other relational database management systems) is highly sensitive to I/O latencies. When I/O operations take excessive amounts of time to complete, the performance of SQL Server degrades, and problems such as blocking and deadlocks might occur. When a thread is waiting on an I/O operation, it might be holding locks. The longer the operation takes to complete, the longer the locks are held, thus causing these types of problems.

Solutions to the Disk Performance Limitation Problem

So how do we solve the problem of disk performance limitations? It is actually quite straightforward. By following these guidelines, you should be able to design an I/O subsystem that performs optimally:

- **Isolate sequential I/O operations.** By isolating components that are sequential in nature on their own disk volume, you can maintain that sequential nature. The transaction log is an example of a sequentially accessed file. If you place more than one sequentially accessed file on the same disk volume, the I/O operations will become random because the disk must seek between the various sequential components.

- **Distribute random I/O operations.** Because the I/O operations are random in nature, you can alleviate the load by adding disk drives. If you build a system with enough disk drives to handle the random I/O load, you should not experience any problems. How many disks to use and how to configure them will be addressed later in this chapter and in Chapter 6.

RAID Overview

As you might imagine, it can become increasingly difficult to manage a system as you add more and more disk drives. Instead of adding tens or hundreds of individual disk drives, many users prefer to use RAID (Redundant Array of Independent Disks). You can implement RAID by using software and existing I/O components, or you can purchase hardware RAID devices. In this section, you will learn about what RAID is and how it works.

As the name implies, RAID takes two or more disk drives and creates an array of disks. To the operating system, this array appears as one *logical disk*. This logical disk is also known as a *disk volume* because it is a collection of disks that appears as one. To the user, to the application, and even to Microsoft Windows 2000 (if hardware RAID is used), the array appears as one disk. In many cases, however, this single logical disk is much larger than any disk you could purchase. Not only does RAID allow you to create large logical disk drives, but many *RAID levels* (configurations) provide disk fault tolerance as well. Fault tolerance allows the RAID logical disk to survive (tolerate) the loss of one or more individual disk drives. In the next few sections, you will learn how this is possible and about the characteristics of various RAID levels.

As was mentioned earlier, RAID can be implemented by using software; in fact, Windows 2000 comes with RAID software. However, this chapter is concerned mostly with hardware-based RAID because of the additional features that it provides. In the next two sections, you will learn about some of these features and the characteristics of the various RAID levels.

I/O Subsystem Concepts

Hardware RAID controllers provide not only the basic RAID functionality but also additional features. The most common of these hardware RAID features is the controller cache. In this section, you will learn about the controller cache, disk drive caches, and the difference between internal and external RAID. In addition, you will learn about the latest in I/O technology, the Storage Area Network. This section also covers some miscellaneous issues concerning RAID controllers and disk drives, as well as bandwidth issues.

Caching Controllers

To improve I/O performance, many vendors offer controllers with caches. A *controller cache* is RAM that resides on the disk controller. This cache serves two purposes:

- **Write caching**   Because there is memory on the controller, it is possible for the controller to tell the operating system (and subsequently SQL Server) that the I/O operation has been completed as soon as it has been written to the cache, thus greatly increasing write performance.

- **Read-ahead caching**   Another use of the controller cache is to read data in addition to the data that was requested. This is in anticipation of that additional data's being requested soon. If it is, the response time will be dramatically shorter.

As you will see later in this chapter, write performance can be crucial, especially if you use RAID level 5. In most cases, the controller cache is of great benefit. There are, however, a couple of things to watch for:

- Don't use write caching without a battery backup. Most caching controllers include a battery or offer one as an option. This battery retains data in the cache in the event of a power failure. Without this battery, the data in the cache would be lost, and the database might become corrupted.

- In rare situations where the RAID array is run near capacity, write caching can actually hurt read performance. This is because of the priority within the controller that writes are given in order to empty the cache.

Controller caches can enhance the performance of your I/O subsystem under certain conditions. By understanding the various RAID levels and their performance characteristics, you will be better able to configure these controllers to perform optimally for your particular application and requirements.

Disk Drive Caches

Most disk drives also contain a memory cache. This cache is smaller than the controller cache. It can hold a few requests at a time, allowing the disk drive itself to do elevator sorting. However, because the cache is so small (usually a few kilobytes), it cannot be used for large read-aheads or to cache large amounts of data. Many RAID controller vendors and SCSI controller vendors do not allow you to modify the state of this cache. However, some RAID manufacturers do allow you to turn this cache on or off.

Internal vs. External RAID

There are two basic types of RAID systems: internal and external. These terms refer to where, in the configuration, the RAID logic lies. With most systems, the RAID logic resides on the controller, which resides in the chassis that houses the computer system. This is referred to as an internal RAID system. In an external RAID system, the RAID logic resides in the storage unit or units that house the disk drives. A representation of these types of systems is shown in Figure 5-5. Each type of system has its own properties and characteristics. However, the differences between internal and external RAID are not really central to this chapter. These two types of controllers are presented only for completeness.

In the next section, you will learn about the various RAID levels. These levels further distinguish RAID controllers.

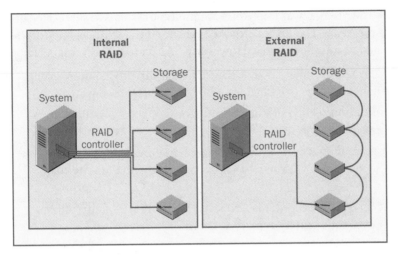

Figure 5-5. *Internal vs. external RAID.*

Storage Area Networks

One of the newest technologies on the market is the Storage Area Network (SAN). A *SAN* is basically a large external RAID system that shares out the storage among several systems. This is why the term "network" is used in the name. A SAN allows you to consolidate storage and reduce costs while managing and supporting the system from a central location.

The concept of a SAN is fairly straightforward. An external RAID system connects a host bus adapter (HBA) directly to a RAID subsystem. As Figure 5-6 shows, a SAN connects multiple HBAs through a switch to at least one external RAID system. With this setup, all of the systems on the SAN can access the RAID subsystem.

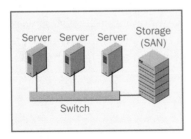

Figure 5-6. *A SAN system.*

When this book was written, it was impossible for multiple systems to share a logical disk drive within the SAN. The SAN software segmented the storage, and logical drives were allocated to specific systems. However, a SAN can offer several benefits:

- **Clustering** The SAN is easily clustered because it already is an external RAID controller. The servers can share all of the RAID intelligence.

- **Storage consolidation** Having one central storage facility reduces storage maintenance problems.

- **Reduction of wasted space** Rather than reserving an extra disk drive for each system, you can put the extra space to productive use by many systems.

- **Fault tolerance** All of the systems accessing the SAN can share online spares, which can immediately replace a failed disk drive.

Controller and Bus Bandwidth Issues

In addition to considering disk drive limitations, you should consider bandwidth limitations of the I/O bus (usually SCSI or Fibre Channel). Because buses run at a specified clock speed and have a certain data width (32 bits, 64 bits, and so on), the maximum throughput is fixed. Your requirements can meet or exceed the bandwidth of the controller, the PCI bus, or the controller I/O bus. You can avoid this by spreading your controllers among several PCI buses in your system. Most new computer systems contain three or more PCI buses.

High-End I/O Subsystems

Companies that require 99.99 percent or more system uptime and maximum performance will often turn to vendors like EMC. These vendors offer sophisticated I/O subsystems that include gigabytes of cache capacity and multiple data paths (channels) from the computer system to the disk drive. These multiple channels guarantee a level of redundancy. If a single component in the system were to fail (including an I/O channel, a controller, or the cache), the subsystem would continue to function. If sized carefully, these subsystems can offer the highest level of performance and reliability.

Elevator Sorting

Elevator sorting is a method of making random I/O operations more efficient. When random I/O requests are issued to disks, the heads must randomly move in and out of the disk drive. This random operation causes latencies, as was described earlier. Many RAID controllers support elevator sorting to make random seeks more efficient. If elevator sorting is supported and multiple I/O operations are queued up on the controller, the operations can be sorted to reduce head movement. The advantages of elevator sorting resemble those of using an elevator to move people from one floor to another.

Imagine that an elevator serviced floors in the order in which the people on the elevator pushed the buttons. The elevator might pass floors where it could more efficiently let people on and off. A real elevator is more efficient because it stops on floors where it is needed. Elevator sorting algorithms do the same thing. If more than one I/O operation is in the queue, the controller will take the most efficient path to empty the queue, as Figure 5-7 illustrates.

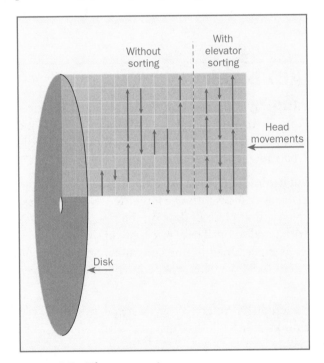

Figure 5-7. *Elevator sorting.*

As you can see, elevator sorting can make disk seeking more efficient. Overall seek times are reduced—perhaps at the expense of some individual seek times. However, in order for elevator sorting to occur, you must have several or even many I/O operations outstanding on the controller or disk drive where the sorting is to occur. This situation can often arise when the I/O subsystem is overloaded. In many cases, an optimally running disk drive has only one or two I/O operations outstanding, making elevator sorting a moot point.

Disk Reliability

Disks are one of the few components in a computer system that is at least partly mechanical. The disk drive spins at a high rate and operates at a high temperature. Components include several motors and bearings that eventually wear out. Included in the disk drive specifications is *duration for mean time between failures* (MTBF). The figure for duration indicates how long a disk is expected to last on average. However, this number is only an average. Some disk drives last longer than others that have the same MTBF estimate. A typical modern disk drive might have an MTBF of 1,000,000 hours, or 114 years. This is a long time; however, some disks with that rating will last much longer, and some will fail early on. The point is that disks have mechanical components, and they are thus subject to wear and tear and eventual failure.

Overview of Common RAID Levels

The main characteristic of a RAID array is that two or more physical disk drives are combined to form a logical disk drive, which appears to Windows 2000 (and Performance Monitor) as one physical disk drive. A logical disk drive can hold many hundreds of gigabytes, even though 100-GB disk drives don't exist (yet!).

Most of the RAID levels that will be described here use *data striping*. Data striping combines the data from two or more disks into one larger RAID logical disk, which is accomplished by placing the first piece of data on the first disk, the second piece of data on the second disk, and so on. These pieces are known as *stripes*, or *chunks*. The size of the stripe is determined by the controller. Some controllers allow you to configure the stripe size, whereas other controllers have a fixed stripe size.

The individual piece of data on each disk is referred to as a stripe, or chunk, but the combination of all of the chunks across all disk drives is also referred to as the stripe, as shown in Figure 5-8.

Thus, the term *stripe* can be used to describe the piece of data on a specific disk drive, as in *the disk stripe*, or to refer to the set of related data, as in *the RAID stripe*. Keep this in mind as you read this chapter and others that refer to RAID.

The RAID level identifies the configuration type and therefore the characteristics of a RAID array other than internal or external logic. One of the most important of these characteristics is *fault tolerance*. Fault tolerance is the ability of a RAID system to continue to function after a disk drive has failed. Fault tolerance is the

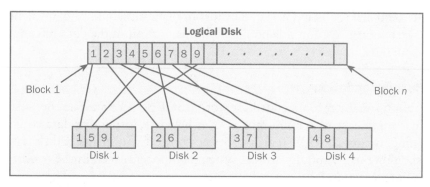

Figure 5-8. *RAID stripes.*

primary purpose of RAID controllers. Because your data is valuable, you must protect it against a disk failure. In this section, you will learn about the most common RAID levels: how they work, what fault tolerance they provide, and how quickly they perform. There are other RAID levels that are rarely used; only the most popular ones will be mentioned.

RAID 0

RAID 0 is the most basic RAID level, offering disk striping only. A chunk is created on each disk drive, and the controller defines the size of the chunk. As Figure 5-9 illustrates, a round-robin method is used to distribute the data to each chunk of each disk in the RAID 0 array to create a large logical disk.

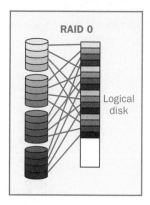

Figure 5-9. *RAID 0.*

Although RAID 0 is considered a RAID level, technically, there is no redundancy at this level. Because there is no redundancy, there is no fault tolerance. If any disk fails in a RAID 0 array, all data is lost. The loss of one disk would be equivalent to losing every fourth word in this book. With this portion of the data missing, the array is useless.

RAID 0 Recommendations

RAID 0 is not normally recommended for storing SQL Server data files. Because the data in the database is so important to your business, losing that data could be devastating. Because a RAID 0 array does not protect you against a disk failure, you shouldn't use it for any critical system component, such as the operating system, a transaction log, or database files.

> **Note**   A disk drive spins at a high rate and operates at a high temperature. Because the disk is a mechanical component, it eventually will fail. Thus, it is important to protect SQL Server data files from that failure by creating a fault-tolerant system.

RAID 1

RAID 1 is the most basic fault-tolerant RAID level. RAID 1, also known as mirroring, duplicates your data disk. As Figure 5-10 shows, the duplicate contains all of the information that exists on the original disk. In the event of a disk failure, the mirror takes over; thus, you lose no data.   Because all the data is held on one disk (and its mirror), no striping is involved. Because RAID 1 uses the second disk drive to duplicate the first disk, the total space of the RAID 1 volume is equivalent to the space of one disk drive. Thus, RAID 1 is costly in that you must double the number of disks and you get no additional disk space in return, but you do get a high level of fault tolerance.

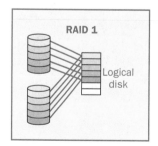

Figure 5-10. *RAID 1.*

For a RAID 1 volume, an I/O operation is not considered complete until the controller has written data to both disk drives. Until that happens, a "fault" (disk failure) cannot be tolerated without loss of data. Once that data has been written to both disk drives, the data can be recovered in the event of a failure in either disk. This means that if writing the data to one disk takes longer than writing the same data to the other disk, the overall latency will equal the greater of the two latencies.

The fact that the write goes to both disks also reduces the performance of the logical disk drive. When calculating how many I/O operations go to each disk drive in the array, you must multiply the number of writes by two. Reads occur on only one disk. Disks might perform at different rates because the heads on one disk might be in a position different from that of the heads on the other disk; thus, a seek might take longer. Because of a performance feature of RAID 1 known as *split seeks*, the disks' heads might be in different positions.

Split seeks allow the disks in a RAID 1 volume to read data independently of each other. Split seeks are possible because reads occur on only one disk of the volume at a time. Most controller manufacturers support split seeks. Split seeks increase performance because the I/O load is distributed to two disks instead of one. However, because the disk heads are operating independently and because they both must perform the write, the overall write latency is the longer latency between the two disks.

RAID 1 Recommendations

RAID 1 offers a high degree of fault tolerance and high performance. RAID 1 is a great solution when one disk drive can hold all of the data. Some recommendations for using RAID 1 are as follows:

- Use RAID 1 for the disk that contains your operating system because rebuilding it takes so much time. RAID 1 is a good choice also because the operating system can usually fit on one disk.
- Use RAID 1 for the transaction log. Typically, the SQL Server transaction log can fit on one disk drive. In addition, the transaction log performs mostly sequential writes. Only rollback operations cause reads from the transaction log. Thus, you can achieve a high rate of performance by isolating the transaction log on its own RAID 1 volume.
- Use write caching on RAID 1 volumes. Because a RAID 1 write will not be complete until both writes have been done, performance of writes can be improved through the use of a write cache. When using a write cache, be sure that it is battery–backed up.

As you will see later in this chapter, you can use other fault-tolerant solutions if more than one disk is required. RAID 1 is great when fault tolerance is required and one disk is sufficient.

RAID 5

RAID 5 is a fault-tolerant RAID level that uses parity to protect data. Each RAID stripe creates parity information on one disk in the stripe. Along with the other disks in the RAID stripe, this parity information can be used to re-create the data on any of the other disk drives in the stripe. Thus, a RAID 5 array can tolerate the loss of one disk drive in the array. The parity information is rotated among the various disk drives in the array, as Figure 5-11 shows.

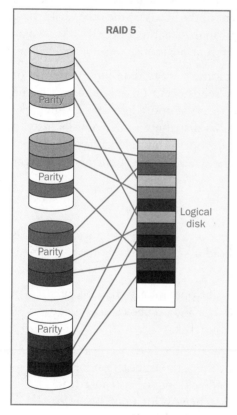

Figure 5-11. *RAID 5.*

The advantage of RAID 5 is that the space that is available in this RAID level is equal to $n - 1$, where n is the number of disk drives in the array. Thus, a RAID 5 array made up of 10 disk drives will have the space of 9 disks, making RAID 5 an economical, fault-tolerant choice.

Unfortunately, there are performance penalties associated with RAID 5. Maintaining the parity information requires additional overhead. When data is written to a RAID 5 array, both the target disk stripe and the parity stripe must be read, the parity must be calculated, and then both stripes must be written out. Therefore, a RAID 5 write actually incurs four physical I/O operations, as you will see.

RAID 5 Parity Explained

In RAID 5, a parity bit is created on the data in each stripe on all of the disk drives. A parity bit is an additional piece of data that, when created on a set of bits, determines what the other bits are. This parity bit is created by adding up all of the other bits and determining which value the parity bit must contain to create either an even or odd number. The parity bit, along with all of the remaining bits, can be used to determine the value of a missing bit.

Let's look at an example of how parity works. For this example, we will consider a RAID 5 system with five disk drives. Each disk drive is essentially made up of a number of bits, starting from the first part of the stripe on the disk and ending at the end part of the stripe on the disk. The parity bit is based on the bits from each disk drive.

In this example, we will consider the parity to be even; thus, all of the bits must add up to 0. If the first bit on the first disk drive is 0, the first bit on the second drive is 1, the first bit on the third drive is 1, and the first bit on the fourth drive is 1, the parity must be 1 in order for these bits to add up to an even number, as Table 5-2 shows.

Table 5-2.   An example of RAID parity

Disk 1 Bit 1	Disk 2 Bit 1	Disk 3 Bit 1	Disk 4 Bit 1	Disk 5 Parity bit	Sum of bits
0	1	1	1	1	4 (even)

So think of the parity as being created on single bits. Even though the disk stripe contains many bits, you make the data recoverable by creating a parity on the single bits.

As you can see from Table 5-2, the parity is actually created on individual bits in the stripes. Even though the disk drives are broken up into chunks or stripe pieces that might be 64 KB or larger, the parity can be created only at the bit level, as shown here. Parity is actually calculated with a more sophisticated algorithm than that just described.

So let's say, for example, that Disk 3 fails. In this case, the parity bit plus the bits from the other disk drives can be used to recover the missing bit from Disk 3 because they must all add up to an even number.

Creating the Parity   As you have seen in this section, the RAID 5 parity is created by finding the sum of the same bits on all of the drives in the RAID 5 array and then creating a parity bit so that the result is even. Well, as you might imagine, it is impractical for an array controller to read all of the data from all of the drives each time an I/O operation occurs. This would be inefficient and slow.

When a RAID 5 array is created, the data is initially zeroed out, and the parity bit is created. You then have a set of RAID 5 disk drives with no data but with a full set of parity bits.

From this point on, whenever data is written to a disk drive, both the data disk and the parity disk must first be read from. The new data is compared with the old data, and if the data for a particular bit has changed, the parity for that bit must be changed. This is accomplished with an exclusive OR (XOR) operation. Thus, only the data disk and the parity disk, not all of the disks in the array, need to be read. Once this operation has been completed, both disk drives must be written out because the parity operation works on entire stripes. Therefore, for each write to a RAID 5 volume, four physical I/O operations are incurred: two reads (one from data and one from parity) and two writes (back to data and back to parity). But with a RAID 5 array, the parity is distributed, so this load should be balanced among all the disk drives in the array.

RAID 5 Recommendations

Because of the additional I/O operations incurred by RAID 5 writes, this RAID level is recommended for disk volumes that are used mostly for reading. Because the parity is distributed among the various disks in the array, all disks are used for read operations. Because of this characteristic, the following is recommended:

- Use RAID 5 on read-only volumes. Any disk volume that does more than 10 percent writes is not a good candidate for RAID 5.

- Use write caching on RAID 5 volumes. Because a RAID 5 write will not be completed until two reads and two writes have occurred, the response time of writes can be improved through the use of a write cache. (When using a write cache, be sure that it is battery–backed up.) However, the write cache is not a cure for overdriving your disk drives. You must still stay within the capacity of those disks.

As you can see, RAID 5 is economical, but you pay a performance price. You will see later in this chapter how high that price can be.

RAID 10

RAID 10 is a combination of RAID 0 and RAID 1. RAID 10 involves mirroring a disk stripe. Each disk will have a duplicate, but each disk will contain only a part of the data, as Figure 5-12 illustrates. This level offers the fault tolerance of RAID 1 and the convenience and performance advantages of RAID 0.

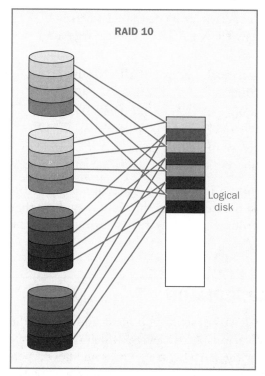

Figure 5-12. *RAID 10.*

As with RAID 1, each RAID 10 write operation will incur two physical I/O operations—one to each disk in the mirror. Thus, when calculating the number of I/O operations per disk, you must multiply the writes by two. As with RAID 1, the RAID10 I/O operation is not considered completed until both writes have been done; thus, the write latency might be increased. But, as with RAID 1, most controllers support split seeks with RAID 10.

RAID 10 offers a high degree of fault tolerance. In fact, the array can survive even if more than one disk fails. Of course, the loss of both sides of the mirror cannot be tolerated. If the mirror is split across disk cabinets, the loss of an entire cabinet can be tolerated.

RAID 10 Recommendations

RAID 10 offers high performance and a high degree of fault tolerance. RAID 10 should be used when a large volume is required and more than 10 percent of the I/O operations are writes. RAID 10 recommendations include the following:

- Use RAID 10 whenever the array experiences more than 10 percent writes. RAID 5 does not perform as well as RAID 10 with a large number of writes.
- Use RAID 10 when performance is critical. Because RAID 10 supports split seeks, you get premium performance.
- Use write caching on RAID 10 volumes. Because a RAID 10 write will not be completed until both writes have been done, performance of writes can be improved through the use of a write cache. Write caching is safe only when used in conjunction with battery–backed up caches.

RAID 10 is the best fault-tolerant solution in terms of protection and performance, but it comes at a cost. You must purchase twice the number of disks that are necessary with RAID 0. If your volume is mostly read, RAID 5 might be acceptable.

RAID Level Performance Comparison

To properly configure and tune your RAID system, you must understand the performance differences between the various RAID levels, which the previous section outlined. By understanding how the RAID system works and how it performs under various conditions, you will be able to tune your I/O subsystem better. This section will compare in detail the various performance characteristics that you have seen in the previous section.

Read Performance

The RAID level you choose will not significantly affect read performance. When read operations are performed on a RAID volume, each drive contributes to the volume's performance. Because random I/O operations are typically the most problematic, they will be covered here. You can maximize sequential performance by isolating the sequential I/O operations on their own volume. Let's look at random-read performance under the various RAID levels:

- RAID 0 volumes spread data evenly among all the disks in the array. Thus, random I/O operations should be spread equally among all the disk drives in the system. If we estimate that a particular disk drive can handle 85 random I/O operations per second, a RAID 0 array of 10 disk drives should be able to handle 850 I/O operations per second.

- RAID 1 volumes support split seeks, so both disk drives perform read operations. Thus, a RAID 1 volume can support twice the number of reads that a single disk can, or 170 I/O operations per second. If reads occur more frequently than that, performance will suffer.

- RAID 5 arrays spread the data evenly among all of the disk drives in the array. Even though one disk drive is used for parity in each stripe, because the I/O operations are random in nature, all drives are typically used. Thus, as with the RAID 0 array, the read capacity of a RAID 5 array is 85 I/O operations per second times the number of disk drives in the array. An array running at more than that will reduce SQL Server performance.

- RAID 10 arrays, like RAID 1 arrays, support split seeks. The maximum read performance is therefore equivalent to the number of disk drives times 85 I/O operations per second. You might be able to initiate I/O operations more frequently, but they will not be completed as quickly as you request them.

As you can see, calculating the read capacity of a RAID array is fairly straightforward. By adding enough disk drives to support your I/O requirements and staying within these limitations, you will optimize your system's performance.

Write Performance

The type of RAID controller you use will dramatically affect write performance. Again, because random I/O operations are typically the most problematic, they will be covered here. You can maximize sequential performance by isolating the sequential I/O operations on their own volume or volumes. Let's look at random-write performance under the various RAID levels.

- RAID 0 is the level most capable of handling writes without performance degradation, but you forfeit fault tolerance. Because RAID 0 does not mirror data or use parity, the performance of RAID 0 is simply the sum of the performance of the individual disk drives. Thus, a RAID 0 array of 10 disk drives can handle 850 random writes per second.

- RAID 1 arrays must mirror any data that is written to the array. Therefore, a single write to the array will generate two I/O operations to the disk drives. So a RAID 1 array has the capacity of a single disk drive, or 85 I/O operations per second.

- RAID 5 arrays are even slower for write operations. A write to a RAID 5 array actually generates two reads from the disks and two writes to the disks. A write to a RAID 5 array generates four physical I/O operations to the disks. Thus, the write capacity of a RAID 5 array is equivalent to the capacity of one-fourth of the disk drives in the array.

- RAID 10 has the same write characteristics as the RAID 1 array does. Each write to the RAID 10 volume generates two physical writes. Thus, the capacity of the RAID 10 array is equivalent to the capacity of one-half of the disk drives in the array.

As you can see, calculating the write capacity of a RAID array is a fairly complex operation. By adding enough disk drives to support your I/O requirements and staying within these limitations, you will optimize your system's performance. In the next section, you will see how to calculate the number of I/O operations per disk under various circumstances.

Disk Calculations

To determine how much load is being placed on the individual disk drives in the system, you must perform some calculations. If you are using a hardware RAID controller, the number of I/O operations per second that Performance Monitor displays is the number of I/O operations that are going to the array. Additional I/O operations that are generated by the controller for fault tolerance are not shown. In fact, Windows 2000 doesn't register that they are occurring, but you must be aware of them for determining the necessary number of disk drives required for optimal performance. The formulas in the following sections can help you determine how many I/O operations are actually going to each disk in the array.

RAID 0

The rate of I/O operations per disk drive in a RAID 0 array is calculated by adding up all the reads and writes to the array and dividing by the number of disks in the array. RAID 0 requires only the following simple and straightforward equation:

```
operations per disk = (reads + writes) / number of disks
```

RAID 1

With RAID 1, the calculation becomes a little more complicated. Because the number of writes is doubled, the number of I/O operations per disk per second is equal to the number of reads plus two times the number of writes, divided by the number of disk drives in the array (two for RAID 1). The equation is as follows:

```
operations per disk = (reads + (2 * writes)) / 2
```

RAID 1 is slower on writes but offers a high degree of fault tolerance.

RAID 5

RAID 5 offers fault tolerance but has a high level of overhead on writes. RAID 5 reads are distributed equally among the various disk drives in the array, but writes actually cause four physical I/O operations to occur. To calculate the number of I/O operations occurring on the individual disk drives, you must add the reads to four times the number of writes before dividing by the number of disk drives. Thus, the equation for RAID 5 is as follows:

```
operations per disk = (reads + (4 * number of writes)) /
    number of disks
```

RAID 10

RAID 10 is slow on writes, as is RAID 1, but RAID 10 offers a high degree of fault tolerance. The calculation for RAID 10 is the same as that for RAID 1. Because writes are doubled, the number of I/O operations per disk is equal to the number of reads plus two times the number of writes, divided by the number of disk drives in the array. The equation is as follows:

```
operations per disk = (reads + (2 * writes)) / number of disks
```

RAID Comparison

Let's compare the RAID levels directly. This might better help you to determine which RAID level is best for your system. When you compare I/O performance across RAID levels, one of the most important factors is the read-to-write ratio. The various RAID levels perform comparably when performing reads; only the write rates differ. You should also consider whether your system needs to be fault tolerant. Finally you should be aware of the various cost/space ratios. Table 5-3 summarizes the various RAID levels.

Table 5-3. RAID levels comparison

RAID Level	Performance	Fault Tolerance	Cost
RAID 0	Best	No fault tolerance	Economical
RAID 1	Good	Good	Expensive
RAID 5	Fast reads, slow writes	OK	Most economical with fault tolerance
RAID 10	Good	Good	Expensive

As you can see, your best choice really depends on your requirements. To see the difference between RAID 5 and RAID 10 at different read/write ratios, look at the following table. Table 5-4 represents 500 I/O operations per second across 10 disk drives with varying read/write ratios.

Table 5-4. RAID 5 and RAID 10 comparison

Read/Write Ratio	RAID 5 I/O Operations (Reads + (4 * Writes)) / Disks	RAID 10 I/O Operations (Reads + (2 * Writes)) / Disks
100% reads 0% writes	(500 + 0) / 10 50 I/O operations per disk	(500 + 0) / 10 50 I/O operations per disk
90% reads 10% writes	(450 + 200) / 10 65 I/O operations per disk	(450 + 100) / 10 55 I/O operations per disk
75% reads 25% writes	(375 + 500) / 10 87.5 I/O operations per disk	(375 + 250) / 10 62.5 I/O operations per disk
50% reads 50% writes	(250 + 1000) / 10 125 I/O operations per disk	(250 + 500) / 10 75 I/O operations per disk
0% reads 100% writes	(0 + 2000) / 10 200 I/O operations per disk	(0 + 1000) / 10 100 I/O operations per disk

As you can see, at about 90 percent reads and 10 percent writes, the disk usage is about even. But for higher percentages of writes, RAID 5 requires much more overhead.

I/O Latencies and SQL Server

SQL Server is especially sensitive to I/O latencies because of the concurrency of transactions within the SQL Server engine. Under normal conditions, tens or hundreds of applications are running against a SQL Server database. To support this concurrency, SQL Server has a complex system of row, page, extent, and table locks, as you will see throughout this book. When a piece of data or a SQL Server resource is locked, other processes must wait for that data or resource to be unlocked.

If I/O operations take excessive amounts of time to complete, these resources will be held for a longer period than normal, further delaying other processing in the system. In addition, this could lead to a greater chance of deadlocks. The longer the I/O takes to complete, the longer the locks are held, and the higher the potential for problems. As a result, individual delays can multiply into a "snowball effect" that cripples the system.

In addition, query processing will be significantly slower. If long table scans are running on your system, for example, hundreds of thousands or even millions of rows will often need to be read in order to complete the task. Even slight variations in performance become dramatic when applied to a million I/O operations. One million operations at 10 ms each will take approximately 2.8 hours to complete. If your system has overloaded the I/O subsystem and each I/O operation is taking 40 ms, the time to complete this query will increase to more than 11 hours.

As you can see, SQL Server performance can be severely degraded by a poorly sized or poorly configured I/O subsystem. By designing your I/O subsystem to work within the capacity of the individual components, you will find that your system's performance will be optimal.

Planning the SQL Server Disk Layout

As you have seen earlier in this chapter, you should configure your I/O system properly in order to avoid overloading it. Overloading the I/O subsystem will cause the I/O latency to increase and degrade SQL Server performance. In this section, you will learn how to build a SQL Server system that can perform within the limitations of your subsystem. The first part of this configuration exercise shows you how to determine the I/O requirements of your system. Then you will plan your system, and finally you will create your system.

Determine I/O Requirements

Determining the I/O requirements of a system that exists only as a concept can be difficult, if not impossible. However, if you can't determine the I/O requirements from hard data, you might be able to gather enough data to make an educated guess. In either case, building an I/O subsystem that cannot expand is not a good idea. Always leave some room for required increases in capacity and performance because sooner or later you will need them.

You should design your system to meet a set of minimum requirements based on the amount of space that you need for data storage and on the level of performance you need. In the next sections, you will see how to determine how many disks these factors require.

Space

The process of determining how much space your database requires is fairly straightforward. The amount of space is equal to the sum of the following:

- Space required for data
- Space required for indexes
- Space required for temporary data
- Space required for the transaction log

The space required for data must include enough space to handle data that is added to your database. Your business and your customers will dictate, to a large degree, the amount your database will grow. To determine what your system's growth rate is, you can check your existing database on a regular basis and calculate the size differences in the amount of space used in the database. This growth rate should be calculated over several months in order to determine trends. You might be surprised by the rate at which your data is growing.

In a system without any history, you can estimate the amount of growth by taking the number of product orders, among other things, and multiplying that by the estimated row size. Doing this for several periods (perhaps months or years) will give you a rough idea of the rate at which the data files will grow. This will not tell you how much your indexes will grow. The amount of index space per data row depends on how the index is constructed and on the amount of data. A complex index takes more space per row of data than a simple index. It is then up to you to determine whether your system should be able to handle growth for two years, five years, or longer. This will allow you to determine how to configure your I/O subsystem for space.

Once you have determined the amount of data in the database, the size of the indexes, the amount of temporary database space required, and the rate of growth, you can determine how much disk space is required. You must then take into account the effects of using RAID fault tolerance. Remember, RAID 1 or RAID 10 (data mirroring) takes up half the disk space of the physical disk drives. RAID 5 takes up the disk space of one disk of the array. Also, remember that the disk size that the manufacturer provides is unformatted space. An un-formatted disk drive that is labeled as a 9.1-GB disk is actually an 8.6-GB disk when formatted.

So once you have calculated the amount of space currently required as well as the amount of growth space required, you must then move to the next step: performance. It is necessary to calculate both space and performance requirements and configure your I/O subsystem accordingly.

Performance

It is not sufficient to simply configure your system to meet the space requirements. As you have seen throughout this chapter, how you configure the I/O subsystem can severely degrade or significantly enhance the performance of your system. However, determining the performance requirements of your I/O subsystem is not nearly as easy as determining the space requirements.

The best way to determine performance requirements is to look at a similar application or system. This data can give you a starting point to use in estimating future requirements. You will learn much more about this in Chapter 6. Assuming that you find a similar system, you can then use data that was gathered from that system and the information given earlier in this chapter to determine the number of disk drives required. Remember to take into account the RAID level that will be used on that I/O subsystem. The next steps are to plan the SQL Server disk layout and then to implement the solution.

Plan the Disk Layout

Planning the layout involves determining where the data will be positioned and then creating SQL scripts to create the database. The advantage of creating databases with SQL scripts, rather than through SQL Server Enterprise Manager, is that you can reuse a script, modifying it if necessary.

The script should take into account the number of logical volumes that your system has, as well as the number of physical disks in those volumes. It is important to balance the database so that each disk drive will handle roughly the same number of I/O operations per second. An unbalanced system will suffer the performance experienced by the slowest volume. You should make sure that the transaction log and the data files are distributed across the disk drives in a way that supports optimal performance.

Planning the Log

The process of planning where to put the transaction log is fairly simple. Using only one data file for the transaction log is often the best approach. If you must add more log files to the database, be sure that they are placed on a RAID 1 or RAID 10 volume. Also, be sure to isolate the transaction log from data or other transaction logs.

Planning the Data Files

The easiest way to configure the I/O subsystem for the data files is to configure each volume with a similar number of similarly sized disk drives. In many cases, you don't need to split the I/O subsystem into multiple volumes. In fact, you might be perfectly happy with one logical volume that spans the entire controller. However, you shouldn't use Windows 2000 striping to span multiple controllers because it adds too much overhead.

> **Tip** For your data files, span as many disk drives per controller as you can. This will allow the controller to distribute the data among multiple disks. Do not use Windows 2000 striping to span multiple controllers. This incurs too much CPU overhead.

If you use multiple controllers, you should simplify the configuration by using similar striping with the same number of disk drives on each controller. If you can't use the same number of disk drives on each of your controllers, you can use proportional filling to properly populate the database.

For example, if you use two volumes, one with 20 disk drives and the other with 10 disk drives, you should create a filegroup with two data files. (You will learn more about using files and filegroups in Chapter 9.) The first data file should go on the 20-disk volume and be twice as big as the data file on the 10-disk volume. As data is loaded, SQL Server will load twice as much data into the first data file as it loads into the second data file. This should keep the I/O load per disk drive approximately the same.

Implement the Configuration

Once you have developed your SQL scripts to create the database, it is necessary only to run them and to view the result. If you made a mistake and the database was not created as planned, now is the time to fix it, not after the data has been loaded and users are accessing the system. The use of SQL scripts allows you to modify the scripts and to run them again and again as necessary. An example of a script that uses multiple files within a filegroup to spread the database among several controllers is shown here.

```
--
-- SQL script to create a database over several files
-- d:, e:, and f: for data. e: and f: have twice the number
-- of disk drives as d:, so they get allocated twice the
-- database size as d:. l: is used for the log.
--

CREATE DATABASE demo
ON
PRIMARY ( NAME = demo1,
   FILENAME = 'd:\data\demo_dat1.mdf',
   SIZE = 100MB,
   MAXSIZE = 200,
   FILEGROWTH = 20),
( NAME = demo2,
   FILENAME = 'e:\data\demo_dat2.ndf',
   SIZE = 200MB,
   MAXSIZE = 200,
   FILEGROWTH = 20),
( NAME = demo3,
   FILENAME = 'f:\data\demo_dat3.ndf',
   SIZE = 200MB,
   MAXSIZE = 200,
   FILEGROWTH = 20)
LOG ON
( NAME = demolog1,
   FILENAME = 'l:\data\demo_log1.ldf',
   SIZE = 100MB,
   MAXSIZE = 200,
   FILEGROWTH = 20)
GO
```

The information in this chapter, especially in this section, should help you to create an optimal I/O subsystem for your SQL Server system. The next section contains several tips and recommendations to help you with both creating and fixing subsystems.

I/O Subsystem Tips and Recommendations

This section presents tips and recommendations for how you can best utilize RAID controllers in your system. Some of these tips and recommendations have been mentioned earlier, and some are new. Ideally, some of them will help you to better configure and utilize your RAID array. By following these guidelines and carefully monitoring your system, you should be able to avoid performance problems.

- Isolate the SQL Server transaction log onto its own RAID 1 or RAID 10 volume. I/O operations to the transaction log are almost 100 percent sequential and almost 100 percent writes. The only time the transaction log handles random I/O is during a rollback operation. If the data needed for a rollback is no longer cached, the information must be read from the transaction log.

- Configure enough drives to keep the data file volumes at fewer than 85 I/O operations per second per disk. You can accomplish this by simply adding more disk drives to the array until you have enough. If the I/O operations are random, which they usually are, they will spread out among all of the disk drives in the array.

- Configure data file volumes as RAID 5 if writes are less than 10 percent and as RAID 10 if writes are greater than 10 percent of the total I/O operations.

- Regularly monitor the number of I/O operations per second per disk. If the disks approach their limits, add more disk drives.

- Spread controllers out among the available PCI slots in your system. Don't double up on a PCI bus unless you need to.

- Use Windows 2000 RAID only in systems where CPU time is plentiful. Software RAID produces a fair amount of overhead, which can slow down a system that is short on CPU cycles.

Summary

As you have seen in this chapter, the I/O subsystem is an extremely important component of your database system. You have learned how a disk drive works and what its limitations are. By knowing the limits of the disk drive, you can configure your system to work within those limits. By knowing the characteristics of the RAID levels, you can now configure your system to take advantage of those characteristics. When designing your system, you must carefully size and tune the I/O subsystem. I/O tuning is all about capacity. By working within the capacity of the various components, you can achieve optimal system performance.

Chapter 6
Capacity Planning

Capacity planning involves figuring out the resources your system requires and deciding how to maximize the productivity of those resources. It also involves planning for the growth of your network to make future hardware and software additions less disruptive and less costly. In this chapter, you'll learn the basics of this important step in creating your system.

Types of Capacity Planning

Capacity planning comes in two forms: pre-capacity planning and post-capacity planning. *Pre-capacity planning,* or *sizing,* involves anticipating the hardware requirements necessary to process your workload within a specified time, as spelled out in the Service Level Agreements (SLA). SLAs are set up to ensure that the response times (the time it takes for an activity or transaction to complete) of certain functions are maintained.

> **Note** An SLA is a condition of operation agreed upon by all organizations involved with the system in question, developed to ensure high performance and smooth operation of the system. For example, an SLA might be developed to ensure that the system meets a certain response time for a query. This response time is agreed upon by the users, the operations group, the applications group, and the performance group.

Also, a certain amount of reserve capacity (space allocated for CPU processing power, space available on a disk drive, or available memory) is set aside to maintain the response times of these activities under steady state operation and peak load conditions. In pre-capacity planning, there is no real performance data to work with because the system is not yet functioning. You must use whatever other information is available. The results will vary depending on the accuracy of this information. For example, the database group that is designing the system can provide details about the database layout and the initial size. The applications group that is designing the application and the various queries that are associated with the application can provide information about how these queries will use system resources. The management group will have information about the number of concurrent users and the number of queries they will put through the system. All this information will give details as to the workload (so you can guess at the number of CPUs), the database size (so you will know how many disk drives you will need), and so on.

Post-capacity planning, or *predictive analysis,* is a complex and ongoing study of hardware and software resource consumption on a system that is already set up and running. Post-capacity planning ensures adequate preparation for workload growth in relation to system resources. These studies are primarily established to provide data to the database administrator (DBA). The DBA uses this data to justify system alterations designed to maintain the level of system performance defined in the SLA. In this chapter, we will look at the two kinds of capacity planning—post-capacity planning and pre-capacity planning—and examine their similarities and differences.

In a typical post-capacity planning scenario, you perform the analysis using historical performance data stored in a database. Through this analysis, you can project trends in the normal growth of CPU utilization (the amount of time a CPU is busy during an observation period), disk usage, memory usage, and network usage. You will also be able to project sudden rises in CPU, disk, and memory utilization caused by the addition of new users to the system. These studies can be extremely detailed and can involve profiling the activities of specific users, enabling you to project rises in system utilization due to the addition of users.

Post-capacity planning studies offer other highly useful features in addition to predictive analysis, including the ability to project "what if" scenarios on workloads. Armed with data regarding how resources are used by the various types of users, you can also add specific types of users to the system workload scenario (such as accounts payable personnel) to predict exactly what kind of resource consumption would take place. This predictive analysis gives the system manager ample time to obtain the necessary hardware before the new users are added to the system, thus averting any degradation of system performance or response time.

Tuning information can also be obtained through post-capacity planning studies. Tuning information, such as information about disk I/Os going to the drive arrays that process queries, is derived from historic performance data and can be used to determine changes in the system configuration that are needed to increase performance. This information can show bottlenecks in performance such as too much activity to one drive array over another. For example, adding users will result in more database table accesses. The number of tables users access and how often they access them can be monitored and tracked. This information can be useful in determining whether the relocation of some of these tables will prevent a potential bottleneck in the disk subsystem.

History of Capacity Planning

In the early years of multiple-user computers, the concepts of capacity planning and performance were not widely understood or developed. By the early 1970s, a sizing project simply involved finding customers who were running an application that "ran like" the target customer application. Finding these customers was difficult, and matching companies or organizations and their application use was even more challenging.

In the mid-1970s, customers and application suppliers developed an analysis methodology, running a specific benchmark or workload to guess at the optimal initial size of a machine. They built an application similar to that of the customers in question and ran it on similar hardware to gather performance statistics. These statistics were then used to determine the best-size machine to meet the customer's needs. This process also enabled "what if" scenarios to be run with the benchmark to determine what size machine would be required if more users, application processes, or data were added to the system. The one drawback to this process was that it was expensive. These early benchmarks, originally developed to simulate customers' usage patterns, began to be used mostly by system vendors as marketing tools, to sell systems and to compare the relative performance of competing hardware offerings.

During this period, analysts were developing methods of predicting usage on an existing system. On the surface, this process seemed less challenging, but it proved to be just as difficult because tested methodologies did not exist, nor were there tools available to collect the necessary data. Computer scientists such as Dr. Jeffrey Buzen, the father of capacity planning, were still developing theories on usage and determining how to perform these calculations.

By the 1980s, the early benchmark simulations had evolved into standard benchmark loads, such as the ST1 benchmark, the TP1 benchmark, and the Debit/Credit benchmark, but the emphasis was on finding the fastest performing hardware for promotional usage instead of on developing a standard application workload that could be used to size and maintain systems. Customers still could not use these benchmark offerings for system hardware comparisons because their situations were all different. Customer demand led to the formation of a computer industry consortium, the Transaction Processing Performance Council. The council specified standardized transaction loads for over 45 hardware and software manufacturers. These benchmarks could often show relative capabilities of hardware and database software; unfortunately, they were not useful for sizing an application workload.

Note The council benchmarks were not useful for sizing because they did not reflect a real workload; more often they were designed to show performance, such as how many transactions were going through the system at a given time. The transactions were of short duration and did very little work, so very large quantities of them could be processed. These large quantities of processed transactions would give the impression that the systems these benchmarks were running on were very powerful, when in reality they only seemed that way because of the workload design.

At the same time, client/server computing and the use of relational database technology was maturing, and the need for predicting the initial size of a system and for capacity planning was growing. Most modern applications are now written based on client/server architecture. Servers are usually used as central data storage devices, and the user interface is usually run locally on a desktop machine or on a remote Web site. This cost-effective strategy for using expensive server processing power takes advantage of the GUIs with which customers are already accustomed. With heavy utilization of the servers running database applications, these servers are now the focus for most sizing projects and capacity planning studies.

To date, the application simulation benchmark remains the most common method used for sizing servers, and collecting historical performance data and using capacity planning techniques on this data is still the most accurate way of predicting the future capacity of a machine. Although the process is expensive and time-consuming, customers can achieve a fairly significant degree of accuracy if they simulate the exact usage of the server. However, because large projects may require a multimillion-dollar investment on the part of the customer or the vendor, only the largest customers can usually gain access to systems for this kind of testing. Clearly a method is required to perform in-depth, accurate system sizing and capacity planning for small to average-size systems. For such systems, some easy calculations and a general knowledge of system usage are all you need to be able to size and predict usage to 90 percent accuracy.

Transaction Processing

In this section, we'll look at how to analyze the CPU, memory, and disk usage trends of a database server in order to select the proper system for a given application. A database server performs only database functions; in terms of its workload, the server performs only transactions. When a SELECT or UPDATE statement is executed, the database server interprets the statement as a series of read and write operations. In fact, any transaction can be broken down into database reads and writes. At this atomic level, a database server processes I/Os. We should select a system that can handle both the type and volume of transactions and the I/Os those transactions will generate. The two main transaction types are Online Transaction Processing (OLTP) and Decision Support System (DSS).

OLTP Transactions

An OLTP transaction is a workload unit that is usually expected to run in a short period of time because it deals with the database in real time or in online mode. In other words, these transactions will update the database constantly, based on the most current information available, so that the next user can rely on that information being the most current. For example, in an order entry system, all the information pertaining to inventory is kept in tables spread across a disk system, and the database is on line. Any user has access to the database information. Database tables such as *Item_Table* or *Stock_Level_Table* contain the most current information about the types and quantity of the items that are sold. That way, when an order for a certain quantity of a specific item is received, you can access the database tables to determine whether the item is available and the quantity of the item in stock, to prevent overselling of an item.

A typical sizing scenario for a transaction processing system such as this involves conducting an interview to gather specific information. During the interview, you might talk to the database designer, the application designer, and the management staff representative. They could provide input and feedback on the expected number of transactions to be processed and the time of day during which the transactions will be expected to be processed (for example, 25,000 transactions should be processed within the 8-hour workday), the number of concurrent users, and the peak operation period (or peak utilization period)—the period in a processing day in which the system is most stressed. The interview is probably the most important part of the sizing process.

Note When you are designing an OLTP system, choose hardware with enough transaction processing capacity to accommodate the peak utilization period. That way you are automatically accommodating the worst-case scenario.

Real World Automated Teller Machines

Let's look at the example of an automated teller machine (ATM) system. Say you've been hired by a national bank to design an ATM system for their Chicago branch. In the interview, you might discover that the peak utilization period for a network of ATMs is between the hours of 11:00 AM and 2:00 PM—coincidentally, the time range when most people go to lunch. With this information, you can choose a transaction processing system with enough capacity to accommodate this peak utilization period.

DSS Transactions

The second type of transaction system is DSS. DSS transactions involve large returns of information and take much longer to process than OLTP transactions. A DSS transaction can take hours, or even days, to process. An example of a DSS system is an inventory archive system, in which little writing to the database occurs except when an update is taking place. These systems usually provide information to management staff so that they can make important decisions—concerning, for example, business growth or levels of stock on hand. As another example, the U.S. Air Force uses a DSS system to inform high-level personnel about the current status, location, and weaponry of its jet fighters, bombers, and personnel.

As mentioned, a DSS transaction is usually not completed in the same time frame as an OLTP transaction—DSS transactions take much longer to process because of the amount of data they gather. Whereas an OLTP transaction will gather the data required by a unique key (such as a customer number), it starts and ends the query with only the information pertaining to that key. In DSS, the query does not start with a unique key; instead, it starts at the beginning of the database table and continues through all the data to the end of the table. A DSS transaction will also include any table joins, linking to other tables to get further information.

Note When you are designing a DSS system, choose large data block sizes so that more records will fit per I/O transfer, causing less I/O activity.

In this type of system, the performance analyst will expect to see the utilization of CPUs and other system resources at nearly 100 percent, so the concern is not what utilization the system is running at, but how long the system will take to process the query. A rule of thumb for designing a DSS system is to throw as much hardware at it as is reasonable. In other words, don't just have enough disks on hand to handle the space needed for the database, but plan to lay out the database across multiple volumes in order to disperse the I/O activity. Memory is not really a consideration here because there will not be much cache activity. (DSS transactions involve full table scans, which means they start at the top of the table and work their way down.)

Real World   Quarterly Sales
Suppose you are compiling quarterly sales figures for a corporate report. You need to gather information pertaining to the sales of items during that quarter within all regions that the sales organization covers. This search involves first linking to the beginning of the *region* table to get to the first *customer* table. After the first customer name is retrieved, a link to the *customer order* table is established to determine what items were ordered during this time period. The search continues with the second customer name, then the third, and so on. After all the data for the customers for that region is scanned, the next *customer* table (by region) is retrieved and the process continues. This processing usually takes many hours to complete.

Principles of Capacity Planning

When you cannot define the peak utilization period, pre-capacity planning is usually accomplished by estimating the transaction activity expected during steady state processing.

Note   "Steady state" refers to the expected utilization of CPU during the course of your working day. For example, if you expect a CPU utilization of 55 percent during the course of the day, that is steady state. If during that same day, your system experiences a utilization of 90 percent for one hour, that is the peak utilization period.

Once you know the maximum number of transactions you expect to complete in a processing day and the length of your processing day, you can calculate the average number of transactions per unit of time. However, since you don't know the actual rate at which the transactions will occur, you should size your system with a built-in reserve capacity. *Reserve capacity* refers to a certain portion of system processing power left in reserve to accommodate the more stressed workload periods.

Post-capacity planning on an order entry system involves the constant monitoring of key performance counters to record what the system has done in the past and what it is doing currently. This information is usually stored in a database and is used in general reporting of the performance, capacity consumption, and available reserve capacity. A database application such as Microsoft Excel can be used to generate graphs, spreadsheets, and transaction activity reports, which can be used to predict the machine's resource use.

CPU Utilization

Another reason to build and maintain a machine with reserve capacity relates to the "knee of the curve" theory. Simply stated, this theory predicts that utilization has a direct effect on queues, and because queue lengths are directly related to response time (in fact, queue length is part of the response time equation), utilization has a direct effect on response time. The knee of the curve is the point at

Real World   Utilization and Response Times at the Supermarket

Say you go to the supermarket at 3:00 AM, pick up the items you need, and carry them to the checkout counter. At this time in the morning, no one is in line in front of you, so the utilization of that cashier is 0 percent and the queue length (number of people in front of you) is also 0. Your response time will be equal to your service time. This means that your service time—in this case, the time it takes to complete the transaction of tallying your purchases and paying the bill—is all the time it will take to complete this task.

Imagine the same scenario at 5:00 PM, a much busier time for a supermarket. Now when you arrive at the checkout counter, eight people are in line in front of you (that is, the queue length is 8). Your response time now is equal to the sum of the individual service times for all eight people ahead of you (which will vary depending on the number of items they are purchasing, whether they are paying by check or with cash, and so on), plus your own service time. The utilization of the cashier is also much higher at 5:00 PM than at 3:00 AM, which has a direct effect on the length of the queue and therefore on your overall response time.

which factors like response time and queue length switch from linear growth to exponential growth or the point at which they begin growing asymptotically (to infinity).

Linear Growth vs. Exponential Growth

Normally, we try to keep a system running linearly—that is, so that the growth of the queue will be linear. As illustrated in Figure 6-1, *linear growth* is the even, incremental growth of queues in relation to utilization growth. The rule of thumb is that as long as CPU utilization remains below 75 percent, queue growth will remain linear.

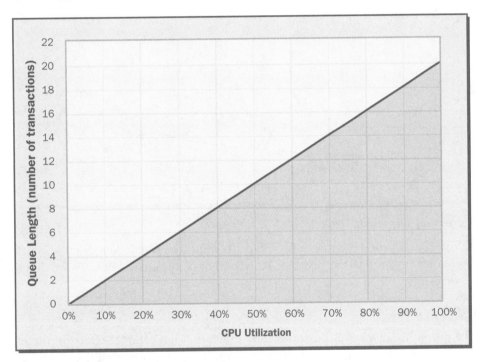

Figure 6-1. *Linear growth of CPU utilization.*

Sometimes, however, a CPU is utilized in a steady state of above 75 percent. This scenario has certain drawbacks—in particular, this high utilization causes exponential growth of queue lengths. *Exponential growth* is geometrically increasing growth, as shown in Figure 6-2.

Note For the figures in this chapter, the service time of a transaction has been set to 0.52 second, and every transaction is assumed to have the same service time.

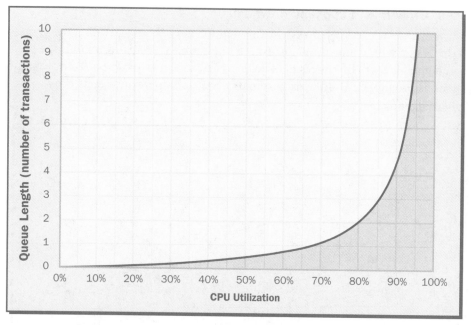

Figure 6-2. *Exponential growth of CPU utilization.*

Notice that at about 75 percent CPU utilization, the queue length curve shifts from linear growth to exponential growth (that is, the curve becomes an almost vertical line).

Response Time

The graph in Figure 6-3 illustrates how utilization has a direct effect on the response times. Notice that similar curves occur in the response time graph and the queue length graph. The dramatic increase in response times shown in both graphs demonstrates why you never want to run your CPUs in a steady state of over 75 percent utilization. This is not to say that you can never run your CPUs above 75 percent, but the longer you do so, the more negative impact you will experience in terms of queue length and response time. Not exceeding the knee of the curve—in this case, 75 percent utilization—is one of the most important principles of sizing and should be considered when you are determining the number of CPUs your sys-tem will require. For example, suppose you are sizing a system that you calculate will produce an anticipated total processor utilization factor of 180 per-cent. You could endure the horrendous performance of such a system, or you could run two CPUs at 90 percent utilization—15 percentage points above the knee of the curve. It would be better, however, to run three CPUs at about 60 percent, keeping the utilization 15 percentage points below the knee of the curve.

This principle also applies to other elements of your system, such as disks. Disks do not have the same knee of the curve as processors do—the knee of the curve for disks tends to occur at 85 percent utilization. This 85 percent threshold ap-plies to both the size and I/O capability of the disk drive. For example, a 9-GB disk should not contain more than 7.65 GB of data stored at any given time. This data limit will allow for growth, but more important it will help keep down re-sponse time because a disk at full capacity will have longer seek times, adding to the overall response time. By the same principle, if a disk drive has an I/O capa-bility of 70 I/Os per second, you would not want to have a constant I/O arrival

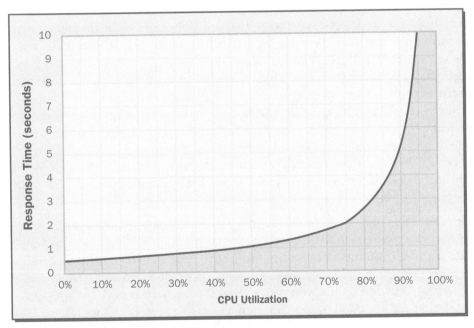

Figure 6-3. *Response time vs. CPU utilization.*

rate of more than 60 I/Os per second in a steady state of operation. By following this principle, you can minimize your overall response times and get the most out of your system because you will not be using your processors or disks at maximum utilization. Your system will also retain a reserve capacity for peak utilization periods.

Note Remember that for optimal performance, keep your CPU utilization below 75 percent and your disk utilization below 85 percent.

Page Faulting

Not exceeding the knee of the curve is an important principle for sizing processors and disks, but what about memory? To help size memory, we use the principle of page faulting. Page faults are a normal system function and are used to retrieve data from the disk. If the system needs a certain code or data page and that page exists in memory, a logical I/O event occurs, meaning that the code or data is read from memory and the transaction that needed the code or data is processed.

But what if the needed code or data page is not in memory? In that case, we must perform a physical I/O to read the needed page from the disk. This task is accomplished via page faulting. The system will issue a page fault interrupt when a needed code or data page is not in its working set in main memory. The page fault instructs another part of the system to retrieve the code or data from the physical disk—in other words, if the code or data page your system is seeking is not in memory, the system will issue a page fault to instruct another part of the system to perform a physical I/O and go to the disk to retrieve it. A page fault will not cause the page to be retrieved from the disk if that page is on the standby list, and hence already in main memory, or if it is in use by another process with which the page is shared.

There are two types of physical I/Os: user and system. A *user physical I/O* occurs when a user transaction asks to read data that is not found in memory. A simple data transfer from the disk to memory occurs. This transfer is usually handled by some sort of data flow manager combined with disk controller functions. A *system physical I/O* occurs when the system requires a code page for a process it is running and the code page is not in memory. The system issues a page fault interrupt, which prevents processing until the required data has been retrieved from disk. After this retrieval, processing continues. Both physical I/O conditions will prolong response time because the retrieval time for data found in memory is rated in microseconds (millionths of seconds) whereas physical I/Os are rated in milliseconds (thousandths of seconds). Since page fault activities cause physical I/Os, which prolong response time, we will achieve better system performance by minimizing page faults.

Three types of page faults can occur in your system:

Operating system page faults   If the system is executing operating system code and the next code address is not in memory, the system will issue an operating system page fault interrupt to retrieve the next code address from the disk. For a code address fault, the transfer of the code data goes from the disk to memory, requiring a single physical I/O to complete.

Application code page faults   If the system is executing any other code and the next code page is not in memory, the system will issue a page fault interrupt to retrieve the next code page from the disk. For these page faults, the transfer of the code data goes from the disk to memory, requiring a single physical I/O to complete.

Page fault swap   In the case of a data page that has been modified (known as a "dirty" page), a two-step page fault known as a *page fault swap* is used, causing the system not only to retrieve the new data from the disk, but also to write the current data in memory out to the disk. This two-step page fault requires two physical I/Os to complete, but it will ensure that any changed data is saved. If swapping occurs often enough, it can be the single most damaging factor in response time. Remember that page fault transfers occur in whole pages, even if only a few bytes are actually needed. Page fault swaps take more time than page faults because they incur twice as many physical I/Os. For this reason, you should minimize the number of page fault swaps in your system.

When you are estimating the minimum memory requirement for a new system, always try to anticipate the total memory that you will need to process the workload by finding the memory specifications of all processes (including the operating system and database engines) that will run on your system. And don't forget about page faults. To maintain a system's memory, information about page fault activity should be collected and stored as part of the performance database. Predictive analysis should be performed on this data to project when you will require additional memory. A comfortable margin of available memory should be maintained for peak usage. When you are planning a system, try to maintain 5 to 10 percent additional memory over what is required for the processes that will be running.

Note   You cannot remove all page faulting from your system, but you can minimize it. You should add memory when you experience more than two page faults per second. Performance monitors (such as the counter for page faults per second) are described in the following section.

Capacity Planning for Memory

When considering the adequate capacity planning of memory, you need certain pieces of information, including the number of concurrent users that will be on the system, the transaction workload type, and of course the operating system type. In sizing, you would typically start by conducting an interview. In this case, we are sizing a database server, so information pertaining to the memory usage and client application utilization do not affect database server size. You might decide against interviewing the application designer, but that would be a mistake.

The database server processes requests from users for information needed to complete transactions. To size a database server's memory, you need to know the number of concurrent user connections and the number of transaction I/Os that will be generated by those users. These I/Os are in the form of read and write operations. The application designer is necessary during the interview to provide information pertaining to the various transactions and the I/Os they will generate.

When calculating the proper amount of memory for your system, you must also take into account things like desirable cache hit rate and page faulting. Consider the following typical scenario: You are involved in sizing a system for a database server that will be used for an OLTP order entry system and need to know the number of concurrent users that will be generating the workload. This piece of information will help you decide the amount of memory that you will need. For example, you know that 50 concurrent users will be on the system at any given time. For this system, you will need 25 MB of memory just for the users.

Note   Generally, you should allow 500 KB of memory for each user because 500 KB is what the shadow process needs. The *shadow process* is the user process that is present for each user on the system.

Next you need to know the operating system that will be used. In this case, the operating system is Microsoft Windows 2000, which uses about 20 MB of memory. This brings your total memory up to 45 MB so far. You also need to know the size of the database executable that you are going to use—in this case, Microsoft SQL Server, which uses 5.5 MB. The total memory required is now 50.5 MB.

The final piece of information you need is the size of the database processing area. This area consists of two elements: the log area and the database cache. The log area holds the information about write activity that is taking place. This area is extremely important because if a system failure occurs during the processing of a transaction, the information held in the log area will be used to restore the "before" image—the image of the database before the failure occurred. The log area is also referred to as the audit trail.

The database cache is a special area of your system. All the data processed by your system will pass through this area. The larger the database cache, the greater your cache hit rate. The cache hit rate is the rate at which your system finds the data it is looking for in memory—obviously, you want the greatest cache hit rate you can get. If the desired information is not resident in cache memory, a cache fault occurs. A cache fault is similar to a page fault in that the desired information must be retrieved by the system and put in cache memory. So, a cache area that is too small will cause physical I/Os to occur because the system must access the disk to retrieve data not present in the cache. These physical I/Os will of course increase the response time of the transaction.

To calculate cache size, use the following formula:

cache size = (cache block size) * (number of blocks in cache)

The *cache block size* is the amount of data that will be transferred per I/O. Remember that SQL Server has a preset cache block size of 8 KB. The *number of blocks in cache* is simply how many blocks you want the cache to hold. In OLTP, choose a smaller block size because the transfer will be small and the smaller the block size, the less time the transfer will take. In DSS transfers, the block size should be much larger because the transfer will be much larger and the larger block size will reduce the number of I/Os.

Note   No set cache size can guarantee a 90 percent or better cache hit rate. A good rule of thumb is a cache size of about 25 MB for a small system, 70 MB for a medium system, and 215 MB for a large system. Systems with very large databases (around 300 GB) can require as much as 3 GB of cache to achieve a desired cache hit rate.

From the information we've collected so far, we can calculate the minimum amount of memory we should require. The following formula is commonly used for calculating the minimum memory required by a system:

minimum memory =(system memory) + (user memory) +
(database process memory)

Here *system memory* is the amount of memory required by the operating system and SQL Server, *user memory* is the 500 KB allotted for each concurrent user, and *database process memory* is the memory needed by the log and cache.

This relatively simple equation can be used for calculating the minimum memory required for normal operation of both OLTP and DSS applications. With a DSS system, we would select a larger block size because a DSS application performs full table scans in sequential read mode. This capability allows more records to be read per physical I/O. Also with DSS systems, cache will not be used because all the I/Os will be physical.

In an OLTP application system, you should check the cache hit rate when the system is installed. A high cache hit rate will help ensure that your system will have the best possible response time and performance.

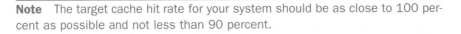

Note The target cache hit rate for your system should be as close to 100 percent as possible and not less than 90 percent.

Collecting Memory Usage Data

When a sized system is configured and tuned, you should routinely collect performance data for memory usage. You can use this data to help ensure that the system you have created meets the SLA requirements for items such as response times and memory or CPU utilization. This data collection can be done simply by using Microsoft Performance Monitor for the Microsoft Windows NT environment.

Note Microsoft Performance Monitor is called System Monitor in Microsoft Windows 2000.

Remember that this is a capacity planning analysis and therefore should have a large reporting interval. The duration of the measurement should be in hours—in most cases, 24 hours—and the reporting interval should be set to 24 hours as well. One record per day written to the performance database is adequate for capacity planning studies. The performance criteria, called *counters,* that you select for monitoring will be averaged over the reporting interval period. The memory counters you can select for your capacity planning studies are contained in the *Memory* object. (In Performance Monitor, an object is a selection of counters.)

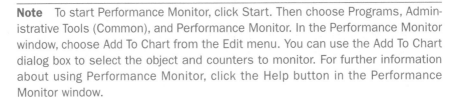

Note To start Performance Monitor, click Start. Then choose Programs, Administrative Tools (Common), and Performance Monitor. In the Performance Monitor window, choose Add To Chart from the Edit menu. You can use the Add To Chart dialog box to select the object and counters to monitor. For further information about using Performance Monitor, click the Help button in the Performance Monitor window.

These counters include the following:

- **Page Faults/sec** This counter contains the average number of page faults that occur in the system per second. Remember that a page fault occurs when a requested code or data page is not in working or standby memory.

- **Cache Faults/sec** This counter contains the average number of cache faults that occur in the system per second. Remember that cache faults occur whenever the Cache Manager does not find a file's page in the immediate cache.

- **Pages/sec** This counter contains the average number of pages read from the disk or written to the disk by the system per second. This value is the sum of two other counters—Pages Input/sec and Pages Output/sec. The count includes paging traffic on behalf of the system cache to access file data for applications and pages read to and from noncached mapped memory files. Use this counter if you are concerned about excessive memory pressure (also known as *thrashing*) and the excessive paging that may result.

- **Available Memory** This counter indicates the amount of unused memory remaining in the system. This memory can be used as additional memory for database or system usage. Available Memory is the most important counter for memory planning.

> **Note** The Available Memory counter is not part of Performance Monitor. It can be retrieved from the Task Manager by selecting the Performance tab and observing the available memory during the peak utilization period. (To access the Task Manager, right-click on the taskbar and select Task Manager from the context menu.)

At a minimum, you should select Available Memory and Page Faults/sec as part of an overall capacity planning data collection process.

Analyzing Memory Data

Once your data has been collected, the information can be graphed to predict the future. The graph in Figure 6-4 illustrates predictive analysis. In this example, data has been collected for available memory from October 22, 1999,

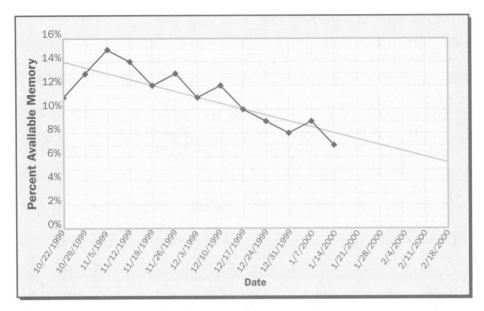

Figure 6-4. *Linear memory predictive analysis.*

through January 14, 2000. Using Microsoft Excel, this data was graphed and a trend line calculated. The jagged line represents the actual usage history; the straight line indicates the linear trend this usage is taking. As you can see, the analysis predicts that by February 18, 2000, this system will have less than 6 percent available memory.

The graph in Figure 6-5 illustrates the increase of page faults for the same period and also the increase that will likely occur as the available memory decreases. Notice that data has been collected for page faults per second for the same time period as available memory. Again using Microsoft Excel, this data was recorded and then graphed, and again the jagged line represents the actual usage history and the straight line indicates the linear trend this usage is taking. In this case, the graph predicts that by February 18, 2000, this system will have over 6 page faults per second. This value serves as an indicator that by that date, response times in general will probably be increasing as well, an indication that the SLA for response times might be violated. This method of predictive analysis is a simple and effective way of keeping track of your memory resources.

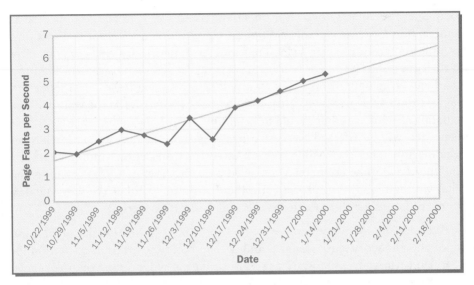

Figure 6-5. *Linear page fault predictive analysis.*

Capacity Planning for the Processor

Now that we have sized and analyzed the memory, it's time to do the same for the processor. At this point, we can make the following assumptions about the system:

- The application and database design schema is complete.
- The target steady state CPU utilization is less than 75 percent.
- Expected cache hit rate is at least 90 percent.
- No disk drive will exceed 85 percent usage of space or I/O activity.
- The server is running only a database.
- Distribution of disk I/Os is even across all drives.

We've made use of these assumptions as guidelines and thresholds for sizing memory, but for anticipating capacity for the CPU, we need additional information. This information can be provided by the database designer and the application designer.

Anticipating the capacity of a CPU on a database server is not as complicated as you might think. Remember that a database server is only processing transactions. The application is running on a client machine, so application sizing does not enter into the equation. The server will be processing requests from users in the form of read and write operations—that is, it will be processing I/Os. The application designer can provide pertinent information about the nature of the transactions. The database designer can provide information pertaining to the tables and their indexes that will be affected by these transactions. So the task at hand will be to determine how many I/Os will be generated by the transactions and in what time frame they have to be completed. We need to know how many transactions the system will be required to process and the definition of either the working day in terms of hours for this system or the peak utilization period.

As we've seen, it's always preferable to size for the peak utilization period because it represents the worst-case scenario and we can build the machine to accommodate it. Unfortunately, in most cases this information will not be available, so we are forced to use the information we have pertaining to steady state. To gain a deeper understanding of the transactions that we will be processing, we need access to the transaction anatomy, or profile, which will help us determine the numbers of reads and writes (I/Os) that will be generated and enable us to calculate the anticipated CPU utilization. We get this information from our interview with the database designers and the application designers. First we need to know how many transactions of each type will go through the system, and then we need to determine the number of I/Os that will be generated. This calculation will provide an estimate of the CPU workload.

For an existing system, the user can profile transactions by running each of the transactions one at a time and tracking them using Performance Monitor to determine the number of I/Os generated. This "real" information can be used to adjust the speed, type, and number of CPUs in use.

So far, we have talked about sizing the CPU in terms of I/Os generated by user transactions. I/Os can also be generated by the fault tolerance equipment that may be in use. These additional I/Os must also be considered when you are sizing the CPU.

Fault Tolerance

Most computer companies today provide fault tolerance through the support of RAID (Redundant Array of Inexpensive Disks) technology. (See Chapter 5 for an in-depth description of RAID technology.) Remember that the most commonly used RAID levels are as follows:

- **RAID 0** Single disk drive
- **RAID 1** Mirrored disk drive
- **RAID 5** Multiple disk drives and data striping

Because RAID 0 requires a single disk, it has a single point of failure—in other words, if the disk drive fails, you will lose the data on that disk drive and therefore the entire database. A RAID 0 array is shown in Figure 4-1. RAID 1 provides a mirror image of the database disk drive. If a disk drive fails, you have a backup data drive complete with all the data that was on the failed disk drive. If you specify RAID 1, users get the added benefit of *split seeks* (covered in Chapter 5), which enable the system to search both drives simultaneously, greatly accelerating search speed and thereby reducing your transaction response time. A RAID 1 array is shown in Figure 4-2.

The choice of RAID level directly affects the number of disk I/Os because different RAID levels alter the number of writes to the disk. For example, RAID 1 requires twice as many writes as RAID 0. If the user describes a transaction as having 50 reads and 10 writes and wants to use RAID 1, the number of writes increases to 20.

If a RAID 0 configuration has two designated disk drives, a comparable RAID 5 configuration would have three disk drives. In a RAID 5 configuration, a parity stripe is used that contains information about the data on the other two drives that can be used to rebuild a failed disk's data. A RAID 5 array is shown in Figure 4-4. This database protection scheme comes with a performance cost as well as a dollar cost. Each write under RAID 5 will add twice the number of reads and twice the number of writes for each transaction processed because each transaction must be written to two disks, and the parity stripe must be read, altered to incorporate the new data, and then written. This redundancy will lengthen the transaction response time slightly.

To calculate the number of I/Os for the various RAID levels, you can use the following equations.

For RAID 0:

number of I/Os = (number of reads per transaction) +
(number of writes per transaction)

If a transaction has 50 reads and 10 writes, the total number of I/Os using RAID 0 is 60.

For RAID 1:

> *number of I/Os = (number of reads per transaction) +*
> *(2 * (number of writes per transaction))*

If a transaction has 50 reads and 10 writes, the total number of I/Os using RAID 1 is 70.

For RAID 5:

> *number of I/Os = 3 * (number of I/Os per transaction)*

If a transaction has 50 reads and 10 writes, the total number of reads would be 150 and the total number of writes would be 30. The total number of I/Os using RAID 5 is therefore 180.

The increase of I/Os is a function of the disk controller and is transparent to the user, who does not need to make adjustments to the application. Remember that your RAID selection directly affects the number of I/Os that will be processed. This increase of reads and writes should be considered, as it will affect the utilization factors of the CPUs and the quantity of disks chosen during sizing.

Once you have calculated the total number of reads and writes due to user transactions and added the additional I/Os due to the RAID levels you have selected, you have all the information you need to calculate the CPU utilization. The following formula is used to determine the CPU utilization of a proposed system:

> *CPU utilization = (throughput) * (service time) * 100*

Here *throughput* is the number of I/Os to be processed per second, and *service time* is the amount of time spent processing a typical I/O transaction. This formula simply states that utilization is the total number of I/Os the system processes per second multiplied by the time it takes to perform each task, multiplied by 100 to get a percentage.

To determine the number of CPUs needed for the system, the following steps should be performed on every transaction that will be processed as part of this workload.

1. Calculate the total number of reads that will be going through the system by using the following formula:

   > *total reads = (reads per transaction) **
   > *(total number of transactions)*

2. Determine how many of these reads will be physical I/Os and how many will be logical I/Os by using the following formulas:

*total logical reads = (total reads) * (cache hit rate)*
total physical reads = (total reads) – (total logical reads)

3. Convert the total number of each read type to reads per second by using the following formulas:

   logical reads/sec = (total logical reads) / (work period)
   physical reads/sec = (total physical reads) / (work period)

   The *work period* should be the length of time, in seconds, in which the work is to be performed.

4. Calculate the amount of CPU time that was used for each of the read functions by using the following formulas:

   *logical read time = (logical reads/sec) * (logical read time)*
   *physical read time = (physical reads/sec) * (physical read time)*

   The *logical read time* is the time it takes to process a logical read. The *physical read time* is the time it takes to process a physical read. These read times can be obtained using Performance Monitor. (See the sidebar "Obtaining Read Times" at the end of this list for directions.)

Note   Typical values for read times are 0.002 second for the physical read time variable and 0.001 second for the logical read time variable.

5. Calculate the CPU utilization for the various read functions using the following equation:

   *utilization = (throughput) * (service time) * 100*

   You can break this down into logical and physical read utilization as follows:

   *logical read utilization = (logical reads/sec) * (logical read time)*
   *physical read utilization = (physical reads/sec) * (physical read time)*

   This information can be used to determine whether there is too much physical read utilization. You can then adjust the cache size so that you will have more logical reads.

6. Calculate the total number of writes that will be going through the system by using the following formula, where the RAID factor is the total number of expected writes that your workload will perform during the processing period:

   *total writes = (writes per transaction) * (total number transactions) *
   (RAID factor increase)*

7. Now find the number of writes per second that will be passing through the system by performing the following calculation:

   writes/sec = (total writes) / (work period)

   Again, the *work period* should be the length of time, in seconds, in which the work is to be performed.

8. Determine the total CPU time that was used to process the writes by performing the following calculation:

   *CPU write time = (writes/sec) * (CPU write time)*

9. Calculate the write utilization by using the following formula:

   *write utilization = (writes/sec) * (CPU write time) * 100*

10. Calculate the total CPU utilization for the transaction type by using the following formula:

    *CPU utilization = ((logical read utilization) + (physical read utilization) + (write utilization)) * 100*

    This calculation must be performed for each type of transaction that your system allows. For example, if you have a banking system, you might allow withdrawals, deposits, and balance inquiries. You must perform these utilization calculations separately for each of these three types of transactions to accurately size the CPUs for your system.

11. Finally, calculate the total processor utilization by using the following formula:

    total CPU utilization = sum of all transaction utilizations

    If the *total CPU utilization* is over the 75 percent threshold, you should add more CPUs to your system. Additional CPUs will reduce the *total CPU utilization* according to the following formula:

    total CPU utilization (>1 CPU) = (total CPU utilization) / (number of CPUs)

    Add enough CPUs to bring the *total CPU utilization* below 75 percent. For example, if *total CPU utilization* is 180 percent, you would use three CPUs. The resulting *total CPU utilization* would then be 60 percent for the three-CPU system.

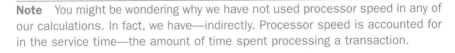

Note You might be wondering why we have not used processor speed in any of our calculations. In fact, we have—indirectly. Processor speed is accounted for in the service time—the amount of time spent processing a transaction.

Obtaining Read Times

You can obtain the read times for your system through Performance Monitor. Turn on Diskperf by entering the following command in an MS-DOS window:

```
diskperf -y
```

Next start Performance Monitor, and look in the *Physical Disk* object for the Avg. Disk sec/Read and Avg. Disk sec/Write counters. Note that these counters give you the average read times for physical reads. Don't worry about these times for logical reads.

Collecting Usage Data for a Single CPU

When your system is implemented, you will need to track CPU usage much as you tracked memory usage. Performance Monitor contains many counters related to individual CPU usage. These counters are contained in the *Processor* object. The following counters will be the most useful for sizing purposes:

- **% Processor Time**   The percentage of the elapsed time that a processor is busy executing instructions. An *instruction* is the basic unit of execution in a computer, a *thread* is the object that executes instructions, and a *process* is the object created when a program is run. This counter can be interpreted as the fraction of time spent doing useful work.

- **% Privileged Time**   Percentage of processor time spent in Privileged mode. The Windows NT service layer, the Executive routines, and the Windows NT Kernel all execute in Privileged mode; device drivers for most devices other than graphics adapters and printers also execute in Privileged mode.

- **% User Time**   Percentage of processor time spent in User mode. All application code and subsystem code executes in User mode. The graphics engine, graphics device drivers, printer device drivers, and the Window Manager also execute in User mode. Code executing in User mode cannot damage the integrity of the Windows NT Executive, Kernel, or device drivers.

- **% Interrupt Time**   Percentage of elapsed time spent by the processor handling hardware interrupts. Interrupts are executed in Privileged mode, so interrupt time is a component of % Privileged Time. This counter can help determine the source of excessive time being spent in Privileged mode.

- **Interrupts/sec** This counter contains the average number of device interrupts the processor experiences per second. A device interrupts the processor when it has completed a task or when it otherwise requires attention. Devices that may generate interrupts include the system timer, the mouse, data communication lines, network interface cards, and other peripheral devices. Normal thread execution is suspended during interrupts, and an interrupt may cause the processor to switch to another, higher priority thread. Clock interrupts are frequent and periodic and create a background of interrupt activity.

Not all of these counters are required to conduct a capacity planning study—the counters you select will be determined by the depth of the study you are conducting. At the very least, the % Processor Time counter should be used.

Collecting Usage Data for Multiple CPUs

You can also retrieve system-averaged data for multiple CPUs via Performance Monitor. Use the *System* object, which includes the following counters, among others:

- **% Total Processor Time** Sum of the % Processor Times for each processor divided by the number of processors in the system.
- **% Total Privileged Time** Sum of the % Privileged Times for each processor divided by the number of processors in the system.
- **% Total User Time** Sum of the % User Times for each processor divided by the number of processors in the system.
- **% Total Interrupt Time** Sum of the % Interrupt Times for each processor divided by the number of processors in the system.
- **Total Interrupts/sec** Average number of device interrupts that the processors experience per second. This counter provides an indication of how busy system devices are on a computer-wide basis.

Analyzing CPU Data

The data you obtain using these counters can be used to predict rises in a specific CPU's utilization and therefore increased response times from that CPU. Figure 6-6 shows CPU utilization over time. Notice that the utilization trend for the CPU is rising; it will reach the 75 percent threshold by February 18, 2000.

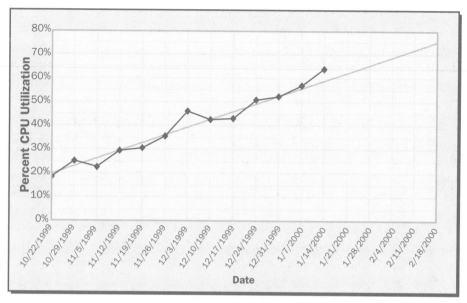

Figure 6-6. *Linear CPU utilization predictive analysis.*

Note   The more data points you collect, the more accurate your prediction.

Capacity Planning for the Disk Subsystem

Now that we have sized the memory and the processor, it's time to size the disk subsystem. Sizing this part of the system is easy because we have already calculated most of the information we require. First we need the total number of I/Os that will be processed through the system. We already have this information from the processor sizing. Second we need the size of the database. This information can be provided by the database designer. When you are sizing the disk subsystem, it is important to realize that you are sizing for either the size of the database or the number of I/Os per second, whichever yields the greater number of disk drives.

Many people are surprised to learn how many disk drives they need for their database. However, additional drives provide more access points to the data. If you have only one access point to the data, you have created a bottleneck. Since all transactions must pass through this bottleneck, response times will increase. The rule of thumb is to have as many access points to the data as you can. If you have more access points to the data, you are less likely to encounter the bottlenecks that might occur with fewer drives. You might also be generating many I/Os per second and might require more disks to accommodate the I/O load than are necessary for the database size.

For example, suppose you have a database system that is 10 GB in size and is generating 140 I/Os per second. Using the 85 percent rule for disk space utilization, you would need one approximately 12-GB drive to accommodate the size of the database. Now, looking at the drive requirement from an I/O point of view, if the disk drives were rated at 70 I/Os per second, three disk drives would be needed to accommodate the number of I/Os per second based on using only 85 percent of the I/O capacity of each drive. Therefore, since I/O capacity analysis yields the greatest result—three disk drives—we should use three disk drives (that total 12 GB, as we calculated earlier), each rated at 70 I/Os per second.

Note that this is the minimum configuration—you can use more higher-capacity drives if you want. Also note that this analysis ignores effects due to RAID configuration.

> **Note** When you are sizing a disk subsystem, always apply the 85 percent usage rule to both the size of the database and to the number of I/Os per second that users will generate. Use whichever calculation results in the larger number of drives. Also remember that 85 percent is the absolute maximum usage the disk should ever see. In practice, use a number lower that 85 percent. And remember that too many I/Os per second on the disk drives will cause bottlenecks and therefore prolonged response times.

Now let's take a more detailed look at how to determine the proper number of disk drives needed for your system, taking the RAID configuration into account. You'll need to store three major components: Windows 2000 and SQL Server, the log files, and the database itself. You'll calculate the number of drives you need for each component and then add the three numbers to obtain the total number of drives needed for your system.

Disk Drives for Windows 2000 and SQL Server

First you need to calculate the number of disk drives needed to support the first component—the Windows 2000 Server operating system and the SQL Server database. Usually, you will want these disk drives to be a separate volume set to RAID 1 (mirrored disk drives) for the fastest possible recovery. The number of disk drives may vary depending on size, but usually the Windows 2000 Server operating system and the SQL Server database system can fit on a single disk. Our simple calculation would look like this:

*opsys and SQL disks = (Windows 2000 Server and SQL disk) ∗
(RAID factor increase)*

In this case, the result would be *two* for mirrored disk drives. (Windows NT and SQL Server are on one disk, and that disk is mirrored in a RAID 1 volume.) Setting the operating system volume to RAID 5 or RAID 0 is not recommended. You must have at least two initial disk drives to use RAID 5, and you will want the fastest possible recovery for the operating system and the database executable.

Disk Drives for the Log Files

Second, you need to calculate the number of disk drives necessary to support your system's log files. This number depends largely on the total number of writes per second your transactions will cause. Remember that the information contained on these disks is of the most important kind—these disks provide the audit trails, or "before" images, that will be needed if anything happens to your database. Audit trails enable you to back out of partially complete transactions caused by disk failure. Calculating the number of writes that will take place was done during the processor sizing. Using arbitrary values, say a transaction resulted in 1,500,000 writes using a RAID 0 volume. Given that the RAID level that should be used for the log disk drives is RAID 1, we're looking at 3,000,000 writes over an 8-hour period, or 104.16 writes per second. (Remember that using RAID 1 results in twice as many writes per transaction as RAID 0.) To calculate the number of drives needed, use the following formula:

log disks = (writes/sec) / (disk I/O capability)

Remember that the *disk I/O capability* should be 85 percent of its rated maximum. Also, be sure to round up to the next whole number after dividing *writes/ sec* by *maximum disk I/O*. And finally, be sure to adjust the *writes/sec* value for any increase in write activity due to the specified RAID level. If we use the 85 percent ceiling for the number of writes allowed on a disk drive that has a capacity of 70 I/Os per second, we would need 1.7 disk drives; rounded up, that would mean two disk drives.

Disk Drives for the Database

The final step is calculating the number of disk drives that will be required for the database. Remember to calculate the number of drives required based on both the size of the database and the number of I/Os per second, and to use whichever results in the larger number of drives.

For Database Size

To determine the number of disk drives that are required to accommodate the database size, use the following formula:

database disks = (data size) / (disk size) + (RAID factor increase)

Remember that the *disk size* should be 85 percent of its rated maximum. Also remember to use the same units (for example, KB and MB) for the *data size* and *disk size*. The *RAID factor increase* is the number of extra drives required to support fault tolerance. For RAID 1, this value is equal to the number of disks required to store the database; for RAID 5, one extra drive is needed. For our 10-GB database using RAID 5, we would need two 12-GB disk drives.

Note RAID 5 is recommended for database drives.

For Database I/O

The number of disk drives required to accommodate I/Os can alter the database disk recommendation drastically, as we saw in our earlier simple example. To calculate this value, follow these steps:

1. Calculate the total number of read I/Os that will be going through the system by using the following formula:

    *total reads = (reads per transaction) * (total number of transactions)*

    If we assume 500 reads per transaction and 50,000 transactions, we have 25,000,000 total reads.

2. Determine how many of these read I/Os will be physical reads and how many will be logical reads by using the following formulas:

    *total logical reads = (total reads) * (cache hit rate)*
    total physical reads = (total reads) – (total logical reads)

    Assuming a target cache hit rate of 90 percent, we will have 22,500,000 total logical reads and 2,500,000 total physical reads.

3. Convert the total number of physical reads to reads per second by using the following formula:

   physical reads/sec = (total physical reads) / (work period)

   The *work period* should be the length of time, in seconds, in which the work is to be performed. You will need this value for the calculation of CPU utilization later on. In our example, if we use an 8-hour work period, we will have 86.8 physical reads/sec.

4. Now calculate the total number of write I/Os that will be going through the system by using the following formula:

   *total writes = (writes per transaction) * (number of transactions) *
   (RAID factor increase)*

   If we assume 10 writes per transaction using a RAID 5 system, we have (10) * (50,000) * (3), or 1,500,000 total writes.

5. Convert the total number of physical writes to writes per second by using the following formula:

   physical writes/sec = (total physical writes) / (work period)

   In this example, we have 1,500,000 physical writes and an 8-hour work period (28,800 seconds), giving us 52.1 physical writes/sec.

6. Calculate the total number of physical I/Os per second by using the following formula:

   *total physical I/Os per second = (physical reads/sec) +
   (physical writes/sec)*

   In this example, we have 86.8 physical reads/sec and 52.1 physical writes/sec, which gives us 138.9 total physical I/Os per second. Calculate the total number of database disk drives by using the following formula:

   *database disks = (total physical I/Os per second) /
   (disk I/O capability) + (RAID factor increase)*

   Remember to apply the 85 percent rule when determining the *disk I/O capability*, and remember that the *RAID factor increase* is the number of disks required to support fault tolerance. Using 138.9 total physical I/Os, a disk rated at 70 I/Os per second, and RAID 5, we come up with a total of four disk drives—three to support the total I/O and one more for the RAID 5 fault tolerance.

So, based on the database size of 10 GB, we would need at least one disk, but based on I/O activity, we would need three disks. Therefore, to accommodate the database, we will need three drives, the larger number of the two calculations.

Disk Drives Needed for the System

To find the total number of drives needed for the system, we take the sum of the parts. We need two disk drives for Windows 2000 Server and SQL Server, two disk drives for the log files, and four disk drives for the database, giving us a total requirement of eight drives for the entire system.

Real World Leave Some Elbow Room

Most designers use the thresholds (75 percent CPU utilization, 85 percent disk utilization, and so on) as the maximum utilizations. In most cases, you will want to use lesser values. Of course, this choice is not always entirely up to the designer. Outside influences, such as the company's hardware budget, can affect design decisions. A good target for a system is 65 percent maximum CPU utilization and 70 percent disk utilization. However, you should use whatever percentages you find optimal for the types of systems you design.

Collecting Disk Usage Data

Once the system is set up and operational, you should collect disk usage data to keep apprised of any changes that might be necessary. The system might expand to more users (and thus more transactions), the requirement for the database might change (resulting in a larger database size), and so on.

When performing post-capacity planning studies on disk usage, you should track the following counters in Performance Monitor. These counters can be found in the *PhysicalDisk* object:

- **% Disk Time**   Percentage of elapsed time that the selected disk drive is busy servicing read or write requests.

- **% Disk Read Time**   Percentage of elapsed time that the selected disk drive is busy servicing read requests.

- **% Disk Write Time**   Percentage of elapsed time that the selected disk drive is busy servicing write requests.

- **Avg. Disk Read Queue Length**   Average number of read requests that were queued for the selected disk during the sample interval.

- **Avg. Disk Write Queue Length**   Average number of write requests that were queued for the selected disk during the sample interval.

- **Avg. Disk Queue Length**   Average number of both read and write requests that were queued for the selected disk during the sample interval. It is the sum of the previous two items.

- **Disk I/O Count Per Second**   I/O activity to the disk array per second averaged over the measurement period. This counter is not directly available through Performance Monitor; to arrive at this value, you simply add together the values of two other counters that are available— Disk Reads/sec and Disk Writes/sec.

- **Disk Space Used**   Amount of disk space currently being used by either the database or the operating system. This counter is not available through Performance Monitor; use the Disk Administrator to access this information.

- **Disk Space Available**   Amount of disk space currently available. This counter is not available through Performance Monitor; use the Disk Administrator to access this information.

To start the Disk Administrator, click Start, and then choose Programs, Administrative Tools (Common), and finally Disk Administrator. For further information about using the Disk Administrator, click the Help button in the Disk Administrator window.

Analyzing Disk Usage Data

Analyzing disk usage information is a simple process. For example, if we were analyzing a system, we would collect data about available disk space to determine how much space is free. Figure 6-7 shows the usage of the database in terms of available MB.

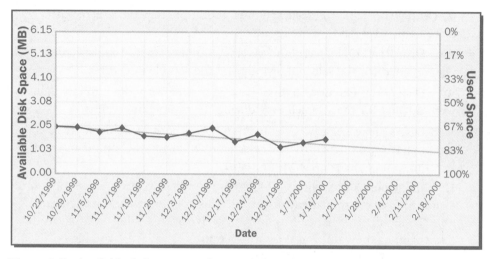

Figure 6-7. *Available disk space predictive analysis.*

As you can see, at the beginning of the analysis we have about 2.05 MB of free space out of 6.15 MB, which means that the disk is about 67 percent full. By January 14, 2000, we are down to about 1.5 MB, meaning that the disk is about 75 percent full. Using Microsoft Excel to plot a trend line, we estimate that by February 18, 2000, we will have only about 1.3 MB of available space, meaning that the disk will be about 83 percent full. At this point, the DBA might want to purchase additional disk space.

Capacity Planning for the Network

We've saved the network aspect of capacity planning for last because you can't get much capacity planning information from inside the system. Performance Monitor does not provide any counters to reveal network performance data, so sizing a network can be difficult. Given that the network is usually the weakest link in the system chain, try to be realistic in your estimations.

To size the network, you'll need to consider how many concurrent users will be on the system, how many messages are going through per second, and how many bytes per second on average these messages will contain. Based on this information, you can develop some estimates for the necessary minimum bit capacity of the network. For example, a proposed system might transmit the following amounts of data: 10 users will each transmit 25 messages per minute. Each of these messages is 259 bytes in length. We can estimate that the 250 total messages generate 64,750 bytes per minute, or 51,800 bits per minute, or 8633.33 bits per second. A small network would be adequate for this workload. You can use the following formula to estimate network size:

*network size = (messages/sec) * (message length) * (bits per byte)*

This calculation will give you an idea of how large (in bits per second) the transmission line should be.

This is about all we can do as far as the network is concerned, aside from monitoring network usage. Besides, in most situations you will be given a network to use; you can't really choose another network unless the given network will not support your system.

Collecting Network Usage Data

When you are performing post-capacity planning studies on the network, you should track the Bytes/Sec Through Network Interface performance counter in Network Monitor. This counter represents the percentage of time the data line is busy.

Note   Instructions for installing Network Monitor can be found in the Windows 2000 Server Help topic "Installing Network Monitor."

Analyzing Network Usage Data

To analyze network data, first calculate the line capacity (*network size*) as shown above, and then examine the Bytes/Sec Through Network Interface counter. Using these two values, the following formula will give you the total network utilization:

network utilization = (bytes/sec through the network) /
*(network size) * 100*

Figure 6-8 shows an example of linear growth for a network by graphing network utilization vs. date.

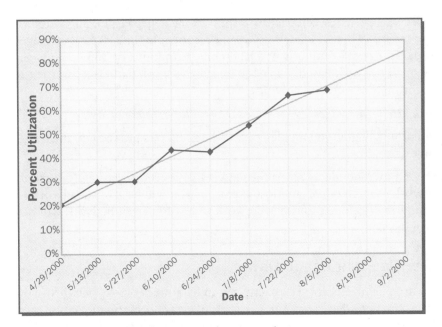

Figure 6-8. *Network utilization predictive analysis.*

This graph indicates that this particular network segment will reach maximum capacity on September 2, 2000. Again, the more data points you put on the graph, the more accurate the prediction will be.

Choosing the Data to Collect

There is no set quantity of counters that should be collected for post-capacity planning. The counters you use depend on the data you are analyzing and the degree of detail you want. In addition to the counters that we have described so far, Performance Monitor provides many other performance counters that you might find useful in certain situations. We'll look at one such situation here—collecting information about processes.

Collecting Process Data

Process information can be valuable when you are profiling a workload activity. Profiling a workload means determining what work each user is actually performing. Performance Monitor provides a variety of counters for this purpose. These counters are similar to the counters in the *Processor* object, but in this case they are used to collect process data. These counters can be found in the *Process* object and include the following:

- **% Processor Time**   Percentage of elapsed time during which all of the threads of this process used the processor to execute instructions. Code executed to handle certain hardware interrupts or trap conditions may be counted for this process.

- **% User Time**   Percentage of elapsed time this process's threads have spent executing code in User mode.

- **% Privileged Time**   Percentage of elapsed time that this process's threads have spent executing code in Privileged mode.

- **Page Faults/sec**   Rate of page faults by the threads executing in this process.

- **Elapsed Time**   Total elapsed time (in seconds) the process has been running.

Analyzing Process Data

Analyzing this information is not as complex as you might think. For example, if we were analyzing a system's processes to determine what kind of work was being performed, we would collect process data using a counter such as % Processor Time. This counter would indicate how much of the system is devoted to a certain function. Figure 6-9 shows the user process growth in a *CalProc* query, which is used by an accounts payable department.

This information is helpful because we can predict what will happen if we add more accounts payable users. In the graph, the trend line shows that utilization is rising and will be up to 30 percent by February 18, 2000. Assuming 10 accounts payable users, we could estimate that each user is responsible for 3 percent utilization in February. We can then deduce that if we add 3 users in February, we will be at approximately 39 percent utilization for the *CalProc* query.

When determining what to measure, it is important to decide what you are analyzing, as this will determine the measurement configuration you use. If your post-capacity study is ongoing, remember that you don't want to contribute to any performance problems—that is, if you decide that you want to measure everything and set a small measurement interval, you're going to be adding to any performance problems that may already exist. The smaller your measurement interval, the more often your record will be written to the disk, and if you're measuring a large number of counters this record will be very large. Multiple records are the way to go when your performance analysis necessitates having a smaller interval to trap performance problems. However, a single record written per day is fine for capacity studies.

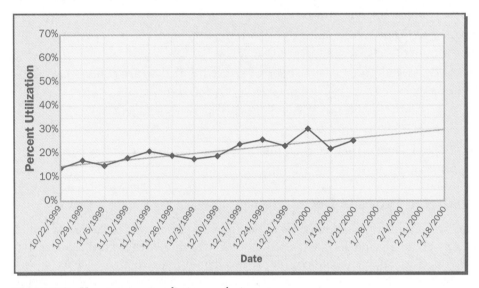

Figure 6-9. *User process predictive analysis.*

Table 6-1 provides a list of the counters you should use for a good basic capacity planning study. Remember that not all these counters reside in Performance Monitor. Available Memory can be retrieved using the Task Manager. Disk Space Used and Disk Space Available can be retrieved using the Disk Administrator.

Table 6-1. Counters available in Performance Monitor

Object	Counters
Processor	% Processor Time (individual CPU statistics)
System	% Total Processor Time (averaged over all CPUs)
PhysicalDisk	% Disk Time (for all disk arrays configured) Avg. Disk Queue Length
Memory	Page Faults/second Available Memory
Network Segment	Total Bytes Received/second

This configuration provides a good starting place for performing predictive analysis on your system. All the necessary elements are present to give information about CPU utilization and disk, memory, and network usage without putting excessive stress on the system and while maintaining a smaller database. As you get more involved in the study, you can add counters to extend the information that you can provide.

Summary

Industry has too few capacity planners and a whole lot of systems that could use this service. Performance problems do not have to be a way of life. With some common sense, the right information, and some of the calculations explained in this chapter, you can easily track and predict the capacity of resources.

Chapter 7
Installing Microsoft SQL Server

If you have finished the preinstallation steps in Chapters 4 and 5 and have properly sized your system, as explained in Chapter 6, you are ready to install Microsoft SQL Server 2000. This chapter guides you through the installation process and reviews upgrading from earlier versions. Finally, so you can make use of SQL Server in a client/server environment, the process of installing the client utilities on your client computers is reviewed in detail.

Server Installation

There are three ways to install SQL Server. You can perform a local, remote, or unattended installation. A local installation installs SQL Server onto the computer that you are currently using. With a remote installation, you can install SQL Server onto another computer that is on your network. An unattended installation allows you to install SQL Server without your having to be present to respond to any prompts. Instead, you store all prompt replies in a file ahead of time, and the setup program automatically reads these replies as it needs them.

Each of the three installation options is described in this chapter. If this is your first time installing SQL Server 2000, perform a local installation before you try either of the other two options. That way, you will be familiar with the general installation procedure.

Local Installation

If you've done your preinstallation homework, as described in Chapters 4, 5, and 6, the installation process will run a lot more smoothly. For a local installation, follow these simple steps to get SQL Server installed and running on your server:

1. Place your SQL Server CD in your server's CD drive. If your server's operating system is set up to automatically start CDs, the Microsoft SQL Server 2000 setup dialog box appears, as shown in Figure 7-1. Otherwise, you will need to manually run the Autorun.exe program (located in the top-level directory of the CD).

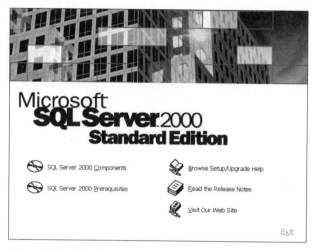

Figure 7-1. *The SQL Server setup dialog box.*

2. If you have not installed the required operating system service packs or the required version of Microsoft Internet Explorer, or if you simply want to examine the list of prerequisites, click SQL Server 2000 Prerequisites to display the SQL Server 2000 Prerequisites dialog box.

   Click the appropriate operating system to view its prerequisites, and then click the prerequisite you would like to install. If you have all the appropriate software already loaded, go to step 3.

Note If you need to install Microsoft Internet Explorer or the service packs required by Microsoft Windows 2000 or Microsoft Windows NT 4, you might be required to reboot your system and rerun Autorun.exe before you can proceed with the SQL Server installation.

   Once the prerequisites have been installed, return to the master setup dialog box by clicking Back.

3. Click SQL Server 2000 Components to begin installing SQL Server.

4. The Install Components dialog box appears, as shown in Figure 7-2. Click Install Database Server to begin installing the primary SQL Server components.

5. The SQL Server 2000 Installation Wizard welcome dialog box appears. If you are running any other programs, you should close them. Click Next to continue the installation process.

6. The Computer Name dialog box appears. Click Local Computer and then click Next.

7. The SQL Server 2000 Installation Selection dialog box appears. Click Create A New Instance Of SQL Server and click Next to continue.

Figure 7-2. *The Install Components dialog box.*

8. The User Information dialog box appears. Verify that your name and company name are correct. Click Next to continue.

9. The Software License Agreement dialog box appears. Click Yes to accept the license agreement and continue the installation process.

10. The CD Key dialog box appears. Enter the 25-character CD key found on the yellow sticker on your CD jewel case, and click Next.

11. The Installation Definition dialog box appears. Click Server And Client Tools and then click Next.

12. The Instance Name dialog box appears. If you want to name this instance of SQL Server something different from the default, clear the Default check box and type the name you want. Click Next to continue the installation process.

13. The Setup Type dialog box appears, as shown in Figure 7-3. You can select a Typical, Minimum, or Custom installation. The Typical installation includes all of the options except for the Development Tools and Full-Text Search options. The Custom installation allows you to add those options as well as to remove any options that you do not desire. The Minimum installation is equivalent to the Typical installation without the Upgrade Tools, Books Online, and Management Tools options.

    In most cases, you'll want to perform a Typical installation, so we will click Typical in our practice installation. You can also specify where to install the program and data files for SQL Server by clicking the Browse buttons in the Destination Folder group box. Click Next to continue.

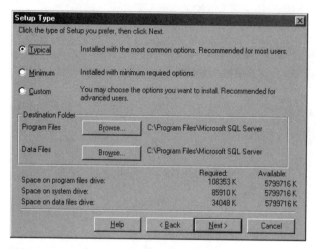

Figure 7-3. *The Setup Type dialog box.*

14. The Services Accounts dialog box appears, as shown in Figure 7-4. You can use either a Windows NT or Windows 2000 user account, or the Administrator account. In either case, the account must have Log On As A Service rights. If you are unsure how to create these user accounts, consult your system administrator or your Windows NT or Windows 2000 documentation. Type the name and password of the account you created for the SQL Server service in the appropriate text boxes here. If you are installing SQL Server on a stand-alone workstation, click Use The Local System Account. Click Next to continue.

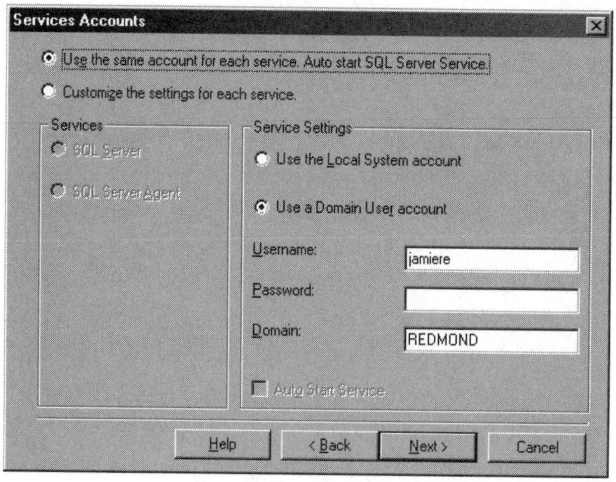

Figure 7-4. *The Services Accounts dialog box.*

15. Next the Authentication Mode dialog box appears, as shown in Figure 7-5. This dialog box determines the level of security for your SQL Server installation. You can choose Windows Authentication Mode or Mixed Mode. If you select Windows Authentication Mode, all user rights to the database are inherited from the Windows User Security settings. If you select Mixed Mode, you can define and administer database security separately. If you select Mixed Mode, you must set a password for the sa, or SQL Server system administrator, account. You can choose to leave this password blank, but doing so will severely lessen the security of your SQL Server installation. After you select an authentication mode, click Next to continue.

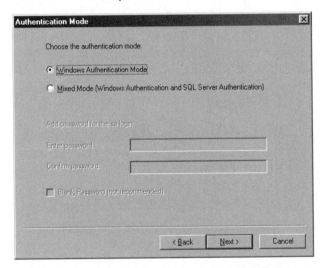

Figure 7-5. *The Authentication Mode dialog box.*

16. The Start Copying Files dialog box appears. Click Next to continue.

17. The Licensing Mode dialog box appears. You have two options for licensing your SQL Server clients. You can license the clients per seat or per processor.

    Per seat licensing requires a Client Access License for each client computer that will access the server. Once a computer is licensed, it can access any computer running SQL Server 2000 on the network at no additional charge. Per processor licensing requires a license for every processor on which SQL Server will execute. For example, if you are running SQL Server on a four-processor machine, you need to purchase four processor licenses to use all four processors. You could choose to limit SQL Server to just two of the four processors. In that case, you would be required to purchase only two processor licenses.

After you have purchased the appropriate number of processor licenses, you are allowed to connect an unlimited number of clients.

Click Continue to begin installing the SQL Server application and data files. SQL Server will install the required files on your system and configure the necessary components. The installation might take just a few minutes, or it might take longer, depending on the speed of your system.

18. Once installation is complete, the Setup Complete dialog box appears. Click Finish to complete the installation process.

Congratulations! You have installed SQL Server on your server!

Remote Installation

If you want to use your computer to install SQL Server on a server over the network, you'll want to perform a remote installation. A remote installation differs slightly from a local installation. The following steps detail how to perform a remote installation.

1. Perform steps 1 through 5 of the instructions for a local installation.

2. In the Computer Name dialog box, click Remote Computer and type the computer name of the remote system. Click Next to continue.

3. The SQL Server 2000 Installation Selection dialog box appears. Click Create A New Instance Of SQL Server and then click Next to continue.

4. The User Information dialog box appears. Verify that your name and company name are correct. Click Next to continue.

5. The Software License Agreement dialog box appears. Click Yes to accept the license agreement and continue with the installation process.

6. The CD Key dialog box appears. Enter the 25-character CD key found on the yellow sticker on your CD jewel case, and click Next.

7. The Remote Setup Information dialog box appears, as shown in Figure 7-6.

   Type the account name, password, and domain for the computer you wish to install SQL Server on. Ensure that the account that you are using has the authority to install software on the computer. You must also type in the Target Path text box the installation path on the remote computer. The installation path must be in Universal Naming Convention (UNC) format, for example, \\remoteserver\c$\Program Files\Microsoft SQL Server. Click Next to continue.

8. The Installation Definition dialog box appears. Click Server And Client Tools and then click Next.

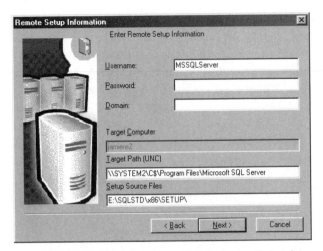

Figure 7-6. *The Remote Setup Information dialog box.*

9. The Instance Name dialog box appears. If you want to name this instance of SQL Server something different from the default, clear the Default check box and type the name you want. Click Next to continue the installation process.

10. The Setup Type dialog box appears. As with a local installation, with a remote installation, you can select a Typical, Minimum, or Custom installation. The Typical installation includes all of the options except for the Development Tools and Full-Text Search options. The Custom installation allows you to add those options as well as to remove any options that you do not desire. The Minimum installation is equivalent to the Typical installation without the Upgrade Tools, Books Online, and Management Tools options.

11. In most cases you'll want to perform a Typical installation, so we will click Typical in our practice installation. You can also specify where to install the program and data files for SQL Server by clicking the Browse buttons in the Destination Folder group box. Click Next to continue.

    The Services Accounts dialog box appears, as shown in Figure 7-4. Type the name and password of the account you created for the SQL Server service in the appropriate text boxes here. (If you didn't create a separate account, you can use the Windows NT or Windows 2000 Administrator account and password.) Click Next to continue.

12. The Authentication Mode dialog box appears. This dialog box determines the level of security for your SQL Server installation. You can choose Windows Authentication Mode or Mixed Mode. When you

select Windows Authentication, all user rights to the database are inherited from Windows User Security. If you select Mixed Mode authentication, you can define and administer database security separately. If you select Mixed Mode authentication, you must set a password for the SQL Server system administrator ("sa" in the dialog box) account. You can choose to leave this password blank, but doing so will severely lessen the security of your SQL Server installation. After you select an authentication mode, click Next to continue.

13. The Licensing Mode dialog box appears. As with a local installation, with a remote installation, you have two options for licensing your SQL Server clients. You can license the clients per server or per seat. See step 16 of the local installation procedure for more information on the two licensing methods.

14. Once the SQL Server installation process has connected to the remote computer and verified that the connection can be established, the remote installation will proceed just as the local installation did. All of the selections and options are chosen in the same manner as with the local installation.

During the SQL Server remote installation process, SQL Server creates a file called Sqlstp.log. This file resides in your %Systemroot% folder on a Windows NT or Windows 2000 system. The %Systemroot% folder is typically C:\Winnt. This file lists each step executed as well as any errors or trouble the installation process encountered. If, by chance, the remote installation fails, this file can aid in the troubleshooting process.

Unattended Installation

SQL Server provides utilities that allow the installation process to be automated. These utilities enable you to perform an installation without being present, which is especially useful when installing SQL Server on a large number of servers. The steps for creating an unattended installation are as follows:

1. From the command prompt, change directories to the CD-ROM drive.

2. Run one of the batch (.bat) files that have been provided for unattended installation. These files are as follows:

   - Sqlins.bat, for performing a Typical installation of SQL Server on Windows 95/98, Windows NT, or Windows 2000. This batch file uses the initialization file Sqlins.iss.

- Sqlcst.bat, for performing a Custom installation of SQL Server on Windows 95/98, Windows NT, or Windows 2000. This batch file uses the initialization file Sqlcst.iss.

- Sqlcli.bat, for installing the client utilities. These utilities are installed using the initialization file Sqlcli.iss. The client utilities are installed to the C:\Program Files\Microsoft SQL Server\80\ folder.

- Sqlrem.bat, for removing all SQL Server components from the system. You must specify the SQL Server installation folder as a parameter.

Prior to running the appropriate batch file, you can customize the associated .iss file for your particular systems. For example, you might want to change the licensing mode from the default of per server to per seat. To accomplish this, you would change the [License] section of the appropriate .iss file from License-Mode=PERSERVER to LicenseMode=PERSEAT.

Upgrading from Earlier Versions

If your site already contains Microsoft SQL Server 6.5 or Microsoft SQL Server 7 data, you can painlessly upgrade the data to SQL Server 2000. For upgrading SQL Server 6.5 installations, you will use the Version Upgrade Wizard. SQL Server 7 installations are upgraded automatically during the setup process for SQL Server 2000.

Upgrading from SQL Server 7 to SQL Server 2000

The process that upgrades SQL Server 7 data to SQL Server 2000 format is an integral component of the SQL Server 2000 installation. Once the installation process has completed, SQL Server 2000 runs a series of upgrade scripts on the SQL Server 7 data. Depending on the number of databases and tables you are upgrading, this process might take some time. You will see status messages as the upgrade process progresses. Figure 7-7 shows an example of an upgrade status message box.

Running script procsyst.sql (5 of 19)

Figure 7-7. *SQL Server 7 upgrade status.*

Upgrading from SQL Server 6.5 to SQL Server 2000

Before starting the SQL Server Upgrade Wizard to upgrade SQL Server 6.5 data to SQL Server 2000 formats, you will need to verify that the items in the following checklist are correct in your SQL Server 6.5 installation:

- Verify that the *user connections* parameter in *sp_configure* has a runtime value of at least 25. The new network libraries might require more than the default of 15 connections to perform the upgrade.
- Ensure that all of your SQL Server 6.5 database files, including the master database, are backed up.
- Run all database consistency checks (using DBCC) on your SQL Server 6.5 databases to ensure that they are in a consistent state.
- Set your tempdb to at least 10 megabytes (MB). The recommended size is 25 MB, but 10 MB will suffice.
- Disable all startup stored procedures you have enabled.
- Stop all replication services and make sure that the replication log is empty.
- Install SQL Server 6.5 Service Pack 3 or later, if you haven't already.

To upgrade SQL Server 6.5 data to SQL Server 2000 formats (after you have installed SQL Server 2000), complete the following steps:

1. Click Start, point to Programs, point to Microsoft SQL Server-Switch, and then click SQL Server Upgrade Wizard to display the welcome screen of the SQL Server Upgrade Wizard, as shown in Figure 7-8. Click Next to begin the upgrade process.

2. The Data And Object Transfer screen of the SQL Server Upgrade Wizard appears, as shown in Figure 7-9. By default, the SQL Server Upgrade Wizard will convert all database objects and data from SQL Server 6.5 to SQL Server 2000 format. To verify that this conversion was successful, select the Validate Successful Object Data Transfer check box. The verification can be time consuming, but it is best to make this check.

   If you are concerned about the consistency of your converted data, select the Exhaustive Data Integrity Verification check box. This option will cause the conversion process to take even more time but will ensure the highest level of integrity. If you have not recently run the SQL Server 6.x DBCC, you should select this option to ensure that database corruption will not affect the conversion process. If you have a tape drive present in your system, an option will be provided to use tape rather than named pipes as the data transfer method. Click Next to continue.

Figure 7-8. *The welcome screen of the SQL Server Upgrade Wizard.*

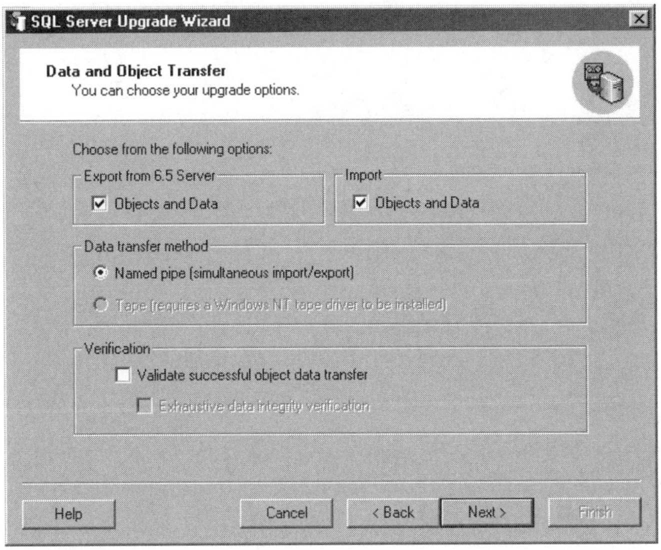

Figure 7-9. *The Data And Object Transfer screen.*

3. The Logon screen of the SQL Server Upgrade Wizard appears, as shown in Figure 7-10. You select the server name from the drop-down list and type the SQL Server system administrator password for the SQL Server 6.5 database you are converting. You must also type the SQL Server system administrator password for the target SQL Server 2000 database. If you want any startup arguments for either server, type them in the appropriate Optional Startup Arguments text box. These options can include trace flags. If you choose not to include startup arguments, leave these text boxes blank. (For additional information, go to the Books Online index and look up "startup options.") Click Next to continue.

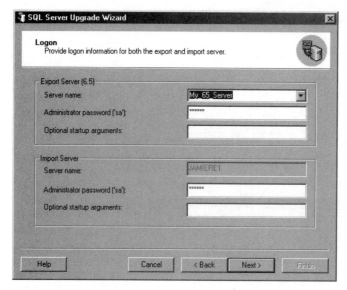

Figure 7-10. *The Logon screen of the SQL Server Upgrade Wizard.*

4. A SQL Server Upgrade Wizard screen displays a message warning that the SQL Server Upgrade Wizard needs to stop and restart your SQL Server 6.5 and SQL Server 2000 databases and that there should not be any users logged on to either database server while the conversion is being performed. Click Yes to continue.

Note   At this point, the system will switch between SQL Server 6.5 and SQL Server 2000.

5. The Code Page Selection screen appears. This screen lets you specify the scripting code page (which determines the character set) to use for the conversion. Unless you have a special need for character sets other than those your system has previously been set up for, you should accept the default setting. Click Next to continue.

6. The SQL Server Upgrade Wizard communicates with your SQL Server 6.5 database to determine the available databases to convert and displays a list of these databases in the Upgrade Databases To SQL Server 2000 screen, as shown in Figure 7-11.

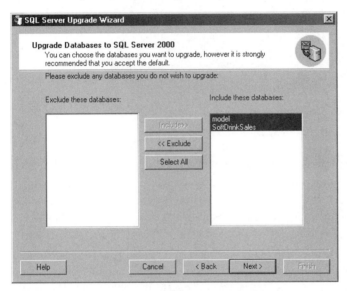

Figure 7-11. *The Upgrade Databases To SQL Server 2000 screen.*

The databases to be converted appear in the list box on the right. To exclude a database from the conversion process, select its name in the Include These Databases list box and then click Exclude. The excluded database will then appear in the list box on the left. Unless you won't be using a particular database any longer, there is no reason to exclude any databases. Click Next to continue.

7. The Database Creation screen appears, as shown in Figure 7-12. This screen lets you specify how your databases are created. Typically, you will want the default configuration. Change the configuration if you want to specify a new location for the data files. Click Next to continue.

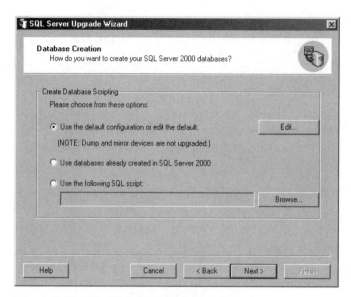

Figure 7-12. *The Database Creation screen.*

Note For the default configuration, SQL Server creates files that are large enough to hold the data and objects (as they are loaded in the SQL Server 6.5 databases) to be converted. However, it does not create any free space for these files. A log file is also created for each converted database. You can change the name and file path for the log files, the initial file size, and the growth increment by clicking Edit.

The second option for creating the databases is Use Databases Already Created In SQL Server 2000. With this option, you will create the data and log files with SQL Server 2000 before you start the Upgrade Wizard, and SQL Server will use those databases for the converted data.

The third option is to use an SQL script for your database file creation. This script should contain the CREATE DATABASE statement needed to create the data and log files you will use for the conversion. Click Browse to locate this script.

The second and third options are not recommended because you must use the same database names for SQL Server 2000 that you used in SQL Server 6.5, and the SQL Server 2000 files might take more disk space than the original SQL Server 6.5 files. If you use the default option, SQL Server will estimate this data growth for you.

8. The System Configuration screen appears, as shown in Figure 7-13. This screen lets you specify which system objects and settings to transfer to your new database. If you select the Server Configuration check

box, all logins and remote login registrations are converted. If you select the SQL Executive Settings check box, all scheduled tasks are converted. If you select the Replication Settings check box, the replication support will be converted. (The Replication Settings check box is disabled in our example because replication was not used in our SQL Server 6.5 data- bases, so nothing is available to transfer here. Database replication is covered in Chapter 26.)

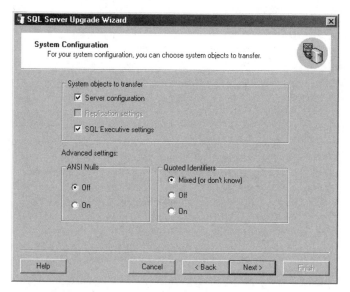

Figure 7-13. *The System Configuration screen.*

Under Advanced Settings on the Upgrade Wizard, you can set the ANSI Nulls option and the Quoted Identifiers option. ANSI Nulls affects the comparisons that use null values. If this is set to On, the comparison op- erators (= and <>) will always return *NULL* when one of the operator's arguments is *NULL*. If it is set to Off, these operators return *TRUE* if both arguments are *NULL*, and the operators return *FALSE* if one ar- gument is *NULL* and the other argument is *NOT NULL*.

The Quoted Identifiers option determines how SQL Server 2000 will handle double quotation marks. If this option is set to On, double quota- tion marks indicate an identifier such as a column name. If it is set to Off, the marks indicate a character string, just as single quotation marks do. If you click Mixed, SQL Server 2000 will convert the objects with Quoted Identifiers set as it was under SQL Server 6.5. If you are not sure about this option, it is best to click Mixed. Click Next to continue.

9. After a short delay, the Completing The SQL Server Upgrade Wizard screen appears, as shown in Figure 7-14. This screen enables you to review all of the conversion options you have selected. If you need to make any changes, click Back and change your settings. Otherwise, click Finish to proceed with the conversion process.

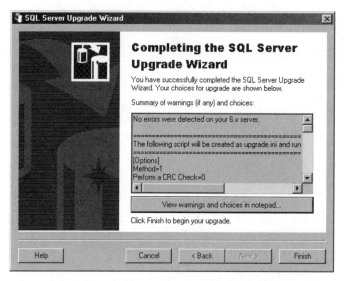

Figure 7-14. *The Completing The SQL Server Upgrade Wizard screen.*

10. The SQL Server Upgrade Script Interpreter dialog box appears, as shown in Figure 7-15. This dialog box displays a running list of the items upgraded, allowing the administrator some feedback on the progress of the upgrade process.

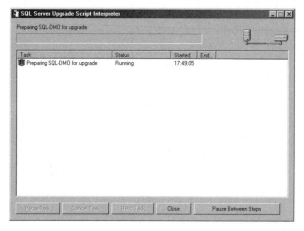

Figure 7-15. *The SQL Server Upgrade Script Interpreter dialog box.*

> **Note**   Depending on the size of the databases you are converting and whether you choose to extensively verify your converted databases, this conversion process could take several hours.

When the upgrade process is complete, the Upgrade Complete dialog box appears. Click OK to dismiss the dialog box, and then click Close to close the SQL Server Upgrade Script Interpreter dialog box.

Congratulations! You have just upgraded your SQL Server 6.5 database to SQL Server 2000.

Client Installation

Installing SQL Server client files is as simple as installing SQL Server itself. To install the SQL Server client files on a client computer, follow these steps:

1. Perform steps 1 through 9 as outlined earlier in the "Local Installation" section.

2. When the SQL Server 2000 Installation Definition dialog box appears, click Client Tools Only and then click Next to continue.

3. In the Select Components dialog box that appears, select the desired options and click Next. You can select Management Tools, Client Connectivity, Books Online, Development Tools, Code Samples, or any combination of these options. By default, the Management Tools, Client Connectivity, Books Online, and Development Tools options are selected.

4. When the Start Copying Files dialog box appears, click Next to continue.

Summary

By now you can probably see that a bit of planning can pay off with a smooth installation of SQL Server 2000. Conversion from an earlier version of SQL Server can also be a quick and painless process if you use the tools provided to you by SQL Server 2000. Now that you have SQL Server 2000 installed, you need to know how to create and manage your databases. That process begins with SQL Server Enterprise Manager. In Chapter 8, you'll learn how to manage and configure your SQL Server service and server processes, as well as how to start, stop, and pause the SQL Server service.

Chapter 8
Managing Microsoft SQL Server Services

As soon as you get Microsoft SQL Server 2000 installed, you can begin using it. But before you can log on and begin building your database, you must know how to start up the SQL Server service and its components—SQL Server Agent, Microsoft Distributed Transaction Coordinator, and Microsoft Search. This chapter describes these components, which run as separate services in addition to the SQL Server service. The chapter also shows you how to start, stop, and manage these services using three tools—SQL Server Service Manager, SQL Server Enterprise Manager, and Microsoft Windows 2000 Service Control Manager.

> **Note** This chapter focuses on running SQL Server 2000 on Microsoft Windows 2000, although it also runs on Microsoft Windows NT 4. SQL Server runs as an executable file on Microsoft Windows 98, which does not support services.

It's important that you know how to manage the SQL Server service using Enterprise Manager. Note that this chapter gives a mere introduction to Enterprise Manager. Many tasks that you can accomplish with Enterprise Manager will be shown, as they apply, in the remaining chapters. These tasks include creating databases and objects, configuring server options, configuring and managing replication, and managing backups. Here we will focus on using Enterprise Manager to manage the SQL Server service and other services.

SQL Server Services

A *service* is a program or process that performs a specific function to support other programs. When you start SQL Server, the SQL Server service starts up on Windows NT or Windows 2000. This service manages database files, processes Transact-SQL (T-SQL) statements, allocates resources among concurrent user connections, ensures data consistency, and much more. If you install one or more instances of SQL Server, the service name for each instance of SQL Server is MSSQL$*InstanceName*, where $*InstanceName* is the instance name you designated at installation time. The corresponding SQL Server Agent service for an instance is called SQLAGENT$*InstanceName*. For multiple instances of SQL Server, however, there will be only one installation each of Microsoft Distributed Transaction Coordinator and Microsoft Search.

The three component services are provided with your licensed copy of SQL Server. SQL Server Agent is installed by default when you install SQL Server. If you don't have Microsoft Distributed Transaction Coordinator and Microsoft Search installed, you can run the SQL Server installation program again to install those components, which are called DTC Client Support and Full-Text Search, respectively. Now let's see what support each of these services provides.

SQL Server Agent supports scheduling and executing jobs, alerts, notifications, and database maintenance plans. Without this service, you will find your job as administrator much more difficult, if not impossible. SQL Server Agent allows you to automate routine database maintenance tasks. For example, you can create a job to automatically perform a database backup every night at 1 A.M. and another job to perform transaction log backups every 30 minutes. To keep checks on your system performance, you can create a performance condition alert to inform you if the server CPU utilization goes above 90 percent. SQL Server Agent must be running to perform these kinds of tasks. This service can be configured to start up automatically when SQL Server starts, or it can be started manually. You should configure it to start automatically to ensure that your scheduled jobs, alerts, and notifications will be able to execute. See Chapter 30 to learn how to create a database maintenance plan and Chapter 31 to learn how to set up jobs, alerts, and notifications using SQL Server Agent.

Microsoft Distributed Transaction Coordinator is a transaction manager that provides the capability of including different sources of data, including data from remote databases, in your client application transactions. This means that a single transaction can update data on multiple remote servers. This transaction manager ensures that all updates will be made permanent on all data sources if the transaction is committed or, in case of an error, ensures that the modifications will be rolled back on all data sources. See Chapter 25 for more details about using Microsoft Distributed Transaction Coordinator.

The Microsoft Search service starts up when you start Microsoft Search, which supports full-text indexing and searching. Full-text indexing allows more complex searches to be performed on character string data. For example, you can search for words that are in close proximity to a given word, or you can search for strings that contain a particular phrase.

As stated earlier in this chapter, there are several tools you can use to stop and start the SQL Server services: SQL Server Service Manager, SQL Server Enterprise Manager, and Windows 2000 Service Control Manager. First let's look at SQL Server Service Manager, which can be used to control the services for SQL

Server, SQL Server Agent, Microsoft Distributed Transaction Coordinator, and Microsoft Search.

Using SQL Server Service Manager

To start or stop the SQL Server services using SQL Server Service Manager, follow these steps. (The SQL Server service can also be paused, as you will see below.)

1. Click Start, point to Programs, point to Microsoft SQL Server, and then choose Service Manager to display the Service Manager application, shown in Figure 8-1.

Figure 8-1. *The SQL Server Service Manager.*

2. The local server name and the SQL Server service name appear in the Server and Services drop-down lists. In the Server drop-down list, select the name of the server whose services you want to control. (Note that you can use Service Manager to manage a server across the network.) In the Services drop-down list, select the specific service you want to control: SQL Server (MSSQLSERVER), Microsoft Distributed Transaction Coordinator (Distributed Transaction Coordinator), Microsoft Search (Microsoft Search), or SQL Server Agent (SQLSERVERAGENT).

3. You can then start or stop the selected service by clicking the appropriate button. If you have selected the SQL Server service, you also have the option of pausing the service. The symbol in the circle (slightly below and to the left of center in the dialog box) shows the current state of the selected service. If SQL Server is in a paused state, click Start/Continue to resume the service. Pausing SQL Server prevents users from logging on and gives you time to ask users to complete their work and log off before you stop the server. If you stop SQL Server without pausing, all server processes are terminated immediately. Stopping SQL Server prevents new connections and disconnects users who are connected.

4. While you are running Service Manager, the display is updated every 5 seconds. To change the update interval, click the small icon in the upper left corner of the dialog box to reveal the System menu, and choose Options to display the SQL Server Service Manager Options dialog box, as shown in Figure 8-2.

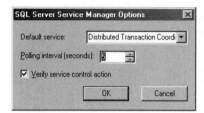

Figure 8-2. *The SQL Server Service Manager Options dialog box.*

In the Polling Interval box, you can specify a new polling interval time for the services. If you select the Verify Service Control Action check box, Service Manager will verify any action you take to start, stop, or pause the services by prompting you with a dialog box. The polling interval and verification settings will be set the same for each of the four services.

Note If the SQL Server and SQL Server Agent services are not configured to start automatically, you must start them manually.

Using Windows 2000 Service Control Manager

You can also start and stop SQL Server services using Windows 2000 Service Control Manager, either locally or remotely. You can even configure the SQL Server services to start automatically each time your system is started. To automatically start the SQL Server services from Windows 2000 Service Control Manager, follow these steps:

1. Click Start, point to Programs, point to Administrative Tools, and then choose Services to start Service Control Manager, as shown in Figure 8-3.

2. Scroll down through the Service list box to find Distributed Transaction Coordinator, Microsoft Search, MSSQLSERVER or SQLSERVER-AGENT. Right-click the service for which you want to configure the startup option, and then choose Properties from the shortcut menu to display the Properties window, as shown in Figure 8-4.

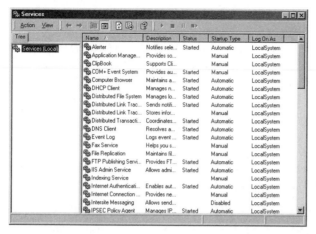

Figure 8-3. *The Windows 2000 Service Control Manager.*

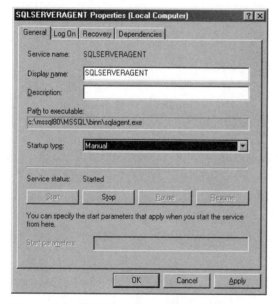

Figure 8-4. *The Properties window for SQL Server Agent.*

3. In the Startup Type drop-down list, select Automatic, Manual, or Disabled. Selecting Automatic will cause the service to start automatically each time you start your system. Selecting Manual will require you to manually start up the service when you want to use it. Selecting Disable will prevent that service from starting—either automatically or manually. Click OK to save your configuration.

4. There are three other tabs in the Properties window. The Log On tab allows you to specify the account that the selected service should log on as. The Recovery tab allows you to set options that should occur in case the selected service fails. The Dependencies tab shows you which services the selected service depends on and which services depend on the selected service, if any. For example, the SQL Server Agent service depends on the SQL Server service. The SQL Server Agent service cannot start if the SQL Server service is stopped.

Using SQL Server Enterprise Manager

Enterprise Manager is part of the Microsoft Management Console (MMC). MMC is a central application that is used to manage all aspects of a system running Windows 2000 Server. In Windows 2000 and in future versions of Windows, MMC will play an increasingly important role in the management of Microsoft BackOffice applications such as Microsoft Exchange Server, Microsoft Proxy Server, Microsoft Site Server, Microsoft Systems Management Server, and Microsoft SNA Server.

Managing SQL Server

Enterprise Manager is the most complete tool for configuring and managing your SQL Server installation. Whereas Service Manager allows you only to start, pause, or stop a service, Enterprise Manager allows you to stop and start a server, and it also enables you to perform the following tasks:

- Register your server
- Configure local and remote servers
- Configure and manage a multiple-server installation
- Set up login security and add users, system administrators, and operators
- Assign a system administrator (sa) password
- Create and schedule jobs
- Create alerts and configure SQL Server to communicate to system administrators through e-mail
- Set up and manage databases, tables, indexes, views, stored procedures, rules, triggers, defaults, backup devices, and error logs
- Manage other SQL Server services

Enterprise Manager, shown in Figure 8-5, is your one-stop shop for managing all these tasks and more. The remainder of this chapter will help you get started using Enterprise Manager. Later chapters will show you how to use Enterprise Manager to perform more advanced SQL Server tasks.

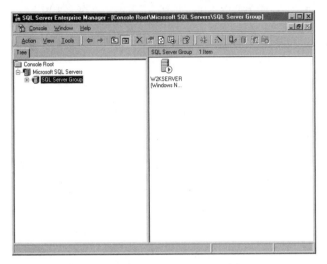

Figure 8-5. *The SQL Server Enterprise Manager.*

The following list describes four tasks that you can perform using Enterprise Manager. You must perform these tasks before you begin using your SQL Server installation for the first time. We will examine each of these tasks in detail in the sections that follow this list.

- **Create a server group.**   By creating a server group, you can restrict access to information to only that group. Accounts with similar resource needs can and should be gathered into groups to simplify account administration.

- **Register your server.**   You must register your server with MMC before you can begin to manage it.

- **Access your server.**   Once your server is registered, you can view and configure a number of properties. If you have a multiple-server environment, you can use Enterprise Manager to manage and configure the servers from a single location.

- **Change the default system administrator password.**   When SQL Server is installed, the default system administrator account is configured with no password. You should specify a password before you begin to use SQL Server.

Creating Server Groups

Enterprise Manager enables you to create groups of servers to help with your administrative tasks. Server groups help you organize a related set of servers for easy access—much like folders help you organize related files. You can then perform actions that will affect every server in the group by using one command, rather than by repeating the command for each server. By default, when you installed SQL Server, a SQL Server group was created, called SQL Server Group. To create a server group, follow these steps:

1. Click Start, point to Programs, point to Microsoft SQL Server 2000, and then choose Enterprise Manager to start the Enterprise Manager application.

2. The left side of the Enterprise Manager window shows the server group folders as subfolders of Microsoft SQL Servers, and the right side of the window contains the server group icons. To create a SQL Server group, right-click the Microsoft SQL Servers folder and then choose New SQL Server Group from the shortcut menu that appears.

3. Type a name for the new server group in the Server Groups dialog box that appears, as shown in Figure 8-6. If you click Sub-group Of, you can select the group of which your new server group will be a sub-group. If you click Top Level Group, your new server group will be a top-level SQL Server group, on the same level as SQL Server Group. Click OK to save your new group.

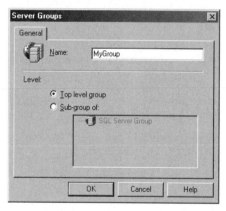

Figure 8-6. *The Server Groups dialog box.*

Registering Your Server

After you have created a SQL Server group, you can register your local or remote servers as members of the group. To register a server, follow these steps:

1. Right-click a server group icon in the right-hand pane of the Enterprise Manager window. (If the Microsoft SQL Servers heading is expanded, you can also right-click the group folder name in the left pane.) Choose New SQL Server Registration from the shortcut menu.

2. The Register SQL Server Wizard welcome screen appears. For many of the routine management tasks you will perform using Enterprise Manager, a wizard is provided to help you through the process. Click Next to continue the registration process.

3. The Select A SQL Server screen appears, as shown in Figure 8-7. The SQL Server installations available on your network are displayed in the Available Servers list box. Select the servers you want to register (or type a server name in the text box), and then click Add to move the server name to the Added Servers list box. After you have completed your selections, click Next.

4. The Select An Authentication Mode screen appears. Select the type of security you want to use to connect to your SQL Server installation. SQL Server security is reviewed in detail in Chapter 34. (If you performed a Typical installation, SQL Server is already configured to use the Windows NT authentication mode.) Click Next to continue.

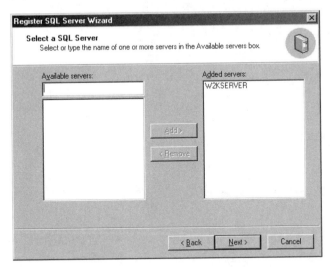

Figure 8-7. *The Select A SQL Server screen.*

5. The Register SQL Server Wizard - Select SQL Server Group screen appears, as shown in Figure 8-8. You can select an existing group to which you can add your server or create a top-level server group for your server. If you want to add the server to an existing group, click the

first option in the screen, and then select the group name from the drop-down list. If you want to create a group, click the second option and then type the group name in the text box. Click Next to continue.

6. The Completing The Register SQL Server Wizard screen appears. The listed server will be registered. If you need to make any changes, click Back; otherwise, click Finish to complete the registration process.

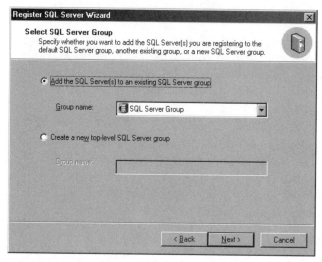

Figure 8-8. *The Select SQL Server Group screen.*

7. The Register SQL Server Messages dialog box appears (Figure 8-9), confirming that your registration was successful. Click Close to close this dialog box.

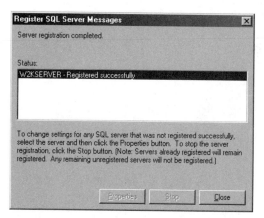

Figure 8-9. *The Register SQL Server Messages dialog box.*

Accessing Your Server

Once you have successfully registered your server using Enterprise Manager, you can access all of its properties, databases, and objects. To view the properties and objects of the newly registered server, first expand the server group name in the left-hand pane of the Enterprise Manager window. A list of all the servers in the group appears. Then expand the server name to display its properties and objects, as shown in Figure 8-10. (Later chapters will explain in detail how to manage and configure these properties.)

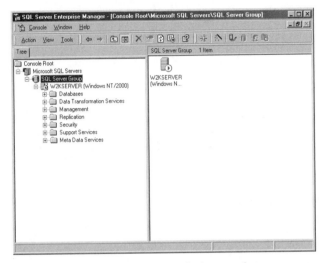

Figure 8-10. *The properties and objects of a server.*

Changing the Default Passwords

All SQL Server installations have a built-in administrative account, the sa account. (The term "sa" is short for "system administrator.") On new SQL Server installations, the sa user account is not assigned a password. To ensure the highest level of security for your SQL Server installation, you should assign a password to the sa account. To do so, follow these steps:

1. As the previous section outlines, access the server whose sa password you want to change.

2. Expand the Security folder and then click Logins to display the installed SQL Server user accounts in the right-hand pane, as shown in Figure 8-11.

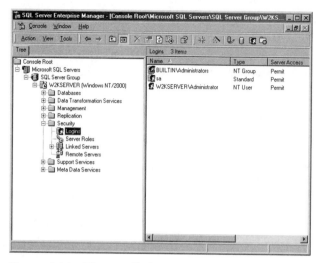

Figure 8-11. *The installed SQL Server user accounts.*

3. Right-click the sa user account and then choose Properties from the shortcut menu that appears. The SQL Server Login Properties window appears (Figure 8-12).

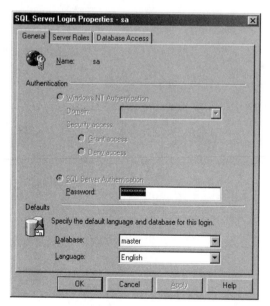

Figure 8-12. *The SQL Server Login Properties window.*

You can specify several other settings via the SQL Server Login Properties window. We will describe these features in Chapter 34.

4. Type a new password in the Password text box, and then click OK to display the Confirm Password dialog box.

5. Retype the password and then click OK. You have just taken a critical step in securing your SQL Server installation.

Caution   Be sure to remember the password you have chosen. If you forget your password, you will have to reinstall SQL Server.

Managing Other Services

Enterprise Manager can also be used to manage the SQL Server component services: SQL Server Agent, Microsoft Distributed Transaction Coordinator, and Microsoft Search. It is the only tool available to manage these services, aside from Service Control Manager and SQL Service Manager, which allow you only to start and stop the component services, as we mentioned earlier.

SQL Server Agent

Enterprise Manager provides a user-friendly interface for managing SQL Server Agent. To access the properties of the SQL Server Agent service, follow these steps:

1. In Enterprise Manager, expand the server you want to access, and then expand the Management folder, as shown in Figure 8-13.

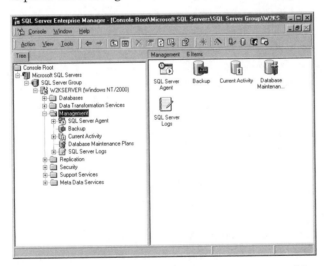

Figure 8-13. *The Management folder in Enterprise Manager.*

2. Right-click SQL Server Agent in the left pane or right-click the SQL Server Agent icon in the right pane, and you will see the shortcut menu. From this menu, you can stop or start the SQL Server Agent service; view the error log; start the wizards to make this server a master or target for running jobs; create a job, an alert, or an operator; or view the Properties window. These options will be described in more detail in Chapter 31.

3. From the shortcut menu, choose Properties. The SQL Server Agent Properties window appears, as shown in Figure 8-14.

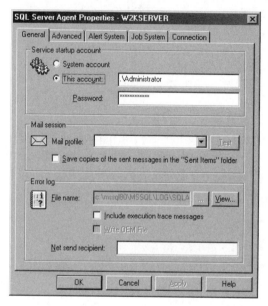

Figure 8-14. *The SQL Server Agent Properties window.*

4. In this window, you can configure various options for the SQL Server Agent service by clicking the various tabs: General, Advanced, Alert System, Job System, and Connection. At the bottom of the window, there is a Help button that explains in detail each option on the displayed tab.

Microsoft Distributed Transaction Coordinator

The only options for Microsoft Distributed Transaction Coordinator in Enterprise Manager are to stop and start the service. To do this, expand the server you want to access and then expand the Support Services folder, as shown in Figure 8-15.

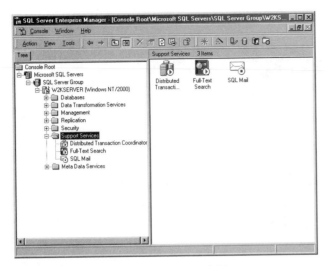

Figure 8-15. *The Support Services folder.*

Right-click Distributed Transaction Coordinator in the left or right pane. You can choose either Start or Stop from the shortcut menu to start or stop this service.

Microsoft Search

To access the menu options for the Microsoft Search service, open the Support Services folder, as shown in the previous section, and then right-click Full-Text Search in either the left or right pane. From this menu, you can stop or start the service, clean up full-text catalogs, or view the service's properties.

Summary

SQL Server Service Manager and Enterprise Manager are the two primary management tools of every SQL Server administrator. In this chapter, we reviewed the basic steps required to manage and configure your SQL Server installation and SQL Server services. (More advanced administration topics are discussed in Part V.) Now you're ready to begin creating your own databases and tables. As you'll see in the next two chapters, SQL Server Enterprise Manager will also be an important component for creating and managing these databases and tables.

Chapter 9
Creating Databases

Once you have installed Microsoft SQL Server 2000 and then designed your database and disk layout, you are ready to create a database. SQL Server 2000 uses the improved methods for storing data and managing space that were introduced in SQL Server 7. Earlier versions of the product used logical devices and segments of a fixed size for data placement; SQL Server 2000 uses files and filegroups that can be configured to grow or shrink automatically. This chapter examines files and filegroups in detail and shows you how to manage database growth. You'll also learn three methods for creating databases, how to view database information, and how to delete a database.

Database Structure

Each SQL Server 2000 database is created from a set of operating system files. These files can be grouped together into filegroups to improve data manageability, data placement, and performance. In this section, you'll learn about SQL Server files and filegroups and examine their role in database creation.

Files

As mentioned, a SQL Server database is made up of a set of operating system files. A database file can be either a *data file* or a *log file*. Data files are used to store data and objects, such as tables, indexes, views, triggers, and stored procedures. There are two types of data files: primary and secondary. Log files are used to store transaction log information only. Log space is always managed separately from data space and can never be part of a data file.

Every database must be created with at least one data file and one log file, and files may not be used by more than one database—that is, databases cannot share files. The following list describes the three types of files that a database can use.

- **Primary data file** A primary data file contains all of the startup information for the database and its system tables and objects. It points to the rest of the files created in the database. It can also store user-defined tables and objects, but it is not required to do so. Each database must have exactly one primary file. The recommended file extension is .mdf.

- **Secondary data files** Secondary data files are optional. They can hold data and objects that are not in the primary file. A database might not have any secondary files if all its data is placed in the primary file. You can have zero, one, or multiple secondary files. Some databases need multiple secondary files in order to spread data across separate disks. (This is different from RAID, as we'll see in the following section.) The recommended file extension is .ndf.

- **Transaction log files** A transaction log file holds all of the transaction log information used to recover the database. Every database must have at least one log file and can have multiple log files. The recommended file extension is .ldf.

 Note The maximum file size for a SQL Server database is 32 terabytes (TB) for data files and 4 TB for log files.

A simple database might have one primary data file, which is large enough to hold all data and objects, and one transaction log file. A more complex database might have one primary data file, five secondary data files, and two transaction log files. How, then, could the data be spread across all the data files? The answer is that filegroups can be used to arrange data.

Filegroups

Filegroups enable you to group files for administrative and data placement purposes. (They are similar to segments in Microsoft SQL Server versions 6.5 and earlier.) Filegroups can improve database performance by allowing a database to be created across multiple disks, multiple disk controllers, or RAID systems. (RAID is described in Chapter 5.) You can create tables and indexes on specific disks by using filegroups, thus enabling you to direct the I/O for a certain table or index to specific physical disks, controllers, or arrays of disks. We'll look at some examples of this process later in this section.

There are three types of filegroups. The main characteristics of these filegroups are outlined in the following list:

- **Primary filegroup**   Contains the primary data file and all other files not put into another filegroup. System tables—which define the users, objects, and permissions for a database—are allocated to the primary filegroup for that database. SQL Server automatically creates the system tables when you create a database.

- **User-defined filegroups**   Includes any filegroups defined by the user during the process of creating (or later altering) the database. A table or an index can be created for placement in a specific user-defined filegroup.

- **Default filegroup**   Holds all pages for tables and indexes that do not have a specified filegroup when they are created. The default filegroup is, by default, the primary filegroup. Members of the db_owner database role can switch the default status from one filegroup to another. Only one filegroup at a time can be the default—again, if no default filegroup is specified, the primary filegroup automatically remains the default. The ALTER DATABASE command is used to change the default filegroup. The syntax for this Transact-SQL (T-SQL) command is shown here:

```
ALTER DATABASE database_name MODIFY FILEGROUP filegroup_name
  DEFAULT
```

(You'll learn how to use T-SQL in Part III.) You might want to change the default filegroup to be one of your user-defined filegroups so that any objects created in your database will automatically be created in the filegroup you specified without your having to specify it every time.

To improve performance, you can control data placement by creating tables and indexes in different filegroups. For example, you might want to place a table that is heavily used in one filegroup on a large disk array (made up of 10 disk drives, for example) and place another table that is less heavily used in another filegroup located on a separate, smaller disk array (made up of 4 disk drives, for example). Therefore, the more heavily accessed table will be spread across the greater number of disks, allowing more parallel disk I/O. If you are not using RAID and you have multiple disk drives, you can still make use of filegroups. For example, you can create a separate file on each disk drive, placing each file in a separate user-defined filegroup. This allows you to place each table and index in a specific file (and on a specific disk) by designating the filegroup when you create the table or index. Figure 9-1 shows a sample arrangement: one primary data file in the primary filegroup on the C drive, one secondary data file in each of the user-defined filegroups (*FG1* and *FG2*) on the E and F drives, and one log file on the G drive. You can then create tables and indexes in either user-defined filegroup—*FG1* or *FG2*.

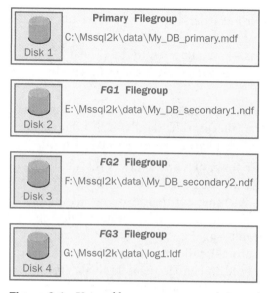

Figure 9-1. *Using filegroups to control data placement.*

Or you might use one user-defined filegroup to spread data across several disks. Figure 9-2 shows a user-defined filegroup (*FG1*) that includes two secondary data files, one on drive E and one on drive F (with the log file on drive G and the primary file on drive C). Again, in this case, we are assuming each database file is created on a single physical disk drive; there is no hardware RAID involved. Tables and indexes created in the user-defined filegroup will be spread across the two disks, as a result of SQL Server's proportional filling strategy.

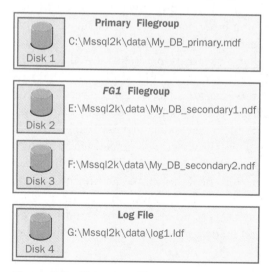

Figure 9-2. *Using one filegroup to spread data across several disks.*

If you use a RAID system, you might need to spread the data from a larger-than-average table across multiple logical disk arrays configured on two or more RAID controllers. You do this by creating a user-defined filegroup that includes a file on each of those controllers. Say you have created two secondary data files, each on a different array of disks, with each logical array made up of eight physical disks and configured with RAID 5. The two arrays are on separate RAID controllers. To create a table or an index across both controllers (thus across all 16 disk drives), define a single user-defined filegroup in which to place both files, and then create the table or index in that filegroup. Figure 9-3 shows the user-defined filegroup, *FG1*, that spans 16 physical disks, or two logical RAID disk arrays. It also shows the primary data file on another controller (with RAID 1) and the log file on yet another controller (with RAID 10).

SQL Server enables you to optimally distribute your data across disk drives because it automatically stripes, or distributes, data proportionally across all the files in a filegroup. "Striping" is the term used to describe distributing data across more than one database file. SQL Server file striping is independent of RAID disk striping, and it can be used alone or in conjunction with RAID, as we saw in our previous examples.

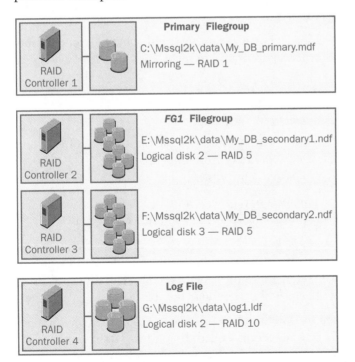

Figure 9-3. *Spreading a user-defined filegroup across multiple RAID controllers.*

To stripe data, SQL Server writes data to a file in an amount proportional to the free space in that file as compared with the free space in other files. Space is allocated for tables and indexes in extents. An *extent* is a unit of 8 pages, and each page is 8 kilobytes (KB), for a total of 64 KB per extent. For example, if 5 extents need to be allocated between file F1, which has 400 megabytes (MB) free, and file F2, which has 100 MB free, 4 extents are allocated to F1, and 1 extent is allocated to F2. Both files will become full at about the same time, allowing for a better distribution of I/O across the disks. Proportional striping will occur whether files F1 and F2 are in a user-defined filegroup or in the primary filegroup. If all the files in a filegroup are defined with the same initial size, data will be spread evenly across the files as it is loaded. This method of creating files with the same initial size in a filegroup is the recommended one for evenly distributing data across drives, in an attempt to allow for evenly distributed I/Os as well.

Another benefit of using filegroups is that SQL Server allows you to perform database backups based on a file or filegroup. If your database is too large to back up all at one time, you can back up just certain portions. This technique will be covered in detail in Chapter 32.

Rules and Recommendations

You should have a well-developed strategy for the use of files and filegroups before creating your database. In order to do that, you must know the following SQL Server 2000 rules:

- Files and filegroups cannot be used by more than one database.
- A file can be a member of only one filegroup.
- Data and transaction log information cannot be part of the same file. Log space is always managed separately from data space.
- Transaction log files are never part of a filegroup.
- Once a file is created as part of a database, it cannot be moved to another filegroup. If you want to move a file, you must delete and re-create it.

In addition to these rules, there are specific methods of using files and filegroups that are known to work well. Here are some general recommendations for using files and filegroups that will help you design your database:

- Most databases perform well with only a primary data file and one transaction log file. This is the recommended design for databases that are not particularly I/O intensive. If you have an I/O-intensive system that requires many disk drives, you will probably want to use user-defined filegroups to allow you to spread the data across disks or disk arrays for parallel I/O performance.

- Always place log files on separate physical disks from the disks containing data files, as explained in Chapter 5.

- If you do need to use multiple data files, use the primary data file for system tables and objects only, and create one or more secondary data files for user data and objects.

- Create files and filegroups across as many physical disks as are available to allow a greater amount of parallel disk I/O and to maximize performance.

- Place nonclustered indexes for heavily used tables in a separate filegroup on different physical disks from the disks containing the table data itself. This technique also allows for parallel disk I/O. (Indexes are covered in Chapter 17.)

- Place different tables that are used in the same query on different physical disks, if possible, to allow parallel disk I/O while the search engine is searching for data.

The last two items might not hold true for a system using RAID volumes with many disk drives. If you have many disk drives, you might do just as well or better to spread the indexes and tables across as many drives as are available, to achieve the greatest amount of parallel I/O possible for each table and index.

Automatic File Growth

SQL Server allows files to grow automatically when necessary. When a file is created, you can specify whether to allow SQL Server to automatically grow the file. Allowing automatic growth, which is the default when you are creating a database, is recommended, as it saves the administrator the burden of manually monitoring and increasing file space.

A file is created with an initial size. When that initial space is filled, SQL Server will increase the file size by a specified amount, known as the *growth increment*. When this new space fills, SQL Server will allocate another growth increment. The file will continue to grow at the specified rate, as needed, until the disk is full or until the maximum file size (if one is specified) is reached.

Note Automatic file growth is different from proportional filling. With automatic file growth, SQL Server automatically increases the size of a file when the file becomes full. With proportional filling, SQL Server places data in files in proportion to how much space the files have available but does not increase the files' size.

The *maximum file size* is just that—the maximum size to which a file is allowed to grow. This value is also specified at file creation but can be revised later using Enterprise Manager or the ALTER DATABASE command. If no maximum size is set for a file, SQL Server will continue to grow the file until all available disk space is filled. To avoid running out of disk space and causing SQL Server to receive errors, set a maximum size for each file. If a file does ever reach its maximum size, you can increase the maximum size by using the ALTER DATABASE statement. Or you can create another file on the same disk if space is still available on that disk, or on a different disk. Be sure that the new file is in the same filegroup as the original file. If a file is allowed to grow without restriction (per the default) until all the available disk space is used up, you will need to create a file on another disk that has free space.

As a rule, you should use automatic file growth and maximum file sizes. When you create a database, specify the largest size to which you think the files will ever grow. Even though automatic file growth is available, you should still monitor database growth on a regular basis—daily or weekly, perhaps—for your own records. You could keep the growth information in a spreadsheet, for example. With this information, you can extrapolate to estimate how much disk space will be needed for the next month, the next year, the next five years, and so on. By monitoring space, you should know if your files have experienced automatic growth and when or if you should alter the database to add more files. This continual space evaluation will help you avoid hitting the maximum file size or using up all the available disk space.

System Databases

When you install SQL Server, four system databases are created: the master, tempdb, model, and msdb databases. These databases are described in the following list:

- **master**   Records the system level information, SQL Server initialization information, and configuration settings for SQL Server. This database also records all login accounts, the existence of all other databases, and the location of the primary file for all user databases. Always keep a recent backup of the master database.

- **tempdb**   Holds temporary tables and temporary stored procedures. This database is also used for other temporary storage needs of SQL Server, such as for sorting data. A clean copy of the tempdb database is re-created at its default size every time SQL Server is started. It then grows automatically, as necessary. If you need a large amount of tempdb space, you can increase the database's default size by using the ALTER DATABASE command.

- **model**   Serves as a template for all other databases created on the system, including tempdb. When a database is created, the first part of it is created as a copy of the contents of the model database. The rest of the database is filled with empty pages. The model database must exist on the system because it is used to re-create tempdb every time SQL Server is started. You can alter the model database to include user-defined data types, tables, and so on. If you alter the model database, each database you create will have the modified attributes.

- **msdb**   Holds tables that SQL Server Agent uses for scheduling jobs and alerts and for recording operators. (*Operators* are individuals who are assigned responsibility for jobs and alerts.) This database also holds tables used for replication.

Each of these system databases has its own primary data file and log file. The databases are stored in the folder you specified for system files during SQL Server installation.

Database Creation

SQL Server provides three methods for creating a database: the Create Database Wizard, SQL Server Enterprise Manager, and T-SQL commands that can be saved in a file and run as a script. All three methods will be described in the sections that follow.

The Create Database Wizard has some limitations you should be aware of. The wizard places all data files it creates on a single drive in one folder that you specify. You cannot put data files in different physical locations (neither on different drives nor in different folders) if you use the wizard. You can place log files on a drive or in a folder separate from the data files but, again, in only one physical location. User-defined filegroups cannot be specified, and all files inherit the same growth options. Because of these limitations, the Create Database Wizard is the best choice if you need only a primary data file and a transaction log file in your database. (On the other hand, you can always add files and filegroups to the database later if you need them.)

You should use Enterprise Manager or a T-SQL script to create your database if you have secondary data files that you want to place on a disk drive different from that containing the primary data file, if you want to add user-defined filegroups, or if you need different growth options for the various files.

Using the Create Database Wizard

For novice database builders, the Create Database Wizard might be the easiest method; if it fits your needs despite the limitations mentioned earlier, by all means, use it. Follow these steps to use the Create Database Wizard to create a database:

1. Start SQL Server Enterprise Manager, and select the server on which you want to create your database. To select the server, begin by expanding the Microsoft SQL Servers folder. (Click the plus sign to the left of the folder name.) Expand the SQL Server Group folder, and then click the name of the server you want to use. From the Tools menu, select Wizards. Expand Database, as shown in Figure 9-4.

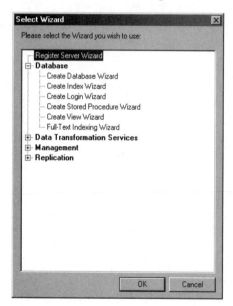

Figure 9-4. *The Select Wizard screen.*

2. Double-click Create Database Wizard to begin the Create Database Wizard, which is shown in Figure 9-5.

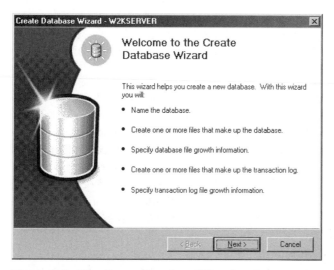

Figure 9-5. *The Create Database Wizard welcome screen.*

3. Click Next to go to the Name The Database And Specify Its Location screen, as displayed in Figure 9-6. Type the name of the database you want to create and the path locations where you want to store your data files and your log files. These locations must contain a valid drive and a folder that already exists on your local system. If you click the browse […] button to the right of one of the bottom two text boxes, you can search for and select a folder. Once you have named your database and located the path where the data and log files should be, click Next to continue.

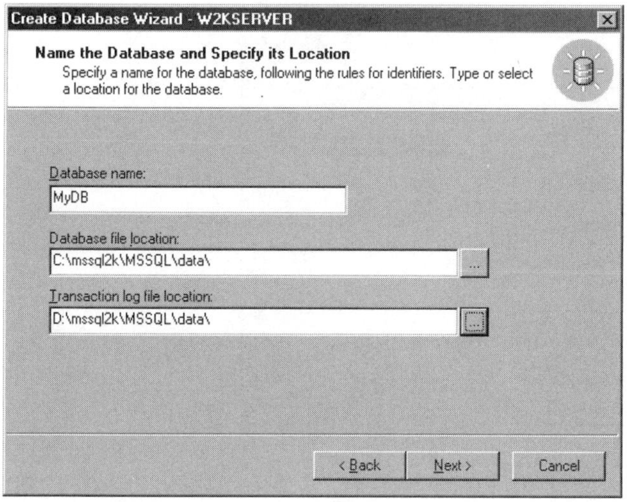

Figure 9-6. *The Name The Database And Specify Its Location screen.*

Note The remainder of the figures in this section show the creation of a database named MyDB that has a primary data file on C:\mssql2k\MSSQL\data and one log file on D:\mssql2k\MSSQL\data.

4. The Name The Database Files screen is displayed (Figure 9-7). In this screen, you can type the name and initial size for each of your database files. The primary database file is automatically created and given the database name as a prefix in its name. You can either accept this name or type a different one. The primary data file has an .mdf extension. If you have some idea of how big your database files should be, type an initial-size value now. Otherwise, leave the default size; you can modify it later using Enterprise Manager or the ALTER DATABASE command. Any files you create in addition to the first, or primary, file will be secondary files and will automatically be given the .ndf extension. All files created here will be placed in the primary filegroup. There is no option to create user-defined filegroups with the Create Database Wizard.

   In our example, we left the default primary file, MyDB_Data, and we added a secondary file, MyDB_Data2. Both these files will be placed in the same location you specified in step 3. (Do not continue if putting all data files on the same drive and in the same folder and filegroup is not what you want. Instead, use one of the other methods shown in the following sections for creating a database.) Click Next to continue.

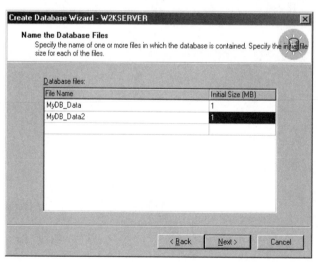

Figure 9-7. *The Name The Database Files screen.*

5. The Define The Database File Growth screen is displayed (Figure 9-8). As mentioned earlier in this chapter, SQL Server can automatically increase the size of your database as needed, which helps to reduce maintenance overhead. In general, you should select the automatic file growth feature (Automatically Grow The Database Files) because it requires little performance overhead; otherwise, you will need to manually adjust the size of your database, as necessary. If you click Automatically Grow The Database Files, you can specify how the database file should increase: either in fixed megabyte chunks or as a percentage of its current size. Remember that the database file will grow only as needed. You can also restrict the database to a maximum size or let it grow without restriction. The settings in this screen will apply to each database file you created in step 4. You cannot use the Create Database Wizard to configure growth settings for individual files. Click Next to continue.

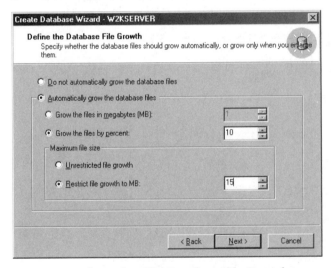

Figure 9-8. *The Define The Database File Growth screen.*

6. The Name The Transaction Log Files screen appears. This screen looks the same as the Name The Database Files screen, but this version is for the log file. Be careful to not get the screens mixed up.

   As you did in step 4 for your database files, type the name and initial size for your transaction log. (Remember that a transaction log contains a record of all database modifications for recoverability in case of system failure.) The first transaction log file is automatically created and given the database name as a prefix in its name. You can accept this name or type a different one. The transaction log data is stored in a file with the

.ldf extension. You can add more log files on different drives, if needed. If you have some idea of how big the transaction log will be, type a value now. Otherwise, keep the default size; you can modify it later using Enterprise Manager or the ALTER DATABASE command. Click Next to continue.

7. The Define The Transaction Log File Growth screen is displayed. This screen looks the same as the Define The Database File Growth screen, but here we are defining growth options for the log file. As you could in step 5, you can select Automatically Grow The Database Files, and if you want, you can specify the growth parameters and maximum file size. Click Next to continue.

8. The Completing The Create Database Wizard screen, shown in Figure 9-9, is displayed. Review the information you have specified for your new database. If it is acceptable, click Finish to complete your database creation; otherwise, click Back and make any necessary changes.

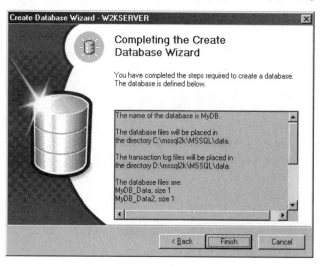

Figure 9-9. *The Completing The Create Database Wizard screen.*

9. Once your database has been created, a Create Database Wizard message box appears to inform you that the database has been successfully created. Click OK to close this message box.

10. Another message box appears, asking whether you would like to create a maintenance plan for your new database. Creating a maintenance plan is recommended to ensure that your database performs well, is regularly backed up in case of system failure, and is checked for inconsistencies. But because we won't cover maintenance plans until Chapter 30, click No to finish.

Using Enterprise Manager

SQL Server Enterprise Manager enables you to create more complex databases than does the Create Database Wizard. You can specify growth options for each file created, rather than for all the files as a group, and you can create user-defined filegroups. To create a database using Enterprise Manager, complete the steps outlined in the following list. In this example, we will create a sample database named MyDB, with a primary data file, three secondary data files (which reside in the same user-defined filegroup), and one log file.

1. Open Enterprise Manager. In the left pane, expand the SQL Server group that contains the name of the server you want to build the database on, and then expand the server node itself. Then right-click the Databases folder and choose New Database.

2. The Database Properties window opens, with the General tab in front, as shown in Figure 9-10. Type the name of the database in the Name box.

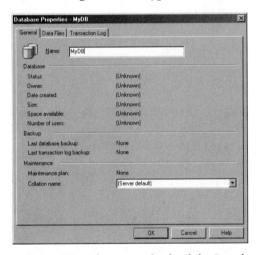

Figure 9-10. *The General tab of the Database Properties window.*

3. Click the Data Files tab. As shown in Figure 9-11, Enterprise Manager automatically creates the primary data file, with the name of your database as a prefix and with *PRIMARY* as the filegroup. You can change the name, location, and size of the primary file, but you cannot change the filegroup for the primary data file. Type the filename (logical name), location (physical name), size, and filegroup for each data file you want to create. For each data file other than the primary file, you can type a user-defined filegroup name, and that filegroup will be created for you.

In our example, we created the secondary data file MyDB_Data2 in the filegroup *My_FG*.

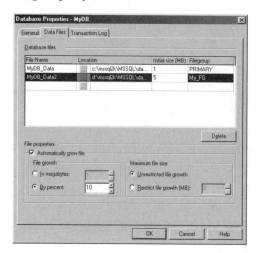

Figure 9-11. *The Data Files tab of the Database Properties window.*

The location for each file is by default the folder on the drive on which SQL Server is installed. You can change this setting by typing a new path or by using the browse button.

4. In the File Properties area at the bottom of the window, you can select automatic-growth options on a per-file basis. Select the name of the file for which you want to set growth options. Select the Automatically Grow File check box to enable automatic growth for that file. You can then specify the growth increment in megabytes or as a percentage of free space left in the file. You can also specify a maximum file size by clicking Restrict File Growth and entering a limit in megabytes, or you can leave the file size unrestricted. You can set these options as you create each file, or you can leave the defaults and set them later using the Enterprise Manager Database Properties window. If you need to delete a file from the list, select the name of the file and press the Delete key.

5. After you have finished configuring all the data files, click the Transaction Log tab in the Database Properties window to configure the transaction log files. Log files are configured in the same way as data files, except that you cannot select a filegroup for log files because they do not belong to any filegroup. Type the filename (logical name), the location (physical name), and the initial size for the log file or files. Also, choose the automatic-growth options for the log files as described step 4 for data files.

6. When you have all the files defined as you want them, click OK. SQL Server will create the database. Go back to Enterprise Manager and click the Databases folder for the server you just added a database to. In the right pane of Enterprise Manager, you'll see that SQL Server has added an icon for that database.

Using T-SQL Commands

You might prefer to create or alter your databases by using T-SQL commands or scripting rather than by using a graphical user interface (GUI). Creating your own scripts can be useful when you create databases. Let's say you create the database but then realize you specified the wrong location for a file. You can drop the database and start over. If you used a T-SQL script to create the database, you will be able to edit it and rerun it quickly, instead of having to reenter all the data into a GUI. You can also run the same script if you need to create the database on another system, such as a warm backup system.

On the other hand, Enterprise Manager can be used to generate T-SQL scripts for database creation (as well as for the creation of all database objects) but only after a database has already been created. The Enterprise Manager scripts will include all of the current database option settings, which can be useful; therefore, you might prefer to use the generated scripts. Whether you decide to write your own scripts or to use generated scripts, it is good to understand the T-SQL code used to create a database. In this section, we will review the T-SQL commands for creating a database. These commands can be typed into a file to create a script. Specifically how to create and run a script is explained in Chapter 13.

Real World   A Simple Database

In the following example, we'll create a database named MyDB that contains a primary data file (MyDB_root); one secondary data file (MyDB_data1), which remains in the primary filegroup by default; and one transaction log file (Log_data1). The SQL statements for creating the MyDB database are shown here:

```
CREATE DATABASE MyDB
ON
(NAME = MyDB_root,              --Primary data file
FILENAME = 'c:\mssql2k\MSSQL\data\mydbroot.mdf',
SIZE = 8MB,
MAXSIZE = 9MB,
FILEGROWTH = 100KB),
```

```
(NAME = MyDB_data1,          --Secondary data file
FILENAME = 'c:\mssql2k\MSSQL\data\mydbdata1.ndf',
SIZE = 1000MB,
MAXSIZE = 1500MB,
FILEGROWTH = 100MB)
LOG ON
(NAME = Log_data1,           --Log file
FILENAME = 'e:\log_files\logdata1.ldf',
SIZE = 1000MB,
MAXSIZE = 1500MB,
FILEGROWTH = 100MB)
```

Notice that, in this example, the primary and secondary data files are both on the C drive and the log file is on the E drive. As mentioned, you should always physically separate data files from log files to improve disk I/O performance.

Also, notice that the recommended file extensions—.mdf, .ndf, and .ldf—were used. The SIZE, MAXSIZE, and FILEGROWTH options can be specified in kilobytes or megabytes; the default is megabytes.

More Info To learn more about the CREATE DATABASE statement, check the Books Online index for the topic "Create Database."

Real World   A More Complex Database

The database example in this section is based on a system with several disk drives or several arrays of disks (in a RAID system). The term "disk" will be used to refer to either a single disk drive or an array of disk drives acting as a RAID volume. Several files are created, each on a separate disk. Each file is placed in one of two filegroups. Our database will be named "Sales" and will contain the following files:

- A primary data file, Sales_root.mdf
- Three secondary data files, customer_data1.ndf, customer_data2.ndf, and customer_data3.ndf, in the filegroup *customers_group*
- Two secondary data files, product_data1.ndf and product_data2.ndf, in the filegroup *products_group*
- One log file, log_data1.ldf

The code for creating the Sales database is shown here. Because we will be creating user-defined filegroups, we will include the keyword FILEGROUP with this CREATE DATABASE command.

```
CREATE DATABASE Sales
ON PRIMARY                   --Explicitly states primary
                             --filegroup (optional)
(NAME = Salesroot,           --Primary data file
FILENAME = 'c:\mssql2k\MSSQL\data\salesroot.mdf',
SIZE = 8MB,
MAXSIZE = 10MB,
FILEGROWTH = 1MB),
FILEGROUP customers_group    --Filegroup for next files
(NAME = customer_data1,      --Secondary data file
FILENAME = 'd:\mssql2k\MSSQL\data\customerdata1.ndf',
SIZE = 800MB,
MAXSIZE = 1000MB,
FILEGROWTH = 100MB),
(NAME = customer_data2,      --Secondary data file
FILENAME = 'e:\mssql2k\MSSQL\data\customerdata2.ndf',
SIZE = 800MB,
MAXSIZE = 1000MB,
FILEGROWTH = 100MB),
(NAME = customer_data3,      --Secondary data file
FILENAME = 'f:\mssql2k\MSSQL\data\customerdata3.ndf',
SIZE = 800MB,
MAXSIZE = 1000MB,
FILEGROWTH = 100MB),
FILEGROUP products_group     --Filegroup for next files
(NAME = product_data1,       --Secondary data file
FILENAME = 'g:\mssql2k\MSSQL\data\product_data1.ndf',
SIZE = 500MB,
MAXSIZE = 700MB,
FILEGROWTH = 100MB),
(NAME = product_data2,       --Secondary data file
FILENAME = 'h:\mssql2k\MSSQL\data\product_data2.ndf',
SIZE = 500MB,
MAXSIZE = 700MB,
FILEGROWTH = 100MB)
LOG ON
(NAME = logdata1,            --Log file
FILENAME = 'i:\log_files\logdata1.ldf',
SIZE = 800MB,
MAXSIZE = 1000MB,
FILEGROWTH = 200MB)
```

As the comments in this code indicate, the primary filegroup can be explicitly stated before the primary data file is defined. The primary filegroup is the default. The other two filegroups, *customers_group* and *products_group*, are defined immediately before the files that will be placed in them. All of the files listed after a filegroup definition will be placed in that filegroup until another filegroup is defined or the LOG ON clause is reached.

Also, notice the drive letters for each file. Each file is created on a different disk to allow data to be spread across disks when the tables and indexes are created in the filegroups. For instance, a table created in the *customers_group* filegroup will have its data striped across the disks that hold the customer_data1.ndf, customer_data2.ndf, and customer_data3.ndf files. The log file is also on a separate disk, with no data files, to allow the log to perform sequential writes.

If you do not want SQL Server to automatically grow a file, set FILEGROWTH=0 so that the file will be allowed to fill only its initial size. You might choose this setting if you have a table that is static—in other words, a table that does not grow. In this case, MAXSIZE would not need to be specified in the statement. The maximum size would be the initial SIZE setting.

> **Note** If you're familiar with SQL Server versions 6.5 and earlier, you'll notice that you no longer use the DISK INIT command to create logical devices before creating the database. The use of files replaces logical devices.

Database Viewing

After you have created a database, you can use Enterprise Manager to browse and view the objects in it. You can also view information about a database by running SQL commands with command-line OSQL. Here, you will learn to use both methods of viewing.

Using Enterprise Manager

To view database information using Enterprise Manager, follow these steps:

1. In Enterprise Manager, expand (by clicking the plus signs) the lists for the SQL Server group, the name of the server on which the database resides, and the Databases folder, as shown in Figure 9-12.

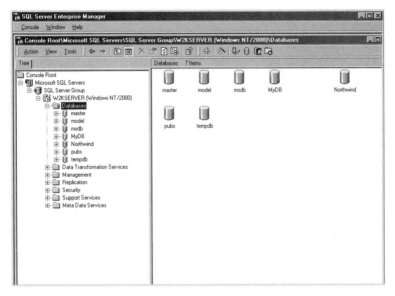

Figure 9-12. *Enterprise Manager with the Databases folder expanded.*

2. Click the desired database name to display the objects the database contains, as shown in Figure 9-13.

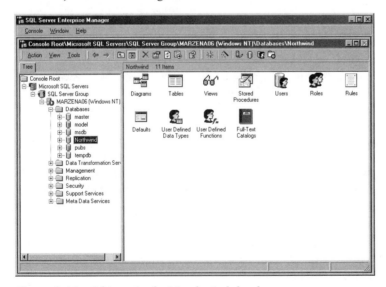

Figure 9-13. *Objects in the Northwind database.*

Using SQL

You can also view database information in a command prompt window or in Query Analyzer by running T-SQL commands. To view database information by using command-line SQL, open a command prompt window and make a connection to SQL Server with OSQL, as in the following example:

```
OSQL -U<username> -P<password> -S<servername>
```

When you type this command, put your own user name, password, and server name in place of the words in angle brackets. (And don't include the angle brackets.)

To use Query Analyzer, click Start, point to Programs, point to Microsoft SQL Server, and then choose Query Analyzer. Now type the T-SQL commands either in the Query Analyzer window or at the OSQL prompt. Run the following SQL commands to list database information:

```
Use MyDB            --Specifies the database context to use
GO
Sp_helpfile        --Shows information for all files in the database
GO                 --Give a filename to see just that file information.
Sp_helpdb MyDB     --Same as above plus shows the space allocated for
                   --the database
GO
Sp_helpfilegroup   --Shows filegroup information for this database
GO                 --Give a filegroup name to see its information only.
Sp_helpdb          --Shows database information for all databases
GO
```

 More Info You can find more details about these commands and what their output means in SQL Server Books Online.

Database Deletion

At some point, you might want to remove a database. Keep in mind that this is a one-way street—once you delete a database, the only way you can retrieve it is by restoring a backup version. It is safest, then, to back up the database before you delete it, just in case you might need it again in the future. You can delete a database by using Enterprise Manager or T-SQL commands.

Using Enterprise Manager

As mentioned in Chapter 8, Enterprise Manager allows you to perform administration on your databases as well as to view information. To permanently delete a database and all of its files by using Enterprise Manager, follow these steps:

1. In Enterprise Manager, expand the SQL Server group and then expand the name of the server on which the database is installed.

2. Expand the Databases folder to view the available databases.

3. Right-click the name of the database you want to delete, and then choose Delete from the shortcut menu. The Delete Database message box appears, as shown in Figure 9-14. It asks if you want to delete the backup-and-restore history of this database as well as delete the database. If you select this option, all backup-and-restore information in the backup-and-restore history tables that reside in the msdb database will be deleted. If you want to keep this data, clear the check box. Click Yes to confirm the deletion.

Note You cannot delete the master database.

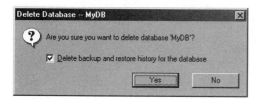

Figure 9-14. *The Delete Database message box.*

Using SQL

You can also administer databases by using T-SQL commands. These can be run in Query Analyzer or in the command prompt window, as mentioned earlier. To delete a database using T-SQL, open either Query Analyzer, as described earlier, or a command prompt window, and make a connection to SQL Server through OSQL, as shown in the following example:

```
OSQL -U<username> -P<password> -S<servername>
```

Remember that deleting a database is a permanent action. The T-SQL command used for deleting a database is DROP DATABASE. The commands to delete the MyDB database and all of its files are shown here:

```
USE master          --You must use the master database to run the DROP
GO                  --DATABASE command.
DROP DATABASE MyDB  --The only parameter is the name of
                    --the database to be removed.
GO
```

After deleting a database, you should make a new backup of the master database so it will have the current information about user databases and so it doesn't include information about the database you just deleted. Also, note that a database cannot be deleted while users are accessing it. All users must disconnect from a database before it is deleted.

Summary

In this chapter, you have expanded your knowledge of SQL Server 2000 data and log files, filegroups, and automatic file growth. You now know how to create databases using the Create Database Wizard, SQL Server Enterprise Manager, and T-SQL commands. You also know two methods for viewing database and file information, as well as how to delete a database. Now you're ready to start creating tables in your database—the topic of Chapter 10.

Chapter 10
Creating Database Tables

Once you have created a database (with files and filegroups), the next step is to create the objects, called tables, that allow you to organize and store your data. This chapter examines the major decisions involved in creating a database table. Creating a table can be a slightly complicated process because many options are available. We will first look at the basic requirements for a table and then explore some of the options, giving examples as we go.

In this chapter, you'll learn about system and user-defined data types, how to place tables in filegroups, null values, and the IDENTITY property. You'll also learn how to create a table using Enterprise Manager and Transact-SQL (T-SQL). Other important table creation issues are touched on here, including constraints, defaults, and indexes; these topics will be described in more detail in later chapters.

Caution Be sure to familiarize yourself with this material before you begin creating your tables.

Laying the Groundwork

As you begin to design your database tables, you must make several decisions regarding their structure. These decisions include determining what pieces of data need to be stored in your tables and how your tables should relate to each other. This process will help you envision the big picture before you get into the details of creating the tables. The following list provides an overview of these design decisions:

- What data will each table contain?
- What columns should be created to hold the data, and what should they be named?
- What are the requirements for the range of data that a column should be allowed to hold, and what Microsoft SQL Server 2000 data type should be used for each column?

- Are there any columns that must be allowed to contain null values, or can defaults be used instead? (Allowing null values requires more processing overhead than does using defaults.)
- Which columns will be primary keys, and which will be foreign keys?
- What kinds of constraints should be used?
- What type of index or indexes (clustered or nonclustered) should the table have, and on which column or columns should these indexes be defined?
- Which users should have access to which tables?

Try to resolve as many of these design issues as possible, and track them on paper or with online diagrams to understand the overall design of your database tables before you create them. You should also find out from your users how the data will be accessed. For example, find out if a particular table data will be read-only or if inserts, deletes, and updates will be performed. Determine which queries will be performed most often and which columns will need to be retrieved. Establish what information is really needed in the database and what is not necessary to store. This information will help you decide how to build tables and indexes, what constraints might be needed, where defaults might be useful, and more. Now let's begin learning how to create tables from the ground up.

Reviewing Table Basics

In this section, we'll review some simple but important concepts about tables. We include a sample database table to introduce you to the basic elements of a table, and you'll learn about system data types and how to create and delete user-defined data types.

Defining a Database Table

A *table* is an object in a database that stores data in a collection of rows and columns. A table is defined by the columns it contains. Data can thus be organized in a spreadsheet-like format, as illustrated in Table 10-1, which shows a sample database table named *Product_Info*. (In our examples, we will create this table in the MyDB database, which we created in Chapter 9.)

The *Product_Info* table is used to store information about each product that is for sale in a store. When a product becomes available for sale, its data is added as a new row in this table. The table contains five columns of information: *Product_ID*, *Product_Name*, *Description*, *Price*, and *Brand_ID*. Table 10-1 shows a sampling of three rows of data from the *Product_Info* table. (The T-SQL command used to create this table, without any data, is shown in the section "Selecting the Correct Data Type" later in this chapter. See Chapter 20 for details on using the INSERT command to insert data into a table.)

Table 10-1. *Product_Info* database

Product_ID	Product_Name	Description	Price	Brand_ID
1	Five-foot tent	For one or two persons	80.00	12
2	Mini-stove	Kerosene-fueled	20.00	33
3	Backpack	Steel-framed	60.00	15

We'll return to this sample database table throughout this chapter to illustrate more complex aspects of table creation. But first we'll continue to explain the basics you'll need to know to create a table.

To define a table, you must decide what columns to define and what type of data, such as character or numerical data, each column is allowed to hold. You should also decide on an allowable range for that data—for example, you could decide to allow up to 30 characters or 4-byte numbers. You specify these attributes by assigning each column a *data type,* which is a set of attributes that determine what type and range of data that column can hold. SQL Server provides a number of system data types you can use, or you can create your own by building on the system types. (You can't change a system data type, but you can create a completely new type.)

Using System Data Types

As mentioned, you specify a data type for each column of a table. Assigning a data type to a column sets the following attributes:

- The kind of data the column can contain, such as characters, integers, or images
- The size or length of the data in a column
- The precision of the number (for numeric data types only)—that is, the number of digits a number can contain
- The scale of the number (for numeric data types only)—that is, the number of digits that can be stored to the right of the decimal point

Data types can also affect columns for views, parameters in stored procedures, variables, and T-SQL functions that return one or more data values. The built-in data types provided by SQL Server are defined in Table 10-2. SQL Server 2000 introduces three data types—*bigint, sql_variant,* and *table.* (With a few exceptions, noted in this table, the same data types are used for all of the mentioned objects.)

Table 10-2. System data types in SQL Server 2000

Data type	Description	Storage size
bigint	An 8-byte integer (whole number).	8 bytes
binary[(n)]	Fixed-length binary data of *n* bytes, where *n* is a value from *1* through *8000*. Use *binary* when data entries in a column are expected to be close to the same size.	*n* + 4 bytes
bit	Integer data type that can be a value of *1*, *0*, or *NULL*. Bit columns cannot have indexes on them.	1 byte for a table with up to 8-bit columns, 2 bytes for a table with 9-bit through 16-bit columns, and so on
char[(n)]	Fixed-length non-Unicode character data with length of *n* characters, where *n* is a value from *1* through *8000*.	*n* bytes
cursor	A reference to a cursor. Can be used only for variables and stored procedure parameters.	Not applicable
datetime	Date and time data from January 1, 1753 through December 31, 9999, with accuracy to 3.33 milliseconds.	8 bytes
decimal[(p,[s])] or *numeric[(p,[s])]*	Fixed-precision and fixed-scale numbers. (The data type *numeric* is a synonym for *decimal*.) Precision (*p*) specifies the total number of digits that can be stored, both to the left and to the right of the decimal point. Scale (*s*) specifies the maximum number of digits that can be stored to the right of the decimal point. Scale must be less than or equal to precision. The minimum precision is *1*, and the maximum precision is *28* unless SQL Server is started with the *–p* parameter, in which case, precision can be up to *38*.	5 through 17 bytes, depending on precision
float[(n)]	Floating-precision numerical data that can range from *–1.79E +308* through *1.79E +308*. The value *n* is the number of bits used to store the mantissa of the float number and can range from *1* to *53*.	4 through 8 bytes, depending on precision
image	Used for variable-length binary data longer than 8000 bytes, with a maximum of $2^{31} - 1$ bytes. An *image* column entry is a pointer to the location of the *image* data value. The data is stored separately from the table data.	16 bytes for the pointer
integer or *int*	Integer (whole number) data from -2^{31} (*–2,147,483,648*) through $2^{31} - 1$ (*2,147,483,647*).	4 bytes
money	Monetary data values from -2^{63} (*–922,337,203,685,477.5808*) through $2^{63} - 1$ (*922,337,203,685,477.5807*), with accuracy to one ten-thousandth of a monetary unit.	8 bytes

Data type	Description	Storage size
nchar[(n)]	Fixed-length Unicode character data of *n* characters, where *n* is a value from *1* through *4000*. Unicode characters use 2 bytes per character and can support all international characters.	2 bytes × the number of characters entered
ntext	Variable-length Unicode data with a maximum length of 2^30 − 1 (1,073,741,823) characters. The column entry for *ntext* is a pointer to the location of the data. The data is stored separately from the table data.	16 bytes for the pointer and 2 bytes × the number of characters entered for the data
nvarchar	Variable-length Unicode data of *n* characters, where *n* is a value from *1* through *4000*. Recall that Unicode characters use 2 bytes per character and can support all international characters.	2 bytes × the number of characters entered
real	Floating-precision numerical data that can range from ?3.40E+38 through 3.40E+38. The synonym for *real* is *float(24)*.	4 bytes
smalldatetime	Date and time data from January 1, 1900 through June 6, 2079, with accuracy to the minute (less precise than the *datetime* data type).	4 bytes
smallint	Integer data from −2^15 (−32,768) through 2^15 − 1 (32,767).	2 bytes
smallmoney	Monetary data values from −214,748.3648 through 214,748.3647, with accuracy to one ten-thousandth of a monetary unit.	4 bytes
sql_variant	Allows values of different data types. The data value and data describing that value—its base data type, scale, precision, maximum size, and collation—are stored in this column.	Size varies
sysname	A special, system-supplied, SQL Server user-defined data type. The *sysname* data type is defined by SQL Server as *nvarchar(128)*, which means that it can contain 128 Unicode characters (or 256 bytes). Use *sysname* to refer to columns that store object names.	256 bytes
table	Similar to using a temporary table—the declaration includes a column list and data types. Can be used to define a local variable or for the return value of a user-defined function.	Varies with table definition
text	Used for variable-length non-Unicode character data longer than 8000 bytes. A *text* column entry can hold up to 2^31 − 1 characters. It is a pointer to the location of the data value. The data is stored separately from the table data.	16 bytes for the pointer
timestamp	A *timestamp* column is automatically updated every time a row is inserted or updated. Each table can have only one *timestamp* column.	8 bytes

(continued)

Table 10-2. *continued*

Data type	Description	Storage size
tinyint	Integer data from 0 through 255.	1 byte
unique-identifier	Stores a 16-byte binary value that is a globally unique identifier (GUID).	16 bytes
varbinary	Variable-length binary data of *n* bytes, where *n* is a value from *1* through *8000*. Use *varbinary* when data entries in a column are expected to vary considerably in size.	Actual length of data entered + 4 bytes
varchar[(n)]	Variable-length non-Unicode character data with a length of *n* characters, where *n* is a value from *1* through *8000*.	Actual length of data entered

Selecting the Correct Data Type

Selecting the correct data type for each column is important when creating tables. You want the range of values that you need to store in the column to be permitted, and you want to reject values that should not be permitted (such as a character value in a column that requires a number). Data types will take care of this for you. Two questions can help guide you in choosing data types:

- Is the data type appropriate for the kind of data you need to store?
- Should you use a fixed-length or a variable-length data type?

Selecting the appropriate data type is a fairly straightforward process. The data that will be entered in a column must conform to the data type specified for that column. Therefore, you should select the data type that best covers the range of values your column might hold over the lifetime of your application, while limiting the amount of wasted space. *Wasted space* is space that is allocated for a column entry but not used. For example, suppose you have a column that will need to hold only integer values that range from *1* through *100*. The *integer* data type would certainly allow those values, but each integer takes up 4 bytes of space. The *tinyint* data type allows values from 0 through 255, and it takes up only 1 byte of space. In this case, *tinyint* would be the best choice because it would save disk space when storing that column's data.

Next you must determine whether to use fixed-length or variable-length data types. If all of the values in a column will be near the same size, a fixed-length data type is more efficient because of the overhead involved with variable-length types. Generally, variable-length data types are appropriate when you expect a wide variance in the length of the data stored in the column and when the column data will not change often. Variable-length data types include *varchar, nvarchar, varbinary, text, ntext,* and *image.* Using variable-length data types can result in significant storage space savings. For example, if you define a fixed-length data type that is big enough to store the largest possible value in a column, all smaller values in that column will take up the same big amount of storage space as the largest value does. This results in a huge waste of space if only a small percentage of rows hold the largest value. If the majority of rows will hold a smaller value, the extra space used to hold those smaller values is wasted space. On the other hand, if you define a variable-length data type, the shorter values will take up only the space they need. But again, variable-length data types will require more processing overhead. So if you don't need the variable-length type, use fixed-length. If it makes sense to use a variable-length type because of the space savings, by all means, use it.

So how do you make choices about data type and length for your tables? Follow the preceding guidelines, and make the choices that best fit your application needs. In general, try not to be wasteful with space when you set your column lengths, and don't forget to consider future requirements.

Creating the *Product_Info* Table Using System Data Types

Before we continue, let's take a look at the T-SQL CREATE TABLE command, which can be used to create the *Product_Info* table shown in Table 10-1 earlier in this chapter. For this example, we will use only system data types and fixed-length columns.

When you issue T-SQL commands to create a table, the table will be created in whichever database you are currently using. To use a particular database, run the USE *database_name* command, as shown in the following code. In this example, our database is named MyDB. The keyword GO indicates that any previous commands should now be executed. (See Chapter 13 for more details about using T-SQL.)

```
USE MyDB
GO
CREATE TABLE Product_Info
(
Product_ID      smallint,
Product_Name    char(20),
Description     char(30),
Price           smallmoney,
Brand_ID        smallint
)
GO
```

Let's look at what happens in the preceding code. After the CREATE TABLE command is given, the table name *Product_Info* is specified. Between the parentheses, each column is then defined by listing the column name followed by its data type. The lengths for the two *char* data types are set at *20* and *30* because most names will be 20 characters or fewer and most descriptions will be 30 characters or fewer. *Product_ID* and *Brand_ID* are both set to the data type *smallint* instead of *tinyint* or *int* because we anticipate more than 255 products and brand types (the maximum value for *tinyint*) yet fewer than *32,767* (the maximum value for *smallint*). Because we will not need values above *32,767*, we would be wasting space if we used the *int* type.

Working with User-Defined Data Types

User-defined data types, or alias data types, are system data types that have been customized. Customizing, or defining, a data type is useful when you have several tables that must store the same type of data in a column and you want to ensure that the corresponding columns in each table have exactly the same type, length, and nullability. You can define a data type with a descriptive name for ease of programming and consistency. Then you can use the data type when you create the various tables.

For example, suppose we have another table—this one named *Brands*—in the same database as the one the *Product_Info* table is in. The *Brands* table will have a *Brand_ID* column that corresponds to the *Brand_ID* column in the *Product_Info* table, and the *Brands* table will provide the brand name and other pertinent brand information. To ensure that the *Brand_ID* columns in the two tables have the same data type and do not allow null values, you could create a user-defined data type and assign it to both columns. Now imagine that you have several tables with columns that need to have the same attributes. You might not remember whether you used *smallint* or *tinyint* for that column in one table or whether you allowed null values. If you had defined a data type with a descriptive name, you would not have to worry what its attributes were each time you used it, and you would be assured that your data types would be consistent among tables.

Note When you define a data type in a particular database, it can be used in only that database. However, if you define the data type in the model database (the template for all other databases), it will exist in all new databases.

Creating User-Defined Data Types Using Enterprise Manager

You might want to create data types for data such as phone numbers, postal codes, social security numbers, and any other data that you can define clearly and that you will use in more than one database table. When you define a data type, you must supply the following pieces of information:

- The name of the data type
- The system data type on which the new data type is based
- The data type's nullability—that is, whether it allows null values (discussed in more detail in the section "Using Null Values" later in this chapter)

Once you have decided on these details, you are ready to create the data type. To create a user-defined data type using Enterprise Manager, follow these steps:

1. In Enterprise Manager, expand a SQL Server group (by clicking the plus sign next to the folder), and then expand a server.

2. Expand the Databases folder and then expand a database. Your Enterprise Manager window will look similar to the window shown in Figure 10-1.

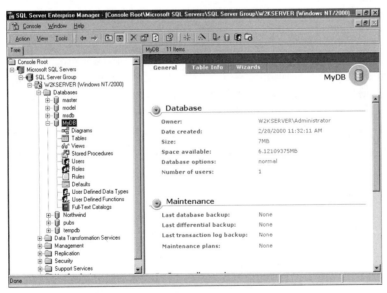

Figure 10-1. *Defining a data type using Enterprise Manager.*

3. Right-click User Defined Data Types and choose New User Defined Data Type from the shortcut menu. The User-Defined Data Type Properties window appears.

4. Type the name of the new data type in the Name text box. We'll name our example *brand_type*, as shown in Figure 10-2.

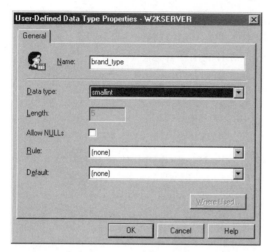

Figure 10-2. *The User-Defined Data Type Properties window.*

5. Next you must specify the SQL Server system data type and length that describe your user-defined field. In this example, we are defining a data type for our *Brand_ID* column, so we'll choose the *smallint* data type, with a default length value of 5. (If we had created a character data type, you would be allowed to specify the length.)

6. If your data type should allow null values, select the Allow NULLs check box. (For more information about null values, see the section "Using Null Values" later in this chapter.)

7. If your data type should use any predefined rules or defaults, select them from their respective list boxes. (Rules and defaults are described in detail in Chapter 16.)

8. Click OK to save your new data type.

Deleting User-Defined Data Types Using Enterprise Manager

If you have created a user-defined data type and are no longer using it (or if you made a mistake when creating it and you want to create it again), you can delete it. To delete a user-defined data type, follow these steps:

1. In Enterprise Manager, locate the user-defined data type you want to delete. (Expand a SQL Server group, expand a server, expand the Databases folder, and then expand the database that contains the data type you want to delete.)

2. Click the User Defined Data Types folder. The user-defined data types in your database will be displayed in the right-hand pane, as shown in Figure 10-3.

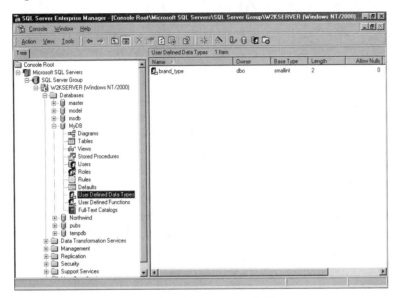

Figure 10-3. *The User Defined Data Types folder.*

3. Right-click the user-defined data type you want to delete and then choose Delete from the shortcut menu that appears. The Drop Objects dialog box appears (Figure 10-4).

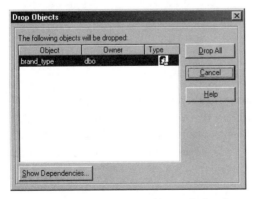

Figure 10-4. *The Drop Objects dialog box.*

4. Before you actually delete the data type, click Show Dependencies to display the Dependencies dialog box, shown in Figure 10-5.

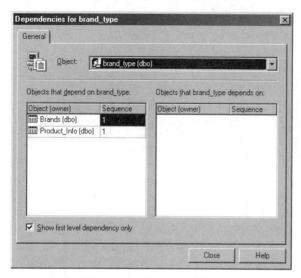

Figure 10-5. *The Dependencies dialog box.*

The list box on the left side of the Dependencies dialog box displays the database objects that depend on your user-defined data type, and the list box on the right displays the objects that your data type depends on. If your data type is being used by any tables or objects (as the data type in our case is), you will not be allowed to delete it—when you try to do so (by following step 5), an error message will appear, as shown in Figure 10-6.

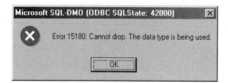

Figure 10-6. *The error message that appears if you attempt to delete a data type that is in use.*

5. If your data type has no dependency problems, close the Dependencies dialog box and then click Drop All in the Drop Objects dialog box to delete the data type. Don't worry—only the data types shown in the Drop Objects dialog box, not all your user-defined data types, will be deleted.

Creating and Deleting User-Defined Data Types Using T-SQL

The system stored procedure *sp_addtype* is a T-SQL command used to add a user-defined data type. Running the command while you are using the model database will enable all new user-defined databases to use the new data type because they are created with the same attributes as the model database. Running the command while you are using a user-defined database will enable the new data type to be used in only that database. (Remember, to use a particular database, you must run the USE *database_name* command.) The following T-SQL command creates the user-defined data type *brand_type* in the model database:

```
USE model
GO
sp_addtype brand_type, 'smallint', 'NOT NULL'
GO
```

The three parameters for *sp_addtype* are the name of the user-defined data type, the system data type the new data type is based on, and the nullability of the new data type. This new data type, *brand_type*, will appear in all new user-defined databases. If you created the user-defined data type in a user database and you want to see the new type in Enterprise Manager, choose Refresh from the Enterprise Manager Action menu.

To drop a user-defined data type that is not in use, run the *sp_droptype* command in the database in which the data type is defined. The following T-SQL command drops the user-defined data type *brand_type* from the model database. (Again, if you create this data type in a user database and want Enterprise Manager to show that the type was dropped, choose Refresh from the Enterprise Manager Action menu.)

```
USE model
GO
sp_droptype brand_type
GO
```

Creating the *Product_Info* and *Brands* Tables Using User-Defined Data Types

Let's return to our database table example. We will re-create the *Product_Info* table, using the new user-defined data type, *brand_type*, and then we will create the *Brands* table. It will have a *Brand_ID* column just as the *Product_Info* table has, and we will use the same user-defined type, *brand_type*. First we must drop the old *Product_Info* table so we can re-create it. The code to perform all these operations appears at the top of the following page.

```
USE MyDB
GO
DROP TABLE Product_Info
GO
CREATE TABLE Product_Info
(
Product_ID      smallint,
Product_Name    char(20),
Description     char(30),
Price           smallmoney,
Brand_ID        brand_type
)
GO
CREATE TABLE Brands
(
Brand_ID        brand_type,
Brand_Name      char(30),
Supplier_ID     smallint
)
GO
```

By assigning the *brand_type* data type to the *Brand_ID* columns of both tables, we are guaranteed that the columns will have the same attributes. We don't have to remember the specifics of the underlying data type, but now we can use this data type for all *Brand_ID* columns.

Who needs to keep track of these user-defined types? The database administrator (DBA) will need to know what user-defined types were used in order to understand whether they are correct and were used properly. (The DBA was probably the person who defined them to begin with, though.) And the application programmer will need to know how these data types are defined when he or she is writing application code. But end users will not need to know about user-defined data types because they will not know the difference.

Creating Tables in a Filegroup

SQL Server lets you specify which filegroup you want each table and its data to be placed in—assuming that you have created one or more user-defined filegroups. If no filegroup is specified at table creation, tables will be placed in the primary filegroup unless another filegroup has been assigned to be the default filegroup. (Filegroups are used to place files and indexes on a particular disk or array of disks. See Chapter 9 for more information about how and why table data is placed in files and filegroups.)

Creating the *Product_Info* Table in a Filegroup

Suppose we create the MyDB database with a filegroup named *product_group* that contains one secondary data file that is on a different disk drive (E) from the disk drive housing the primary filegroup (C). This technique allows us to physically separate our data tables from the SQL Server system tables. We'll also create the log file on a different drive (F) to separate log I/O. (Creating databases and using filegroups is explained in Chapter 9.) The commands might look like this:

```
USE master
GO
CREATE DATABASE MyDB
ON PRIMARY                       --Explicitly states primary
                                 -- filegroup (optional)
(NAME = MyDBroot,                --Primary data file
FILENAME = 'c:\mssql2k\MSSQL\data\mydbroot.mdf',
SIZE = 8MB,
MAXSIZE = 10MB,
FILEGROWTH = 1MB),
FILEGROUP product_group          --Filegroup for next file
(NAME = MyDBdata1,               --Secondary data file
FILENAME = 'e:\mssql2k\MSSQL\data\mydbdata1.ndf',
SIZE = 1000MB,
MAXSIZE = 1500MB,
FILEGROWTH = 100MB)
LOG ON
(NAME = Logdata1,                --Log file
FILENAME = 'f:\log_files\logdata1.ldf',
SIZE = 1000MB,
MAXSIZE = 1500MB,
FILEGROWTH = 100MB)
GO
```

We can now create the *Product_Info* table in the *product_group* filegroup using the CREATE TABLE command, as shown here:

```
USE MyDB
GO
CREATE TABLE Product_Info
(
Product_ID      smallint,
Product_Name    char(20),
Description     char(30),
Price           smallmoney,
Brand_ID        brand_type
)
on product_group
GO
```

The table and all data inserted in the table will be placed on drive E, the drive on which *product_group* was defined. Thus, the *Product_Info* table data will have a dedicated drive for its I/O, as long as no other tables are created in this same filegroup.

Using Null Values

A *null value* is an unknown value that we refer to as *NULL*. The *nullability* of a column refers to the ability of the column to accept or reject null values. A null value in a column usually indicates that no entry has been made into that column for a particular row of data because the value is either not known, not applicable, not defined, or to be added at a later time. Null values are neither empty values nor *0* values; their true values are unknown—so no two null values are equal.

A nullable column might be needed if information that you need is not available yet—for example, a customer's middle initial. What should the column contain in a record for someone who does not have a middle name and therefore no middle initial? If *NULL* is allowed in that column, a null value in that record would be true and would make sense—it would let you know that the information is not applicable.

As a general rule, avoid allowing null values. They cause more complexity in queries and updates, and some options, such as primary keys and the IDENTITY property, cannot be used on a nullable column.

More Info For more information, display the Books Online index entry for Null Values, and then select the topic "Comparison Search Conditions." Also see the section "Adding the IDENTITY Property" later in this chapter.)

An excellent alternative to allowing *NULL*s in a column is to define a default value for the column. When a value is not specified for a row insert, the default value is entered into the column. (See Chapter 16 for more information about using defaults.) If you do define a column to allow null values, a *NULL* can be entered into that column in one of two ways:

- If a row is inserted into the table but no data value is specified for the nullable column, SQL Server will assign it the value *NULL* (unless a default value has been specified for that column).

- A user can type the word "NULL," without quotation marks so that it will not be confused with the character string "NULL."

Creating the *Product_Info* Table Using *NULL*s

Returning to our *Product_Info* table example, let's add the null options to each column definition. If you want a column to allow null values, add *NULL* after the data type. If you do not want null values allowed, add *NOT NULL* after the data type. It is a good practice to always specify whether a column should allow null values—except when you are using a user-defined data type that has already been defined with *NULL* or *NOT NULL*. Doing this will help get you into the habit of considering what the nullability should be for columns.

> **More Info**   To learn what the default nullability will be when *NULL* or *NOT NULL* is not specified, see the "CREATE TABLE" topic in Books Online and scroll down to the section "Nullability Rules Within a Table Definition." Explicitly specifying *NULL* or *NOT NULL* takes precedence over these rules.

In our *Product_Info* table example, let's allow only the product description column to accept null values. We do not have to specify nullability for the *brand_type* data type, as its nullability was defined (as *NOT NULL*) when we created the user-defined data type. The new CREATE TABLE statement will look like this:

```
USE MyDB
GO
DROP TABLE Product_Info
GO
CREATE TABLE Product_Info
(
Product_ID      smallint NOT NULL,
Product_Name    char(20) NOT NULL,
Description     char(30) NULL,
Price           smallmoney NOT NULL,
Brand_ID        brand_type

)
GO
```

Now, if a product description is not specified but all four other values are, when you enter a product's data, the new row will be inserted in the table with a *NULL* for the *Description* column entry. You must enter values for the four other columns *Product_ID*, *Product_Name*, and *Price*, *Brand_ID*, which do not accept *NULL*s. If one of these columns is empty, the attempted entry of the new row will not succeed.

Adding the IDENTITY Property

When you create a table, you can specify a column as an identity column by adding the IDENTITY property to the column definition. If a column is created with the IDENTITY property, SQL Server automatically generates a row value for that column, based on a seed value and an increment value. The *seed* is a value that will be the identity value for the first row inserted into the table. The *increment* is the amount by which SQL Server will increase the identity value for successive inserts. Each time a row is inserted, SQL Server assigns the current identity value to the row's identity column. The next row inserted will receive an identity value that is an increment greater than the current highest identity value. This way, each inserted row receives a unique identity value. The identity property is useful for columns where each row in the column should have a unique ID, such as the *Product_ID* column. It is easier to let SQL Server generate the identity value for rows inserted than to track what value should be inserted next. An identity column is commonly used as a primary key constraint in the table to uniquely identify a row. (See Chapter 16 to learn about primary key constraints.)

For example, if you specify IDENTITY(0, 10), the first row inserted will get an identity column value of *0*, the second row will get *10*, the third row will get *20*, and so on. The default seed and increment values, if none are specified, are (1, 1). You must specify either both parameters or none. Identity columns cannot have default values and cannot allow null values. Only one identity column is allowed per table.

By default, identity columns cannot have data inserted directly into them and they cannot be updated. If you want to reinsert a row that was deleted and want to keep the original identity value for that row, you can override the default setting by using the following statement:

```
SET IDENTITY_INSERT tablename ON
```

This statement will enable you to insert a row and assign the value you want for its identity column. After you have finished, you should disallow identity column inserts by running the following command:

```
SET IDENTITY_INSERT tablename OFF
```

SQL Server will then take the highest identity value for the column at that time and use it as the seed it must increment for the next inserted row.

Adding the IDENTITY Property to the *Product_Info* Table

Let's add the IDENTITY property to the *Product_Info* table. Instead of entering data values for the column *product_ID*, we'll make it an identity column and let

SQL Server automatically generate the identity values to ensure uniqueness. The T-SQL code for creating the table is shown here:

```
USE MyDB
GO
DROP TABLE Product_Info
GO
CREATE TABLE Product_Info
(
Product_ID      smallint IDENTITY(1, 1) NOT NULL,
Product_Name    char(20) NOT NULL,
Description     char(30) NULL,
Price           smallmoney NOT NULL,
Brand_ID        brand_type

)
GO
```

The *product_ID* column will now receive values starting at *1*, with an increment of *1* for each successive row that is inserted into the table. Adding the IDENTITY property ensures that each product will be assigned a unique identification number without a user being required to enter one. The choice of *1* for the increment is arbitrary. Whatever increment you use, the identity values will be unique.

Creating a Table Using Enterprise Manager

Now that you understand the basic elements of creating tables using SQL Server, let's step through an example of using Enterprise Manager to create a table. Before you begin this process, however, it is critical to remember that when you're designing your own databases, you should design all your database tables and their relationships *before* you begin to actually create them. To create a database table by using Enterprise Manager, follow these steps:

1. In Enterprise Manager, expand a SQL Server group and then expand a server.
2. Expand the Databases folder to view the available databases.
3. Expand the database in which you want to work—in this case, MyDB.
4. Right-click the Tables folder and then choose New Table from the shortcut menu that appears. The New Table window appears, as shown (maximized) in Figure 10-7.

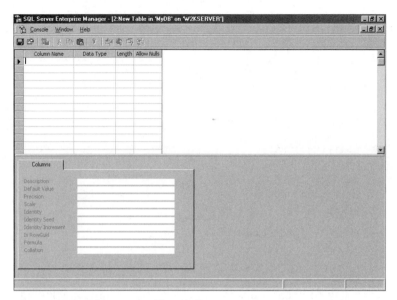

Figure 10-7. *The New Table window.*

The New Table window contains a spreadsheet-like grid. Each row in the grid represents a column in your table. Each column in the grid represents a different attribute of the table column—data type, length, or nullability.

Note You should adopt standards when naming your table columns. It really doesn't matter what type of naming convention you adopt, but be consistent. Every time you use the same column in different tables, use exactly the same name. This consistency will help avoid confusion when you are performing queries.

5. Define each of the columns in your database table—working in one row at a time—by typing the name in the Column Name column, choosing the data type from the pull-down menu in the Data Type column, choosing the length where applicable (such as for character data types), and pressing the Shift key in or clicking in the Allow Nulls column to toggle the check mark (to allow or disallow null values, respectively). The *Product_Info* table is shown in Figure 10-8. Notice that we chose our user-defined data type *brand_type* for the *Brand_ID* column. But also notice that, by default, the check mark in the Allow Nulls column is turned on, even for our *brand_type* data type, which was created not to allow null values. You should turn off this check mark here to be consistent with the data type's intended nullability.

The data in your table rows will be physically stored in the order in which you have defined your columns. If you want to insert a column definition row in this grid between two existing rows, right-click the

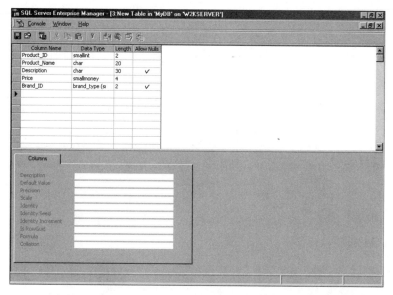

Figure 10-8. *Defining columns in the New Table window.*

row just below where you want to insert a new row and choose Insert Column from the shortcut menu that appears. To delete a row, right-click the appropriate row and choose Delete Column from the shortcut menu. In the *Product_Info* table example, we'll set the *Product_ID* column as the primary key column by right-clicking the *Product_ID* column name and choosing Set Primary Key from the shortcut menu. A key icon will appear next to that column name, as shown in Figure 10-9. (Primary keys and other constraints are discussed in Chapter 16.)

6. At the bottom of the window is a tab labeled "Columns." This tab allows you to change some attributes of the column that is selected at the top. For example, we selected the *Brand_ID* column and then assigned a description and a default value of *0* for it in the Columns tab below, as shown in Figure 10-10.

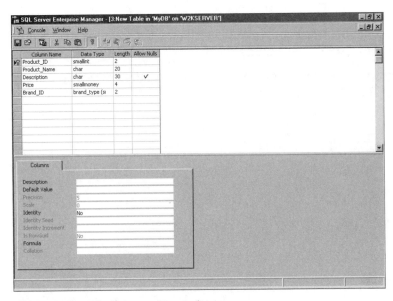

Figure 10-9. *The Primary Key indicator.*

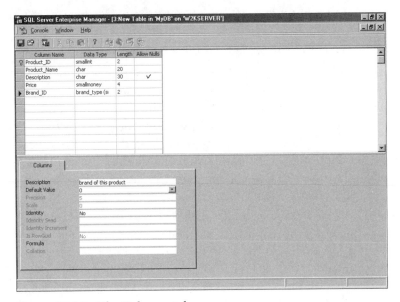

Figure 10-10. *The Columns tab.*

7. You can create other constraints and indexes on the table by right-clicking any column name and choosing Indexes/Keys, Relationships, Constraints, or Properties from the shortcut menu, or by clicking the Table And Index Properties icon next to the Save icon on the toolbar. Any of these methods

will get you to the Properties window, shown in Figure 10-11. Your table name will appear as Table1, Table2, or something similar. Ours is named Table2. You can change this name, as shown in the next step, when you save your table. There are four tabs in this window. These will be explained in more detail throughout the book.

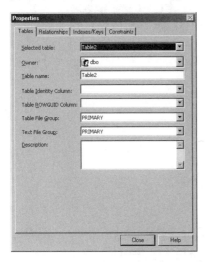

Figure 10-11. *The Properties window for tables and indexes.*

8. To name this new table, click the Save icon and a dialog box will appear where you can type the table name. Type the name you want and click OK, and the table you have designed will be created and its information saved. You can close the New Table window now, and you will see your table name appear in the right-hand pane of Enterprise Manager.

Summary

In this chapter, you've learned the basics of creating a table, including using and defining data types, placing tables in filegroups, using null values, and adding the IDENTITY property. There's still plenty more to learn about other attributes and properties you can add to a table. You can add and delete columns, add constraints and indexes, and alter a table in other ways, even after it has been created. It is best to have your table in its final form before adding any data, but this might not always be possible, or you might find that you need to add an index or a constraint you hadn't thought of before. Chapter 15 demonstrates several ways to alter tables using T-SQL. In the next few chapters, you'll learn about installation and setup of the network and about Microsoft Cluster Server. These chapters will help you get your SQL Server system through its final stages of setup.

Chapter 11

Configuring Microsoft SQL Server on the Network

After you have installed Microsoft SQL Server 2000, you must configure your system on the network. By now, you or the administrator of your Microsoft Windows NT or Microsoft Windows 2000 system has probably already configured the desired network protocol. If this has not been done, you can easily configure a network protocol via Control Panel. The protocol you choose is usually dictated by corporate guidelines or by other systems that are already configured on your network. Although some performance and functionality differences exist among the protocols, most protocols are adequate for your needs.

In this chapter, you'll learn how to configure the various networking components for SQL Server, including the network hardware layer, the network protocol layer, and the SQL Server net-library layer. In addition, you'll be introduced to the database connectivity components—DB-LIB, and Open Database Connectivity (ODBC)—as well as the ODBC connection-pooling features. Finally you will learn how to monitor the network to determine whether SQL Server is experiencing a network bottleneck.

Overview of Network Services

Communication between SQL Server clients and servers requires various software and hardware layers. Each layer serves a specific purpose. Let's take a brief look at each of these layers; their functions will be described more fully later in this chapter.

The top layer is the SQL Server application programming interface (API). One of the following serves as the API layer:

- DB-LIB (an older API specific to SQL Server)
- ODBC (can connect to SQL Server or other database products)
- OLE DB (for ActiveX programmers)
- Open Data Services (ODS)

The API functions on top of a network library layer, which comprises one or more net-libraries, or net-libs. Net-libraries transform SQL Server instructions and data into system calls that communicate with the underlying network protocol layer. Net-libraries are SQL Server components, whereas the network protocol layer is a component of the operating system. You can choose from among the following net-libraries:

- Named pipes
- TCP/IP
- Multiprotocol
- NWLink IPX/SPX
- AppleTalk
- Banyan VINES

Just as the network library layer can contain more than one net-library, the network protocol layer can contain more than one protocol, and each net-library communicates with one or more protocols. The network protocol layer is the operating system component that speaks the network protocol language. The SQL Server calls and data are encapsulated within network calls that can be transmitted across the network in this layer. With the exception of multiprotocol, each network protocol supports a particular net-library with the same name. The multiprotocol option utilizes the remote procedure call (RPC) facility of Windows 2000 and Windows NT. It supports TPC/IP sockets, NWLink IPX/SPX, and named pipes simultaneously.

It is quite common for a Windows NT or Windows 2000 Server to run several network protocols simultaneously. These protocols will be described in more detail in the section "Network Libraries" later in this chapter.

The lowest communication layer consists of the network hardware and device drivers. This layer is usually independent of the network protocol layer, but a few dependencies exist. For example, some devices support only certain network protocols. Many network technologies are available, and more are constantly being created. The network hardware layer can consist of multiple technologies, including the following:

- Ethernet
- Token ring
- Asynchronous Transfer Mode (ATM)
- Fiber optics
- Modem

The communication layers exist on both the client side and the server side, as illustrated in Figure 11-1. As you can see, quite a bit of processing is required to go from an ODBC call down to actual transmission. In this chapter, we'll examine not only how the various layers are supposed to function but also how to troubleshoot problems.

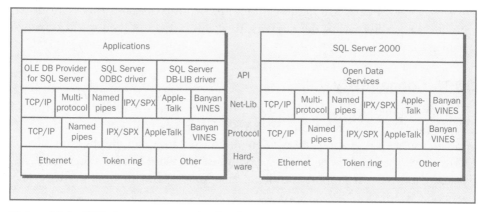

Figure 11-1. *SQL Server communication layers.*

SQL Server APIs

To communicate with SQL Server, your applications must speak SQL Server's language. One means of communication is to use one of the tools provided with SQL Server, such as command-line OSQL or the SQL Server Query Analyzer (ISQLW). These tools can be useful for simple queries, but they are not useful for day-to-day application processing. For example, the people who process inventory, accounts payable, and accounts receivable can work more productively using a graphical user interface than they can typing in SQL statements. In fact, most users of such applications don't know SQL. In general, developers use an API to write applications that connect to SQL Server. APIs provide calls that can be used to execute various database functions.

SQL Server provides a number of APIs, including DB-LIB, ODBC, and OLE DB. DB-LIB is the original SQL Server API; it is available for both Microsoft SQL Server and Sybase products. ODBC is a newer and more flexible language that can be used to communicate with any number of relational database management system (RDBMS) products. OLE DB and several other APIs are also available for programmers to use with SQL Server. This section describes the various APIs.

DB-LIB Connectivity

DB-LIB has been a part of SQL Server since the product's first release, in 1988, and DB-LIB is the original API for SQL Server programming. Although DB-LIB has always been an integral part of SQL Server, a move is on to migrate to ODBC as the primary API. C and C++ as well as Microsoft Visual Basic support DB-LIB. DB-LIB calls are made in the application code and then sent down through the net-library, to the network protocol layer, and then to the network hardware layer.

ODBC Connectivity

ODBC is a standard API developed by Microsoft to facilitate the connection of PCs running Windows to various RDBMS's. By programming to the ODBC API, you can use the same application to communicate with any number of systems. ODBC is versatile but is perhaps not the most efficient API for every RDBMS. Typically, native APIs support additional functionality and are optimized for their particular RDBMS's.

ODBC is used to support additional connectivity via the Internet using Active Server Pages (ASP). Support is also included for ActiveX, Microsoft Foundation Classes (MFC), and Extensible Markup Language (XML). The level of support for ODBC has increased dramatically in the last few years, making it a great API for products that support multiple RDBMS's.

The ODBC API has the same form regardless of the RDBMS to which you will connect, but the ODBC driver does not. You must obtain a unique ODBC driver for each RDBMS that you will use. This driver translates ODBC into the native RDBMS network protocol. Newer versions of the RDBMS typically require new ODBC drivers in order to function optimally, but backward compatibility is usually maintained. With DB-LIB, a specific net-library is typically used, whereas with ODBC, usually the multiprotocol net-library is used. This library facilitates the connection of ODBC applications to the server without requiring you to choose a specific protocol.

ODBC Connection Pooling

The ability to pool connections from within an application was introduced with ODBC 2.*x*. Normally, an application creates an additional connection from the application layer to the database each time a different user logs in to the application. This process can be inefficient because establishing and maintaining a connection to the database involves quite a bit of overhead.

A connection pool allows other threads within an application to use existing ODBC connections without requiring a separate connection. This capability can be especially useful for Internet applications that might repeatedly connect. Applications that require connection pooling must register themselves when they are started.

When an application requests an ODBC connection, the ODBC Connection Manager determines whether a new connection will be initiated or an existing connection reused. This determination is made outside the control of the application. The application thread then works in the usual manner.

Once the thread has finished with the ODBC connection, the application makes a call to release the connection. Again, the ODBC Connection Manager takes control of the connection. Also, if a connection has been idle for a certain amount of time, the ODBC Connection Manager will close it.

More Info   For more information about ODBC connection pooling, consult the *Microsoft ODBC Software Development Kit (SDK).*

Other APIs

A number of other APIs can enable your applications to communicate with SQL Server. These APIs include OLE DB, ODS, SQL–Distributed Management Framework (SQL-DMF), SQL–Distributed Management Objects (SQL-DMO), and SQL-Namespace (SQL-NS). In general, each of these protocols supports a specific function or market segment that requires its own programming interface.

More Info   For more information about specialized APIs, consult SQL Server 2000 Books Online.

Network Libraries

The SQL Server net-library layer translates API calls into protocol-specific calls and then passes them down to the network protocol layer. You manage the net-library layer on your client systems by using the Client Network Utility and on your server by using the Server Network Utility. These utilities enable you to add or remove net-libraries on both the server and each client system. The net-library or net-libraries enabled on the client systems must be available on the server for SQL Server communication to occur. A single network can accommodate several protocols at one time. For example, a set of client systems can communicate to

SQL Server via named pipes, while on the same network other clients can communicate to SQL Server via TCP/IP.

The SQL Server 2000 Server Network Utility

It is common to configure several protocols on the server system. By default, the named pipes and TCP/IP net-libraries are installed on the server. To configure additional net-libraries on the server, follow these steps:

1. Start the Server Network Utility by clicking Start, pointing to Programs, pointing to Microsoft SQL Server, and finally choosing Server Network Utility. The SQL Server Network Utility dialog box appears, as shown in Figure 11-2.

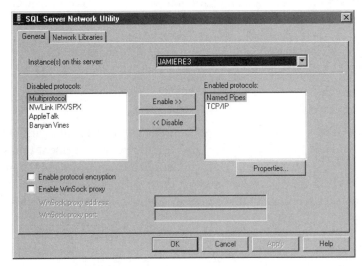

Figure 11-2. *The General tab of the SQL Server Network Utility dialog box.*

2. The SQL Server Network Utility dialog box contains two tabs: General and Network Libraries. The General tab is used to enable and disable network protocols. The enabled protocols appear in the right-hand list in the order in which SQL Server attempts to utilize them. The General tab allows the following operations:

   • Enabling additional protocols by first selecting one or more protocols from the list of disabled protocols and then clicking Enable

   • Disabling protocols by selecting one or more protocols from the list of enabled protocols and then clicking Disable

- Modifying the properties of an enabled protocol by selecting the protocol name and clicking Properties
- Enabling protocol encryption via the Secure Sockets Layer (SSL)
- Enabling WinSock proxy support

The Network Libraries tab is for informational purposes only. From the Network Libraries tab, you can view the version numbers and the dates on which the net-libraries were most recently modified, as shown in Figure 11-3.

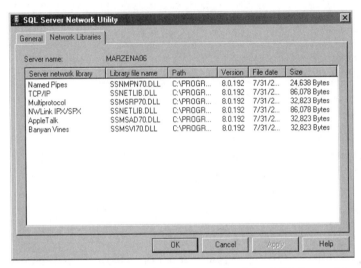

Figure 11-3. *The Network Libraries tab of the SQL Server Network Utility dialog box.*

The SQL Server 2000 Client Network Utility

On the other side of the network connection is the client system, which is configured in much the same way as the server system is. To configure the client system, follow these steps on the client system:

1. Start the Client Network Utility by clicking Start, pointing to Programs, pointing to Microsoft SQL Server, and finally choosing Client Network Utility. The SQL Server Client Network Utility dialog box, shown in Figure 11-4, performs some of the same functions as the SQL Server Network Utility dialog box, but the client utility provides many more options.

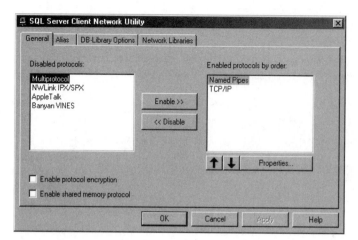

Figure 11-4. *The General tab of the SQL Server Client Network Utility dialog box.*

Although the SQL Server Network Utility dialog box simply lists a number of net-libraries and their connection parameters, the SQL Server Client Network Utility dialog box allows you to specify which protocols are enabled by default on the client as well as to specify server aliases. The enabled protocols are listed on the General tab in the order in which they'll be used. For example, in Figure 11-4, the enabled protocols are, in order, named pipes and TCP/IP. In our example, the client will attempt to connect to the server via named pipes first. If that is unsuccessful, the client will then attempt to connect to the server by using TCP/IP. If that fails, the client will produce a connection error message.

A *server alias* enables you to override the enabled-protocols list and use a specific protocol only. There will be no escalation if the connection is not successful on the specified protocol. If you have multiple servers that do not use a common protocol, you should put the most common protocol at the top of the list of enabled protocols. This will minimize the amount of potential retry time while you establish connections.

You can easily enable or disable protocols. To enable a protocol, simply select the desired protocol from the list of disabled protocols, and then click Enable. To disable a protocol, select the desired protocol from the enabled-protocols list, and then click Disable.

You can modify the properties of an enabled protocol by selecting it from the Enabled Protocols By Order list and then clicking Properties. However, the default values are optimal for almost every network.

From the General tab, you can also enable protocol encryption, which protects the data as it crosses the network. This option is available with the multiprotocol protocol only.

2. To define a server alias, click the Alias tab. Any existing server aliases are listed on the tab. To add an alias, click Add. The Add Network Library Configuration dialog box appears, as shown in Figure 11-5.

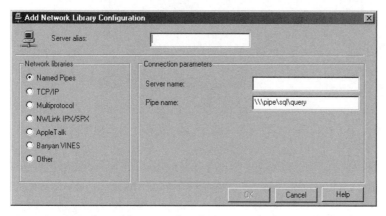

Figure 11-5. *The Add Network Library Configuration dialog box.*

3. In this dialog box, you can add an alias that specifies a particular protocol. This network protocol must be configured on the client system and must be specified here in order to allow the client to communicate using the protocol. The SQL Server client will use the net-library and connection parameters that you set up here when it attempts to connect to the alias. Unless your application attempts to connect to a server through an alias, the default enabled protocols will be used.

4. The DB-Library Options tab of the SQL Server Client Network Utility dialog box is shown in Figure 11-6. This tab displays information about DB-LIB and contains the following check boxes: Automatic ANSI To OEM Conversion, and Use International Settings. The first option lets you enable automatic conversion from ANSI to OEM character sets when you are communicating with SQL Server. The second option lets you get date, time, and currency formats from the system rather than using hard-coded values.

These options typically do not need to be disabled. They require little overhead, and they add functionality.

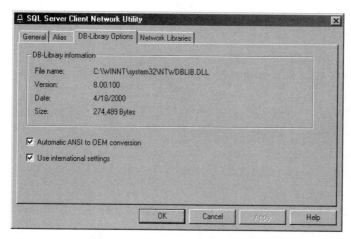

Figure 11-6. *The DB-Library Options tab of the SQL Server Client Network Utility dialog box.*

5. The SQL Server Client Network Utility dialog box also includes a Network Libraries tab, as shown in Figure 11-7. As with the tab of the same name in the SQL Server Network Utility, this tab simply shows you the available net-libraries and their version numbers.

Most connection problems arise when the net-libraries are not set in the proper order on the client system. If you are experiencing connectivity problems, check the net-library settings first.

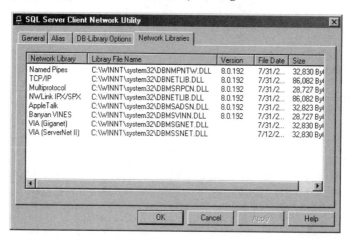

Figure 11-7. *The Network Libraries tab of the SQL Server Client Network Utility dialog box.*

SQL Server Net-Libraries and Protocols

As mentioned earlier, SQL Server supports a number of net-libraries: named pipes, TCP/IP, multiprotocol, NWLink IPX/SPX, AppleTalk, Banyan VINES, VIA (Giganet), and VIA (ServerNet II). Each net-library corresponds to a different network protocol or set of protocols. This section provides a brief overview of each net-library.

The network protocol on which you run SQL Server will likely be determined by corporate standards or legacy systems. All SQL Server commands and functions are supported across all network protocols; however, some protocols are faster than others. In addition, some protocols support routing and name services that others do not.

Named Pipes

Microsoft developed the named pipes protocol several years ago. Named pipes is supported in two modes: local and remote. The local named pipes protocol is used when the client and server are on the same system, and remote named pipes is used when the client and server are on different systems. When a connection is established via named pipes, the SQL Server network utilities determine whether to use a local named pipe or a remote named pipe.

Named pipes is the default client protocol, and it is one of the default network protocols on Windows NT 4 Server and Windows 2000 systems. On Microsoft Windows 95 and Microsoft Windows 98 systems, named pipes is not an option. On these systems, the server-side protocols are TCP/IP, multiprotocol, and shared memory. Although named pipes is an efficient protocol, it is not usually used for large networks because it does not support routing and gateways. It is also not preferred for use with a slower network. Named pipes requires significantly more interaction between the server and the client than do other protocols, such as TCP/IP.

TCP/IP

TCP/IP is one of the most popular network protocols because of the number of platforms on which it runs, its acceptance as a standard, and its high speed. It is also the network protocol used for the Internet. The TCP/IP net-library is one of the highest performing of the SQL Server net-libraries. TCP/IP's speed and its rich feature set make it a good choice.

Multiprotocol

The multiprotocol net-library was new with SQL Server 7 and carries over to SQL Server 2000. This net-library is actually a combination of several net-libraries. As such, it is not as efficient as a single net-library, but it offers more flexibility. The multiprotocol net-library supports the TCP/IP, NWLink IPX/SPX, and named pipes protocols. When you use the multiprotocol net-library, the first protocol that the client and server have in common is used. When a client might connect to various servers running different protocols, multiprotocol is an ideal choice.

NWLink IPX/SPX

NWLink IPX/SPX is an ideal protocol to use when you are integrating SQL Server 2000 systems into a Novell NetWare network because it performs the integration seamlessly. IPX/SPX has been around for quite a while, and it has high performance and stability.

AppleTalk

AppleTalk is the network protocol developed by Apple Computer and used for Apple systems. Windows NT and Windows 2000 support AppleTalk, which allows Windows NT and Windows 2000 servers and clients to seamlessly integrate into an AppleTalk environment.

Banyan VINES

The Banyan VINES net-library supports systems on a VINES network. This net-library allows you to integrate Windows clients and servers into a VINES environment.

VIA (Virtual Interface Architecture)

This protocol comes in two flavors, Giganet and ServerNet II. It is well suited for clustered servers.

Choosing a Net-Library

Your choice of net-library will be based on the protocols your network is using. Connection problems usually occur when the net-libraries on the server and on the client are not in sync. If you have trouble connecting to your server, check the net-library definitions on both sides. Also, try connecting to the server using another program such as PING or Microsoft Windows Explorer to determine whether the problem is SQL Server related or is caused by the network itself.

Network Components and SQL Server Performance

The network is divided into two layers: the software layer, which houses the network protocols, and the hardware layer. For the purposes of this book, the hardware layer includes the software drivers necessary to run the hardware. These network layers are independent of each other and can each have more than one component. For example, it is possible to run both TCP/IP and IPX/SPX over the same network card, as well as to run multiple network cards with the same protocol. This structure is illustrated in Figure 11-8.

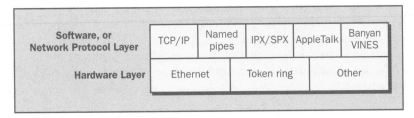

Software, or Network Protocol Layer	TCP/IP	Named pipes	IPX/SPX	AppleTalk	Banyan VINES
Hardware Layer	Ethernet		Token ring		Other

Figure 11-8. *The network layers.*

Each network layer has its own characteristics and performance considerations. As mentioned, there are several reasons for choosing a particular protocol or network hardware component. Usually, this choice is made based on your business rules and how each system is connected to other systems in your network. This book will not try to convince you to run a particular protocol or to use particular network hardware. In this section, we'll examine the software-related and hardware-related factors that might affect SQL Server functionality and performance.

The Software Layer—Network Protocols

As mentioned, the network protocols include named pipes, TCP/IP, NWLink IPX/SPX, AppleTalk, and Banyan VINES. Essentially, all the network protocols function in about the same manner as far as SQL Server is concerned. If a network isn't functioning or performing as you expect, the problem most likely resides in the hardware layer.

Connectivity problems, on the other hand, usually occur at either the net-library layer or the network protocol layer. If you are having problems connecting a SQL Server client to a SQL Server 2000 server, try connecting in some other manner—for example, by using Windows Explorer. If you can connect via Windows Explorer but not via SQL Server, your problem probably relates to SQL Server. Be sure that you are trying to connect using the appropriate network protocol. If multiple protocols are configured, it is sometimes hard to figure out which one you are using. If you can connect to the server via PING, Internet Explorer, or some other external source, the problem is most likely in your selection of net-libraries.

Regardless of which network protocol you use, a number of performance issues can arise at the hardware level. By configuring your system to stay within the limits of your network, you should experience few problems.

The Hardware Layer

You'll need to understand the hardware layer to determine where network performance problems are occurring. The physical hardware layer and the protocol layers are independent, which means that you can run various network protocols on any number of network hardware devices. The networking hardware you choose helps determine the performance of the network. The amount of traffic that the network can handle depends on both the type of the network and the speed of the network.

Network Bandwidth

Network bandwidth measures the amount of data that a network can transmit in a specified amount of time. Network bandwidth is sometimes stated in the name of the network hardware itself, as in 10BaseT and 100BaseT, which indicate a 10-megabit per second (Mbps) bandwidth and a 100-Mbps bandwidth, respectively.

This measurement of network throughput can sometimes be deceiving, however. For most network hardware, the rate at which a particular network adapter can transmit data decreases as the size of the transmission decreases because each network transmission takes a certain amount of overhead. For example, the amount of overhead necessary to transmit 64 kilobytes (KB) of data is approximately the same amount of overhead that is necessary to transmit 2 KB of data. RDBMS's, including SQL Server, typically deal with transmissions of small amounts of data. Thus, the amount of data that your server can handle might be smaller than the bandwidth of the network hardware.

Ethernet

Perhaps the most popular network hardware is Ethernet, although many other options are available. Ethernet speeds have increased over the last few years and will continue to increase. Xerox, DEC, and Intel developed Ethernet in 1976. In the early days, when coaxial cable, or coax, was used, Ethernet had a bandwidth of approximately 3 Mbps. This bandwidth increased with the introduction of 10BaseT technology, which boosted the network bandwidth to 10 Mbps, and then 100BaseT technology increased it again, to 100 Mbps. Soon, Gigabit Ethernet will be available, which offers 1-Gbps bandwidth. This comparison is shown in the following table.

Network	Bandwidth
Coax Ethernet	3 Mbps
10BaseT	10 Mbps
100BaseT	100 Mbps
Gigabit Ethernet	1000 Mbps

Although the bandwidth of Ethernet networks is skyrocketing, Ethernet suffers from a serious problem: multiple Ethernet adapters might try to transmit data at the same time. If two or more adapters transmit at precisely the same time, a collision will occur. Each of the adapters involved in the collision must wait and then attempt to transmit the data again. Although the amount of time lost is small, these delays can add up. The more collisions that occur, the longer you will wait for retransmission.

The chance of a collision increases as network traffic increases. If the amount of traffic approaches the capacity of the network, the chance of a collision is quite high, as Figure 11-9 illustrates. Performance degrades when collisions occur. It is important to monitor network traffic and to watch for collisions. For example, you can follow a rule of thumb not to exceed 75 percent of the network's band-width. Of course, your network will have brief periods of heavy usage during which traffic exceeds this value, but you don't want it to exceed this limit for long periods of time.

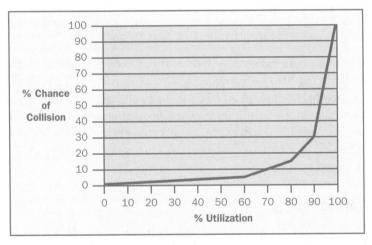

Figure 11-9. *The relationship between the chance of collision and network utilization.*

Token Ring

A *token ring* network gives each member of the ring a chance to communicate with other members by passing a token. The token allows only one system at a time to transmit data on the network. With this type of architecture, you can utilize almost the entire bandwidth of the network without causing undue delays in communication.

Token ring, like Ethernet, encompasses a number of technologies, each offering a different bandwidth, as shown in the following table. But because token ring is a series of point-to-point connections and no collisions can occur, almost the entire bandwidth can be used. As is Ethernet technology, token ring technology is constantly improving.

Network	Bandwidth
IEEE 802.3	token ring 1, 4, or 16 Mbps
IEEE 802.5	100 Mbps
Gigabit	token ring 1000 Mbps

Many other network hardware options are available, including ATM and fiber optics.

Network Monitoring

As we've seen, the type and speed of the network hardware you choose can affect the overall performance of your database system. If you try to transmit more data than your network can handle at one time, data transmissions will queue up and will be delayed. This delay will, in turn, slow down the entire system.

You can get an idea of the maximum performance of the network based on the hardware that is installed. You also have an idea of where performance problems can occur. Using this information, you can often solve problems by simply adding network cards. The first step in finding network problems is to periodically monitor the network. You can use the data you collect to determine whether you are experiencing a network problem and to then develop a solution to any problems that you might experience.

Monitoring Performance

Monitoring the network is not always as easy as you might think. It is usually necessary to purchase additional network-monitoring hardware or software to be able to effectively monitor the network. A couple of factors determine whether such purchases are necessary, as discussed in the next two paragraphs.

First, all the database servers and clients on your physical network might not be using the same protocols. For example, a system that is running TCP/IP on Ethernet will be able to detect (at the operating system level) only traffic that is TCP/IP in nature. IPX/SPX packets will be filtered out at the device driver level. Typically, custom device drivers and network layers are required by network-monitoring software.

Second, the network card itself filters out data that is not intended for your particular machine; therefore, not all of the network data is transmitted up to the driver or operating system. To view all network activity, you must apply a custom device driver and network layer. Thus, a typical workstation is not usually able to monitor all the traffic on the physical network without your making some modifications.

Once you have installed network-monitoring hardware or software or both, you can get a good idea of the amount of traffic your network is handling. This traffic might be directed at your systems, but sometimes traffic occurs as a result of routing or configuration problems. (The topic of debugging network hardware problems is beyond the scope of this book.) After you have your network-monitoring system in place, look at the following items:

- **Utilization**   How much data is being transmitted across the network? How does this amount compare with the bandwidth of the network hardware?

- **Packet sizes**   How big are the network transmissions? Are they large, efficient transmissions or small ones?

- **Collisions (if applicable)**   Are you experiencing a large number of collisions? If so, why?

- **Errors**   Do you have many damaged transmissions that need to be retransmitted? This can be an indication of faulty network adapters or cabling.

Determining Whether You Have a Problem

Once you have collected the performance data, you will need to determine whether you have a problem. This is not always easy. Network performance problems do not usually manifest themselves in failures; rather, the effect is degraded performance. To determine whether you are experiencing a problem, you will have to compare the data extracted from monitoring with the configuration information for your network.

It is usually a good idea not to exceed 75 percent of the network's bandwidth. If the majority of network transmissions are small, you might want to reduce this percentage; handling many small transmissions requires more overhead than handling a few large transmissions. In an Ethernet network, this reduction will in turn reduce the number of collisions. Response time to network requests will decrease, resulting in a faster network.

Some problems are a little more obvious to detect than bandwidth issues. Check for a high rate of collisions and errors. If you are close to the 75 percent threshold and collisions are high, you might be nearing the capacity of your network. If network traffic is relatively light and collisions are high, you might be experiencing hardware errors.

Also, check for transmission errors. Transmission errors generally indicate faulty hardware. The hardware in question can be anything from a network card to cables, routers, bridges, and so on. Once a problem is identified, it's time to call in a network expert.

Finding Solutions to Network Problems

You can solve bandwidth problems in a number of ways, depending on the specific problem. You might be able to solve the problem by purchasing more or different hardware, segmenting the network, or even redesigning the application.

One way to reduce your percentage of network utilization is to increase the network's bandwidth. Moving from 10BaseT to 100BaseT increases the bandwidth tenfold. This solution is simple and easy, but it can be expensive. Let's look at alternatives.

If you are seeing too much traffic on the network, it might be time to divide the network into subnets, based on departments or workgroups. By subnetting, you can create a network for each office or department instead of having the entire company on the same network. This process will reduce the number of systems on a single network and thus reduce the traffic. Sometimes, the network will grow slowly over a long period of time, and you might not notice additional traffic until a problem occurs. The use of subnets might be the best solution to alleviate network congestion.

Another solution is to look at the network usage from a functional standpoint. Is the network being used for good reasons? Are the applications returning too much data? It is always a good idea to look at the SQL Server client applications to be sure that they are not requesting more rows than users need. Using queries that return the minimum number of rows is an easy way to reduce network traffic if you have many users.

As you can see, there can be a variety of problems and thus a variety of solutions. Don't be afraid to look at all the possibilities. Logic errors in applications can sometimes manifest themselves as network bandwidth problems. Scheduling problems can also arise—for example, it's not a good idea to back up your network during the busiest time of day.

Summary

In this chapter, you've learned the basics of SQL Server networking and how to configure SQL Server on the network. You've seen the layering system that SQL Server uses, from the API to the net-library to the network protocol and finally to the network hardware. Each of these layers is independent, but they all fit together in various configurations. You have a great deal of flexibility in your choice of APIs, net-libraries, protocols, and even hardware solutions. And remember to periodically check network traffic to avoid performance problems before they start. We'll discuss common performance problems in Chapter 36. In Chapter 12, we will switch topics: you'll learn how to configure SQL Server 2000 with Microsoft Cluster Services to develop a high-availability system.

Chapter 12
Microsoft SQL Server and Microsoft Cluster Services

In recent years, Microsoft SQL Server systems have moved off the desktop, out of the workgroup, and into the back office. As these systems become larger and more critical to business operations, the need has arisen to make them more stable, easier to administer remotely, and more tolerant of failures. To meet this need, Microsoft has devoted a tremendous amount of time and effort to reducing software bugs and improving support. Microsoft has improved administration tools and remote administration capabilities, and it has developed technologies such as Microsoft Cluster Services (MSCS). A *cluster* is a group of computers that back each other up in the case of malfunction. In this chapter, you'll learn how MSCS works and how to configure it, as well as how to plan for disasters and recover from them. MSCS itself cannot make your system fault tolerant. You must combine this technology with careful planning to make your system capable of recovering from failures.

Note MSCS is included with Microsoft Windows 2000 Advanced Server, Windows 2000 Datacenter Server, and Microsoft Windows NT 4 Enterprise Edition.

Types of Failure

As a database administrator, your primary job is to keep the database up and running during specific time periods, which are usually outlined in a service level agreement. This service level agreement probably specifies the amount of uptime your system must provide, as well as performance rates and recovery time in the event of a failure. Using MSCS can increase the amount of uptime and decrease recovery time. Although server hardware, Windows 2000, Windows NT, and SQL Server are usually stable and reliable, components sometimes fail. In fact, a variety of types of failures can occur in a complex computer system, including the following:

- **Disk drive failure** Disk drive technology has improved, but a disk drive is still a mechanical device and, as such, is subject to wear. The disk drive is one of the most common areas of failure.

- **Hardware component failure** Hardware failures can occur because of wear and tear on the components, primarily from heat. Even the best-made computer equipment can fail over time.

- **Software component failure** Some software flaws are discovered only under rare conditions. Your system might run for months or years until a specific set of conditions uncovers a problem. In addition, adding applications to a stable environment might modify a critical library or file and cause problems.

- **External failure** A system can fail because of external causes, such as power outages. Whether your system can survive such a failure depends on whether you are using an uninterruptible power supply (UPS) and redundant power sources.

- **Human error** Clustering does not usually protect a system against failures caused by human error (such as accidentally deleting a table or a Windows NT file system partition).

Failures are unavoidable. The issue of how to best prepare for some of these failures will be our focus in this chapter.

Overview of MSCS

MSCS is a built-in service of Windows 2000 Advanced Server, Windows 2000 Datacenter Server, and Windows NT 4 Enterprise Edition. MSCS is used to form a server cluster, which, as mentioned earlier, is a group of independent servers working collectively as a single system. The purpose of the cluster is to preserve client access to applications and other resources in the event of a failure or planned outage. If one of the servers in the cluster is unavailable for any reason, the resources and applications move to another node in the cluster.

When we talk about clustered systems, we generally use the term "high availability" rather than "fault tolerant." Traditionally, the term "fault tolerant" refers to a specialized system that offers an extremely high level of redundancy, resilience, and recovery. This type of system normally uses highly specialized software to provide a nearly instantaneous recovery from any single hardware or software failure. Fault-tolerant systems are significantly more expensive than systems without fault tolerance. Clustered systems, which offer high availability, are not as costly as fault-tolerant systems. Clustered systems are generally composed of standard server hardware and a small amount of cluster-aware software in the operating system. As the availability needs of the installation increase, systems can be added to the cluster with relative ease. Though a clustered system does not guarantee continuous operation, it does provide greatly increased availability for most mission-critical applications.

A system running MSCS provides high availability and a number of other benefits. Some of the benefits of running MSCS are described here:

- **High availability**   System resources, such as disk drives and IP addresses, are automatically transferred from a failed server to a surviving server. This is called *failover*. When an application in the cluster fails, MSCS automatically starts the application on a surviving server, or it disperses the work from the failed server to the remaining nodes. Failover happens quickly, so users experience only a momentary pause in the service.

- **Failback**   When a failed server is repaired and comes back on line, MSCS automatically rebalances the workloads in the cluster. This is called *failback*.

- **Manageability**   The Cluster Administrator software allows you to manage the entire cluster as a single system. You can easily move applications to different servers within the cluster by dragging the cluster objects in Cluster Administrator. You can move data in the same manner. These drag-and-drop operations can be used to manually balance server workloads or to "unload" a server to prepare it for planned downtime and maintenance. Cluster Administrator also allows you to monitor (from anywhere in the network) the status of the cluster, each node, and all the resources available. Figure 12-1 shows an example of the Cluster Administrator window.

- **Scalability**   As the demands of the system increase, MSCS can be reconfigured to support the increase. Nodes can be added to the cluster when the overall load exceeds the capabilities of the cluster.

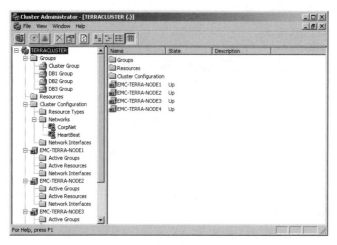

Figure 12-1. *Windows 2000 Cluster Administrator.*

Basic Concepts

MSCS reduces downtime by providing failover between multiple systems using a server interconnect and a shared disk system, as Figure 12-2 illustrates. The server interconnect can be any high-speed connection, such as an Ethernet network or other networking hardware. The server interconnect acts as a communication channel between the servers, allowing information about the cluster state and configuration to be passed back and forth. The shared disk system allows the database and other data files to be equally accessed by all of the servers in the cluster. This shared disk system can be SCSI, SCSI over Fibre Channel, or other proprietary hardware. The shared disks can be either stand-alone disks or a RAID system. (RAID systems are described in Chapter 5.)

Caution If the shared disk system is not fault tolerant and a disk subsystem fails, MSCS will fail over to another server, but the new server will still use the same failed disk subsystem. Be sure to protect your disk drives by using RAID, because these mechanical devices are the components most likely to fail.

Once a system has been configured as a cluster server, it is transformed from a traditional server into what is called a virtual server. A *virtual server* looks like a normal server, but the actual physical identity of the system has been abstracted away. Because the computer hardware that makes up this virtual server might change over time, the user does not know which actual server is servicing the application at any given moment. Therefore, the virtual server, not a particular set of hardware, serves user applications.

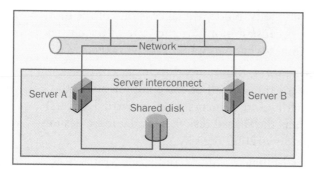

Figure 12-2. *A Windows 2000 cluster.*

A virtual server exists on a network and is assigned an IP address used in TCP/IP. This address can switch from one system to another, enabling users to see the virtual server regardless of what hardware it is running on. The IP address will actually migrate from one system to another to maintain a consistent presentation of the virtual server to the outside world. An application directed to a specific address can still access the address if a particular server fails, even though the address then represents a different server. The virtual server keeps the failover operations hidden from the user, so the user can keep working without knowing what's happening "behind the scenes."

Cluster Components

Several components are required to create a cluster: cluster management software, a server interconnect, and a shared disk system. These components must be configured in conjunction with cluster-aware applications to create a cluster. In this section, you'll learn about the various components and how they work together to create the cluster. In the section "SQL Server Cluster Configuration" later in this chapter, you'll learn how to configure a SQL Server cluster.

MSCS Cluster Management Software

The *cluster management software* is actually a set of software tools used to maintain, configure, and operate the cluster. It consists of the following subcomponents, which work together to keep the cluster functioning and to perform failover if necessary:

- **Node Manager**   Maintains cluster membership and sends out "heartbeats" to members (nodes) of the cluster. (*Heartbeats* are simply "I am alive" messages sent out periodically.) If a node's heartbeats stop, another node will think that this node is no longer functioning and will take steps to take over its functions. Node Manager is one of the most critical pieces of the cluster because it monitors the state of the cluster and its members and determines what actions should be taken.

- **Configuration Database Manager** Maintains the cluster configuration database. This database keeps track of all of the components of the cluster, including the abstract logical elements (such as virtual servers) and physical elements (such as the shared disks). This database is similar to the Windows NT/Windows 2000 registry.

- **Resource Manager/Failover Manager** Starts and stops MSCS. Resource Manager/Failover Manager receives information (such as the loss of a node, the addition of a node, and so on) from Resource Monitor and Node Manager.

- **Event Processor** Initializes the cluster and routes event information among components of the cluster. Event Processor also initiates cluster expansion by directing Node Manager to add a node.

- **Communications Manager** Manages communication between the nodes in the cluster. All nodes in the cluster must communicate with each other constantly to function properly. If the nodes did not have this contact, cluster state information would be lost, and the cluster would not function.

- **Global Update Manager** Communicates cluster state information (including information about the addition of a node to a cluster, the removal of a node, and so on) to all nodes in a cluster.

- **Resource Monitor** Monitors the condition of the various resources in the cluster and provides statistical data. This information can be used to determine whether any failover action needs to be taken in the cluster.

- **Time Service** Ensures that all nodes in the cluster report the same system time. If Time Service were not present, events might seem to occur in the wrong sequence, resulting in bad decisions. For example, if one node thought it was 2 P.M. and contained an old copy of a file and another node thought it was 10 A.M. and contained a newer version of that file, the cluster would erroneously determine that the file on the first system was the most recent.

Server Interconnect

The *server interconnect* is simply the connection between the nodes in the cluster. Because the nodes in the cluster need to be in constant communication (via Time Service, Node Manager, and so on), it is important to maintain this link.

So the server interconnect must be a reliable communication channel between these systems.

In many cases, the server interconnect will be an Ethernet network running TCP/IP or NetBIOS. This setup is adequate, but you might also want to use a proprietary, high-speed interconnect that is much faster than Ethernet. These interconnects are commercially available from many hardware vendors, and some provide communications services as well as shared-disk services. A complete list of approved server interconnect devices is available from the hardware compatibility list on the Microsoft Web site at *http://www.microsoft.com/hcl/*.

Shared Disk System

Another key component of cluster creation is the shared disk system. If multiple computer systems can access the same disk system, another node can take over if the primary node fails. This shared disk system must allow multiple computer systems to have equal access to the same disks—in other words, each of the computers must be able to access all of the disks. In the current version of MSCS, only one system can access the disk at a time, but future versions will allow multiple systems to access the data simultaneously.

Several types of shared disk systems are available, and new disk technology is always being developed. The SCSI disk subsystem has always supported multiple initiators. With multiple initiators, you can have multiple SCSI controllers on the same SCSI bus, which makes SCSI ideal for clustering. In fact, SCSI systems were the first disk subsystems to be used for clustering.

More recent disk technologies, such as Fibre Channel and some proprietary solutions, are designed to support clustering. Fibre Channel systems allow disks to connect over a long distance from the computer system. Most Fibre Channel systems support multiple controllers on the same Fibre Channel loop. Some RAID controllers are designed or have been modified to support clustering. Without modification or configuration changes, most disk controllers will not support clustering.

Controller caches that allow writes to be cached in memory are also an issue with clustering when the cache is located on the controller itself, as shown in Figure 12-3. In this case, each node contains its own cache, and we say that the cache is "in front of" the disk sharing because two caches share the same disk drives. If each controller has a cache and a cache is located on a system that fails, the data in the cache might be lost. For this reason, when you use internal controller caches in a cluster configuration, they should be set as read-only. (Under some conditions, this setting might reduce the performance of some systems.)

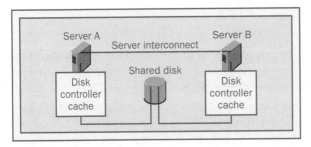

Figure 12-3. *Controller caches in front of disk sharing.*

Other solutions to the shared-disk problem involve RAID striping and caching in the disk system itself. In this configuration, the cache is shared by all nodes, and we say that the cache is "behind" the sharing, as shown in Figure 12-4. Here, the striping mechanisms and the cache are viewed identically by all of the controllers in the system, and both read caching and write caching are safe.

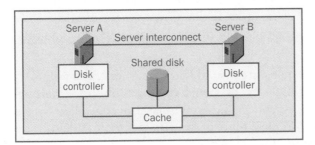

Figure 12-4. *Controller cache behind disk sharing.*

Newer SCSI and Fibre Channel disk subsystems allow the RAID controller to be in the disk enclosure, rather than in the computer system. These systems offer good performance and fault tolerance. In fact, many RAID systems of this type offer fully redundant controllers and caches. Many of the newer RAID systems use this type of architecture. Let's look at some disk subsystems in detail.

I/O Subsystems As mentioned, various types of I/O subsystems support clustering. The three main types of I/O subsystems are as follows:

- **SCSI JBOD** This is a SCSI system with multiple initiators (controllers) on a SCSI bus that address JBOD (short for "just a bunch of disks"). In this setup, the disks are individually addressed and must be either configured into a stripe using Windows 2000 striping or addressed individually. This subsystem is not recommended.

- **Internal RAID**   A RAID controller is used in each server. The disadvantage of this subsystem is that the RAID logic is on the board that goes in the server and thus the controller caches must be disabled.

- **External RAID**   The RAID controller is shared by the systems in the cluster. The cache and the RAID logic are in the disk enclosure, and a simple host bus adapter (HBA) is used to communicate with the external controller.

The next two sections address only the two RAID solutions. The SCSI JBOD solution is not advisable unless the cluster is small and cost is a major issue.

Internal RAID   Internal RAID controllers are designed such that the hardware that controls the RAID processing and the cache reside in the host system. With internal RAID, the shared disk system is shared behind the RAID striping, as shown in Figure 12-5.

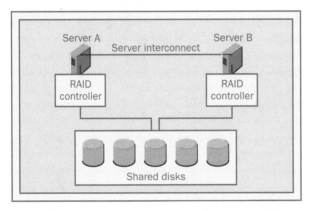

Figure 12-5. *Internal RAID controller.*

Because the cache is located on the controller, which is not shared, any data in the cache when the system fails will not be accessible. This is a big problem when a relational database management system (RDBMS) is involved. When SQL Server writes data to disk, that data has been recorded in the transaction log as having been written. When SQL Server attempts to recover from a system failure, these data blocks will not be recovered because SQL Server thinks that they have already been written to disk. In the event of a failure in this type of configuration, the database will become corrupted.

Therefore, vendors certify their caching RAID controllers for use in a cluster by disabling the cache (or at least the write cache). If the cache has been disabled,

SQL Server will not be signaled that a write operation has been completed until the data has actually been written to disk.

> **Note** SQL Server performs all writes to disk in a nonbuffered, noncached mode. Regardless of how much file system cache is available, SQL Server will not use it. SQL Server completely bypasses the file system cache, as do most RDBMS products.

In certain situations, using the controller cache can provide a great performance benefit. This is particularly true when you are using a RAID 10 or RAID 5 configuration because writes incur additional overhead with these RAID levels. To use a controller write cache in a cluster configuration, you must use an external RAID system so that the cache is shared and data is not lost in a failover.

External RAID In an external RAID system, the RAID hardware is outside the host system, as shown in Figure 12-6. Each server contains an HBA whose job is to get as many I/O requests as possible out to the RAID system as quickly as possible. The RAID system determines where the data actually resides.

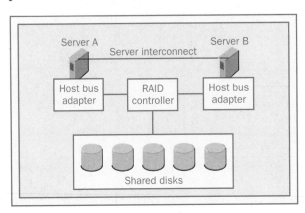

Figure 12-6. *External RAID subsystem.*

An external RAID subsystem is sometimes referred to as "RAID in the cabinet" or "RAID in the box" because RAID striping takes place inside the disk cabinet. The external RAID subsystem has many advantages. Not only is it an ideal solution for MSCS, but it's also a great solution overall. The advantages of the RAID-in-the-cabinet approach include the following:

- **Allows easier cabling** Using internal RAID, you need multiple cables— one for each disk cabinet—coming from the RAID controller. With external RAID, you run one cable from the HBA to the RAID controller and then you run cables from the controller to form a daisy chain connecting each of the disk cabinets, as illustrated in Figure 12-7. External RAID makes it easy to connect hundreds of drives.

- **Allows RAID redundancy**   Many of the external RAID solutions allow one storage controller to communicate with both a primary and a secondary RAID controller, allowing full redundancy and failover.

- **Allows caching in a cluster**   You can configure a caching RAID solution much more easily using external RAID. If you use external RAID, you can enable both caching and fault tolerance without having to worry about cache consistency between controllers (because there is only one cache and one controller). In fact, using the write cache is safe if you use external RAID controllers. You still run some risks if you are caching RDBMS data, but you reduce those risks if you use external RAID controllers. Be sure that your external RAID system vendor supports mirroring of caches. Mirrored caches provide fault tolerance to the cache memory in case a memory chip fails.

- **Supports more disk drives**   In the case of large or high-performance systems, it is sometimes necessary to configure a large number of drives. The need for a large number of drives was illustrated in Chapter 6, where you learned how to size the system; you'll see it again in Chapter 36, when you learn about common performance problems. External RAID devices let you connect hundreds of disks to a single HBA. Internal RAID systems are limited to a few dozen drives per controller, as are SCSI systems.

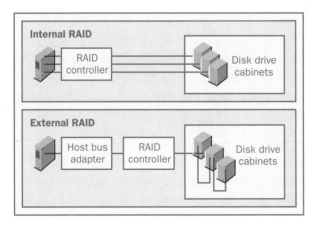

Figure 12-7. *Internal RAID cabling vs. external RAID cabling.*

Of the disk subsystems available today that support clustering, external RAID cabinets are preferable for large clusters. Of course, cost might be a consideration, and some clusters are too small to justify using external RAID. But, in the long run, an external RAID solution will provide the best performance, reliability, and manageability for your cluster.

Cluster Application Types

Applications that run on systems running MSCS fall into one of four categories:

- **Cluster-unaware applications** Applications of this type do not have any interaction with MSCS. Although they might run adequately under normal conditions, they might not perform well if a failure occurs, forcing them to fail over to another node.

- **Cluster-aware applications** These applications are aware of MSCS. They take advantage of MSCS for performance and scalability. They react well to cluster events and generally need little or no attention after a component fails and the failover occurs. SQL Server 2000 is an example of a cluster-aware application.

- **Cluster management applications** Applications of this type are used to monitor and manage the MSCS environment.

- **Custom resource types** These applications provide customized cluster management resources for applications, services, and devices.

Figure 12-8 illustrates the application types and their interaction with MSCS.

MSCS Modes

You can run SQL Server 2000 cluster support and MSCS in different modes. In *active/passive mode*, one server remains in standby mode, ready to take over in the event of a system failure on the primary server. In *active/active mode*, each server runs a different SQL Server database. In the event of a failure on either of the servers, the other server takes over. In this case, one server ends up running two databases. In this section, we'll examine the advantages and the disadvantages of using each of these modes.

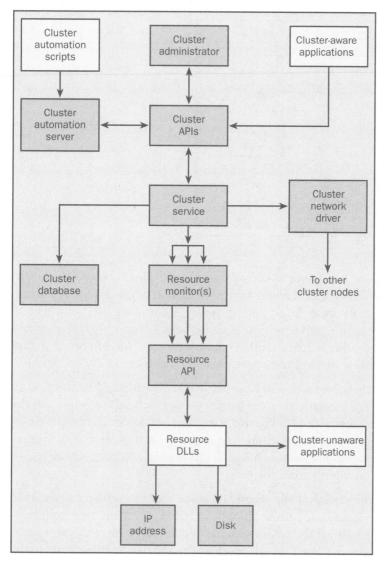

Figure 12-8. *Application types and MSCS.*

Active/Passive Clusters

An active/passive cluster uses the primary node to run the SQL Server application, and the cluster uses the server in the secondary node as a backup, or standby, server, as illustrated in Figure 12-9.

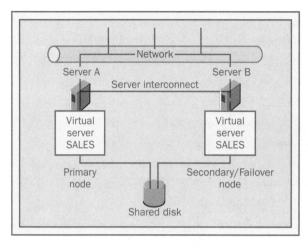

Figure 12-9. *Active/passive cluster.*

In this configuration, one server is essentially unused. This server might go for months without ever being called into action. In fact, in many cases, the backup server is never used. Because the secondary server is not being used, it might be seen as a costly piece of equipment that is sitting idle. Because this server is not available to perform other functions, other equipment might have to be purchased in order to serve users, making the active/passive mode potentially expensive.

Although the active/passive mode can be expensive, it does have advantages. With the active/passive configuration, if the primary node fails, all resources of the secondary node are available to take over the primary node's activity. This reliability can be important if you're running mission-critical applications that require a specific throughput or response time. If this is your situation, active/passive mode is probably the right choice for you.

It is highly recommended that the secondary node and the primary node have identical hardware (that is, the same amount of RAM, the same type and number of CPUs, and so on). If the two nodes have identical hardware, you can be certain that the secondary system will perform at nearly the same rate as the primary system. Otherwise, you might experience a performance loss in the event of a failover.

Active/Active Clusters

In an active/active cluster, each server can run applications while serving as a secondary server for another node, as illustrated in Figure 12-10.

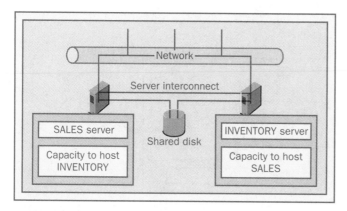

Figure 12-10. *An active/active cluster.*

Each of the two servers acts both as a primary node for some applications and as a secondary node for the other server's applications. This is a more cost-effective configuration because no equipment is sitting idle, waiting for another system to fail. Both systems are actively serving users. In addition, a single passive node can act as a secondary node for several primary nodes.

One disadvantage of the active/active configuration is that, in the event of a failure, the performance of the surviving node will be significantly reduced because of the increased load on the secondary node. The surviving node now has to run not only the applications it was running originally but also the applications from the primary node. In some cases, performance loss is unacceptable, and the active/passive configuration is required.

Examples of Clustered Systems

In this section, we'll look at four sample clustered systems that use MSCS. These examples will help you decide what type of cluster best suits your needs and environment.

Example 1—High-Availability System with Static Load Balancing

This system provides high availability for multiple applications on the cluster. It does, however, sacrifice some performance when only one node is on line. This system allows the maximum utilization of the hardware resources because each node is being accessed. Figure 12-11 illustrates the configuration of this cluster, which is an active/active cluster.

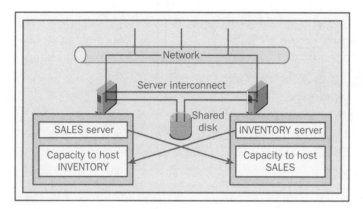

Figure 12-11. *High-availability cluster with static load balancing.*

Each node of this cluster advertises its own set of resources to the network in the form of virtual servers. Each node is configured with some excess capacity so that it can run the other node's applications when a failover occurs. Which client services from the failed node will be available depends on the resources and the server capacity.

Example 2—Hot Spare System with Maximum Availability

This system provides maximum availability and performance across all the system resources. The downside to this configuration is the investment in hardware resources that, for the most part, are not used. One of the nodes acts as the primary node and supports all client requests. The other node is idle. This idle node is a dedicated hot spare and is accessed only when a failover occurs. If the primary node fails, the hot spare node immediately takes over all operations and continues to service the client requests. Figure 12-12 illustrates the configuration.

This configuration is best suited for the most mission-critical applications. If your company depends on sales over the Internet, your Web/commerce server could be run in this configuration. Because business depends on the system's being up and running, it is easier to justify the hardware expense associated with having an idle system.

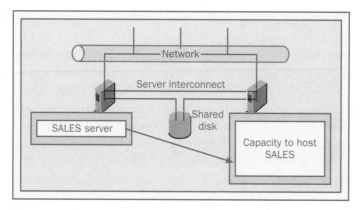

Figure 12-12. *Hot spare system with maximum availability.*

Example 3—Partial Server Cluster

The partial server cluster configuration demonstrates how flexible MSCS can be. In this system, only selected applications are allowed to fail over. As shown in Figure 12-13, you can specify that some applications will be available when their node is down but that others won't.

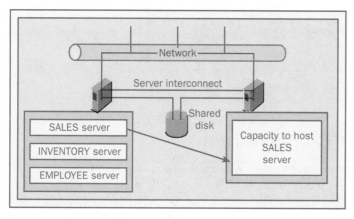

Figure 12-13. *Partial server cluster.*

This configuration is ideal when you need to maximize hardware resource usage but still provide limited failover capability for mission-critical applications. In addition, this configuration supports applications that are not cluster aware while providing failover for applications that are cluster aware.

Example 4—Virtual Server Only, with No Failover

Our final sample system is not a true cluster, but it does exploit MSCS and its support of virtual servers. This configuration, illustrated in Figure 12-14, is a way of organizing and advertising resources. The virtual server feature allows you to specify meaningful and descriptive names for resources, rather than the normal list of server names. In addition, MSCS will automatically restart an application or a resource after a server failure. This feature is useful with applications that do not provide an internal mechanism for restarting themselves. Implementing the configuration described in this example is also excellent preparation for true clustering. Once you have defined the virtual servers on a single node, you can easily add a second node without changing the server definitions.

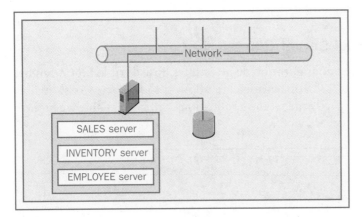

Figure 12-14. *Virtual server only, with no failover.*

SQL Server Cluster Configuration

After you have installed and configured MSCS, the next step is to configure SQL Server for clustering. As mentioned, SQL Server 2000 is cluster aware and is designed to make use of clustering. In this section, we will first look at planning a cluster, and we will then review the steps you must perform to configure SQL Server on a cluster.

 Note To gain all the benefits of MSCS, the application must be cluster aware. As mentioned, a cluster-aware application is one that understands the cluster architecture and is able to fail over in the event of a failure. Not all applications are cluster aware and cluster capable "out of the box."

Planning Your Configuration

The first step in planning a SQL Server cluster is determining the type of hardware to be used and the mode of operation in which the cluster will run. The cluster can comprise systems with many hardware configurations, and it can operate in active/passive mode or active/active mode. The mode determines the amount and type of hardware you will need.

Active/passive cluster configurations should consist of identical systems, each capable of handling the entire workload. Because the active/passive mode does not use the secondary system during normal operation, nor does it use the primary system after a failure has occurred, the performance of the virtual server will remain constant. Users will not experience any performance change if the primary system fails over to an identical secondary system.

Active/active cluster configurations should consist of two systems that are each running a specific workload. If a failure occurs, the surviving system will take over the workload of the failed system. In this case, two workloads will then be running on a single system, offering lower performance to all users. If you have planned carefully, the performance delivered by this system will still remain within acceptable limits, but that performance is not guaranteed. In planning the active/active cluster configuration, you must prepare for some performance loss by planning to eliminate some services or by warning users that performance will be degraded in the event of a failover.

The next step you must perform when you are configuring SQL Server for a cluster is to check and possibly change several SQL Server settings. The next three sections examine these settings.

Setting the Recovery Time

In tuning SQL Server, you might have set the configuration parameter *recovery interval* to something other than the default value of 0. Changing this setting will increase the time between checkpoints and improve performance but will also increase recovery time. (The system must recover after it has failed over.) In a clustered system, the default value of 0, which specifies automatic configuration, should not be changed. (Having a system to which another system can fail over is the primary reason for using MSCS and should outweigh performance considerations.) This setting will cause a checkpoint to occur approximately every minute, and the maximum recovery time will also be about one minute.

More Info   For more information, check the Books Online index for "recovery interval option."

Note A checkpoint operation causes all modified data in the SQL Server cache to be written to disk. Any modified data that has not been written to disk at the time of a system failure will be cleaned up by SQL Server at startup by rolling forward committed transactions and rolling back noncommitted transactions.

Configuring SQL Server for Active/Passive Clusters

To create an active/passive cluster configuration, you might have to change one setting in SQL Server. If your secondary server is identical to the primary server, no change is necessary. If the secondary server has fewer resources than the primary server, you should set the SQL Server configuration parameter *min server memory* to *0*. This setting instructs SQL Server to allocate memory based on available system resources.

More Info For more information, check the Books Online index for "min server memory option."

Configuring SQL Server for Active/Active Clusters

In an active/active cluster configuration, you must set the SQL Server configuration parameter *min server memory* to *0*. If this configuration parameter is set to Manual, SQL Server might over-allocate memory after a failover. Because Windows 2000 is a virtual-memory system, it is possible to allocate more memory than is physically available. In fact, this problem frequently arises, causing paging. For example, if each SQL Server system allocated 75 percent of the system's memory and a failover occurred, the combined SQL Server services would demand 150 percent of the available memory, essentially bringing the system to a standstill.

Installing SQL Server for Clustering

The process of installing SQL Server for clustering is similar to the SQL Server installation process described in Chapter 7. Before starting the installation process for the cluster, you need to decide where SQL Server will be installed. You should install the SQL Server files on a shared disk drive controlled by the primary server. You should set both the SQL Server installation path and the master database installation path to this shared drive. You should also specify the network protocol under which you want the cluster to run. The following steps outline the installation procedure for SQL Server clustering:

1. Place your SQL Server 2000 CD in your CD-ROM drive. If your system is set up to automatically start CDs, the main SQL Server 2000 setup dialog box appears, as Figure 12-15 shows. Otherwise, you will need to manually run the Autorun.exe program (located in the top-level directory on the CD).

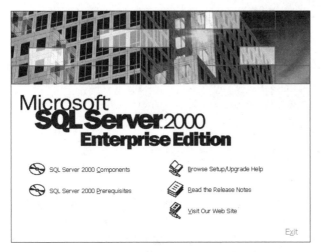

Figure 12-15. *The SQL Server setup dialog box.*

2. If you have not installed the required operating system service packs or the required version of Microsoft Internet Explorer, or if you simply want to examine the list of prerequisites, click SQL Server 2000 Prerequisites to display the SQL Server 2000 Prerequisites dialog box.

   Click the appropriate operating system to view its prerequisites, and then click the prerequisite you would like to install. If you have all the appropriate software already loaded, go directly to step 3.

Note   You must install MSCS before starting the SQL Server cluster installation.

3. Click SQL Server 2000 Components. The SQL Server 2000 Installation Wizard welcome screen appears. If you are running any other Windows programs, you should close them. Click Next to continue with the installation process.

4. In the Computer Name screen, click Virtual Server and type a virtual server name, as shown in Figure 12-16. Click Next to continue.

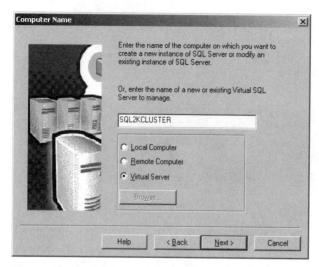

Figure 12-16. *The Computer Name screen.*

5. The User Information screen appears. Verify that your name and your company name are correct. Click Next to continue.

6. The Software License Agreement screen appears. Click Yes to accept the license agreement and to continue with the installation process.

7. In the Setup screen, type the 25-digit CD key, which you can find on the yellow sticker in your CD liner notes or on the CD sleeve. Click OK to continue.

8. Next the Failover Clustering screen appears, as Figure 12-17 shows. Type the IP address for the virtual server, and then click Add. MSCS supplies the subnet address. Click Next to continue.

9. In the Cluster Management screen, review the cluster definition SQL Server provides. By default, the local computer is set as the preferred node. Any other available nodes appear in the Additional Node box. Verify the settings and click Next to continue.

10. When the Remote Information screen appears, type the administrator user ID and password that is valid for all selected nodes in the cluster.

11. In the Instance Name screen, accept the default name or specify a named instance of SQL Server. If you want to specify a named instance, clear the Default check box and type the desired name for the instance. Click Next to continue.

Note   You cannot name an instance DEFAULT, MSSQLSERVER, or any other name that is a SQL Server reserved keyword.

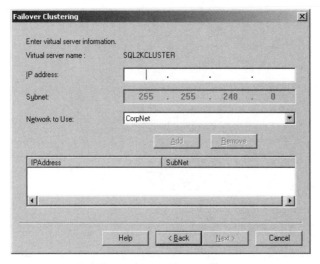

Figure 12-17. *The Failover Clustering screen.*

12. In the Setup Type screen, select the type of installation you want. By default, the SQL Server setup program will install SQL Server in the first available shared disk resource. If you want to install it in another location, click Browse under the Data Files heading, and specify a path to a different shared disk resource. Click Next to continue.

13. Next the Authentication Mode screen appears, as Figure 12-18 shows. The setting you choose in this screen determines the level of security for your SQL Server installation. You can choose to use Windows Authentication Mode or Mixed Mode Authentication. If you select Windows Authentication Mode, all user rights to the database are inherited from the Windows User Security settings. If you select Mixed Mode Authentication, you can define and administer user security for the database separately. If you select Mixed Mode Authentication, you must set a password for the sa, or SQL Server system administrator, account. You can choose to leave the sa password blank, but this will severely lessen the security of your SQL Server installation.

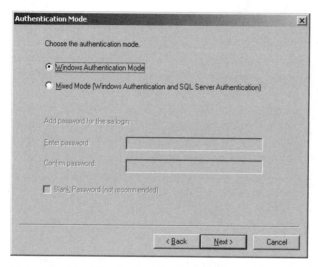

Figure 12-18. *The Authentication Mode screen.*

14. In the Start Copying Files screen, click Next.

15. The Licensing Mode screen appears. You have two options for licensing your SQL Server clients. You can license the clients per server or per seat. Per server licensing requires you to assign each Client Access License to a particular server, and it allows one connection to that server. The maximum number of client computers that can connect to a server at any time equals the number of Client Access Licenses you have assigned to that server. If you select per server, you must specify the number of Client Access Licenses for concurrent connections that you have purchased for that server.

Per seat licensing mode requires a Client Access License for each computer that will access any of your servers running SQL Server. Once a computer is licensed, it can access any computer running SQL Server 2000 on the network at no additional charge.

If you are unsure which licensing mode to choose, click Per Server. The license agreement allows you a one-time, one-way option to change from per server licensing mode to per seat licensing mode.

Click Continue to begin installing the SQL Server application and data files. The SQL Server setup program will install the required files on your system and configure the necessary components. The installation might take just a few minutes, or it might take longer, depending on the speed of your system.

16. When the Setup Complete screen appears, select the option to restart your computer and click Finish.

As you can see, the SQL Server cluster is simple to configure. Once you have configured the cluster, no other configuration steps are necessary. Clients will access SQL Server through an IP address that will be reassigned as part of the failover. The remaining programming issues that you might need to consider are described in the following section, "Beyond MSCS."

Using a Three-Tier Application

Most applications establish a direct connection to a database. The application submits transactions, and the database responds to those transactions. In the event of a system failure, the transaction times out and the application fails. In many cases, this is the best setup—if the transaction is not completed, you want the application to fail. If you implement a failover cluster, however, the database soon becomes available and able to respond to transactions after a failure. By carefully designing a three-tier application, you can help ensure that the application will take advantage of this fast restoration of service.

In a three-tier application, the middle layer can detect that the server has stopped responding, wait a specified amount of time, and resubmit the transaction. The user will experience a longer delay waiting for the transaction to be completed, but the delay might be preferable to the transaction failing. To succeed, the application must be able to detect that the connection to the server has failed and must know to reconnect. And the application should inform the end user that this process is taking place by displaying a message box or by using some other means.

With a three-tier application, seamless failover is possible. The application must be cluster aware and must know that the virtual server will soon be up and functioning. Using a three-tier application framework in conjunction with MSCS can provide both application and data robustness.

Beyond MSCS

We've examined the basics of MSCS and how SQL Server works within that architecture. We've also seen how SQL Server can survive some types of catastrophic hardware and software failures and be back up and running transactions in a short time. To achieve this degree of fault tolerance, you must not only enable

MSCS but also take other measures. Two important steps are to perform regular and effective backups and to prepare a disaster recovery plan. The procedures for backing up your system and preparing a disaster recovery plan are described in detail in Chapters 32 and 33. Clustering servers and creating RAID storage are not alternatives to performing backups. In many cases, neither of these technologies can help you if your system crashes and you have not performed a backup. These situations can include the following types of failures:

- **Hardware failures** In rare cases, hardware failures can corrupt data. If the primary system experiences a hardware failure that corrupts the database, the secondary server will fail over to a corrupted database.

- **Software failures** Regardless of how well software has been developed and tested, occasional bugs can sneak in. If one of these rare software bugs corrupts the database, failover to that database will be of no avail. RAID technology will simply offer a fault-tolerant copy of corrupted data.

- **Human error** Users commonly delete their data by mistake. Neither clustering technology nor RAID will solve this problem.

In Chapters 32 and 33, you'll learn more about planning for a disaster and enabling your system to survive one. The preceding examples simply illustrate the fact that clusters and failover serve specific purposes and are only two weapons in the battle to provide constant data access and data integrity.

Summary

In this chapter, you've learned about the various clustering configurations, the hardware and software you'll need to create clusters, and the SQL Server cluster configuration process. You've also seen that MSCS will help you in several situations but that it is not the be-all and end-all of system fault tolerance. You must also use a fault-tolerant disk subsystem and implement a backup scheme. MSCS, along with a good disaster recovery strategy, can offer maximum uptime and system reliability. In the next chapter, we examine Transact-SQL, an enhanced version of SQL that is available in SQL Server 2000.

Part III
Using Microsoft SQL Server

Chapter 13

Introduction to Transact-SQL and SQL Query Analyzer

In this chapter, you'll be introduced to the basic concepts of Structured Query Language (SQL) and Transact-SQL (T-SQL) and to the differences between the two languages. This chapter explains data definition language (DDL) and data manipulation language (DML) and includes examples of each. We'll also take a look at the new features of T-SQL for Microsoft SQL Server 2000. And you'll learn how to use the various SQL Server utilities—including command-line T-SQL and the SQL Query Analyzer—to create and manage database objects. You'll also learn about creating scripts that contain T-SQL statements.

What Is SQL?

SQL is a database query and programming language used for accessing data and for querying, updating, and managing relational database systems. Both the American National Standards Institute (ANSI) and the International Organization for Standardization (ISO) have defined standards for SQL. ANSI is an organization of industry and business groups that develops trade and communication standards for the United States. ANSI is also a member of ISO and of the International Electrotechnical Commission (IEC). ANSI publishes U.S. standards that correspond to international standards. In 1992, ISO and IEC published an international standard for SQL called SQL-92. ANSI published a corresponding standard, ANSI SQL-92, in the United States. ANSI SQL-92 is sometimes referred to as ANSI SQL. Although different relational databases use slightly different versions of SQL, most comply with the ANSI SQL standard. SQL Server uses the superset of ANSI SQL-92 known as T-SQL, which conforms to the SQL-92 standard defined by ANSI.

The SQL language contains statements that fit into two main programming language categories: DDL and DML. We'll look at these language categories in the following sections.

DDL

DDL is used to define and manage database objects such as databases, tables, and views. (Views are explained in Chapter 18.) DDL statements usually include CREATE, ALTER, and DROP commands for each object. For example, the statements CREATE TABLE, ALTER TABLE, and DROP TABLE are used to initially create a table, alter its properties (by adding or deleting columns, for instance), and drop a table, respectively, as we'll see in the next few paragraphs.

The CREATE TABLE Statement

Let's use DDL to create a sample table named *Customer_Data* in the MyDB database. We'll use the *Customer_Data* table in later examples in this chapter. As mentioned, the CREATE TABLE statement is used to create a table. The sample table is defined with four columns, as shown here:

```
Use MyDB
CREATE TABLE Customer_Data
(customer_id  smallint,
first_name    char(20),
last_name     char(20),
phone         char(10))
GO
```

This statement creates the structure for the *Customer_Data* table; the table is empty until data is inserted or bulk copied into it. For more details on database table creation, see Chapter 10.

The ALTER TABLE Statement

The ALTER TABLE statement is used to alter the definition or the attributes of a table. In this example, ALTER TABLE has been used to add a column, *middle_initial*, to the existing *Customer_Data* table:

```
ALTER TABLE Customer_Data
ADD middle_initial char(1)
GO
```

Now the table definition includes five columns instead of the original four. For more details on using ALTER TABLE, see Chapter 15.

The DROP TABLE Statement

The DROP TABLE statement is used to delete a table definition and all of the data, indexes, triggers, constraints, and permission specifications for that table. To drop our *Customer_Data* table, use the following command:

```
DROP TABLE Customer_Data
GO
```

For more details on the DROP TABLE statement, see Chapter 15.

DML

DML is used to manipulate the data contained in database objects, using statements such as INSERT, SELECT, UPDATE, and DELETE. These statements allow you to select rows of data by performing queries, insert new rows of data, modify existing rows of data, and delete unwanted rows of data, respectively. This section gives basic examples of each. For more advanced uses of these statements, see Chapters 14 and 20.

The INSERT Statement

An INSERT statement is used to insert a row of data into a table or view. For example, if you want to add a new customer to the sample *Customer_Data* table, your INSERT statement might look like this:

```
INSERT INTO Customer_Data
(customer_id, first_name, last_name, phone)
VALUES (777, 'Frankie', 'Stein', '4895873900')
```

Notice the list of column names in the second line of the preceding SQL statement. Listing these column names specifies in which column the data values will be placed, in corresponding order. For example, the first data value will be placed into the first column listed, *customer_id*, the second value will go into the second column listed, and so on. Because we have listed the values to be inserted in the same order in which the columns were defined when the table was created, we do not have to specify the column names at all. We could use the following INSERT statement instead:

```
INSERT INTO Customer_Data
VALUES (777, 'Frankie', 'Stein', '4895873900')
```

> **Caution**   If you use this form of the INSERT statement and the values to be inserted are not listed in the order in which the columns were created, the values might be placed in the wrong columns (if the data being inserted is compatible with the data types of the columns). If the data is not compatible with the data types, you will receive an error.

The SELECT Statement

A SELECT statement is used to retrieve data from a table or tables. The columns listed and the WHERE clause of the statement determine which data is retrieved. For example, say you want to retrieve the *customer_id* and *first_name* column values from the *Customer_Data* table created earlier. In addition, you want this data only for each row that has the value *Frankie* in the *first_name* column. The SELECT statement would look like this:

```
SELECT customer_id, first_name FROM Customer_Data
WHERE first_name = 'Frankie'
```

If one row was found to meet the criteria of the SELECT statement, the results might look like this:

```
customer_id       first_name
-------------     ------------
777               Frankie
```

The UPDATE Statement

An UPDATE statement is used to update, or change, a value or values in a row or rows of a table. For example, if the customer Frankie Stein called and wanted to change his first name in the records to Franklin, the UPDATE statement to change his first name would look like this:

```
UPDATE Customer_Data
SET first_name = 'Franklin'
WHERE last_name = 'Stein' and customer_id=777
```

We included the customer ID in the WHERE clause to make sure that if there are other customers with the same last name of Stein, their first names would not be updated also—only the customer whose ID is 777 will get his name updated.

Note When you are writing UPDATE statements, be sure to provide sufficient filters in the WHERE clause so that you do not unintentionally update rows that you should not be updating.

The DELETE Statement

A DELETE statement is used to delete a row or rows of data from a table. You can even delete all rows from a table. To delete all rows from the *Customer_Data* sample table, you could use one of the following statements:

```
DELETE FROM Customer_Data
```

```
DELETE Customer_Data
```

The FROM keyword before the table name is always optional in the DELETE statement; otherwise, the two statements are identical.

To delete the rows from the *Customer_Data* table in which the value in the *customer_id* column is less than *100*, use the following statement:

```
DELETE FROM Customer_Data
WHERE customer_id < 100
```

Now that we've had a quick overview of the DDL and DML statements provided by SQL, let's take a look at T-SQL.

What Is T-SQL?

T-SQL is an enhancement of the standard SQL programming language. It is the primary language used for communications between applications and SQL Server. T-SQL provides the DDL and DML capabilities of standard SQL, plus extended functions, system stored procedures, and programming constructs (such as IF and WHILE) to allow more flexibility in programming. The capabilities of T-SQL continue to grow with new versions of SQL Server. Let's look at some of the new features of T-SQL.

A Review of New T-SQL Features

Numerous additions and enhancements were made to T-SQL in Microsoft SQL Server 7, including new stored procedures, system tables, functions, data types, statements, and options for existing statements. These remain the same in SQL Server 2000, so we will review them here (in case you are not yet familiar with them from SQL Server 7). There are far too many features to describe them all in detail here, however, so we'll look at just a few examples in each category.

> **More Info**   For a complete list of features, refer to the topic "New Features in Transact-SQL" in SQL Server Books Online. To display this topic, on the Contents tab, click Transact-SQL Reference, and then click New Features In Transact-SQL.

System Stored Procedures

System stored procedures are provided by SQL Server to perform administrative and other tasks that involve updating system tables and to retrieve information from system tables. System stored procedures are installed with SQL Server; their names begin with *sp_* (for "stored procedure") or *xp_* (for "extended stored procedure"). These procedures are stored in the master database and are owned by the system administrator, but many of them can be executed from any user-defined database to retrieve information from the system tables in that particular database. When you execute a system stored procedure, it operates on the system tables in the current database.

More Info See the topic "Extended Stored Procedures" in Books Online for more information about this type of procedure.

Many system stored procedures were added in SQL Server 7, and they are now available in SQL Server 2000 as well. Table 13-1 describes a few of these system stored procedures that you might find helpful.

Table 13-1. Procedures introduced in SQL Server 7 and included in SQL Server 2000

System stored procedure	Description
sp_cycle_errorlog	Closes the current error log file, renames it errorlog.1 (and, if necessary, renames the old errorlog.1 as errorlog.2, and so on), and starts a new error log file
sp_helpfile	Returns the physical names and attributes of the files associated with the current database
sp_helpfilegroup	Returns the names and attributes of the filegroups associated with the current database
sp_helprole	Returns information about the roles in the current database
sp_help_alert	Reports information about the alerts defined for the server
sp_start_job	Instructs the SQL Server Agent to begin execution of a job

Not only do some of these stored procedures provide immediate information, but they can also be used to save important information about your user databases for later use. For example, the procedures that return information about a user database might prove useful when they are run as T-SQL scripts and the output is saved to a file. You could run and save the output from *sp_helpfile*, *sp_helpfilegroup*, and *sp_helpdb* (this latter stored procedure is an oldie) in a particular database, in case you ever need to rebuild that database and want to know how the files, filegroups, and database options were originally created and configured. A listing of the remainder of the new system stored procedures (introduced in SQL Server 7) can be found in the "New Features in Transact-SQL" topic in Books Online.

System Tables

System tables are used to store SQL Server configuration information and definitions of objects, users, and permissions for all databases. Each user database has its own system tables, which hold information for that database. System tables that hold server-level configuration information are found in only the master database. You should use system stored procedures to access system tables rather than access the tables directly. A list of the new system tables first featured in SQL Server 7 can be found in the "New Features in Transact-SQL" topic in Books Online. Some interesting new system tables include the following:

- *backupfile*   This table resides in the msdb database. It records a row of information for every log backup or database file backup. This information includes the file ID, the filegroup that the file belongs to, and the physical drive letter for the file.

- *restorehistory*   This table resides in the msdb database. It records a row of information for each restore operation, whether it be a file restore or a database restore. The information includes the date and time the restore occurred, the destination database, the point in time to which the data was recovered, and the type of restore.

- *sysfiles*   This table is a virtual table, which means it cannot be updated directly. It contains information about each database file, such as the physical and logical filenames, the size and maximum size for the file, and the growth increment, if any.

Caution   Always use system stored procedures to access system tables. The system stored procedures provide a layer of insulation that can keep you from altering data you should not alter. If you access system tables by hand, you run the risk of rendering your database useless by inadvertently altering important system information.

Functions

SQL Server's built-in functions provide a quick and easy way to accomplish certain tasks. Several new T-SQL functions were made available in SQL Server 7 and are included in SQL Server 2000. Knowing which functions are available to you can make SQL Server application programming a little easier. A complete list of the new functions can be found in the "New Transact-SQL Functions" topic in Books Online. Here are just a few new functions that you might find useful:

- **NEWID**   Creates a globally unique identifier (GUID) of type *uniqueidentifier*. You would use this function to assign a value to a column of that type. Usage: NEWID(). (No parameters are needed.)

- **YEAR**   Returns an integer that represents the year part of a date. Usage: YEAR(*date*). Example: the statement SELECT YEAR('07/11/01') returns the value *2001*.

- **MONTH**   Returns an integer that represents the month part of a date. Usage: MONTH(*date*). Example: the statement SELECT MONTH('07/11/01') returns the value 7.

- **DAY**   Returns an integer that represents the day part of a date. Usage: DAY(*date*). Example: the statement SELECT DAY('07/11/01') returns the value *11*.

- **FILE_NAME**   Returns the logical name of a file that corresponds to the given file ID number. Usage: FILE_NAME(*file_id_number*). Example: The statement SELECT FILE_NAME(4) returns the name of the file that has an ID of *4*. If no file in the database has that file ID, *NULL* is returned.

Data Types

Several new data types were added with SQL Server 7, and a size extension was added to some existing data types. In addition to including these changes, three more new data types were added for SQL Server 2000. Most of these data types were discussed in Chapter 10. Here is a list of the data type changes in SQL Server 7 that are also included in SQL Server 2000:

- A new *cursor* data type has been added for cursor variables. For more information about cursors, see the topic "Cursors" in Books Online.

- Three new Unicode data types—*nchar*, *nvarchar*, and *ntext*—have been added. Unicode characters use 2 bytes per character and can support all international characters.

- A new *uniqueidentifier* data type has been added for storing GUIDs.

- The maximum length for character data and binary strings has been expanded to 8000 bytes. This length applies to the *char*, *varchar*, *binary*, and *varbinary* types.

And the three new data types for SQL Server 2000 are as follows:

- *bigint*   Stores an 8-byte integer.

- *sql_variant*   Allows values of different data types in the same column. The data value itself and data describing its value—its base data type, scale, precision, maximum size, and collation—are stored in a column of this type.

- *table*   Works in similar ways as a temporary table does; the declaration includes a column list and data types. This data type can be used to define a local variable or for the return value of a user-defined function.

Statements

SQL Server 7 included many new T-SQL statements and new options added to existing statements, which, again, are also part of SQL Server 2000. These statements correspond to some of the features introduced in SQL Server 7. For example, the ALTER DATABASE statement includes the following new options for files and filegroups: MODIFY FILE, ADD FILEGROUP, MODIFY FILEGROUP, REMOVE FILE, and REMOVE FILEGROUP. Also related to filegroups, the new statement DBCC CHECKFILEGROUP checks the allocation and structural integrity of all tables in a given filegroup.

SQL Server 7 and SQL Server 2000 include two additional DBCC statements: DBCC SHRINKFILE and DBCC SHRINKDATABASE. The former shrinks the size of a given data file, and the latter shrinks all data files in a given database, freeing up unused disk space.

SQL Server 7 and SQL Server 2000 have an improved backup-and-restore architecture. The new BACKUP statement allows full or partial database backups and log backups, and the new RESTORE statement allows full or partial database backups and log backups to be restored. These take the place of the DUMP and LOAD statements from previous versions of SQL Server. For a complete list of the new statements and options available for SQL Server 7 and SQL Server 2000, see the "New Features in Transact-SQL" topic in Books Online. See Chapters 32 and 33 for details about backing up and restoring databases.

How to Use T-SQL

In addition to using T-SQL in your application programs (a topic that is beyond the scope of this book), you can execute interactive T-SQL statements by using one of three SQL Server utilities—ISQL, OSQL, or Query Analyzer—or you can create and execute T-SQL scripts.

The ISQL Utility

The ISQL utility communicates with SQL Server through DB-LIB and enables you to execute interactive T-SQL statements, stored procedures, and script files. Because DB-LIB remains at the SQL Server 6.5 level of functionality, the ISQL application does not support some SQL Server 2000 features. For example, ISQL cannot retrieve data of the Unicode *ntext* data type.

The OSQL Utility

The OSQL utility was new in SQL Server 7 and remains as a replacement for ISQL in SQL Server 2000. These two utilities are essentially the same, except that OSQL uses Open Database Connectivity (ODBC) instead of DB-LIB to communicate with SQL Server, and OSQL supports all of the SQL Server 2000 features. The functionality of OSQL and ISQL is otherwise the same, and SQL Server 2000 supports both utilities, but you should use OSQL in place of ISQL to avoid the problem just mentioned.

To execute OSQL from a command prompt window (from an MS-DOS prompt), you simply run the OSQL.exe program with the appropriate parameters, as shown here:

```
osql -U username -P password -S servername
```

After OSQL makes a connection to SQL Server, the following numbered prompt appears:

```
1>
```

At this prompt, you can type a T-SQL statement, as shown here:

```
1>    sp_helpdb master
2>    go
```

This statement will cause the information about the master database to appear. The GO keyword is not a T-SQL statement; it is a command recognized by ISQL, OSQL, and Query Analyzer that signals the end of a batch of T-SQL statements. The results from an interactive query such as this are displayed in the command prompt window.

If you mistype in OSQL, you can start over at the 1> prompt by using the OSQL command RESET, as shown here:

```
1>    sp_helpbd
2>    reset
1>    sp_helpdb
2>    go
```

To stop the OSQL utility, type *QUIT* or *EXIT*. You can terminate a command or query while it is still running, without exiting the OSQL utility, by pressing Ctrl+C.

The $-U$, $-P$, and $-S$ parameters are not the only parameters that the OSQL utility recognizes. For a full description of all the other parameters that the OSQL utility recognizes and for additional information about OSQL, see the topic "osql Utility" in Books Online.

The Query Analyzer

You can use the Query Analyzer to display a graphical user interface (GUI)–based tool where you can execute T-SQL statements or scripts and get the results in a formatted output. You can also perform some index and query analysis with this tool. Some people prefer using Query Analyzer to running statements in an MS-DOS prompt window. To run Query Analyzer, follow these steps:

1. Start Query Analyzer using one of the following three methods:

    • Type *isqlw* at a command prompt.

    • Open Enterprise Manager and choose SQL Query Analyzer from the Tools menu.

    • From the Start menu, point to Programs, point to Microsoft SQL Server, and then choose Query Analyzer.

   The Connect To SQL Server dialog box appears (unless you are already connected to the server), as shown in Figure 13-1.

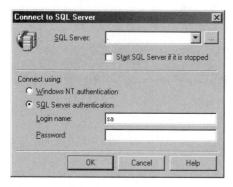

Figure 13-1. *The Connect To SQL Server dialog box.*

2. Select the name of the server you want to connect to from the SQL Server drop-down list. A period in this box stands for the local server. Type your logon information, and if you want SQL Server to start automatically if it is not currently started, select the check box next to that option. Click OK. The opening window of the Query Analyzer will appear, as shown in Figure 13-2.

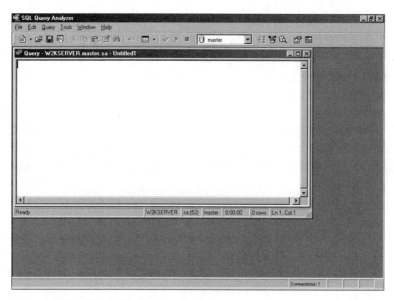

Figure 13-2. *The SQL Query Analyzer.*

3. Type any T-SQL statement or stored-procedure call in the query window, as shown in Figure 13-3. Note that the query window has now been maximized to occupy the entire Query Analyzer window.

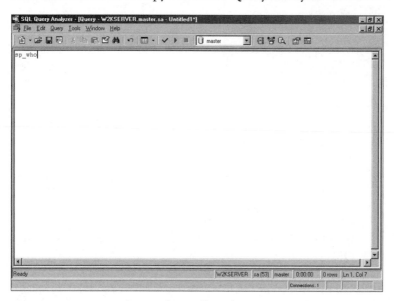

Figure 13-3. *A stored-procedure call in the query window of the Query Analyzer.*

4. To execute this statement, click the Execute Query button (the triangular green arrow pointing to the right) on the toolbar, or press Ctrl+E. The results will appear in the results pane, as shown in Figure 13-4.

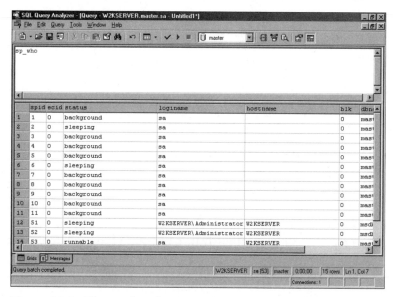

Figure 13-4. *The results of a query shown in the Query Analyzer.*

5. To use Query Analyzer to load and run T-SQL scripts that you created previously, click the Load SQL Script button (the yellow folder) on the toolbar or choose Open from the File menu, and then browse for the desired file. The entire script will appear in the top pane of the query window. Click the Execute Query button to run the script.

Note   Many other options are available with Query Analyzer, including some new ones for SQL Server 2000. (See Chapter 35 for more details.)

T-SQL Scripting

Creating your own scripts is a great way to run T-SQL statements or stored procedures when you might need to run them more than once. A *script* is simply a file that contains the T-SQL you want to execute. It can be one statement or a series of statements. One suggestion: when you are creating T-SQL scripts, give them the file extension .sql so that you can quickly identify them.

The following code shows the statements in a sample script. The script calls several system stored procedures that gather a variety of information about the MyDB database and its files, filegroups, and tables (*Customer_Data* and *Product_Info*). Let's assume that the script has been saved in the file MyDB_info.sql:

```
use MyDB
go
sp_helpdb MyDB
go
sp_helpfilegroup
go
sp_spaceused Customer_Data
go
sp_spaceused Product_Info
go
```

To run this script via the command line, you can use the *–i* and *–o* options of OSQL. The *–i* option is followed by the name of the input script file to run, and the *–o* option is followed by the name of the output file to direct the results into—in this case, MyDB_info.out. Let's also use the *–e* option to have the original T-SQL statements echoed into the output file for clarity. For example, to run the preceding script as the system administrator, enter the following code at the command prompt:

```
osql -U sa  -P  -i MyDB_info.sql  -o MyDB_info.out  -e
```

Check the output file to verify that the script worked as you intended. Using T-SQL scripts in this way allows you to save output to a file so that you can view it later, as you wish—maybe to compare results of running the script before and after some change to the database. Also, scripting is useful when you want to run a statement or statements more than once.

Another way to run a script without entering this OSQL command every time is to create a .cmd file with the OSQL command in it. In this case, we could name the file MyDB_info.cmd, and it would contain the OSQL command we just typed. Be sure that the input and output files' filenames have directory paths specified if they are not in the same directory as the .cmd file. Now you can either run the command MYDB_INFO from a command prompt or double-click the MyDB_info.cmd filename in Microsoft Windows Explorer.

You can also run T-SQL scripts in the Query Analyzer. To run our script, MyDB_info.sql, open the file by choosing Open from the File menu in Query Analyzer and then browsing to select the file. Then click Open and the script code will appear in the top pane. Click the Execute Query button or press Ctrl+E to execute the statements. The output for each statement will appear in the order in which it was executed, as shown in Figure 13-5. Notice that the top two tables of results are both from the *sp_helpdb* stored procedure.

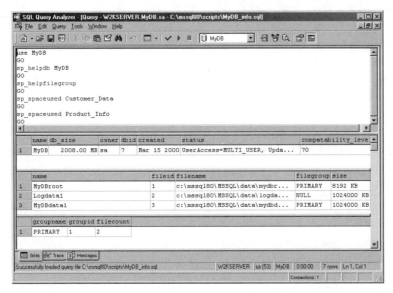

Figure 13-5. *The results of a script run in the Query Analyzer.*

Summary

In this chapter, you've learned the basics of SQL and T-SQL and you've seen some examples of simple DDL and DML statements. You learned how to run T-SQL statements by various methods—using ISQL, OSQL, SQL Query Analyzer, and T-SQL scripting. You'll find even more information about using T-SQL in the next two chapters and in Chapter 25.

Chapter 14

Retrieving Data Using Transact-SQL

In this chapter, you'll learn how to use the Transact-SQL (T-SQL) SELECT statement to retrieve data. The chapter will also cover the many optional clauses, search conditions, and functions that can be used within the SELECT statement. These elements will help you write queries that return only the data you need.

The SELECT Statement

Although the SELECT statement is used primarily to retrieve specific data, it can also be used to assign a value to a local variable or to call a function, as you'll see in the section "Other Uses for SELECT" at the end of this chapter. A SELECT statement can be simple or complex—complex is not necessarily better. Try to make your SELECT statements as simple as possible while still retrieving the results you need. For example, if you need data from only two columns of a table, include only those two columns in the SELECT statement to minimize the amount of data that must be returned.

After you have decided what data you need from which tables, you can determine which other options, if any, you should use. These options can include specifying which columns should be in the WHERE clause to make use of your indexes, specifying whether the returned data should be sorted, and specifying whether you want only distinct values returned. For more information about optimizing your queries, see Chapter 35.

Let's begin by examining the various options for the SELECT statement and reviewing examples of each. The sample databases used in this chapter, pubs and Northwind, were created for you automatically when you installed Microsoft SQL Server 2000. To familiarize yourself with the pubs and Northwind databases, use SQL Server Enterprise Manager to examine the database tables.

The syntax for the SELECT statement consists of several clauses, most of which are optional. A SELECT statement must include at least a SELECT clause and a FROM clause. These two clauses identify which column or columns of data to retrieve and from which table or tables to retrieve the data, respectively. For example, a simple SELECT statement to retrieve the authors' first and last names from the *authors* table in the pubs database might look like this:

```
SELECT    au_fname, au_lname
FROM      authors
```

If you're using command-line OSQL (described in Chapter 13), don't forget the GO command, which executes the statement. The complete T-SQL code for the preceding SELECT statement—if you are using OSQL—is shown here:

```
USE       pubs
SELECT    au_fname, au_lname
FROM      authors
GO
```

Note Because keywords are not case sensitive, you can use any capitalization system you want. It's a good idea to be consistent just to make your code easier to read. For this reason, the examples in this book use uppercase letters for keywords.

When you run the SELECT statement interactively—for example, using OSQL or SQL Query Analyzer—the results are displayed in columns, with column headings for clarity. (See Chapter 13 for an introduction to T-SQL and a discussion of OSQL and Query Analyzer.)

The SELECT Clause

The SELECT clause consists of a required select list and possibly some optional arguments. The *select list* is the list of expressions or columns that you specify in the SELECT clause to indicate which data should be returned. The optional arguments and the select list are described in this section.

Arguments

The following two arguments can be used in the SELECT clause to control which rows are returned:

- **DISTINCT**   Returns only unique rows. If the select list contains several columns, the rows will be considered unique if the corresponding values in at least one of the columns differ. For two rows to be duplicates, they must contain identical values in every column.

- **TOP *n* [PERCENT]**   Returns only the first *n* rows from the result set. If PERCENT is specified, only the first *n* percent of the rows are returned. When PERCENT is used, *n* must be between *0* and *100*. If the query includes an ORDER BY clause, the rows are ordered first and then the first *n* or first *n* percent are returned from the ordered result set. (ORDER BY clauses are described in the section "The ORDER BY Clause" later in this chapter.)

The following T-SQL code shows our sample SELECT statement run three times, each time with a different argument. The first query uses the DISTINCT argument, the second query uses the TOP 50 PERCENT argument, and the third query uses the TOP 5 argument.

```
SELECT    DISTINCT au_fname, au_lname
FROM      authors
GO

SELECT    TOP 50 PERCENT au_fname, au_lname
FROM      authors
GO

SELECT    TOP 5 au_fname, au_lname
FROM      authors
GO
```

The first query returns 23 rows, each of which is unique. The second query returns 12 rows (approximately 50 percent, rounded up), and the third query returns 5 rows.

The Select List

As mentioned, the select list is the list of expressions or columns that you specify in the SELECT clause to indicate which data should be returned. An expression can be a list of column names, functions, or constants. The select list can include several expressions or column names, separated by commas. The preceding examples use the following select list:

```
au_fname, au_lname
```

The *, or Wildcard Character   You can use the asterisk (*), or wildcard character, in the select list to return all columns from all tables and views named in the FROM clause of the query. For example, to return all columns of all rows from the *sales* table in the pubs database, use the following query:

```
SELECT    *
FROM      sales
GO
```

The section "Cross Joins" later in this chapter describes what happens when more than one table is listed in the FROM clause of a SELECT statement that contains the wildcard character.

IDENTITYCOL and ROWGUIDCOL   To retrieve the values of an identity column from a table, you can simply use the IDENTITYCOL expression in the select list. The following example queries the Northwind database, which has an identity column defined in the *Employees* table:

```
USE      Northwind
GO
SELECT   IDENTITYCOL
FROM     Employees
GO
```

The result set looks something like this:

```
EmployeeID
----------
3
4
8
:
9
```

```
(9 rows affected)
```

Notice that the column heading in the result set matches the name of the column in the table that has the IDENTITY property—in this case, *EmployeeID*.

In a similar manner, you can use the ROWGUIDCOL expression in the select list to retrieve values from the globally unique identifier (GUID) column—that is, the column that has the ROWGUIDCOL property. A column must be of the data type *uniqueidentifier* to have the ROWGUIDCOL property.

Column Aliases   Using a column alias in the select list allows you to specify the column heading that you want to appear in the result set. You can use an alias to clarify the meaning of the data in an output column, to assign a heading to a column that is used in a function, and to refer to an ORDER BY clause.

When two or more columns with the same name exist in different tables, you might want to include the table name in the column heading of the output for clarity. For an example using a column alias, let's look at the *lname* column in the *employee* table of the pubs database. You could issue the following query:

```
USE      pubs
GO
SELECT   lname
FROM     employee
GO
```

If you made such a query, you would get the following results:

```
lname
--------
Cruz
Roulet
Devon
⋮
O'Rourke
Ashworth
Latimer
```

(43 rows affected)

To display the heading "Employee Last Name" instead of the original heading, *lname*, in the result set (to emphasize the fact that the last name is from the *employee* table), use the AS keyword, as shown here:

```
SELECT   lname AS "Employee Last Name"
FROM     employee
GO
```

The output from this command is shown here:

```
Employee Last Name
------------------
Cruz
Roulet
Devon
⋮
O'Rourke
Ashworth
Latimer
```

(43 rows affected)

You can also use a column alias with other types of expressions in the select list and as a reference column in an ORDER BY clause. Suppose you have a function call in the select list. To assign a column alias that describes the output from the function, use the AS keyword after the function call. If you do not use an alias with a function, there will be no column heading at all. For example, the following statement assigns the column heading "Maximum Job ID" for the output of the MAX function:

```
SELECT   MAX(job_id) AS "Maximum Job ID"
FROM     employee
GO
```

The column alias is enclosed in quotation marks because it contains multiple words with spaces between them. If the alias does not include spaces, you do not have to enclose it in quotation marks, as you'll see in the next example.

You can reference a column alias that was assigned in the SELECT clause as an argument in the ORDER BY clause. This technique is useful when the select list contains a function whose results need to be sorted. For example, the following command retrieves the quantity of books sold at each store and sorts the output by quantity. The alias assigned in the select list is used in the ORDER BY clause.

```
SELECT   SUM(qty) AS Quantity_of_Books, stor_id
FROM     sales
GROUP BY stor_id
ORDER BY Quantity_of_Books
GO
```

In this case, we did not enclose the alias in quotation marks because it contains no spaces.

If we had not assigned a column alias for *SUM(qty)* in this query, we could have used *SUM(qty)* instead of the alias in the ORDER BY clause. This technique, shown in the next example, will provide the same output, but with no column heading for the *sum* column:

```
SELECT   SUM(qty), stor_id FROM sales
GROUP BY stor_id
ORDER BY SUM(qty)
GO
```

Remember that a column alias is used to assign a heading to a column for output purposes; it does not affect the results of the query in any way.

The FROM Clause

The FROM clause contains the names of the tables and views from which the data is pulled. Every SELECT statement requires a FROM clause, except when the select list contains no column names—only constants, variables, and arithmetic expressions. You've already seen some simple examples of the FROM clause, but FROM clauses can also contain derived tables, joins, and aliases.

Derived Tables

A *derived table* is the result set from a SELECT statement nested in the FROM clause. The result set of the nested SELECT statement is used as a table from which the outer SELECT statement selects its data. The following query uses a derived table to find the names of any stores that honor at least one type of discount:

```
USE      pubs
GO
SELECT   s.stor_name
FROM     stores AS s, (SELECT stor_id, COUNT(DISTINCT discounttype)
                       AS d_count
                       FROM     discounts
                       GROUP BY stor_id) AS d
WHERE    s.stor_id = d.stor_id AND
         d.d_count >= 1
GO
```

If you run this command, you should see one row selected, which means that only one store in the database, Bookbeat, offers any discount.

Notice that this query uses shorthand for the table names (*s* for the *stores* table and *d* for the *discounts* table). This shorthand, called a *table alias*, is described in the section "Table Aliases" later in this chapter.

Note   You cannot have a derived table in a WHERE clause. A SELECT statement in a WHERE clause is used as a search condition. See the section "The WHERE Clause and Search Conditions" later in this chapter for details.

Joined Tables

A *joined table* is a result set from the join operation performed on two or more tables. Several types of joins can be performed on tables: inner joins, full outer joins, left outer joins, right outer joins, and cross joins. Let's look at each of these joins in detail.

Inner Joins   An *inner join* is the default join type; it specifies that only table rows matching the ON condition should be included in the result set and that any unmatched rows should be discarded. To specify a join, use the JOIN keyword. Use the ON keyword to identify the search condition on which to base the join. The following query joins the *stores* and *discounts* tables to show which stores offer a discount and the type of discount. (By default, this is an inner join, which means that only rows matching the ON search condition are returned.)

```
SELECT    s.stor_id, d.discounttype
FROM      stores s JOIN discounts d
ON        s.stor_id = d.stor_id
GO
```

The result set looks like this:

```
stor_id  discounttype
-------  ------------------
8042     Customer Discount
```

As you can see, only one store offers a discount, and it has only one type of discount. The only row returned is the one whose *stor_id* from the *stores* table has a matching *stor_id* from the *discounts* table. That particular *stor_id* and its associated *discounttype* are returned.

Full Outer Joins A *full outer join* specifies that the unmatched rows (rows that do not meet the ON condition) as well as the matched rows (rows that meet the ON condition) should be included in the result set. For unmatched rows, *NULL* will appear in the column that did not match. In this example, *NULL* means either that a store did not offer any discount, and thus it has a *stor_id* value in the *stores* table but not in the *discounts* table, or that a type of discount in the *discounts* table is not offered by any store. The following query uses the same query as the preceding inner join, but this time, we will specify FULL OUTER JOIN:

```
SELECT    s.stor_id, d.discounttype
FROM      stores s FULL OUTER JOIN discounts d
ON        s.stor_id = d.stor_id
GO
```

The result set looks like this:

```
stor_id  discounttype
-------  ------------------
NULL     Initial Customer
NULL     Volume Discount
6380     NULL
7066     NULL
7067     NULL
7131     NULL
7896     NULL
8042     Customer Discount
```

Only one of the results rows shows a match—the last row. The other rows have *NULL* in one column.

Left Outer Joins   A *left outer join* returns the matching rows plus all the rows from the table that is specified to the left of the JOIN keyword. Using the same query, we specify LEFT OUTER JOIN this time, as shown here:

```
SELECT   s.stor_id, d.discounttype
FROM     stores s LEFT OUTER JOIN discounts d
ON       s.stor_id = d.stor_id
GO
```

The result set looks like this:

```
stor_id discounttype
------- ----------------------------------------
6380    NULL
7066    NULL
7067    NULL
7131    NULL
7896    NULL
8042    Customer Discount
```

This result set includes the rows from the *stores* table that had no matching *stor_id* value in the *discounts* table. (The *discounttype* column for those rows is *NULL*.) The result set also includes the one row that matched the ON condition.

Right Outer Joins   A *right outer join* is the opposite of a left outer join: it returns the matching rows plus all the rows from the table specified to the right of the JOIN keyword. Here is the same query with RIGHT OUTER JOIN specified:

```
SELECT   s.stor_id, d.discounttype
FROM     stores s RIGHT OUTER JOIN discounts d
ON       s.stor_id = d.stor_id
GO
```

The result set looks like this:

```
stor_id discounttype
------- --------------------
NULL    Initial Customer
NULL    Volume Discount
8042    Customer Discount
```

This result set shows the rows from the *discounts* table that do not have a matching *stor_id* value in the *stores* table. (The *stor_id* column for those rows is *NULL*.) The result set also shows the one row that matched the ON condition.

Cross Joins   A *cross join* is the product of two tables when no WHERE clause is specified. When a WHERE clause is specified, the cross join acts like an inner join. Without a WHERE clause, all rows and columns will be returned from both tables in the following manner: each row from the first table will be matched with each row from the second table, so the size of the result set will be the number of rows in the first table multiplied by the number of rows in the second table.

To understand a cross join, let's start with some new examples. First we'll look at a cross join without a WHERE clause, and then we'll look at three examples of cross joins that include WHERE clauses. The following queries show a simple example. Run the three queries and note the number of rows that result from each.

```
SELECT  *
FROM    stores
GO

SELECT  *
FROM    sales
GO

SELECT  *
FROM    stores CROSS JOIN sales
GO
```

> **Note** If you include two tables in the FROM clause, the effect is the same as specifying CROSS JOIN, as in the following example:

```
SELECT  *
FROM    stores, sales
GO
```

To avoid this jumble of information (if it is more than we need), we can add a WHERE clause to narrow the query, as in the following statement:

```
SELECT  *
FROM    sales CROSS JOIN stores
WHERE   sales.stor_id = stores.stor_id
GO
```

This statement returns only the rows that match the search condition in the WHERE clause, which narrows the result set to 21 rows. The WHERE clause forces a cross join to act the same as an inner join. (That is, only rows matching the search condition are returned.) The preceding query returns the rows in the *sales* table, concatenated with the rows from the *stores* table that have the same *stor_id* value. Rows that do not contain a match are not returned.

To further narrow the result set, you can specify from which table to select all rows and columns by adding the table name before the asterisk (*), as in the following query. You can also specify to which table a column belongs by inserting the table name and a dot (.) before any column name.

```
SELECT    sales.*, stores.city
FROM      sales CROSS JOIN stores
WHERE     sales.stor_id = stores.stor_id
GO
```

This query returns all the columns from the *sales* table, with the *city* column from the *stores* table row that has the same *stor_id* value appended. In effect, the result set includes the city of the store where the sale was made appended to the rows in the *sales* table that have a matching *stor_id* value in the *stores* table.

Here is the same query without the * symbol; only the *stor_id* column will be selected from the *sales* table:

```
SELECT    sales.stor_id, stores.city
FROM      sales CROSS JOIN stores
WHERE     sales.stor_id = stores.stor_id
GO
```

Table Aliases

We've already looked at several examples in which a table name alias was used. Specifying the AS keyword is optional. (FROM *tablename* AS *alias* gives the same result as FROM *tablename* *alias*.) Let's look again at the query from the "Right Outer Joins" section, which used aliases:

```
SELECT    s.stor_id, d.discounttype
FROM      stores s RIGHT OUTER JOIN discounts d
ON        s.stor_id = d.stor_id
GO
```

Each of the two tables has a *stor_id* column. To distinguish which table's *stor_id* column you are referring to in the query, you must supply the table name or an alias followed by a dot (.) and then the column name. In this example, the alias *s* is used for the *stores* table, and *d* is used for the *discounts* table. When specifying a column, we must add *s.* or *d.* before the column name to indicate which table contains it. The same query with the AS keyword included looks like this:

```
SELECT    s.stor_id, d.discounttype
FROM      stores AS s RIGHT OUTER JOIN discounts AS d
ON        s.stor_id = d.stor_id
GO
```

The INTO Clause

This brings us to the first truly optional clause for the SELECT statement: the INTO clause. Using the SELECT *<select list>* INTO *<new_tablename>* syntax enables you to retrieve data from a table or tables and place the resulting rows in a new table. The new table is created automatically when you run the SELECT...INTO statement and is defined according to the columns in the select list. Each column in the new table has the same data type as the original column and carries the column name specified in the select list. The user must have CREATE TABLE permission in the destination database to execute SELECT...INTO. See Chapter 34 for information about how to set permissions.

You can use SELECT...INTO to select rows into a temporary table or a permanent table. For a local temporary table (which is visible to only the current connection or user), you must include the pound symbol (#) before the table name. For a global temporary table (which is visible to any user), you must include two pound symbols (##) before the table name. A temporary table is automatically deleted after all users who are using the table have disconnected from SQL Server. To select into a permanent table, you do not need a prefix for the new table name, but the Select Into/Bulk Copy option must be turned on for the destination database. To turn on this option in the pubs database, you can execute the following OSQL statement:

```
sp_dboption pubs, "select into/bulkcopy", true
GO
```

You can also use the SQL Server Enterprise Manager to turn on this option, as follows:

1. Right-click the pubs database name in either pane of the Enterprise Manager and choose Properties from the shortcut menu to display the Pubs Properties window, shown in Figure 14-1. (You might remember this window from Chapter 9, when we created a database and specified file growth options.)

2. Click the Options tab, shown in Figure 14-2, and select Bulk-Logged in the Model drop-down list. Leave all other settings as they are. Click OK.

The following query uses SELECT...INTO to create a new permanent table, *emp_info*, that includes all employees' first and last names and their job descriptions (from the pubs database):

```
SELECT    employee.fname, employee.lname, jobs.job_desc
INTO      emp_info
FROM      employee, jobs
WHERE     employee.job_id = jobs.job_id
GO
```

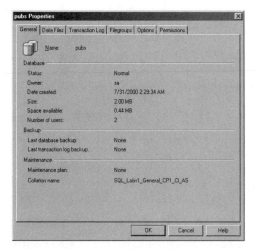

Figure 14-1. *The General tab of the database Properties window.*

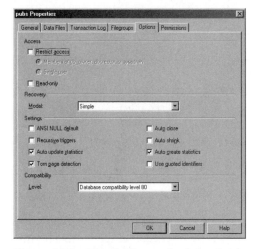

Figure 14-2. *The Options tab of the database Properties window.*

The *emp_info* table will contain three columns—*fname*, *lname*, and *job_desc*—that have the same data types as the columns defined in the original tables (*employee* and *jobs*). If you want the new table to be a local temporary table, the table name must be preceded by a # symbol, as in *#emp_info*; for a global temporary table, use the ## symbol, as in *##emp_info*.

The WHERE Clause and Search Conditions

You can use the WHERE clause to restrict the rows that are returned from a query, according to the search conditions specified. In this section, we'll examine many of the operations that can be used in the search condition.

> **Note** Search conditions are used not only in WHERE clauses for the SELECT statement, but they are also used in UPDATE and DELETE statements. (The UPDATE and DELETE statements will be covered in Chapter 20.)

First let's review some terminology. The search condition can contain an unlimited number of predicates joined by the logical operators AND, OR, and NOT. A *predicate* is an expression that returns a value of *TRUE, FALSE,* or *UNKNOWN*. An *expression* can be a column name, a constant, a scalar function (a function that returns one value), a variable, a scalar subquery (a subquery that returns one column), or a combination of these elements joined by operators. In this section, the term "expression" refers to predicates and expressions.

Comparison Operators

The equality and nonequality operators that can be used with expressions are listed in Table 14-1.

Table 14-1. Comparison operators

Operator	Condition Tested
=	Tests for equality between two expressions
<>	Tests whether two expressions are not equal to each other
!=	Tests whether two expressions are not equal to each other (same as <>)
>	Tests whether one expression is greater than the other
>=	Tests whether one expression is greater than or equal to the other
!>	Tests whether one expression is not greater than the other
<	Tests whether one expression is less than the other
<=	Tests whether one expression is less than or equal to the other
!<	Tests whether one expression is not less than the other

A simple WHERE clause might compare two expressions by using the equality operator (=). For example, the following SELECT statement tests the value in the *lname* column for each row, which is of the *char* data type, and returns *TRUE* if the value is equal to *"Latimer."* (The rows that return *TRUE* will be included in the result set.)

```
SELECT   *
FROM     employee
WHERE    lname = "Latimer"
GO
```

In this case, the query returns one row. The name *Latimer* must be enclosed in quotation marks because it is a character string.

> **Note**   By default, SQL Server will accept either single quotation marks ('') or
> double quotation marks (""), as in *'Latimer'* or *"Latimer"*. The examples in this
> book use double quotation marks only, to avoid confusion. To allow a reserved
> keyword to be used as an object name and force literals to use single quotation
> marks only, use the SET QUOTED_IDENTIFIER option. Set the option to *TRUE*.
> (*FALSE* is the default.)

The following query uses the not equal operator (<>), this time with an *integer* data type column, *job_id*:

```
SELECT    job_desc
FROM      jobs
WHERE     job_id <> 1
GO
```

This query will return the job description text from the row or rows in the *jobs* table that have a *job_id* value not equal to *1*. In this case, 13 rows are returned. If a row has a value of *NULL*, it does not equal *1* or any other value, so rows with null values will be returned as well.

Logical Operators

The logical operators AND and OR test two expressions and return a Boolean value of *TRUE*, *FALSE*, or *UNKNOWN*, depending on the results from the two expressions. The NOT operator negates the Boolean value returned by an expression that follows it. Figure 14-3 shows the return value from each possible AND, OR, and NOT operation. To read the AND and OR tables, find the first expression's result in the left column, find the second expression's result in the top row, and then find the cell in which the row and column meet to see the resulting Boolean value. The NOT table is fairly straightforward. An *UNKNOWN* value could result from an expression that contained *NULL* as an operand.

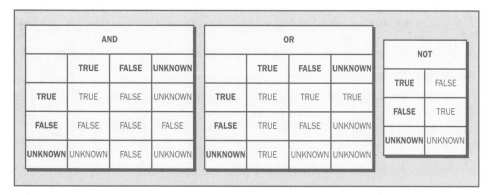

Figure 14-3. *Return values for various AND, OR, and NOT operations.*

The following query uses two expressions in the WHERE clause with the AND logical operator:

```
SELECT    job_desc, min_lvl, max_lvl
FROM      jobs
WHERE     min_lvl >= 100 AND
          max_lvl <= 225
GO
```

As shown in Figure 14-3, for an AND operation to return *TRUE*, both conditions must return *TRUE*. In this query, four rows are returned.

In the next query, an OR operation tests for publishers in either Washington, D.C. or Massachusetts. A row will be returned if either of the tests returns *TRUE* for that row.

```
SELECT    p.pub_name, p.state, t.title
FROM      publishers p, titles t
WHERE     p.state = "DC" OR
          p.state = "MA" AND
          t.pub_id = p.pub_id
GO
```

This query returns 23 rows.

The NOT operation simply returns the negation of the value of the Boolean expression that follows it. For example, to return all book titles for which an author's royalties were not less than 20 percent, you could use the NOT operator in the following manner:

```
SELECT    t.title, r.royalty
FROM      titles t, roysched r
WHERE     t.title_id = r.title_id AND NOT
          r.royalty < 20
GO
```

This query returns the 18 titles for which royalties were equal to or greater than 20 percent.

Other Keywords

In addition to the operators described in the preceding sections, a variety of T-SQL keywords can be used in a search condition. The most commonly used keywords are explained in this section, and examples of their use are given.

LIKE   The LIKE keyword indicates pattern matching in a search condition. *Pattern matching* is testing for a match between a match expression and the pattern specified in the search condition, using the following syntax:

```
<match_expression> LIKE <pattern>
```

If the match expression matches the pattern, a Boolean value of *TRUE* is returned. Otherwise, *FALSE* is returned. The match expression must be of the *character string* data type. If it is not, SQL Server will convert it to the *character string* data type, if possible.

Patterns are really string expressions. A *string expression* is defined as a string of characters and wildcard characters. *Wildcard characters* are characters that take on special meanings when used in a string expression. Table 14-2 lists the wildcard characters that can be used in patterns.

Table 14-2.   T-SQL Wildcard characters

Wildcard Character	Description
%	Percent symbol; matches a string of zero or more characters
_	Underscore; matches any single character
[]	Range wildcard character; matches any single character within the range or set, such as *[m–p]* or *[mnop]*, meaning any of the characters *m, n, o,* or *p*
[^]	Not-in-range wildcard character; matches any single character not within the range or set, such as *[^m–p]* or *[^mnop]*, meaning any character other than *m, n, o,* or *p*

To get a better understanding of using the LIKE keyword and wildcard characters, let's look at some examples. To find all last names in the *authors* table that begin with the letter "S," you could use the following query with the % wildcard character:

```
SELECT    au_lname
FROM      authors
WHERE     au_lname LIKE "S%"
GO
```

The result set will look like this:

```
au_lname
----------
Smith
Straight
Stringer
```

In this query, *"S%"* means return all rows that contain a last name beginning with "S," followed by any number of characters.

> **Note** The examples in this section assume that you are using the default sort order—Dictionary Order, Case-Insensitive. If you have specified another sort order, your results might be different, but the theory of operation for the LIKE keyword will remain the same.

To retrieve the information for an author whose ID starts with the number 724, knowing that each ID is formatted like a social security number (three digits, followed by a dash, followed by two digits, then another dash, and finally four digits), you could use the _ wildcard character, as follows:

```
SELECT    *
FROM      authors
WHERE     au_id LIKE "724-__-____"
GO
```

The result set will contain two rows, with *au_id* values of *724-08-9931* and *724-80-9391*.

Now let's look at an example that uses the [] wildcard. To retrieve the last names of authors starting with "A" through "M," you could use the [] wildcard along with the % wildcard character, as shown here:

```
SELECT    au_lname
FROM      authors
WHERE     au_lname LIKE "[A-M]%"
GO
```

The result set will contain 14 rows of names beginning with "A" through "M" (13, if you are using a case-sensitive sort order).

If we perform a similar query but use the [^] wildcard in place of the [] wildcard character, we will get rows that contain last names that start with letters other than "A" through "M," as shown here:

```
SELECT    au_lname
FROM      authors
WHERE     au_lname LIKE "[^A-M]%"
GO
```

This query returns nine rows.

If you are using a case-sensitive sort order and you want to find all names that fall into a range without regard to case, you could use a query that checks for a lowercase or an uppercase first letter, as shown here:

```
SELECT    au_lname
FROM      authors
WHERE     au_lname LIKE "[A-M]%" OR
          au_lname LIKE "[a-m]%"
GO
```

This result set will include the name "del Castillo," whereas a case-sensitive query that checked for only uppercase "A" through "M" would not.

The LIKE keyword can also be preceded by the NOT operator. NOT LIKE returns rows that do not match the condition specified. For example, to select titles that do not start with the word "The," you could use NOT LIKE in the following query:

```
SELECT    title
FROM      titles
WHERE     title NOT LIKE "The %"
GO
```

This query returns 15 rows.

You can be creative when using the LIKE keyword. But be careful to test your queries to be sure they are returning the data you expect. If you leave out a NOT or a ^ character when you meant to include one, your result set will be the opposite of what you desired. Failing to include the % wildcard character when it is needed will cause incorrect results also. And remember that leading and trailing spaces are also matched exactly.

ESCAPE   The ESCAPE keyword enables you to perform pattern matching for the wildcard characters themselves, such as ^, %, [, and _. Following the ESCAPE keyword, you specify the character you want to use as the escape character, which signals that the following character in the string expression should be matched literally. For example, to search for all rows in the *titles* table that have an underscore in the *title* column, you would use the following query:

```
SELECT    title
FROM      titles
WHERE     title LIKE "%e_%" ESCAPE "e"
GO
```

This query returns no rows because no titles in the database include an underscore.

BETWEEN   The BETWEEN keyword is always used with AND and specifies an inclusive range to test for in a search condition. The syntax is shown here:

```
<test_expression> BETWEEN <begin_expression> AND <end_expression>
```

The result of the search condition will be the Boolean value *TRUE* if *test_expression* is greater than or equal to *begin_expression* and is also less than or equal to *end_expression*. Otherwise, the result will be *FALSE*.

The following query uses BETWEEN to find all the book titles that have a price between $5 and $25:

```
SELECT    price, title
FROM      titles
WHERE     price BETWEEN 5.00 AND 25.00
GO
```

This query returns 14 rows.

You can also use NOT with BETWEEN to find rows that are not in the specified range. For example, to find the book titles whose prices are not between $20 and $30 (meaning that their prices are less than $20 or greater than $30), you would use the following query:

```
SELECT    price, title
FROM      titles
WHERE     price NOT BETWEEN 20.00 AND 30.00
GO
```

When you use the BETWEEN keyword, *test_expression* must have the same data type as *begin_expression* and *end_expression*.

In the preceding example, the *price* column has the data type *money*, so *begin_expression* and *end_expression* must each be a number that can be compared with or implicitly converted to the *money* data type. You could not use *price* as *test_expression* and then use a character string (of the *char* data type) for *begin_expression* and *end_expression*. If you did, SQL Server would return an error message.

Note SQL Server will automatically convert data types when necessary if an implicit conversion is possible. *Implicit conversion* is the automatic conversion of one data type to another, compatible data type. After the conversion, the comparison can be performed. For example, if a column of the *smallint* data type is compared to a column of the *int* data type, SQL Server implicitly converts the data type of the former column to *int* before performing the comparison. If an implicit conversion is not supported, you can use the *CAST* or *CONVERT* function to explicitly convert a column. For a complete chart showing which data types SQL Server will convert implicitly and which ones must be explicitly converted, check the SQL Server Books Online index for "CAST," and then select "CAST and CONVERT (T-SQL)" in the Topics Found dialog box.

Our last example involving the BETWEEN keyword uses strings in a search condition. To find authors' last names that fall alphabetically between the names "Bennet" and "McBadden," you would use the following query:

```
SELECT    au_lname
FROM      authors
WHERE     au_lname BETWEEN "Bennet" AND "McBadden"
GO
```

Because the BETWEEN range is inclusive, the results of this query will include the names "Bennet" and "McBadden," which do exist in the table.

IS NULL   The IS NULL keyword is used in a search condition to select rows that have a null value in the specified column. For example, to find the book titles in the *titles* table that have no data in the *notes* column (that is, the value for *notes* is *NULL*), you would use the following query:

```
SELECT    title, notes
FROM      titles
WHERE     notes IS NULL
GO
```

The result set looks like this:

```
title                                notes
------------------------------------ -------
The Psychology of Computer Cooking   NULL
```

As you can see, the null value in the *notes* column appears as *NULL* in the result set. *NULL* is not the actual value in the column—it simply indicates that a null value exists in that column. (Recall from Chapter 10 that a null value is an unknown value.)

To find the titles that do have data in the *notes* column (titles for which the value of *notes* is not a null value), use IS NOT NULL, as follows:

```
SELECT    title, notes
FROM      titles
WHERE     notes IS NOT NULL
GO
```

All of the 17 rows in the result set will have one or more characters in the *notes* column and therefore do not have null values in the *notes* column.

IN   The IN keyword is used in a search condition to determine whether the given test expression matches any value in a subquery or list of values. If a match is found, a value of *TRUE* is returned. NOT IN returns the negation of the result for IN, and therefore, if the test expression is not found in the subquery or the list of values, *TRUE* is returned. The syntax is as follows:

```
<test_expression> IN (<subquery>)
```

or

```
<test_expression> IN (<list of values>)
```

A *subquery* is a SELECT statement that returns only one column in the result set. The subquery must be enclosed in parentheses. A *list of values* is just that, with the values enclosed in parentheses and separated by commas. The column resulting from either the subquery or the list of values must have the same data type as *test_expression*. SQL Server will perform implicit conversion when necessary.

You could use IN with a list of values to find the job ID numbers of three specific job descriptions, as in the following query:

```
SELECT    job_id
FROM      jobs
WHERE     job_desc IN ("Operations Manager",
                       "Marketing Manager",
                       "Designer")
GO
```

The list of values in this query is as follows: *("Operations Manager", "Marketing Manager", "Designer")*. The query returns the job IDs from rows that have one of these three values in the *job_desc* column. The IN keyword makes your query simpler and easier to read and understand than if you had used two OR operators, as shown here:

```
SELECT    job_id
FROM      jobs
WHERE     job_desc = "Operations Manager" OR
          job_desc = "Marketing Manager"  OR
          job_desc = "Designer"
GO
```

The following query uses the IN keyword twice in one statement—once for a subquery and once for a list of values within the subquery:

```
SELECT    fname, lname      --Outer query
FROM      employee
WHERE     job_id IN ( SELECT job_id      --Inner query, or subquery
                      FROM   jobs
                      WHERE  job_desc IN ("Operations Manager",
                                          "Marketing Manager",
                                          "Designer"))
GO
```

The subquery result set is found first—in this case, a set of *job_id* values. The *job_id* values resulting from the subquery are not returned to the screen; the outer query uses them as the expression for its own IN search condition. The final result set will contain the first and last names of all employees whose job titles are Operations Manager, Marketing Manager, or Designer. Here is the result set:

```
fname                   lname
--------------------    ---------------------------
Pedro                   Afonso
Lesley                  Brown
Palle                   Ibsen
Karin                   Josephs
Maria                   Larsson
Elizabeth               Lincoln
Patricia                McKenna
Roland                  Mendel
Helvetius               Nagy
Miguel                  Paolino
Daniel                  Tonini

(11 rows affected)
```

IN can also be used with the NOT operator. For example, to return the names of all publishers not located in California, Texas, or Illinois, run the following query:

```
SELECT    pub_name
FROM      publishers
WHERE     state NOT IN ("CA",
                        "TX",
                        "IL")
GO
```

This query will return five rows whose *state* column value is not one of the three states in the list of values. If you have the database option *ANSI nulls* set to *ON*, the result set will contain only three rows. This reduction is because two of the five rows from the original result set will have *NULL* as the *state* value, and *NULL*s are not selected when *ANSI nulls* is set to *ON*.

To determine your *ANSI nulls* setting for the pubs database, run the following system stored procedure:

```
sp_dboption "pubs", "ANSI nulls"
GO
```

If *ANSI nulls* is set to *OFF*, change the value to *ON* by using the following statement:

```
sp_dboption "pubs", "ANSI nulls", TRUE
GO
```

To change the value from *ON* to *OFF*, use *FALSE* in place of *TRUE*.

More Info For more information about the effects of the *ANSI nulls* database option, check the SQL Server Books Online index for "sp_dp_option," and then select "sp_db_option (T-SQL)" in the Topics Found dialog box. Also, check the SQL Server Books Online index for "*ANSI nulls,*" and then click the "SET ANSI_NULLS" link at the bottom of the page to display the "SET ANSI_NULLS (T-SQL)" topic.

EXISTS The EXISTS keyword is used to test for the existence of rows in the subquery that follows. The syntax is shown here:

```
EXISTS (<subquery>)
```

If any rows satisfy the subquery, *TRUE* is returned.

To select names of authors who have already published a book, you could use the following query:

```
SELECT    au_fname, au_lname
FROM      authors
WHERE     EXISTS (SELECT au_id
                  FROM    titleauthor
                  WHERE   titleauthor.au_id = authors.au_id)
GO
```

Authors whose names are in the *authors* table but who have not published a book listed in the *titleauthor* table will not be selected. If no rows had been selected in the subquery, the result set for the outer query would be empty. (Zero rows would be selected.)

CONTAINS and FREETEXT The CONTAINS and FREETEXT keywords are used for full-text searching on character-based data type columns. They allow greater flexibility than the LIKE keyword. For example, the CONTAINS keyword enables you to search for words that are not an exact match for but are similar to the specified word or phrase (a "fuzzy" match). FREETEXT enables you to search for words that match (or fuzzy match) part or all of the search string. The words do not have to match the entire search string, nor do they need to be in the same order as the words in the string. These two keywords can be used in many ways and offer a number of options related to full-text searching, topics which are beyond the scope of this chapter.

More Info For more information about the CONTAINS and FREETEXT keywords, check the SQL Server Books Online index for "CONTAINS" and "FREETEXT."

The GROUP BY Clause

GROUP BY is used after the WHERE clause to indicate that the result set rows should be grouped according to the grouping columns specified. If an aggregate function is used in the SELECT clause, an aggregate summary value is calculated for each group and shown in the output. (An *aggregate function* performs a calculation and returns a value; these functions are described in detail in the section "Aggregate Functions" later in this chapter.)

> **Note**   Every column in the select list—except for columns used in an aggregate function—must be specified in the GROUP BY clause as a grouping column; otherwise, SQL Server will return an error message. The output could not be presented in a logical manner if this rule were not enforced, as the specified GROUP BY column must group each column in the select list.

GROUP BY is most useful when an aggregate function is included in the SELECT clause. Let's take a look at a SELECT statement that uses the GROUP BY clause to find the total number sold of each book title:

```
SELECT    title_id, SUM(qty)
FROM      sales
GROUP BY title_id
GO
```

The result set looks like this:

```
title_id
-------- -----------
BU1032          15
BU1111          25
BU2075          35
BU7832          15
MC2222          10
MC3021          40
PC1035          30
PC8888          50
PS1372          20
PS2091         108
PS2106          25
PS3333          15
PS7777          25
TC3218          40
TC4203          20
TC7777          20

(16 rows affected)
```

This query does not contain a WHERE clause—you do not need one. The result set shows a *title_id* column and a summary column with no heading. For each distinct title ID, the total number sold of that title appears in the summary column. For example, the *title_id* value *BU1032* appears twice in the *sales* table—it appears once showing 5 sales in the *qty* column, and it appears again showing 10 sales for a different order. The SUM aggregate function adds these two sales to arrive at the total sales figure of 15, which appears in the summary column. To add a heading to your summary column, use the AS keyword, as shown here:

```
SELECT    title_id, SUM(qty) AS "Total Sales"
FROM      sales
GROUP BY title_id
GO
```

Now the result set will show the heading "Total Sales" over the summary column:

```
title_id  Total Sales
--------  -----------
BU1032             15
BU1111             25
BU2075             35
BU7832             15
MC2222             10
MC3021             40
PC1035             30
PC8888             50
PS1372             20
PS2091            108
PS2106             25
PS3333             15
PS7777             25
TC3218             40
TC4203             20
TC7777             20

(16 rows affected)
```

You can nest groups by including more than one column in the GROUP BY clause. Nesting groups means that the result set will be grouped by each of the grouping columns in the order in which the columns are specified. For example, to find the average price for book titles that are grouped by type and then by publisher, run the following query:

```
SELECT    type, pub_id, AVG(price) AS "Average Price"
FROM      titles
GROUP BY type, pub_id
GO
```

The result set looks like this:

```
type          pub_id Average Price
------------- ------ ------------------------
business      0736                       2.99
psychology    0736                      11.48
UNDECIDED     0877                       NULL
mod_cook      0877                      11.49
psychology    0877                      21.59
trad_cook     0877                      15.96
business      1389                      17.31
popular_comp  1389                      21.48

(8 rows affected)
```

Notice that the psychology and business types occur more than once because they are grouped under different publisher IDs. The *NULL* average price for the UNDECIDED type reflects that no prices were inserted into the table for that type, and therefore, no average could be calculated.

GROUP BY provides an optional keyword, ALL, that specifies that all groups should be included in the result set, even if they do not meet the search condition. The groups that do not have rows that meet the search condition will contain a *NULL* in the summary column so that they can be easily identified. For example, to show the average price for books that have a royalty of 12 percent (and also show books that do not, which will have *NULL* in the summary column) and to group the books by type and then by publisher ID, run the following query:

```
SELECT    type, pub_id, AVG(price) AS "Average Price"
FROM      titles
WHERE     royalty = 12
GROUP BY ALL type, pub_id
GO
```

The result set looks like this:

```
type          pub_id Average Price
------------- ------ ------------------------
business      0736                       NULL
psychology    0736                      10.95
UNDECIDED     0877                       NULL
mod_cook      0877                      19.99
psychology    0877                       NULL
trad_cook     0877                       NULL
business      1389                       NULL
popular_comp  1389                       NULL

(8 rows affected)
```

All types are present in the output and *NULL* appears for the types that do not have a book with a commission of 12 percent.

If we now remove the keyword ALL, the result set will contain only types that have a book with a 12 percent commission, as shown here:

```
type          pub_id Average Price
------------  ------ -----------------------
psychology    0736                     10.95
mod_cook      0877                     19.99

(2 rows affected)
```

The GROUP BY clause is often accompanied by the HAVING clause, which is covered next.

The HAVING Clause

The HAVING clause is used to specify a search condition for a group or an aggregate function. HAVING is most commonly used after a GROUP BY clause for cases in which a search condition must be tested after the results are grouped. If the search condition can be applied before the grouping occurs, it is more efficient to place the search condition in the WHERE clause than to add a HAVING clause. This technique reduces the number of rows that must be grouped. If there is no GROUP BY clause, HAVING can be used only with an aggregate function in the select list. In this case, the HAVING clause acts the same as a WHERE clause. If HAVING is not used in either of these ways, SQL Server will return an error message.

The syntax for the HAVING clause is as follows:

```
HAVING <search_condition>
```

Here, *search_condition* has the same meaning as the search conditions described in the section "The WHERE Clause and Search Conditions" earlier in this chapter. One difference between the HAVING clause and the WHERE clause is that the HAVING clause can include an aggregate function in the search condition, but the WHERE clause cannot.

Note You can use aggregate functions in the SELECT clause and in the HAVING clause, but you can't use them in the WHERE clause.

The following query uses the HAVING clause to select the types of books per publisher that have an average price greater than $15:

```
SELECT    type, pub_id, AVG(price) AS "Average Price"
FROM      titles
GROUP BY  type, pub_id
HAVING    AVG(price) > 15.00
GO
```

The result set looks like this:

```
type           pub_id Average Price
------------   ------ ------------------------
psychology     0877                     21.59
trad_cook      0877                     15.96
business       1389                     17.31
popular_comp   1389                     21.48
```

(4 rows affected)

You can also use logical operators with the HAVING clause. Here, the AND operator has been added to our query:

```
SELECT    type, pub_id, AVG(price) AS "Average Price"
FROM      titles
GROUP BY  type, pub_id
HAVING    AVG(price) >= 15.00 AND
          AVG(price) <= 20.00
GO
```

The result set looks like this:

```
type           pub_id Average Price
------------   ------ ------------------------
trad_cook      0877                     15.96
business       1389                     17.31
```

(2 rows affected)

You could get the same results by using the BETWEEN clause instead of just AND, as shown here:

```
SELECT    type, pub_id, AVG(price) AS "Average Price"
FROM      titles
GROUP BY  type, pub_id
HAVING    AVG(price) BETWEEN 15.00 AND 20.00
GO
```

To use HAVING without a GROUP BY clause, you must have an aggregate function in the select list and in the HAVING clause. For example, to select the sum of the prices for books of type *mod_cook* only if the sum is greater than $20, run the following query:

```
SELECT   SUM(price)
FROM     titles
WHERE    type = "mod_cook"
HAVING   SUM(price) > 20
GO
```

If you try to put the expression *SUM(price) > 20* in the WHERE clause, SQL Server will return an error message. (Aggregate functions are not allowed in the WHERE clause.)

> **Note** Remember, the only time you can use the HAVING clause is when you add a search condition to test the resultant groups from a GROUP BY clause or to test an aggregate function. Otherwise, you should specify the search condition in the WHERE clause.

The ORDER BY Clause

The ORDER BY clause is used to specify the order in which the rows in a result set should be sorted. You can specify either ascending (from lowest to highest) or descending (from highest to lowest) order by using the keywords ASC or DESC. Ascending order is the default if no order is specified. You can specify more than one column in the ORDER BY clause. The results will be ordered by the first column listed. If the first column contains duplicate values, those rows will be ordered according to the second column listed, and so on. This ordering makes more sense when ORDER BY is used with GROUP BY, as you'll see later in this section. First let's look at an example that uses one column in the ORDER BY clause to list authors by last name, in ascending order:

```
SELECT   au_lname, au_fname
FROM     authors
ORDER BY au_lname ASC
GO
```

The result set will be ordered alphabetically by last name. Remember that the case sensitivity of the sort order you set when installing SQL Server will affect how last names such as "del Castillo" will be ordered.

If you want to sort results on more than one column, simply add the column names, separated by commas, to the ORDER BY clause. The following query selects job IDs and employee first names and last names and then displays them ordered by job ID, then last name, and then first name:

```
SELECT   job_id, lname, fname
FROM     employee
ORDER BY job_ifd, lname, fname
GO
```

The result set looks like this:

```
job_id lname                              fname
------ ---------------------------------- --------------------
     2 Cramer                             Philip
     3 Devon                              Ann
     4 Chang                              Francisco
     5 Henriot                            Paul
     5 Hernadez                           Carlos
     5 Labrune                            Janine
     5 Lebihan                            Laurence
     5 Muller                             Rita
     5 Ottlieb                            Sven
     5 Pontes                             Maria
     6 Ashworth                           Victoria
     6 Karttunen                          Matti
     6 Roel                               Diego
     6 Roulet                             Annette
     7 Brown                              Lesley
     7 Ibsen                              Palle
     7 Larsson                            Maria
     7 Nagy                               Helvetius
     : :                                  :
    13 Accorti                            Paolo
    13 O'Rourke                           Timothy
    13 Schmitt                            Carine
    14 Afonso                             Pedro
    14 Josephs                            Karin
    14 Lincoln                            Elizabeth

(43 rows affected)
```

The sort on first names in this query doesn't affect the result set because no two employees have the same last name and the same job ID.

Now let's take a look at an ORDER BY clause with a GROUP BY clause and an aggregate function:

```
SELECT   type, pub_id, AVG(price) AS "Average Price"
FROM     titles
GROUP BY type, pub_id
ORDER BY type
GO
```

The result set looks like this:

```
type          pub_id Average Price
------------- ------ -----------------------
UNDECIDED     0877                      NULL
business      0736                      2.99
business      1389                     17.31
mod_cook      0877                     11.49
popular_comp  1389                     21.48
psychology    0736                     11.48
psychology    0877                     21.59
trad_cook     0877                     15.96

(8 rows affected)
```

The results are sorted in alphabetical order (ascending) by type. Also, notice that in this query, both *type* and *pub_id* must be in the GROUP BY clause because they are not part of an aggregate function. If you had left the *pub_id* column out of the GROUP BY clause, SQL Server would have displayed an error message similar to the one shown in Figure 14-4.

You cannot use aggregate functions or subqueries in the ORDER BY clause. However, if you had given an alias to an aggregate in the SELECT clause, you could use it in the ORDER BY clause, as shown here:

```
SELECT   type, pub_id, AVG(price) AS "Average Price"
FROM     titles
GROUP BY type, pub_id
ORDER BY "Average Price"
GO
```

The result set looks like this:

```
type          pub_id Average Price
------------- ------ -----------------------
UNDECIDED     0877                      NULL
business      0736                      2.99
psychology    0736                     11.48
mod_cook      0877                     11.49
```

psychology	0877	21.59
trad_cook	0877	15.96
business	1389	17.31
popular_comp	1389	21.48

(8 rows affected)

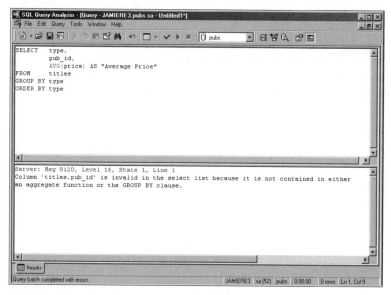

Figure 14-4. *The error message that appears if you do not include* pub_id *in the* GROUP BY *clause.*

Now the results are ordered by average price. *NULL* is considered lowest in the sort order, so it is at the top of the list.

> **Note**   The exact results of an ORDER BY clause will depend on the sort order selected at SQL Server installation.

The UNION Operator

UNION is considered an operator rather than a clause. It is used to combine the results from two or more queries into one result set. You must follow two rules when you use UNION:

- The number of columns must be the same in all queries.
- The data types for the corresponding columns between queries must be compatible.

The columns listed in the SELECT statements joined by UNION correspond in the following manner: the first column of the first SELECT statement will correspond to the first column in each subsequent SELECT statement, the second column will correspond to the second column in each subsequent SELECT statement, and so on. Therefore, you must have the same number of columns in all of the SELECT statements joined by UNION to ensure a one-to-one correspondence.

In addition, the corresponding columns must have compatible data types, meaning either that two corresponding columns must be of the same data type or that SQL Server must be able to implicitly convert one data type to the other. The following example uses UNION to join the result sets from two SELECT statements that retrieve the *city* and *state* columns from both the *publishers* and *stores* tables:

```
SELECT    city, state
FROM      publishers
UNION     SELECT city, state
          FROM    stores
GO
```

The result set is shown here:

```
city                   state
-------------------    -----
Fremont                CA
Los Gatos              CA
Portland               OR
Remulade               WA
Seattle                WA
Tustin                 CA
Chicago                IL
Dallas                 TX
München                NULL
Boston                 MA
New York               NY
Paris                  NULL
Berkeley               CA
Washington             DC

(14 rows affected)
```

Note For the queries in this section, the order of the output might differ depending on the SQL Server sort order you use.

The two columns, *city* and *state*, are of the same data type (*char*) in both the *publishers* and *stores* tables; therefore, no data type conversion is required. The column headings for the UNION result set are taken from the first SELECT statement. If you want to create an alias for a heading, place it in the first SELECT statement, as shown here:

```
SELECT    city AS "All Cities", state AS "All States"
FROM      publishers
UNION     SELECT city, state
          FROM    stores
GO
```

The result set is shown here:

```
All Cities               All States
--------------------     ----------
Fremont                  CA
Los Gatos                CA
Portland                 OR
Remulade                 WA
Seattle                  WA
Tustin                   CA
Chicago                  IL
Dallas                   TX
München                  NULL
Boston                   MA
New York                 NY
Paris                    NULL
Berkeley                 CA
Washington               DC

(14 rows affected)
```

You do not have to use the same columns in both SELECT clauses in a union. For example, you could select *city* and *state* from the *stores* table and select *city* and *country* from the *publishers* table, as shown here:

```
SELECT    city, country
FROM      publishers
UNION     SELECT city, state
          FROM    stores
GO
```

The result set is shown here:

```
city                     country
-------------------- ----------
Fremont                  CA
Los Gatos                CA
Portland                 OR
Remulade                 WA
Seattle                  WA
Tustin                   CA
New York                 USA
Paris                    France
Boston                   USA
München                  Germany
Washington               USA
Chicago                  USA
Berkeley                 USA
Dallas                   USA

(14 rows affected)
```

In this result set, the top six rows make up the results from the query on the *stores* table, and the last eight rows are the results from the query on the *publishers* table. The *state* column has the data type *char*, and the *country* column has the data type *varchar*. Because these are compatible data types, SQL Server will perform an implicit conversion so that both columns are of the *varchar* type. The column headings are *city* and *country*, as they are for the columns listed in the first SELECT statement, but in this result set, a better choice for the *country* column heading might be "State or Country."

You can use one optional keyword with UNION: ALL. If you specify ALL, duplicate rows will be included in the result set—in other words, all rows will be included. If ALL is not specified, the default is to remove duplicate rows from the result set.

You can use ORDER BY in only the last statement of a union, not in each SELECT statement. This limitation ensures that the final result set will be ordered only once for all results. On the other hand, you can use GROUP BY and HAVING in individual statements, as they will affect only the individual result sets and not the final result set. The following union joins the results from two SELECT statements that both have a GROUP BY clause.

```
SELECT    type, COUNT(title) AS "Number of Titles"
FROM      titles
```

```
GROUP BY type
UNION    SELECT    pub_name, COUNT(titles.title)
         FROM      publishers, titles
         WHERE     publishers.pub_id = titles.pub_id
         GROUP BY pub_name
GO
```

The result set is shown here:

```
type                                         Number of Titles
-------------------------------------------- ----------------
Algodata Infosystems                                        6
Binnet & Hardley                                            7
New Moon Books                                              5
psychology                                                  5
mod_cook                                                    2
trad_cook                                                   3
popular_comp                                                3
UNDECIDED                                                   1
business                                                    4

(9 rows affected)
```

This result set shows how many titles have been published by each publisher that has published titles (the first three result rows), and it shows the number of titles in each category. Each GROUP BY was performed on each subquery.

The UNION operator can be used with more than two SELECT statements as well. Take care, when you are creating a union, to ensure that all columns and data types in the queries correspond correctly.

More Info   Documentation for all available T-SQL keywords and arguments is available in SQL Server Books Online.

T-SQL Functions

Now that you are familiar with the basic clauses you can use with the SELECT statement (a few more will be covered in Chapter 20), let's look at some of the T-SQL functions that you can use in the SELECT clause to give you more flexibility in creating queries. These functions are grouped in several categories, including configuration, cursor, date and time, security, metadata, system, system statistical, text and image, mathematical, rowset, string, and aggregate functions. These functions either perform calculations, conversions, or some other operations, or they return certain information. Many functions are available, but in this section, we'll examine only the aggregate functions, which are commonly used.

> **More Info** For more information about this category and the other categories of functions, use the Index tab in SQL Server Books Online to look up "functions."

Aggregate Functions

As mentioned, an aggregate function performs a calculation on a set of values and returns a single value. Aggregate functions can be specified in the select list and are most often used when the statement contains a GROUP BY clause. Some of the preceding examples used the aggregate functions AVG and COUNT. Table 14-3 lists the available aggregate functions.

Table 14-3. Aggregate functions

Function	Description
AVG	Returns the average of the values in an expression; ignores all null values.
COUNT	Returns the number of items (same as the number of rows) in an expression.
COUNT_BIG	Same as COUNT, except it returns the count in a *bigint* data type rather than an *int*.
GROUPING	Returns an additional special column; used only when the GROUP BY clause contains either the CUBE or ROLLUP operator. For more information, use the Index tab in SQL Server Books Online to find "GROUPING keyword."
MAX	Returns the maximum value of an expression.
MIN	Returns the minimum value of an expression.
STDEV	Returns the statistical standard deviation of all values in an expression. This function assumes that the values used in the calculation are a sample of the entire population.
STDEVP	Returns the statistical standard deviation for the population for all values in an expression. This function assumes that the values used in the calculation are the entire population.
SUM	Returns the sum of all the values in an expression.
VAR	Returns the statistical variance of all values in an expression. This function assumes that the values used in the calculation are a sample of the entire population.
VARP	Returns the statistical variance for the population for all values in an expression. This function assumes that the values used in the calculation are the entire population.

The COUNT function has a special use: to count all of the rows in a table. To do this, use *(*)* after *COUNT*, as shown here:

```
SELECT    COUNT(*)
FROM      publishers
GO
```

The result set is shown here:

```
----------
        8
```

This result set indicates that the *publishers* table contains eight rows.

The AVG, COUNT, MAX, MIN, and SUM functions can be used with the optional keywords ALL and DISTINCT. For each of these functions, ALL indicates that the function should be applied to all values in the expression, and DISTINCT indicates that duplicate values should be counted only once in the calculation. The default option is ALL.

The aggregate functions are basically self-explanatory. The following example uses the MAX and MIN functions together in the select list to find the price difference between the most expensive book and the least expensive book:

```
SELECT    MAX(price) - MIN(price) AS "Price Difference"
FROM      titles
GO
```

The result set is shown here:

```
Price Difference
-----------------------
            19.96
```

In this example, SUM is used to find the total quantity of items ordered per store:

```
SELECT    stores.stor_name, SUM(sales.qty) AS "Total Items Ordered"
FROM      sales, stores
WHERE     sales.stor_id = stores.stor_id
GROUP BY  stor_name
GO
```

The result set is shown here:

```
stor_name                                    Total Items Ordered
-------------------------------------------  -------------------
Barnum's                                                     125
Bookbeat                                                      80
```

(continued)

```
Doc-U-Mat: Quality Laundry and Books                        130
Eric the Read Books                                           8
Fricative Bookshop                                           60
News & Brews                                                 90

(6 rows affected)
```

> **Note**   Remember that SQL Server offers many types of functions. If you need to perform a specific operation, check SQL Server Books Online to see whether a built-in function already exists.

Other Uses for SELECT

The SELECT statement is used mainly to perform queries that retrieve data from the database. These queries can be simple or complex. SELECT can also be used to set values for variables or to call functions.

You can use the SELECT statement to set a value for a local variable within a transaction or a stored procedure, although the preferred method is to use the SET statement. Local variables must have an "at" symbol (@) as the first character. For example, to set the local variable *@count* to the value *0* by using SET, use the following statement:

```
SET  @count = 0
GO
```

You can use SELECT to set a local variable to the value returned from a query. For example, to set the local variable *@price* to the maximum value in the *price* column of the items table, use the following statement:

```
SELECT  @price = MAX(price)
FROM    items
GO
```

When you set a local variable within a SELECT statement, it's best if the statement returns one row for the query. If multiple rows are returned, the local variable will be given the value from the last row returned.

You can also use SELECT to call a function, such as the system-provided function GETDATE. The following statement calls GETDATE to retrieve the current date and time:

```
SELECT  GETDATE()
GO
```

GETDATE does not take any parameters, but the parentheses are still necessary.

Summary

In this chapter, we have examined the SELECT statement, the separate clauses that can be included in the SELECT statement and how they can be used, search conditions, and functions. You've learned about logical operators, joins, aliases, pattern matching, grouping and sorting results, and more. We've covered a lot of information, but there's still much more you can do with a SELECT statement. In Chapter 20, we'll look at some of the more advanced options you can use in the SELECT statement, and we'll examine the other data manipulation statements—INSERT, UPDATE, and DELETE. In Chapter 15, we'll look at how to modify database tables.

Chapter 15

Managing Tables Using Transact-SQL and Enterprise Manager

In Chapter 10, you learned how to create a table by defining its columns and data types. Once you've created a table, you can modify it in several ways, even if the table already contains data. This chapter describes some of the ways to modify a table, including altering, adding, dropping, and renaming columns and dropping an entire table. Creating and modifying table constraints (a method for ensuring data integrity) and triggers (a special type of stored procedure that is automatically executed under certain conditions) will be described in Chapters 16 and 22.

In this chapter, we will examine the use of Transact-SQL (T-SQL) and the Microsoft SQL Server 2000 Enterprise Manager in managing your tables. Keep in mind that T-SQL and Enterprise Manager do not provide the same flexibility when you are modifying a table. Enterprise Manager is more helpful because you can perform certain modifications more easily than you can by using T-SQL. Enterprise Manager displays informative error messages and sometimes suggests alternatives when you try to make an illegal modification. One benefit of using T-SQL, however, is that if you run your commands by scripting, you will have a record tracing how and in what order you made the modifications. In this chapter, we'll look at the advantages and the disadvantages of using these two techniques for modifying tables.

Before we begin, we need to create two tables in the MyDB database—*Bicycle_Sales* and *Bicycle_Inventory*—to use for the examples in this chapter. The *Bicycle_Sales* table contains sales information for a used bicycle dealership and includes the following columns: *make_id*, *model_id*, *description*, *year*, *sale_id*, *price*, *quantity*, and *sale_date*. The *make_id* and *model_id* columns are specified together as a foreign key constraint. This constraint references the *make_id* and *model_id* columns in the *Bicycle_Inventory* table, which make up the unique clustered index. As you'll see in Chapter 16, a foreign key constraint can reference only a primary key column or other unique-constraint column of the referenced table. (Constraints will be covered in detail in Chapter 16, and indexes will be explained in Chapter 17.)

The *sale_id* column is declared as the primary key clustered index for the *Bicycle_Sales* table. The CREATE TABLE statement for each of these tables is shown here:

```
USE MyDB
GO
CREATE TABLE Bicycle_Inventory
(
    make_name        char(10)      NOT NULL,
    make_id          tinyint       NOT NULL,
    model_name       char(12)      NOT NULL,
    model_id         tinyint       NOT NULL,
    in_stock         tinyint       NOT NULL,
    on_order         tinyint       NULL,
    CONSTRAINT       MI_clu_indx
    UNIQUE CLUSTERED(make_id, model_id)
)
GO


CREATE TABLE Bicycle_Sales
(
    make_id        tinyint     NOT NULL,    --Used in foreign
                                            --key constraint
    model_id       tinyint     NOT NULL,    --Also used in foreign
                                            --key constraint
    description  char(30)    NULL,
    year         char(4)     NOT NULL,
    sale_id      int         NOT NULL IDENTITY (1,1) PRIMARY KEY CLUSTERED,
    price        smallmoney  NOT NULL,
    quantity     tinyint     NOT NULL,
    sale_date    datetime    NOT NULL,
    CONSTRAINT   sales_inventory_fk FOREIGN KEY (make_id, model_id)
    REFERENCES   Bicycle_Inventory(make_id, model_id)
)
GO
```

Caution Be sure to create the *Bicycle_Inventory* table before you create the *Bicycle_Sales* table. If you attempt to create the *Bicycle_Sales* table first, you'll get an error message. The *Bicycle_Sales* table references *Bicycle_Inventory* via a constraint, so if the *Bicycle_Inventory* table is not present, the constraint cannot be created, and an error will result.

Now that we've created our sample database tables, let's make some modifications, first using T-SQL and then using Enterprise Manager.

Modifying a Table Using T-SQL

In this section, you'll learn how to use T-SQL commands to alter, add, drop, and rename columns in an existing table. The T-SQL command used to perform all table modifications is ALTER TABLE.

Altering Columns

Once you have created a table, you can alter a column's data type, precision (for numeric types), and nullability, and you can add the ROWGUIDCOL property to a column or drop it from a column, all by using the ALTER TABLE command. You can make other column modifications, such as adding a default value, by using other T-SQL commands; these commands will be described in Chapter 16.

Not all columns can be altered. In general, you cannot alter the following types of columns:

- A column that is part of a primary key or foreign key constraint
- A column that is used in replication (Replication is explained in Chapter 26.)
- A column that has a *text*, an *ntext*, an *image*, or a *timestamp* data type
- A computed column
- A ROWGUIDCOL column (You can, however, add or drop the ROWGUIDCOL property for a column.)
- A column used in an index
- A column used in a check or unique constraint (Constraints are explained in Chapter 16.)
- A column used in statistics generation by explicitly executing the CREATE STATISTICS statement (SQL Server–generated statistics are dropped by using ALTER TABLE.)
- A column associated with a default value

All other types of columns can be altered by using the ALTER TABLE statement. In some of the preceding cases, you can remove the restriction on altering the column. For example, you could remove a foreign key or other constraint or delete an index on a column, and if no other restrictions apply, you could then alter that column.

Altering the Data Type

To alter the data type of a column, the original data type must be implicitly convertible to the new data type. A table of allowable conversions can be found under the topic "CAST and CONVERT (T-SQL)" in Books Online. To access this topic, look up "CAST" in the Books Online index, and then select "CAST and CONVERT (T-SQL)" in the Topics Found dialog box.

The command for altering the data type of a column has the following syntax:

```
ALTER TABLE      <table_name>
ALTER COLUMN     <column_name> <new_data_type>
```

You will use less space per row of data if you change the data type for the *sale_date* column of our *Bicycle_Sales* table from the *datetime* type to the *smalldatetime* type. This is because *datetime* takes up 8 bytes, whereas *smalldatetime* takes only 4 bytes. To make this change, use the following command:

```
ALTER TABLE      Bicycle_Sales
ALTER COLUMN     sale_date smalldatetime NOT NULL
GO
```

Any existing table data will be implicitly converted to the new data type, *smalldatetime*. The nullability on this column, *NOT NULL*, has not been changed.

To change the *description* column from the data type *char(30)* to *varchar(20)* (which has a shorter length), use the following command:

```
ALTER TABLE      Bicycle_Sales
ALTER COLUMN     description varchar(20) NULL
GO
```

Note that *char(30)*, the original data type, is implicitly convertible to *varchar(20)*, the new data type, but that *varchar(20)* is shorter. Therefore, for all existing rows, values in the *description* column that are longer than 20 characters will be truncated without warning and will be converted to *varchar(20)*.

Note If you alter a column to a new data type that is shorter than the original data type, the existing rows in the table whose values in that column exceed the length of the new data type will have those values automatically truncated.

Altering Nullability

To alter nullability, you can change a *NOT NULL* column to *NULL*, except for columns in primary key constraints. (By definition, such columns can never allow null values.) You can change a *NULL* column to *NOT NULL* only if no null values exist in the column. If the column contains null values, you could execute an UPDATE statement to change all null values to some value and then make the change from *NULL* to *NOT NULL* for that column. If nullability is not specified for an altered column, the column allows null values by default. Let's look at some examples.

To change the nullability of the *quantity* column to allow null values, execute the following statement:

```
ALTER TABLE    Bicycle_Sales
ALTER COLUMN   quantity tinyint NULL
GO
```

The data type of the column, *tinyint*, remains the same; only the nullability of the column was changed. Now the *quantity* column will allow null values to be inserted. If no value is entered, *NULL* will automatically be inserted. This change will not affect the *quantity* column values in existing rows, but it will allow *NULL*s to be inserted for new rows added to the table.

Now let's change the *description* column to *NOT NULL*. We'll assume that some null values already exist in the column. Therefore, we must first set all null values to some value—in this case, *None*, which is compatible with the column's data type. To test for a value of *NULL*, it is safest not to use the equality operator (=), but rather to use the T-SQL keywords IS NULL or IS NOT NULL. This is because *NULL* is an unknown value, and an equality operation might not be able to match null values, depending on whether the *ANSI nulls* database option is set to *ON* or *OFF*. If this option is set to *OFF*, the equality operator will return *TRUE* for *expression = NULL* if *expression* holds a null value. The operator will return *FALSE* if *expression* does not hold a null value. If this option is set to *ON*, *expression = NULL* will return *UNKNOWN* for all comparisons, and no results will be returned. SQL Server will not return the values that are *NULL,* as you might expect when the option is set to *ON*. IS NULL and IS NOT NULL will behave the same no matter what you have the ANSI_NULLS option set to. To change null values in the *description* column to the value "*None*", use the UPDATE SET statement, as shown here:

```
UPDATE   Bicycle_Sales SET description = "None"
WHERE    description IS NULL
GO
```

Next change the nullability of the *description* column to *NOT NULL*:

```
ALTER TABLE    Bicycle_Sales
ALTER COLUMN   description char(30) NOT NULL
GO
```

Again, we did not change the original *char(30)* data type of this column, only the nullability. You can change both data type and nullability in a single ALTER TABLE command, as shown here:

```
ALTER TABLE    Bicycle_Sales
ALTER COLUMN   description varchar(20) NOT NULL
GO
```

This statement changes the data type and the nullability of the *description* column.

Adding or Dropping the ROWGUIDCOL Property

To add the ROWGUIDCOL property to a column or drop it from a column, use the following syntax:

```
ALTER TABLE    <table_name>
ALTER COLUMN   <column_name> ADD | DROP ROWGUIDCOL
```

You can add the ROWGUIDCOL property only to a column of the type *uniqueidentifier*. Assuming that we have a *uniqueidentifier* column named *unique_id* in our *Bicycle_Sales* table, you would add the ROWGUIDCOL property using the following command:

```
ALTER TABLE    Bicycle_Sales
ALTER COLUMN   unique_id ADD ROWGUIDCOL
GO
```

And you would drop the property using this command:

```
ALTER TABLE    Bicycle_Sales
ALTER COLUMN   unique_id DROP ROWGUIDCOL
GO
```

Adding Columns

You can also add columns to a table using the ALTER TABLE command. A column is defined in much the same way, whether you are creating or altering a table. You must assign the column a name and a data type, and you can optionally assign other attributes, properties, and constraints.

When you add a column that is *NOT NULL*, you must also declare a default value so that the existing rows will be given the default value in the new column. You specify this default value with the keyword DEFAULT. To add a column, use the following syntax:

```
ALTER TABLE    <table_name>
ADD            <column_name> <data_type> <nullability >
DEFAULT        default_value
```

For example, to add a column named *salesperson_id* to the *Bicycle_Sales* table, use the following command. (The new column does not allow null values and has a default value of *0*.)

```
ALTER TABLE    Bicycle_Sales
ADD            salesperson_id tinyint NOT NULL
DEFAULT        0
GO
```

Because the column is declared as *NOT NULL*, all existing rows in the table will be assigned the default value of *0* in the new column.

If we instead add the *salesperson_id* column to the table as *NULL*, as shown here, a default value is optional:

```
ALTER TABLE    Bicycle_Sales
ADD            salesperson_id tinyint NULL
DEFAULT        0    --Optional default value
GO
```

Even if we specify a default value, the existing rows will be assigned *NULL* for the *salesperson_id* column—the default value will apply only to newly inserted rows.

To force the existing rows to be assigned a default of *0* instead of *NULL*, use the WITH VALUES option of DEFAULT, as follows:

```
ALTER TABLE    Bicycle_Sales
ADD            salesperson_id tinyint NULL
DEFAULT        0 WITH VALUES
GO
```

WITH VALUES specifies that all existing rows will be assigned the new default value instead of *NULL* for the new column.

Dropping Columns

You can also use the ALTER TABLE command to drop columns from a table. All data for a dropped column will be deleted from the table. When you are using T-SQL to drop columns, you cannot drop the following types of columns:

- A column used in a primary key, foreign key, unique, or check constraint
- A column used for replication
- A column used in an index (unless the index is dropped first)
- A column bound to a rule
- A column associated with a default value

> **Note** These restrictions still apply, but are handled differently, when you are using Enterprise Manager to drop a column. See the section "Modifying a Table Using Enterprise Manager" later in this chapter for details.

To drop a column from a table, use the following syntax:

```
ALTER TABLE <table_name>
DROP COLUMN <column_name>
```

The following command drops the *description* column from the *Bicycle_Sales* table:

```
ALTER TABLE    Bicycle_Sales
DROP COLUMN    description
GO
```

The *description* column and its values are deleted from all rows in the table.

> **Caution** Be careful when you are dropping columns. You cannot retrieve a dropped column's data without restoring the database from a backup. If transactions had been issued subsequent to your backup, you would also need to apply the transaction log to recover these transactions. You could also recreate the column and supply new values for it.

Renaming Columns

To rename a column using T-SQL commands, you must run the *sp_rename* system stored procedure using the following syntax:

```
sp_rename 'table.original_column_name', 'new_column_name', 'COLUMN'
```

For example, to change the column name *description* to *Bicycle_desc*, you would use the following statement:

```
sp_rename 'Bicycle_Sales.description', 'bicycle_desc', 'COLUMN'
GO
```

The original column name must be specified using the format *table.column*, but the table name should not be included with the new column name.

Modifying a Table Using Enterprise Manager

As mentioned, modifying a table using Enterprise Manager is simpler and gives you more functionality and flexibility than using T-SQL commands. You can make all your modifications either in the Design Table window or using a database diagram. We'll look at the Design Table window method first. To open the Design Table window for our *Bicycle_Sales* table, follow these steps:

1. Expand the MyDB database folder in the left pane of Enterprise Manager.

2. Click Tables to display a list of all tables in MyDB in the right pane, as shown in Figure 15-1.

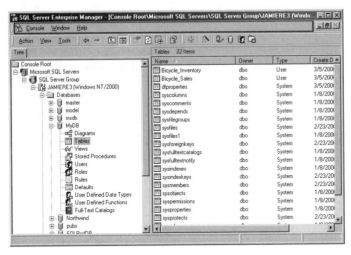

Figure 15-1. *Enterprise Manager.*

3. Right-click the *Bicycle_Sales* table in the right pane. Choose Design Table from the shortcut menu to display the Design Table window, shown in Figure 15-2. This window shows the original, unmodified *Bicycle_Sales* table.

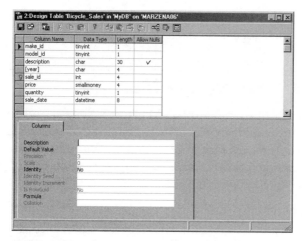

Figure 15-2. *The Design Table window.*

Altering Columns

To alter a column in the Design Table window, simply click in the appropriate cell or check box in the grid and make the desired change. Each row in the grid represents a column in the table. The headings at the top of the grid tell you which property each cell sets.

For some situations in which T-SQL does not allow you to perform certain modifications and returns an error message, Enterprise Manager provides options that guide you through the process of performing the modifications correctly. For example, if you try to change the data length of a column that has a primary key or foreign key constraint using the ALTER TABLE T-SQL command, you will get an error message similar to this:

```
Column or parameter #0: Cannot specify a column width on
data type int.
```

If you use Enterprise Manager, however, you'll see a message box that enables you to change the data length for that column.

For example, to change the data type of the column *make_id* (which has a foreign key constraint that references *make_id* from the *Bicycle_Inventory* table) from *tinyint* to *smallint*, simply click tinyint, click the drop-down arrow to display the Data Type drop-down list, and then select smallint, as shown in Figure 15-3.

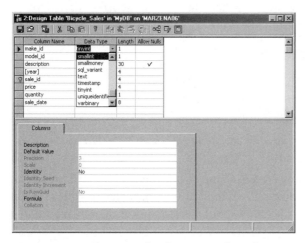

Figure 15-3. *Changing the data type of a column using Enterprise Manager.*

Because the *make_id* column has a foreign key constraint, the Data Type Change Required dialog box appears, as shown in Figure 15-4. Click Yes to automatically convert the *make_id* column in both tables from *tinyint* to *smallint*.

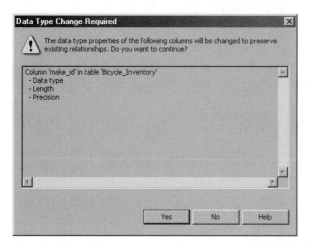

Figure 15-4. *The Data Type Change Required dialog box.*

As with T-SQL, when you alter a data type using Enterprise Manager, the original data type must be implicitly convertible to the new data type. If you try to perform an illegal conversion, Enterprise Manager will return an error message similar to the one displayed in Figure 15-5, which shows the result of an illegal attempt to change the data type for the *sale_date* column from *datetime* to *text*. Click OK to close the error message, and then change the incorrect data type to one that is implicitly convertible.

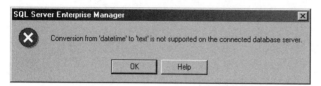

Figure 15-5. *Error message displayed after an attempt to change a data type to one that is not implicitly convertible.*

To save your changes, click the Save Disk button on the toolbar in the Design Table window. The Save dialog box, shown in Figure 15-6, then confirms that the listed tables are to be written to disk. Click Yes to confirm that you want to save your changes.

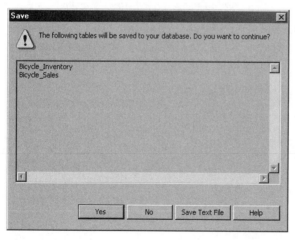

Figure 15-6. *The Save dialog box.*

Adding Columns

To add a column, click in the Column Name column of the first blank row in the Design Table window, type the name of the new column, select its data type, and assign it the appropriate attributes (Allow Nulls, Default Value, Identity, and so on). As shown in Figure 15-7, we've added a column named *salesperson_id* that is of the data type *tinyint*, allows null values, and has a default value of *0*. Click the Save Disk button to save your changes. SQL Server will now add the new column to the table.

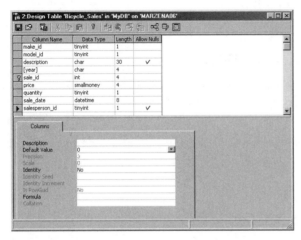

Figure 15-7. *Adding a new column named* salesperson_id.

Dropping Columns

Dropping, or deleting, a column is a simple process with Enterprise Manager. In the Design Table window, simply right-click the column name or any of its attributes (any cell in the same row as the column name), and choose Delete Column from the shortcut menu. The row will be deleted from the table. Remember to click the Save Disk button to save your changes.

Enterprise Manager will warn you when you are attempting to delete a column that is part of a constraint or an index, when the column has a default value, or when it has a rule bound to it. You will see a message box similar to the one shown in Figure 15-8. Clicking Yes will proceed with the column deletion as well as the deletion of all associated relationships.

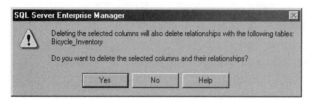

Figure 15-8. *Message box that appears if you attempt to delete a column that has relationships with other columns and tables.*

Creating and Using a Database Diagram

You can also modify tables using a database diagram in Enterprise Manager. To create a database diagram for MyDB with the two sample tables *Bicycle_Sales* and *Bicycle_Inventory*, follow these steps:

1. Expand MyDB in the left pane of Enterprise Manager, and then right-click Diagrams. Choose New Database Diagram from the shortcut menu to display the Create Database Diagram Wizard welcome screen, shown in Figure 15-9.

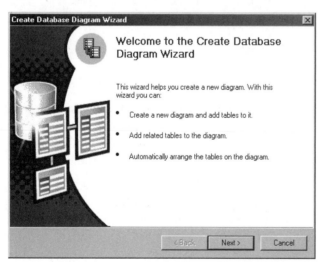

Figure 15-9. *The Create Database Diagram Wizard welcome screen.*

2. Click Next to display the Select Tables To Be Added screen, shown in Figure 15-10. Select the tables you want to include in your diagram from the Available Tables list, and then click Add. In this example, we have added the *Bicycle_Inventory* and *Bicycle_Sales* tables.

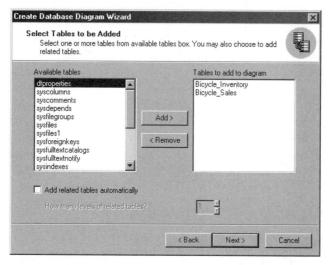

Figure 15-10.   *The Select Tables To Be Added screen.*

3. Click Next to display the Completing The Create Database Diagram Wizard screen. Click Finish if the tables you selected are correct, or click Back and make the necessary changes.

4. After you click Finish, you will see your database diagram, shown in Figure 15-11.

5. Save your diagram with a descriptive name by clicking the Save Disk button and typing a name when prompted.

   The vertical line that ends with a key and connects the two tables in our diagram represents the foreign key constraint relationship between them. To display the relationship label, right-click in the window background and choose Show Relationship Labels from the shortcut menu. The name of the foreign key constraint appears, as shown in Figure 15-12.

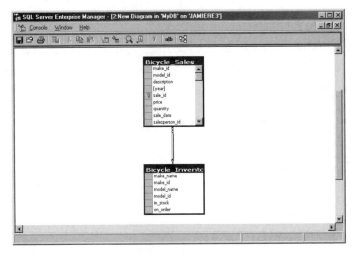

Figure 15-11. *Sample database diagram.*

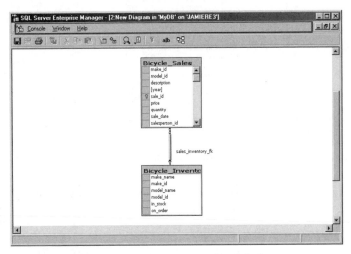

Figure 15-12. *Viewing table relationship labels.*

To select a table, click it; to select more than one table, hold down the Ctrl key and click each table. If you right-click one of the tables and then choose an option from the shortcut menu, that action will be performed on all selected tables. For example, if we select both tables in our database diagram, right-click one of the tables, and then choose Table View and Standard from the shortcut menu, both tables will be modified to display all column properties, as shown in Figure 15-13.

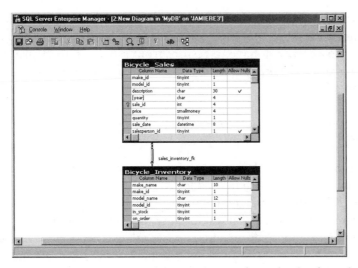

Figure 15-13. *Viewing column properties from the database diagram.*

The column properties display for each table is similar to the Design Table window, and each table can be modified using the same methods as those used with the Design Table window. Simply add or change the column data in the desired cells and save your changes by clicking the Save Disk button. You can also move and resize the tables in the database diagram, display different views of the tables, and more. Experiment with the various shortcut-menu commands. Notice that as soon as you make a change to a table, an asterisk will appear next to that table name to indicate that a change was made.

The Effects of Altering a Table

When you alter a table, any necessary changes to existing data rows will occur immediately upon execution of the ALTER TABLE T-SQL command or, if you're using Enterprise Manager, upon saving the changes. SQL Server puts a lock on the table so that no other users can access it while the changes are being made. A modification that requires a change in all rows of a large database, such as adding a *NOT NULL* column with a default value or dropping a column, might take some time and should be done with care, at a time when user access is at a minimum. When you alter a column by changing its data length, precision, or scale, the table is re-created in the database, and the existing data is converted to the new data type.

All table changes are logged and fully recoverable in the event that a system crash or fatal error occurs during the alteration process. Once the alteration is completed successfully, however, you have to restore from a backup to return the table to its original status. (Backing up and restoring a database are explained in Chapters 32 and 33.)

Dropping a Table

When you drop a table, the table definition and data, indexes, constraints, triggers, and permissions associated with that table are all deleted. Views and stored procedures that reference the dropped table must be dropped explicitly. A table cannot be dropped if it is referenced by a foreign key constraint in another table—in other words, a table cannot be dropped if another table depends on it. Either the constraint or the referenced table must be dropped before the table can be deleted. On the other hand, the table that holds the foreign key constraint can be dropped if no other tables depend on it. In this section, we'll look at how to drop a table using T-SQL and Enterprise Manager.

Using T-SQL to Drop a Table

The T-SQL command used to drop a table has the following syntax:

```
DROP TABLE <table_name>
```

Use DROP VIEW or DROP PROCEDURE to drop views or stored procedures that reference the dropped table. You can drop the views and stored procedures before or after dropping the table. Once a table has been dropped, you cannot retrieve it—you must re-create the entire table, data and all.

To drop the *Bicycle_Inventory* table, which is referenced by a foreign key constraint from the *Bicycle_Sales* table, we must first drop the foreign key constraint, *sales_inventory_fk*, and then drop the table, as shown here:

```
ALTER TABLE       Bicycle_Sales
DROP CONSTRAINT   sales_inventory_fk
GO
DROP TABLE        Bicycle_Inventory
GO
```

If you try to drop the table before removing the foreign key constraint, you will get an error message and the table will not be dropped.

Using Enterprise Manager to Drop a Table

Enterprise Manager provides two methods for dropping a table: using the Drop Objects dialog box or using a database diagram. The Drop Objects dialog box method is best when you are deleting a table that does not have any other tables dependent on it. To use this method, follow these steps:

1. In the left pane of Enterprise Manager, expand the database that contains the table you want to drop and click Tables, and then, in the right pane, right-click the name of the table you want to drop.

2. Choose Delete from the shortcut menu to display the Drop Objects dialog box, shown in Figure 15-14.

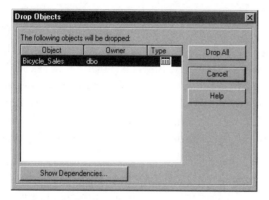

Figure 15-14. *The Drop Objects dialog box.*

3. If the table has any dependent tables, click Show Dependencies to show the Dependencies dialog box (Figure 15-15). Any tables that are dependent on this table will appear in the left list in this dialog box. If there are any dependent tables, you cannot delete this table until those dependencies have been removed.

4. If no other tables are dependent on the selected table, you can delete the table by clicking Drop All in the Drop Objects dialog box.

Figure 15-15. *The Dependencies dialog box for the Bicycle_Sales table.*

To delete a table that does have dependent tables, we'll use the second method: a database diagram. In this example, we'll remove the *Bicycle_Inventory* table, which is referenced in a foreign key constraint by the *Bicycle_Sales* table. This deletion would fail if we used the Drop Objects dialog box method. But if we use a database diagram that shows both tables, we can remove either table and the foreign key constraint will be removed automatically. To delete the *Bicycle_Inventory* table, follow these steps:

1. Open the database diagram in Enterprise Manager by expanding the database you want to use, clicking Diagrams, and then double-clicking the appropriate diagram name in the right pane. Select the name of the table you want to delete—in this case, *Bicycle_Inventory*.

2. Right-click anywhere in the table and choose Delete Table From Database from the shortcut menu. When you are prompted to verify that you want to delete the table from the database, click Yes. The table and the foreign key constraint are removed from the diagram.

3. If you're certain you want to permanently delete this table, save your changes by clicking the Save Disk button. The table will then be deleted from the database. If you change your mind about deleting the table, simply exit the Edit Diagram window without saving your changes by clicking Close. If you then reopen the database diagram, the original data will still be there. No changes take effect until you save your work.

Summary

In this chapter, you've learned how to use T-SQL and Enterprise Manager to modify database tables by altering, adding, dropping, and renaming columns. Along the way, some of the differences between T-SQL functionality and Enterprise Manager functionality have been demonstrated. You've also learned how to create a database diagram using the Create Database Diagram Wizard and how to drop a table and all its data from a database. Other types of modifications can be made to a table, including altering, adding, and dropping constraints and defaults. These modifications will be described in Chapter 16.

Chapter 16
Creating and Using Defaults, Constraints, and Rules

Defaults, constraints, and rules are optional attributes that you can define on database columns and tables. Chapter 15 showed you a little bit about defaults by describing how to add a column with a default value to a table by using the ALTER TABLE command. In this chapter, you'll learn the two methods for creating and modifying defaults. As you'll recall, *defaults* are values inserted into a particular column when no value is explicitly entered. *Constraints* provide methods for identifying valid values for a column (in order to reject invalid values) and for enforcing data integrity within database tables and between related tables. We'll look at the five types of constraints in this chapter, and you'll learn how to create and modify defaults and constraints by using both Transact-SQL (T-SQL) and Microsoft SQL Server Enterprise Manager, although using Enterprise Manager is often simpler.

Defaults

First let's talk about the reason you might want to use defaults for certain table columns by looking at what happens if you don't use a default. If a row is inserted into a table containing columns without default values and the data values for one or more nullable columns are not specifically entered, those nullable columns will be given the value *NULL*. But if a column was defined as *NOT NULL* and you do not supply a value for that column when inserting a row, an error message will be returned, informing you that *NULL* cannot be inserted into the column. This is when defaults come in handy. Defaults can be used to specify a value to be inserted in place of *NULL* so that you do not receive an error message. You should use defaults on your columns instead of allowing null values because operations on nullable columns require more processing overhead than those on non-nullable columns.

Microsoft SQL Server 2000 enables you to define a default for each column in a table. You cannot define a default for columns that have a *timestamp* data type or the IDENTITY or ROWGUIDCOL property, as those columns must have unique values. These column types are not compatible with a default because if a default is used more than once for a column, that column will no longer have unique values. You can assign only one value as the default, and it will be used automatically every time it's needed. And here is an important note about defaults: the value specified as the default definition for a column must be compatible with the data type for that column.

A default definition can be created and modified in several ways. In this section, we'll look at how to define a default value at table creation and how to modify a column to add or change a default, first by using T-SQL and then by using Enterprise Manager. Remember, in Chapter 15 we talked about adding a column with a default value to a table and how this affects the existing rows in the table. You will see a less detailed example of that here. We will also examine the available options and the effects of adding a default to an existing column in a table.

Defining and Modifying Defaults by Using T-SQL

You can define a default on a column by using one of three T-SQL statements: CREATE TABLE, ALTER TABLE, or CREATE DEFAULT. CREATE DEFAULT, which is available in SQL Server 2000 for backward compatibility, creates a *Default* object. When you use this method, SQL Server stores the object apart from the table, so you must bind the object to a column or columns by using the system stored procedure *sp_bindefault*. If you drop the table, the DEFAULT definition will be automatically unbound from the table, but the *Default* object will still exist. If you use the CREATE TABLE or ALTER TABLE method, however, SQL Server will store the DEFAULT definition with the table, and if the table is dropped, the default itself is automatically dropped as well, without your having to perform any extra steps. For this reason, it is generally recommended that you do not use CREATE DEFAULT. Using a *Default* object might be beneficial, however, when the same default will be used for multiple columns.

You should use SQL Query Analyzer to run your T-SQL statements because the output will appear in a GUI. This is easier to read than if you run the statements in a command prompt window.

CREATE TABLE with DEFAULT

Creating a default on a column by using the CREATE TABLE command is the preferred, standard technique. The following statement creates a table in MyDB that has defaults defined for both *columnA*, a *char* type column, and *columnB*, an *int* type column:

```
USE MyDB
CREATE TABLE MyTable
(
columnA   char(15) NULL DEFAULT 'n/a',
columnB   int      NULL DEFAULT 0
)
GO
```

The default value *n/a* for *columnA* is compatible with the *char* data type of that column, and the default value *0* for *columnB* is compatible with the *int* data type. If no value is specified for one or both of these columns when a row is inserted into the table, the default value will be used. Therefore, the only way one of these columns can contain a *NULL* is if *NULL* is explicitly inserted. Null values are allowed because both columns are nullable. If the columns were defined as *NOT NULL*, you could not explicitly insert the value *NULL*.

ALTER TABLE with DEFAULT

To change a DEFAULT definition on a column or add one to a column, you can use the ALTER TABLE command. If a default has already been defined and you want to change it by using this command, you must first drop the existing default by name and then add the new one. (If you use Enterprise Manager, you will not have to perform this step; therefore, you will find that using Enterprise Manager is the easier method. After you have altered a table by using Enterprise Manager, you can, at any time, generate the scripts to re-create the table as well.)

Let's assume you do want to change an existing default. If you created the default by using the CREATE TABLE command or by using Enterprise Manager, which is described later in this chapter, but did not name the default yourself, SQL Server automatically named the default for you. To find out what name the default was assigned by SQL Server so that you can drop the default by using

T-SQL, you can run the *sp_help* stored procedure with the name of the table in which the default exists, such as

```
USE MyDB
GO
sp_help MyTable
GO
```

The names of all the default constraints on *MyTable* appear at the end of the output under the column heading *constraint_name*, as shown in Figure 16-1.

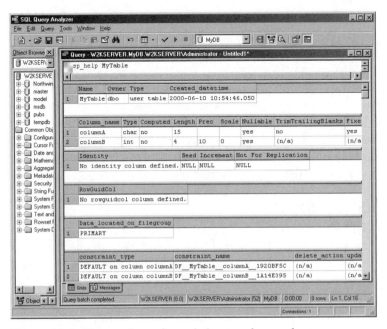

Figure 16-1. *Output from the* sp_help *stored procedure.*

Suppose we want to change the default value for *columnA* from *n/a* to *not applicable*. Remember that we must first drop the existing default and then add the new one. To drop this default, use the following command:

```
ALTER TABLE MyTable
DROP CONSTRAINT DF_MyTable_columnA_1920BF5CGO
```

Now we can add a new default, this time naming it ourselves, by using the following command:

```
ALTER TABLE MyTable
ADD CONSTRAINT DF_MyTable_columnA
DEFAULT 'not applicable' FOR columnA
GO
```

When you change an existing default on a column, all existing rows will keep their original values for that column, even if a value is *NULL*. Only newly inserted rows will use the new default value.

Again, as we saw in Chapter 15, you can also add an entirely new column to an existing table and assign it a default value by using the ALTER TABLE command, as shown here:

```
ALTER TABLE MyTable
ADD columnC tinyint NOT NULL DEFAULT 13
GO
```

Now the *MyTable* sample table has another column, *columnC*, which has a default value of *13*. Because *columnC* is a new column and is defined as *NOT NULL*, any existing data rows in the table will be assigned the default value *13* in the new column.

If the new column allowed *NULL*s, all existing rows would, by default, get *NULL* for the value in the new column. If we wanted the default value inserted for each existing row instead of *NULL*, we would use the WITH VALUES option of DEFAULT, as shown here:

```
ALTER TABLE MyTable
ADD columnC tinyint NULL DEFAULT 13 WITH VALUES
GO
```

WITH VALUES will force all existing rows in *MyTable* to receive the value *13*, instead of the value *NULL*, for the new column.

Now that you know how to create a DEFAULT definition that is stored with a table, let's look at using CREATE DEFAULT. This method creates a *Default* object that is stored apart from the table.

CREATE DEFAULT and *sp_bindefault*

You can also add a default to an existing column or change a default on a column by first creating a *Default* object, using the T-SQL CREATE DEFAULT command. If you create a *Default* object, you can later bind it to a column or to a user-defined data type by using the system stored procedure *sp_bindefault*. As mentioned, this method still exists in SQL Server 2000 for backward compatibility only; it is not the preferred method. It might be useful, however, if you will be using the same default for columns in more than one table.

Let's look at an example that uses CREATE DEFAULT to create a *Default* object that is named *DF_not_applicable* and has a value of *n/a*. The default will be created in the MyDB database and will then be bound to *columnA* of *MyTable* (assuming no defaults exist for the table). The syntax for CREATE DEFAULT is shown here:

```
CREATE DEFAULT default_name AS constant_expression
```

The syntax for *sp_bindefault* is shown here:

```
sp_bindefault 'default_name', table.column | user_defined_datatype
[, futureonly]
```

The parameter *default_name* is the name of the *Default* object. *Table.column* specifies the column to which you want to assign the default.

The following T-SQL statements create our sample *Default* object and bind it to *columnA* of *MyTable*:

```
USE MyDB
GO
CREATE DEFAULT DF_not_applicable AS 'n/a'
GO
sp_bindefault 'DF_not_applicable', 'MyTable.columnA'
GO
```

If a default already exists on *columnA*, SQL Server will return an error message informing you that you cannot bind a default to a column that already has a default. Remove that default first and then bind the new default to the column. (The process of using DROP DEFAULT to remove a *Default* object is described later in this section.)

You can also create a *Default* object and bind it directly to a user-defined data type. Any column that is assigned that particular data type will inherit the default property automatically. You can use the option *futureonly* with *sp_bindefault* when you are binding the *Default* object to a user-defined data type. This option prevents existing columns of that user-defined data type from inheriting the new default; thus, only newly created columns of the user-defined data type will inherit the bound default. If *futureonly* is not specified, SQL Server will bind the default to all existing and newly created columns of that user-defined data type.

For example, let's create a user-defined data type named *area_code* and a *Default* object that is named *DF_area_code* and has the value *786*; we'll then bind this default to the user-defined data type. (Creating user-defined data types was described in Chapter 10.) Because this is a new user-defined data type and therefore no columns of this type yet exist, the *futureonly* option is not required. We'll include it anyway so that we can see the syntax, which simply will have no effect. The statements look like this:

```
sp_addtype 'area_code', 'char(3)', 'NOT NULL'
GO
CREATE DEFAULT DF_area_code AS 786
GO
sp_bindefault 'DF_area_code', 'area_code', 'futureonly'
GO
```

To view the data type and see the default assigned to it, use the system stored procedure *sp_help*, as shown in Figure 16-2.

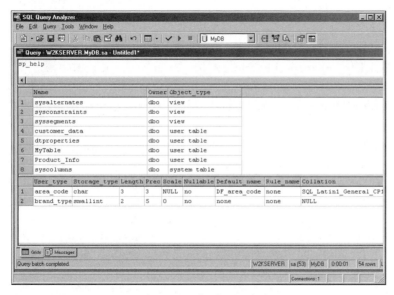

Figure 16-2. *Query Analyzer results for* sp_help.

sp_unbindefault

To unbind a *Default* object from a column or a user-defined data type, use *sp_unbindefault* followed by the table name and column name or by the user-defined data type name. For example, to unbind *DF_not_applicable*, the *Default* object that we previously bound to *columnA* of *MyTable*, use the following statement:

```
sp_unbindefault 'MyTable.columnA'
GO
```

To unbind the default we bound to the user-defined data type *area_code*, use this statement:

```
sp_unbindefault 'area_code'
GO
```

When you do this, all columns that had been assigned the user-defined data type *area_code* no longer have the default property.

You can bind a *Default* object to more than one column by using separate *sp_bindefault* statements. Also, if you unbind a default from a column, you can bind it back again, as long as you do not delete the *Default* object itself. To delete a *Default* object, use the DROP DEFAULT statement, as shown here:

```
DROP DEFAULT DF_area_code
GO
```

Once a *Default* object has been dropped, it cannot be retrieved. You must use CREATE DEFAULT to re-create the object if you want to use it again.

Defining and Modifying Defaults by Using Enterprise Manager

As you saw in Chapter 15, using Enterprise Manager is probably the easiest way to create, view, and modify your database tables. When you create or modify a table or column by using Enterprise Manager, SQL Server automatically takes care of executing the appropriate T-SQL commands to perform the work for you. (For step-by-step instructions on how to create a table by using Enterprise Manager, see Chapter 10.) In this section, we'll look at the specifics of using Enterprise Manager to assign a default definition to a column, modify a default on a column, and create a *Default* object. This is the preferred method. Let's start with examples of assigning and modifying default definitions.

Assigning and Modifying Default Definitions

Suppose we have a table named *Product_Info* in the MyDB database. The table structure is shown in Figure 16-3. (Refer to Chapter 10 for instructions on using Enterprise Manager to create this table.)

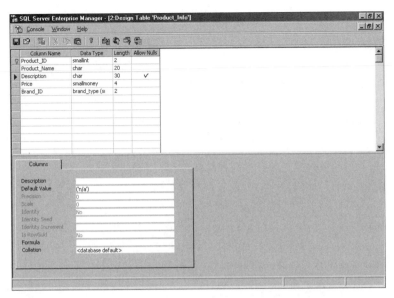

Figure 16-3. *The Design Table window for the* Product_Info *table.*

To define a default, simply click the name of the column to which you want to assign the default, and type the default value next to Default Value on the Columns tab at the bottom of the window. In Figure 16-3, a default value of *'n/a'* has been assigned to the *Description* column; this might be a placeholder value indicating that a description is not yet known for a product. Also, the default value is enclosed in parentheses—Enterprise Manager adds these for you automatically when you save the table.

Changing a default value is just as simple. Replace the original default value with the new default value, and save your work by clicking the Save button. Figure 16-4 shows the *Description* default changed to *'not available'*; Figure 16-5 shows a default of *'general merchandise'* added to *Product_Name*.

Note If you enter a character string for the default value, you must enclose it in single quotation marks or you'll get an error message from SQL Server when you try to save the change.

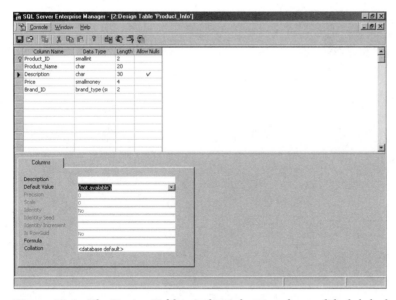

Figure 16-4. *The Design Table window, showing the modified default value.*

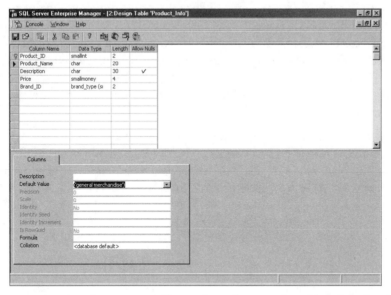

Figure 16-5. *The Design Table window, showing the added default value.*

As with T-SQL, when you create or change a default on an existing column using Enterprise Manager, the existing rows in the table are not affected—only newly inserted rows will use the new default. If you add a new column to the table and assign it a default value, any existing rows of data will get the default value for that new column only if *NULLs* are not allowed. If *NULLs* are allowed, existing rows will be assigned the value *NULL* in the new column. To allow *NULLs* for a new column and also force the default value to be inserted into all existing rows, use the technique described in the section "ALTER TABLE with DEFAULT" earlier in this chapter.

Creating and Managing *Default* Objects

You can also create a *Default* object and view existing *Default* objects by using Enterprise Manager. To view any existing *Default* objects, open Enterprise Manager, expand the server and the database that you want to use, and click Defaults. All existing *Default* objects will appear in the right pane, as shown in Figure 16-6. Notice that the *DF_not_applicable* and *DF_area_code* defaults we created earlier in this chapter by using the CREATE DEFAULT statement are visible.

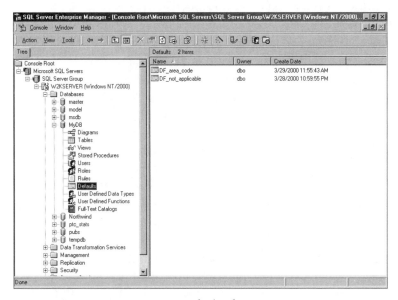

Figure 16-6. *Viewing existing* Default *objects.*

To create a new *Default* object and bind the default to a column or user-defined data type by using Enterprise Manager, follow these steps:

1. Expand the server and the database, right-click Defaults, and choose New Default from the shortcut menu to display the Default Properties window, as shown in Figure 16-7. We'll name the *Default* object *DF_none* and assign it a value of *'none'*. Click OK when you have finished.

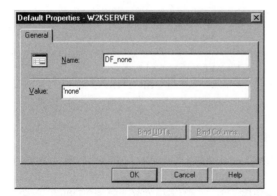

Figure 16-7. *The Default Properties window.*

2. To bind your default to a user-defined data type or to a column, right-click the name of the default (in this case, *DF_none*) in the right-hand pane of Enterprise Manager and choose Properties from the shortcut menu. The Default Properties window will appear again, but now the Bind UDTs (user-defined types) and Bind Columns buttons are available.

   Click Bind UDTs to display the Bind Default To User-Defined Data Types dialog box, as shown in Figure 16-8. This dialog box displays all the user-defined data types. From this list, you can select the user-defined data type to which you want to bind the default. In Figure 16-8, we see the *area_code* and *brand_type* data types. If you have defined more data types, they will appear in your list as well. When you have finished, click Apply and then click OK to return to the Default Properties window. We will choose to not bind our default to a user-defined data type; we will bind it to a column instead, as shown in the next step.

3. To bind the default to a column, click Bind Columns to display the Bind Default To Columns dialog box. Now select the column to which you want to bind the default. First select the table name in the Table drop-down list. Then, in the Unbound Columns list, select the column name to which you want to bind the default. Then click Add. (Figure 16-9 shows this dialog box after the *phone* column from the *customer_data* table was added to the Bound Columns list.)

4. Click OK to return to the Default Properties window, and click OK again to close the Default Properties window.

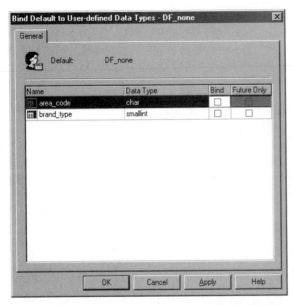

Figure 16-8. *The Bind Default To User-Defined Data Types dialog box.*

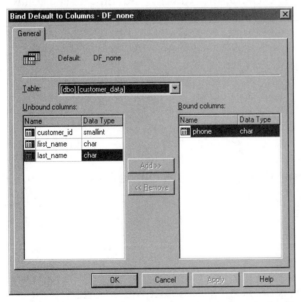

Figure 16-9. *The Bind Default To Columns dialog box.*

To unbind a *Default* object from a user-defined type, from the Default Properties window, open the Bind Default To User-Defined Data Types dialog box as described previously, and simply clear the Bind check box. To unbind a *Default* object from a column, open the Bind Default To Columns dialog box, select the column name, and then click Remove.

To delete a *Default* object, you must first unbind the default from all other objects (as was just described). SQL Server will return an error message if you try to delete a default that is bound to one or more objects. To delete a *Default* object, click Defaults in the left pane of Enterprise Manager, right-click the *Default* object name, choose Delete from the shortcut menu, and then click Drop All in the Drop Objects dialog box that appears.

Constraints

Constraints enforce data integrity automatically. Constraints define rules that determine the data values that are allowed in a column. They allow you to restrict the values that can be entered into a column so that invalid values are not accepted. For example, you could restrict the values of an integer type column to only *1* through *100* by using a constraint. Then any values outside that range could not be inserted into that column. (You would use a CHECK constraint to create this restriction, as shown later.) A constraint on only one column is called a *column constraint*; it restricts only that column's values. A constraint that affects two or more columns is called a *table constraint*; it ensures that the combination of values for the columns in the constraint meets the constraint requirements. The five types of constraints are NOT NULL, UNIQUE, PRIMARY KEY, FOREIGN KEY, and CHECK.

Creating and Modifying Constraints by Using T-SQL

In this section, you'll learn about the use of each type of constraint and how to implement the constraints by using T-SQL. In the following section, you'll learn how to implement the constraints by using Enterprise Manager.

NOT NULL

The NOT NULL constraint is fairly simple—in fact, we've already seen it used in the examples in this chapter and in previous chapters. The NOT NULL constraint is placed on a column to simply prevent null values from being inserted into that column (as opposed to the NULL constraint, which allows null values).

Using T-SQL, you can specify NOT NULL either at the time of table creation or later, when you are modifying a column. (See Chapter 10 for more details on modifying database tables.) You should use NOT NULL instead of NULL whenever possible because operations that deal with null values, such as comparisons, require more processing overhead. As mentioned earlier in this chapter, it is better to use a default, when possible, than to allow null values.

UNIQUE

The UNIQUE constraint ensures that a column or a set of columns will not allow duplicate values—in other words, the uniqueness of the values in the column or set is enforced. To enforce this uniqueness, SQL Server by default creates a unique nonclustered index on the column or columns in the UNIQUE constraint. You can, however, specify whether the index should be clustered or nonclustered. Remember that a table can have only one clustered index.

Note   You'll see the terms "clustered index" and "nonclustered index" used frequently in this chapter. Don't despair if you're unsure of what these terms mean—Chapter 17 describes these types of indexes in detail.

A UNIQUE constraint can be used on any column that is not part of a PRIMARY KEY constraint (covered in the next section), which also enforces unique values. A UNIQUE constraint can be used on columns that allow null values, whereas PRIMARY KEY constraints cannot. Null values are ignored by UNIQUE constraints. A column with a UNIQUE constraint can be referenced by a FOREIGN KEY constraint (described in the section "FOREIGN KEY" later in this chapter). And multiple UNIQUE constraints are allowed on a table, as long as the total number of indexes for that table does not exceed 249 nonclustered and 1 clustered.

To create a UNIQUE constraint on a table by using T-SQL, use the CREATE TABLE or ALTER TABLE command. For example, the following statement creates the *customer* table with a UNIQUE constraint on the *SSN* column as a clustered index:

```
CREATE TABLE customer
(
first_name    char(20) NOT NULL,
mid_init      char(1)  NULL,
last_name     char(20) NOT NULL,
SSN           char(11) NOT NULL UNIQUE CLUSTERED,
cust_phone    char(10) NULL
)
GO
```

The preceding CREATE statement used a column constraint. The following example again creates the *customer* table, this time with an added UNIQUE table constraint, named *UQ_full_name*, on the *first_name*, *mid_init*, and *last_name* columns:

```
CREATE TABLE customer
(
first_name    char(20) NOT NULL,
mid_init      char(1)  NULL,
last_name     char(20) NOT NULL,
SSN           char(11) NOT NULL UNIQUE CLUSTERED,
cust_phone    char(10) NULL,
CONSTRAINT    UQ_full_name UNIQUE NONCLUSTERED (first_name,
              mid_init, last_name)
)
GO
```

A UNIQUE table constraint (a constraint on more than one column) ensures that the combination of values in the columns is unique. In this case, no two customer names that consist of exactly the same first name, last name, and middle initial can be entered into the database. One or two of these columns can be the same, but not all three. Notice that here the UNIQUE table constraint is a nonclustered index because we already have a unique clustered index on *SSN*.

To add a UNIQUE constraint to an existing table, use the ALTER TABLE command. If you try to modify an existing column or columns by adding a UNIQUE constraint, all existing rows in the table must contain unique or null values in the column or columns, or you will get an error message and the UNIQUE constraint will not be added. Let's assume we have created the *customer* table with no constraints at all. Here are the two commands to add both the column and table constraints:

```
ALTER TABLE customer
ADD CONSTRAINT UQ_ssn UNIQUE CLUSTERED (SSN)
GO
```

```
ALTER TABLE customer
ADD CONSTRAINT UQ_full_name UNIQUE NONCLUSTERED (first_name,
    mid_init, last_name)
GO
```

Again, you can add constraints to a table only if the existing data already meets the constraint requirements.

To change an existing UNIQUE constraint on a column or table by using T-SQL, you must first delete the constraint and then re-create it. As you should for defaults, you should use descriptive names for your constraints so that you can find them and drop them easily, without having to determine what names SQL Server assigned to them. As we'll see in the section "Creating and Modifying Constraints by Using Enterprise Manager," when you change a constraint by using Enterprise Manager, SQL Server will automatically delete the old constraint and re-create it when you save the change.

PRIMARY KEY

A PRIMARY KEY constraint is used to specify the *primary key* of a table, which is a column or set of columns that uniquely identifies a row. Because it identifies the row, a primary key column can never be *NULL*. This is the difference between a PRIMARY KEY constraint and a UNIQUE constraint, which allows null values. When you define a PRIMARY KEY constraint on a set of columns, the constraint indicates that the combination of those column values must be unique for each row, which is similar to a UNIQUE constraint on a set of columns. And, like the UNIQUE constraint, the PRIMARY KEY constraint does not allow duplicate values. When a PRIMARY KEY is assigned to a column or a set of columns, a unique index is automatically created on the primary key column or columns. You can also specify either a clustered or nonclustered index for a primary key; a clustered index is the default when none is specified, as long as the table does not already have a clustered index.

A table can have only one PRIMARY KEY constraint. An IDENTITY column makes a good candidate for a primary key, as does any other column or set of columns that is unique for each row. For example, in our sample *customer* table, we could have created the *SSN* column as the primary key instead of creating a UNIQUE constraint on it. The PRIMARY KEY constraint would not allow null values and would enforce unique values in the *SSN* column, and a clustered index would automatically be created on the primary key column. The following T-SQL command shows one way to specify the *SSN* column as the primary key when you are defining a table. This method allows SQL Server to assign a name to the PRIMARY KEY constraint, which is not the preferred method because you might want to delete the key by name later.

```
CREATE TABLE customer
(
first_name    char(20) NOT NULL,
mid_init      char(1)  NULL,
last_name     char(20) NOT NULL,
SSN           char(11) PRIMARY KEY,
cust_phone    char(10) NULL
)
GO
```

As an alternative, you can assign a name to the constraint by adding the CON-STRAINT keyword. To assign the name *PK_SSN* to our PRIMARY KEY constraint, use the following command:

```
CREATE TABLE customer
(
first_name    char(20) NOT NULL,
mid_init      char(1)  NULL,
last_name     char(20) NOT NULL,
SSN           char(11) CONSTRAINT PK_SSN PRIMARY KEY,
cust_phone    char(10) NULL
)
GO
```

You can also specify the PRIMARY KEY constraint after all the table columns have been defined. The column name must be enclosed in parentheses and specified after the CONSTRAINT clause when this syntax is used, as shown here:

```
CREATE TABLE customer
(
first_name    char(20) NOT NULL,
mid_init      char(1)  NULL,
last_name     char(20) NOT NULL,
SSN           char(11),
cust_phone    char(10) NULL,
CONSTRAINT PK_SSN PRIMARY KEY (SSN)
)
GO
```

To add a PRIMARY KEY constraint to a table that does not have a PRIMARY KEY constraint, use the ALTER TABLE command. The following command adds a PRIMARY KEY constraint to the *customer* table:

```
ALTER TABLE customer
ADD CONSTRAINT PK_SSN PRIMARY KEY CLUSTERED (SSN)
GO
```

Here we have included the optional keyword CLUSTERED just to clarify that a clustered index will be created on the primary key column, although this is the default.

To drop a PRIMARY KEY constraint, use the ALTER TABLE command with the DROP CONSTRAINT clause. Here we drop the constraint on the *SSN* column:

```
ALTER TABLE customer
DROP CONSTRAINT PK_SSN
GO
```

Notice that only the constraint name is necessary for the DROP CONSTRAINT clause. To change an existing PRIMARY KEY constraint on a table by using T-SQL commands, you must first drop the existing constraint and then alter the table to add the new constraint. You do this by using the ALTER TABLE…DROP CONSTRAINT and ALTER TABLE…ADD CONSTRAINT statements.

FOREIGN KEY

A FOREIGN KEY constraint defines a *foreign key,* which identifies a relationship between two tables. The foreign key column or columns in one table reference a *candidate key*—one or more columns—in another table. When a row is inserted into the table with the FOREIGN KEY constraint, the values to be inserted into the column or columns defined as the foreign key are checked against the values in the candidate key of the referenced table. If no row in the referenced table matches the values in the foreign key, the new row cannot be inserted. But if the foreign key values to be inserted into the table do exist in the candidate key of the other table, the new row will be inserted. If the value to be inserted into the table with the FOREIGN KEY constraint is *NULL*, it is also allowed.

FOREIGN KEY constraints are also checked when you want to update a row in either the referenced table or the foreign key table. You cannot update a candidate key value nor a foreign key value if doing so will violate the constraint. There is an exception to this rule when you update the referenced table: you can update the table by using the ON UPDATE CASCADE option of the T-SQL CREATE TABLE statement. This option is described in the section "Creating and Modifying Constraints by Using Enterprise Manager" later in this chapter.

Additionally, FOREIGN KEY constraints are checked when you want to delete a row from the referenced table. You cannot delete a row from a referenced table if the value in the foreign key column is referenced by a row in the foreign key table (the table that holds the FOREIGN KEY constraint). In other words, for each row in the foreign key table, a corresponding row in the referenced table must exist, and that row cannot be deleted while it is still referenced. There is also an exception to this rule: you can delete a row from the referenced table by using the ON DELETE CASCADE option of the T-SQL CREATE TABLE statement. This option is also described in the section "Creating and Modifying Constraints by Using Enterprise Manager."

A foreign key can reference only columns that have a PRIMARY KEY or UNIQUE constraint in the referenced table. If you try to create a foreign key that references a column that is not part of one of these constraints, SQL Server will return an error message. Also, the data type and size of the foreign key column or columns must match that of the referenced column or columns.

To get a better understanding of foreign keys, let's look at some examples. First we'll create a table named *items* that has a PRIMARY KEY constraint on the *item_id* column, as shown here:

```
CREATE TABLE items
(
item_name    char(15)      NOT NULL,
item_id      smallint      NOT NULL IDENTITY(1,1),
price        smallmoney    NULL,
item_desc    varchar(30)   NOT NULL DEFAULT 'none',
CONSTRAINT   PK_item_id    PRIMARY KEY (item_id)
)
GO
```

Next we'll create a table named *inventory* with a FOREIGN KEY constraint named *FK_item_id* that references the *item_id* column in the *items* table, as shown here:

```
CREATE TABLE inventory
(
store_id        tinyint     NOT NULL,
item_id         smallint    NOT NULL,
item_quantity   tinyint     NOT NULL,
CONSTRAINT      FK_item_id FOREIGN KEY (item_id)
REFERENCES      items(item_id)
)
GO
```

To see how these two tables are related, we create a database diagram, as shown in Figure 16-10. (Instructions for creating a database diagram can be found in Chapter 15.) In this example, *items* is the referenced table, with a candidate key of *item_id*. This is the only candidate key possible because it is the primary key in the table and the table has no UNIQUE constraints. Remember, only primary key columns and columns with UNIQUE constraints are valid candidate keys. The *inventory* table has a FOREIGN KEY constraint defined on its *item_id* column, creating a foreign key relationship between these two tables. The related columns are both of the data type *smallint*. Defining a FOREIGN KEY constraint in the *inventory* table on the *item_id* column ensures that no *item_id* value can be inserted into the table if that value does not already exist as an *item_id* value in the *items* table. In other words, if an item does not exist in the *items* table, it cannot exist in the *inventory* table. Also, a row cannot be deleted from the *items* table if it is referenced by a row in the *inventory* table. In other words, if an item exists in the *items* table and the *inventory* table, that item cannot be deleted from the *items* table while it exists in the *inventory* table. As you might realize by now, foreign keys are used to help keep a consistent database. In our example, for instance, you do not want information about an item to be allowed in tables when there is no record of that item in the *items* table, which is intended to hold a record for every item available.

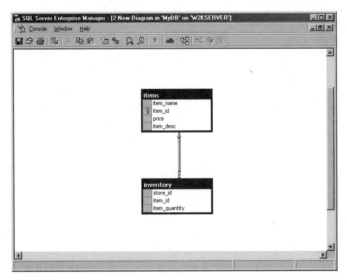

Figure 16-10. *Database diagram showing a foreign key relationship between the* items *and* inventory *tables.*

To modify a FOREIGN KEY constraint by using T-SQL commands, you must first delete the old constraint and then create a new one by using the ALTER TABLE command. This method is similar to the one used to modify a PRIMARY KEY constraint. Here are the commands to first drop the original constraint on the *inventory* table and to then add the new constraint:

```
ALTER TABLE inventory
DROP CONSTRAINT FK_item_id
GO

ALTER TABLE inventory
ADD CONSTRAINT FK_item_id FOREIGN KEY (item_id)
REFERENCES items(item_id)
GO
```

When you add a FOREIGN KEY constraint to an existing table column, SQL Server checks the existing rows in the table to ensure that the foreign key column values, except null values, have matching values in the PRIMARY KEY or UNIQUE constraint column of the referenced table. To create a FOREIGN KEY constraint without allowing SQL Server to validate existing values, you can use the WITH NOCHECK option of ALTER TABLE, as shown here:

```
ALTER TABLE inventory
WITH NOCHECK ADD CONSTRAINT FK_item_id
FOREIGN KEY (item_id)
REFERENCES items(item_id)
GO
```

The WITH NOCHECK option prevents SQL Server from checking the existing rows in the table so that the constraint will be added to the table regardless of what the existing values are. After the constraint is added, SQL Server enforces foreign key integrity for future inserted rows.

Caution Be careful when using the WITH NOCHECK option if you plan to perform updates later on the existing data. An update will fail if attempted on a row containing a value in the foreign key column that does not comply with the constraint.

You can also enable or disable the use of a FOREIGN KEY constraint. If you want to insert a row that does not comply with an existing constraint, you can temporarily disable the constraint, insert the row, and then re-enable the constraint. The NOCHECK keyword indicates that the constraint should be ignored (disabled), and the CHECK keyword indicates that the constraint should be enabled. The following commands disable and re-enable a FOREIGN KEY constraint by using the NOCHECK and CHECK keywords:

```
ALTER TABLE inventory
NOCHECK CONSTRAINT FK_item_id     --Disables the constraint
GO


--INSERT statement goes here
GO


ALTER TABLE inventory
CHECK CONSTRAINT FK_item_id       --Re-enables the constraint
GO
```

> **Caution**   You should not insert a row of data that does not comply with the
> FOREIGN KEY constraint unless absolutely necessary. If you do so, future table
> updates might fail.

CHECK

The CHECK constraint is used to restrict the values allowed in a column to specific values. The values to be inserted or updated in a column are validated if they
return *TRUE* from the specified Boolean search condition in the constraint. For
example, if we wanted to restrict the possible range of values that will be allowed
in the *price* column of the *items* table to *$0.01* through *$500.00*, we would use
the following statement:

```
CREATE TABLE items
(
item_name   char(15)    NOT NULL,
item_id     smallint    NOT NULL IDENTITY(1,1),
price       smallmoney  NULL,
item_desc   varchar(30) NOT NULL DEFAULT 'none',
CONSTRAINT  PK_item_id  PRIMARY KEY (item_id),
CONSTRAINT  CK_price    CHECK (price >= .01 AND
                        price <= 500.00)
)
GO
```

Notice that we allow *NULLs* in the *price* column and that we also have a CHECK
constraint on the column. Because SQL Server can distinguish a null value from
any other type of value, *NULLs* are allowed in the *price* column despite the CHECK
constraint. Also, notice that we gave this constraint the name *CK_price*. As we've
seen, assigning a constraint name makes it easier to later drop and re-create the

constraint by name, using T-SQL. For instance, to change the range of values to *$1.00* through *$1000.00*, use the following statement:

```
ALTER TABLE items
DROP CONSTRAINT CK_price
GO

ALTER TABLE items
ADD CONSTRAINT CK_price CHECK (price >= 1.00 AND
    price <= 1000.00)
GO
```

The second ALTER TABLE command is the same one you would use if you added this constraint for the first time to an existing *items* table. When you are adding a CHECK constraint to an existing table, the same rules apply as when you add a FOREIGN KEY constraint. The existing rows will be checked against the constraint. If they do not all return *TRUE*, the constraint will not be added to the table, and SQL Server will return an error message stating that the ALTER TABLE statement had a conflict because of the CHECK constraint. If you must, use WITH NOCHECK to specify that existing rows should not be validated but that future updates and rows added later should be validated.

> **Caution** Using WITH NOCHECK is not recommended because a later update might fail on a row that does not comply with the constraint.

Here is an example of using WITH NOCHECK when the *CK_price* constraint is added:

```
ALTER TABLE items
WITH NOCHECK ADD CONSTRAINT CK_price
CHECK (price >= 1.00 AND price <= 1000.00)
GO
```

You can also enable and disable a CHECK constraint as you can a FOREIGN KEY constraint, using the CHECK and NOCHECK keywords with ALTER TABLE. You might want to use this technique to insert one price that is out of the specified range but is still valid. The following example disables and then re-enables the *CK_price* CHECK constraint:

```
ALTER TABLE items
NOCHECK CONSTRAINT CK_price       --Disables constraint
GO

--INSERT statement goes here
GO

ALTER TABLE items
CHECK CONSTRAINT CK_price         --Re-enables constraint
GO
```

Note   CHECK and FOREIGN KEY are the only types of constraints that can be disabled and enabled in this manner.

Creating and Modifying Constraints by Using Enterprise Manager

In this section, you'll learn how to create, modify, and delete constraints by using the Enterprise Manager Design Table window and, in the case of FOREIGN KEY constraints, a database diagram. (Instructions for creating a database diagram can be found in Chapter 15.) The Design Table window appears when you create or edit a table by using Enterprise Manager. To create a table, expand the Server and Database folders in the left pane of Enterprise Manager, right-click Tables, and then choose New Table from the shortcut menu. To display the Design Table window for an existing table, first click Tables, right-click the table name in the right pane, and then choose Design Table from the shortcut menu.

Allow Nulls

To specify whether null values should be allowed in a column, simply select or clear the appropriate cell under the Allow Nulls heading in the Design Table window. You can set this option either when you create the table or when you modify it. (For rules on allowing null values, see Chapter 10.) Figure 16-11 shows the Design Table window for the *customer* table we created in the section "Creating and Modifying Constraints by Using T-SQL" earlier in this chapter. As you can see, the *mid_init* and *cust_phone* columns allow null values, but the other three columns do not.

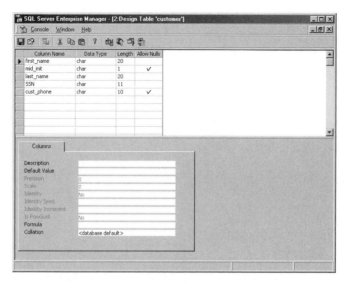

Figure 16-11. *The Design Table window for the* customer *table, with settings in the Allow Nulls column.*

UNIQUE

To create or modify a UNIQUE constraint by using Enterprise Manager, follow these steps:

1. In the Design Table window, click the Table And Index Properties button on the Design Table toolbar (the button to the right of the Save button), and then click the Indexes/Keys tab in the Properties window that appears. Figure 16-12 shows the Indexes/Keys tab of the Properties window for the *customer* table. This tab will show any UNIQUE constraints because they are actually unique indexes.

   This table was created by using the following statement, which includes a UNIQUE constraint as a clustered index on the *SSN* column. (SQL Server automatically named the index *UQ_customer_398D8EEE*; you can see why it is helpful to specify your own constraint and index names.)

```
CREATE TABLE customer
(
first_name    char(20) NOT NULL,
mid_init      char(1)  NULL,
last_name     char(20) NOT NULL,
```

```
SSN            char(11) NOT NULL UNIQUE CLUSTERED,
cust_phone     char(10) NULL
)
GO
```

Figure 16-12. *The Indexes/Keys tab of the Properties window for the* customer *table.*

2. To create a new UNIQUE constraint, begin by clicking the New button
   on the Indexes/Keys tab of the Properties window. Select the names of
   the columns that you want to be part of the constraint, type the name
   of the new constraint, and then select the Create UNIQUE check box.
   Select the Create As CLUSTERED check box if you want this to be the
   clustered index on the table, and specify a fill factor if you want. If you
   do not want SQL Server to automatically recompute this index's statistics periodically, select the check box next to that option as well.

3. You can use the Properties window to modify a UNIQUE constraint—
   for example, you can change the constraint name, specify the columns
   to which the constraint is attached, set the clustered index option, and
   choose the fill factor for the index. (Fill factor is described in detail in
   Chapter 17.) Make any changes you want to this constraint. When you
   are done, click Close and then click the Save button in the Design Table
   window to save your changes.

PRIMARY KEY

You can specify a PRIMARY KEY constraint on one column or on multiple columns. These columns should uniquely identify each row in the table. To specify a PRIMARY KEY, follow these steps:

1. In the Design Table window, select a column by clicking in one of the cells in its row. (You can select multiple columns by holding down the Ctrl key and clicking the gray boxes to the left of the column names.)

2. Right-click one of the selected columns and choose Set Primary Key from the shortcut menu. A small key will appear to the left of the columns you set as the primary key. Figure 16-13 shows the Design Table window for the *customer* table after the *SSN* column was set as the primary key. The UNIQUE constraint was also removed from the *SSN* column by deleting the unique index because it is not necessary to have both a UNIQUE constraint and a PRIMARY KEY constraint on the same column.

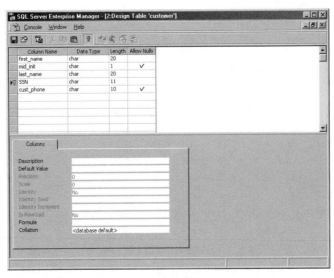

Figure 16-13. *Setting a PRIMARY KEY constraint in the Design Table window.*

3. If you want to change the PRIMARY KEY constraint to another column, simply set the new column as the primary key. You are not required to explicitly remove the original primary key first—SQL Server drops and

re-creates the PRIMARY KEY index for you. You can also modify the PRIMARY KEY index in the Properties window. Again, your changes will take effect when you save your work by clicking the Save button on the toolbar.

Note   If you have modified the PRIMARY KEY constraint on a table that has existing data, the re-creation of the index might take some time. If your table contains a lot of data and you specified a major change in the index, such as changing the columns or the cluster status, you should perform this kind of change during periods of off-peak use of the database, if possible.

FOREIGN KEY

To create or modify a FOREIGN KEY constraint by using Enterprise Manager, you can use the Design Table window, or you can create a database diagram of the tables to be involved in the foreign key relationship. It is always best to create the foreign key relationships at table creation time (or at least before any data is inserted into the tables). You'll see why in the following example. First you'll learn how to use the Design Table window to create a FOREIGN KEY constraint. We will build a foreign key relationship between two tables described earlier in this chapter, *items* and *inventory*. We will re-create the *items* table with a PRIMARY KEY constraint (which we used before) but without the IDENTITY property on the *item_id* column, because we will be working through an example where this column is updated, and you cannot update an IDENTITY column without doing some extra work. We will also re-create the *inventory* table without the FOREIGN KEY constraint so that we can add it later. Here are the CREATE TABLE statements used for both tables:

```
CREATE TABLE items
(
item_name    char(15)      NOT NULL,
item_id      smallint      NOT NULL,
price        smallmoney    NULL,
item_desc    varchar(30)   NOT NULL DEFAULT 'none',
CONSTRAINT   PK_item_id    PRIMARY KEY (item_id)
)
GO
```

(continued)

continued

```
CREATE TABLE inventory
(
store_id         tinyint     NOT NULL,
item_id          smallint    NOT NULL,
item_quantity    tinyint     NOT NULL
)
GO
```

To add a FOREIGN KEY constraint on the *inventory* table, follow these steps:

1. Right-click the *inventory* table name in the right pane of Enterprise Manager and choose Design Table. Right-click in an open space in this window and choose Relationships from the shortcut menu. The Properties window will appear with the Relationships tab open, as shown in Figure 16-14.

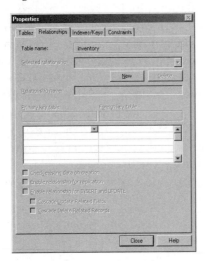

Figure 16-14. *The Relationships tab of the Properties window for the* inventory *table.*

2. Click New. Default data will appear in the window, as shown in Figure 16-15.

3. We select the primary key table to be *items* (instead of *customer*), and we select the *item_id* column for the foreign key relationship between the *items* and *inventory* tables. To do this, just click in one of the empty rows below the table names, and the possible column choices will appear

in a drop-down menu. Once you have selected the appropriate tables for the relationship, the name in the Relationship Name box changes, as shown in Figure 16-16.

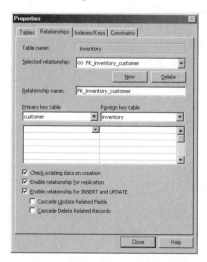

Figure 16-15. *The Relationships tab with default entries after clicking New.*

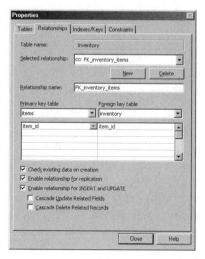

Figure 16-16. *The Relationships tab showing a foreign key relationship between the* items *and* inventory *tables.*

4. Several check boxes appear at the bottom of this window. Sample selections are shown in Figure 16-17. Select the Check Existing Data On Creation option if you want SQL Server to check existing data against the foreign key relationship. If the data does not comply, the constraint creation will fail. Clear this check box only if you have no data yet, you know that the existing data is already compliant with the constraint, or you do not want existing data to comply for a particular reason. This could cause problems if you try to update or delete one of those existing rows later, though.

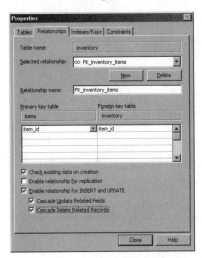

Figure 16-17. *The Relationships tab showing check box options selected.*

5. The next check box is Enable Relationship For Replication. Do not select this if you are not using replication. Even if you are using replication, you still do not need to select this check box because the data will already be checked against the constraint in the original tables, so it should not have to be checked again upon replication. If you do enable the relationship for replication, and if the replication schedules of the two tables in the relationship are not well synchronized, you will receive errors during replication that indicate a row could not be replicated because it violated the foreign key constraint.

6. The next check box is Enable Relationship For INSERT And UPDATE. Selecting this check box means that the FOREIGN KEY constraint will be checked when you perform inserts and updates, as well as deletes. If this is your intent, select this check box. The two check boxes below will become available. They are Cascade Update Related Fields and Cascade Delete Related Records. ("Record" refers to a row of data.)

7. Selecting Cascade Update Related Fields means that if you update the referenced column of the referenced table (such as by updating an *item_id* value in the *items* table), that update will be cascaded to the foreign key table. (In this case, that same *item_id* value will be updated if it exists in the *inventory* table.) Only the column value will be updated; the rest of the information in the row in the foreign key table will remain the same. Selecting this option also allows the update of the referenced column to occur. If you do not select this option, you will not be allowed to update a referenced column if it exists in the table with the foreign key. You will get an error message from SQL Server similar to the following: "UPDATE statement conflicted with COLUMN REFERENCE constraint 'FK_inventory_items'. The conflict occurred in database 'MyDB', table 'inventory', column 'item_id'. The statement has been terminated."

8. Selecting Cascade Delete Related Records means that a delete from the referenced table will be cascaded to the foreign key table. For example, if a row in the *items* tables is deleted and a row in the *inventory* table has the same *item_id* value as the deleted row, that row will be deleted from the *inventory* table as well. This keeps your information consistent. If you do not select this option, you will not be allowed to delete a row from the referenced table if it is referenced by a row in the foreign key table. You will get an error message from SQL Server similar to the following: "DELETE statement conflicted with COLUMN REFERENCE constraint 'FK_inventory_items'. The conflict occurred in database 'MyDB', table 'inventory', column 'item_id'. The statement has been terminated."

9. When you have finished selecting your options, click Close and then click the Save button in the Design Table window to save your changes. Another window will appear stating that the listed tables will be saved to

your database, and it lists the two tables in the foreign key relationship. Click Yes to finish. Then you can close the Design Table window by clicking the Close button in the top right corner of that window (not of the Enterprise Manager window, or you will close Enterprise Manager).

There is another method you can use to create or modify a FOREIGN KEY constraint: the database diagram method. To learn how to create and modify a FOREIGN KEY constraint by using a database diagram, we will develop a diagram using the same two tables we used in the previous example, *items* and *inventory*. First we'll look at a database diagram of these tables without a foreign key relationship, and then we'll add a foreign key. The initial database diagram is shown in Figure 16-18.

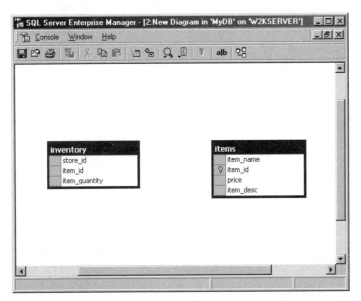

Figure 16-18. *Database diagram for the* items *and* inventory *tables.*

As you can see in Figure 16-18, the *item_id* column in the *items* table is a primary key column. This is the only candidate for a foreign key reference because there are no UNIQUE constraints on the *items* table. To create a foreign key relationship between the *item_id* column in the *inventory* table and the *item_id* column in the *items* table, follow these steps:

1. Click in the far left side of the row (in the gray box) for the *item_id* column in the *items* table, and hold down the mouse button while you drag the cursor to the *inventory* table. (You'll see a dotted line following the cursor.) Release the mouse button when you are pointing to the *item_id* column's row in the *inventory* table. The Create Relationship dialog box will appear, as shown in Figure 16-19. This is similar to the Properties window from the Design Table window, as shown previously. The *item_id* column will appear in each table's column in the dialog box, indicating that the foreign key relationship will be between the two *item_id* columns.

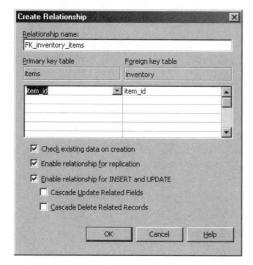

Figure 16-19. *The Create Relationship dialog box showing the proposed foreign key relationship.*

2. You can change the relationship name if you want. Select or clear the check boxes at the bottom of the dialog box to choose the options you want. These options were described earlier in this section.

3. Click OK when you're finished to create the relationship in the diagram, as shown in Figure 16-20. (It is not saved yet.) A line with a key on the end runs from the foreign key table to the referenced table.

4. Click the Save button to save your changes. You will be asked to name the database diagram and then to confirm the changes to the involved tables. Click Yes to finish.

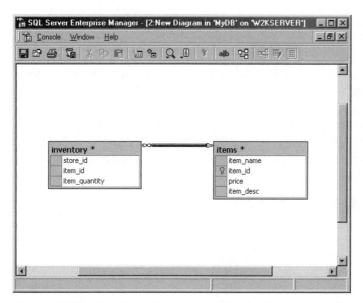

Figure 16-20. *Database diagram showing the foreign key relationship.*

To modify a FOREIGN KEY constraint, you can use the two methods described in this section, in a similar manner. In the Design Table window, simply open the Relationships tab again, make your changes, and save your work. In the database diagram, right-click the foreign key line in the diagram and choose Properties to make changes to the constraint, or choose Delete Relationship From Database to completely delete the constraint. You can then create a new one if you want.

CHECK

To create a CHECK constraint by using the Design Table window, open the Design Table window for the table you want to work with, and follow these steps:

1. Right-click in the Design Table window and choose Properties from the shortcut menu to display the Properties window. Click the Check Constraints tab, shown in Figure 16-21, and click New for the *items* table.

2. Next type the expression you want to use for validating data that is inserted or updated. In our example, we'll add a CHECK constraint on the *price* column of the *items* table so that values only from *$1.00* through *$1000.00* can be inserted into the table, as shown in Figure 16-22.

3. Notice the three check boxes at the bottom. Selecting Check Existing Data On Creation means that the existing data in the table will be checked against the CHECK constraint and that if it does not comply, the constraint will not be created. Selecting Enforce Constraint For

Replication means that the constraint will be checked when the data is replicated. The data should have been checked before it got into the original table, so selecting this option means the data is unnecessarily checked again when it is replicated. Selecting Enforce Constraint For INSERTs And UPDATEs simply means that the CHECK constraint will be enabled. If you do not select this check box, the constraint will be created, but it will not be enabled and thus will have no effect.

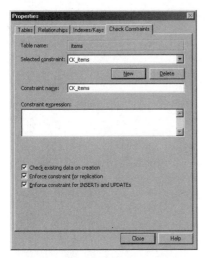

Figure 16-21. *The Check Constraints tab of the Properties window.*

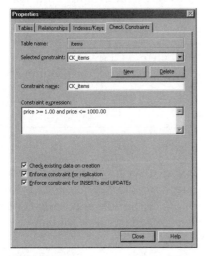

Figure 16-22. *Adding a CHECK constraint on the* price *column of the* items *table.*

4. Click Close and then click the Save button to save the new constraint.

To modify a CHECK constraint, use the Check Constraints tab to modify the name, the expression, and the check box options. In Figure 16-23, the CHECK constraint on the *price* column has been changed from a range of *$1.00* through *$1000.00* to a range of *$1.00* through *$99.00*.

Figure 16-23. *Modifying the CHECK constraint.*

Notice that the Check Existing Data On Creation option is now cleared because the constraint was already created. If you want to verify the existing data against the modified range, select this check box. If the check fails for the existing data, you will get an error message and the constraint will not be modified.

You can also use the Check Constraints tab to delete a CHECK constraint by selecting the name of the constraint you want in the Selected Constraint list box and clicking Delete.

Rule Objects

An alternative to using the CHECK constraint is to create a *Rule* object to restrict the values that can be inserted or updated in a column. The *Rule* object is similar to the *Default* object in that it is created apart from a table and is not deleted when the table is dropped. You must also bind a *Rule* object to a column or to a user-defined type—in this case, by using the *sp_bindrule* system stored procedure. And like the *Default* object, the *Rule* object is available with SQL Server 2000 for backward compatibility. Using the CHECK constraint is the preferred method of restricting column values, but *Rule* objects might be useful when the same rule is needed for many columns or user-defined types.

Creating a *Rule* Object by Using T-SQL

As an example, let's create a *Rule* object that performs the same function as the CHECK constraint we created earlier. Our rule uses the variable name *@price* to refer to the *price* column of the *items* table. The variable name must begin with an "at" symbol (@), but you can choose any name you want. First we'll create the rule, and then we'll bind it to a column, as shown here:

```
USE MyDB
GO
CREATE RULE price_rule AS
(@price >= .01 AND @price <= 500.00)
GO
sp_bindrule 'price_rule', 'items.price', 'futureonly'
GO
```

To unbind the rule and delete it, use the following statement:

```
sp_unbindrule 'items.price'
GO
DROP RULE price_rule
GO
```

The parameters for *sp_bindrule* and *sp_unbindrule* are the same as for *sp_bindefault* and *sp_unbindefault* (described in the section "CREATE DEFAULT and *sp_bindefault*" earlier in this chapter). Each column or user-defined type can have only one rule, although you can assign both a rule and one or more CHECK constraints to the same column or user-defined type. If you do so, SQL Server will apply all of the restrictions to the inserted or updated data.

Creating a *Rule* Object by Using Enterprise Manager

To use Enterprise Manager to create and bind a *Rule* object, follow these steps:

1. Expand the server name and the database name in Enterprise Manager. Right-click Rules, and then choose New Rule from the shortcut menu to display the Rule Properties window. In this example, we will name the rule *price_rule* and will add text, as shown in Figure 16-24. Click OK to create the *Rule* object.

2. To bind the rule, click Rules in the left pane of Enterprise Manager, right-click the name of the new rule, and then choose Properties from the short-cut menu to display the Rule Properties window. As we did earlier when binding *Default* objects, click Bind UDTs to bind the rule to a user-defined data type, or click Bind Columns to bind the rule to a column or columns. For this example, we'll click Bind Columns and select the *price* column of the *items* table to bind the rule to, as shown in Figure 16-25.

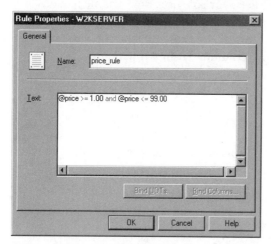

Figure 16-24. *The Rule Properties window for creating a rule.*

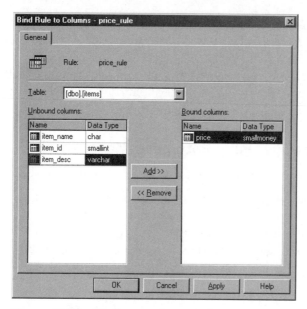

Figure 16-25. *Binding a rule to a column.*

3. Click OK to apply your rule, and then click OK again to close the Rule Properties window.

To delete a rule, you must first unbind the rule from all columns or user-defined types. After you unbind the rule, right-click the rule name, choose Delete from the shortcut menu, and then click Drop All in the Drop Objects dialog box. If the rule is bound to anything when you try to delete it, SQL Server will display an error message and will not delete the rule.

Summary

In this chapter, you learned about defaults and the five types of constraints that can be placed on a column or table, and you learned how to create and modify defaults and constraints by using T-SQL commands and Enterprise Manager. You also learned how to create and modify defaults and rules by using *Default* and *Rule* objects. Defaults provide a way to specify a default value for a column when a specific value has not been assigned. Constraints provide various ways to enforce data integrity in your database. Defaults and constraints are helpful tools when they are thoughtfully applied to your database tables. In Chapter 17, we'll look at how to use indexes in SQL Server, including clustered and nonclustered indexes. Indexes can greatly improve the efficiency of data access.

Chapter 17
Creating and Using Indexes

Indexes are one of the most powerful tools available to the database designer. An *index* is an auxiliary structure that enables you to improve the performance of queries by reducing the amount of I/O activity necessary to retrieve requested data—that is, an index enables Microsoft SQL Server 2000 to locate data by using fewer I/O operations than it would need to look up the data by accessing the database table alone. When you use a database table index to search for a row of data, SQL Server can quickly determine where the data is stored and immediately retrieve that data. Thus, database table indexes are much like indexes in books—they both provide fast access to large amounts of information.

In this chapter, you'll learn the basics of indexing, including how to create an index and the types of indexes that are available with SQL Server. You'll also learn when to use indexes and when not to use them because using an index is not always effective—in some situations, it can actually hurt performance.

What Is an Index?

As mentioned, an index is an auxiliary data structure used by SQL Server to access data. Depending on its type, an index is stored with the data or separate from the data. Regardless of type, all indexes work in the same basic way, which you'll learn about in this section.

In systems without indexes, all data retrieval must be done by using table scans. In a table scan, all of the data in a table must be read and compared with the requested data. Table scans are generally avoided because of the amount of I/O that is generated by this operation—scanning large tables could take a long time and eat up a lot of system resources. By using an index, you can greatly reduce the number of I/O operations, speeding up access to data as well as freeing up system resources for other operations.

A database index is organized in a B-tree structure. Each page in an index is called an index page or an index node. The index structure begins with a root node at the top level. The *root node* marks the beginning of the index; it is the first data accessed when a data lookup occurs. The root node contains a number of index rows. These index rows contain a key value and a pointer to an index page (called a branch node), as illustrated in Figure 17-1. This configuration is necessary because in an average-size data table, an index consists of thousands or millions of index pages. By starting at the root node and traversing the branch nodes, SQL Server can zoom in on the data you want.

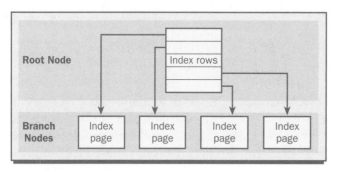

Figure 17-1. *Root node and branch nodes.*

Using a book as an analogy, an index works something like this: suppose the index started with a page that listed the numbers of the pages on which entries beginning with "a," "b," "c," and so on began. Then suppose those pages contained page numbers for entries in the ranges aa-ab, ac-ad, ae-af, and so on, and those pages contained pointers to entries in the ranges aaa-aab, aac-aad, aae-aaf, and so forth. With this arrangement, you could find what you are looking for quickly, with relatively few lookups. This is similar to a database table index, with the first page being the root node.

Like the root node, each branch node contains a number of index rows held in an index page. Each index row points to another branch node or a leaf node, as illustrated in Figure 17-2. The leaf nodes make up the last level of an index. Unlike the root node, each branch node also contains a linked list to other branch nodes on the same level. In other words, the node knows about adjacent nodes as well as lower nodes.

As the name "B-tree" implies, the branch nodes expand out from the root node in treelike fashion. Each group of branch nodes at the same level of the tree structure is known as an *index level*, as illustrated in Figure 17-3. The number of I/O operations that are needed to reach the leaf nodes (the nodes at the lowest level in the tree) is dependent on the number of index levels. If the database table contains only a small amount of data, the root node can point directly to the leaf nodes, and the index need not contain any branch nodes at all (an unlikely situation).

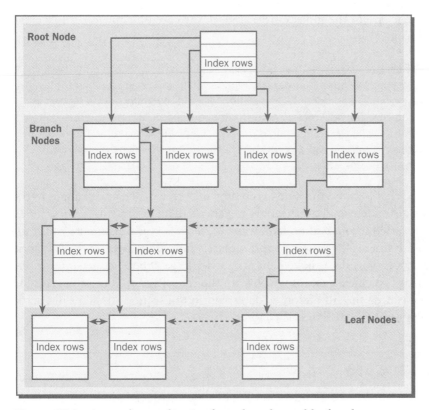

Figure 17-2. *A search tree showing branch nodes and leaf nodes.*

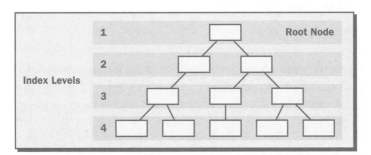

Figure 17-3. *Index levels.*

In a nonclustered index, the leaf node contains the key value and either a Row ID pointing to the desired row in the table or the clustered-index key if there is also a clustered index on the table. And in a clustered index, the data itself is in the leaf node. (Clustered and nonclustered indexes will be described in the section "Types of Indexes" later in this chapter.) The number of rows in a leaf node depends on the size of the index entries and, in the case of a clustered index, the size of the data.

> **Note** A Row ID is a pointer that SQL Server builds automatically from the File ID, the page number, and the data row number. With a Row ID, you can retrieve data with only one additional I/O operation. Because you know which page to retrieve and SQL Server knows where that page resides, the page is read into memory with a single I/O request. The simplicity of this process is the reason why indexes are so efficient at retrieving data and provide such a great performance enhancement.

Keep in mind that because the index is created in sorted order, any changes to the data might cause additional overhead. For example, if an insert causes a new index row to be inserted into a leaf node that is full, SQL Server must make room for the new row. It does so by moving approximately half of the rows in the leaf node to another page. This data movement is called a *page split*. A page split on one level of a tree can cause cascading splits up the tree. Page splits can be avoided by carefully tuning the fill factor, as described in the section "Using Fill Factor to Avoid Page Splits" later in this chapter.

Indexing Concepts

Now that you have a basic understanding of index structure, let's look at some of the more general concepts of indexing. In this section, you'll learn about index keys, index uniqueness, and types of indexes.

Index Keys

An *index key* designates the column or columns that are used to generate the index. The index key is the value that enables you to quickly find the row that contains the data you are interested in, much like an index entry in a book points you to a particular topic in the text. To access the data row by using the index, you must include the index key value or values in the WHERE clause of the SQL statement. How this is accomplished depends on whether the index is a simple index or a composite index.

Simple Indexes

A *simple index* is an index that is defined on only one table column, as illustrated in Figure 17-4. This column must be referenced in the WHERE clause of the SQL statement in order for this index to be used to satisfy the statement.

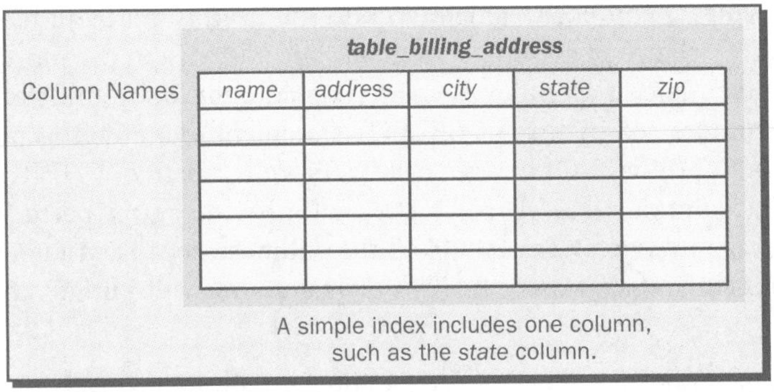

A simple index includes one column,
such as the *state* column.

Figure 17-4. *Simple index.*

Depending on the type of data being stored, the number of unique items in the column, and the type of SQL statements being used, a simple index can be effective. In other cases, a composite index is necessary. For example, if you are indexing an address book with thousands of names and addresses, the *state* column would not be a good candidate for a simple index because there would be many entries for the same state. However, by adding the columns *street* and *city* to the index, thereby making it a composite index, you can make each entry almost unique. This step would be helpful if you used queries that looked up rows according to the address.

Composite Indexes

A *composite index* is an index defined on more than one column, as illustrated in Figure 17-5. A composite index can be accessed by using one or more index keys. With SQL Server 2000, an index can comprise up to 16 columns, and its key columns can be as long as 900 bytes.

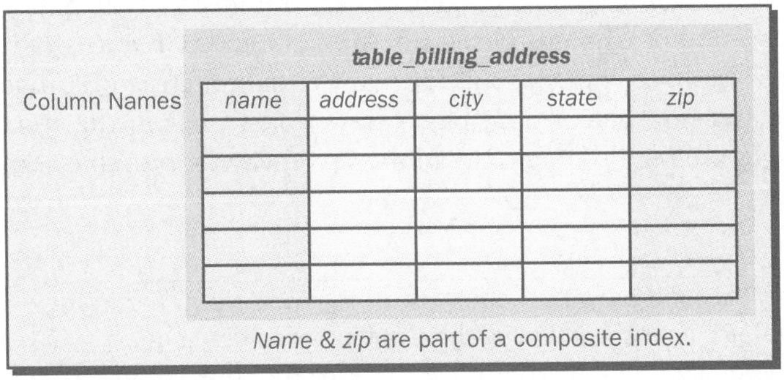

Name & *zip* are part of a composite index.

Figure 17-5. *Composite index.*

For the queries that involve a composite index, you do not need to place all the index keys in the WHERE clause of an SQL statement, but it is wise to use more than one of them. For example, if an index is created on columns a, b, and c of a table, the index can be accessed by using a SELECT statement that contains (a AND b AND c) or (a AND b) or a. Of course, using a more restrictive WHERE clause, such as one that contains a AND b AND c, will provide better performance. It will most likely retrieve fewer rows from the database because it identifies a row more specifically. If you use a AND b or just a, you will initiate an index scan.

An index scan occurs because more than one index entry satisfies the search criteria. In an index scan, the nodes within an index are scanned to retrieve multiple data records. Furthermore, the index partially covers the value that has been selected. For example, if the index has been created on columns a, b, and c and the query specifies only column a, all rows that satisfy that value of a will be returned, for all values of b and c.

Because the columns on which the index is based are ordered numerically, the SQL Server query optimizer can determine the range of index pages that might contain the desired data. Once the starting and ending pages are known, all of the pages that contain the data values will be retrieved, and the data will be scanned to select the requested data.

Real World A Customer Location Table

Suppose we have a table that contains information about the location of customers of our business. An index is created on the columns *state*, *county*, and *city* and is stored in the B-tree structure in the following order: *state, county, city*. If a query specifies the *state* column value as *Texas* in the WHERE clause, the index will be used. Because values for the *county* and *city* columns are not given in the query, the index will return a number of rows based on all of the index records that contain *Texas* as the *state* column value. An index scan is used to retrieve a range of index pages and then a number of data pages based on values in the *state* column. The index pages are read sequentially in the same way that a table scan accesses data pages.

Note The index can be used only if at least one of the index keys are in the WHERE clause of the SQL query. Continuing the previous example, a query with only a name or phone number in the WHERE clause would not use the index.

In most cases, an index scan will be fairly efficient; however, if more than 20 percent of the rows in the table are accessed, it is more efficient to perform a table scan, in which all the rows are read from the table. The efficiency of queries using an index depends on how you use the index (described in the section "Using Indexes" later in the chapter) and on index uniqueness, which we'll look at next.

Index Uniqueness

You can define a SQL Server index as either unique or nonunique. In a *unique index,* each index key value must be unique. A *nonunique index* allows index keys to be duplicated in the table data. The effectiveness, or efficiency, of a nonunique index will depend on the selectivity of the index.

Unique Indexes

A unique index contains only one row of data for each index key—in other words, index key values cannot appear in the index more than once. Unique indexes work well because they guarantee that only one more I/O operation is needed to retrieve the requested data. SQL Server enforces the unique property of an index on the column or combination of columns that make up the index key. SQL Server will not allow a duplicate key value to be inserted into the database. If you attempt to do so, an error will result. SQL Server creates unique indexes when you create either a PRIMARY KEY constraint or a UNIQUE constraint on a table. The PRIMARY KEY and UNIQUE constraints are described in Chapter 16.

An index can be made unique only if the data itself is unique. If the data in a column does not contain unique values, you can still create a unique index by using a composite index. For example, the *last name* column might not be unique, but by combining the data in this column with the *first name* and *middle name* columns, you might be able to create a unique index on the table.

Note   If you attempt to insert a row in a table that will create a duplicate index key value in a unique index, the insert will fail.

Nonunique Indexes

A nonunique index works in the same manner as a unique index except that it can contain duplicate values in the leaf nodes. All duplicate values will be retrieved if they match the criteria specified in the SELECT statement.

A nonunique index is not as efficient as a unique index because it requires additional processing (additional I/O operations) in order to retrieve the requested data. But because some applications require using duplicate keys, it is sometimes impossible to create a unique index. In those cases, a nonunique index is often better than no index at all.

Types of Indexes

There are two types of B-tree indexes: *clustered indexes* and *nonclustered indexes*. A clustered index stores the actual rows of data in its leaf nodes. A nonclustered index is an auxiliary structure that points to data in a table. In this section, we'll look at the differences between these two index types. You'll also be introduced to the full-text index, which is actually more of a catalog than an index, in this section.

Clustered Indexes

As mentioned, a clustered index is a B-tree index that stores the actual row data of the table in its leaf nodes, in sorted order, as illustrated in Figure 17-6. This system offers several benefits and several disadvantages.

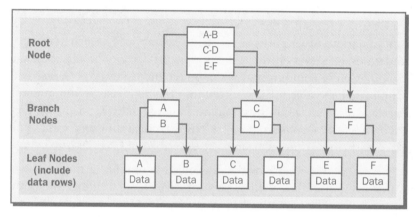

Figure 17-6. *Clustered index.*

Because the data in a clustered index is stored in the leaf nodes, once the leaf node is reached, the data is available, which can result in a smaller number of I/O operations. Any reduction in these operations will yield higher performance for the individual operation and greater overall performance for the system.

Another advantage of clustered indexes is that the retrieved data will be in index-sorted order. For example, if a clustered index is created on the *state, county*, and *city* columns and a query selects all values for which *state ? Texas*, the resulting output will be sorted on *county* and *city* in the order in which the index was defined. This feature can be used to avoid unnecessary sort operations if the application and the database have been carefully designed. For example, if you know that you will always need to sort data in a certain way, using a clustered index means you will not need to perform the sort after the data retrieval.

One disadvantage of using a clustered index is that access to the table always occurs through the index, which can result in additional overhead. SQL Server begins data access at the root node and traverses the index until it reaches the leaf node containing the data. If many leaf nodes are created because of the volume of data, the number of index levels necessary to support that many leaf nodes is also large, which requires more I/O operations for SQL Server to travel from the root node to the leaf node.

Because the actual data is stored in the clustered index, you cannot create more than one clustered index on a table. On the other hand, you can create non-clustered indexes on top of a clustered table. (A clustered table is simply a table that has a clustered index.) You should create your clustered index using the most commonly accessed index keys—doing so will give you the best chance of accessing the data through the clustered index and will thus provide the best performance.

Nonclustered Indexes

Unlike the clustered index, the nonclustered index does not contain actual table data in its leaf nodes. The leaf nodes can contain one of two types of data row location information. First, if there is no clustered index on a table, nonclustered indexes on that table store Row IDs in their leaf nodes, as illustrated in Figure 17-7. Each Row ID points to the actual data row in the table. The Row ID consists of a value that includes the data file ID, the page number, and the row in the page. This value enables quick access to the actual data by pinpointing where the data is stored.

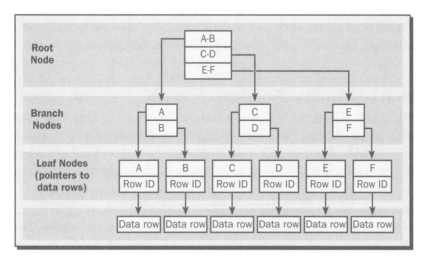

Figure 17-7. *Nonclustered index on a table without a clustered index.*

If there is a clustered index on the table, nonclustered indexes will contain the clustered index key value for that data in the leaf node, as shown in Figure 17-8.

When the leaf node of the nonclustered index is reached, the clustered key value found there is used to search the clustered index, where the data row will be found in its leaf node.

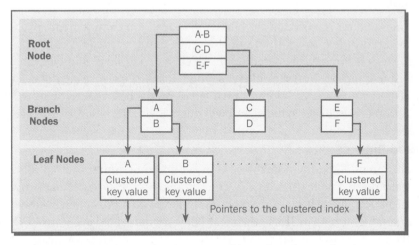

Figure 17-8. *Nonclustered index on a table with a clustered index.*

As mentioned, you can have only one clustered index per table. You can create 249 nonclustered indexes per table, but doing so might not be wise, as explained in the "Index Guidelines" section later in this chapter. It is common to have several nonclustered indexes on various columns in a table. The predicate in the WHERE clause will be used by the query optimizer to determine which index is used.

Full-Text Indexes

As mentioned, a SQL Server full-text index is actually more like a catalog than an index, and its structure is not a B-tree. The full-text index allows you to search by groups of keywords. The full-text index is part of the Microsoft Search service; it is used extensively in Web site search engines and in other text-based operations.

Unlike B-tree indexes, a full-text index is stored outside the database but is maintained by the database. Because it is stored externally, the index can maintain its own structure. The following restrictions apply to full-text indexes:

- A full-text index must include a column that uniquely identifies each row in the table.

- A full-text index also must include one or more character string columns in the table.

- Only one full-text index is allowed per table.
- A full-text index is not automatically updated as B-tree indexes are. That is, in a B-tree index, a table insert, update, or delete operation will update the index. With the full-text index, these operations on the table will not automatically update the index. Updates must be scheduled or run manually.

The full-text index has a wealth of features that cannot be found in B-tree indexes. Because this index is designed to be a text search engine, it supports more than standard text-searching capabilities. Using a full-text index, you can search for words or phrases, single words or groups of words, or words that are similar to each other. You'll learn how to create a full-text index in the section "Using the Full-Text Indexing Wizard" later in this chapter.

Creating Indexes

Creating indexes is not difficult. You create clustered and nonclustered indexes in much the same way, by using wizards provided with Enterprise Manager or by using the SQL command CREATE INDEX. In this section, you'll learn how to create indexes by using these two methods, and you'll also learn about using the fill factor and how to use stored procedures to create a full-text index.

> **Note**   Although the wizards are easy to use, if you will be repeating operations or creating multiple similar databases, you might find scripts more convenient. Scripts allow you to both document and reproduce the build process.

Using the Create Index Wizard

Obviously, if you want to create an index on a table, the table must already exist in the database. You can use the Create Index Wizard to create either a clustered or nonclustered index on a table by following these steps:

1. Open Enterprise Manager, and click the Wizards button on the Tools menu. The Select Wizard dialog box appears. In this example, we'll use the Northwind database.

2. Expand the Database folder, select Create Index Wizard, and then click OK.

3. The Create Index Wizard welcome screen appears, as shown in Figure 17-9. Notice that the name of the server and the name of the database you selected appear in the title bar. In this example, the server W2KSERVER and the Northwind database have been selected.

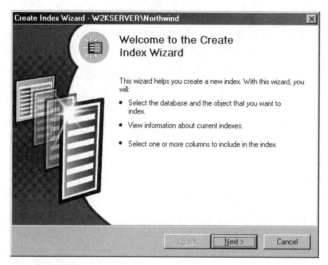

Figure 17-9. *The Create Index Wizard welcome screen.*

4. Click Next to display the Select Database And Table screen, shown in Figure 17-10. Here you can specify the database and the table on which you want to create the index. The default database is the database you selected when you started the wizard. A default table within the database is also listed.

5. Click Next to proceed to the Current Index Information screen, shown in Figure 17-11. This example uses the *Customers* table because it contains a large number of rows. As you can see, quite a few indexes have already been created on the *Customers* table, including one clustered index and four nonclustered indexes. Remember, you can create only one clustered index on a table, thus transforming it into a clustered table.

All of the indexes that have been created on the *Customers* table are simple indexes (there is only one column listed), and each has been created on a different column. When the query optimizer analyzes a query to choose the query execution plan, it will decide which index to use based on the available indexes and on the predicate in the WHERE clause.

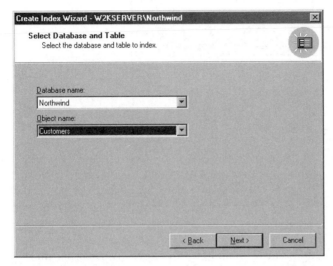

Figure 17-10. *The Select Database And Table screen.*

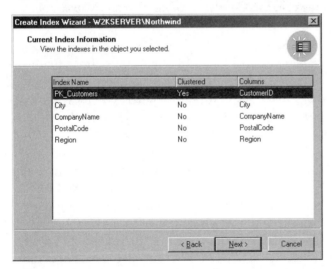

Figure 17-11. *The Current Index Information screen.*

6. Click Next to display the Select Columns screen, shown in Figure 17-12. This screen enables you to choose which columns to include in the index. Don't worry about the order of the columns at this point—you'll be able to change that later.

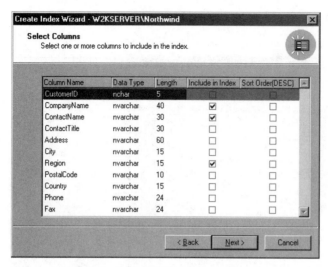

Figure 17-12. *The Select Columns screen.*

7. Specify the columns you want to include in the index by selecting the check boxes to the right of the column names. In this example, we will create a composite index on the *CompanyName*, *ContactName*, and *Region* columns.

8. Click Next to display the Specify Index Options screen, shown in Figure 17-13. This screen enables you to set several important options that determine how the index is created. You can select the Make This A Clustered Index check box to make the new index a clustered index. In this example, the check box used to create a clustered index is shown in the disabled state because a clustered index has already been created on the *Customers* table.

   You can select the Make This A Unique Index option to specify that the index will be a unique index rather than a nonunique index. You can also specify the fill factor: optimal or fixed. Because rows in an index are stored in sorted order, SQL Server might have to move data to maintain this order. The fill factor option enables you to specify how full the newly created index should be in order to leave space for future inserts. The default fill factor (what you get if you click Optimal) is *0*, which specifies full leaf nodes but free space in the upper index nodes. For a more detailed explanation of fill factor, see the section "Using Fill Factor to Avoid Page Splits" later in this chapter.

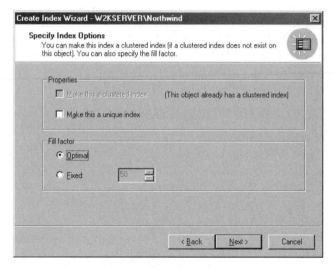

Figure 17-13. *The Specify Index Options screen.*

9. Select your index options and then click Next to display the Completing The Create Index Wizard screen, shown in Figure 17-14. In this screen, you can reorder the columns that make up the index. Select the column you want to move, and click Move Up or Move Down until the column reaches the desired location. You can also assign the index a name in this screen.

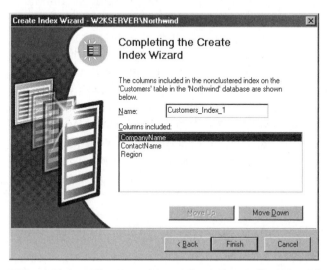

Figure 17-14. *The Completing The Create Index Wizard screen.*

The order of a composite index is important. An SQL statement can take advantage of an index only if the leading portion of the index is in the WHERE clause of the statement. Figure 17-15 shows the same screen with the index renamed to *CustomerAreaIndex* and the columns reordered as *Region*, *CompanyName*, and *ContactName*.

Figure 17-15. *Reordering the index columns.*

With the index columns in this order, an SQL statement must contain *Region* in its WHERE clause in order for the index to be used, because *Region* is the leading column. Of course, the statement could have *Region* and *CompanyName*, or even *Region*, *CompanyName*, and *ContactName* in the WHERE clause. If you can use all three values in the WHERE clause, you will achieve the best performance because you will be performing the fewest I/O operations. It does not matter in what order the column names appear in the WHERE clause.

10. Once you are satisfied with the column ordering, click Finish and the index will be created. This process can take anywhere from a few seconds to several hours, depending on the amount of data, the performance of the system, the performance of the disk drives, and the amount of memory in the system. To create an index on a table, SQL Server must read all of the data in the table, so the time it takes is quite variable.

Caution If you are creating a unique index and duplicate values are found in the index key, the index creation process will fail.

Creating an index by using the Create Index Wizard is easy, but the process has some disadvantages. In particular, because the Create Index Wizard does not maintain information about the tasks you perform while using it, you must go through the process outlined in this section every time you want to create another index. If you create an index by using a script file, you can use the file over and over again. Also, if you want to re-create the database, you must go through the Create Index Wizard all over again for each index in the database. Remember though, after indexes are created, you can generate SQL scripts for them by using Enterprise Manager.

Using Transact-SQL

By using Transact-SQL (T-SQL) to create an index, you can script the command and run it over and over again. You can also modify the index creation script to create other indexes. In addition, this method of creating an index offers you more flexibility because more parameters are available to you. To use this technique to create an index, simply put the T-SQL commands in a file and read the file into OSQL by using the following syntax:

```
Osql -Uusername -Ppassword < create_index.sql
```

This command assumes that the file you created is named create_index.sql. You could also execute the script by using Query Analyzer. (See Chapter 13 for more information about this process.)

To create an index by using T-SQL, you must use the CREATE INDEX command. The syntax for using CREATE INDEX is shown here:

```
CREATE [UNIQUE] [CLUSTERED | NONCLUSTERED]
INDEX index_name ON table_name
(
column_name [, column_name, column_name, … ]
)
[ WITH options ]
[ ON filegroup_name ]
```

The values within the brackets are optional. You can create the index as unique or nonunique, as clustered or nonclustered, with one or more columns, and with the optional parameters listed in Table 17-1. You can also optionally specify a filegroup in which to place the index.

Table 17-1. Optional parameters for use with **CREATE INDEX**

Parameter	Description
PAD_INDEX	When used in conjunction with the *FILL_FACTOR* parameter, indicates that space should be left in the branch nodes, rather than just in the leaf nodes.
FILL_FACTOR ? number	Specifies how full to make each leaf node; a percentage ranging from 0 through 100.
IGNORE_DUP_KEY	Specifies that an insert into a unique index with a duplicate value will be ignored and a warning message will be issued. If *IGNORE_DUP_KEY* is not specified, the entire insert will be rolled back.
DROP_EXISTING	Specifies that the existing index of the same name should be dropped and the index re-created. This parameter enhances performance when you re-create a clustered index on a table that has nonclustered indexes because separate steps are not required to drop and re-create the nonclustered indexes.
STATISTICS_NORECOMPUTE	Specifies that statistics data should not be recomputed. This option is not recommended because if execution plans are based on old data, they probably will be less than optimal. Use this parameter only if you plan on updating statistics manually.

 More Info For further information regarding these optional parameters, go to the Books Online index, look up "CREATE INDEX," and then choose "CREATE INDEX (T-SQL)" from the Topics Found dialog box.

Using T-SQL scripts is preferable to using the Create Index Wizard. Although T-SQL is initially more difficult to use, in the long run, you'll find that it is much easier to create multiple indexes by using T-SQL.

Using Fill Factor to Avoid Page Splits

When updates or inserts are made to a table that has indexes, the index pages must also be updated. Index pages are chained together by pointers from one page to another. There are two pointers, one to the next page and one to the previous page. When an index page is full, an update to the index will cause a change in the pointer chain because a new index page must be inserted between two pages (in a process known as an *index page split*) so that the new information can be put into the right spot in the index chain. SQL Server moves approximately half of the rows in the existing page (where the new data needs to go) to this new index page. The two pages that originally pointed to each other now point to the new page, and the new page points to both of them (forward and back). Now the new index page is pointed to in the right order in the chain, but the index pages are no longer physically in order in the database. (See Figure 17-16.) Eventually, because new index rows are constantly being added to the index (assuming that updates or inserts are occurring) and the index page size is finite, more and more index pages will fill up. When that happens, additional space for new index pages must be found. To create more space, SQL Server continues to perform index page splits, which result in increased system overhead because of additional CPU usage and additional I/O operations. This also causes a fragmented index. The index data is scattered around in the database, causing slower performance.

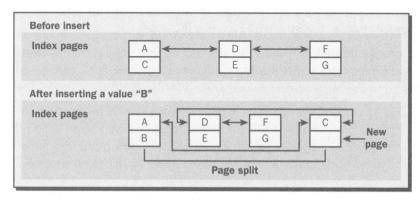

Figure 17-16. *An index page split.*

One way to reduce page splitting and fragmentation is by tuning the fill factor of the index nodes. The *fill factor* specifies the percentage of the node to be filled when you are creating the index, enabling you to leave room for additional index rows. You can specify the fill factor for an index by using the FILL_FACTOR option of the CREATE INDEX T-SQL statement, as described earlier. If a fill factor is not specified in the CREATE INDEX command, the system default will be used. The default is set to whatever value the *sp_configure* parameter *fill factor* is set to. This value was set to *0* when you installed SQL Server.

Note   The *fill factor* parameter affects only how an index is created; changing it has no effect after an index has been built.

The value of the fill factor ranges from *0* through *100*, indicating the percentage of the index page that is filled. A value of *0* is a special case. When *0* is specified, the leaf nodes are completely filled, but the branch nodes and the root node retain some free space. This value is the SQL Server installation default and usually works well.

A fill factor value of *100* specifies that all index nodes be completely filled when the index is created. This value is optimal for indexes on tables that never have new data inserted into them and are not updated. Both the leaf index nodes and the upper level nodes will be completely packed, and any insert will cause a page split. Read-only tables are ideal for this setting, although deleting data would be OK as it does not cause page splits.

A low fill factor value will leave a lot of space for inserts but requires a lot of extra space to create the index. Unless you will be doing constant inserts into the database, a low value for the fill factor is usually discouraged. If too many page splits are occurring, try reducing the value for the fill factor and rebuilding the index to see whether this lowers the number of page splits.

You can find out the number of page splits per second that your system is experiencing by using the Performance Monitor counter Page Splits/Sec. This counter can be found in the *SQL Server: Access Methods* object.

If, over time, page splits do occur and your indexes become heavily fragmented, the solution is to rebuild your indexes. Fragmentation can happen even if you use a fill factor that leaves space in the index pages. Eventually, that space can fill up too. See the section "Rebuilding Indexes" later in this chapter for more information.

Using the Full-Text Indexing Wizard

To use the Full-Text Indexing Wizard to create a full-text index, follow these steps. (The next section will show you how to take advantage of full-text indexes.)

1. In Enterprise Manager, select the table on which you want to create a full-text index. This example uses the *Customers* table of the Northwind database.

2. Click Wizards on the Tools menu. Alternatively, you can expand the database, and click the Wizards tab. The Select Wizard dialog box appears.

3. Expand the Database folder in the Select Wizard dialog box. Select Full-Text Indexing Wizard and click OK. Or, if you used the Wizards tab in the previous step, click Full Text Index. The welcome screen of the Full-Text Indexing Wizard appears, as shown in Figure 17-17.

4. Click Next to go to the Select A Database screen. We'll choose Northwind for our example. (Note: This screen will not appear if you used the Wizards tab, because the database is already selected.)

Figure 17-17. *The Full-Text Indexing Wizard welcome screen.*

5. Click Next to display the Select A Table screen, shown in Figure 17-18. We'll select the *Customers* table. Click Next.

6. The Select An Index dialog box appears. The wizard requires you to select an existing unique index to use in conjunction with the full-text operations. Only one unique index, *PK_Customers*, is available for the *Customers* table.

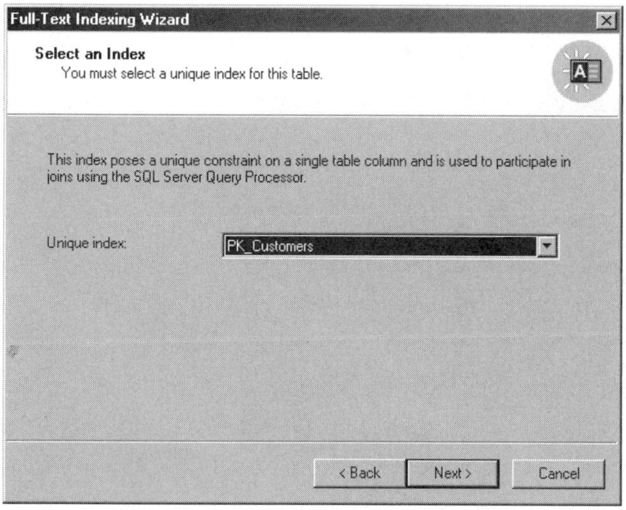

Figure 17-18. *The Select A Table screen.*

7. Click Next to display the Select Table Columns screen. Here you will choose the columns that are eligible for full-text queries. Figure 17-19 shows this screen with a few columns selected.

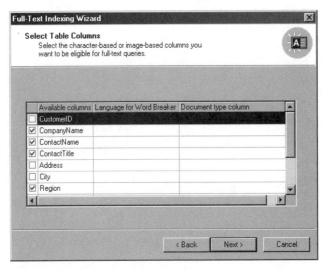

Figure 17-19. *The Select Table Columns screen, with several columns selected.*

8. Click Next to display the Select A Catalog screen, shown in Figure 17-20. This screen lets you choose between using an existing catalog (if there is one) and creating a new catalog. If you are creating a new catalog, be sure to place the catalog where the I/O system can support it and to type a descriptive name in the Name text box.

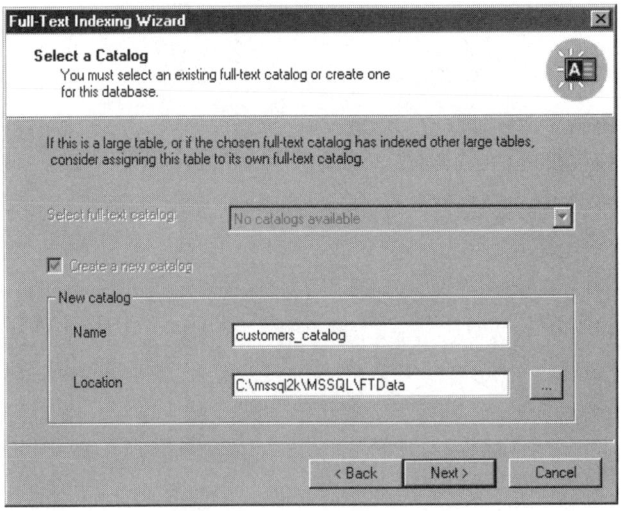

Figure 17-20. *The Select A Catalog screen.*

9. Click Next to display the Select Or Create Population Schedules screen, shown in Figure 17-21. Unlike a B-tree index, the full-text index is not continually updated when data is inserted. The scheduling feature allows you to specify the interval at which updates to the index occur. Here you can choose an existing schedule (if there is one), create a new schedule to populate the index on a table basis or per catalog (a catalog can contain many tables that are enabled for full-text indexing), or choose no schedule at all. If you create a schedule, you can choose full population or incremental population. Full population means that all rows for the table (or for the tables in a catalog) will have index entries created for them (or re-created if they already exist). Full population usually occurs only when a catalog is created. Incremental population means that only the modified rows of data in the table will have their index entries updated. The table must have a *timestamp* column in order for incremental population to work. If not, full population will occur.

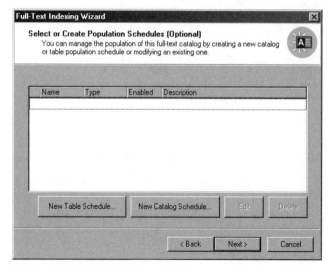

Figure 17-21. *The Select Or Create Population Schedules screen.*

From here, you can click Next to continue or choose to create a schedule. If you click Next without creating a population schedule, the full-text index will be created once only, at the completion of the wizard (rather than being re-created on a periodic basis).

Note   Because the full-text index is not constantly updated with changes to the underlying database, it might be necessary to update it periodically. The scheduling feature allows you to schedule automatic updates to the full-text index. Once this schedule has been created, the index will be updated according to the schedule.

10. Click Next to display the Completing The SQL Server Full-Text Indexing Wizard screen, shown in Figure 17-22. Click Finish, and the Full-Text Indexing Wizard creates the full-text indexing catalog for you. If you have established an update schedule, the schedule will be implemented also. Once the catalog has been created, it is available for use.

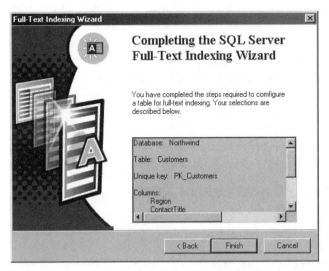

Figure 17-22. *The Completing The SQL Server Full-Text Indexing Wizard screen.*

Creating Full-Text Indexes by Using Stored Procedures

You can also create full-text indexes by using stored procedures. A brief overview of the process of creating a full-text index by using stored procedures is presented here; for the complete syntax, consult SQL Server 2000 Books Online.

1. Call *sp_fulltext_database* with the *enable* parameter to enable full-text support in SQL Server.

2. Call *sp_fulltext_catalog* to create the catalog. This stored procedure must be called with the *create* parameter.

3. Call *sp_fulltext_table* to establish the connection between the catalog and a table/index pair. This stored procedure must be called with the *create* parameter, and you must provide both a table name and the name of the unique index that the full-text index will use.

4. Call *sp_fulltext_column* to add a column that will take part in the full-text index. This stored procedure must be run with the *add* option and the name of the column that will participate in the catalog, and the procedure must be run for each column in the index.

5. Call *sp_fulltext_table* again. This stored procedure must be passed the *activate* parameter in order to activate the catalog with this table.

6. Call *sp_fulltext_catalog* again, this time passing it the *start_full* parameter to start the full population of the catalog, for every row of every table associated with the catalog.

Creating a full-text index by using stored procedures is more complicated than using T-SQL commands to create a B-tree index. However, if you're creating a number of full-text index catalogs, it might be worth the trouble to create a script file to perform this task.

Using the Full-Text Index

Once the full-text index has been created, it's easy to take advantage of it. You can specify T-SQL keywords that take advantage of the full-text indexes: CONTAINS and FREETEXT. The following statement shows how typical string recognition in SQL would be performed if you didn't use a full-text index. As you can see, the LIKE keyword is used in the WHERE clause of the query:

```
SELECT * FROM Customers WHERE ContactName
    LIKE '%PETE%'
```

This statement might not produce the desired result. To use a more user-friendly query and to take advantage of the full-text index, you can use the CONTAINS predicate. The CONTAINS predicate must contain the column name and the desired text, as follows:

```
SELECT * FROM Customers WHERE
    CONTAINS(ContactName, ' "PETE" ')
```

The CONTAINS predicate can find text strings that contain the desired string, such as "PETER" or "PETEY," by using the full-text index.

You can also search full-text indexes by using the FREETEXT keyword. Like CONTAINS, FREETEXT is used in the WHERE clause. FREETEXT can be used to find a word (or related words) whose meaning matches the meaning of a word (or a set of words) given in the FREETEXT call but whose form does not exactly match that of the specified word. This can be done in an SQL statement such as the following:

```
SELECT CategoryName FROM Categories WHERE
    FREETEXT(Description, 'Sweets candy bread')
```

This query might find category names containing such words as "sweetened," "candied," or "breads."

Rebuilding Indexes

SQL Server keeps statistics on each index, which describe its uniqueness, or selectivity, and the distribution of the index key values. The SQL server query optimizer then uses these statistics to determine which index to use, if any, to best satisfy a particular query. Index statistics are periodically updated by default. However, indexes sometimes become fragmented over a long period of time because of page splits, which physically scatter index pages in the database. As a result, performance worsens. An index can also become off balance, meaning that one portion of the tree has more full index pages than another portion of the tree. You can restore balance and continuity by rebuilding the index. Also, index statistics are re-created when the index is rebuilt. But do not drop and re-create an index. Please read on!

Note By default, index statistics are updated, but you can turn this feature on or off by using the stored procedure *sp_autostats*.

Another problem with indexes that have become fragmented occurs when an index has more levels than are necessary. More index levels means more I/O operations per index lookup. By rebuilding an index, you can reduce the number of levels and thus lower the number of I/O operations required for all index lookups.

One method for rebuilding an index involves removing the index by hand and then building the index again. For a small table, this option might be acceptable. But for medium-size to large-size tables, do not use this method. It is best to use the options described in this section for rebuilding an index, which do not involve dropping and creating the index again. Here are some reasons why this is true. When nonclustered indexes are created on a clustered table, the nonclustered indexes are based on the cluster keys. When the clustered index is dropped, the nonclustered indexes must be re-created because there is no longer a clustered index on the table. If the clustered index is then created again on the table, the nonclustered indexes must also be re-created a second time! Again, if you drop and then re-create the clustered index, you must re-create the nonclustered indexes twice: when the clustered index is dropped and when it is re-created. If you use the other methods to rebuild the clustered index, the nonclustered indexes will be re-created only once.

The two methods for rebuilding an index, without dropping and re-creating it, are using CREATE INDEX...DROP_EXISTING and using DBCC DBREINDEX. Both of these options will rebuild an index in a single step, and SQL Server knows to reorganize an existing index. Using these methods enable you to avoid the dropping and re-creating of nonclustered indexes when you rebuild a clustered index. These one-step methods also take advantage of the sorted order of the data currently in the index; this data will not have to be sorted again.

CREATE INDEX...DROP_EXISTING is used to rebuild only one index at a time on a table. DBCC DBREINDEX is used with a database name and a table name to rebuild all of the indexes on that table, without having to execute separate commands for each index. See Books Online for the syntax and options for these two commands.

Updating Index Statistics

If you don't have the time or resources to re-create indexes, you can update the index statistics independently. This technique is not nearly as efficient as rebuilding an index because the index might be fragmented, which might be more of a problem than outdated statistics. And this is assuming that you have turned off automatic statistic updates in SQL Server. (Otherwise, your statistics are being updated periodically anyway.) You can update index statistics manually by using the UPDATE STATISTICS command. The syntax is shown here:

```
UPDATE STATISTICS table_name
[ index_name | (statistics_name [, statistics_name, ...] ]
[ WITH
[ FULLSCAN | SAMPLE number {PERCENT | ROWS} ]
[ ALL | COLUMNS | INDEX ]
[ NORECOMPUTE]
]
```

The values enclosed in brackets are optional. The only required parameter is *table_name*. The optional parameters are described in Table 17-2.

If your system experiences a large number of inserts, updates, and deletes, you should rebuild the indexes occasionally to avoid the performance degradation mentioned earlier. If you cannot rebuild the indexes, you should at least update the statistics periodically.

Table 17-2.   Optional parameters for use with the UPDATE STATISTICS command

Parameter	Description
index_name	Specifies the index to recompute statistics on. By default, statistics for all of the indexes in the table are recomputed. If *index_name* is specified, only that index's statistics are recomputed.
statistics_name	Allows you to specify which statistics to recompute. If this value is not specified, all of the statistics are recomputed.
FULLSCAN	Specifies that all rows in the table be read for statistics gathering. Using this parameter is by far the best way to gather statistics, but it is also the most costly in terms of system resources and time.
*SAMPLE number PERCENT	ROWS*	Specifies either the number or the percentage of rows on which the statistics are based. By default, SQL Server determines the number of rows to sample. This option cannot be used with the *FULLSCAN* option.
*ALL	COLUMN	INDEX*	Specifies whether all statistics, column statistics, or just index statistics are gathered.
NORECOMPUTE	Specifies that statistics are not automatically recomputed in the future. To reestablish automatic statistics recomputation, run the command again without the *NORECOMPUTE* option, or run the *sp_autostats* stored procedure.

Using Indexes

Now that you know how to create indexes, let's look at how indexes are used. The fact that an index exists does not necessarily mean SQL Sever will use it. Whether SQL Server uses an index depends on the index and the SQL statement. In addition, if multiple indexes exist, SQL Server might have a choice of indexes that could be used. In this section, you'll see how SQL Server chooses indexes, and you'll learn how to use hints in order to specify which index to use. You'll also see how to use Query Analyzer to view a query execution plan.

Using Hints

When the SQL Server query optimizer generates a query execution plan, it chooses an index based on which index will provide the best performance—usually the index that will use the fewest I/O operations and retrieve the least number of rows.

Although the query optimizer usually chooses the most efficient query execution plan and access path for your query, you might be able to do better if you know more about your data than the query optimizer does. For example, suppose you want to retrieve data about a person named "Smith" from a table with a column listing last names. Index statistics generalize based on a column. Suppose the statistics show that each last name appears three times on average in the column. This information provides fairly good selectivity; however, you know that the name "Smith" appears much more often than average. If you have an idea about how to better conduct an SQL operation, you can use a hint. A *hint* is simply advice you give to the query optimizer specifying that it should not make the automatic choice.

Several types of hints are available—including join hints, query hints, and table hints—but here we are most interested in table hints. Table hints let you specify how the table is accessed. (Other types of hints are described in Chapter 35.) A table hint can be used to specify the following information:

- **Table scan**   In some cases, you might decide that a table scan would be more efficient than an index lookup or an index scan. A table scan is more efficient when the index scan will retrieve more than 20 percent of the rows in the table—such as when 70 percent of the data is highly selectable and the other 30 percent is "Smith."

- **Which index to use**   You can specify a particular index to be the only index considered. You might not know which index the SQL Server query optimizer would choose without your hint, but you feel the hinted index will perform best.

- **Which group of indexes to select from**   You can suggest several indexes to the query optimizer, and it will use all of them (ignoring duplicates). This option is useful when you know that a set of indexes will work well.

- **Locking method** You can tell the query optimizer which type of lock to use when it is accessing the data from a particular table. If you feel that the wrong type of lock might be chosen for this table, you can specify that the query optimizer should use a row lock, a page lock, or a table lock.

Let's look specifically at a hint that specifies which index to use—an index hint. The following example illustrates an index hint in a T-SQL statement (to use the *Region* index for this query):

```
SELECT *
FROM Customers WITH (INDEX(Region))
WHERE region = 'OR' AND city = 'Portland'
```

Note that the index hint is preceded by the keyword WITH. If you want to specify multiple indexes for SQL Server to use, list them in a T-SQL statement like this:

```
SELECT *
FROM customers WITH (INDEX(Region, City, CompanyName))
WHERE region = 'OR' AND city = 'Portland'
```

An index hint parameter can be either an index name, as you have seen, or an index ID. There are also some special cases for hints, shown in the following table.

Hint	Result
INDEX(0) on a clustered table (clustered index exists on the table)	Forces a clustered index scan
INDEX(1) on a clustered table	Forces a clustered index scan or seek
INDEX(0) on a nonclustered table (no clustered index on the table)	Forces a table scan
INDEX(1) on a nonclustered table	Interpreted as an error

You can view the result of using a hint by executing your queries using SQL Server Query Analyzer.

Using Query Analyzer

In Chapter 13, you learned that Query Analyzer is a useful tool included with SQL Server 2000. We're going to look at this tool again to see how it can show us which index was used in a query execution plan. Query Analyzer can also be used for any of the following tasks:

- **Performing SQL queries** You can execute SQL statements and view the results with an easy-to-use GUI.

- **Parsing queries** By parsing an SQL statement without executing it, you can find and correct any errors.
- **Displaying an estimated execution plan** By displaying the execution plan, you can see how variations of the query affect the execution cost. This can be valuable in optimizing SQL statements by allowing you to rewrite your SQL statement and to see whether the cost changes.
- **Performing index analysis** An index analysis will tell you whether using an index will decrease the cost of a query's execution.

To experiment with using Query Analyzer, load the following T-SQL statement into Query Analyzer:

```
SELECT *
FROM customers
WHERE region = 'OR' AND city = 'Portland'
```

Now examine the Estimated Execution Plan after choosing Display Estimated Execution Plan from the Query menu. You can see in Figure 17-23 that the index *City* is used.

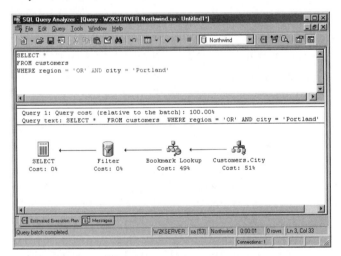

Figure 17-23. *The Estimated Execution Plan without a hint using the* City *index.*

Now let's add a hint that instructs SQL Server to use the *Region* index. The query now looks like this:

```
SELECT *
FROM customers WITH (INDEX(Region))
WHERE region = 'OR' AND city = 'Portland'
```

The Estimated Execution Plan for this query is shown in Figure 17-24. Notice that the *Region* index is now used.

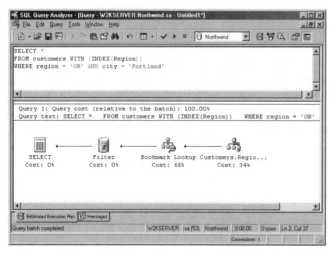

Figure 17-24. *The Estimated Execution Plan with the hint to use the* Region *index.*

SQL Query Analyzer is quite useful and convenient for running SQL statements, not only by providing a GUI, but also by allowing you to parse and analyze the SQL statements. For operations that can be performed using scripting, you can save your work in Query Analyzer to a file by choosing Save As from the File menu.

Designing Effective Indexes

The effectiveness—defined as the maximum efficiency and performance—of an index is determined by the design of the index and of the SQL statements that take advantage of it. It's not enough to just create indexes; you must also tailor the SQL statements to indexes' strengths. An index is used only when one or more of the index keys are included in the WHERE clause of the SQL statement. In this section, you'll learn the properties of a good index, as well as the best and worst times to create indexes.

Characteristics of an Effective Index

As we've seen, a good index helps you to retrieve your data by using fewer I/O operations and system resources than a table scan. Because an index scan requires traversing the tree to find an individual value, using an index is not efficient when you are retrieving large amounts of data.

Note   If a query accesses more than 20 percent of the rows in a table, a table scan is more efficient than using an index.

An effective index retrieves only a few rows—in fact, most queries end up using only a few rows anyway. To perform effectively, an index should be designed with good selectivity. The *selectivity* of an index is based on the number of rows per index key value. An index with poor selectivity has multiple rows per index key value; an index with good selectivity has a few rows or one row per index key value. A unique index has the highest selectivity. The selectivity of the index is stored within the index distribution statistics. You can view the selectivity of an index by using the command DBCC SHOW_STATISTICS. An index with good selectivity is more likely to be used by Query Optimizer.

You can enhance the selectivity of an index by using multiple columns to create a composite index. Several columns with poor selectivity can be joined in a composite index to form one index that has good selectivity. Although a unique index provides the best selectivity, be sure to choose an index type that fits your data model. For example, if you have several entries for the last name "Smith" in a *Customers* table, you won't be able to create a unique index on last names, but you might still find such an index useful.

When to Use Indexes

Indexes are best suited for tasks such as the following:

- **Queries that specify a narrow search criteria**   These queries should retrieve only a few rows that match the specific criteria.

- **Queries that specify a range of values**   These queries should also retrieve a small number of rows.

- **Searches that are used in a join**   Columns that are often used as join keys are good candidates for indexes.

- **Searches that retrieve data in a specific order**   If the resulting data set is to be sorted in the order of a clustered index, the sort is not necessary, because the resulting data is returned presorted. For example, if the clustered index is on the *lastname, firstname* columns and the application requires sorting by last name and then first name, it is not necessary to add the ORDER BY qualifiers.

Indexes should be used cautiously and sparingly on tables that have a large number of insert, update, and delete operations performed on them because each operation that changes the data must update the index pages as well.

Index Guidelines

You should follow a number of index guidelines to increase both the efficiency and the performance of the system:

- **Use indexes in moderation.**   A few indexes can be quite useful, but too many indexes can adversely affect the performance of the system. Because the indexes must be maintained, every time an insert, update, or delete operation is performed on the table, the index must be updated. If there are very many of these operations, the overhead of maintaining the index can be quite high.

- **Don't index small tables.**   It is sometimes much more efficient to perform table scans if the table is small (say, a few hundred rows). The additional overhead of the index is not worth the benefit.

- **Use as few index key columns as necessary to achieve good selectivity.** The fewer columns, the better, but not at the expense of selectivity. An index with a few columns is called a *narrow index,* and an index with many key columns is called a *wide index*. Narrow indexes take up less space and require less maintenance overhead than do wide indexes.

- **Use covering queries whenever possible.**   A *covering query* is one in which all of the desired data is held in the index keys—that is, all of the index keys are also the selected columns. With a covering query, only the index is accessed; the table itself is bypassed. A *covering index* is an index in which all of the table columns are included. For example, if the index is on columns *a* and *b* and *c* and the SELECT statement is requesting data from only those columns, only the index needs to be accessed.

Summary

Using indexes can be a great way to improve database performance. In this chapter, you have learned about SQL Server indexes, including index terminology and concepts, the index creation process, and the ways in which indexes are used. You've learned about clustered and nonclustered indexes, unique and nonunique indexes, and full-text indexes. We examined page splitting and fill factor concepts, rebuilding indexes, and updating index statistics. In Chapter 18, you'll learn how to create and use views, another type of auxiliary structure used to create a subset or superset of a table.

Chapter 18
Creating and Using Views

In Chapter 17, you learned about indexes, auxiliary structures that exist separately from the database data but that relate to accessing the data. In other words, an index is an independent structure, but it is integrally tied to the data. In this chapter, we'll look at another auxiliary database structure: views. A view, like an index, exists independently of the data but is closely tied to that data. A view is used to filter, or process, data before users access it. In this chapter, you'll learn more about what a view is, how views are related to data, and why and when views are used, and you'll learn how to create and manage views. In addition, we will examine some view enhancements in Microsoft SQL Server 2000.

What Is a View?

A *view* is a virtual table that is defined by a query consisting of a SELECT statement. This virtual table is made up of data from one or more real tables, and to users, a view looks like an actual table. In fact, a view can be treated exactly like a regular table. Users can reference these virtual tables in Transact-SQL (T-SQL) statements in the same way tables are referenced. SELECT, INSERT, UPDATE, and DELETE operations can be performed on a view.

In reality, a view is stored simply as a predefined SQL statement. When the view is accessed, the SQL Server query optimizer merges the currently executing SQL statement with the query that was used to define the view.

The advantage of using views is that views with different attributes can be created without having to duplicate the data. Views are useful in a number of situations. As we will see later in this chapter, they can be used for data security, for ease of presentation of data, and for logical presentation of data. They can also be used to merge partitioned data.

View Concepts

Now that you have a basic understanding of what views are, let's look at them more closely. In this section, you'll learn about the types of views, the advantages of using views, and the restrictions SQL Server places on the use of a view.

Types of Views

Several types of views can be created, each of which has its advantages in certain situations. Which type of view you create is entirely dependent on what you want to use the view for. You can create views in any of the following forms:

- **Subset of table columns**   A view can consist of one or more columns in a table. Probably the most common type of view, it can be used for data simplification or security.

- **Subset of table rows**   A view can contain as few or as many rows as desired. This type of view is also useful for security.

- **Join of two or more tables**   You can create a view by using a join operation. Complex join operations can be simplified when a view is used.

- **Aggregate information**   You can create a view that contains aggregated data. This type of view is also used to simplify complex operations.

Examples of how to use these types of views are presented in the section "Using T-SQL to Create a View" later in this chapter.

Views can also be used to consolidate partitioned data. Data in a large table can be partitioned across multiple smaller tables for easier management, and then views can be used to merge these tables into a larger virtual table for easier accessibility.

Advantages of Views

One advantage of using views is that they always provide up-to-date data. The SELECT statement that defines a view is executed only when the view is accessed, so all changes to the underlying table are reflected in the view.

Another advantage of using views is that a view can have a different security level than that of the underlying table. The query that defines the view is run under the security level of the user who created the view. Thus, you can use a view to mask off data that you do not want certain classes of users to see. We'll look at an example of this feature in the section "Subset of Columns" later in this chapter.

View Restrictions

SQL Server places a few restrictions on view creation and use. These restrictions include the following:

- **Column limitation**   A view can reference up to 1024 columns in a table. If you need to reference more columns than this, you'll have to use some other method.

- **Database limitation**   A view can be created on a table only in the database the view creator is accessing.

- **Security limitation**   The creator of the view must have access to all of the columns referenced in the view.

- **Data integrity rules**   Any updates, modifications, and so on to the view cannot violate data integrity rules. For example, if a view's underlying table does not allow null values, the view does not allow them either.

- **Nested-view levels limitation**   Views can be built on other views—in other words, you can create a view that accesses other views. Views can be nested to 32 levels.

- **SELECT statement limitation**   A view's SELECT statement cannot contain an ORDER BY, a COMPUTE or COMPUTE BY statement, or the INTO keyword.

Note   For more information regarding view restrictions, go to the Books Online Index and look up "Creating a View" and then choose "Creating a View" from the Topics Found dialog box.

Creating Views

Views, like indexes, can be created in a number of ways. You can create a view by using the CREATE VIEW T-SQL statement. This method is preferable if there is any chance that you will be creating more views in the future, because you can put the T-SQL statements in a script file and then edit and use the file over and over again. SQL Server Enterprise Manager provides a graphical environment in which you can create a view. Finally you can use the Create View Wizard when you need to be walked through the view creation process, which can be useful for the novice and expert alike.

Using T-SQL to Create a View

Creating views by using T-SQL is a straightforward process: you run CREATE VIEW to create a view, using ISQL, OSQL, or SQL Server Query Analyzer. As mentioned, using T-SQL commands in a script is preferable because the commands can be modified and reused. (You should also store your database definitions in scripts in case you need to re-create your database.)

The CREATE VIEW command has the following syntax:

```
CREATE VIEW view_name [(column, column, ...)]
[WITH ENCRYPTION]
AS
your SELECT statement
[WITH CHECK OPTION]
```

When you create a view, you can activate two options that change the view's behavior. You activate these options by including the optional keywords WITH ENCRYPTION or WITH CHECK OPTION or both in the T-SQL statement. Let's look at these options more closely.

The WITH ENCRYPTION keyword specifies that the view definition (the SELECT statement that defines the view) be encrypted. SQL Server uses the same encryption method to encrypt SQL statements that is used for passwords. This security technique can be useful if you don't want certain classes of users to know which tables are being accessed.

The WITH CHECK OPTION keyword specifies that data modification operations performed on a view must adhere to the criteria contained within the SELECT statement that defined the view. For example, a data modification operation performed on a view to create a table row that is not visible within the view would not be allowed. Suppose a view is defined to select information about all finance department employees. If WITH CHECK OPTION is not included, you can modify the *department* column value from *finance* to a value indicating another department. If this keyword is specified, this modification would not be allowed because changing a row's *department* value would make this row no longer accessible from the view. The WITH CHECK OPTION keyword specifies that you cannot make a row inaccessible from the view by making a change within the view.

The SELECT statement can be modified to create whatever view you want. It can be used to select a subset of columns or a subset of rows, or it can be used to perform a join operation. In the following sections, you'll learn how to use T-SQL to create the various types of views.

Subset of Columns

A view consisting of a subset of columns can be useful when you need to provide security for a table that should be only partially accessible to users. Let's look at an example. Suppose a corporate employee database consists of a table named *Employee* that contains the data columns shown in Figure 18-1.

Employee					
name	dept	phone	office	manager_id	salary

Figure 18-1. *The* Employee *table.*

Most of this data is sensitive and should be viewed by only certain employees. It would be useful, however, to allow all employees to view some of the data. Creating a view that gives all employees access to only certain data will address this issue. The view could also be used to avoid duplicating employee data in other database tables.

To create a view on the *Employee* table that can access only the *name*, *phone*, and *office* columns, use the following T-SQL statement:

```
CREATE VIEW emp_vw
AS
   SELECT  name,
           phone,
           office
   FROM    Employee
```

The resulting view will contain the columns shown in Figure 18-2. Although these columns also exist in the underlying table, users who access the data through this view can see the columns only in the view. Because the view can have a different security level than that of the underlying table, the view can allow access to anyone while the underlying table remains secure. In other words, you can restrict access to the *Employee* table to only the human resources department, for example, while allowing all employees to use the view.

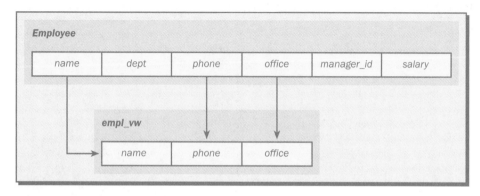

Figure 18-2. *The* emp_vw *view.*

Subset of Rows

A view that consists of a subset of rows can be used to restrict access by restricting the rows that are available to users. Suppose our *Employee* table was populated with data, as shown in Figure 18-3. In this example, instead of restricting the columns, we will restrict the rows by specifying them in a WHERE clause, as shown here:

```
CREATE VIEW emp_vw2
AS
  SELECT  *
  FROM    Employee
  WHERE   Dept = 1
```

Employee					
name	dept	phone	office	manager_id	salary
Dick Bridgforth	1	232-7115	3	10	35000
Mary Weeks	2	232-7116	1	12	40000
Jack Reding	1	244-8171	6	17	55000
Patti Campbell	3	325-1746	4	14	20000
Karen Reding	2	232-7114	8	10	48000
Jackson Reding	1	232-7219	7	17	60000
Sharon Reding	2	325-7394	3	18	50000

Figure 18-3. *The* Employee *table with data.*

The resulting view will contain only the rows that list an employee who works in the human resources department, or department 1, as shown in Figure 18-4. This view would be useful when employees in the human resources department should have access to the records of employees in their area. A subset-of-rows view, like a subset-of-columns view, can be assigned a different security level than that of the underlying table or tables.

Employee

name	dept	phone	office	manager_id	salary
Dick Bridgforth	1	232-7115	3	10	35000
Mary Weeks	2	232-7116	1	12	40000
Jack Reding	1	244-8171	6	17	55000
Patti Campbell	3	325-1746	4	14	20000
Karen Reding	2	232-7114	8	10	48000
Jackson Reding	1	232-7219	7	17	60000
Sharon Reding	2	325-7394	3	18	50000

emp_vw2

Dick Bridgforth	1	232-7115	3	10	35000
Jack Reding	1	244-8171	6	17	55000
Jackson Reding	1	232-7219	7	17	60000

Figure 18-4. *The emp_vw2 view.*

Joins

By defining joins in a view, you can simplify the T-SQL statements used to access data when the statements would contain a JOIN statement. Let's work through an example. Suppose we have two tables, *Manager* and *Employee2*, as shown in Figure 18-5.

Manager	
id	mname
10	Pat Bridgforth
12	Alex Reding
14	Steven Weeks
17	Ginger Shaw
18	Pam Horton

Employee2	
ename	manager_id
Mary Weeks	12
Dick Bridgforth	10
Patti Campbell	14
Karen Reding	10
Sharon Reding	18

Figure 18-5. *The* Manager *and* Employee2 *tables.*

The following statement joins the *Employee2* and *Manager* tables into a single virtual table:

```
CREATE VIEW org_chart
AS
   SELECT    Employee2.ename,
             Manager.mname
   FROM      Employee2, Manager
   WHERE     Employee2.manager_id = Manager.id
   GROUP BY Manager.mname, Employee2.ename
```

In this example, the two tables are joined on the *manager_id* value. The resulting data, contained in the view *org_chart*, is grouped by manager name, as shown in Figure 18-6. Notice that if a manager is listed in the *Manager* table but no employees listed in the *Employee2* table work for that manager, no entry for that manager appears in the view. There is also no entry in the view for an employee who is listed in the *Employee2* table but has no corresponding manager listed in the *Manager* table. To users, all that is visible is a virtual table listing employees and managers.

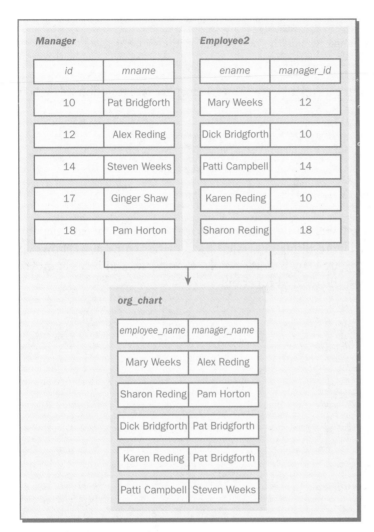

Figure 18-6. *The* org_chart *view.*

Aggregation

Aggregation views can be useful in many ways, such as for retrieving departmental averages and sums. For example, for budgeting purposes, you could use an aggregate view to view the amount of money each department in your corporation pays in salaries. You can also accomplish this task by using a T-SQL query. The advantage of using a view is that users can run it without knowing how to use aggregate functions and T-SQL queries.

> **Note**   The SQL Server aggregate functions perform calculations on a set of values and return a single value. The aggregate functions include AVG, COUNT, MAX, MIN, and SUM.

The following statement sets up a view that uses an aggregate function (SUM) on the *Employee* table:

```
CREATE VIEW sal_vw
AS
    SELECT    dept,
              SUM(salary)
    FROM      Employee
    GROUP BY dept
```

In this example, the view sets up a virtual table that shows the total each department pays in salaries. The resulting data is grouped by department, as shown in Figure 18-7. This aggregate view is quite simple. Your views can be as complex as necessary to perform the desired function.

sal_vw	
dept	SUM(salary)
1	150000
2	138000
3	20000

Figure 18-7. *The* sal_vw *view.*

Partitioning

Views are commonly used to merge partitioned data into a single virtual table. Partitioning is used to reduce the size of tables and indexes. To partition data, you create multiple tables to replace one table and assign each new table a range of values from the original table. For example, instead of having one large database table that stores data about your company's sales transactions, you can create many small tables that each hold one week's worth of data and then use a view to combine them to see the transaction history. The multiple small tables and their indexes are more manageable than one large database table and its index would be. Furthermore, you can easily drop older data by deleting an underlying table of obsolete data. Let's look at this concept in more detail.

The view shown in Figure 18-8 looks like one large table to users, but underneath are many tables, each with its own index. (In fact, a clustered date index would be appropriate here.)

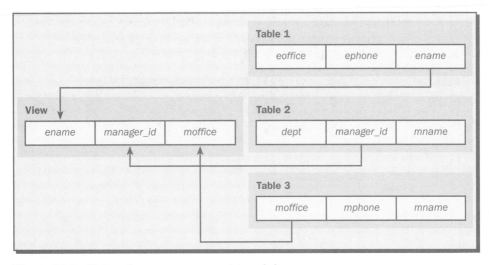

Figure 18-8. *Using views to merge partitioned data.*

As mentioned, partitioning creates a much more manageable system for the DBA, and merging partitioned data simplifies the data for users.

To create a view that consolidates partitioned data, or a partitioned view, you must first create the partition tables. These tables will most likely contain sales data. Each table will store data for a particular period, usually a week or a month. Once you create these tables, you can use a UNION ALL statement to create a view that contains all of the data. For example, suppose you have four tables, named *table_1*, *table_2*, *table_3*, and *table_4*. The following statement creates one large virtual table that includes all the data from these tables:

```
CREATE VIEW partview
AS
  SELECT * FROM table_1
  UNION ALL
  SELECT * FROM table_2
  UNION ALL
  SELECT * FROM table_3
  UNION ALL
  SELECT * FROM table_4
```

Now all of the data is available in one table, but it is still manageable. As new partitions are created and older ones are dropped, the view will need to be re-created.

Using Enterprise Manager to Create a View

In this section, we will use Enterprise Manager to create a view in the Northwind database. The following steps will guide you through this process:

1. In the Enterprise Manager window, expand the Databases folder for the server on which the sample database Northwind resides and click Northwind, as shown in Figure 18-9.

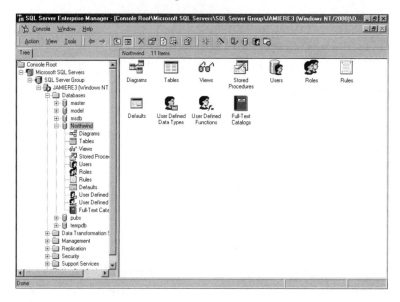

Figure 18-9. *Information about the Northwind database.*

2. Right-click Northwind in the left-hand pane. Point to New in the short-cut menu that appears, and then choose View. The New View window appears, as shown in Figure 18-10. You use this window to define the view name, the table columns used in the view, and the underlying table structure.

    The New View window consists of the following four panes:

    *   **Diagram pane**   Shows the table data that is used to create the view. Columns can be selected from within this pane.

    *   **Grid pane**   Shows the columns that have been selected from the table or tables that make up the view. Columns can be selected from within this pane.

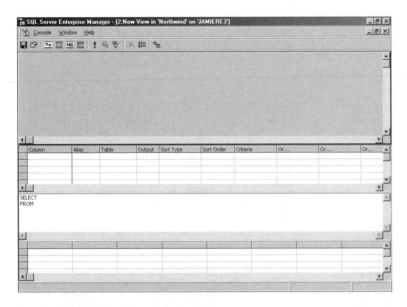

Figure 18-10. *The New View window.*

- **SQL pane** Shows the SQL statement that is used to define the view. SQL Server generates this SQL statement for you when you drag items in the Diagram pane and select columns in the Grid pane.

- **Results pane** Shows the rows that have been retrieved from the view. This information gives you an idea of what the data looks like.

You can specify which panes are visible by clicking the corresponding buttons on the New View window's toolbar. The other buttons on this toolbar provide some important options. The following list describes all the toolbar buttons, starting from the left side of the toolbar:

- **Save** Saves the view.

- **Properties** Enables you to change the view's properties. Clicking this button displays the Properties window, which includes the Distinct Values and Encrypt View options.

- **Show/Hide Panes (four buttons)** Let you show or hide the four panes of the New View window.

- **Run** Runs the query and displays the results in the Results pane. This test can be used to verify that the query is performing correctly.

- **Cancel Execution And Clear Results** Clears the Results pane.

- **Verify SQL** Tests the query against the underlying table to validate the SQL statement.

- **Remove Filter**   Removes any filters that have been defined.
- **Use GROUP BY**   Adds a GROUP BY clause to the statement in the SQL pane.
- **Add Table**   Lets you add a table to the query.

3. Modify the SELECT statement in the SQL pane to match the SELECT statement shown in Figure 18-11. The view will consist of the columns *CompanyName*, *ContactName*, and *Phone*. Once you have typed the SELECT statement, click the Verify SQL button to verify that the query is valid. If it is, you must click OK in the dialog box that appears to allow Enterprise Manager to fill in the Diagram and Grid panes. Your New View window will look like the window shown in Figure 18-11.

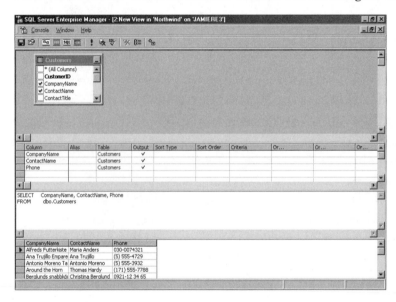

Figure 18-11. *The filled-in New View window.*

4. Once you have finished verifying that the view behaves as intended (by using the Results pane) and have made any necessary changes, close the New View window. At this point, a dialog box appears asking whether you want to save the view. If you click Yes, you will be prompted to supply a name for the view. Type a descriptive name for your view, and save it by clicking OK.

Your view is now available for use. You can use Enterprise Manager to set the properties of the new view, including permissions. The View Properties window is described in the section "Altering and Dropping Views" later in the chapter.

Using the Create View Wizard to Create a View

To use the Create View Wizard to create a view, follow these steps:

1. In Enterprise Manager, choose Wizards from the Tools menu, expand the Database folder in the dialog box that appears, select Create View Wizard, and click OK. The Create View Wizard welcome screen appears, as shown in Figure 18-12.

Figure 18-12. *The Create View Wizard welcome screen.*

2. Click Next to display the Select Database screen. This screen lets you specify the database for which you will be creating the view—in this case, the Northwind database.

3. Click Next to display the Select Objects screen, shown in Figure 18-13. Here you can select one or more tables to be referenced in the view. If you are creating a simple view, you can select a single table. To create a view on a join, choose multiple tables.

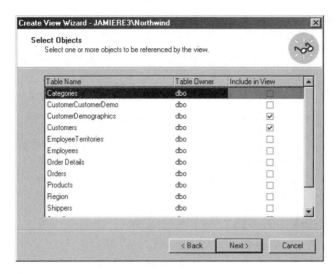

Figure 18-13. *The Select Objects screen.*

4. Click Next to display the Select Columns screen, shown in Figure 18-14. Here you can select the columns you want to use in the view—in this example, the *CompanyName*, *ContactName*, and *Phone* columns have been selected.

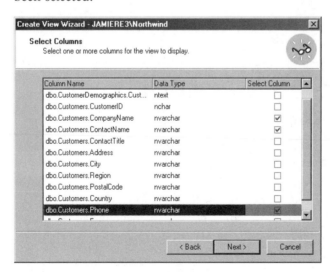

Figure 18-14. *The Select Columns screen.*

5. Click Next to display the Define Restriction screen. This screen is used to define an optional WHERE clause to restrict the rows in the database that are selected in the view.

6. Click Next to display the Name The View screen, shown in Figure 18-15. Type a name for the view in the View Name text box.

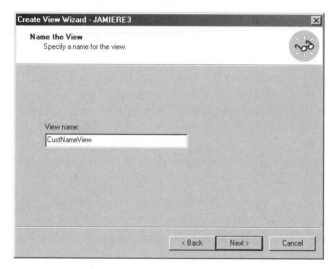

Figure 18-15. *The Name The View screen.*

7. Click Next to display the Completing The Create View Wizard screen, shown in Figure 18-16. This screen enables you to save the view, backtrack and make changes, or cancel the view creation. Once you click Finish, the view will be available for use.

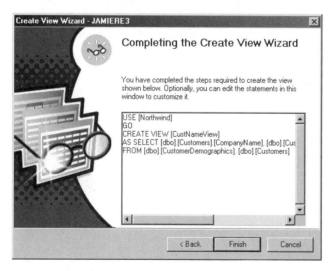

Figure 18-16. *The Completing The Create View Wizard screen.*

Tips for Views

When you are creating a view, remember that a view is made up of an SQL statement that accesses the underlying data, and that you control this SQL statement. Also keep in mind the following guidelines, which can help improve the performance, manageability, and usability of your databases:

- **Use views for security.** Rather than re-creating a table to provide access to only certain data in the table, create a view that contains the columns and rows you want to make accessible. Using a view is an ideal way to restrict some users to one portion of the data and other users to a different portion of the data. By using a view instead of building a table that must be populated from an existing table, you do not increase the amount of data and you maintain security.

- **Take advantage of indexes.** Remember that when you use a view, you are still accessing the underlying tables and therefore the indexes on those tables. If a table has a column that is indexed, be sure to include that column in the WHERE clause of the view's SELECT statement. Only if the column is part of the view and is used in the WHERE clause can the index be used for selecting data. For example, if the *Employee* table has an index on the *dept* column and this column is included in the view, the index can be used.

- **Partition your data.** Views are especially useful in enabling you to partition data, which can reduce the amount of time needed to rebuild indexes and manage the virtual table by reducing the size of the individual components. For example, if an index rebuild on a single large table takes two hours, you could partition the data into four smaller tables for which the index rebuild time is much shorter. You could then define a view that transparently combines the individual tables. With large tables that store historical data, this technique can be quite useful.

Altering and Dropping Views

You drop and alter views by using either Enterprise Manager or T-SQL commands. The Enterprise Manager method is easier, as it is when you carry out other SQL Server procedures, but T-SQL commands provide repeatability. In this section, we'll look at both methods.

Using Enterprise Manager to Alter and Drop Views

To alter and drop views by using Enterprise Manager, follow these steps:

1. In Enterprise Manager, expand the Databases folder on the desired server, expand the database containing the view you want to drop or alter, and then click Views to display the views in the right pane of the window, as shown in Figure 18-17.

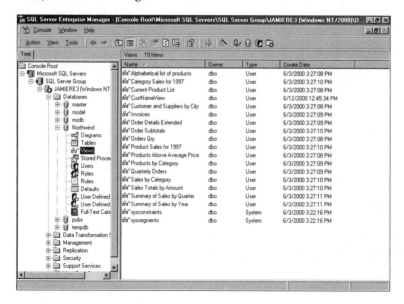

Figure 18-17. *Displaying views in the Enterprise Manager window.*

2. Right-click the name of the view you want to modify or drop. A shortcut menu appears, as shown in Figure 18-18. To delete a view, choose Delete from this menu. To alter a view, choose Design View.

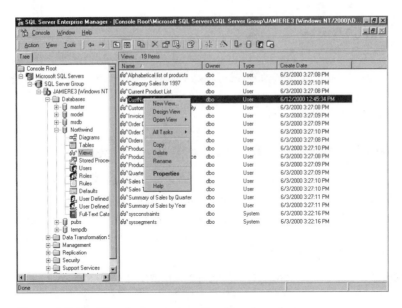

Figure 18-18. *The shortcut menu for the selected view.*

3. If you choose Delete, the Drop Objects dialog box appears, as shown in Figure 18-19. Click Show Dependencies to view the underlying structure of the view. Here you will see what tables the view depends on. If the selected view is a join or a union view, you will see all of the tables involved; if it is a column or a row view, you will see only one table. When you are ready to drop the selected view, click Drop All in the Drop Objects dialog box.

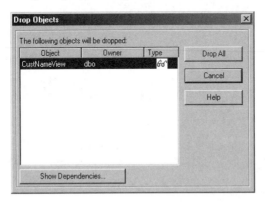

Figure 18-19. *The Drop Objects dialog box.*

If you choose Design View from the shortcut menu, the Design View window appears, as shown in Figure 18-20. Notice the similarity to the New View window we saw in Figure 18-10. You can use the Design View window to modify your view in the same way you used the New View window to create the view.

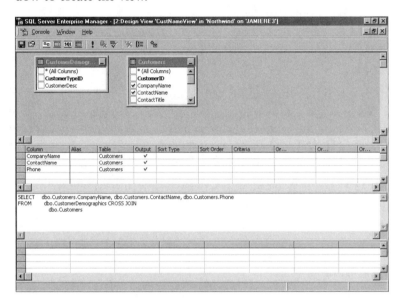

Figure 18-20. *The Design View window.*

4. Once you have made any necessary modifications to the view, close the Design View window by clicking the window's Close button. You will then be prompted to save the view.

When you have finished modifying the view, you can set the view's permissions. First open the View Properties window by right-clicking the view name in Enterprise Manager and choosing Properties from the shortcut menu. Then click Permissions to display the permissions for the view. The process of setting permissions is described in detail in Chapter 34.

As you can see, modifying a view by using Enterprise Manager is easy. However, if you are modifying or dropping a large number of views, T-SQL can be much more convenient to use because it can be scripted.

Using T-SQL to Alter and Drop Views

To alter views by using T-SQL, use the ALTER VIEW command. The ALTER VIEW command is similar to the CREATE VIEW command and has the following syntax:

```
ALTER VIEW view_name [(column, column, ...)]
[WITH ENCRYPTION]
AS
your SELECT statement
[WITH CHECK OPTION]
```

The only difference between the ALTER VIEW and CREATE VIEW commands is that the CREATE VIEW command will fail if the view already exists, whereas the ALTER VIEW command will fail if the named view does not exist. (The optional keywords WITH ENCRYPTION and WITH CHECK OPTION are covered in the section "Using T-SQL to Create a View" earlier in this chapter.)

To see how the ALTER VIEW command works, let's return to our partitioning example (introduced in the section "Partitioning"). To drop an older partition and add a new partition, we could alter the view as follows:

```
ALTER VIEW partview
AS
  SELECT * FROM table_2
  UNION ALL
  SELECT * FROM table_3
  UNION ALL
  SELECT * FROM table_4
  UNION ALL
  SELECT * FROM table_5
```

The modified view will look much like it did before the ALTER VIEW command was run, but now a different set of data will be selected. The view no longer uses *table_1* and now uses *table_5*.

To drop a view, use the DROP VIEW command. The syntax of the DROP VIEW command, which is quite simple, is shown here:

```
DROP VIEW view_name
```

As you can see, the Enterprise Manager and T-SQL command methods are both straightforward and easy to use. Choose the technique that best suits your needs.

View Enhancements in SQL Server 2000

SQL Server 2000 includes two view enhancements: partitioned views now are updatable and distributable, and views can now be indexed like tables. Let's explore these enhancements in a little more detail.

Updatable, Distributed Partitioned Views

In Microsoft SQL Server versions 7 and earlier, data in views was static and reflected the actual state of the underlying table or tables. In SQL Server 2000, an update performed on a partitioned view will modify both the view and the underlying table or tables. In addition, partitioned views can span multiple SQL Server 2000 systems. Partitioned views can be used to implement a federation of database servers. A *federation* is a group of servers that are each administered independently but that share the processing load of the entire system. When you create a federation of servers, you partition data across the servers, which allows you to scale out the system. A federation of database servers can grow to support the largest e-commerce Web sites or enterprise database systems. Figure 18-21 shows a sample configuration for a federation of database servers.

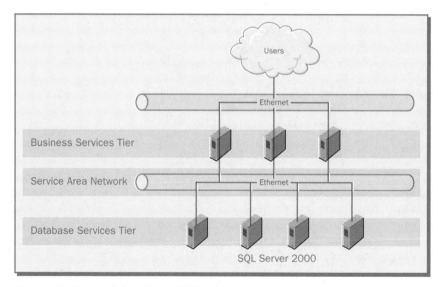

Figure 18-21. *A federation of SQL Server systems.*

Before you can implement a partitioned view, you must partition your table horizontally. You replace the original table with several smaller member tables. You give each of these member tables the same number of columns as you gave the original table, and you assign each column the same attributes (such as data type, size, and collation) as you assigned the corresponding column in the original table. If you are creating the partitioned view to be distributed, you put each member table on a separate member server. To maintain a greater degree of transparency, you should name each member table of the member databases the same on each member server. Though this is not a requirement, it makes overall management of the system easier.

When you design the member tables, you partition them horizontally. Each member table stores a horizontal slice of the original data. This partitioning is generally based on a range of key values. The range is based on the actual data values in the partitioning column. The value range for each member table is enforced by a CHECK constraint on the partitioning column. Keep in mind when you are partitioning your data that these data ranges cannot overlap. Let's look at an example of a horizontal partition. In this example, we will partition the *Customer* table into four member tables, and we'll place each table on a different server. Each server will hold 3000 records of the *Customer* table. The constraints are shown in the following CREATE TABLE statements:

```
Server 1:
CREATE TABLE Customer_Table_1
   (CustomerID        INTEGER PRIMARY KEY
                      CHECK (CustomerID BETWEEN 1 AND 3000),

   .     (Additional column definitions)
   .

Server 2:
CREATE TABLE Customer_Table_2
   (CustomerID        INTEGER PRIMARY KEY
                      CHECK (CustomerID BETWEEN 3001 AND 6000),

   .     (Additional column definitions)
   .

Server 3:
CREATE TABLE Customer_Table_3
   (CustomerID        INTEGER PRIMARY KEY
                      CHECK (CustomerID BETWEEN 6001 AND 9000),

   .     (Additional column definitions)
   .

Server 4:
CREATE TABLE Customer_Table_4
   (CustomerID        INTEGER PRIMARY KEY
                      CHECK (CustomerID BETWEEN 9001 AND 12000),

   .     (Additional column definitions)
   .
```

After you have created the member tables, you can define a distributed partitioned view on each member server. All views should have the same name to preserve application transparency. The distributed partitioned view allows any query running on any member server to execute as though all the referenced data is local to the query. In other words, if you run a query on a member server that references data on any other member server, the data is transparently returned to the query.

In order to preserve data transparency, you will need to create linked-server definitions on each member server. These definitions provide a member server with all the appropriate connection information for all the other federation member servers. This allows the partitioned view on a server to access data on the other member servers. You create the linked-server definitions via T-SQL commands or in Enterprise Manager.

Linking Servers by Using T-SQL

The syntax of the T-SQL command used to create a linked-server definition is as follows:

```
sp_addlinkedserver [ @server = ] 'server'
                   [ , [ @srvproduct = ] 'product_name' ]
                   [ , [ @provider = ] 'provider_name' ]
                   [ , [ @datasrc = ] 'data_source' ]
                   [ , [ @location = ] 'location' ]
                   [ , [ @provstr = ] 'provider_string' ]
                   [ , [ @catalog = ] 'catalog' ]
```

The stored procedure *sp_addlinkedserver* has the following arguments:

- *@server*   The system name of the linked server. If there are multiple instances of SQL Server on the server, you must specify the name as *server_name\instance_name*.

- *@srvproduct*   The product name of the OLE DB provider. If you are linking a SQL Server 2000 system to another SQL Server 2000 system, you do not need to specify *@srvproduct*.

- *@provider*   The unique programmatic identifier of the OLE DB provider previously specified in *@srvproduct*. If you are linking a SQL Server 2000 system to another SQL Server 2000 system, you do not need to specify *@provider*.

- *@datasrc*   The name of the data source as interpreted by the OLE DB provider. If you are linking a SQL Server 2000 system to another SQL Server 2000 system, you do not need to specify *@datasrc* unless you are connecting to a specific instance on the linked server. If so, you must specify *server_name\instance_name* for the data source.

- **@location** The location of the database as interpreted by the OLE DB provider. If you are linking a SQL Server 2000 system to another SQL Server 2000 system, you do not need to specify *@location*.

- **@provstr** The OLE DB provider–specific string that identifies a unique data source. If you are linking a SQL Server 2000 system to another SQL Server 2000 system, you do not need to specify *@provstr*.

- **@catalog** The catalog used when making the connection to the OLE DB provider.

For example, the following T-SQL commands will create linked-server definitions for communications between Servers 1, 2, 3, and 4.

Server 1:

```
sp_addlinkedserver 'Server2'
sp_setnetname 'Server2', 'sql-server-02'
sp_addlinkedserverlogin Server2, 'false', 'sa', 'sa'
sp_addlinkedserver 'Server3'
sp_setnetname 'Server3', 'sql-server-03'
sp_addlinkedserverlogin Server3, 'false', 'sa', 'sa'
sp_addlinkedserver 'Server4'
sp_setnetname 'Server4', 'sql-server-04'
sp_addlinkedserverlogin Server4, 'false', 'sa', 'sa'
```

Server 2:

```
sp_addlinkedserver 'Server1'
sp_setnetname 'Server1', 'sql-server-01'
sp_addlinkedserverlogin Server1, 'false', 'sa', 'sa'
sp_addlinkedserver 'Server3'
sp_setnetname 'Server3', 'sql-server-03'
sp_addlinkedserverlogin Server3, 'false', 'sa', 'sa'
sp_addlinkedserver 'Server4'
sp_setnetname 'Server4', 'sql-server-04'
sp_addlinkedserverlogin Server4, 'false', 'sa', 'sa'
```

Server 3:

```
sp_addlinkedserver 'Server1'
sp_setnetname 'Server1', 'sql-server-01'
sp_addlinkedserverlogin Server1, 'false', 'sa', 'sa'
sp_addlinkedserver 'Server2'
sp_setnetname 'Server2', 'sql-server-02'
sp_addlinkedserverlogin Server2, 'false', 'sa', 'sa'
sp_addlinkedserver 'Server4'
sp_setnetname 'Server4', 'sql-server-04'
sp_addlinkedserverlogin Server4, 'false', 'sa', 'sa'
```

Server 4:

```
sp_addlinkedserver 'Server1'
sp_setnetname 'Server1', 'sql-server-01'
sp_addlinkedserverlogin Server1, 'false', 'sa', 'sa'
sp_addlinkedserver 'Server2'
sp_setnetname 'Server2', 'sql-server-02'
sp_addlinkedserverlogin Server2, 'false', 'sa', 'sa'
sp_addlinkedserver 'Server3'
sp_setnetname 'Server3', 'sql-server-03'
sp_addlinkedserverlogin Server3, 'false', 'sa', 'sa'
```

Two statements were used in addition to the *sp_addlinkedserver* T-SQL statement. These statements are required to facilitate the distributed partitioned view processing. The call to *sp_setnetname* connects the linked-server name in SQL Server with the network name of the server hosting the database. In the preceding example, the linked-server name of Server2 is on the server with the network name of sql-server-02. We also specified the credentials to use for logon to the linked server. The call to *sp_addlinkedsrvlogin* instructs SQL Server to use the specified user ID and password for accessing the linked server.

Linking Servers by Using Enterprise Manager

Enterprise Manager also provides a method for linking servers. To use this method, follow these steps:

1. In Enterprise Manager, expand the Security folder for your server, as shown in Figure 18-22.

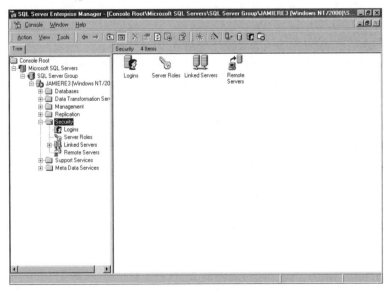

Figure 18-22. *Expanding a server's Security folder.*

2. Right-click Linked Servers in the left-hand pane. Choose New Linked Server from the shortcut menu that appears. The Linked Server Properties window appears, as shown in Figure 18-23.

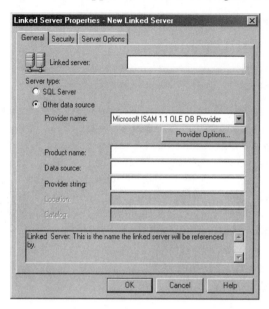

Figure 18-23. *The General tab of the Linked Server Properties window.*

3. In the Linked Server text box, type the name of the SQL server you would like to link. Select the SQL Server option, as illustrated in Figure 18-24.

4. Click the Security tab. Type the local login name to use and either select the Impersonate check box or type a remote name and password. Figure 18-25 shows a local login name entered.

5. Click OK to complete the linked-server definition.

The linked server is now available for use. You can also use Enterprise Manager to modify or delete the linked server's properties. In addition, you can use Enterprise Manager to view the tables and views available on the linked server.

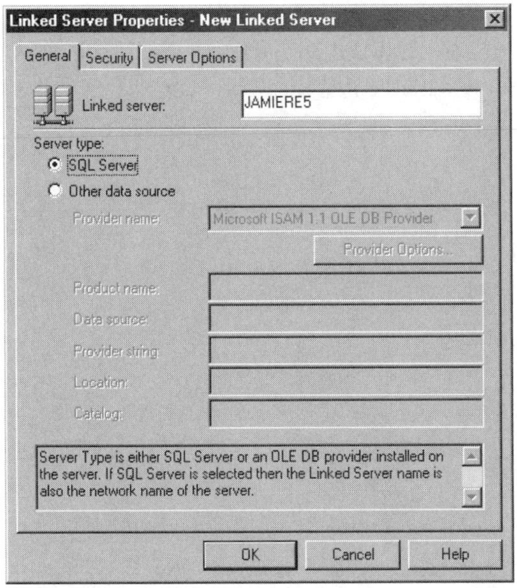

Figure 18-24. *Selecting the linked-server type.*

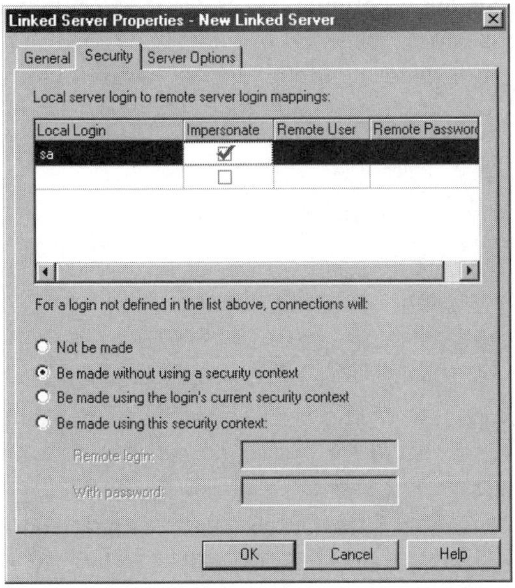

Figure 18-25. *The Security tab of the Linked Server Properties window.*

Creating the View

Once all the linked-server definitions are in place, you can create the actual view. The following example creates a view called *sales* that combines sales data from the *sales* table on four servers:

```
CREATE VIEW sales
AS
  SELECT * FROM /*Server1.bicycle.dbo.*/1_sales
    UNION ALL
      SELECT * FROM Server2.bicycle.dbo.1_sales
    UNION ALL
      SELECT * FROM Server3.bicycle.dbo.1_sales
    UNION ALL
      SELECT * FROM Server4.bicycle.dbo.1_sales
GO
```

Indexed Views

SQL Server 2000 also enables you to create an index on a view. Because a view is simply a virtual table, it has the same general form as an actual database table. You create the index by using the same CREATE INDEX T-SQL command that you use to create an index on a table. (This command is covered in Chapter 17.) The only difference is that rather than specifying a table name, you specify a view name. For example, the following T-SQL command creates a clustered index on a view called *partview*:

```
CREATE UNIQUE CLUSTERED INDEX partview_cluidx
   ON partview (part_num ASC)
   WITH FILLFACTOR=95
ON partfilegroup
```

Creating indexes on views has several impacts on performance. Obviously, an index on a view will improve performance when you are accessing data in the view, just as an index on a table improves performance.

Also, when you create an index on a view, SQL Server stores the view result set in memory and will not have to materialize it for future queries. The term "materializing" refers to the process SQL Server uses to dynamically merge the data needed to build a view result set each time a query references a view. (Remember, a view is a dynamic structure.) The process of materializing a view can substantially increase the overhead required to satisfy a query. The impact on performance caused by repeatedly materializing a view can be significant if the view is complex or includes large amounts of data.

In addition, when you create an index on a view, the SQL Server query optimizer automatically uses the index in queries that do not directly name the view in the FROM clause of a SELECT statement. In other words, when an existing query in an application or a stored procedure might benefit from the indexed view, the query optimizer will apply the indexed view to satisfy the query.

These benefits do not come without a price. Indexed views can be more complex for SQL Server to maintain over time. Each time an underlying table of a view is modified, SQL Server has to update the view result set and potentially the index on that view. Because the scope of a view's index can be larger than that of any one table's index—for example, if a view encompasses several large tables—the overhead associated with maintaining a view and its index can negate any benefit that queries gain from the indexed view. Because of this additional maintenance overhead, you should create indexes only on those views where the advantage provided by the improved speed in retrieving the results outweighs the disadvantage caused by the increased maintenance overhead. Views that generally should be indexed are those in which the underlying data is rather static, those whose result set processes a large number of rows, and those referenced by a large number of queries.

Summary

In this chapter, you've learned that a view is an auxiliary data structure that can be used to create virtual tables. These virtual tables look like actual database tables, but they're really just stored SQL queries. These queries are joined with other queries to access the underlying table or tables.

You can reference a view in T-SQL statements in the same way you reference tables. Views can be used as a security measure to shield sensitive data. They can also provide an easier way to access data. What's more, views enable the logical presentation of data. You can also use views to create a virtual table from individual partitions.

In this chapter, you've also learned about a few restrictions and guidelines that apply to using views. And you've seen that in certain situations, you should create indexes on your views. In Chapter 19, we'll look at transactions and transaction locking.

Chapter 19
Understanding Transactions and Transaction Locking

This chapter explains the fundamentals of transactions and transaction locking. In this chapter, you'll learn what a transaction is, what properties Microsoft SQL Server 2000 requires for valid transactions, how transaction modes are used to specify the beginning and the end of a transaction, and how to commit and roll back transactions. We'll also look at the types and modes of locking that SQL Server uses when performing transactions and at the concepts of blocking and deadlocking. The chapter ends with some table-level locking hints that you can use in your transactions.

What Is a Transaction?

A *transaction* is a series of operations that are performed as one logical unit of work. Transactions allow SQL Server to ensure a certain level of data integrity and data recoverability. The *transaction log,* which every database must have, keeps a record of all transactions that make any type of modification (insert, update, or delete) to the database. SQL Server uses this transaction log to recover data in case of errors or system failures.

The integrity of a transaction depends in part on the SQL programmer. The programmer must know when to start and end the transaction and in what sequence to make data modifications to ensure logical consistency and meaningfulness of data. We'll cover how to begin and end transactions in later sections. Now that you know what a transaction is, let's take a look at the properties required for a valid transaction.

ACID Properties

A transaction must meet four requirements to qualify as a valid transaction. These requirements are known as the *ACID properties*. "ACID" is an acronym for "atomicity, consistency, isolation, and durability." SQL Server provides mechanisms to help ensure that a transaction meets each of these requirements.

Atomicity

SQL Server ensures that all data modifications in a transaction are completed as a group if the transaction is successful or that none of the modifications occur if the transaction is not successful—in other words, SQL Server ensures the *atomicity* of your transactions. The transaction must be performed as an atomic unit—thus the term "atomicity." For a transaction to be successful, every step (or statement) in the transaction must succeed. If one of the steps fails, the entire transaction fails, and any modifications made since the transaction started will be undone. SQL Server provides a transaction management mechanism that automatically performs the task of determining whether a transaction has succeeded or failed and undoes any data modifications, as necessary, in the case of a failure.

Consistency

SQL Server also ensures the consistency of your transactions. *Consistency* means that all data remains in a consistent state—that the integrity of the data is preserved—after a transaction finishes, regardless of whether the transaction failed or was completed successfully. Before a transaction begins, the database must be in a consistent state, which means that the integrity of the data is upheld and that internal structures, such as B-tree indexes and doubly linked lists, are correct. And after a transaction occurs, the database must be in a consistent state—a new state if the transaction succeeded or, if the transaction failed, the same consistent state it was in before the transaction started.

Consistency is also a transaction management feature provided by SQL Server. If your data is consistent and your transactions maintain logical consistency and data integrity, SQL Server will ensure the consistency of the data after a transaction. When you are using data replication in a distributed environment, various levels of consistency can be achieved that range from eventual transactional convergence (or latent consistency) to immediate transactional consistency. The level of consistency will depend on the type of replication you use. For more information about replication, see Chapters 26, 27, and 28.

Isolation

Isolation means that the effects of each transaction are the same as if the transaction were the only one in the system; in other words, modifications made by a transaction are isolated from modifications made by any other concurrent transaction. In this way, a transaction will not be affected by a value that has been changed by another transaction until the change is committed. If a transaction fails, its modifications will have no effect because the changes will be rolled back. SQL Server enables you to adjust the isolation level of your transactions. A transaction's isolation behavior depends on the isolation level you specify.

Note   When a transaction is committed, all of its modifications are made a permanent part of the database. When a transaction is rolled back, the changes are rescinded, and the database functions as if the transaction had never occurred.

Levels of Isolation

SQL Server supports four levels of isolation. A *level of isolation* is a setting that determines the level at which a transaction is allowed to accept inconsistent data—that is, the degree to which one transaction is isolated from another. A higher isolation level increases data accuracy, but it can reduce the number of concurrent transactions. On the other hand, a lower isolation level will allow more concurrency but will result in reduced data accuracy. The isolation level you specify for a SQL Server session determines the locking behavior for all SELECT statements performed during that session (unless you set the isolation level to another level). Locking behavior is described in the section "Transaction Locking" later in this chapter. The four levels of isolation, from lowest to highest, are listed here:

- **Read uncommitted**   Lowest level of isolation. At this level, transactions are isolated just enough to ensure that physically corrupted data is not read.

- **Read committed**   Default level for SQL Server. At this level, reads are allowed only on committed data. (*Committed data* is data that has been made a permanent part of the database.)

- **Repeatable read**   Level at which repeated reads of the same row or rows within a transaction will achieve the same results. (Until a transaction is completed, no other transactions can modify the data.)

- **Serializable**   Highest level of isolation; transactions are completely isolated from each other. At this level, the results achieved by running concurrent transactions on a database are the same as if the transactions had been run serially (one at a time in some order).

Concurrent Transaction Behavior

To better understand each isolation level, we must first look at three types of behaviors that can occur when you are running concurrent transactions. These behaviors are as follows:

- **Dirty read** A read that retrieves uncommitted data. A dirty read occurs when one transaction modifies data and a second transaction reads the modified data before the first transaction has committed the changes. If the first transaction rolls back the changes, the second transaction will have retrieved data that is not in the database.

- **Nonrepeatable read** Inconsistent results obtained by repeated reads. A nonrepeatable read occurs when a single row of data is read more than once within a transaction, and between the reads, a separate transaction makes an update to that row. Because the first transaction's repeated reads will retrieve different data, the results were not repeatable within that transaction.

- **Phantom read** A read that occurs when a transaction attempts to retrieve a row that does not exist when the transaction begins but that is inserted by a second transaction before the first transaction finishes. If the first transaction again looks for the row, it will find that the row has suddenly appeared. This new row is called a *phantom row*.

Table 19-1 lists the types of behaviors each isolation level allows. As you can see, read uncommitted is the least restrictive isolation level, and serializable is the most restrictive. As mentioned, the default SQL Server isolation level is read committed. As the level of isolation increases, SQL Server will hold more restrictive locks, for longer periods of time. And since the isolation level affects the locking behavior for SELECT statements, isolation affects the locking mode used on data that is being read. Locking modes are described in the section "Transaction Locking" later in this chapter.

Table 19-1. Isolation level behaviors

	Behavior Allowed		
Isolation Level	Dirty Read	Nonrepeatable Read	Phantom Read
Read uncommitted	Yes	Yes	Yes
Read committed	No	Yes	Yes
Repeatable read	No	No	Yes
Serializable	No	No	No

Setting the Isolation Level

You can set the isolation level to be used for an entire SQL Server user session by using Transact-SQL (T-SQL) statements or through functions in your application. You can also specify a locking hint in a query to override the set isolation level for that transaction. Locking hints are given in the section "Locking Hints" later in this chapter. To set the isolation level by using T-SQL or in a DB-LIB application, use the SET TRANSACTION ISOLATION LEVEL statement, and specify one of the four isolation levels. The syntax is as follows:

```
SET TRANSACTION ISOLATION LEVEL
  READ UNCOMMITTED
  | READ COMMITTED
  | REPEATABLE READ
  | SERIALIZABLE
GO
```

More Info   For other types of applications, such as those using ODBC, ADO, or OLE-DB, look up "ACID properties" in the Books Online index and select "Adjusting Transaction Isolation Levels" in the Topics Found dialog box.

Once you have set the isolation level for a session, subsequent transactions in that SQL Server session will perform locking that ensures this isolation level. To find out which isolation level SQL Server is currently using as the default, use the DBCC USEROPTIONS command. The syntax for this command is simply the command name:

```
DBCC USEROPTIONS
```

This command returns only the options that a user has set or that are active. If you do not set the isolation level (leaving it at the SQL Server default level), you will not see the isolation level when you run the DBCC USEROPTIONS command. If you do specify a level other than the default, however, you will see the isolation level. For example, if you execute the following statements, the isolation level will be shown in the output from DBCC USEROPTIONS:

```
USE pubs
GO
SET TRANSACTION ISOLATION LEVEL SERIALIZABLE
GO
DBCC USEROPTIONS
GO
```

The results returned from the DBCC USEROPTIONS command will look something like this:

```
Set Option                      Value
-------------------------------------------
textsize                        64512
language                        us_english
dateformat                      mdy
datefirst                       7
quoted_identifier               SET
arithabort                      SET
ansi_null_dflt_on               SET
ansi_defaults                   SET
ansi_warnings                   SET
ansi_padding                    SET
ansi_nulls                      SET
concat_null_yields_null         SET
isolation_level                 serializable

(13 row(s) affected)
```

You can use locking hints at the table level to override the default isolation level, but you should use this technique only when absolutely necessary and if you fully understand how it will affect your transactions. For more details about the available locking hints, see the section "Locking Hints" later in this chapter.

Durability

The last ACID property is durability. *Durability* means that once a transaction is committed, the effects of the transaction remain permanently in the database, even in the event of a system failure. The SQL Server transaction log and your database backups provide durability. If SQL Server, the operating system, or a component of the server fails, the database will automatically recover when SQL Server is restarted. SQL Server uses the transaction log to replay the committed transactions that were affected by the system crash and to roll back any uncommitted transactions.

If a data drive fails and data is lost or corrupted, you can recover the database by using database backups and transaction log backups. If you plan your backups well, you should always be able to recover your system from a failure. Unfortunately, if your backup drives fail and you lose the backup that is needed to recover the system, you might not be able to recover your database. See Chapters 32 and 33 for details about backing up and restoring your database and transaction logs. Now that you understand the properties of a transaction, let's look at how to begin and end a transaction.

Transaction Modes

A transaction can be started in one of three modes: autocommit, explicit, or implicit. The default mode for SQL Server is autocommit. Let's take a look at what each of these modes means.

Autocommit Mode

In *autocommit mode*, each T-SQL statement is committed when it finishes—there is no need for any additional statements to control transactions with this mode. In other words, each transaction consists of just one T-SQL statement. Autocommit mode is useful when you are executing statements by interactive command line, using OSQL or SQL Server Query Analyzer, because you do not have to worry about explicitly starting and ending each transaction. You know that each statement will be treated as its own transaction by SQL Server and will be committed as soon as it is finished. Every connection to SQL Server will use autocommit mode until you start an explicit transaction by using BEGIN TRANSACTION or until you specify implicit mode. Once the explicit transaction is ended or implicit mode is turned off, SQL Server returns to autocommit mode.

Explicit Mode

Explicit mode is used most often for programming applications and for stored procedures, triggers, and scripts. When you are executing a group of statements to perform a task, you might need to determine at what point the transaction should start and end so that either the entire group of statements succeeds or the entire group's modifications are rolled back. When you explicitly identify the beginning and the end of a transaction, you are using *explicit mode*, and the transaction is referred to as an *explicit transaction*. You specify an explicit transaction by using either T-SQL statements or API functions. This section explains only the T-SQL method; API functions are beyond the scope of this book.

More Info For information about explicit transactions using ADO and OLE-DB, look up "explicit transactions" in the Books Online index and select "Explicit Transactions" in the Topics Found dialog box. Note that the ODBC API does not support explicit transactions, but only implicit and autocommit transactions.

Real World **Using an Explicit Transaction**

Let's look at a situation in which you would need to use an explicit transaction to start and end a task. Suppose we have a stored procedure named *Place_Order* that handles the database task of placing a customer's order for an item. The steps in this procedure include selecting the customer's current account information, entering the new order ID number and the item ordered, calculating the price of the order plus taxes, updating the customer's account balance to reflect the total price, and checking whether the item is in stock.

We want all of these steps to be completed together or none of them to be completed so that the data will remain consistent in the database. To achieve this, we will group the statements that handle these tasks into an explicit transaction. If we do not group the statements, we could get inconsistent data. For example, if the network connection from the client to the server is broken off after the step that enters the new order number is executed but before the customer balance is updated, the database will be left with a new order for the customer but no charge on the customer's account. In this case, SQL Server commits each statement as soon as it finishes, leaving the stored procedure half-completed at the time of the network disconnect. But if the steps are defined within one explicit transaction, SQL Server automatically rolls back the entire transaction upon disconnection, and the client can later reconnect and execute the procedure again. For more details, see the section "Transaction Rollbacks" later in this chapter.

Using explicit transactions when your task consists of several steps, as in the preceding example, is also beneficial because whether or not you specify your own ROLLBACK statements, SQL Server will automatically roll back your transactions when a severe error occurs, such as a break in communication across the network, a database or client system crash, or a deadlock. (Deadlocks are covered in the section "Blocking and Deadlocks" later in this chapter.) The T-SQL statement used to start a transaction is BEGIN TRANSACTION. You specify the end of a transaction by using either COMMIT TRANSACTION or ROLLBACK TRANSACTION. You can optionally specify a name for a transaction in the BEGIN TRANSACTION statement, and you can then refer to the transaction by name in the COMMIT TRANSACTION or ROLLBACK TRANSACTION statement. The syntax for these three statements is shown here:

```
BEGIN TRAN[SACTION] [tran_name | @tran_name_variable]

COMMIT [TRAN[SACTION] [tran_name | @tran_name_variable]]

ROLLBACK [TRAN[SACTION] [tran_name | @tran_name_variable
        | savepoint_name | @savepoint_name_variable]]
```

Committing Transactions

As mentioned, a committed transaction is one in which all modifications performed by the transaction are made a permanent part of the database. Before a transaction can commit, a record of its modifications and a commit record are written to the database transaction log. Thus, modifications that are a permanent part of the database can be in one of two locations: either the modifications are actually written to disk and thus are literally in the database, or they are in the data cache, and the transaction log can thus roll forward this transaction in the case of a failure so the transaction will not be lost.

All resources used by a transaction, such as locks, are released when the transaction commits. A transaction will commit successfully if each of its statements is successful. Here is a small explicit transaction, named *update_state*, that updates the *state* column value to *XX* in the *publishers* table for all publishers that have *NULL* in that column:

```
USE pubs
GO
BEGIN TRAN update_state

UPDATE publishers SET state = 'XX'
WHERE state IS NULL
COMMIT TRAN update_state
GO
```

If you run this transaction, you should see two rows affected. To return the table to its original state (as if a rollback had occurred instead of the commit), run the following transaction:

```
USE pubs
GO
BEGIN TRAN undo_update_state

UPDATE publishers SET state = NULL
WHERE state = 'XX'
COMMIT TRAN undo_update_state
GO
```

Again, you should see two rows affected. The transaction names *update_state* and *undo_update_state* used with COMMIT TRAN are ignored by SQL Server—transaction names serve simply as an aid to the programmer for identifying which transaction is being committed. SQL Server automatically commits the latest uncommitted transaction that started before the commit, regardless of whether a transaction name is specified.

Creating Nested Transactions

SQL Server allows *nested transactions*, or transactions within a transaction. With nested transactions, you should explicitly commit each inner transaction so SQL Server knows that an inner transaction has finished and will be able to release resources used by that transaction once the outer transaction commits. If resources are locked, other users will not be able to access them. Although you must include a COMMIT statement for each transaction, SQL Server will not actually commit the inner transactions until the outermost transaction has committed successfully; at the same time, SQL Server releases all resources used by the inner and outer transactions. If the outermost transaction fails to commit, none of the inner transactions will commit, and the outer transaction and all inner transactions will be rolled back. If the outer transaction commits, all inner transactions will commit. In other words, SQL Server basically ignores any COMMIT statements within inner nested transactions, in the sense that the inner transactions do not commit, and instead waits for the final commit or rollback of the outer transaction to determine the completion status of all inner transactions. (This is explained further in the Real World examples that follow.)

Also, in nested transactions, if a ROLLBACK statement is executed within the outer transaction or any of the inner transactions, all transactions are rolled back. It is not valid to include an inner transaction name with a ROLLBACK statement—if you do, SQL Server will return an error. Include the name of the outermost transaction, no name at all, or a savepoint name. (Savepoints are explained in the "Savepoints" section later in this chapter.)

Real World Using a Nested Transaction

Let's look at an example of a nested transaction that includes a stored procedure. The stored procedure contains an explicit transaction and is called from within another explicit transaction. Therefore, the transaction in the stored procedure becomes an inner nested transaction. The following code shows the statements used to create the stored procedure and the transaction that calls the stored procedure. (For simplicity, this example uses a PRINT statement rather than the real data modification statements.)

```
USE MyDB
GO
CREATE PROCEDURE Place_Order    --Creates the stored procedure
AS
BEGIN TRAN place_order_tran
PRINT 'SQL Statements that perform order tasks go here'
COMMIT TRAN place_order_tran
GO

BEGIN TRAN Order_tran           --Begins the outer transaction
PRINT 'Place an order'
EXEC Place_Order                --Calls the stored procedure, which
                                --begins the inner transaction
COMMIT TRAN Order_tran          --Commits the inner and outer
                                --transactions
GO
```

After you execute this code, you will see both PRINT statements as output. The *place_order_tran* transaction must have a COMMIT statement within the stored procedure to mark the end of that transaction, but it will not actually commit until the *Order_tran* transaction commits. Whether *place_order_tran* will be committed or rolled back depends entirely on whether *Order_tran* commits.

Although SQL Server does not actually commit inner transactions upon encountering their COMMIT statements, it does update the @@TRANCOUNT system variable for each COMMIT statement encountered. This variable keeps track of the number of active transactions per user connection. When no active transactions are present, @@TRANCOUNT is 0. As each transaction begins (using BEGIN TRAN), @@TRANCOUNT is increased by 1. As each transaction is committed, @@TRANCOUNT is decreased by 1. When @@TRANCOUNT reaches 0, the outermost transaction commits. If a ROLLBACK statement is executed within the outer transaction or any of the inner transactions, @@TRANCOUNT is set to 0. Remember, you should commit each inner transaction so that @@TRANCOUNT can be decremented properly. You can test the value of @@TRANCOUNT to determine whether any active transactions are present. To see the value of @@TRANCOUNT, use the statement SELECT @@TRANCOUNT.

Real World **Using @@*TRANCOUNT***

Let's look at an example of how SQL Server uses the @@*TRANCOUNT* variable. Assume that you have a nested transaction that consists of two transactions, one inner transaction and an outer transaction, as in the preceding example. After both transactions have begun but before either has been committed, the value of @@*TRANCOUNT* is 2. The outer transaction will not be able to commit because @@*TRANCOUNT* has a nonzero value. When the inner transaction COMMIT statement is encountered, SQL Server decrements @@*TRANCOUNT* to 1. When SQL Server encounters the COMMIT statement for the outer transaction, @@*TRANCOUNT* is decremented to 0, and the outer and inners transactions will actually commit.

The following code builds on our previous example but includes retrievals of @@*TRANCOUNT* values:

```
USE MyDB
GO
DROP PROCEDURE Place_Order
GO
CREATE PROCEDURE Place_Order        --Creates the stored procedure.
AS
BEGIN TRAN place_order_tran         --TRANCOUNT is incremented.
PRINT 'SQL Statements that perform order tasks go here'
SELECT @@TRANCOUNT as TRANCOUNT_2
COMMIT TRAN place_order_tran        --TRANCOUNT is decremented.
GO

SELECT @@TRANCOUNT as TRANCOUNT_initial
BEGIN TRAN Order_tran               --TRANCOUNT is incremented.
PRINT 'Place an order'
SELECT @@TRANCOUNT as TRANCOUNT_1
EXEC Place_Order                    --Calls the stored procedure,
                                    --which begins the inner transaction.
SELECT @@TRANCOUNT as TRANCOUNT_3
COMMIT TRAN Order_tran              --TRANCOUNT is decremented.
SELECT @@TRANCOUNT as TRANCOUNT_4
GO
```

If you run these statements, you will see a series of @@*TRANCOUNT* values displayed in this order: *0, 1, 2, 1, 0*.

Note For explicit transactions that use BEGIN TRAN, you must commit each transaction explicitly. When you use nested transactions, SQL Server will not be able to commit the outermost or innermost transactions until all the inner transactions have been explicitly committed with a COMMIT statement.

Implicit Mode

In *implicit mode,* a transaction automatically begins whenever certain T-SQL statements are used and will continue until explicitly ended with a COMMIT or ROLLBACK statement. If an ending statement is not specified, the transaction will be rolled back when the user disconnects. The following T-SQL statements will begin a new transaction in implicit mode:

- ALTER TABLE
- CREATE
- DELETE
- DROP
- FETCH
- GRANT
- INSERT
- OPEN
- REVOKE
- SELECT
- TRUNCATE TABLE
- UPDATE

When one of these statements is used to begin an implicit transaction, the transaction will continue until it is explicitly ended, even if another of these statements is executed within the transaction. After the transaction has been explicitly committed or rolled back, the next time one of these statements is used, a new transaction is started. This process continues until implicit mode is turned off.

To set the implicit transaction mode to ON, you can use the following T-SQL command:

```
SET IMPLICIT_TRANSACTIONS {ON | OFF}
```

ON activates the mode, and *OFF* deactivates it. When implicit mode is deactivated, autocommit mode is used.

Implicit transactions are useful when you are running scripts that perform data modifications that need to be protected within a transaction. You can turn on implicit mode at the beginning of the script, perform the necessary modifications, and then turn off the mode at the end. To avoid concurrency problems, disable implicit mode after making data modifications and before browsing through data. If the next statement after a commit is a SELECT statement, it will start a new transaction in implicit mode, and the resources will not be released until that transaction is committed.

Transaction Rollbacks

A rollback can occur in one of two ways: as an automatic rollback by SQL Server or as a manually programmed rollback. In certain cases, SQL Server will do the rollback for you. But to have logical consistency in your programs, you must explicitly call the ROLLBACK statement when needed. Let's look at these two methods in more detail.

Automatic Rollbacks

As mentioned earlier in this chapter, if a transaction fails because of a severe error, such as a loss of network connection while the transaction is being run or a failure of the client application or computer, SQL Server will automatically roll back the transaction. A rollback reverses all modifications the transaction performed and frees up any resources the transaction used.

If a run-time statement causes an error, such as a constraint or rule violation, by default, SQL Server automatically rolls back only the particular statement in error. To change this behavior, you can use the SET XACT_ABORT statement. Setting XACT_ABORT to *ON* tells SQL Server to automatically roll back a transaction in the event of a run-time error. This technique is useful when, for instance, one statement in your transaction fails because it violates a foreign key constraint and—because that statement failed—you do not want any of the other statements to succeed. By default, XACT_ABORT is set to *OFF*.

SQL Server also uses automatic rollback during recovery of a server. For example, if you have a power loss while running transactions and the system is rebooted, when SQL Server is restarted, it will perform automatic recovery. Automatic recovery involves reading from the transaction log information to replay committed transactions that did not get written to disk and to roll back transactions that were in flight (not committed yet) at the time of the power loss.

Programmed Rollbacks

You can specify a point in a transaction at which a rollback will occur by using the ROLLBACK statement. The ROLLBACK statement terminates the transaction and reverses any changes that were made. If you cause a rollback in the middle of a transaction, the rest of the transaction will be ignored. If the transaction is an entire stored procedure, for example, and the ROLLBACK statement occurs within the stored procedure, the stored procedure is rolled back and processing resumes at the next statement in the batch after the stored procedure call.

If you want to roll back a transaction based on the number of rows that are returned by a SELECT statement, use the @@ROWCOUNT system variable. This variable contains the number of rows returned from a query or affected by an update or a delete. If the specific number of rows does not matter but you simply need to find out whether a row or rows exist for a specific condition, you can use the IF EXISTS statement with the SELECT statement. This statement will not return any rows of data but returns *TRUE* or *FALSE*. If the result is *TRUE*, the statement that follows will be executed; if it returns *FALSE*, the statement that follows will not be executed. The IF EXISTS statement can use an ELSE clause also.

Let's look at an example using the IF EXISTS...ELSE clause. The following transaction updates royalty amounts in the *roysched* table for two royalty rates (16 percent and 15 percent), but if either of the royalty rates to be updated does not exist, neither UPDATE command will be executed. The transaction uses the ROLLBACK statement to ensure this outcome.

```
BEGIN TRAN update_royalty        --Begin the transaction.
USE pubs
IF EXISTS (SELECT titles.title, roysched.royalty FROM titles, roysched
WHERE titles.title_id = roysched.title_id
AND roysched.royalty = 16)
UPDATE roysched SET royalty = 17 WHERE royalty = 16    --13 rows exist.
ELSE
ROLLBACK TRAN update_royalty     --ROLLBACK is not executed.

IF EXISTS (SELECT titles.title, roysched.royalty FROM titles, roysched
WHERE titles.title_id = roysched.title_id
AND roysched.royalty = 15)        --No rows exist.
BEGIN
UPDATE roysched SET royalty = 20 WHERE royalty = 15
COMMIT TRAN update_royalty
END
ELSE                              --ROLLBACK is executed.
ROLLBACK TRAN update_royalty
GO
```

In this transaction, the first IF EXISTS (SELECT...) statement finds some rows that exist, and therefore the first UPDATE command is executed (showing 13 rows affected). The second SELECT statement returns 0 rows, and therefore the second UPDATE command is not executed, but ROLLBACK TRAN *update_royalty* is executed. Because ROLLBACK reverses all modifications to the beginning of the transaction, the first update was rolled back. If you execute the first SELECT statement again, you will still see 13 rows with *royalty* set to *16*, which was the original state of the database when we started this transaction. Again, the update to set *royalty* to *17* was reversed, or rolled back, because of the ROLLBACK statement.

> **Note** Some new keywords were used in this transaction: IF, ELSE, BEGIN, and END. These keywords will be described in detail in Chapter 20.

A transaction cannot be rolled back after it commits. (Remember, an inner transaction isn't really committed until the outer one commits.) For an explicit rollback of a single transaction to occur, ROLLBACK must be called before COMMIT. In the case of nested transactions, once the outermost transaction has committed (and therefore the inner transactions also commit), none of the transactions can be rolled back. As mentioned, you cannot roll back only the inner transactions; instead, the entire transaction (all inner transactions and the outer transaction) must be rolled back. Therefore, if you include a transaction name in the ROLLBACK statement, be sure to use the outermost transaction's name to avoid confusion and to avoid getting an error from SQL Server. There is a way to get around having to roll back an entire transaction, which allows you to keep some of the modifications: you can use savepoints.

Savepoints

You can avoid having to roll back an entire transaction by using a savepoint to roll back to a certain point in a transaction, rather than to the beginning of the transaction. All modifications up to the savepoint will remain in effect and will not be rolled back, but the statements that are executed after the savepoint (which you must specify in the transaction) and up to the ROLLBACK statement will be rolled back. The statements following the ROLLBACK statement will then continue to be executed. If you later roll back the transaction without specifying a savepoint, all modifications will be reversed to the beginning of the transaction as usual; the entire transaction will be rolled back. Note that when a transaction is being rolled back to a savepoint, SQL Server does not release locked resources. They will be released when the transaction commits or upon a full-transaction rollback.

To specify a savepoint in a transaction, use the following statement:

```
SAVE TRAN[SACTION] {savepoint_name | @savepoint_name_variable}
```

Position a savepoint in the transaction at the location you want to roll back to. To roll back to the savepoint, use ROLLBACK TRAN with the savepoint name, as shown here:

```
ROLLBACK TRAN savepoint_name
```

You can have more T-SQL statements after the ROLLBACK statement to continue with the transaction. Remember to include a COMMIT statement or another ROLLBACK statement after the first ROLLBACK statement in order for the entire transaction to be completed.

> **More Info**   For more information about savepoints and a good example of using them, look up "Save Transaction" in the Books Online index and select "Save Transaction (T-SQL)" in the Topics Found dialog box.

Transaction Locking

SQL Server uses an object called a *lock* to prevent multiple users from making modifications to a database at the same time and to prevent a user from retrieving data that is being changed by another user. Locking helps to ensure logical integrity of transactions and data. Locks are managed internally by SQL Server software and are acquired on a per-user-connection basis. When a user acquires (or owns) a lock on a resource, the lock indicates that the user has the right to use that resource. Resources that can be locked by a user include a row of data, a page of data, an extent (8 pages), a table, or an entire database. For example, if the user holds a lock on a data page, another user cannot perform operations on that page that would affect the operations of the user owning the lock. So a user could not update a data page that is currently locked and being retrieved by another user. Nor can a user acquire a lock that would conflict with a lock already held by another user. For instance, two users could not both have locks to update the same page at the same time. The same lock cannot be used by more than one user.

SQL Server's locking management automatically acquires and releases locks, according to users' actions. No action by the DBA or the programmer is needed to manage locks. However, you can use programming hints to indicate to SQL Server which type of lock to acquire when performing a particular query or database modification; these are covered in the section "Locking Hints" later in this chapter.

In this section, we'll look at the levels of granularity of locks as well as at locking modes. But first let's examine some of the locking management features that enhance SQL Server performance.

Locking Management Features

SQL Server supports row-level locking—the ability to acquire locks on a row in a data page or an index page. Row-level locking is the finest level of locking granularity that can be acquired in SQL Server. This lower level of locking provides many online transaction processing (OLTP) applications with more concurrency. Row-level locking is especially useful when you are performing row inserts, updates, and deletes on tables and indexes.

In addition to providing the row-level locking feature, SQL Server provides ease of administration for lock configuration. You do not need to set the *locks* configuration parameter manually to determine the number of locks available for SQL Server use. By default, if more locks are needed, SQL Server will dynamically allocate more, up to a limit set by SQL Server memory. If locks were allocated but are no longer in use, SQL Server will deallocate them. SQL Server is also optimized to dynamically choose which type of lock to acquire on a resource—usually row-level locking for inserts, updates, and deletes, and page locking for table scans. The next section explains the levels of locking in more detail.

More Info   See Chapter 30 for more information about the *locks* configuration option.

Levels of Locking

Locks can be acquired on a number of resources; the type of resource determines the granularity level of the lock. Table 19-2 lists the resources that SQL Server can lock, ordered from the finest to the coarsest level of locking granularity.

Table 19-2. Lockable resources

Resource	Type of Locking	Description
Row ID	Row level	Locks an individual row in a table
Key	Row level	Locks an individual row in an index
Page	Page level	Locks an individual 8-KB page in a table or an index
Extent	Extent level	Locks an extent, a group of 8 contiguous data pages or index pages
Table	Table level	Locks an entire table
Database	Database level	Locks an entire database

As the granularity level becomes coarser, concurrency decreases. For example, locking an entire table with a certain type of lock can block that table from being accessed by any other users. But overhead will decrease because fewer locks are used. As the granularity level becomes finer—in page-level and row-level locking, for example—concurrency increases because more users are allowed to access various pages or rows in a table at one time. In this case, overhead also increases because more locks are required when many rows or pages are being accessed individually.

SQL Server automatically chooses the type of lock that will be appropriate for the task, while minimizing the overhead of locking. SQL Server also automatically determines a lock mode for each transaction involving a locked resource; these modes are covered next.

Lock Modes

A *lock mode* specifies how a resource can be accessed by concurrent users (or concurrent transactions). Each type of lock is acquired in one of these modes. Six modes of locking are available: shared, update, exclusive, intent, schema, and bulk update.

Shared

Shared lock mode is used for read-only operations such as operations you perform by using the SELECT statement. This mode allows concurrent transactions to read the same resource at the same time, but it does not allow any transaction to modify that resource. Shared locks are released as soon as the read is finished unless the isolation level has been set to repeatable read or higher, or unless a locking hint that overrides this behavior was specified in the transaction.

Update

Update lock mode is used when an update might be performed on the resource. Only one transaction at a time can obtain an update lock on a resource. If the transaction does make a modification (because, for example, the search condition found rows to modify), the update lock is converted to an exclusive lock (described next); otherwise, it is converted to a shared lock.

Exclusive

Exclusive lock mode is used for operations that modify data, such as updates, inserts, and deletes. When an exclusive lock is held on a resource by a transaction, no other transaction can read or modify that resource. This lock mode prevents the same data from being updated at the same time by concurrent users, which might cause invalid data.

Intent

Intent lock mode is used to establish a locking hierarchy. For example, an intent lock at the table level indicates that SQL Server intends to acquire a lock on one or more pages or rows in that table. Generally, if a transaction needs to acquire an exclusive lock on a resource, SQL Server first checks whether any intent locks exist for that resource. If an intent lock is held by a transaction that is waiting for that resource, the second transaction cannot acquire the exclusive lock. If there is no transaction that is holding an intent lock and is waiting for that resource, the transaction can acquire the exclusive lock on it. There are three types of intent lock modes, as follows:

- **Intent shared**   Indicates that a transaction intends to put a shared lock on a resource

- **Intent exclusive**   Indicates that a transaction intends to put an exclusive lock on a resource

- **Shared with intent exclusive**   Indicates that a transaction intends to put a shared lock on some resources and an exclusive lock on other resources

For details concerning these mode types, look up "shared lock mode" in the Books Online index and select "Understanding Locking in SQL Server" in the Topics Found dialog box.

Schema

Schema lock mode is used when a table schema change operation, such as the addition of a column to a table, is executed or when queries are being compiled. Two types of schema locks exist for these cases: schema modification (Sch-M) and schema stability (Sch-S). A schema modification lock is used when a table data definition language (DDL) operation is performed. A schema stability lock is used for compiling queries. When a query is compiled, other transactions can run and acquire locks on the table at the same time, even exclusive locks, but DDL statements cannot be executed on the table when there is a schema stability lock.

Bulk Update

Bulk update lock mode is used when you are bulk copying data into a table with the TABLOCK hint specified or when you set the *table lock on bulk load* option by using *sp_tableoption*. The purpose of the bulk update lock is to allow processes to bulk copy data concurrently into the same table, while preventing access to that table by any processes that are not performing a bulk copy.

Blocking and Deadlocks

Blocking and deadlocks are two additional problems that can appear with concurrent transactions. They can cause major problems for a system and can slow and even halt performance. These problems can be handled in the application, or SQL Server will deal with them as best it can; they will be described here only so that you will be aware of them and understand the concepts. Avoiding and resolving blocking and deadlock issues is the responsibility of the programmer.

Blocking occurs when one transaction is holding a lock on a resource and a second transaction requires a conflicting lock type on that resource. The second transaction must wait for the first transaction to release its lock—in other words, it is blocked by the first transaction. Blocking usually occurs when a transaction holds a lock for an extended period, causing a chain of blocked transactions that are waiting for other transactions to finish so that they can obtain their required locks—a condition referred to as *chain blocking*. Figure 19-1 shows an example of chain blocking.

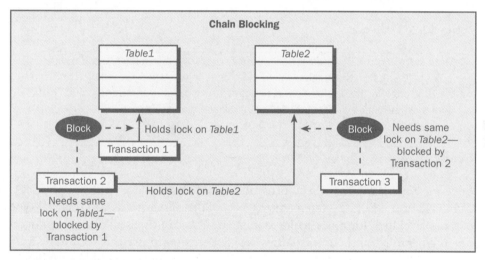

Figure 19-1. *Chain blocking.*

A *deadlock* differs from a blocked transaction in that a deadlock involves two blocked transactions waiting for each other. For example, assume that one transaction is holding an exclusive lock on *Table_1* and a second transaction is holding an exclusive lock on *Table_2*. Before either exclusive lock is released, the first transaction requires a lock on *Table_2* and the second transaction requires a lock on *Table_1*. Now each transaction is waiting for the other to release its exclusive lock, yet neither transaction will release its exclusive lock until a commit or roll-back occurs to complete the transaction. Neither transaction can be completed because it requires a lock held by the other transaction in order to continue—deadlock! Figure 19-2 illustrates this scenario. When a deadlock occurs, SQL Server will terminate one of the transactions, and that transaction will have to be run again.

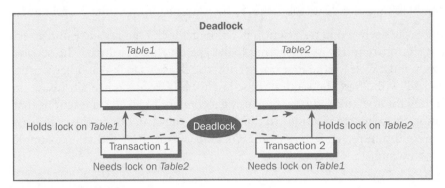

Figure 19-2. *Deadlock.*

More Info For basic information about how to avoid blocking and deadlocks, look up "Blocks" in the Books Online index and select "Understanding and Avoiding Blocking" in the Topics Found dialog box. Also, look up "Deadlocks" in the Books Online index and select "Avoiding Deadlocks and Handling Deadlocks."

Locking Hints

Locking hints are T-SQL keywords that can be used with SELECT, INSERT, UPDATE, and DELETE statements to direct SQL Server to use a preferred type of table-level lock for a particular statement. You can use locking hints to over-ride the default transaction isolation level. You should use this technique only when absolutely necessary because if you're not careful, you could cause block-ing or deadlocks.

Let's look at a situation where using a locking hint could be useful. Suppose you are using the default read committed isolation level for all transactions. With read committed, when a transaction performs a read, a shared lock is held on the re-source only until the read is completed, and then the shared lock is released. Therefore, if a transaction reads the same data twice, the results might differ between reads because another transaction could have obtained a lock and up-dated the same data between the first and second read.

To avoid the repeated read problem, you could specify the serializable isolation level, but doing so will cause SQL Server to hold all shared locks needed for SELECT statements in all transactions until each transaction is completed. In other words, shared locks will be held on the table specified in a transaction's SELECT statement for the entirety of the transaction. If you do not want to enforce serializability on all your transactions, you can add a locking hint to a specific query. The HOLDLOCK locking hint in a SELECT statement instructs SQL Server to hold all shared locks on the table specified in a transaction's SELECT statement until the end of the transaction, despite the isolation level. Thus, if the transaction performed a repeated read, the data would be consistent (not changed by another transaction). The isolation level is not affected for other transactions when you use a locking hint.

> **Note** The SQL Server query optimizer automatically determines the most efficient execution plan and lock types for a query. Because the query optimizer automatically selects the correct locking type or types, locking hints should be used only if they are well understood and only when absolutely necessary, as they might adversely affect concurrency.

The following list describes the available table-level locking hints:

- **HOLDLOCK**   Holds a shared lock until the completion of a transaction, rather than releasing it as soon as the table, page, or row of data is no longer required. Equivalent to using the SERIALIZABLE locking hint.
- **NOLOCK**   Applies only to the SELECT statement. Does not obtain shared locks and does not honor exclusive locks; it will read data that is held exclusively by another transaction. This hint allows for reads of uncommitted data (dirty reads).
- **PAGLOCK**   Uses a page-level lock where a single table-level lock would normally be used.
- **READCOMMITTED**   Performs a scan with the same locking behavior as that of a transaction using the read committed isolation level (the default isolation level for SQL Server).
- **READPAST**   Applies only to the SELECT statement and only to rows locked using row-level locking. Skips rows locked by other transactions that would normally be in the result set; returns results without these locked rows. Can be used only with transactions running at the read committed isolation level.
- **READUNCOMMITTED**   Is equivalent to NOLOCK.

- **REPEATABLEREAD** Performs a scan with the same locking behavior as that of a transaction using the repeatable read isolation level.
- **ROWLOCK** Uses row-level locks instead of page-level or table-level locks.
- **SERIALIZABLE** Performs a scan with the same locking behavior as that of a transaction using the serializable isolation level. Equivalent to HOLDLOCK.
- **TABLOCK** Uses a table-level lock rather than a page-level or row-level lock. SQL Server holds this lock until the end of the statement.
- **TABLOCKX** Uses an exclusive lock on a table. Careful! This hint prevents other transactions from accessing the table.
- **UPDLOCK** Uses update locks instead of shared locks while reading a table. This hint allows other users to only read the data and allows you to update it, thus ensuring that no other user has updated the data since you last read it.

You can choose to combine compatible locking hints, such as TABLOCK and REPEATABLEREAD, but you cannot combine conflicting hints, such as REPEATABLEREAD and SERIALIZABLE. To indicate a table-level locking hint, include the hint within parentheses after the table name in the T-SQL statement. The following statement is an example of using the TABLOCKX hint in a SELECT statement:

```
USE pubs
SELECT COUNT(ord_num)
FROM sales (TABLOCKX)
WHERE ord_date > "Sep 13 1994"
GO
```

The TABLOCKX hint directs SQL Server to hold an exclusive table-level lock on the *sales* table until the statement is completed. This hint ensures that no other transaction can modify data in the *sales* table while the query is counting the orders from that table. Be careful with this kind of hint because blocking other transactions from this table might cause other transactions to wait, and slower response times and chained blocking might result. Again, use table-level locking hints only when absolutely necessary.

Summary

In this chapter, you've learned about transactions, including the ACID properties of a transaction and the modes used to specify the beginning and the end of a transaction. You've also learned about SQL Server locking management features, levels of locking, and locking modes. We've also taken a look at blocking, deadlocks, and the use of locking hints. You should now have a good understanding of basic transactions and transaction locking methods. Chapter 20 expands on the introduction to T-SQL presented in Chapter 13 and will show you how to use the INSERT, UPDATE, and DELETE T-SQL statements, as well as the other statements you might need when writing transactions and stored procedures.

Chapter 20
Understanding Advanced T-SQL

This chapter covers in detail the Transact-SQL (T-SQL) statements used to modify data that were introduced in earlier chapters; it also describes the T-SQL keywords you can use to control programming flow. You can use these statements and keywords anywhere T-SQL is used—in command lines, scripts, stored procedures, batches, and application programs. In particular, we'll look at the data manipulation statements INSERT, UPDATE, and DELETE (which were touched on in Chapter 13) and the programming constructs IF...ELSE, WHILE, and CASE.

Before we begin our main topic, let's create a table, *items*, to use for our examples. (We'll create this table in the MyDB database.) The T-SQL commands used to create the *items* table are shown here:

```
USE MyDB
GO
CREATE TABLE items
(
item_category  CHAR(20)     NOT NULL,
item_id        SMALLINT     NOT NULL,
price          SMALLMONEY   NULL,
item_desc      VARCHAR(30)  DEFAULT 'No desc'
)
GO
```

The *item_id* column is a good candidate for the IDENTITY property. (See the "Adding the IDENTITY Property" section in Chapter 10 for more information about this property.) But because you cannot explicitly insert values into an identity column, we're not using IDENTITY here. This way, we'll have more flexibility with the examples that use the INSERT statement.

The INSERT Statement

The INSERT statement, introduced in Chapter 13, is used to add a new row or rows to a table or a view. The basic syntax for the INSERT statement is shown here:

```
INSERT [INTO] table_name [(column_list)] VALUES
    expression | derived_table
```

The INTO keyword and the *column_list* parameter are optional. The *column_list* parameter specifies which columns you are inserting data into; these values will have a one-to-one correspondence (in order) with the values listed in the expression (which can be simply a list of values). Let's look at some examples.

Inserting Rows

The following code example demonstrates how to insert a single row of data into the *items* table:

```
INSERT INTO items
    (item_category, item_id, price, item_desc)
VALUES ('health food', 1, 4.00, 'tofu 6 oz.')
GO
```

Because we specified a value for each column in the table and listed these values in the same order as their corresponding columns were defined in the table, we would not have to use the *column_list* parameter at all. But if the values were not in the same order as the columns, you could get the wrong data in a column or receive an error. For example, if you try to run this next statement, you will get the error message that follows it:

```
INSERT INTO items
VALUES (1, 'health food', 4.00, 'tofu 6 oz.')
GO
Server: Msg 245, Level 16, State 1, Line 1
Syntax error converting the varchar value 'health food' to a column
of data type smallint.
```

This message is returned and the row is not inserted because we ordered the values incorrectly. We tried to insert the item ID into the *item_category* column, and the item category into the *item_id* column. The values were not compatible with the data types for those columns. If they had been compatible, SQL Server would have allowed us to insert the row, whether or not the values were in the proper place.

To see how the one row that we inserted in the table appears, query the table to select all rows, by using the following SELECT statement:

```
SELECT * from items
GO
```

You will get the following result set:

```
item_category    item_id price    item_desc
---------------  ------- -------- ------------
health food         1     4.00    tofu 6 oz.
```

When the *items* table was created, the *price* column was defined to allow null values, and the *item_desc* (description) column was assigned a default value of *No desc*. If no value is specified in the INSERT statement for the *price* column, a *NULL* will be inserted in that column for the new row. If no value is specified for the *item_desc* column, the default value *No desc* will be inserted in that column for the new row.

Omitting Column Values

In the first sample INSERT statement in the preceding section, we could have omitted values as well as column names for the columns *price* and *item_desc* because those columns have default values. If we omit a value for a column, we must specify the remaining columns in *column_list* because otherwise, SQL Server will match the listed values to the columns in the order in which the columns were defined in the table.

For example, suppose we leave out the *price* column value and do not specify any value for *column_list*, such as in this query:

```
INSERT INTO items
VALUES ('junk food', 2, 'fried pork skins')
GO
```

SQL Server will attempt to insert the value given for *item_desc* (*fried pork skins*; the third value in the list of values) into the *price* column (the third column in the table). An error will result because *fried pork skins* is a *char* data type value, while *price* is a *smallmoney* data type. These are incompatible data types. The error message will look something like this:

```
Msg 213, Level 16, State 4, Server NTSERVER, Line 1
Insert Error: Column name or number of supplied values
does not match table definition.
```

Imagine what could have happened to table integrity had *fried pork skins* been a value of a data type compatible with the data type specified for *price*. SQL Server would have unknowingly inserted the value into the wrong column, and the table data would have inconsistent data.

Remember that a value inserted in a table or view must be of a data type compatible with the column definition. Also, if a row being inserted violates a rule or constraint, you'll get an error message from SQL Server, and the insert will fail.

To avoid incompatible data type errors, order the names in *column_list* to match the order of the corresponding values, as shown here:

```
INSERT INTO items
    (item_category, item_id, item_desc)
VALUES ('junk food', 2, 'fried pork skins')
GO
```

Because we did not specify the price, the *price* column will get a *NULL* for this row. Now execute the following SELECT statement:

```
SELECT * FROM items
```

You should see the following result set (which now includes the two rows we inserted). Notice the *NULL* in the *price* column.

item_category	item_id	price	item_desc
health food	1	4.00	tofu 6 oz.
junk food	2	NULL	fried pork skins

Now let's add another row, without specifying values for either the *price* or the *item_desc* column, as shown here:

```
INSERT INTO items
    (item_category, item_id)
VALUES ('toys', 3)
GO
```

The result set for this row alone can be found by using this query:

```
SELECT * FROM items WHERE item_id = 3
```

The result set will appear as follows:

item_category	item_id	price	item_desc
toys	3	NULL	No desc

Notice the *NULL* in the *price* column and the *No desc* in the *item_desc* column. You can change these values by using the UPDATE statement, as you'll see later in this chapter.

The four types of columns for which SQL Server will automatically provide a value when one is not specified are columns that allow null values, columns with a default value, identity columns, and *timestamp* columns. We have seen what happens with nullable columns and columns with default values. An identity column gets the next available identity value, and a *timestamp* column gets the current timestamp value. (These types of columns are described in Chapter 10.) In most cases, you cannot manually insert data values into these two types of columns.

> **Note**   Exercise caution when performing an INSERT operation on a table. Be sure that the data you are inserting is being put in its intended column. Make sure you thoroughly test any T-SQL code before you use it to access or modify any important data.

Adding Rows from Another Table

You can also insert rows into a table from another table. You do this by using a derived table in the INSERT statement or by using the EXECUTE clause with a stored procedure that returns rows of data.

> **Note**   A *derived table* is the result set from a SELECT statement nested in the FROM clause of another T-SQL statement. For a more detailed explanation, see Chapter 14.

To perform an insertion by using a derived table, let's first create a second small table named *two_newest_items*, into which we will insert rows from the *items* table. The CREATE TABLE statement for the new table is shown here:

```
CREATE TABLE two_newest_items
(
item_id     SMALLINT    NOT NULL,
item_desc   VARCHAR(30) DEFAULT 'No desc'
)
GO
```

To insert the two most recent *item_id* and *item_desc* column values from the *items* table into the *two_newest_items* table, use the following INSERT statement:

```
INSERT INTO two_newest_items
    (item_id, item_desc)
SELECT TOP 2 item_id, item_desc FROM items
ORDER BY item_id DESC
GO
```

Notice that instead of using a value list in this INSERT statement, we used a SELECT statement. This SELECT statement returns data from an existing table, and that returned data is used as the value list. Also, notice that we did not use parentheses around the SELECT statement—parentheses would cause a syntax error to be returned.

We can query this new table for all rows by using this query:

```
SELECT * FROM two_newest_items
```

The following result set will appear:

```
item_id item_desc
------- ------------
3       No desc
2       fried pork skins
```

Notice that we included the ORDER BY *item_id* DESC clause in the INSERT statement. This clause tells SQL Server to order the results by *item_id* in descending order.

If we create the SELECT statement in the preceding insertion example as a stored procedure and use the EXECUTE statement with a stored procedure name, we'll get the same results we got in that example. (Stored procedures are explained in Chapter 21.) To do that, we first delete all existing rows in the *two_newest_items* table by using the DELETE statement so we can start with an empty table. (For details, see the section "The DELETE Statement" later in this chapter.) Then we create a stored procedure named *top_two* and use it with the EXECUTE statement to insert two new rows into the *two_newest_items* table. The T-SQL statements to perform these actions are as follows:

```
DELETE FROM two_newest_items
GO
CREATE PROCEDURE top_two
AS
SELECT TOP 2 item_id, item_desc FROM items
ORDER BY item_id DESC
GO
```

```
INSERT INTO two_newest_items
    (item_id, item_desc)
EXECUTE top_two
GO
```

The two rows that were inserted in the previous example are deleted, and then the INSERT statement inserts two new rows (containing the same data) by using the stored procedure *top_two*.

More Info You can also specify table hints with the INSERT statement. For details about which hints can be used with the INSERT statement, use the Search tab of Books Online to search for "Locking Hints" and select the topic "Locking Hints."

The UPDATE Statement

The UPDATE statement is used to modify or update existing data. The basic syntax for the UPDATE statement is shown here:

```
UPDATE table_name SET column_name = expression
    [FROM table_source] WHERE search_condition
```

Updating Rows

Building on our sample table, *items*, we'll first update the *junk food* row that we inserted earlier without a price. To identify the row, specify *fried pork skins* in the search condition. To set (update) the price to $2, use the following statement:

```
UPDATE items SET price = 2.00
WHERE item_desc = 'fried pork skins'
GO
```

Now select the *junk food* row by using this query:

```
SELECT * FROM items
WHERE item_desc = 'fried pork skins'
GO
```

The output for the *junk food* row appears as follows, with the original *NULL* value for *price* replaced by *2.00*:

```
item_category    item_id  price      item_desc
---------------  -------  ---------  ----------------
junk food        2        2.00       fried pork skins
```

To increase the price of this item by 10 percent, you would run the following statement:

```
UPDATE items SET price = price * 1.10
WHERE item_desc = 'fried pork skins'
GO
```

Now if you select the *junk food* row, you will notice the price has been changed to $2.20 ($2 multiplied by 1.10). The prices of the other items have not changed.

You can update more than one row by using an UPDATE statement. For example, to update all the rows in the *items* table by increasing their *price* values by 10 percent, run the following statement:

```
UPDATE items SET price = price * 1.10
GO
```

Now if you examine the *items* table, it will look like this:

```
item_category    item_id price      item_desc
---------------- ------- ---------- ----------------
health food      1       4.40       tofu 6 oz.
junk food        2       2.42       fried pork skins
toys             3       NULL       No desc
```

Rows with a value of *NULL* for *price* will not be affected because $NULL * 1.10 = NULL$. This is not a problem; you will not get an error.

Using the FROM Clause

The UPDATE statement enables you to use the FROM clause to specify a table to be used as the source of data in an update. The table source list can include table names, view names, rowset functions, derived tables, and joined tables. Even the table that is being updated can be used as a table source. To see how this process works, let's first create another small sample table. The CREATE TABLE statement for our new table, named *tax*, and an INSERT statement to insert a row with a value of *5.25* for the *tax_percent* column are shown here:

```
CREATE TABLE tax
(
tax_percent     real                NOT NULL,
change_date     smalldatetime       DEFAULT getdate()
)
GO
INSERT INTO tax
    (tax_percent) VALUES (5.25)
GO
```

The *change_date* column will get the current date and time from its default GETDATE function because a date was not explicitly inserted.

Next let's add a new, nullable column, *price_with_tax*, to our original *items* table, as shown here:

```
ALTER TABLE items
ADD price_with_tax smallmoney NULL
GO
```

Next we want to update the new *price_with_tax* column to contain the result of *items.price * tax.tax_percent* for all rows in the *items* table. To do so, use the following UPDATE statement with a FROM clause:

```
UPDATE items
SET price_with_tax = i.price +
    (i.price * t.tax_percent / 100)
FROM items i, tax t
GO
```

The two rows in the *items* table that have a value in the *price* column now have a calculated value in the *price_with_tax* column. The row that has a *NULL* for *price* is not affected, and its *price_with_tax* entry is *NULL* as well, because a null value multiplied by anything is *NULL*. The result set for all rows in the *items* table (including all of the modifications we have made so far) now looks like this:

```
item_category   item_id price      item_desc        price_with_tax
-------------   ------- --------   --------------   --------------
health food     1       4.40       tofu 6 oz.       4.63
junk food       2       2.42       fried pork skins 2.55
toys            3       NULL       No desc          NULL
```

If you add items to the table, you could run the preceding UPDATE statement again, but that would repeat the same update on rows that already have a value for *price_with_tax*, which would waste processing time. You can use the WHERE clause of the UPDATE statement so that only rows that currently have a *NULL* in the *price_with_tax* column are updated, as shown here:

```
UPDATE items
SET price_with_tax = i.price +
    (i.price * t.tax_percent / 100)
FROM items i, tax t
WHERE i.price_with_tax IS NULL
GO
```

This UPDATE statement is a good candidate for a trigger that would be executed when a value is inserted into the *price* column. A *trigger* is a special type of stored procedure that is automatically executed upon certain conditions. Triggers will be discussed in detail in Chapter 22.

Using Derived Tables

Another way to use the UPDATE statement is with a derived table, or subquery, in the FROM clause. The derived table is used as input for the outer UPDATE statement. For this example, we will use the *two_newest_items* table in the subquery and the *items* table in the outer UPDATE statement. We want to update the two newest rows in the *items* table to contain a *price_with_tax* value of *NULL*. By querying the *two_newest_items* table, we can find the *item_id* values of the rows that need to be updated in the *items* table. The following statement achieves this:

```
UPDATE items
SET price_with_tax = NULL
FROM (SELECT item_id FROM two_newest_items) AS t1
WHERE items.item_id = t1.item_id
GO
```

The SELECT statement serves as a subquery, whose results are put into a temporary derived table called *t1*, which is then used in the search condition (the WHERE clause). The results from the subquery give us the *item_id* values 2 and 3. Thus, the two rows in the *items* table with an *item_id* column value of 2 or 3 are affected. The row with an *item_id* value of 3 already had a *NULL* in the *price_with_tax* column, so it does not change values. The row with an *item_id* value of 2 does get its *price_with_tax* value changed to *NULL*. The result set showing all rows in the *items* table after this update looks like this:

```
item_category   item_id price      item_desc         price_with_tax
--------------- ------- ---------  ----------------- --------------
health food     1       4.40       tofu 6 oz.        4.63
junk food       2       2.42       fried pork skins  NULL
toys            3       NULL       No desc           NULL
```

More Info For details about additional options that can be used with the UP-DATE statement, such as table hints and query hints, check the Books Online index for "UPDATE" and select the subtopic "Described."

The DELETE Statement

The DELETE statement is used to remove (delete) a row or rows from a table or view. DELETE does not affect the table definition; it simply deletes rows of data from the table. The basic syntax for the DELETE statement is shown here:

```
DELETE [FROM] table_name | view_name
    [FROM table_sources] WHERE search_condition
```

The first FROM keyword is optional, as is the second FROM clause. Rows are not deleted from the table sources in the second FROM clause; they are deleted from only the table or view specified after DELETE.

Deleting Individual Rows

By using the WHERE clause with DELETE, you can specify certain rows to delete from a table. For example, to delete all rows from the *items* table that have an *item_category* value of *toys*, run the following statement:

```
DELETE FROM items
WHERE item_category = 'toys'
GO
```

This statement deletes one row from our *items* table.

You can use a second FROM clause with one or more table sources to specify other tables and views that can be used in the WHERE search condition. For example, to delete rows from the *items* table that correspond to the rows in the *two_newest_items* table, run the following statement:

```
DELETE items
FROM two_newest_items
WHERE items.item_id = two_newest_items.item_id
GO
```

Notice that in this statement we left out the first optional FROM keyword. The two rows in the *two_newest_items* table have *item_id* values of 2 and 3. The *items* table contains *item_id* values of 1 and 2, so the row with 2 as its *item_id* value (the one that matched the search condition) gets deleted. The two rows in the *two_newest_items* table (the table source) are not affected.

Deleting All Rows

To delete all rows from a table, use DELETE without a WHERE clause. The following DELETE statement will delete all rows in the *two_newest_items* table on the next page.

```
DELETE FROM two_newest_items
GO
```

The *two_newest_items* table is now an empty table—it contains no data. If you want to delete the table definition as well, use the DROP TABLE command, as follows. (This command is explained in Chapter 15.)

```
DROP TABLE two_newest_items
GO
```

More Info To learn more ways of using the DELETE statement, such as using joined tables as table sources and using table and query hints, check the Books Online index for "DELETE" and select the subtopic "Described."

Programming Keywords

Several helpful programming-construct keywords can be used with T-SQL statements to control program flow. These constructs can be used within batches (a group of T-SQL statements that are executed at one time), stored procedures, scripts, and ad hoc queries. (The examples in this section use the pubs database.)

IF...ELSE

The IF...ELSE construct is used to impose conditions that determine which T-SQL statements will execute. The syntax for IF...ELSE is shown here:

```
IF Boolean_expression
T-SQL_statement | block_of_statements
[ELSE T-SQL_statement | block_of_statements]
```

A *Boolean expression* is one that returns either *TRUE* or *FALSE*. If the expression in the IF clause returns *TRUE*, the subsequent statements are executed, but the ELSE clause and its statements are not executed. If the expression returns *FALSE*, only the statements after the ELSE keyword are executed. The variable *block_of_statements* simply refers to more than one T-SQL statement. When a block of statements is used, you must provide the keywords BEGIN and END to specify the beginning and the end of each block, whether the block is in the IF clause, the ELSE clause, or both.

You can have an IF clause without an ELSE clause. Let's look first at an example that uses IF alone. The following code will test an expression, and if the expression returns *TRUE*, the subsequent PRINT statement will be executed:

```
IF (SELECT ytd_sales FROM titles
    WHERE title_id = 'PC1035') > 5000
PRINT 'Year-to-date sales are
    greater than $5,000 for PC1035.'
GO
```

The IF expression will evaluate to *TRUE* because the *ytd_sales* value for the row with *title_id* = "*PC1035*" is *8780*. The PRINT statement will be executed, and "Year-to-date sales are greater than $5,000 for PC1035" will be printed to the screen.

Now let's add an ELSE clause to the preceding example and change the > *5000* to > *9000*. The code is shown here:

```
IF (SELECT ytd_sales FROM titles
    WHERE title_id = 'PC1035') > 9000
PRINT 'Year-to-date sales are
    greater than $9,000 for PC1035.'
ELSE
PRINT 'Year-to-date sales are
    less than or equal to $9,000 for PC1035.'
GO
```

In this case, the PRINT statement after the ELSE clause will be executed because the IF expression returns *FALSE*.

Let's take this example a step further and add a block of statements after the IF clause and a block after the ELSE clause. Which message will be printed and which query will then be performed will depend on whether the IF condition is *TRUE* or *FALSE*. Here is the code:

```
IF (SELECT ytd_sales FROM titles WHERE title_id = 'PC1035') > 9000
BEGIN
    PRINT 'Year-to-date sales are
        greater than $9,000 for PC1035.'
    SELECT ytd_sales FROM titles
        WHERE title_id = 'PC1035'
END
ELSE    --ytd_sales must be <= 9000.
BEGIN
    PRINT 'Year-to-date sales are
        less than or equal to $9,000 for PC1035.'
    SELECT price FROM titles
        WHERE title_id = 'PC1035'
END
GO
```

The IF expression evaluates to *FALSE*, so the statements between BEGIN and END in the ELSE clause are executed. The PRINT statement is executed first, and then the SELECT statement is executed, showing that the book costs $22.95.

You can also use nested IF statements after an IF clause or after an ELSE clause. For example, to use nested IF...ELSE statements to determine what range the average *ytd_sales* value for all titles falls into, run the following code:

```
IF (SELECT avg(ytd_sales) FROM titles) < 10000
    IF (SELECT avg(ytd_sales) FROM titles) < 5000
        IF (SELECT avg(ytd_sales) FROM titles) < 2000
            PRINT 'Average year-to-date sales are
            less than $2,000.'
        ELSE
        PRINT 'Average year-to-date sales are
            between $2,000 and $4,999.'
    ELSE
    PRINT 'Average year-to-date sales are
        between $5,000 and $9,999.'
ELSE
PRINT 'Average year-to-date sales are greater
    than $9,999.'
GO
```

When you run this code, you will see the following warning message twice in the output: "Warning: Null value eliminated from aggregate." This message means simply that the null values that exist in the *ytd_sales* column were not counted as values when the average was calculated. The final result from this code will be "Average year-to-date sales are between $5,000 and $9,999" because the average is $6,090. Be careful when using nested IF statements. It's easy to mix up which IF belongs with which ELSE, or to leave an IF without a corresponding ELSE. Using tabs for spacing, as in the preceding query, makes it easier to see which IF...ELSE pairs belong together.

WHILE

The WHILE construct is used to test a condition that causes the repeated execution of a statement or block of statements while the condition is *TRUE*. This is commonly known as a WHILE loop because the code inside the WHILE construct is repeated in loop fashion. The syntax is shown here:

```
WHILE Boolean_expression
SQL_statement | block_of_statements
[BREAK] SQL_statement | block_of_statements
[CONTINUE]
```

As in IF...ELSE clauses, you specify a block of statements in a WHILE loop by using BEGIN and END. The BREAK keyword causes an exit from the WHILE loop, and execution will continue with any statements after the end of the WHILE loop. If the WHILE loop is nested within other WHILE loops, the BREAK keyword causes an exit from only the WHILE loop in which it is contained; any statements outside the loop, as well as the outer loops, will continue to execute. The CONTINUE keyword in a loop specifies that the statements between the BEGIN and END keywords for that WHILE loop should restart, ignoring any other statements after CONTINUE.

Let's look at an example that uses a simple WHILE loop to repeatedly execute one UPDATE statement. The condition in this WHILE loop tests whether the average value of the *royalty* column is less than *20*. If the test returns *TRUE*, the *royalty* column is updated by increasing all royalties by 5 percent. The WHILE condition is then checked again, and the update is repeated until the average value of the *royalty* column is *20* or higher. The code is as follows:

```
WHILE (SELECT AVG(royalty) FROM roysched) < 20
UPDATE roysched SET royalty = royalty * 1.05
GO
```

Because the average value of the *royalty* column was originally *15*, this WHILE loop is executed 21 times before the average value reaches *20*; the loop then terminates because the test condition returns *FALSE*.

Now let's look at an example that uses BEGIN, BREAK, CONTINUE, and END in a WHILE loop. We will loop through the UPDATE statement until the average royalty exceeds 25 percent. If, however, during the loop, the maximum royalty in the table exceeds 27 percent, we will break out of the loop no matter what the average is. We'll also add a SELECT statement after the end of the WHILE loop. Here is the T-SQL code:

```
WHILE (SELECT AVG(royalty) FROM roysched) < 25
BEGIN
UPDATE roysched SET royalty = royalty * 1.05
IF (SELECT MAX(royalty)FROM roysched) > 27
BREAK
ELSE
CONTINUE
END
SELECT MAX(royalty) AS "MAX royalty" FROM roysched
GO
```

This loop will execute only one time because a *royalty* value greater than 27 already exists in the table. The UPDATE statement is executed once because the average royalty is less than 25 percent. Then the IF statement is tested and returns *TRUE*, so BREAK is executed, causing an exit from the WHILE loop. Program execution then continues with the statement following the END keyword, the last SELECT statement.

Remember that you can also use nested WHILE loops, but keep in mind that a BREAK or CONTINUE keyword applies only to the loop from which it was called, not to outer WHILE loops.

CASE

The CASE keyword is used to evaluate a list of conditions and return one of multiple possible results. Which result is returned will depend on which condition is equal to another specified condition or is true. Common uses for CASE are to replace a code or an abbreviated value with a more readable value, and to categorize values, as will be shown in our examples in this section. The two formats for the CASE construct are called simple and searched. The *simple* format specifies an input expression value after CASE that will be tested for equality with the value in the WHEN expression or expressions. The *searched* format tests a Boolean expression for *TRUE* or *FALSE* rather than testing for equality with a value. Let's first look at the simple format. The syntax for a simple-format CASE clause is shown here:

```
CASE input_expression
    WHEN when_expression THEN result_expression
    [WHEN when_expression THEN result_expression…n]
    [ELSE else_result_expression]
END
```

The result expression value will be returned if the corresponding WHEN expression value is equal to the input expression value. The expressions are compared in the order in which they are listed in the CASE clause. If no match is made, the ELSE result expression value will be returned if one is specified, or *NULL* is returned if an ELSE result expression value is not specified. Note that in the simple-format CASE clause, the input expression value and the WHEN expression value must have the same data type or allow implicit conversion.

This example uses a simple-format CASE clause within a SELECT statement. The *payterms* column of the *sales* table contains one of these values for each row: *Net 30*, *Net 60*, *On invoice*, or *None*. This T-SQL statement allows an alternative (easier to understand) value to be displayed in the *payterms* column:

```
SELECT 'Payment Terms' =
CASE payterms
    WHEN 'Net 30' THEN 'Payable 30 days
        after invoice'
    WHEN 'Net 60' THEN 'Payable 60 days
        after invoice'
    WHEN 'On invoice' THEN 'Payable upon
        receipt of invoice'
    ELSE 'None'
    END,
title_id
FROM sales
ORDER BY payterms
GO
```

This CASE clause tests the value of *payterms* for each row specified in the SELECT statement. The result expression value is returned when the WHEN expression value equals the value in *payterms*. The results from the CASE clause appear in the *Payment Terms* column in the result set, as shown here:

```
Payment Terms                                  title_id
-----------------------------------------      --------
Payable 30 days after invoice                  PC8888
Payable 30 days after invoice                  TC3218
Payable 30 days after invoice                  TC4203
Payable 30 days after invoice                  TC7777
Payable 30 days after invoice                  PS2091
Payable 30 days after invoice                  MC3021
Payable 30 days after invoice                  BU1111
Payable 30 days after invoice                  PC1035
Payable 60 days after invoice                  PS1372
Payable 60 days after invoice                  PS2106
Payable 60 days after invoice                  PS3333
Payable 60 days after invoice                  PS7777
Payable 60 days after invoice                  BU7832
Payable 60 days after invoice                  MC2222
Payable 60 days after invoice                  PS2091
Payable 60 days after invoice                  BU1032
Payable 60 days after invoice                  PS2091
Payable upon receipt of invoice                PS2091
Payable upon receipt of invoice                BU1032
Payable upon receipt of invoice                BU2075
Payable upon receipt of invoice                MC3021

(21 row(s) affected)
```

Now let's look at the second CASE clause format, the searched format. The syntax for the searched-format CASE clause is shown here:

```
CASE
    WHEN Boolean_expression THEN result_expression
    [WHEN Boolean_expression THEN result_expression…n]
    [ELSE else_result_expression]
END
```

The difference between the simple-format CASE clause and the searched-format CASE clause is that the searched-format CASE clause does not have an input expression value after the CASE keyword; it has Boolean expressions after the WHEN keywords to test for *TRUE* or *FALSE* rather than for equality. A searched-format CASE clause tests the Boolean expression values and displays the corresponding result expression value for the first Boolean expression value that returns *TRUE*. (The expressions are tested in the order in which they are listed.)

For example, the CASE clause within the following SELECT statement will test each row for its *price* value and will return a character string based on the price range in which the price of the book falls:

```
SELECT 'Price Range' =
    CASE
        WHEN price BETWEEN .01 AND 10.00
            THEN 'Inexpensive: $10.00 or less'
        WHEN price BETWEEN 10.01 AND 20.00
            THEN 'Moderate: $10.01 to $20.00'
        WHEN price BETWEEN 20.01 AND 30.00
            THEN 'Semi-expensive: $20.01 to $30.00'
        WHEN price BETWEEN 30.01 AND 50.00
            THEN 'Expensive: $30.01 to $50.00'
        WHEN price IS NULL
            THEN 'No price listed'
        ELSE 'Very expensive!'
    END,
title_id
FROM titles
ORDER BY price
GO
```

The result set is shown here:

```
Price Range                      title_id
-------------------------------- --------
No price listed                  MC3026
No price listed                  PC9999
Inexpensive: $10.00 or less      MC3021
Inexpensive: $10.00 or less      BU2075
```

```
Inexpensive: $10.00 or less      PS2106
Inexpensive: $10.00 or less      PS7777
Moderate: $10.01 to $20.00       PS2091
Moderate: $10.01 to $20.00       BU1111
Moderate: $10.01 to $20.00       TC4203
Moderate: $10.01 to $20.00       TC7777
Moderate: $10.01 to $20.00       BU1032
Moderate: $10.01 to $20.00       BU7832
Moderate: $10.01 to $20.00       MC2222
Moderate: $10.01 to $20.00       PS3333
Moderate: $10.01 to $20.00       PC8888
Semi-expensive: $20.01 to $30.00 TC3218
Semi-expensive: $20.01 to $30.00 PS1372
Semi-expensive: $20.01 to $30.00 PC1035

(18 row(s) affected)
```

> **Note**   In these two CASE clause examples, we inserted a comma after the END keyword because the entire CASE clause was used as part of *column_list* in the SELECT clause along with *title_id*. In other words, the entire CASE clause was simply an entry in *column_list*. This is the most common use of the CASE keyword.

Other Keywords

The additional T-SQL keywords available for controlling programming flow are listed here:

- **GOTO** *label*   Directs processing to continue at *label* as defined in GOTO

- **RETURN**   Exits unconditionally from a query or procedure

- **WAITFOR**   Sets a delay or a specific time for a statement to execute

> **More Info**   For details about how to use these keywords, check the Books Online index for "GOTO," "RETURN," and "WAITFOR" and examine the topics listed in the Topics Found dialog box.

Summary

In this chapter, you have learned to use the INSERT, UPDATE, and DELETE T-SQL statements. You have also learned about the T-SQL keywords IF, ELSE, WHILE, BEGIN, END, and CASE, which are used to control programming flow. In Chapter 21, you'll learn how to create stored procedures in which you can use these statements and constructs.

Chapter 21
Creating and Managing Stored Procedures

In this chapter, you'll learn about Microsoft SQL Server 2000 stored procedures and how to use them. First we'll look at the types of stored procedures used in SQL Server. Then you'll learn how to create and manage your own stored procedures and how to define parameters and variables. You can use four methods to create stored procedures. This chapter describes how to use Transact-SQL (T-SQL), SQL Server Enterprise Manager, and the Create Stored Procedure Wizard. The fourth method of creating stored procedures, using SQL Distributed Management Objects (SQL-DMO), will not be covered here because it pertains to application programming. As you'll see, the three methods explained in this chapter require that you know the same T-SQL code, so pay close attention to the description of the first method, in the section "Using the CREATE PROCEDURE Statement."

What Is a Stored Procedure?

A *stored procedure* is a collection of T-SQL statements that SQL Server compiles into a single execution plan. This plan is stored in the procedure cache area of memory when the stored procedure is first executed so that the plan can be used repeatedly; SQL Server does not have to recompile it every time the stored procedure is run. T-SQL stored procedures are similar to procedures in other programming languages in that they can accept input parameters, return output values as parameters, or return success or failure status messages. All of the statements in the procedure are processed when the procedure is called. Stored procedures are used to group the T-SQL statements and any associated logic needed to perform a task. Since they are stored as a procedural unit, stored procedures can be used to allow different users to repeat the same task consistently, even across multiple applications. Stored procedures also provide a single point of control for a task, which helps to ensure that any business rules are consistently and correctly enforced.

Your application can communicate with SQL Server in two ways—you can code the application to send the T-SQL statements from the client to SQL Server, or you can create stored procedures, which are stored and run at the server. If you send your T-SQL statements from the client application to the server, the statements will be sent across the network and recompiled by SQL Server each time they are run. If you use stored procedures, you can execute the stored procedures by calling them from your application with one statement. As mentioned, the first time a stored procedure is executed, it is compiled and its execution plan is created and stored in memory. SQL Server will then use this execution plan when the procedure is called again, without recompiling it. Therefore, when several T-SQL statements are needed to perform a task or when a statement is processed frequently, using a stored procedure can reduce network traffic and can be more efficient and faster than sending each statement over the network from the client to the server.

Stored procedures can improve performance in other ways. For example, using stored procedures for testing server conditions can improve performance by reducing the amount of data that must be passed between the client and the server and by reducing the amount of processing done on the client. To test for a condition from within a stored procedure, you program conditional statements (such as the IF and WHILE constructs, covered in Chapter 20) into the stored procedure. The logic for this test will be handled at the server through the stored procedure, so you don't have to code that logic into the application itself, and the server does not have to return intermediate results to the client to test the condition. You can also call stored procedures from scripts, batches, and interactive command lines by using the T-SQL statements shown in the examples later in this chapter.

Stored procedures also provide easy database access for users. Users can access the database without having to know the architectural details of the tables and without directly accessing table data—they simply execute the procedures that perform the required tasks. In this way, stored procedures help to ensure that the business rules are protected.

Stored procedures can accept input parameters, use local variables, and return data. Stored procedures can return data by using output parameters, return codes, result sets from SELECT statements, or global cursors. You'll see examples of these techniques (except using global cursors) in later sections.

More Info You can find information about using cursors and global cursors by searching for "Cursors" in the Search tab of Books Online and selecting the topics "Cursors" (in the Transact-SQL Reference) and "DECLARE CURSOR (T-SQL)."

There are three types of stored procedures: system stored procedures, extended stored procedures, and simple user-defined stored procedures. *System stored procedures* are supplied by SQL Server and have the prefix *sp_*. They are used to manage SQL Server and to display information about databases and users. System stored procedures were introduced in Chapter 13. *Extended stored procedures* are dynamic-link libraries (DLLs) that SQL Server can dynamically load and execute. They are generally written in C or C++, and they execute routines external to SQL Server. Extended stored procedures have the prefix *xp_*. *Simple user-defined stored procedures* are created by the user and customized to perform whatever task the user wants.

Note   You should not use the *sp_* prefix when you create simple user-defined stored procedures. When SQL Server encounters a stored procedure that has the *sp_* prefix, it first looks for that stored procedure in the master database. So if you create a stored procedure named *sp_myproc* in the MyDB database, for example, SQL Server will look for the procedure in the master database before it looks in any user databases. It would be more efficient to name the procedure simply *myproc*.

In this chapter, we'll focus on simple user-defined stored procedures. Before we begin learning about these procedures, however, we'll briefly go over some basic facts about extended stored procedures. Extended stored procedures allow great flexibility and extensibility in the SQL Server environment. They allow you to create your own external routines in C, C++, or other programming languages. Extended stored procedures are executed in the same manner as the other two types of stored procedures. You can pass parameters to extended stored procedures, like you can to the other types of stored procedures, and they can return result sets, status messages, or both.

As mentioned, extended stored procedures are DLLs that SQL Server dynamically loads and executes. They run directly in the address space of SQL Server, and you program them by using the SQL Server Open Data Services API.

You write extended stored procedures outside SQL Server. Once you complete an extended stored procedure, you register it in SQL Server, either by using T-SQL commands or via Enterprise Manager.

More Info   For additional information about and examples of extended procedures, look in SQL Server Books Online.

Creating Stored Procedures

In this section, we'll look at three methods for creating a stored procedure: using the T-SQL CREATE PROCEDURE statement, using Enterprise Manager, and using the Create Stored Procedure Wizard. Whichever method you choose, make sure that you execute each procedure to test it, and then edit and re-create the procedure, as necessary, until it functions the way you want it to.

Using the CREATE PROCEDURE Statement

The basic syntax for the CREATE PROCEDURE statement is shown here:

```
CREATE PROC[EDURE] procedure_name
                [ {@parameter_name data_type} ] [= default] [OUTPUT]
                [,...,n]
AS t-sql_statement(s)
```

Let's create a simple stored procedure. This stored procedure will select (and return) three columns of data for each row in the *Orders* table with a date in the *ShippedDate* column later than the date in the *RequiredDate* column. Note that a stored procedure can be created in only the database that is currently being accessed, so we must first specify the database via the USE statement. Before we create the procedure, we will also determine whether a stored procedure with the name we want to use already exists. If one does exist, we will drop it, and then we will create a new procedure with the same name. The T-SQL code used to create this procedure is shown here:

```
USE Northwind
GO

IF EXISTS (SELECT name
           FROM    sysobjects
           WHERE   name = "LateShipments" AND
                   type = "P")
DROP PROCEDURE LateShipments
GO

CREATE PROCEDURE LateShipments
AS
SELECT RequiredDate,
       ShippedDate,
       Shippers.CompanyName
FROM   Orders, Shippers
WHERE  ShippedDate   > RequiredDate AND
       Orders.ShipVia = Shippers.ShipperID
GO
```

When you run this T-SQL code, the stored procedure will be created. To run the stored procedure, simply call it by name, as shown here:

```
LateShipments
GO
```

The *LateShipments* procedure will return 37 rows of data.

If the statement that calls the procedure is part of a batch of statements and is not the first statement in the batch, you must use the EXECUTE (which can be abbreviated as "EXEC") keyword with the procedure call, as in the following example:

```
SELECT getdate()
EXECUTE LateShipments
GO
```

You can use the EXECUTE keyword even if the procedure is run as the first statement in a batch or if it is the only statement you are running.

Using Parameters

Now let's add an input parameter to our stored procedure so that we can pass data into the procedure. To specify input parameters in a stored procedure, list the parameters, preceding each one with an @ symbol, as in *@parameter_name*. You can specify up to 1024 parameters in a stored procedure. For our example, we will create a parameter called *@shipperName*. When we then run the stored procedure, we enter a shipping company name, and the query will return rows for only that shipper. Here is the T-SQL code used to create the new stored procedure:

```
USE Northwind
GO

IF EXISTS (SELECT name
           FROM   sysobjects
           WHERE  name = "LateShipments" AND
                  type = "P")
DROP PROCEDURE LateShipments
GO

CREATE PROCEDURE LateShipments @shipperName char(40)
AS
SELECT RequiredDate,
       ShippedDate,
       Shippers.CompanyName
FROM   Orders, Shippers
WHERE  ShippedDate         > RequiredDate AND
```

(continued)

continued

```
        Orders.ShipVia        = Shippers.ShipperID AND
        Shippers.CompanyName = @shipperName
GO
```

To run this stored procedure, you must supply an input parameter. If you don't, SQL Server will display an error message similar to the following:

```
Procedure LateShipments, Line 0 Procedure 'LateShipments'
expects parameter '@shipperName', which was not supplied.
```

To return the qualifying rows for the shipper Speedy Express, run the following statement:

```
USE Northwind
GO


EXECUTE LateShipments "Speedy Express"
GO
```

You will see 12 rows returned from this stored-procedure call.

You can also supply a default value for a parameter, which will be used if no parameter is entered in the procedure call. For example, to use the default of *United Package* for our stored procedure, change the procedure's creation code to look like this. (Only the CREATE PROCEDURE line has been changed.)

```
USE Northwind
GO
IF EXISTS (SELECT name
           FROM    sysobjects
           WHERE   name = "LateShipments" AND
                   type = "P")
DROP PROCEDURE LateShipments
GO

CREATE PROCEDURE LateShipments @shipperName char(40) = "United Package"
AS
SELECT RequiredDate,
       ShippedDate,
       Shippers.CompanyName
FROM    Orders, Shippers
WHERE   ShippedDate            > RequiredDate AND
        Orders.ShipVia        = Shippers.ShipperID AND
        Shippers.CompanyName = @shipperName
GO
```

Now when you run *LateShipments* without providing an input parameter, the procedure will use the default, *United Package*, for *@shipperName*, and it will return 16 rows. Even when a default parameter has been defined, you can provide an input parameter, which will override the default.

To return the value of a parameter in a stored procedure to the calling program, use the OUTPUT keyword after the parameter name. To save the value in a variable that can be used in the calling program, use the OUTPUT keyword when calling the stored procedure. To see how this works, let's create a new stored procedure that selects the unit price for a specified product. The input parameter, *@prod_id*, will be a product ID, and the output parameter, *@unit_price*, will be the returned unit price. A local variable named *@price* will be declared in the calling program and will be used to save the returned value. Here is the code used to create the *GetUnitPrice* stored procedure:

```
USE Northwind
GO

IF EXISTS (SELECT name
           FROM    sysobjects
           WHERE   name = "GetUnitPrice" AND
                   type = "P")
DROP PROCEDURE GetUnitPrice
GO

CREATE PROCEDURE GetUnitPrice @prod_id int, @unit_price money OUTPUT
AS
SELECT @unit_price = UnitPrice
FROM    Products
WHERE   ProductID = @prod_id
GO
```

You must declare the variable in the calling program before you can use it in the stored-procedure call. For example, in the following code, we first declare the *@price* variable and assign it the data type *money* (which must be compatible with the output parameter data type), and then we execute the stored procedure:

```
DECLARE @price money
EXECUTE GetUnitPrice 77, @unit_price = @price OUTPUT
PRINT CONVERT(varchar(6), @price)
GO
```

The PRINT statement returns the value *13.00* for *@price*. Note that we used the CONVERT statement to convert the value of *@price* to the *varchar* data type so that we could print it as a string, as a character data type, or as a type that can be implicitly converted to character—which is required for the PRINT statement.

Also, notice also that different names were used for the output variables in the stored procedure and in the calling program so that you could better follow the placement of the variables in the example and to show that the names can be different.

You can also specify an input value for an output parameter when you execute a stored procedure. This means that the value will be entered into the stored procedure, which can modify the value or use it for operations; then the value is returned to the calling program. To send an input value to an output parameter, simply assign a value to the variable in the calling program before you execute the procedure, or execute a query that retrieves a value into a variable and then send that variable to the stored procedure. Now let's take a look at using local variables within a stored procedure.

Using Local Variables Within Stored Procedures

As shown in the preceding section, the DECLARE keyword is used to create local variables. You must specify the local variable's name and data type when you create it, and you must precede the variable name with an @ symbol. When you declare a variable, its value is initially set to *NULL*.

Local variables can be declared in a batch, in a script (or calling program), or in a stored procedure. Variables are often used in stored procedures to hold values that will be tested in a condition statement and to hold values that will be returned by a stored-procedure RETURN statement. Variables in stored procedures are also frequently used as counters. The scope of a local variable in a stored procedure is from the point at which the variable is declared until the stored procedure exits. Once the procedure exits, that variable can no longer be referenced.

Let's look at an example of a stored procedure that contains local variables. This procedure inserts five rows into a table by using the WHILE loop construct. First we will create a sample table, *mytable,* and then we will create the stored procedure, *InsertRows.* The local variables we will use in the procedure are *@loop_counter* and *@start_val,* which we will declare together and separate by a comma. The following T-SQL code creates the table and the stored procedure:

```
USE MyDB
GO

CREATE TABLE mytable
(
    column1 int,
    column2 char(10)
)
```

```
GO

CREATE PROCEDURE InsertRows @start_value int
AS
DECLARE @loop_counter int, @start_val int
SET     @start_val = @start_value - 1
SET     @loop_counter = 0
WHILE (@loop_counter < 5)
   BEGIN
       INSERT INTO mytable VALUES (@start_val + 1, "new row")
       PRINT (@start_val)
       SET @start_val = @start_val + 1
       SET @loop_counter = @loop_counter + 1
   END
GO
```

Now let's execute this stored procedure with a start value of *1*, as shown here:

```
EXECUTE InsertRows 1
GO
```

You'll see five values printed for *@start_val*: *0, 1, 2, 3*, and *4*. Select all rows from *mytable* by using the following statement:

```
SELECT *
FROM    mytable
GO
```

After we execute this SELECT statement, the output looks like this:

```
column1      column2
-----------  --------
1            new row
2            new row
3            new row
4            new row
5            new row
```

After the stored procedure is completed, the two variables *@loop_counter* and *@start_val* can no longer be accessed. You will receive an error message if you try to print them by using the following T-SQL statement:

```
PRINT (@loop_counter)
PRINT (@start_val)
GO
```

The error message will be similar to this:

```
Msg 137, Level 15, State 2, Server JAMIERE3, Line 1
Must declare the variable '@loop_counter'.
Msg 137, Level 15, State 2, Server JAMIERE3, Line 2
Must declare the variable '@start_value'.
```

The same rules concerning the scope of a variable apply when you are running a batch of statements. As soon as the GO keyword is issued (which marks the end of the batch), any local variables declared within the batch are no longer accessible. The scope of the local variable is only within the batch. To better understand these rules, let's look at a stored-procedure call from an earlier example:

```
USE Northwind
GO

DECLARE @price money
EXECUTE GetUnitPrice 77, @unit_price = @price OUTPUT
PRINT CONVERT(varchar(6), @price)
GO

PRINT CONVERT(varchar(6), @price)
GO
```

The first PRINT statement prints the *@price* local variable from within the batch. The second PRINT statement attempts to print it again outside the batch, but the statement will return an error message. The output will be similar to the following:

```
13.00

Msg 137, Level 15, State 2, Server JAMIERE3, Line 2
Must declare the variable '@price'.
```

Note that the first PRINT statement was successful. (It printed the value *13.00*.)

You might want to use the BEGIN TRANSACTION, COMMIT, and ROLL-BACK statements within a stored procedure that has more than one T-SQL statement. Doing so indicates which statements should be grouped as one transaction. See Chapter 19 for information about transactions and the use of these statements.

Using RETURN

You can return from any point in a stored procedure to the calling program by using the RETURN keyword to exit unconditionally from the procedure. RETURN can also be used to exit from a batch or statement block. When RETURN is executed in a stored procedure, execution stops at that point in the procedure and returns to the next statement in the calling program. The statements following RETURN in the procedure are not executed. You can also return an integer value by using RETURN.

First, let's look at an example of using RETURN to simply exit from a stored procedure. We will create a modified version of the *GetUnitPrice* procedure that checks whether an input value is provided and, if one is not, prints a message to the user and returns to the calling program. To do this, we will define the input parameter with a default value of *NULL* and will then see whether the value is *NULL* within the procedure, which would indicate that no value was entered. Here is the code to drop and re-create this procedure:

```
USE Northwind
GO

IF EXISTS (SELECT name
           FROM   sysobjects
           WHERE  name = "GetUnitPrice" AND
                  type = "P")
DROP PROCEDURE GetUnitPrice
GO

CREATE PROCEDURE GetUnitPrice @prod_id int = NULL
AS
IF @prod_id IS NULL
   BEGIN
      PRINT "Please enter a product ID number"
      RETURN
   END
ELSE
   BEGIN
      SELECT UnitPrice
      FROM   Products
      WHERE  ProductID = @prod_id
   END
GO
```

Now let's run *GetUnitPrice* without entering an input value and see the results. You must specify the EXECUTE statement to run the stored procedure because the statement that calls the procedure is not the first of this batch. Use the following code:

```
PRINT "Before procedure"
EXECUTE GetUnitPrice
PRINT "After procedure returns from stored procedure"
GO
```

Your output will look like this:

```
Before procedure
Please enter a product ID number
After procedure returns from stored procedure
```

The second PRINT statement is included to demonstrate that when RETURN is executed from the stored procedure, the batch continues at the PRINT statement.

Now let's look at using RETURN to return a value to the calling program. The value returned must be an integer. It can be a constant or a variable. You must declare a variable in the calling program in order to store the return value for later use in the calling program. For example, this next procedure will return a value of *1* if the unit price of the product specified in the input parameter is less than $100; otherwise, it will return *99*.

```
CREATE PROCEDURE CheckUnitPrice @prod_id int
AS
IF (SELECT UnitPrice
    FROM    Products
    WHERE   ProductID = @prod_id) < 100
    RETURN 1
ELSE
    RETURN 99
GO
```

To call this stored procedure and to be able to make use of the return value, declare a variable in the calling program and set it equal to the return value of the stored procedure (using the *ProductID* value of *66* for the input parameter), as follows:

```
DECLARE @return_val int
EXECUTE @return_val = CheckUnitPrice 66
IF (@return_val = 1) PRINT "Unit price is less than $100"
GO
```

The results will show the statement "Unit price is less than $100" because the unit price for the specified product is $17 and because, therefore, the returned value is *1*. Make sure that you specify an integer data type when you declare the variable used to hold the return value because RETURN requires the value to be an integer.

Using SELECT to Return Values

You can also return data from a stored procedure by using the SELECT statement within the procedure. You can return the result set from a SELECT query or return the value of a variable.

Let's work through a couple of examples. First we'll create a new stored procedure called *PrintUnitPrice*, which returns the unit price for the product specified (by its product ID) in the input parameter. The code is as follows:

```
CREATE PROCEDURE PrintUnitPrice @prod_id int
AS
SELECT ProductID,
       UnitPrice
FROM   Products
WHERE  ProductID = @prod_id
GO
```

Call this procedure with *66* as the input parameter value, as shown here:

```
PrintUnitPrice 66
GO
```

Your results will look like this:

```
ProductID    UnitPrice
----------- -----------------------
        66                    17.00
(1 row(s) affected)
```

To return variable values by using the SELECT statement, use SELECT followed by the variable name. In the following example, we re-create the *CheckUnitPrice* stored procedure to return a variable value, and we specify an output-column heading:

```
USE Northwind
GO

IF EXISTS (SELECT name
           FROM    sysobjects
           WHERE   name = "CheckUnitPrice" AND
                   type = "P")
DROP PROCEDURE CheckUnitPrice
GO

CREATE PROCEDURE CheckUnitPrice @prod_id INT
AS
DECLARE @var1 int
IF (SELECT UnitPrice
    FROM    Products
    WHERE   ProductID = @prod_id) > 100
    SET     @var1 = 1
ELSE
    SET     @var1 = 99
SELECT "Variable 1" = @var1
PRINT "Can add more T-SQL statements here"
GO
```

Call this procedure with 66 as the input parameter value, as shown here:

```
CheckUnitPrice 66
GO
```

The output from running this stored procedure looks like this:

```
Variable 1
-----------
        99

(1 row(s) affected)

Can add more T-SQL statements here
```

We printed the statement "Can add more T-SQL statements here" to see the difference between returning a value by using SELECT and returning a value by using RETURN. RETURN will end the stored procedure wherever it is called, but SELECT will return its result set, and the stored procedure will then continue to execute.

In the previous example, if we had not specified an output-column heading and had simply used *SELECT @var1* instead, we would have seen the output with no heading, as follows:

```
-----------
99

(1 row(s) affected)
```

Using Enterprise Manager

Now that you know how to use T-SQL to create stored procedures, let's look at how to use Enterprise Manager to create them. To create a stored procedure by using Enterprise Manager, you still must know how to write the T-SQL statements. Enterprise Manager simply provides you with a graphical interface in which to create your procedure. We'll practice this method by re-creating the *InsertRows* stored procedure, as explained in the following steps:

1. To delete the stored procedure, first expand the MyDB database folder in the left pane of Enterprise Manager and click the Stored Procedures folder. All stored procedures in that database will appear in the right-hand pane. Right-click the *InsertRows* stored procedure (it should exist

already—we created it earlier in this chapter) and choose Delete from the shortcut menu. (You can also rename or copy the stored procedure through this shortcut menu.) The Drop Objects dialog box appears, as shown in Figure 21-1. Click Drop All to delete the stored procedure.

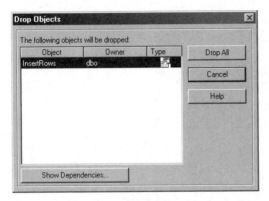

Figure 21-1. *The Drop Objects dialog box.*

2. Right-click the Stored Procedures folder and choose New Stored Procedure from the shortcut menu. The Stored Procedure Properties window appears, as shown in Figure 21-2.

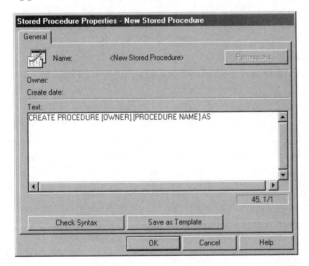

Figure 21-2. *The Stored Procedure Properties window.*

3. In the Text box on the General tab, replace [OWNER].[PROCEDURE NAME] with the name of the stored procedure—in this case, *InsertRows*. Then type the T-SQL code for the stored procedure. Figure 21-3 shows the Stored Procedure Properties window after the T-SQL code for *InsertRows* has been added.

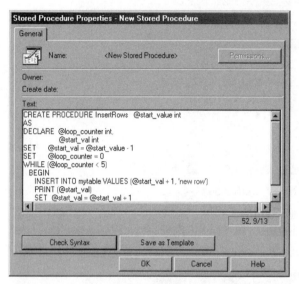

Figure 21-3. *The T-SQL code for the new stored procedure.*

4. Click Check Syntax to have SQL Server point out any T-SQL syntax errors in the stored procedure. Correct any syntax errors found, and click Check Syntax again. Once the syntax check is successful, you will see the message box shown in Figure 21-4. Click OK.

Figure 21-4. *The message box indicating that the stored-procedure syntax check was successful.*

5. Click OK in the Stored Procedure Properties window to create your stored procedure and to return to Enterprise Manager. Click the Stored Procedures folder in the left-hand pane of Enterprise Manager to display the new stored procedure in the right-hand pane, as shown in Figure 21-5.

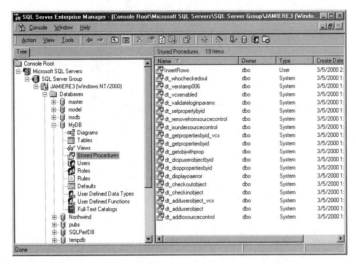

Figure 21-5. *The new stored procedure in Enterprise Manager.*

6. To assign execute permission for the new stored procedure to users, right-click the stored-procedure name in the right-hand pane of Enterprise Manager and choose Properties from the shortcut menu. In the Stored Procedure Properties window that appears, click Permissions. The Object Properties window appears, as shown in Figure 21-6. Select the boxes in the EXEC column for the users or database roles that you want to allow to execute this stored procedure. In this example, three users have been given execute permission for the *InsertRows* stored procedure.

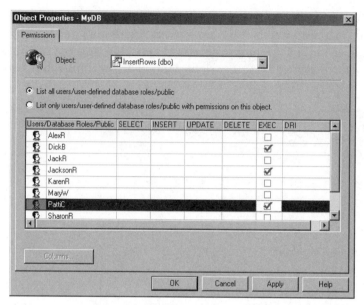

Figure 21-6. *The Permissions tab of the Object Properties window.*

7. Click Apply and then click OK to set the permissions you selected and to return to the Stored Procedure Properties window. Click OK to finish.

You can also use Enterprise Manager to edit a stored procedure. To do so, right-click the name of the procedure and choose Properties from the shortcut menu. Edit the procedure in the Stored Procedure Properties window (the same window shown in Figure 21-3), check the syntax by clicking Check Syntax, click Apply, and then click OK.

Additionally, you can use Enterprise Manager to manage permissions on a stored procedure. To do so, right-click the stored-procedure name in Enterprise Manager, point to All Tasks in the shortcut menu, and then choose Manage Permissions. You can also create a publication for replication (described in Chapter 26), generate SQL scripts, and display dependencies for the stored procedure from the All Tasks submenu. If you choose to generate SQL scripts, SQL Server will automatically create a script file (with the name you specify) that will contain the definition of the stored procedure. Then you can re-create the procedure, as necessary, by using the script.

Using the Create Stored Procedure Wizard

The third method for creating stored procedures, using the Create Stored Procedure Wizard, gives you a head start by providing a skeleton of T-SQL code for you to build on when writing your procedures. You can use the wizard to create a stored procedure to insert, delete, or update table rows. The wizard does not help with procedures that retrieve rows from a table.

The wizard lets you create multiple stored procedures in one database without exiting and restarting the wizard. However, to create a procedure in a different database, you must run the wizard again. To run the wizard, follow these steps:

1. In Enterprise Manager, choose Wizards from the Tools menu to display the Select Wizard dialog box. Expand the Database folder and select Create Stored Procedure Wizard, as shown in Figure 21-7.

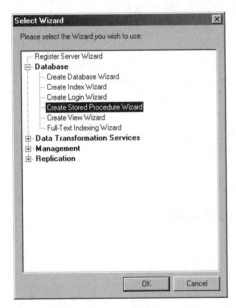

Figure 21-7. *The Select Wizard dialog box.*

2. Click OK to display the Create Stored Procedure Wizard welcome screen, shown in Figure 21-8.

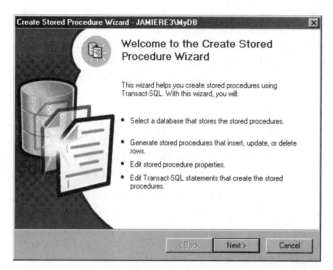

Figure 21-8. *The Create Stored Procedure Wizard welcome screen.*

3. Click Next to display the Select Database screen. Select the name of the database in which you want to create the stored procedure.

4. Click Next to display the Select Stored Procedures screen, shown in Figure 21-9. Here you will see a list of all the tables in the selected database, with three columns of check boxes. These columns represent the three types of stored procedures you can create using the wizard: stored procedures that insert, delete, or update data. Select the appropriate check boxes in the columns next to each table name.

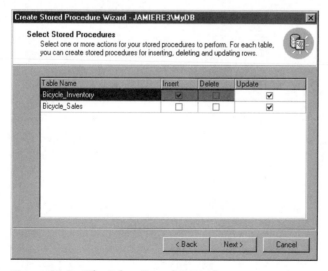

Figure 21-9. *The Select Stored Procedures screen.*

This example shows two tables that have been used throughout this book. As you can see, the *Bicycle_Inventory* table has been assigned two procedures: an insert procedure and an update procedure. As shown in the subsequent steps, you will be able to modify the procedures before they are actually created.

Note   One stored procedure can perform multiple data modifications, but the Create Stored Procedure Wizard starts each modification type as a separate stored procedure. You can alter any of the procedures the wizard sets up by adding more T-SQL code.

5. Click Next to display the Completing The Create Stored Procedure Wizard screen, shown in Figure 21-10. This screen lists the names and descriptions of all stored procedures that will be created when you finish the wizard.

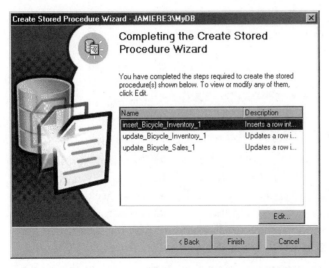

Figure 21-10. *The Completing The Create Stored Procedure Wizard screen.*

6. To rename and edit a stored procedure, begin by selecting its name in the Completing The Create Stored Procedure Wizard screen and then clicking Edit to display the Edit Stored Procedure Properties window, shown in Figure 21-11. The window includes a list of the columns in the table that the procedure will affect. The columns that have a check mark in the Select column will be used in the stored procedure.

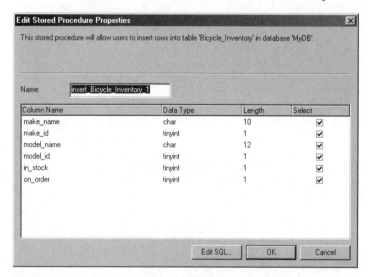

Figure 21-11. *The Edit Stored Procedure Properties window.*

This example shows six columns in the *Bicycle_Inventory* table that can be affected by the insert procedure, which is currently named *insert_Bicycle_Inventory_1*. Each table column has a check mark in the Select column. The check marks indicate that values for all six columns will need to be entered into the stored procedure when it is executed and that the stored procedure will insert the six values into all six columns.

7. To rename the stored procedure, delete the existing name in the Name text box, and replace it with the new name.

8. To edit the stored procedure, click Edit SQL to display the Edit Stored Procedure SQL dialog box, shown in Figure 21-12. Here you can view the T-SQL code for the stored procedure. As you can see, the T-SQL here is quite basic. In this example, the five parameters you list when you call the stored procedure will be the values inserted as the new row in the table. To edit the code, simply type your changes in the text box. When you have finished your edits, click Parse to check for any syntax errors, correct any errors, and then click OK to return to the Completing The Create Stored Procedure Wizard screen.

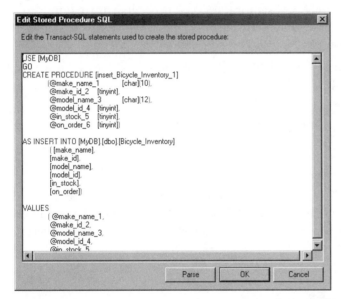

Figure 21-12. *The Edit Stored Procedure SQL dialog box.*

9. After making your changes, if any, and verifying the code, click Finish to create the stored procedures. Don't forget to set permissions on each of the stored procedures after the procedures are created. (See the section "Using Enterprise Manager" earlier in the chapter for instructions on setting permissions.)

As you can see, the wizard is not extremely helpful. If you know how to write the T-SQL code, you might as well use scripts or Enterprise Manager to create your stored procedures.

Managing Stored Procedures by Using T-SQL

Now that you know how to create stored procedures, let's look at how to use T-SQL commands to alter, drop, and view the contents of a stored procedure.

The ALTER PROCEDURE Statement

The ALTER PROCEDURE T-SQL statement is used to alter a stored procedure created by the use of CREATE PROCEDURE. When you use ALTER PROCEDURE, the original permissions set for the stored procedure are maintained, and any dependent stored procedures or triggers are not affected. (A dependent procedure or trigger is one that calls a procedure.)

The syntax for the ALTER PROCEDURE statement is similar to the syntax for CREATE PROCEDURE:

```
ALTER PROC[EDURE] procedure_name
                  [ {@parameter_name data_type} ] [= default] [OUTPUT]
                  [,...,n]
AS t-sql_statement(s)
```

In the ALTER PROCEDURE statement, you must rewrite the entire stored procedure, making the desired changes. For example, let's re-create the stored procedure *GetUnitPrice*, which we used in an earlier example, and alter the procedure to add a condition to check for unit prices greater than $100, as shown here:

```
USE Northwind
GO

IF EXISTS (SELECT name
           FROM   sysobjects
           WHERE  name = "GetUnitPrice" AND
                  type = "P")
DROP PROCEDURE GetUnitPrice
GO

CREATE PROCEDURE GetUnitPrice @prod_id    int,
                              @unit_price money OUTPUT
AS
SELECT @unit_price = UnitPrice
FROM   Products
WHERE  ProductID = @prod_id
GO

ALTER PROCEDURE GetUnitPrice @prod_id    int,
                             @unit_price money OUTPUT
```

```
AS
SELECT @unit_price = UnitPrice
FROM    Products
WHERE   ProductID = @prod_id AND
        UnitPrice > 100
GO
```

Now let's grant execute permission on the stored procedure to the user DickB, with the following statement:

```
GRANT EXECUTE ON GetUnitPrice TO DickB
GO
```

As stated previously, if we alter the stored procedure, the permission will be maintained. Let's alter the procedure to select rows whose *UnitPrice* column value is greater than *200*, instead of *100*, as follows:

```
ALTER PROCEDURE GetUnitPrice @prod_id     int,
                             @unit_price money OUTPUT
AS
SELECT @unit_price = UnitPrice
FROM    Products
WHERE   ProductID = @prod_id AND
        UnitPrice > 200
GO
```

The user DickB will still have execute permission on the stored procedure after this ALTER PROCEDURE statement is run.

The DROP PROCEDURE Statement

The T-SQL DROP PROCEDURE statement is simple—it deletes a stored procedure. You cannot restore a stored procedure after you drop it. If you want to use a deleted procedure, you must totally re-create it by using the CREATE PROCEDURE statement. All permissions on the dropped stored procedure will be lost and will have to be regranted. Here's an example that uses DROP PROCEDURE to drop the *GetUnitPrice* procedure:

```
USE Northwind
GO

DROP PROCEDURE GetUnitPrice
GO
```

Note   To drop a stored procedure, you must be using the database in which it resides. Remember that to use a database, you execute the USE statement followed by the database name.

The *sp_helptext* Stored Procedure

The *sp_helptext* system stored procedure enables you to view the definition of a stored procedure and the statement that was used to create the procedure. (It can also be used to print the definition of a trigger, a view, a rule, or a default.) This capability is useful when you want to quickly recall the definition of a procedure (or one of the other objects just mentioned) while you're using ISQL, OSQL, or SQL Query Analyzer. You might also direct the output to a file to create a script of the definition that can be used to edit and re-create the procedure, as needed. To use *sp_helptext*, you must provide the name of your user-defined stored procedure (or other object name) as the parameter. For example, to view the statements used earlier to create the *InsertRows* procedure, use the following command. (Again, you must be using the database in which the procedure resides for this command to work.)

```
USE MyDB
GO
sp_helptext InsertRows
GO
```

The output looks like this:

```
Text
-------------------------------------------------------------
CREATE PROCEDURE InsertRows    @start_value int
AS
DECLARE   @loop_counter int,
          @start_val    int
SET       @start_val = @start_value - 1
SET       @loop_counter = 0
WHILE (@loop_counter < 5)
   BEGIN
      INSERT INTO mytable VALUES (@start_val + 1, 'new row')
      PRINT (@start_val)
      SET  @start_val    = @start_val + 1
      SET  @loop_counter = @loop_counter + 1
   END
```

Summary

In this chapter, you've learned what system stored procedures and user-defined stored procedures are and why they are used. You've also learned how to create stored procedures by using T-SQL code, Enterprise Manager, and the Create Stored Procedure Wizard, and you've seen the differences among these methods. Additionally, you've learned how to use parameters and variables and how to execute stored procedures. We also looked at the T-SQL statements used to alter, drop, and view the text of a stored procedure. In Chapter 22, we'll look at triggers, a special type of stored procedure that is executed automatically under certain conditions.

Chapter 22
Creating and Using Triggers

Triggers are a special class of stored procedure. In this chapter, you'll learn what triggers do and when you should use them. You'll also learn about the trigger enhancements that Microsoft SQL Server 2000 provides. You'll practice two methods for creating triggers: using Transact-SQL (T-SQL) statements and using SQL Server Enterprise Manager. And you'll learn how to manage and modify triggers.

What Is a Trigger?

A *trigger* is a special type of stored procedure that is executed automatically by SQL Server when a table is modified by any one of the three statements: UPDATE, INSERT, or DELETE. Triggers, like other stored procedures, can contain simple or complex T-SQL statements. Unlike other types of stored procedures, triggers execute automatically when specified data modifications occur and cannot be executed manually by name. When a trigger executes, it is said to have *fired*. A trigger is created on one database table, but it can access other tables and objects in other databases. Triggers cannot be created on temporary tables or system tables, only on user-defined tables or views. The table on which a trigger is defined is called a *trigger table*.

There are five types of triggers: UPDATE, INSERT, DELETE, INSTEAD OF, and AFTER. Like their names imply, an UPDATE trigger fires when an update is performed on a table, an INSERT trigger fires when data is inserted into the table, and a DELETE trigger fires when data is deleted from a table. An INSTEAD OF trigger is executed instead of an insert, update, or delete operation. The AFTER trigger fires after a triggering action and provides a mechanism to control the execution order of multiple triggers.

The update, insert, and delete operations are known as data modification events. You can create a trigger that will fire at the occurrence of more than one data modification event. For example, you can create a trigger that will fire when either an UPDATE or INSERT statement is executed, which we'll refer to as an UPDATE/INSERT trigger. You can even create a trigger that will fire when any of the three data modification events occurs (an UPDATE/INSERT/DELETE trigger).

You should know some other general rules about triggers. These rules are listed here:

- Triggers are executed only after the statement that causes them to fire is completed. For example, an UPDATE trigger won't fire until the UP-DATE statement is completed.

- If a statement attempts to perform an operation that violates a constraint on a table or causes some other error, the associated trigger will not fire.

- A trigger is included as part of a single transaction with the statement that invokes it. Therefore, a rollback statement can be called from within the trigger and will roll back both the trigger and the data modification event. Also, if a severe error occurs, such as a user discon-nect, SQL Server will automatically roll back the entire transaction.

- A trigger fires only once for a statement, even if that statement affects many rows of data.

When a trigger fires, the results, if any, are returned to the calling application, just as with stored procedures. Normally, results are not returned from an INSERT, an UPDATE, or a DELETE statement (which are the statements that could cause the trigger to fire). Results are normally returned from SELECT queries. Thus, to avoid having results returned to the application from within a trigger, elimi-nate the use of SELECT statements and variable assignments in the trigger defi-nition. If you do want results to be returned from within a trigger, you must code special handling into the application wherever modifications to the table contain-ing the trigger are allowed so that the application receives the returned data and handles it properly.

If you need to assign a variable within a trigger, use the statement SET NOCOUNT ON at the beginning of the trigger to prevent any result rows from being returned. The SET NOCOUNT statement specifies whether to return a message indicating how many rows were affected by a query or statement (for example, "23 rows affected"). By default, SET NOCOUNT is set to OFF, which means that the affected-rows message is returned. Note that this setting does not affect the return of any actual results from a SELECT statement; it affects only the rowcount messages returned.

Trigger Enhancements in SQL Server 2000

SQL Server 2000 includes two new triggers: the INSTEAD OF trigger and the AFTER trigger. The INSTEAD OF trigger is executed instead of the triggering SQL statement. This overrides the action of the triggering statement. You can specify one INSTEAD OF trigger per INSERT, UPDATE, or DELETE statement. The INSTEAD OF trigger can be specified on a table, a view, or both. You can cascade INSTEAD OF triggers by defining views on views, where each view has a separate INSTEAD OF trigger. INSTEAD OF triggers are not allowed on updatable views that include the WITH CHECK option. Before you specify an INSTEAD OF trigger on one of these views, you must remove the WITH CHECK option from the updatable view by using the ALTER VIEW command. See Chapter 18 for more information on creating views.

The AFTER trigger is fired after *all* operations specified in the triggering SQL statement or statements have executed successfully. This includes all referential cascade actions and constraint checks. If you have multiple AFTER triggers defined on a table for a particular statement or set of statements, you can specify which trigger will fire first and which trigger will fire last. If you have more than two triggers defined, you can specify the firing order of only the first and last to fire. Any other triggers are fired randomly. You set this firing order via the *sp_settriggerorder* T-SQL statement.

In addition to providing new triggers, SQL Server 2000 allows you to specify triggers on views as well as tables. Previous versions of SQL Server allowed triggers to be specified on tables only. Triggers on views function exactly as do those defined on tables.

When to Use Triggers

Triggers, like constraints, can be used to maintain data integrity and business rules, but a trigger should not replace a constraint where a constraint alone is sufficient. (Constraints are explained in Chapter 16.) For example, you don't need to create a trigger that checks for the existence of a value in a primary key column in one table to determine whether a value can be inserted into a corresponding column of another table—a FOREIGN KEY constraint would work best in this situation. However, you would create a trigger to cascade changes throughout related tables in the database. For example, you might create a DELETE trigger on the *title_id* column in the *titles* table of the pubs database that would delete rows in the *sales*, *roysched*, and *titleauthor* tables when a corresponding row in *titles* is deleted. (We'll see how to create this DELETE trigger in the next section.)

You can also use triggers to enforce more complex checks on data than are possible when you use the CHECK constraint. (CHECK constraints are explained in detail in Chapter 16.) This complexity is possible because triggers can reference columns in tables other than the table on which they are defined, whereas CHECK constraints are limited to a single table.

Triggers are also useful for performing multiple actions in response to one data modification event. If you create multiple triggers for a single type of data modification event, all of the triggers will fire when that event occurs. (Remember, if multiple triggers are defined on a table or view and for an event, each trigger must have a unique name.)

You can create a single trigger that will fire for multiple types of data modification events. The trigger will fire once each time an event for which it is defined occurs. Therefore, a trigger that is defined on a specified table or view for inserts, updates, and deletes will fire each time any of these events occurs on the table or view.

SQL Server creates two special, temporary tables when you create a trigger. You can reference these tables when you write the T-SQL code that composes the trigger definition. These tables are always in memory and are local to the trigger, and each trigger can access only its own temporary tables. A trigger's temporary tables are copies of the database table on which the trigger is defined. You can use the temporary tables to see the effect a data modification event had on the original table. You will see examples of these special tables (called the *deleted* and *inserted* tables) in the next section.

Creating Triggers

Now that you know what triggers are and when they are used, let's move on to the specifics of creating triggers. In this section, we'll look first at the T-SQL method of creating triggers and then at the Enterprise Manager method. To use Enterprise Manager to create triggers, you will need to know T-SQL coding, just as you do when you use Enterprise Manager to create other types of stored procedures.

Using the CREATE TRIGGER Statement

To use T-SQL to create a trigger, you use the CREATE TRIGGER statement. (The Enterprise Manager method uses this statement as well.) The basic syntax of the CREATE TRIGGER statement is as follows:

```
CREATE TRIGGER trigger_name
ON {table | view}
[WITH ENCRYPTION]
{FOR | AFTER | INSTEAD OF}
  {[DELETE] [,] [INSERT] [,] [UPDATE]}
    [WITH APPEND]
    [NOT FOR REPLICATION]
AS
    sql_statement [...n]
```

As you can see, you can create a trigger for an INSERT, an UPDATE, a DELETE, an INSTEAD OF, or an AFTER statement or for any combination of the five. You must specify at least one option with the FOR clause. This clause indicates which type of data modification event (or types of events), when performed on the specified table, will cause the trigger to fire.

The SQL statements after the AS keyword will be performed when the trigger is called. You can include multiple statements here, including programming constructs such as IF and WHILE. The following statements are not allowed in a trigger definition:

- ALTER DATABASE
- CREATE DATABASE
- DISK INIT
- DISK RESIZE
- DROP DATABASE
- LOAD DATABASE
- LOAD LOG
- RECONFIGURE
- RESTORE DATABASE
- RESTORE LOG

Using the *deleted* and *inserted* Tables

As mentioned, you have access to two temporary tables, the *deleted* and *inserted* tables, when you create a trigger. They are referred to as tables, but they are different from true database tables. They are stored in memory—not on disk.

The two tables have the same structure (the same columns and types of data) as the table on which the trigger is defined. The *deleted* table holds copies of rows affected by the execution of a DELETE or an UPDATE statement. The rows that are deleted from the trigger table are transferred to the *deleted* table. The data in the *deleted* table can then be accessed within the trigger. The *inserted* table holds copies of the rows added to the trigger table by the execution of an INSERT or UPDATE statement. The rows are added simultaneously to the trigger table and the *inserted* table. Because an UPDATE statement is treated as a DELETE followed by an INSERT, when an UPDATE statement is used, the old row values are copied into the *deleted* table and the new row values are copied into the trigger table and the *inserted* table.

If you try to examine the contents of the *deleted* table within a trigger that fires because an INSERT statement executes, the table will be empty, but no error will occur. The execution of an INSERT statement will not cause any row values to be copied into the *deleted* table. Similarly, if you attempt to examine the contents of the *inserted* table within a trigger that fires because a DELETE statement executes, you will see that the *inserted* table is empty. The execution of a DELETE statement will not cause any row values to be copied into the *inserted* table. Again, you will not cause an error to occur by looking at these tables when they are empty; so if you want to use the tables to see the effect of a modification, make sure you choose the correct table to access within your triggers.

Note The values in the *inserted* and *deleted* tables are accessible only within the trigger. Once the trigger is completed, these tables are no longer accessible.

Creating Your First Trigger

To see how a trigger functions, let's create a simple table with a trigger defined on it that prints a statement whenever an update occurs. The T-SQL code for creating this table is as follows:

```
USE MyDB
GO
CREATE TABLE Bicycle_Inventory
(
        make_name       char(10)      NOT NULL,
        make_id         tinyint       NOT NULL,
        model_name      char(12)      NOT NULL,
        model_id        tinyint       NOT NULL,
        in_stock        tinyint       NOT NULL,
        on_order        tinyint       NULL,
)
GO

IF EXISTS (SELECT name
          FROM    sysobjects
          WHERE   name = "Print_Update" AND
                  type = "TR")
```

```
DROP TRIGGER Print_Update
GO

CREATE TRIGGER Print_Update
ON Bicycle_Inventory
FOR UPDATE
AS
PRINT "The Bicycle_Inventory table was updated"
GO
```

To test our trigger, let's insert a row into the table and then update it:

```
INSERT INTO Bicycle_Inventory VALUES ("Trek",1,"5500",5,1,0)
GO

UPDATE Bicycle_Inventory
SET    make_id = 2
WHERE  model_name = "5500"
GO
```

The message "The Bicycle_Inventory table was updated" is returned because the execution of the UPDATE statement fired the trigger. In this example, we defined our trigger to display a message so we could see that the trigger was executed. Normally, you do not want a trigger to return output. In certain circumstances, however, you might find it helpful to have a trigger that returns output. For example, suppose you create an UPDATE trigger that executes its statements only if a specified column receives a certain value, but the update does not appear to be working correctly. If you add a PRINT statement within the trigger that prints the column's value before the other trigger statements are executed, it might help in determining whether the problem lies in the logic of the trigger or in the data being updated.

Creating a DELETE Trigger

Now let's look at a more complex example—a DELETE trigger that cascades changes through related tables. We'll create a trigger that will delete rows from the *sales*, *roysched*, and *titleauthor* tables of the pubs database when a corresponding row is deleted from the *titles* table. We'll use the *deleted* table to indicate which rows to delete from the related tables. (Remember that when a row is deleted from a trigger table, it is copied to the *deleted* table; then you can examine the contents of the *deleted* table and delete all corresponding entries in the other tables.) For this trigger to work, we would have to drop the FOREIGN KEY constraints from the *titleauthor*, *roysched*, and *sales* tables that reference the *title_id* column in the *titles* table. In this example, let's create the trigger as if these FOREIGN KEY constraints did not exist. If you do attempt to delete a row from the *titles* table without removing the FOREIGN KEY constraints, you will get an error message from SQL Server, and the delete will fail.

Note If you don't mind altering your pubs database, try deleting the FOREIGN KEY constraints on your own and then creating this trigger. It's easiest to delete FOREIGN KEY constraints by using a database diagram in Enterprise Manager. (This process is explained in Chapter 16.) Be sure to delete the FOREIGN KEY constraints that reference *title_id*.

The T-SQL code for this trigger is shown here:

```
USE pubs
GO
IF EXISTS (SELECT name
           FROM    sysobjects
           WHERE  name = "Delete_Title" AND
                  type = "TR")
DROP TRIGGER Delete_Title
GO

CREATE TRIGGER Delete_Title
ON titles
FOR DELETE
AS
DELETE sales
FROM    sales, deleted
WHERE   sales.title_id = deleted.title_id
PRINT   "Deleted from sales"
DELETE roysched
FROM    roysched, deleted
WHERE   roysched.title_id = deleted.title_id
PRINT   "Deleted from roysched"
DELETE titleauthor
FROM    titleauthor, deleted
WHERE   titleauthor.title_id = deleted.title_id
PRINT   "Deleted from titleauthor"
GO
```

To test the trigger, use a DELETE statement such as this:

```
DELETE titles
WHERE   title_id = "PC1035"
GO
```

If you execute this DELETE statement, the trigger will fire (assuming that you deleted the foreign key relationships mentioned earlier). You'll see the rows-affected message for the data modification event on the *titles* table, followed by the messages specified in the three PRINT statements from the trigger and the number of rows affected in the other three tables; this output is shown here:

```
(1 row(s) affected)

Deleted from sales

(5 row(s) affected)

Deleted from roysched

(1 row(s) affected)

Deleted from titleauthor

(1 row(s) affected)
```

Another use of the *deleted* table in a trigger is to save all deleted rows from a table to a backup table for later data analysis. For instance, to store the deleted rows from the *roysched* table in a new table called *roysched_backup*, use the following code:

```
USE pubs
GO
CREATE TABLE roysched_backup
(
        title_id        tid NOT NULL,
        lorange         int NULL,
        hirange         int NULL,
        royalty         int NULL
)

CREATE TRIGGER tr_roysched_backup
ON roysched
FOR DELETE
AS
INSERT INTO roysched_backup SELECT * FROM deleted
GO

SELECT * FROM roysched_backup
GO
```

Notice that we gave the backup table the same column names and data types as we gave the original table. You can use different column names for *roysched_backup*, but you should use the same data types for the two tables to ensure compatibility.

Creating an INSERT Trigger

In this example, we'll create an INSERT trigger (a trigger that fires when an INSERT statement executes) on the *sales* table. This trigger will update the *ytd_sales* column in the *titles* table when a row is inserted into *sales*, by adding to it the value that was inserted into the *sales* table's *qty* column. The trigger queries the *inserted* table to obtain the *qty* value that was inserted into the *sales* table. We'll include a SELECT * statement in the trigger that will show us what the *inserted* table contains. Here is the T-SQL code for this trigger:

```
USE pubs
GO
IF EXISTS (SELECT name
           FROM    sysobjects
           WHERE   name = "Update_ytd_sales" AND
                   type = "TR")
DROP TRIGGER Update_ytd_sales
GO

CREATE TRIGGER Update_ytd_sales
ON sales
FOR INSERT
AS
SELECT *
FROM    inserted
UPDATE titles
SET    ytd_sales = ytd_sales + qty
FROM    inserted
WHERE  titles.title_id = inserted.title_id
GO
```

Notice that we used the FROM *table_source* (FROM inserted) clause in the UPDATE statement to indicate that the *qty* value should come from the *inserted* table. Now run the following INSERT statement to view the results from this trigger:

```
INSERT INTO sales VALUES(7066, 1, "March 7, 2000", 100, "Net 30", "BU1111")
GO
```

You will see the following results. The first set of results shows the row selected from the *inserted* table, and the second "1 row(s) affected" message is from the UPDATE statement.

stor_id	ord_num	ord_date	qty	payterms	title_id
7066	1	2000-03-07 00:00:00.000	100	Net 30	BU1111

(1 row(s) affected)

(1 row(s) affected)

Creating an UPDATE Trigger

Next let's create an UPDATE trigger that will check the *price* column when the
titles table is updated to verify that the price of a book has not increased by more
than 10 percent. If it has, a ROLLBACK statement is issued that will roll back
the trigger and the statement that called it. If the trigger fires from within a larger
transaction, the entire transaction will be rolled back. The *deleted* and *inserted*
tables are used in this example to test for the price change. The trigger definition
is shown here:

```
USE pubs
GO
IF EXISTS (SELECT name
           FROM    sysobjects
           WHERE   name = "Update_Price_Check" AND
                   type = "TR")
DROP TRIGGER Update_Price_Check
GO

CREATE TRIGGER Update_Price_Check
ON titles
FOR UPDATE
AS
DECLARE @orig_price money, @new_price money
SELECT  @orig_price = price from deleted
PRINT   "orig price ="
PRINT   CONVERT(varchar(6),@orig_price)
SELECT  @new_price = price from inserted
PRINT   "new price ="
PRINT   CONVERT(varchar(6),@new_price)
IF (@new_price > (@orig_price * 1.10))
BEGIN
    PRINT "Rollback occurred"
    ROLLBACK
END
ELSE
PRINT "Price is OK"
GO
```

To test this trigger, first run the following statements to check the current price of the book whose title ID is BU1111:

```
SELECT price
FROM   titles
WHERE  title_id = "BU1111"
GO
```

The price is $11.95. Next, attempt to increase the price by 15 percent, using this statement:

```
UPDATE titles
SET    price = price * 1.15
WHERE  title_id = "BU1111"
GO
```

You will see the following results:

```
orig price =
11.95
new price =
13.74
Rollback occurred
```

The trigger fired, printing the original price and the new price and—because the price increase was more than 10 percent—issuing a rollback.

Now let's check the price again to verify that the modification was rolled back. Use the following T-SQL code:

```
SELECT price
FROM   titles
WHERE  title_id = "BU1111"
GO
```

The price has been reset to $11.95, so the modification was indeed rolled back.

Now let's increase the price by 9 percent and verify that the change in price takes effect. The T-SQL code for this modification is as follows:

```
UPDATE titles
SET    price = price * 1.09
WHERE  title_id = "BU1111"
GO

SELECT price
FROM   titles
WHERE  title_id = "BU1111"
GO
```

The price is changed to $13.03, and because the increase is less than 10 percent, the trigger does not initiate a rollback.

When you create an UPDATE trigger, you can specify that the trigger perform certain statements only if a particular column or certain columns are updated. For example, let's re-create the preceding trigger, this time using an IF UPDATE clause to specify that the trigger check the *price* column only when the *price* column itself is updated:

```
USE pubs
GO
IF EXISTS (SELECT name
           FROM    sysobjects
           WHERE   name = "Update_Price_Check" AND
                   type = "TR")
DROP TRIGGER Update_Price_Check
GO

CREATE TRIGGER Update_Price_Check
ON titles
FOR UPDATE
AS
IF UPDATE (price)
BEGIN
    DECLARE @orig_price money, @new_price money
    SELECT  @orig_price = price
    FROM    deleted
    PRINT   "orig price ="
    PRINT   CONVERT(varchar(6),@orig_price)
    SELECT  @new_price = price
    FROM    inserted
    PRINT   "new price ="
    PRINT CONVERT(varchar(6),@new_price)
    IF (@new_price > (@orig_price * 1.10))
    BEGIN
        PRINT "Rollback occurred"
        ROLLBACK
    END
    ELSE
    PRINT "Price is OK"
END
GO
```

Now if an update is made to one or more columns in the *titles* table and does not include the *price* column, this trigger will skip the statements between the BEGIN and END keywords in the outer IF statement, in effect skipping over the entire trigger.

To test this trigger, run the following T-SQL statement, which updates the year-to-date sales (the value in the *ytd_sales* column) for the book whose *title_id* column value is *BU1111*.

```
UPDATE titles
SET    ytd_sales = 123
WHERE  title_id = "BU1111"
GO
```

Notice that the output does not include any of the messages specified in the trigger's PRINT statements. The trigger fired because we updated the *titles* table. Because the update was to the *ytd_sales* column, not to the *price* column, the outer IF condition returned *FALSE*. Therefore, the statements in the trigger were not executed. This technique prevents SQL Server from processing unnecessary statements.

Creating an INSTEAD OF Trigger

The INSTEAD OF trigger gives you control of what happens when an INSERT, an UPDATE, or a DELETE function occurs. The INSTEAD OF trigger is used primarily when updating a union view. Normally, union views are not updatable, because SQL Server would not know which underlying table or tables to modify. To get around this, you define an INSTEAD OF trigger on the view to modify the underlying tables. Let's look at an example.

The following T-SQL statements create a view called *TitlesByAuthor*, which references the *authors*, *titles*, and *titleauthor* tables. (See Chapter 18 for more information on creating views.)

```
USE pubs
GO

CREATE VIEW TitlesByAuthor
AS
SELECT authors.au_id, authors.au_lname, titles.title
FROM   authors INNER JOIN
       titleauthor ON authors.au_id = titleauthor.au_id INNER JOIN
       titles ON titleauthor.title_id = titles.title_id
GO
```

Now that we have created a view, we'll use the following T-SQL code to display all the rows (also shown here) that meet the view criteria:

```
USE pubs
GO

SELECT *
FROM    TitlesByAuthor
GO
```

```
au_id        au_lname        title
-----------  --------------  -------------------------------------------
---
238-95-7766  Carson          But Is It User Friendly?
724-80-9391  MacFeather      Computer Phobic AND Non-Phobic Individuals:
756-30-7391  Karsen          Computer Phobic AND Non-Phobic Individuals:
267-41-2394  O'Leary         Cooking with Computers:
724-80-9391  MacFeather      Cooking with Computers:
486-29-1786  Locksley        Emotional Security: A New Algorithm
648-92-1872  Blotchet-Halls  Fifty Years in Buckingham Palace Kitchens
899-46-2035  Ringer          Is Anger the Enemy?
998-72-3567  Ringer          Is Anger the Enemy?
998-72-3567  Ringer          Life Without Fear
486-29-1786  Locksley        Net Etiquette
807-91-6654  Panteley        Onions, Leeks, and Garlic:
172-32-1176  White           Prolonged Data Deprivation: Four Case Studi
427-17-2319  Dull            Secrets of Silicon Valley
846-92-7186  Hunter          Secrets of Silicon Valley
712-45-1867  del Castillo    Silicon Valley Gastronomic Treats
274-80-9391  Straight        Straight Talk About Computers
267-41-2394  O'Leary         Sushi, Anyone?
472-27-2349  Gringlesby      Sushi, Anyone?
672-71-3249  Yokomoto        Sushi, Anyone?
213-46-8915  Green           The Busy Executive's Database Guide
409-56-7008  Bennet          The Busy Executive's Database Guide
722-51-5454  DeFrance        The Gourmet Microwave
899-46-2035  Ringer          The Gourmet Microwave
213-46-8915  Green           You Can Combat Computer Stress!

(25 row(s) affected)
```

If you attempt to delete the row from this view in which the *au_lname* value is *Carson*, you will get the following message:

```
Server: Msg 4405, Level 16, State 1, Line 1
View or function 'TitlesByAuthor' is not updatable because the
FROM clause names multiple tables.
```

To get around this condition, let's create an INSTEAD OF trigger to handle the delete operation. The following T-SQL statements create an INSTEAD OF trigger called *Delete_It*:

> **Note** The following code does not actually delete a row from the *authors* table in the pubs database. It simply renames the row for the purposes of this example.

```
USE pubs
GO

IF EXISTS (SELECT  name
           FROM    sysobjects
           WHERE   name = 'Delete_It' AND
                   type = 'TR')
DROP TRIGGER Delete_It
GO

CREATE TRIGGER Delete_It
ON TitlesByAuthor
INSTEAD OF DELETE
AS
PRINT   'Row from authors before deletion...'
SELECT  au_id, au_lname, city, state
FROM    authors
WHERE   au_lname = 'Carson'
PRINT   'Deleting row from authors...'
UPDATE  authors
SET     au_lname = 'DELETED'
WHERE   au_lname = 'Carson'
PRINT   'Verifying deletion...'
SELECT  au_id, au_lname, city, state
FROM    authors
WHERE   au_lname = 'Carson'
GO
```

Now when we issue the T-SQL statements to delete *Carson* from the view, the INSTEAD OF trigger will fire, and we will receive the following output:

```
Row from authors before deletion...
au_id       au_name          city                  state
----------- ---------------- --------------------- -----
238-95-7766 Carson           Berkeley              CA

(1 row(s) affected)
Deleting row from authors...
(1 row(s) affected)
Verifying deletion...
au_id       au_name          city                  state
----------- ---------------- --------------------- -----

(0 row(s) affected)
```

Using AFTER Triggers

As mentioned earlier in this chapter, an AFTER trigger is simply a trigger that fires after a specified data modification event is completed. If you have more than one AFTER trigger defined on a table for a particular event or set of events, you can specify which trigger will fire first and which trigger will fire last. Any other triggers defined on the table for that event or set of events will fire in a random order. The first and last triggers are specified via the *sp_settriggerorder* T-SQL statement. The syntax of the statement is as follows:

```
sp_settriggerorder [@triggername =] 'triggername',
                    [@order=] {'first' | 'last' | 'none'}
```

Let's look at an example. Suppose we have four triggers defined on a table: *MyTrigger*, *MyOtherTrigger*, *AnotherTrigger*, and *YetAnotherTrigger*. We want to ensure that after the triggering event, *AnotherTrigger* fires first and *MyTrigger* fires last. We issue the following T-SQL statements:

```
sp_settriggerorder @triggername = 'AnotherTrigger', @order = 'first'
go
sp_settriggerorder @triggername = 'MyTrigger', @order = 'last'
go
sp_settriggerorder @triggername = 'MyOtherTrigger', @order = 'none'
go
sp_settriggerorder @triggername = 'YetAnotherTrigger', @order = 'none'
go
```

The 'none' designation for *MyOtherTrigger* and *YetAnotherTrigger* instructs SQL Server to fire these triggers randomly after *AnotherTrigger* fires and before *MyTrigger* fires. Because this random firing is the default behavior for triggers, you need not explicitly execute *sp_settriggerorder* for the triggers that will randomly fire.

Using Nested Triggers

Nested triggers are triggers that are fired by other triggers. They differ from recursive triggers, which fire themselves. A nested trigger is initiated when a data modification event within another trigger fires the nested trigger. Like SQL Server 7, SQL Server 2000 allows triggers to be nested up to 32 levels deep. One trigger fires a second trigger, which, in turn, fires a third trigger, and so on, up to the thirty-second trigger. Nested triggers are enabled by default in SQL Server 2000. You can specify whether SQL Server should allow nested triggers by setting the *nested triggers* server configuration parameter. To disable nested triggers, for example, run the following command:

```
sp_configure "nested triggers", 0
GO
```

Setting the value to *0* disables nested triggers; setting it to *1* enables them.

Let's look at an example of using nested triggers. In this example, we'll create nested triggers that will perform cascading deletes when a book title is deleted from the *titles* table. In the section "Creating a DELETE Trigger," we created a single trigger that performs this operation. First we'll drop the trigger from the earlier example so it will not fire. Then we'll create three triggers. The second and third triggers will be nested triggers. The first one fires the second, which fires the third. Here is the code:

```
USE pubs
GO
IF EXISTS (SELECT name
           FROM    sysobjects
           WHERE   name = "Delete_Title" AND
                   type = "TR")
DROP TRIGGER Delete_Title
GO

CREATE TRIGGER TR_on_titles
ON titles
FOR DELETE
AS
DELETE sales
FROM   sales, deleted
WHERE  sales.title_id = deleted.title_id
PRINT  "Deleted from sales"
GO
```

```
CREATE TRIGGER TR_on_sales
ON sales
DELETE roysched
FROM   roysched, deleted
WHERE  roysched.title_id = deleted.title_id
PRINT  "Deleted from roysched"
GO

CREATE TRIGGER TR_on_roysched
ON roysched
DELETE titleauthor
FROM   titleauthor, deleted
WHERE  titleauthor.title_id = deleted.title_id
PRINT  "Deleted from titleauthor"
GO
```

To execute these triggers successfully, you must delete the FOREIGN KEY constraints on the tables specified in the triggers (as you did in the section "Creating a DELETE Trigger"). To test whether all of the triggers execute, run the following DELETE statement:

```
DELETE
FROM   titles
WHERE  title_id = "PS7777"
GO
```

You will see the following result set:

```
(2 row(s) affected)

(1 row(s) affected)

Deleted from titleauthor

(2 row(s) affected)

Deleted from roysched

(2 row(s) affected)

Deleted from sales

(1 row(s) affected)
```

When a failure occurs at any level in a set of nested triggers, the entire transaction is canceled, and all data modifications are rolled back to the beginning of the transaction.

Using Enterprise Manager

To create a trigger by using Enterprise Manager, you simply type your T-SQL statements in the Trigger Properties window. To use this method, follow these steps:

1. In Enterprise Manager, right-click the name of the table on which you want to create the trigger. In the shortcut menu that appears, point to All Tasks and then choose Manage Triggers from the All Tasks submenu. The Trigger Properties window appears, as shown in Figure 22-1.

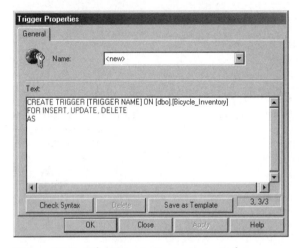

Figure 22-1. *The Trigger Properties window.*

2. Type the T-SQL code for your trigger in the Text box. Figure 22-2 shows the Trigger Properties window, containing T-SQL code for a sample trigger called *Print_Update*.

3. Click Check Syntax to verify the syntax. If the syntax of your T-SQL code is correct, you will see the dialog box shown in Figure 22-3. If not, make the required corrections. Click Apply to create the trigger. The name of the new trigger now appears in the Name drop-down list. Figure 22-4 shows the list, with the name of our sample trigger appearing in it.

4. The Trigger Properties window remains open, enabling you to create additional triggers on the table. If you do not have more triggers to create, click Close.

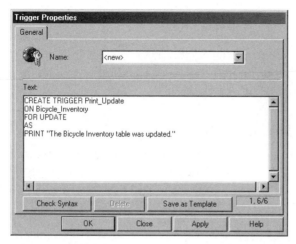

Figure 22-2. *The Trigger Properties window with trigger code inserted.*

Figure 22-3. *The dialog box indicating a successful syntax check.*

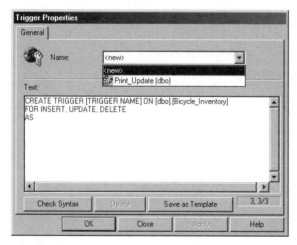

Figure 22-4. *The name of the newly created trigger in the Name drop-down list.*

Managing Triggers

Now that you know how to create a trigger, you need to learn how to manage triggers. In this section, we'll look first at the T-SQL method of managing triggers and then at the Enterprise Manager method.

Managing Triggers by Using T-SQL

Several T-SQL commands are available to help you manage triggers. You can view trigger code, view the triggers that exist on a particular table, alter trigger code, drop triggers, and enable or disable triggers. All of these options are described in this section.

Viewing Trigger Code

Two system stored procedures provide information about triggers: *sp_helptext* and *sp_helptrigger*. Use the procedure *sp_helptext* followed by a trigger name to display the code used to create that trigger. For example, to view the definition of the *Print_Update* trigger created earlier, use the following command:

```
USE MyDB
GO
sp_helptext Print_Update
GO
```

The output looks like this:

```
Text
-------------------------------------------------
CREATE TRIGGER Print_Update
ON Bicycle_Inventory
FOR UPDATE
AS
PRINT "The Bicycle Inventory table was updated."
```

Viewing the Triggers Existing on a Table

To view the triggers that exist on a particular table (or to see if no triggers exist), use the *sp_helptrigger* stored procedure followed by the table name. To view the triggers on the sample table *MyTable*, use the following command:

```
USE MyDB
GO
sp_helptrigger MyTable
GO
```

The output is shown here:

```
trigger_name trigger_owner isupdate isdelete isinsert isafter isinsteadof
------------ ------------- -------- -------- -------- ------- -----------
Print_Update dbo           1        0        0        1       0

(1 row affected)
```

The output shows the name of the trigger, the owner of the trigger, and the type of data modification event (or types of events) that will fire the trigger. The output columns isupdate, isdelete, isinsert, isafter, and isinsteadof contain the value *1* if the trigger fires for the type of data modification event indicated by the column name, or *0* if it does not. More than one column will contain a value of *1* if the trigger fires for more than one type of data modification event.

Using ALTER TRIGGER

To change the definition of a trigger, you can either drop and re-create the trigger or use the ALTER TRIGGER statement. This statement uses the same syntax as the CREATE TRIGGER statement. You must redefine the entire trigger if you modify it. For example, to alter our sample trigger *Print_Update* to fire upon the execution of either an INSERT statement or an UPDATE statement that affects *Bicycle_Inventory*, use the following code:

```
USE MyDB
GO
ALTER TRIGGER Print_Update
ON Bicycle_Inventory
FOR UPDATE, INSERT
AS
PRINT "Bicycle_Inventory was updated or a row was inserted"
GO
```

The old version of the trigger no longer exists; it has been replaced by the altered version. Now if you either update *Bicycle_Inventory* or insert data into it, the trigger will fire. Examples of the statements used to perform these operations are shown here:

```
INSERT INTO Bicycle_Inventory VALUES ("Trek",1,"Lance S.E.",1,0,1)
GO


UPDATE Bicycle_Inventory
SET    in_stock = 1
WHERE  model_name = "Lance S.E."
GO
```

Using DROP TRIGGER

To delete a trigger from a table, use the DROP TRIGGER statement. You can drop a trigger that you no longer need. The syntax for this statement is shown here:

```
DROP TRIGGER trigger_name
```

To drop our sample trigger *Print_Update*, use the following statement:

```
USE Bicycle_Inventory
GO
DROP TRIGGER Print_Update
GO
```

Now if you attempt to view the triggers that exist on the table *MyTable* by using the following T-SQL code, you will see that none exist:

```
USE MyDB
GO
sp_helptrigger MyTable
GO
```

Note If you delete a table, all triggers on that table are automatically deleted as well.

Enabling and Disabling Triggers

You can use the ALTER TABLE statement to enable or disable a trigger without deleting the trigger definition from the table. Because each trigger is defined on a certain table, we use the ALTER TABLE statement instead of ALTER TRIGGER. Let's re-create the first sample trigger in this chapter to use as an example:

```
USE MyDB
GO
IF EXISTS (SELECT name
          FROM    sysobjects
          WHERE name = "Print_Update" AND
                type = "TR")
DROP TRIGGER Print_Update
GO

CREATE TRIGGER Print_Update
ON Bicycle_Inventory
FOR UPDATE
AS
PRINT "The Bicycle_Inventory table was updated"
GO
```

At creation time, the trigger is automatically enabled. To disable the trigger so that it never fires (until re-enabled), but so its definition will still exist, as is, on the table, use the DISABLE TRIGGER option, as follows:

```
ALTER TABLE Bicycle_Inventory
DISABLE TRIGGER Print_Update
GO
```

Now when an update occurs on *Bicycle_Inventory*, the *Print_Update* trigger does not fire. It will not fire again until it is explicitly re-enabled with the ENABLE TRIGGER option, as follows:

```
ALTER TABLE Bicycle_Inventory
ENABLE TRIGGER Print_Update
GO
```

The ENABLE TRIGGER and DISABLE TRIGGER clauses are useful when you want to stop a trigger from firing but you want to retain the trigger in case you need to use it later. Your trigger definition remains intact, so you don't have to re-create the trigger later; you only have to re-enable it.

Managing Triggers by Using Enterprise Manager

With Enterprise Manager, you can manage your triggers through a graphical interface. However, you still need to know how to write the T-SQL code.

Deleting a Trigger

To delete a trigger by using Enterprise Manager, follow these steps:

1. Open the Trigger Properties window by right-clicking a table name, pointing to All Tasks in the shortcut menu that appears, and then choosing Manage Triggers from the All Tasks submenu.

2. In the Trigger Properties window, select the trigger name from the Name drop-down list, and click Delete.

3. A confirmation dialog box appears, as shown in Figure 22-5. Click Yes to delete the trigger you selected.

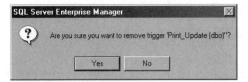

Figure 22-5. *The dialog box in which you confirm a trigger deletion.*

Modifying a Trigger

To modify a trigger by using Enterprise Manager, follow these steps:

1. Open the Trigger Properties window by right-clicking a table name, pointing to All Tasks in the shortcut menu that appears, and then choosing Manage Triggers from the All Tasks submenu.

2. Select the trigger name from the Name drop-down list.

3. Edit the T-SQL code in the Text box. Use Ctrl+Tab to indent the text. You can use the CREATE TRIGGER or ALTER TRIGGER statement. In either case, SQL Server will delete the existing trigger and re-create it for you. You can even use CREATE TRIGGER followed by the same trigger name as the existing name. You will not get an error in this case, as you would when using interactive OSQL or ISQL. When you have finished your edits, click Apply. SQL Server will then automatically modify the trigger definition.

Summary

In this chapter, you have learned about the special type of stored procedure called a trigger and about the five types of triggers that can be created on a table: DELETE, INSERT, UPDATE, INSTEAD OF, and AFTER. You've also learned how to create and manage these triggers by using T-SQL and Enterprise Manager. In Chapter 23, you'll learn how to access SQL Server 2000 from the Internet by using technologies such as ADO and XML.

Chapter 23

Accessing Microsoft SQL Server from the Internet

The introduction of Microsoft SQL Server 2000 on the Microsoft Windows 2000 operating system platform makes publishing SQL Server databases on the Internet easier. The combination of Windows 2000 and Microsoft Internet Information Server (IIS) 5 provides an extensive array of components and interfaces that can be used to connect to and interact with your SQL Server 2000 databases. This chapter introduces you to the basic concepts of accessing Microsoft SQL Server from the Internet using a variety of methods. Since this book is not a development book, this chapter is designed to provide an overview of the various access methods. Many good books on the market can give you the programming details.

This chapter begins by describing Internet programming concepts and the default Internet programming interfaces available with Windows 2000. You will be introduced to the basics of ODBC programming and ADO. You will also be introduced to ISAPI and ASPs as methods of accessing SQL Server. Finally you will be introduced to XML, what it is and how to use it. This chapter covers many topics but should help you understand basic tools for programming for the Internet.

Internet Programming Concepts

In this section, you will learn the basics of connecting Internet-enabled applications to SQL Server. These applications contain two different interfaces, both of which are necessary because they perform different tasks: they are the interface for the user and the interface for SQL Server. This section introduces you to the connection between the application and SQL Server and covers IIS and ODBC connection methods.

Using Windows 2000 and IIS 5 as an Internet Platform

By using Windows 2000 and IIS 5 as the platform for Internet applications, developers have unrivaled access to the features of SQL Server. Developers can take advantage of such features as server-side scripting with integrated database access, Open Database Connectivity (ODBC) data sources, OLE DB (a powerful set of Component Object Model [COM] interfaces for universal data access), and a Web application architecture known as Internet Server API (ISAPI) (an extremely strong competitor of traditional Common Gateway Interface [CGI] applications).

Using ODBC Data Sources

ODBC is undoubtedly the database interface of choice for the Microsoft Windows platform. Through ODBC, developers can access a wide variety of heterogeneous data sources, from simple text files to Microsoft Excel spreadsheets to Microsoft Access and SQL Server databases. ODBC provides a common yet powerful layer of abstraction for the database programmer.

Developing Internet applications using SQL Server is no exception. ODBC data sources provide the primary means of accessing SQL Server databases through Web servers. They do so through a set of OLE DB COM objects referred to as ActiveX Data Objects (ADO). ADO provides an object-oriented–interface access into ODBC data sources, which is an easier method than using the ODBC C API. With ADO, developers can instantiate simple objects representing database connections, commands (such as SQL statements or stored procedures), and recordsets, which are analogous to client-side cursors and which have much of the same functionality as server-side database cursors. All of these database objects and interfaces make Internet development using SQL Server almost trivial while providing some of the more powerful features available within ODBC, such as connection pooling.

The most important aspect of an ODBC-based Web application is the proper use of connection pooling. *Connection pooling* enables a middle-tiered application to maintain and share connections into SQL Server databases. Shared connections remain open for a specified duration and can be shared by users. Establishing connections is often a resource-intensive operation and can incur lots of overhead on the database server. Because Web servers and associated

Internet applications handle a great deal of traffic, establishing and, more important, re-establishing connections should be minimized through database connection pooling. The results are quicker connection times for users and a reduction in the resource overhead on the database server. By default, IIS 5 activates database connection pooling.

> **Note**   When using ODBC data sources and ADO, you should use ADO connection objects on a per-page basis. By creating connection objects only when the page needs them and releasing them when they are no longer needed, as opposed to using an entire user session object, the database connection can be released back to the pool more quickly for another connection to use. This will drastically reduce the amount of time users of your Internet application must wait for a connection.

Choosing a Network Library

Although SQL Server supports network libraries such as named pipes and Banyan VINES, you should use TCP/IP as your network library when deploying a SQL Server database on the Internet. TCP/IP provides network flexibility and the fastest connectivity and best performance of any network library option in SQL Server. (Network libraries are explained in Chapter 11.)

By using TCP/IP as your network library, you are limited to using standard security as your SQL Server security method. This method uses SQL Server logins for authentication. Using integrated security, which is not supported by TCP/IP and which uses Windows 2000 accounts for authentication, offers better security and is arguably the most efficient means of maintaining centralized account management in the enterprise. However, using integrated security can worsen performance in several ways.

First the effectiveness of ODBC connection pooling can be severely hampered if you use integrated security. When integrated security is implemented, each user authenticating through the Web server into the database server uses a unique login. The performance benefit provided by connection pooling is lost because for a pooled connection to be reused, a request for the connection must include a login and password identical to those used by the existing connection.

Second, connections based on the network library most commonly used with integrated security, named pipes, are generally slow. Using named pipes also poses problems for connection pooling. You can use connection pooling in conjunction with named pipes by mapping the Anonymous account to a valid SQL Server login, but most implementations use challenge/response or basic authentication from the Web server to enforce individual connections into SQL Server. This effectively negates any performance improvement connection pooling might have offered.

If SQL Server is installed on a machine other than the Web server, using integrated security also limits the available authentication options. Challenge/response authentication cannot be used, and the only available options are basic authentication and anonymous authentication. Allowing anonymous authentication in an otherwise secure system on the Internet is generally not advised, and, as mentioned, using basic authentication limits the benefits of connection pooling.

Using ISAPI to Access SQL Server

ISAPI is a set of function calls that are designed to provide Internet application developers with a powerful method of extending the functionality of IIS. ISAPI applications offer outstanding performance and low-level control. In fact, ISAPI applications can outperform other Web applications available for IIS. Also, through ISAPI, the developer has access to the entire array of Win32 API functions.

ISAPI applications are implemented as dynamic-link libraries (DLLs) that come in two flavors: extensions and filters. Because DLLs are typically natively compiled code, they execute much faster than any interpreted code or scripting language. If fast performance and scalability are important features in your Internet application, at the expense of ease of programming and modification, an ISAPI extension or filter is the best option. The next two sections describe ISAPI extensions and filters in detail, and the section that follows explains the limitations of programming and using ISAPI applications.

ISAPI Extensions

ISAPI extensions are implemented as DLLs and are loaded into either the IIS process space or a separate process space. You have this option for each ISAPI extension you install on your Web server. If application stability is an issue, extensions should be loaded into a separate process space to prevent a faulty ISAPI extension from crashing the entire Web server. This is a possibility with experimental or untested ISAPI extensions.

An ISAPI extension is referenced by using the virtual location of the .dll file in the URL. Here is an example: *http://www.mydomain.com/SampleISAPI.dll*.

When referenced this way, the ISAPI extension is loaded into memory if it has not already been loaded, and the extension handles the entire request, with IIS acting as a simple intermediary to transfer data to and from the client browser. One possible use for this approach would be implementing a custom search engine for an Internet site.

ISAPI Filters

ISAPI filters are also implemented as DLLs, but they are loaded into the IIS process space when the Web server is started and stay in memory until it is shut down. ISAPI filters can be configured to receive any number of filter event notifications, which occur for every Hypertext Transfer Protocol (HTTP) request that IIS processes and for every HTTP response that IIS generates. When an ISAPI filter is loaded, the filter communicates with IIS—via a special structure it passes—which types of events the filter should be notified of. Each time an such an event happens, an event notification is posted to each ISAPI filter that registered interest in that event.

ISAPI filters are quite powerful and can be used to implement compression or encryption, custom authentication, Web traffic logging and analysis, and even server-side scripting engines. You can create an ISAPI filter that examines each Web page set to be delivered to a client, looks for special markup tags, and acts in accordance with those instructions, much like an Active Server Pages (ASP) page does.

The ability to examine and modify every incoming and outgoing data stream makes ISAPI filters highly powerful and flexible. However, if ISAPI filters are used too much, overall site performance and scalability will be drastically diminished. For example, if every single input and output page is filtered, this filter activity may be too great a load for the system to handle, since it does incur overhead. Great care must be taken to ensure work performed by ISAPI filters is minimized. For example, in a custom encryption scheme, the filter should perform encryption, while IIS should read data from and write data to the client. This reduces the number of tasks that the ISAPI filter must carry out.

Limitations of ISAPI

The ISAPI technology can provide the best performance available, but it has a few disadvantages. Developing ISAPI extensions and filters requires more time than developing scripted pages because ISAPI extensions and filters are generally written in C or C++, and for the same reason maintenance difficulties increase as well. A change to an ISAPI extension or filter requires a recompile of the entire application, not just the replacement of a file. And even though ISAPI extensions and filters generally run faster than do their server-side scripting counterparts, they offer no absolute guarantee of perfect scalability. Finally, certain programming abstractions that most server-side scripting developers take for granted, most notably the session object, are surprisingly absent in ISAPI programming. ISAPI programming is performed at a significantly lower level than server-side scripting.

Using ASP to Access SQL Server

ASP is a server-side scripting environment that developers can use to create interactive, dynamic Web pages, which they can use to build powerful Web applications. An ASP file is a text file with the extension .asp and can contain any combination of text, HTML tags, and server-side scripts. Although ASP is purely server side, developers can include client-side script with their HTML code, which is not processed by the Web server but rather by the client browser.

When a Web server receives a request for an ASP file, the Web server processes server-side scripts contained in special tags in the file to build a Web page. The result is a pure HTML file, which, again, can include client-side script components. This file is then sent to the client browser. The client browser renders these components on the screen. None of the ASP source code is ever transferred to the client. It is all parsed and stripped at the server. Users cannot view the script commands that created the page they are viewing.

In addition to containing server-side scripts, ASP files can contain calls to COM components that perform a multitude of tasks, including database access, and can implement business logic objects that can be shared across several development environments.

ASP is designed to be language neutral. Developers skilled in working with scripting languages such as Microsoft Visual Basic Scripting Edition (VBScript), Microsoft JScript, or Perl will find developing ASP files a familiar process. ASP pages can use a scripting language for which the Web server has an installed, COM-compliant scripting engine. A *scripting engine* is a program that processes the commands written in a particular language. IIS includes scripting engines for the popular VBScript (based on Visual Basic) and JScript (the Microsoft implementation of the European Computer Manufacturers Association [ECMA] 262 language specification) languages. Scripting engines for popular languages such as Perl are available from third-party vendors.

ASP has several advantages over conventional CGI applications. As mentioned, developers who are already familiar with VBScript or JScript will not have to learn a new language such as C or Perl. ASP offers enhanced functionality by providing objects for user sessions, requests, and responses, which make developing personalized content much easier. Additionally, an ASP file requires much less time and code in order to process and collect HTML form information and store it in a database than does a full-blown CGI application written and compiled in C. And because all ASP code is embedded directly in the HTML document, maintainability is increased.

Using XML to Access SQL Server

"XML" stands for "Extensible Markup Language," but XML is not actually a language. Rather it is a system for defining other languages and a common syntax for expressing structure in data. Unlike HTML, which is a markup language used strictly for specifying how a Web document is presented, XML specifies the content and structure of a document. *Structured data* is data that is tagged for its content or use.

XML is inherently extensible. Developers use XML to define data within Web pages, and the level of detail is limited only by the needs of the developer. For example, a developer would use <AUTHOR> or <TITLE> tags to describe information about books and publications. If additional definitions are needed, the developer could add <RETAILPRICE>, <PUBLISHER>, or even <ISBN> tags.

Using XML is similar to building a table in a database, which involves determining which data elements, or columns, are necessary to fully describe the data rows in the table for the needs of the application.

Because XML does not describe presentation, an XML document can be written once and then displayed in a variety of ways using different devices: through a Web browser, a cellular phone, an in-car display for automobiles, and so forth. Each of these devices might have specific display requirements: a computer monitor might display 800 × 600 pixels, whereas a wireless Internet device might support only 200 × 200 pixels. Because XML defines only the structure and content of the document, each device will be able to render a version of the document specifically tailored for its display by using its own integrated XML browser. Unlike HTML documents, XML documents can be useful long after the authoring and display technologies available when they were written become obsolete.

The real strength of XML is its ability to interact with the Document Object Model (DOM), an interface that defines the mechanisms for accessing data in a document. Using DOM, developers can script dynamic content in a standardized way. For example, developers can use DOM to cause a specific piece of content to behave in a certain way. Small effects can be added by using this method, such as a piece of text—say, a book's title in an XML tag called <TITLE>—that changes colors as the user's pointer moves over it and that is a hyperlink to an online bookstore. Achieving such effects is currently not such a trivial task, with proprietary DOMs and style sheet specifications currently the trend, but new DOM standards from the World Wide Web Consortium (W3C) will help XML developers maintain true platform independence.

XML is also fast becoming a standard for exchanging data and documents. XML is being used to exchange data between heterogeneous database systems on the Internet. For instance, an automobile parts supplier could use XML to exchange inventory data with an automobile manufacturer, even though the two might be using two completely different database systems on two different platforms. Because XML describes how data is structured, it can bridge the two otherwise incompatible systems seamlessly.

Summary

In this chapter, you've learned about the fundamentals of developing Internet applications by using SQL Server and IIS 5 on the Windows 2000 operating system platform. A wide variety of development choices are available, ranging from scripting environments such as ASP to compiled code options like ISAPI extensions and filters. Each of these options has its advantages and disadvantages. When you choose the tools for developing your large-scale Internet application, examine carefully the trade-offs each option presents in order to avoid later problems.

Chapter 24
Loading the Database

After you create your database and database tables, you are ready to load your data. Several methods of loading data into a database are available; which method you choose depends on what the source of your data is, what sort of processing you want to perform on the data, and where you are loading the data. In this chapter, we'll look at the following methods of loading a database:

- **Using Bulk Copy Program (BCP)**   BCP is an external program provided with Microsoft SQL Server 2000 to facilitate the loading of data files into a database. BCP can also be used to copy data out of a SQL Server table into a data file.

- **Using the BULK INSERT command**   The BULK INSERT Transact-SQL (T-SQL) command lets you copy large quantities of data from a data file into a SQL Server table, from within SQL Server. Because this command is an SQL statement (run within ISQL, OSQL, or Query Analyzer), the process runs as a SQL Server thread. You cannot use this command to copy data from SQL Server into a data file.

- **Using Data Transformation Services (DTS)**   DTS is a set of tools provided with SQL Server that makes copying data into and out of SQL Server an easy task. DTS includes a wizard for importing data and a wizard for exporting data.

Note   Although staging tables do not provide a method of loading data, they are commonly used in database loading.

Each of these methods has different capabilities and characteristics. You should be able to find at least one method that suits your needs.

Note   Recovering a database from a backup file can also be considered a form of database loading, but because database backup and recovery are discussed in Chapters 32 and 33, these topics are not covered here.

Certain database configuration parameters are common to BCP and the BULK INSERT statement. These database parameters define how bulk copies are performed. These settings must be made before any load operation is performed.

You might find these additional actions useful:

- **The SELECT...INTO statement**   This statement is used to copy data from one table into another table.

- **Staging tables**   Staging tables are temporary tables commonly used to transform data within a database. You can use these tables to facilitate the loading process and to modify data during the loading process.

Load Operation Performance

In this section, we'll look at three configuration options commonly used to improve the performance of load operations. Two of these options affect logging during bulk copy operations, and the other option affects locking. A *bulk copy* is an operation in which data is copied in large chunks; copying large chunks of data at one time is the most efficient way to reproduce data.

Logging Options

SQL Server uses a sophisticated logging mechanism to ensure that data is not lost in the event of a system failure. Logging is essential to the integrity of the data within the system, but it can significantly increase the load on the system. You can reduce the load on your system by reducing the amount of data that is logged during bulk loads.

> **Note**   After a system failure, SQL Server will recover the database. All transactions that were not committed at the time of the failure will be rolled back (undone). All transactions that were committed at the time of the failure will be rolled forward (recovered). This rolling back or rolling forward will return the system to the state it was in before the failure occurred. Backup and recovery are described in detail in Chapters 32 and 33.

By default, all database insert operations are completely logged, enabling both rolling forward and rolling back of inserted data in the event of a system failure. By disabling full logging of bulk copies (that you perform by using BCP, the BULK INSERT statement, or the SELECT...INTO statement), you can reduce the amount of data logged, but only rollback operations will be supported. This option will improve the performance of bulk copies, but it will require the entire database-loading process to be restarted in the event of a system failure because the logging normally used for recovery is not done. This option will apply to staging tables only if you load these tables by using the bulk load methods described earlier.

Full logging of these bulk copy operations is disabled when all of the following conditions are met:

- The database option SELECT INTO/BULKCOPY is set to *TRUE*. Here is the syntax of the command using the *sp_dboption* stored procedure:

  ```
  exec sp_dboption database_name, "select into/bulkcopy", TRUE
  ```

- You can also configure this option with SQL Server Enterprise Manager. See Chapter 8 for details about Enterprise Manager.

- The table that data is being loaded into is not replicated. (Replication is explained in Chapters 26, 27, and 28.)

- The TABLOCK hint is specified. (See the section "Optional Parameters" later in this chapter for more information about this hint.) If the table that data is being loaded into has indexes defined, SQL Server does not require you to specify the TABLOCK hint.

Another database option, *trunc. log on chkpt*, disables the saving of log records while the option is set to *TRUE*. When this option is set to *TRUE*, the transaction log will be truncated whenever a checkpoint occurs. This improves bulk copy performance, but it means that you will not be able to perform either a forward or backward recovery in the event of a system failure.

Caution If you enable the *trunc. log on chkpt* option (by setting it to *TRUE*), you should do so only when you initially load data into the database. Completely disabling logging affects the entire database and can render the system unrecoverable. Thus, this option should never be used on a production system during normal operations, when recovery is important. If you do set the *trunc. log on chkpt* option to *TRUE*, be sure to disable it after you finish the loading operation.

To set this option by using a stored procedure, use *sp_dboption* with the following parameters:

```
exec sp_dboption database_name, "trunc. log on chkpt", TRUE
```

Note You can set additional options on the Options tab of the database Properties window, shown in Figure 24-1. Restrict Access limits access to specific roles or to a single user. Read Only disallows write access to the database. ANSI NULL Default specifies whether nullable columns are set to NULL or NOT NULL by default. Recursive Triggers simply enables recursive firing of triggers. Auto Update Statistics enables SQL Server to rebuild any out-of-date statistics during optimization. Torn Page Detection allows removal of incomplete pages. Auto Close specifies that the database be shut down after all its resources are freed and all users have logged off. Auto Shrink specifies that SQL Server will shrink database files periodically. Auto Create Statistics enables SQL Server to automatically build statistics during optimization. And Use Quoted Identifiers enforces ANSI rules regarding quotation marks.

Figure 24-1. *The Options tab of the database Properties window.*

Locking Option

You can also improve bulk copy performance by enabling the *table lock on bulk load* option. This option allows the use of a single table lock instead of numerous row locks for a bulk copy operation. You set the *table lock on bulk load* option by using the *sp_tableoption* stored procedure with the following parameters:

```
exec sp_tableoption "table_name", "table lock on bulk load", TRUE
```

(Remember to reset the *trunc. log on chkpt* parameter after the load has been completed.) Because the *table lock on bulk load* option affects the locking mode of the table only during a bulk load, no performance degradation occurs when you are not doing bulk loads.

Note To take advantage of the *table lock on bulk load* option, you must use the TABLOCK setting.

Bulk Copy Program

Using BCP, you can copy data from a data file into SQL Server or you can copy data from SQL Server into a data file. BCP is useful for transferring data into SQL Server from other databases as well as for transferring user-generated data. In this section, you'll learn how to use BCP and its options and how to format data so that you can copy it into and out of SQL Server by using BCP.

BCP Syntax

BCP is a command-line executable program that is invoked from the command prompt window. BCP requires certain parameters and offers many optional parameters for you to use. The format of the BCP command is shown here. (All the required and optional parameters are shown.)

```
bcp  {[[database_name.][owner].]{table_name | view_name} | "query"}
     {in | out | queryout | format} data_file
     [-m max_errors] [-f format_file] [-e error_file]
     [-F first_row] [-L last_row] [-b batch_size]
     [-n] [-c] [-w] [-N] [-V (60 | 65 | 70)] [-6]
     [-q] [-C code_page] [-t field_term] [-r row_term]
     [-i input_file] [-o output_file] [-a packet_size]
     [-S server_name[\instance_name]] [-U login_id] [-P password]
     [-T] [-v] [-R] [-k] [-E] [-h "hint [,...n]"]
```

Required Parameters

The required parameters specify the data extraction and insertion locations, among other things. As mentioned, using BCP, you can extract data from a data file and insert it into a SQL Server table (or view), or you can extract data from a table (or view) and insert it into a data file.

You specify the table or view used in the bulk copy operation in one of two ways. First, you can use the *table/view_definition* parameter. The simplest definition consists of the table or view name. As shown in the preceding command, you have the option of specifying the name of the database where the specified table or view resides, the owner of the table or view, or both. If you do not specify a database name, this is the default database specified in the user's login definition. See Chapter 34 for more information about user definitions.

Alternatively, you can specify the table or view by using a query. When you use this method, you are specifying which data will be extracted from the table or view. (The *table/view_definition* parameter can be used to specify the table or view used for data extraction or insertion.) This query must be enclosed in double quotation marks and can consist of a SELECT statement with or without clauses such as ORDER BY. If you specify a query definition, you must also specify the *queryout* parameter (discussed in Table 24-1).

The location of the data file used in the bulk copy operation is specified by the *data_file* parameter. This must be a valid path.

Finally, you must specify one or more of the parameters listed in Table 24-1.

Table 24-1.   The bulk copy directional specifiers

Parameter	Description
In	Specifies that the bulk copy operation will copy data from the data file into the table or view in the SQL Server database.
Out	Specifies that the bulk copy operation will extract data from the SQL Server table or view and insert it into the data file.
Queryout	Specifies that data will be extracted from the SQL Server database by means of the defined query. The bulk copy will then copy the data that the query selects into the data file.
Format	Specifies that BCP will create a format file in addition to performing the bulk copy operation. The formatting options (–n, –c, –w, –6, or –N) and the table or view delimiters are used to create the format file. The *format* parameter must be accompanied by the –f option. The format file allows you to store the BCP definitions so that you do not need to repeat them when you subsequently use BCP.

Optional Parameters

You can use the optional parameters listed in Table 24-2 to modify the way in which BCP performs bulk copies.

Table 24-2.   The optional bulk copy directional specifiers

Parameter	Description
–a *packet_size*	Specifies the number of bytes per network packet sent between the client and the server.
–b *batch_size*	Specifies the number of rows to be included in a batch. Each batch is copied as one transaction. By default, all of the rows in the data file are copied as one batch, using one commit. You might want to specify this option when you perform bulk inserts so that table locks are released as batches are processed, thus allowing other processing.
–c	Specifies that BCP use a character data type.
–e *err_file*	Specifies the path of an error file in which BCP errors are logged.
–f *format_file*	Specifies the path of a format file that BCP has used previously. A format file is created if BCP is run with the *format* option specified, as described earlier. If the format file is used, other formatting options need not be included.

Table 24-2. *continued*

Parameter	Description
–h "*hint* [,.*n*]"	Specifies hints to use during the bulk copy. These hints can be any of the following:
	• **ORDER** (*column* [ASC I DESC]) Specifies that the data in the column indicated is sorted.
	• **ROWS_PER_BATCH** = *number* Specifies the number of rows per batch. This option is similar to –b but should not be used in conjunction with –b. The –b option sends the specified batch of rows to SQL Server as one transaction. When –b is not specified, the entire data file is sent to SQL Server as one transaction and ROWS_PER_BATCH is used to help SQL Server estimate the size of the load. This information is used to optimize the load internally.
	• **KILOBYTES_PER_BATCH** = *number* Specifies the approximate number of kilobytes per batch. This option is similar to –b but uses kilobytes rather than the number of rows to specify batch size.
	• **TABLOCK** Specifies that a table-level lock be used for the duration of the bulk load. This technique significantly improves performance by reducing lock contention on the table.
	• **CHECK_CONSTRAINTS** Specifies that constraints be checked during the bulk load. The default behavior is to ignore constraints.
–i *input_file*	Specifies the name of the response file. The response file contains responses to the questions asked by BCP when the database is running in interactive mode.
–k	Specifies that empty columns get null values rather than default values.
–m *max_errors*	Specifies how many errors can occur before BCP terminates. If this option is not included, the default value is *10*.
–n	Specifies that BCP use native data types.
–o *output_file*	Specifies the output file that receives BCP output. This output file is a normal text file that you can read by using Microsoft Notepad or other utilities.
–q	Specifies that quoted identifiers be required for table and view names that contain non-ANSI characters such as spaces.
–r *row_term*	Specifies the row terminator. The default is the newline character.
–t *field_term*	Specifies the field terminator, also known as the delimiter. The default is the tab character.
–v	Prints the version number of and copyright information about BCP.
–w	Specifies that BCP use Unicode characters.
–C *code_page*	Specifies the code page of the data in the data file.
–E	Specifies that the file being copied contains values for identity columns.

(continued)

Table 24-2. *continued*

Parameter	Description
–F *first_row*	Specifies the first row to start the bulk copy. If no row is specified, the first row will be row 1. This option is useful if you want to skip header information in the data file.
–L *last_row*	Specifies the last row to perform the bulk copy. The default value of 0 specifies that the last row to be copied will be the last row in the data file. This option is useful if you want to copy only a certain number of rows.
–N	Specifies that BCP use native data types for noncharacter data and Unicode for character data.
–P *password*	Specifies the password for the login ID used in the –U option.
–R	Specifies that currency, date, and time data use the regional format of the client system.
–S *server_name*	Specifies the name of the server to copy into.
–T	Specifies that a trusted connection be used. The *login_id* and *password* variables are not needed if this option is used; the network user credentials are used.
–U *login_id*	Specifies the user login ID to copy the data under.
–V *60	65	70*	Performs the bulk copy using data types from an earlier version of SQL Server. This option should be used with the –c and –n options.
–6	Specifies that BCP use Microsoft SQL Server 6 or Microsoft SQL Server 6.5 data types.

As you can see, numerous options and combinations of options can be used to take advantage of BCP. The best way to begin learning how these options can be used is to work through examples of using BCP, which we'll do next.

Using BCP

In this section, we'll look at several examples of using BCP to load data into and out of SQL Server. These examples don't cover every possibility, but they should give you a good idea of the variety of modes and methods of operation available with BCP.

You can use BCP from the command-line as described earlier, or you can use BCP in a more interactive fashion. To invoke BCP without having any additional interaction with the program, you must specify the –n, –c, –w, or –N parameter. If none of these parameters is specified, BCP will operate in the interactive mode.

Note All of the following examples use the *Customers* table from the Northwind database.

Loading Data Using BCP Interactively

Using BCP in interactive mode to load data is somewhat difficult because this technique requires you to specify column lengths and types. You do not have to do this when you use command-line options, as described in the next section. Although using BCP in interactive mode to load data is not recommended, we'll look at an example of this technique so that you will have a thorough understanding of how BCP works. In this example, we'll copy data from the file data2.file into the *Customers* table of the Northwind database, writing errors to the file err.file. You must have previously created the data file data2.file. This file contains the data you want to load into the *Customers* table. To start the interactive session as the system administrator, enter the following command:

```
bcp Northwind.dbo.Customers in data2.file -e err.file -Usa
```

You will then be prompted for a password. Enter the system administrator (sa) password.

Next BCP will require you to provide information regarding the data you want to copy. A sample BCP interactive session follows. Note that user input appears in bold type.

```
Enter the file storage type of field CustomerID [nchar]: char
Enter prefix-length of field CustomerID [1]: 0
Enter length of field CustomerID [26]: 5
Enter field terminator [none]: ,

Enter the file storage type of field CompanyName [nvarchar]: char
Enter prefix-length of field CompanyName [1]: 0
Enter length of field CompanyName [189]: 40
Enter field terminator [none]: ,

Enter the file storage type of field ContactName [nvarchar]: char
Enter prefix-length of field ContactName [1]: 0
Enter length of field ContactName [143]: 30
Enter field terminator [none]: ,

Enter the file storage type of field ContactTitle [nvarchar]: char
Enter prefix-length of field ContactTitle [1]: 0
Enter length of field ContactTitle [143]: 30
Enter field terminator [none]: ,

Enter the file storage type of field Address [nvarchar]: char
Enter prefix-length of field Address [1]: 0
Enter length of field Address [283]: 60
Enter field terminator [none]: ,
```
(continued)

continued

```
Enter the file storage type of field City [nvarchar]: char
Enter prefix-length of field City [1]: 0
Enter length of field City [73]: 15
Enter field terminator [none]: ,

Enter the file storage type of field Region [nvarchar]: char
Enter prefix-length of field Region [1]: 0
Enter length of field Region [73]: 15
Enter field terminator [none]: ,

Enter the file storage type of field PostalCode [nvarchar]: char
Enter prefix-length of field PostalCode [1]: 0
Enter length of field PostalCode [49]: 10
Enter field terminator [none]: ,

Enter the file storage type of field Country [nvarchar]: char
Enter prefix-length of field Country [1]: 0
Enter length of field Country [73]: 15
Enter field terminator [none]: ,

Enter the file storage type of field Phone [nvarchar]: char
Enter prefix-length of field Phone [1]: 0
Enter length of field Phone [115]: 24
Enter field terminator [none]: ,

Enter the file storage type of field Fax [nvarchar]: char
Enter prefix-length of field Fax [1]: 0
Enter length of field Fax [115]: 24
Enter field terminator [none]: ,

Do you want to save this format information in a file? [Y/n]: Y
Host filename [bcp.fmt]: data.fmt


Starting copy...
SQLState = S1000, NativeError = 0
Error = [Microsoft][ODBC SQL Server Driver] Unexpected EOF
encountered in BCP data-file

5 rows copied.
Network packet size (bytes): 4096
Clock Time (ms.): total        51 Avg        10 (98.04 rows
per sec.)
```

As you can see, you must know many of these values before you begin. An error message was generated when BCP reached the end of the file because we did not specify the number of rows to be copied.

Loading Data Using BCP with Command-Line Options

As mentioned, you will find it much easier to use BCP to load data when you use the command-line options. In the example in this section, we'll use BCP to load data from a data file that is made up of tab-delimited character columns. We'll use the –c option to specify that the data is in character format in the data file. The use of the –c option also makes BCP run in noninteractive mode. The following command copies 25 lines of data from the file data.file into the *Customers* table in the Northwind database:

```
bcp Northwind.dbo.Customers in data.file -e err.fil -c -Usa
```

Because the –c option specifies character data, you do not have to provide the field length and prefix length. Assuming that you have created data.file with 25 rows and tab-delimited character data corresponding to the columns in the *Customers* table, and that you have entered the sa password, the session should look something like this. (Your network packet size and clock time numbers might differ.)

```
Starting copy...

25 rows copied.
Network packet size (bytes): 4096
Clock Time (ms.): total       80 Avg       3 (312.50 rows
per sec.)
```

In this example, the direction of the copy was set to *in* to indicate that data be transferred into the database. It's always a good idea to specify an error file because it provides you with a log of any error encountered during the BCP session. If you do not specify an error file, the errors will be sent to your screen and will eventually scroll out of view.

Loading Data Using the *format* Option

In our first example in the "Using BCP" section, we created a format file named data.fmt. Rather than entering all of the formatting options such as storage type, prefix length, field length, and field terminator by hand, you can use this format file. You invoke this file by using the –f (*format*) option, as shown here:

```
bcp Northwind.dbo.Customers in data2.file -e err.fil -f data.fmt
-L 5 -Usa
```

Assuming that you have entered the sa password and created data2.file, the session should look something like this:

```
Starting copy...

5 rows copied.
Network packet size (bytes): 4096
Clock Time (ms.): total        50 Avg        10 (100.00 rows
per sec.)
```

In addition to including the –f option, this example includes the –L option. The –L option indicates the last row to copy from the input file. In this example, the fifth row was the last row to be processed. This specification eliminates the EOF error message seen in the earlier example.

Extracting Data Using BCP Interactively

Using BCP in interactive mode to copy data out of a database is easier than using it interactively to copy data into a database because when you extract data, BCP will fill in the field-length options for you. Let's use the following command to interactively copy data out of the *Customers* table in the Northwind database:

```
bcp Northwind.dbo.Customers out dataout.dat -e err.fil -U sa
```

After you enter this command and the sa password, the session will proceed. A sample session follows. (User input is shown in bold type.)

```
Enter the file storage type of field CustomerID [nchar]: char
Enter prefix-length of field CustomerID [1]: 0
Enter length of field CustomerID [26]:
Enter field terminator [none]: ,

Enter the file storage type of field CompanyName [nvarchar]: char
Enter prefix-length of field CompanyName [1]: 0
Enter length of field CompanyName [189]:
Enter field terminator [none]: ,

Enter the file storage type of field ContactName [nvarchar]: char
Enter prefix-length of field ContactName [1]: 0
Enter length of field ContactName [143]:
Enter field terminator [none]: ,

Enter the file storage type of field ContactTitle [nvarchar]: char
Enter prefix-length of field ContactTitle [1]: 0
Enter length of field ContactTitle [143]:
Enter field terminator [none]: ,
```

continued
```
Enter the file storage type of field Address [nvarchar]: char
Enter prefix-length of field Address [1]: 0
Enter length of field Address [283]:
Enter field terminator [none]: ,

Enter the file storage type of field City [nvarchar]: char
Enter prefix-length of field City [1]: 0
Enter length of field City [73]:
Enter field terminator [none]: ,

Enter the file storage type of field Region [nvarchar]: char
Enter prefix-length of field Region [1]: 0
Enter length of field Region [73]:
Enter field terminator [none]: ,

Enter the file storage type of field PostalCode [nvarchar]: char
Enter prefix-length of field PostalCode [1]: 0
Enter length of field PostalCode [49]:
Enter field terminator [none]: ,

Enter the file storage type of field Country [nvarchar]: char
Enter prefix-length of field Country [1]: 0
Enter length of field Country [73]:
Enter field terminator [none]: ,

Enter the file storage type of field Phone [nvarchar]: char
Enter prefix-length of field Phone [1]: 0
Enter length of field Phone [115]:
Enter field terminator [none]: ,

Enter the file storage type of field Fax [nvarchar]: char
Enter prefix-length of field Fax [1]: 0
Enter length of field Fax [115]:
Enter field terminator [none]: ,

Do you want to save this format information in a file? [Y/n]: n
Host filename [bcp.fmt]:

Starting copy...

96 rows copied.
Network packet size (bytes): 4096
Clock Time (ms.): total     10 Avg      0 (9600.00 rows per sec.)
```

This interactive BCP session creates a tab-delimited file (remember that tab delimiters are the default delimiter) that you can view using Notepad. This file is a text file, and all of the data is character data. Unfortunately, BCP does not add a newline character at the end of each line. Thus, if you do view the file by using Notepad, you will see one extremely long line of data.

Extracting Data Using BCP with Command-Line Options

In order to create a more readable data file that is tab-delimited and ends each line with a newline character, use the –c option, as shown here:

```
bcp Northwind.dbo.Customers out dataout.dat -e err.fil -c -U sa
```

After you enter this command and the sa password, the session will proceed, as follows:

```
Starting copy...

96 rows copied.
Network packet size (bytes): 4096
Clock Time (ms.): total       1 Avg       0 (96000.00 rows per sec.)
```

Extracting Data Using the *queryout* Option

Our final example uses the *queryout* option to extract data. This option enables you to specify a query when copying data out of the SQL Server database. This query selects certain data, and only that data will be copied. The *queryout* option is fairly easy to use—just remember to enclose your query in double quotation marks, as shown here:

```
bcp "SELECT CustomerID, CompanyName FROM Northwind..Customers"
queryout dataout.dat -e err.fil -c -U sa
```

As usual, enter the sa password; the session will appear as follows:

```
Starting copy...

96 rows copied.
Network packet size (bytes): 4096
Clock Time (ms.): total       1 Avg       0 (96000.00 rows per sec.)
```

The output from this query is a tab-delimited, row-terminated data file consisting of two columns: *CustomerID* and *CompanyName*. This technique is useful when you want to extract only certain database columns or rows.

The BULK INSERT Statement

The T-SQL BULK INSERT statement is similar to BCP in that both can be used to bulk copy data into the SQL Server database from a data file. Unlike BCP, however, BULK INSERT cannot be used to extract data from SQL Server databases. This limitation reduces its functionality, but because the BULK INSERT statement is run as a thread within SQL Server, the need to send data from one program to another is eliminated, which improves the performance of data loading. Thus, the BULK INSERT statement loads data more efficiently than does BCP.

BULK INSERT Syntax

Like BCP, the BULK INSERT statement has several required parameters and many optional parameters. You invoke BULK INSERT from within SQL Server (using ISQL, OSQL, or SQL Server Query Analyzer) by using the following command. (All of the required and optional parameters are shown here.)

```
BULK INSERT [['database_name'.]['owner'].]
            {'table_name' | 'view_name' FROM 'data_file' }
    [WITH (
            [BATCHSIZE [ = batch_size ]]
            [[,] CHECK_CONSTRAINTS ]
            [[,] CODEPAGE [ = 'ACP' | 'OEM' | 'RAW' | 'code_page' ]]
            [[,] DATAFILETYPE [ = {'char'|'native'|
                                   'widechar'|'widenative' }]]
            [[,] FIELDTERMINATOR [ = 'field_terminator' ]]
            [[,] FIRSTROW [ = first_row ]]
            [[,] FIRETRIGGERS [ = fire_triggers ]]
            [[,] FORMATFILE [ = 'format_file_path' ]]
            [[,] KEEPIDENTITY ]
            [[,] KEEPNULLS ]
            [[,] KILOBYTES_PER_BATCH [ = kilobytes_per_batch ]]
            [[,] LASTROW [ = last_row ]]
            [[,] MAXERRORS [ = max_errors ]]
            [[,] ORDER ( { column [ ASC | DESC ]}[ ,...n ])]
            [[,] ROWS_PER_BATCH [ = rows_per_batch ]]
            [[,] ROWTERMINATOR [ = 'row_terminator' ]]
            [[,] TABLOCK ]
            )]
```

Required Parameters

The location of the data file is specified by the *data_file* parameter. This value must be a valid path.

The database location where the data is inserted is defined by either a table definition or a view. As you can see in the preceding command, you can also specify the table or view owner, the database name, or both. If you attempt to use the BULK INSERT command to insert data into a view, you can affect only one of the base tables referenced in the FROM clause of the view.

Optional Parameters

You can use the optional parameters and keywords listed in Table 24-3 to modify the behavior of BULK INSERT. As you will see, the options available with the BULK INSERT statement are similar to those available with BCP.

Table 24-3. The optional parameters for BULK INSERT

Optional Parameter	Description
BATCHSIZE = *size*	Specifies the number of rows in a batch. Each batch is one transaction.
CHECK_CONSTRAINTS	Specifies that constraint checking be performed. The default behavior is to ignore constraints.
CODEPAGE [= 'ACP' | 'OEM' | 'RAW' | *'code_page'*]	Specifies the code page of the data in the data file. This option is useful only with *char*, *varchar*, and *text* data types.
DATAFILETYPE [= 'char' | 'native' | 'widechar' | 'widenative']	Specifies the type of data in the data file; by default, this value is *char*. Other options include *native* (native database data types), *widechar* (Unicode characters), and *widenative* (same as *native*, except *char*, *varchar*, and *text* are stored as Unicode).
FIELDTERMINATOR [= *field_term*]	Specifies the field terminator used with *char* and *widechar* data types. By default, this value is the tab character, \t.
FIRSTROW [= *first_row*]	The number of the first row to copy. The default is *1*. This parameter is useful if you want to skip header information in the data file.
FORMATFILE [= *format_file*]	Specifies the path of a format file.
KEEPIDENTITY	Specifies that values for an identity column are present in the data files being imported.
KEEPNULLS	Specifies that empty columns retain null values.

Table 24-3.   *continued*

Optional Parameter	Description
KILOBYTES_PER_BATCH [= *number*]	Specifies the approximate number of kilobytes per batch used in the bulk copy.
LASTROW [= *last_row*]	Specifies the last row on which to perform bulk insert. The default is *0*. This option is useful if you want to insert only a certain number of rows.
MAXERRORS [= *max_errors*]	Specifies how many errors can occur before the insert terminates. The default value is *10*.
ORDER (*column* [ASC I DESC])	Specifies that the data in the column indicated be sorted in the specified order.
ROWS_PER_BATCH [= *rows_per_batch*]	Specifies the number of rows per batch. Each batch is copied as one transaction. By default, all the rows in the data file are inserted as one batch, using a single commit. You might want to specify this option when you perform bulk inserts so that table locks are released as batches are performed, thus allowing other processing to take place.
ROWTERMINATOR [= *row_term*]	Specifies the row terminator for *char* and *widechar* data types. The default is the newline character, \n.

Using BULK INSERT

Now let's look at two examples of how to use the BULK INSERT statement. In both examples, we'll load data from the character file data.file (which we used in earlier examples) into the *Customers* table of the Northwind database.

> **Note**   Remember that the BULK INSERT statement can be used only to insert data into a database; it cannot be used to extract data. Because BULK INSERT does not offer the variety of modes of operation that BCP does, only a couple of examples are provided here.

To load the data into the database, use the following T-SQL statement:

```
BULK INSERT Northwind..Customers FROM 'C:\data.file'
WITH
    (
    DATAFILETYPE = 'char'
    )
GO
```

You can add as many options as you want. In the following example, more optional parameters are used:

```
BULK INSERT Northwind..Customers FROM 'C:\data.file'
WITH
    (
    BATCHSIZE = 5,
    CHECK_CONSTRAINTS,
    DATAFILETYPE = 'char',
    FIELDTERMINATOR = '\t',
    FIRSTROW = 5,
    LASTROW = 20,
    TABLOCK
    )
```

This statement will load only rows 5 through 20 from the data file. The field terminator is specified to be the tab character (even though this is the default). This example also specifies that constraints be checked during the bulk insert process and allocates a table lock for the duration of the load. The transactions that perform the load will be done in batches of five rows each.

Data Transformation Services

DTS, which is part of SQL Server Enterprise Manager, is designed to help you easily import data into the database and export data out of the database. DTS consists of two wizards: the Import Wizard and the Export Wizard. In this section, we'll look at how to use these wizards.

Import Wizard

You can use the Import Wizard to import data into the database from various data sources. Unlike BCP and the BULK INSERT T-SQL statement, the Import Wizard can import data from sources other than data files. To use the Import Wizard, follow these steps:

1. In Enterprise Manager, expand a server group and click the name of the server you want to import data into. From the Tools menu, choose Wizards. In the Select Wizard dialog box that appears, expand the Data Transformation Services folder, click DTS Import Wizard, and then click OK. Alternatively, right-click the name of the server, point to All Tasks, and then click Import Data. The Data Transformation Services Import/Export Wizard welcome screen appears, as shown in Figure 24-2.

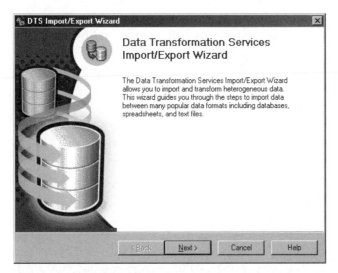

Figure 24-2. *The Data Transformation Services Import/Export Wizard welcome screen.*

2. Click Next to display the Choose A Data Source screen, shown in Figure 24-3.

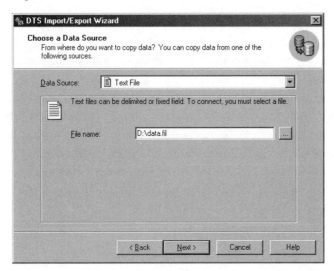

Figure 24-3. *The Choose A Data Source screen.*

Here you select a data source from the Source drop-down list. Figure 24-3 shows Text File selected. You can choose from the following data source options:

- dBase
- Microsoft Access
- Microsoft Data Link
- Microsoft Excel
- Microsoft Visual FoxPro
- Other ODBC data source
- Other OLE DB data source
- Paradox
- Data files

These selections depend in part on the ODBC drivers you have installed on your system. For example, if you have an Oracle ODBC driver installed, OLE DB provider for Oracle will also be listed as an option. The Choose A Data Source screen will change based on the data source you select. Whichever source you choose, you will need to enter file and sometimes logon information.

3. Click Next to display the Select File Format screen, shown in Figure 24-4. (The Select File Format screen is shown only when Text File is chosen.) This screen allows you to select a file format. The options on the screen are described here:

- The Delimited and Fixed Field option buttons allow you to choose the format of the input file, and a particular delimiter character or a fixed width.
- The File Type drop-down list allows you to specify whether the input file is an ANSI-format, OEM-format, or Unicode-format file.
- The Row Delimiter drop-down list lets you specify which character is used to terminate each row in the input file.

- The Text Qualifier drop-down list can be used to specify text in a delimited file.

- The Skip Rows spin box allows you to specify how many rows at the beginning of the input file to skip.

- The First Row Has Column Names check box specifies that the first row is not data; it is a label and is skipped.

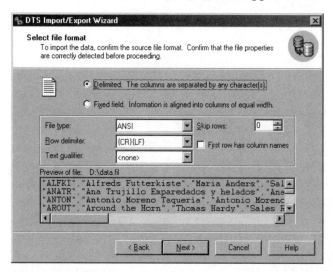

Figure 24-4. *The Select File Format screen.*

4. Choose the delimited file format, {CR}{LF} for the delimiter, and no text qualifier. Then click Next to display the Specify Column Delimiter screen, shown in Figure 24-5. (If you click Fixed Field instead of Delimited, the Fixed Field Column Positions screen appears.) This screen provides a convenient way of specifying the column delimiter because you receive instant feedback based on your choice, which shows whether you have chosen the appropriate delimiter. You can use commas, tabs, semicolons, or any other delimiter. When you select the delimiter, rows appear in the Preview pane. This lets you see whether you have chosen the best delimiter based on the data in the file.

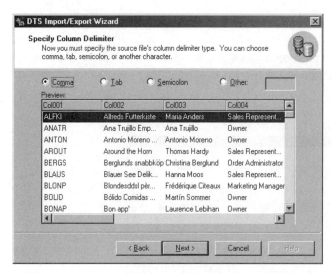

Figure 24-5. *The Specify Column Delimiter screen.*

5. After you select a delimiter, click Next to display the Choose A Destination screen, shown in Figure 24-6. This screen lets you select a database to import the data into. You must specify the SQL Server ODBC destination (the ODBC alias for the database) as well as a server and a database. In this example, we'll specify the Northwind database. You must also choose an authentication type: Windows or SQL Server authentication. If you use SQL Server authentication, you must type a SQL Server username and password in the appropriate text boxes. (SQL Server security is described in detail in Chapter 34.) If you type an invalid username or password, you can retry by clicking Refresh. To modify additional properties, including security options and the connection time-out, click Advanced and make your selections in the screen that appears. These properties do not usually need to be modified.

6. Click Next to display the Select Source Tables And Views screen, shown in Figure 24-7. From this screen, you choose the table into which the data is to be loaded by selecting it from the drop-down list in the Destination column. You can preview the data by clicking Preview. And you can use the Select All and Deselect All buttons to easily select all or no tables from the list.

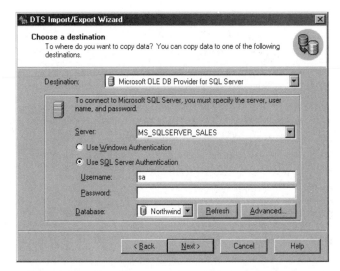

Figure 24-6. *The Choose A Destination screen.*

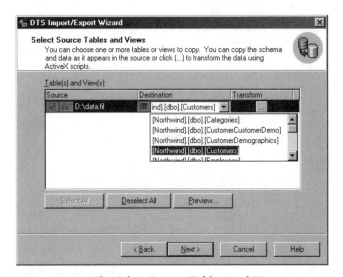

Figure 24-7. *The Select Source Tables And Views screen.*

7. From this same screen, you can access the transformation services. The transformation services allow you to transform the data (change columns and so forth) while you are performing the import. To transform data, first click the Transform button (the button showing three dots under the label Transform) to open the Column Mappings And Transformations dialog box, shown in Figure 24-8. On the Column Mappings tab, you can choose to create a new table or to delete rows from or append rows to an existing table. The Append Rows To Destination Table option is the default. If you choose to create a table, the Edit SQL button will allow you to view and modify the SQL statement that you used to create the table.

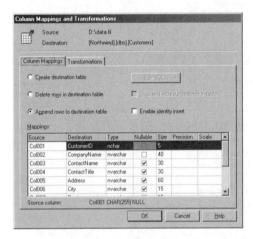

Figure 24-8. *The Column Mappings tab of the Column Mappings And Transformations dialog box.*

8. Click the Transformations tab to view the transformation options, shown in Figure 24-9. On this tab, you can choose to copy directly into the columns or to transform information as it is copied. Transformation services such as precision conversion (16-bit to 32-bit, 32-bit to 16-bit) are specified here. Conversion of null values can also be performed (NOT NULL to NULL, NULL to NOT NULL).

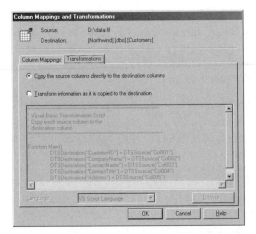

Figure 24-9. *The Transformations tab of the Column Mappings And Transformations dialog box.*

9. Click OK to close this dialog box, and click Next to display the Save, Schedule, And Replicate Package screen, shown in Figure 24-10. This screen lets you run the import now or schedule it for a later time. You can also save the DTS package so that you can run this import again later. To do this, select the Save DTS Package check box, which appears in the Save area at the bottom of the screen. This will save the transformation services settings you made.

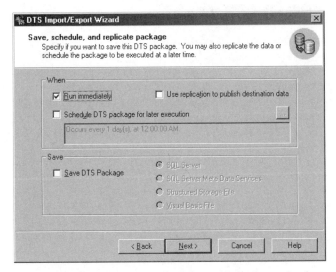

Figure 24-10. *The Save, Schedule, And Replicate Package screen.*

10. Click Next to display the Completing The DTS Import/Export Wizard screen, shown in Figure 24-11. Click Finish to run the import.

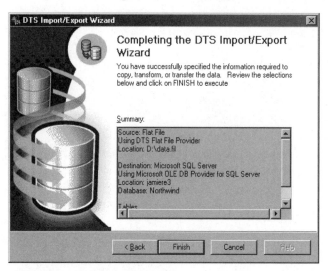

Figure 24-11. *The Completing The DTS Import/Export Wizard screen.*

11. After you click Finish, you will see the Executing Package screen, shown in Figure 24-12. A message box then appears informing you that the data copy is completed or that an error occurred.

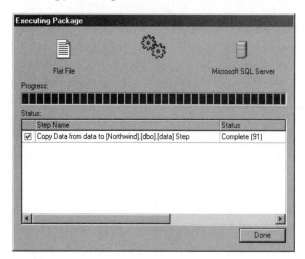

Figure 24-12. *The Executing Package screen.*

As you can see, the DTS Import Wizard makes performing an import of data easy. However, if you were performing this task repeatedly, creating a script would be more effective because it could be reused quickly and easily. You create a script file by saving the BULK INSERT statement to an .sql file.

Export Wizard

You can use the Export Wizard to export data from the database into external data destinations. Unlike BCP, the Export Wizard can export data to destinations other than data files. To use the Export Wizard, follow these steps:

1. In Enterprise Manager, expand a server group and click the name of the server you want to export data from. From the Tools menu, choose Wizards. In the Select Wizard dialog box that appears, expand the Data Transformation Services folder, click DTS Export Wizard, and then click OK. Alternatively, right-click the name of the server, point to All Tasks, and then click Export Data. The Data Transformation Services Import/Export Wizard welcome screen appears, as shown in Figure 24-13.

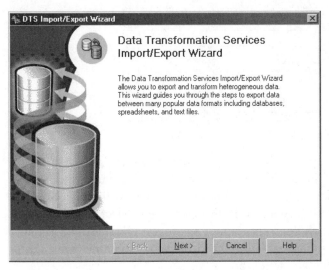

Figure 24-13. *The Data Transformation Services Import/Export Wizard welcome screen.*

2. Click Next to display the Choose A Data Source screen, shown in Figure 24-14. This screen lets you specify a data source. You can keep the default setting, Microsoft OLE DB Provider For SQL Server, or you can select Microsoft ODBC Driver For SQL Server. Either option will connect to SQL Server. Other options can be used to export data from other database products. Next select a database—in this case, the Northwind database. You can also set advanced options, such as the connection timeout, network address, net-libraries, and workstation ID, in the dialog box that appears when you click Advanced. These options typically do not need to be modified, however.

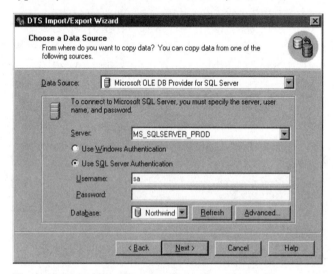

Figure 24-14. *The Choose A Data Source screen.*

3. Click Next to display the Choose A Destination screen, shown in Figure 24-15. The screen options will vary depending on the data type of the destination you choose; however, in most cases, you will be required to enter logon and file information. In this case, we'll select Text File as the destination, which does not require any logon information, so that we can save the database table in text form. Type the name of the destination file in the File Name textbox.

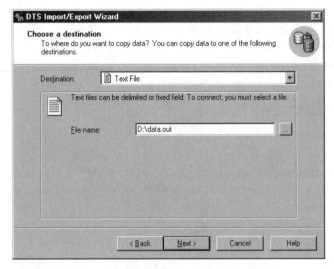

Figure 24-15. *The Choose A Destination screen.*

4. Click Next to display the Specify Table Copy Or Query screen, shown in Figure 24-16. This screen simply lets you specify whether the entire table will be exported or whether the export will be performed by using a query. If you had chosen another SQL Server database as the output destination, a third option—Copy Objects And Data Between SQL Server Databases—would be available.

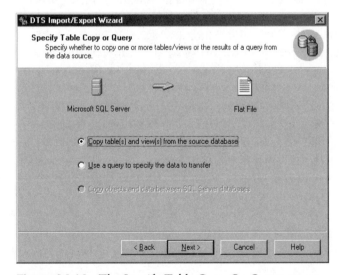

Figure 24-16. *The Specify Table Copy Or Query screen.*

If you click Use A Query To Specify The Data To Transfer and click Next, the Type SQL Statement screen will appear, as shown in Figure 24-17. Here you can type the SQL statement that will select the data you want to export. This query can select subsets of columns or rows, or it can select the entire table, as shown in this example.

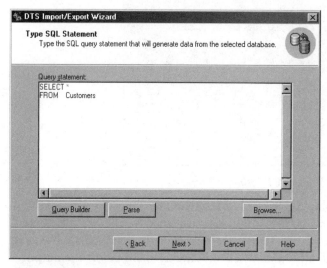

Figure 24-17. *The Type SQL Statement screen.*

5. Click Next to display the Select Destination File Format screen, shown in Figure 24-18. (The Source drop-down list does not appear when you access this screen from the Type SQL Statement screen.) Here you can specify several formatting options for the destination file, including whether the file should be a delimited or a fixed-field file. When you are finished selecting the formatting options, click Next.

   If you click Copy Table(s) And View(s) From The Source Database in the Specify Table Copy Or Query screen and click Next, the Select Destination File Format screen will appear (Figure 24-18). (In this case, the Source drop-down list appears.) In this screen, you select the source table and you select formatting options for the destination file. When you are finished making your selections, click Next.

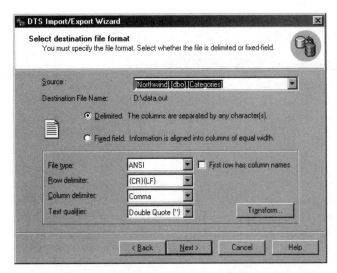

Figure 24-18. *The Select Destination File Format screen.*

6. After you click Next in the Select Destination File Format screen, the Save, Schedule, And Replicate Package screen appears, as shown in Figure 24-19. Here you select when you want to run the job and whether you want to save a DTS package for future use. This screen is similar to its counterpart in the Import Wizard.

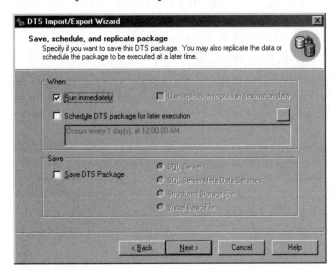

Figure 24-19. *The Save, Schedule, And Replicate Package screen.*

7. Click Next to display the Completing The DTS Import/Export Wizard screen, as shown in Figure 24-20. Click Finish to run the export.

Figure 24-20. *The Completing The DTS Import/Export Wizard screen.*

8. Once you click Finish in the Export Wizard, the data export process begins. The Executing Package screen appears (Figure 24-21), as it does in the Import Wizard. A message box then appears telling you whether the job has succeeded or failed.

Both the Import Wizard and the Export Wizard are easy to use and configure and can make a sometimes difficult job easier. But remember that if you will be performing these operations repeatedly, it is worth the extra effort to script them. You can create a script containing a BULK INSERT T-SQL statement to perform an import operation, and you can use a SELECT statement, with the output redirected to a data file, to handle an export operation.

Note While we used a text file-to-database table transfer in the preceding Import Wizard example and a table-to-text file transfer in the Export Wizard example, these wizards support many other types of data transfers. The wizards are especially useful for transferring data between databases or other entities.

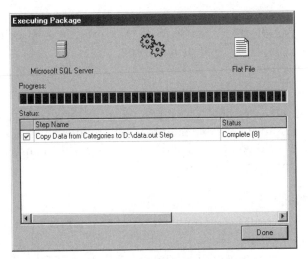

Figure 24-21. *The Executing Package screen.*

Staging Tables

Staging tables are temporary tables that you create to load data into SQL Server, to process and manipulate that data, and to copy that data into the appropriate table or tables within the database. In this section, you'll learn how and when to use staging tables.

Staging Table Basics

A staging table is a temporary storage area in the database into which you can copy data. You can then use T-SQL to process that data into the desired format by performing operations, such as joins, that involve the staging table and existing tables.

By letting you process data during the loading process, staging tables enable you to overcome certain limitations of data-loading methods. Most data-loading techniques allow the data to be simply copied into the database, without any processing. By using DTS, you can perform some data transformations, but you cannot make changes based on the data in the database. The main benefit of using staging tables is that they give you the ability to perform join operations based on information either in the staging table itself or in existing tables.

Using Staging Tables

In this section, we'll look at three examples of using staging tables: merging and loading a table, loading and splitting a table, and loading unique values into a table. These examples should help you understand how staging tables can benefit you when you load data into your database.

Merging and Loading a Table

Consider a table in a data mart that is a combination of two tables from online transaction processing (OLTP) systems. This table has columns A, B, C, D, and E; columns A, B, and C exist in one table, and columns C, D, and E exist in another table. The two input tables can both be staged, and a join operation can be used to load the table into the data mart. This operation is shown in Figure 24-22.

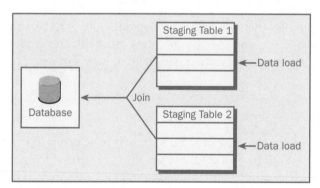

Figure 24-22. *Using staging tables for joins.*

Loading and Splitting a Table

The corollary to our first example is a scenario in which one table is being loaded into several tables in the data mart, which might occur for normalization purposes. This task can be easily accomplished by copying the data into the staging table and using two queries to load the staging table into the data mart tables, as shown in Figure 24-23.

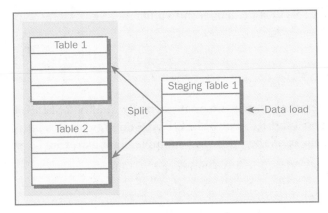

Figure 24-23. *Using staging tables for data splits.*

Loading Unique Values into a Table

You can load unique values into a table by bulk copying the data to be loaded into a staging table and then using a T-SQL statement to insert data into the main table only if that data does not already exist in the table. This option is useful when you are loading data that might invalidate some business rules. To copy unique values from a staging table, use the NOT IN statement, as shown here:

```
INSERT  INTO table ( columnA, columnB )
SELECT  columnA, columnB
FROM    staging_table
WHERE   columnA NOT IN ( SELECT columnA
                         FROM   table )
```

This rather convoluted T-SQL statement simply loads those rows from the staging table into the main table that do not have a *columnA* value that matches one in the main table, thus ensuring that no duplicate values will be inserted.

The SELECT...INTO Statement

Using the SELECT...INTO statement is not really a method of loading the database, but rather a way to create new tables from existing tables or from staging tables. The SELECT...INTO statement cannot be used to populate an existing table.

Note For the SELECT...INTO statement to have permission to work, the database option *select into/bulkcopy* must be set to *TRUE*. To set this option, use the following T-SQL statement:

```
exec sp_dboption <database_name>, "select into/bulkcopy", TRUE
```

The syntax of the SELECT...INTO statement is shown here:

```
SELECT <column_list>
INTO   <new_table_name>
<select_clause>
```

The *select_clause* variable refers to statements that normally qualify a SELECT statement, such as FROM and WHERE. The SELECT...INTO statement is fairly straightforward and easy to use, as the following example demonstrates:

```
exec sp_dboption "example", "select into/bulkcopy", TRUE
GO

SELECT order_id,
       contact_id,
       item_id,
       item_description,
       amount INTO newsales
FROM   stage
GO

exec sp_dboption "example", "select into/bulkcopy", FALSE
GO
```

Here the database name is "example," and the table that is created is *newsales*. The table from which the data is extracted is *stage*.

Summary

In this chapter, you have learned how to load the SQL Server database by using BCP, the BULK INSERT statement, and DTS. You've also been introduced to staging tables, which can be useful under some circumstances. And you've learned how to use the SELECT...INTO statement. These utilities and techniques should serve you well because loading the database is a major task for the DBA. In Chapter 25, you'll learn about Distributed Transaction Coordinator and Microsoft Transaction Server.

Part IV
Built-In Server Features

Chapter 25

Component Services and Microsoft Distributed Transaction Coordinator

In this chapter, you'll learn about Microsoft Distributed Transaction Coordinator (MS DTC), a product designed to allow multiple data sources to be accessed from the same database transaction in a way that ensures data integrity. As you will see in this chapter, MS DTC has many uses, and many types of applications require the services it provides.

MS DTC is a part of Component Services, a collection of products and technologies included in Microsoft Windows 2000 that have evolved from several Microsoft Windows NT services. Specifically, Component Services is based on Component Object Model (COM) and Distributed COM (DCOM), Microsoft Transaction Server, Microsoft Internet Information Server, and Microsoft Message Queue Server. In Windows 2000 Component Services, the COM and DCOM models have evolved to the next level, COM+. The COM+ applications and other system services make up Windows 2000 Component Services.

Before describing MS DTC in detail, this chapter provides an introduction to the technologies that Component Services comprises. This overview should give you enough information to decide whether you can take advantage of these technologies in your environment.

Overview of Component Services

Component Services is made up of a number of separate products and utilities that are managed via the same management console. The Component Services management console is a Microsoft Management Console (MMC) snap-in. Component Services includes the following utilities and products:

- COM+ application services
- MS DTC
- Event Viewer services
- System services
- Microsoft Message Queuing

To run the Component Services management utility, click Start, point to Programs, point to Administrative Tools, and then choose Component Services. The Component Services administration console appears, as shown in Figure 25-1.

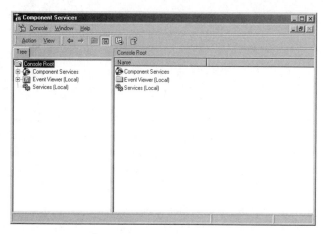

Figure 25-1. *The Component Services administration console.*

COM+ Application Services

COM+ applications are applications that have been designed and built with Microsoft's COM+ specification. COM+ is an extension to the COM model, which facilitates the creation and deployment of distributed applications within an enterprise. With the improvements provided in COM+, you can more easily enhance security and provide queuing components within your application.

You can administer and configure COM+ application components from the Component Services administration console. To access your COM+ applications, expand Component Services, Computers, My Computer, and then COM+ Applications, as shown in Figure 25-2.

As you can see, COM+ applications that have been registered are shown here. By expanding these COM+ applications, you can access the application components.

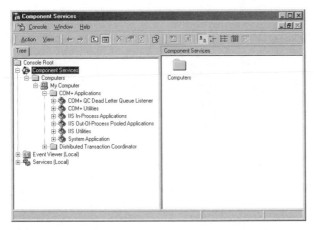

Figure 25-2. *Viewing COM+ applications in the Component Services administration console.*

MS DTC

As you can see in the preceding figure, beneath the COM+ Applications folder in the Component Services administration console is a folder for MS DTC. MS DTC is covered in detail later in this chapter, so it will not be covered here.

Event Viewer Services

The Event Viewer services are the follow-on to the Event Viewer utility that was provided with Windows NT. Like Windows NT Event Viewer, the Event Viewer services in Windows 2000 Component Services enable you to access event logs. All application, security, and system errors and information messages are logged to these event logs. You should check these logs occasionally. To view events, expand the Event Viewer folder, as shown in Figure 25-3, and click the name of the event log that you want to browse.

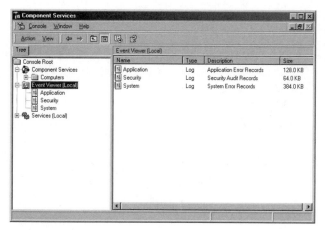

Figure 25-3. *Expanding the Event Viewer folder to view application, security, and system events.*

System Services

The system services component of Component Services is the follow-on to the Services utility that was provided with Window NT. This component, like the Windows NT Services utility, enables you to view and administer all the services that are configured on your system. To view system services, expand the Services folder, as shown in Figure 25-4.

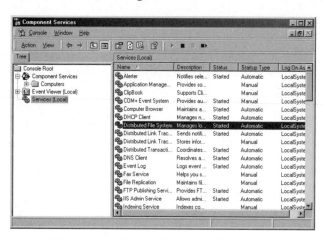

Figure 25-4. *Expanding the Services folder to view system services.*

To start up or shut down a service, right-click the name of that service and choose the desired option from the shortcut menu that appears. These options are shown in Figure 25-5.

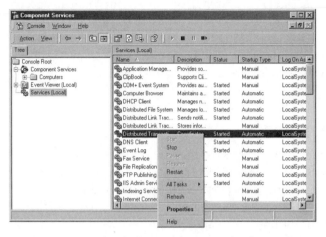

Figure 25-5. *Right-clicking a service to display options.*

To view or change the properties of a service, you can either choose Properties from the menu shown in the preceding figure or double-click the name of the service. In either case, the service's Properties window appears, as shown in Figure 25-6.

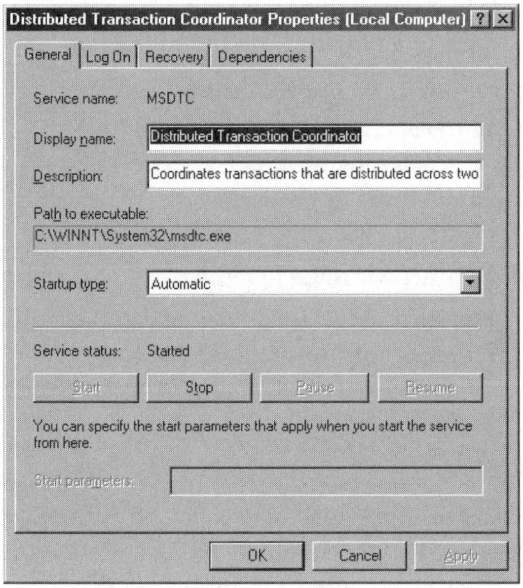

Figure 25-6. *The General tab of a service's Properties window.*

From the General tab of this window, you can change the startup property of the service and stop or pause the service, as applicable. From the other tabs, you can change how that service logs on to Windows 2000. This setting can be highly important for services such as MS DTC and SQL Server Agent. You can specify whether or not they startup automatically when the system starts and you can alter the account that SQL Server and MS DTC use. In addition, you can specify what actions will be taken in the event of a failure in the service, and you can view what other services this service depends on and what services depend on this service.

Microsoft Message Queuing

Although Microsoft Message Queuing (MSMQ) is not shown in the Component Services management console, it can be considered a part of Component Services because Microsoft Message Queuing uses MS DTC for external transactions. Microsoft Message Queuing allows the passing of messages between different applications, different systems, or both. Message Queuing can send transactional and nontransactional messages. Applications use Message Queuing to pass durable messages between servers. A *durable message* is a message that will not be lost in the event of a system loss, such as a power failure. In the event that the system temporarily loses power, MSMQ will resume the message queuing when power is resumed. Microsoft Message Queuing uses a store-and-forward method of sending messages, which keeps messages in the queue even if a network disruption occurs. Other features of Message Queuing include the following:

- **Connectionless messaging**   A connection does not have to be established in order for Message Queuing to send a message. In addition, messages can be routed; thus, different network protocols can be bridged.

- **Dynamic queue administration**   Queues can be added or modified without the need to shut down and restart Message Queuing.

- **Prioritization of messages**   Messages sent by Message Queuing can have different priorities, thus allowing more important messages to be sent first.

- **Cluster support**   Message Queuing is cluster aware, supporting both active/active and active/passive clusters.

- **Integration with Active Directory directory services**   This allows Message Queuing to utilize the directory service within Active Directory.

- **Interoperability with MSMQ 1**   Message Queuing can interoperate with MSMQ 1, which is the predecessor to Message Queuing.

- **Integration with Windows 2000 security**   This allows for the use of the enhanced security features within Windows 2000.

- **Message backup and restore**   Messages can be backed up, and they can be restored in the event of a system failure.

- **MMC snap-in administration**   As with many other Management utilities, the administration is now done from within an MMC snap-in.

As you can see, the Microsoft Message Queuing system has many aspects. However, this chapter focuses on MS DTC, which is the transactional message component of Microsoft Message Queuing.

Microsoft Distributed Transaction Coordinator

As mentioned, MS DTC is a part of Windows 2000 Component Services. (The last incarnation of MS DTC was included with SQL Server 7.) Component Services also includes COM+. COM+ is used when nontransactional communication is needed, and MS DTC is used when transactional communication is needed.

MS DTC is used mainly to manage distributed transactions. A *distributed transaction* is a transaction that uses data from two or more databases. These databases can be on separate computer systems, or they can be on the same system. Transactions between tables in the same database are not considered distributed transactions. Transactions between databases on the same system can be initiated as standard (nondistributed) transactions; however, SQL Server executes them as distributed transactions.

Overview of MS DTC

Many applications require the coordination of transactions that involve multiple data sources. Coordination is necessary when multiple data sources are involved in a transaction because it guarantees that the transaction is executed in an atomic fashion. In other words, coordination ensures that the individual transactions (occurring in the various data sources) that compose the larger transaction all succeed or all fail. If one part of a transaction succeeds and another fails, inconsistency problems and data loss can result. The MS DTC service provides this coordination for you. (Without this service, developers would be responsible for coming up with some sort of distributed transaction scheme for their applications.) MS DTC does this by performing a two-phase commit.

The two-phase commit is not a new technique, nor is it specific to SQL Server. Two-phase commit technology has been around for many years, but its reliability and performance have improved. In addition, the flexibility of the two-phase commit has been enhanced. In fact, a distributed transaction using a two-phase commit can be performed between a SQL Server database and an Oracle database. Because the two databases both support two-phase commits and access protocols such as ODBC, the distributed transaction is possible.

A *two-phase commit* is a commit operation split into two parts: the first part is the prepare phase, which is followed by the commit phase. These phases are initiated by a COMMIT command from the application, which signals MS DTC to perform the two-phase commit. MS DTC coordinates the operation with the systems involved in the distributed transaction by communicating with SQL Server on its own system and with MS DTC on the other systems. MS DTC components that handle two-phase commits are known as *resource managers*.

Once the COMMIT command is issued, MS DTC signals the resource managers to execute the prepare phase of the two-phase commit. In the *prepare phase,* all of the functions necessary for the commit to occur are performed, including flushing out buffers and writing transaction log records. The operations performed in this phase are similar to the operations involved in a standard commit operation. The only difference is that during the prepare phase, SQL Server does not mark the transaction as committed, nor does it release all of the resources and locks that the transaction used. After all of the actions necessary for the transaction to commit on a data source are completed, the resource manager for that data source returns a success signal to the transaction manager. When success signals have been returned from all the data sources, the commit phase can be initiated.

In the *commit phase,* the commit actually takes place on the distributed systems. If all of the resource managers signal a successful commit phase, a notification is sent to the application. If any of the resource managers fail, a notification is sent to the other resource managers to perform a rollback operation. This failure is then reported to the application. In the event that communication between the systems is interrupted, the transaction eventually times out, and a rollback is initiated. If any system involved in the distributed transaction fails, all systems involved in that distributed transaction perform a rollback.

Examples of Using MS DTC

In this section, we'll look at two Real World examples that demonstrate how the coordination services of MS DTC are critical when distributed transactions are used. These examples show what can happen if some transactions in a distributed transaction succeed and others fail.

Real World **Bank Transactions**

Suppose you are choosing a way in which computer systems at two banks perform transactions when money is transferred between the banks. Two basic transactions must be performed by these systems when a customer requests an electronic transfer: money must be removed from account 1 at bank A and added to account 2 at bank B.

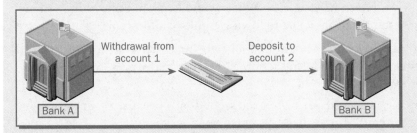

How does this electronic transfer happen? If both accounts were at the same bank, this transfer could be performed by simply updating data in the database on one system. But because the accounts in our example are at different banks, the transfer involves initiating a remote transaction. The transaction, which comprises two transactions, can be initiated by either of the two systems involved in the transaction, or it can be initiated by a third system (a client system).

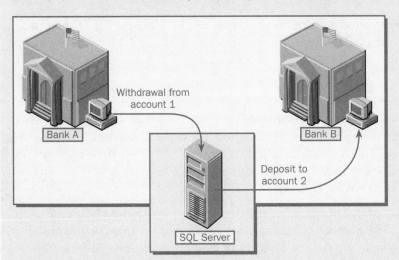

These two transactions can be executed by a teller initiating a program that runs a series of SQL statements on the third (client) computer system. These SQL statements perform the operations on the following page.

1. Update account 1 on system A by removing n dollars
2. Commit transaction
3. Update account 2 on system B by adding n dollars
4. Commit transaction

This technique will work as long as no problems occur on any of the systems, but it is not a safe way to transfer money. What would happen if one of the systems fails during these operations? The following results could occur:

- The first transaction fails because of an error on either system A or the client system. The second transaction is thus not performed, so no money is transferred.

- The first transaction succeeds, but the second fails because of an error on either system B or the client system. The money is lost.

The second result is certainly not an acceptable option. Here's a better way of conducting this transaction:

1. Update account 1 on system A by removing n dollars.
2. Update account 2 on system B by adding n dollars.
3. Commit both transactions as a set. Either both commit or neither commits.

MS DTC enables you to perform these operations. By using the MS DTC service, you can specify which distributed transactions are committed as a set. These transactions will either all commit or all be rolled back.

Real World   **E-Commerce Applications**

Many e-commerce applications are designed to handle thousands of online users and numerous concurrent transactions. Companies that use these applications often run them on multiple systems. Using a single computer system can be unsuitable for many reasons, including the following:

- **The capacity of one system is insufficient.**   Any computer system has limitations. The number of transactions performed by an e-commerce application might exceed the capacity of a single system.

- **Business logic.**   It might make sense from a business perspective to put different functions on different systems. For example, a company might want user information on one system and product information on another system.

- **Outsourcing is used.**   E-commerce functions are sometimes outsourced. For example, a company could hire another company to perform billing.

When multiple systems (or multiple databases on the same system) are used, distributed transactions are initiated to access information in the systems (or databases). If MS DTC is not used, atomicity might be impossible to guarantee.

Let's look at an e-commerce transaction that uses distributed transactions. In this example, the customer wants to use her credit card to purchase a product, a new water bowl for her dog, from an imaginary company named Piercetronics. Let's deconstruct this transaction into its major components.

Note   There are many ways to perform e-commerce transactions. The method described in the following list is not necessarily the best way of performing e-commerce transactions but is rather a simple method that was chosen to make this example easier to understand.

1. The customer establishes a connection to Piercetronic's Web server. At this point, she is most likely looking at static Web pages and is not actually connecting to the database.
2. She browses around for a while and finally finds the water bowl that she wants to purchase. She then puts it into her shopping cart.
3. Placing the item into the shopping cart will require two database operations to be carried out:
   a. A lookup must be performed to find out whether the customer is a return customer or a new customer. If she is a return customer, her account ID is retrieved. (Some applications do this at purchase time.)
   b. The item is inserted into a shopping-cart table.
4. When the customer indicates she is ready to check out, a database transaction or set of transactions begins in order to perform the following operations:
   a. The shopping-cart table is read in order to find the item that the customer is purchasing.
   b. The order table has a new row inserted that contains the order.
   c. The customer database is accessed to update the customer's account so that she can be billed for this order. Because in this example customer account information is stored in a database separate from the database containing the order table, the transaction is escalated to a distributed transaction.

d. The record in the shopping-cart table is deleted at this point. (However, some applications purge the shopping-cart table at a later time, in a batch operation.)

e. Once both the account table and the order table are updated, the transaction can be committed. Thus, the distributed transaction is finished.

5. At a later time, employees at Piercetronic's warehouse will access the database and put together the order for shipment. More specifically, the following transactions occur:

a. The order table is queried and the order is retrieved.

b. The item is pulled off a shelf and put in a box for shipment.

c. Piercetronic's system connects to a credit card processor to charge the customer's card. This transaction is a distributed transaction because the charge is recorded locally as well. (Some applications bill the customer's card when he or she checks out, but this is not the typical procedure, as getting credit card approval usually takes longer than the transaction can be held open.)

d. In a distributed transaction, the order table is updated and the database containing account information is updated to reflect the shipment.

6. The package arrives and the customer's dog has a new water dish to drink from.

If any of the components had failed during these distributed transactions and if Piercetronics had not been using MS DTC, which enables two-phase commits, several problems could have occurred, including the following:

- The customer's credit card could have been charged for an item that she never received.

- Her order could have been placed and shipped without a charge to her credit card.

- The order table could have been updated to indicate the product was shipped, when the shipping never occurred.

So you can see the necessity of making sure that either all systems are updated or no systems are updated in a distributed transaction. Without the coordination of these transactions, the databases could become inconsistent and several problems could occur.

MS DTC Properties

As mentioned, the MS DTC service runs within SQL Server to coordinate transactions. It performs complex handshaking and error checking to ensure that the proper sequences of events occur. Without MS DTC, you will find that coordinating updates on server systems and guaranteeing consistency can be complicated.

You can invoke MS DTC by using one of the following methods:

- Invoking a remote procedure that is a distributed transaction
- Using Transact-SQL (T-SQL) commands to promote your SQL statements to a distributed transaction
- Updating data on multiple OLE DB data sources
- Embedding MS DTC commands in your application

If you use one of the first three methods, the distributed transaction is initiated from within SQL Server on the same system on which your transaction is initiated, as shown in Figure 25-7. The SQL Server instance running on the server on which the transaction is initiated will perform all of the operations necessary to invoke MS DTC to handle the distributed transaction—no user intervention is necessary. SQL Server will handle all of the details for you.

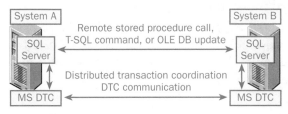

Figure 25-7. *MS DTC communication in a distributed transaction initiated from within SQL Server.*

If you use the fourth method, embedding MS DTC commands within your application, the client application and the SQL Server network interface will communicate with MS DTC as well as with SQL Server. The SQL Server client will help coordinate the distributed transaction. The architecture of this distributed transaction is shown in Figure 25-8.

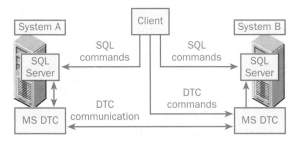

Figure 25-8. *MS DTC communication in a distributed transaction initiated by embedding MS DTC commands within an application.*

Programming MS DTC

Because this book is not geared toward developers, you will not find here all the specifics concerning how to initiate and program distributed transactions. This section simply lists ways in which you can initiate distributed transactions and shows you how to test MS DTC by running a simple transaction.

You can initiate a distributed transaction by performing one of the following actions:

- **Accessing a remote data source from within a transaction** If you do this, the transaction will be escalated to a distributed transaction. Any distributed query within a transaction will escalate that transaction.

- **Explicitly issuing a BEGIN DISTRIBUTED TRANSACTION command** This will explicitly create a distributed transaction.

- **Using the REMOTE_PROC_TRANSACTIONS SQL Server configuration option** This will immediately escalate transactions to distributed transactions if a remote stored procedure is called.

- **Calling OLE DB or ODBC functions** OLE DB and SQL Server include syntax for initiating distributed transactions.

You can test MS DTC by initiating a distributed transaction via T-SQL. You initiate the distributed transaction by using the T-SQL command BEGIN DISTRIBUTED TRANSACTION, and you complete it by using the COMMIT command, as shown in the following example:

```
BEGIN DISTRIBUTED TRANSACTION
SELECT EmployeeID FROM Northwind.dbo.Employees
SELECT emp_id FROM pubs.dbo.employee
GO
COMMIT
GO
```

Enter just the first four lines of the preceding code. By delaying the COMMIT command and the final GO command, you will be able to view the transaction on the Transaction List folder of the Distributed Transaction Coordinator folder, which is in the Component Services MMC administration console. To view this folder expand Component Services, expand Computers and then My Computer, and finally expand Distributed Transactions Coordinator in the Component Services MMC administration console. After you view the transaction, enter the final two lines of the T-SQL code. Notice that the transaction, now committed, no longer appears on the Transaction List tab. Of course, most distributed transactions are more complex than this one, involving updates and inserts, but this example is easy to run and does not alter any database tables.

Distributed transactions will typically be invoked from within a program by using ODBC or DB-LIB API calls to start and terminate each transaction. Distributed transactions are programmed in much the same way as other transactions, except that the connection must be opened with Autocommit turned off so that each SQL statement does not commit automatically. MS DTC will handle the two-phase commit whenever the application ends the transaction with either a COMMIT or a ROLLBACK option.

More Info   For more information about SQL Server application development, see *Inside Microsoft SQL Server 7.0* (Microsoft Press, 1999), by Ron Soukup and Kalen Delaney. If you are using Microsoft Visual Basic, see *Hitchhiker's Guide to Visual Basic and SQL Server* (Microsoft Press, 1998), by William Vaughn.

Administering MS DTC

By default, MS DTC is installed along with Windows 2000. All you have to do is enable the technology. You can start MS DTC in two ways: by using SQL Server Service Manager or by using the system services component of Component Services, which was described earlier in this chapter. You invoke the SQL Server Service Manager utility by clicking Start, pointing to Programs, pointing to Microsoft SQL Server, and then choosing Service Manager. This utility is shown in Figure 25-9.

Figure 25-9. *Using SQL Server Service Manager to start MS DTC.*

If Distributed Transaction Coordinator is not shown in the Services box, select it from the drop-down list. Click Start/Continue to start the service, and click Stop to stop it. You should also select the check box that indicates whether MS DTC will start when the operating system starts.

Monitoring MS DTC

In order to monitor MS DTC, you must use the Component Services administration console. Start up the console (as described earlier in this chapter), and expand Component Services, Computers, My Computer, and Distributed Transaction Coordinator, as shown in Figure 25-10.

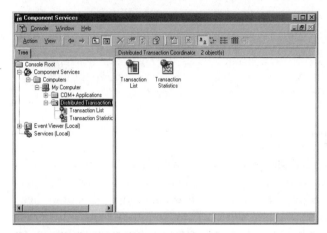

Figure 25-10. *The Distributed Transaction Coordinator folder in the Component Services administration console.*

You will see two options in this folder: Transaction List and Transaction Statistics.

Transaction List

The Transaction List view, shown in Figure 25-11, allows you to view a list of distributed transactions that are currently running on your system. You can view the properties of a transaction, and you can actually resolve a transaction by forcing it to commit or abort. You do this by right-clicking the transaction and choosing the appropriate option from the shortcut menu that appears.

Transaction Statistics

The Transaction Statistics view, shown in Figure 25-12, enables you to view distributed-transaction information such as the number of transactions in progress and the maximum number of active transactions. This information gives you an overview of the distributed-transaction activity occurring on your system. It can also be helpful for planning future capacity.

As you have seen, monitoring distributed transactions is not difficult. And, as you have seen earlier in the chapter, creating and running distributed transactions is easy as well.

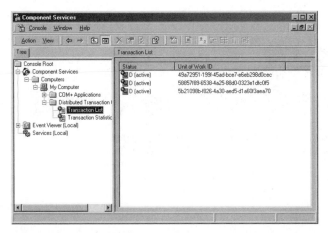

Figure 25-11. *The Transaction List view showing MS DTC transactions.*

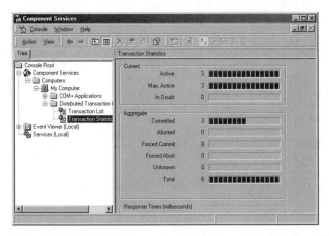

Figure 25-12. *The Transaction Statistics view showing MS DTC transactions.*

Summary

In this chapter, you've learned how MS DTC works and how to create distributed transactions. You've also gotten an overview of the Component Services products and technologies that are provided with Windows 2000. In addition, you have seen how to administer the parts of Component Services. In the next several chapters, you will learn about SQL Server replication.

Chapter 26

Microsoft SQL Server Replication: Overview and Snapshot Replication

Microsoft SQL Server database replication technology is designed to help you distribute data and stored procedures among the servers in your company. Replication allows you to configure systems to copy data to other systems automatically. Using database replication, you can copy as much or as little data as you want, and you can allocate data among as many systems as you want. Because the replication process is automatic and because during replication a database stores data about the state of the replication as well as the replicated data, there is no danger in losing data. If a replication procedure is interrupted (say, due to a power failure), replication resumes from the point of failure as soon as the systems are running normally again.

Because replication is a complex process, three chapters in this book are devoted to the topic of replication. In this chapter, you will learn about the basics of replication and about the snapshot replication method. In Chapter 27, you will learn about transactional replication, and in Chapter 28, you will learn about merge replication. These three chapters provide the information you need to thoroughly understand SQL Server replication, including understanding how to configure, administer, and use replication technology.

What Is Database Replication?

Database replication is the act of copying, or replicating, data from one table or database to another table or database. Using this technology, you can distribute copies of an entire database to multiple systems throughout your company, or you can distribute selected pieces of the database. When SQL Server replication technology is used, the task of copying and distributing data is automated. No user intervention is needed to replicate data once replication has been set up and configured. Because the data replication and processing is done from within a SQL Server database, there is additional stability and recoverability. If a failure occurs during replication (or while any other SQL Server transaction is being performed), operations resume at the point of failure once the problem is fixed. Because of this, many people prefer replication to other methods of moving data between systems.

You have many options for configuring replication on your network. For example, you can specify how much or how little data will be replicated. You can specify whether the replicated copies will be read-only or can be modified. And you can specify how often the data is to be replicated. We'll explore these and other options in the section "Configuring Snapshot Replication" later in this chapter, and similar sections in the next two chapters.

Replication Concepts

In this section, you'll learn about basic database replication concepts. We'll look at the publish-and-subscribe metaphor, the three types of replication, replication data, data propagation, and replication agents.

Replication Components

Microsoft SQL Server 2000 replication is based on the publish-and-subscribe metaphor first used to implement replication in SQL Server 6. This metaphor consists of three main concepts: publishers, distributors, and subscribers. A *publisher* is a database system that makes data available for replication. A *distributor* is the database system that contains the distribution database, or pseudodata, used to maintain and manage the replication. A *subscriber* is a database system that receives replicated data and stores the replicated database.

Publishers

The publisher consists of a Microsoft Windows system hosting a SQL Server database. This database provides data to be replicated to other systems. In addition, the SQL Server database keeps track of which data has changed so that it can be effectively replicated. The publisher also maintains information about which data is configured for replication. Depending on the type of replication that is chosen, the publisher does some work or little work during the replication process. This will be explained in further detail later in this chapter.

A replicated environment can contain multiple subscribers, but any given set of data that is configured for replication, called an article, can have only one publisher. (Articles are described in more detail in the section "Replication Data" later in this chapter.) Having only one publisher for a particular set of data does not mean that the publisher is the only component that can modify the data—the subscriber can also modify and even republish the data. However, this can get a little tricky, as you will see in this chapter and the next two chapters.

Distributors

In addition to containing the distribution database, servers acting as distributors store metadata, history data, and other information. In many cases, the distributor is also responsible for distributing the replication data to subscribers. The publisher and the distributor are not required to be on the same server. In fact, you will likely use a dedicated server as a distributor. Each publisher must be assigned a distributor when it is created, and a publisher can have only one distributor. This arrangement is described in more detail in the section "Configuring Publishing and Distribution" later in this chapter.

> **Note**   *Metadata* is data about data. Metadata is used in replication to keep track of the state of replication operations. It is also the data that is propagated by the distributor to other members of the replication set and includes information about the structure of data and the properties of data, such as the type of data in a column (numeric, text, and so on) or the length of a column.

Subscribers

As mentioned, subscribers are the database servers that store the replicated data and receive updates. Subscribers can also make updates and serve as publishers to other systems. For a subscriber to receive replicated data, it must subscribe to that data. Subscribing to replication involves configuring the subscriber to receive that data. A subscription is the database information to which you are subscribing. You'll learn more about the relationships between the components in the section "Configuring Snapshot Replication" later in this chapter.

Types of Replication

SQL Server offers three types of replication: snapshot, transactional, and merge. These replication types offer varying degrees of data consistency within the replicated database, and they require different levels of overhead.

Snapshot Replication

Snapshot replication is the simplest replication type. With snapshot replication, a picture, or snapshot, of the database is taken periodically and propagated to subscribers. The main advantage of snapshot replication is that it does not involve continuous overhead on publishers and subscribers. That is, it does not require publishers to continuously monitor data changes, and it doesn't require the continuous transmission of data to subscribers. The main disadvantage is that the database on a subscriber is only as current as the last snapshot.

In many cases, as you will see later in this chapter, snapshot replication is sufficient and appropriate—for example, when source data is modified only occasionally. Information such as phone lists, price lists, and item descriptions can easily be handled by using snapshot replication. These lists can be updated once per day during off hours.

Transactional Replication

Transactional replication can be used to replicate changes to the database. With transactional replication, any changes made to articles (a set of data configured for replication) are immediately captured from the transaction log and propagated to the distributors. Using transactional replication, you can keep a publisher and its subscribers in almost exactly the same state, depending on how you configure the replication.

Transactional replication should be used when it is important to keep all of the replicated systems current. Transactional replication uses more system overhead than snapshot replication because it individually applies each transaction that changes data in the system to the replicated systems. However, transactional replication keeps the systems in a more up-to-date state than do snapshot and merge replication. Transactional replication is covered in detail in Chapter 27.

Merge Replication

Merge replication is similar to transactional replication in that it keeps track of the changes made to articles. However, instead of individually propagating transactions that make changes, merge replication periodically transmits a batch of changes. Because merge replication transmits data in batches, it is also similar to snapshot replication. (Although with snapshot replication, all data configured for replication, not just changes, is propagated.) Merge replication is covered in detail in Chapter 28.

Replication Data

You group data to be replicated in an object called a publication. A *publication* is made up of one or more articles. Let's look at articles and publications in more detail.

Articles

As mentioned, an *article* is an individual set of data that is to be replicated. An article can be an entire table, a subset of a table consisting of certain columns or rows, or a stored procedure. You create subsets by using filters. A filter that is used to create a subset consisting of rows is called a *horizontal filter*. A filter that is used to create a subset consisting of columns is known as a *vertical filter*. Horizontal and vertical filters are covered in more detail later in this chapter.

> **Note**   Filters are defined and work differently in merge replication than in snapshot and transactional replication. This is covered in detail in this chapter and in the next two chapters.

Publications

A publication is a set of articles grouped together as a unit. Publications provide the means to replicate a logical grouping of articles as one replication object. For example, you can create a publication to be used to replicate a database consisting of multiple tables, each of which is defined as an article. It is more efficient to replicate a database by replicating the entire database in one publication than by replicating tables individually.

A publication can consist of a single article, but it almost always contains more than one article. However, a subscriber can subscribe only to publications, not to articles. Therefore, if you want to subscribe to a single article, you must configure a publication that contains only that article and then subscribe to that publication.

Push and Pull Subscriptions

Replicated data can be propagated in a number of ways. All propagation methods are based on either push subscriptions or pull subscriptions. A subscriber can support a mixture of push and pull subscriptions simultaneously.

Push Subscriptions

If you set up a push subscription, the distributor is responsible for providing updates to the subscribers. Updates are initiated without any request from the subscriber. A push subscription is useful when centralized administration is desired because the distributor, rather than multiple subscribers, controls and administers replication. In other words, the initiation and the scheduling of the replication are handled on the distributor.

Push subscriptions allow you a lot of flexibility in scheduling replication. Push subscriptions can be configured to propagate changes immediately after they are made or to perform updates on a regular schedule. You'll learn more about these options in the section "Configuring Snapshot Replication" later in this chapter.

Pull Subscriptions

Pull subscriptions allow subscribers to initiate replication. Replication can be initiated either via a scheduled task or manually. Pull subscriptions are useful if you have a large number of subscribers and if the subscribers are not always attached to the network. Because subscribers initiate pull subscriptions, subscribers not always connected to the network can periodically connect and request replication data. This can also be useful in reducing the number of connection errors reported on the distributor. If the distributor tries to initiate replication to a subscriber that does not respond, an error will be reported. Thus, if the replication is initiated on the subscriber only when it is attached, no errors will be reported.

Replication Agents

Several agents are used to perform the actions necessary to move the replicated data from the publisher to the distributor and finally to the subscriber: the Snapshot Agent, the Log Reader Agent, the Distribution Agent, the Merge Agent, and the Queue Reader Agent. In this section, you'll learn what these agents do and how to manage them.

Snapshot Agent

The Snapshot Agent is used for creating and propagating the snapshots from the publisher to the distributor (or snapshot location). The Snapshot Agent creates the replication data (the snapshot) and creates the information that is used by the Distribution Agent to propagate that data (the metadata). The Snapshot Agent stores the snapshot on the distributor (or anywhere that you specify). The Snapshot Agent is also responsible for maintaining information about the synchronization status of the replication objects; this information is stored in the distribution database.

The Snapshot Agent is dormant most of the time and might periodically activate, based on the schedule that you have configured, and perform its tasks. Each time the Snapshot Agent runs, it performs the following tasks:

1. The Snapshot Agent establishes a connection from the distributor to the publisher. If a connection is not available, the Snapshot Agent will not proceed with creating the snapshot. Once the connection has been established, the Snapshot Agent locks all of the articles involved in the replication to ensure that the snapshot is a consistent view of the data. (For this reason, it is not a good idea to schedule snapshots during periods of peak usage.)

2. The Snapshot Agent establishes a connection from the publisher to the distributor. Once this connection has been established, the Snapshot Agent engineers a copy of the schema for each article and stores that information in the distribution database. This data is considered metadata.

3. The Snapshot Agent takes a snapshot of the actual data on the publisher and writes it to a file at the snapshot location. The snapshot location does not necessarily need to be on the distributor. If all systems involved in the replication are SQL Server systems, the file is stored as a native bulk copy program. (Bulk copying is covered in Chapter 24.) If mixed types of systems are involved in the replication, the data is stored in text files. At this point, synchronization information is set by the Snapshot Agent.

4. After the data has been copied, the Snapshot Agent updates information in the distribution database.

5. The Snapshot Agent releases the locks that it has held on the articles and logs the snapshot into the history file.

As you can see, the Snapshot Agent is responsible for only creating the snapshot; it does not distribute it to subscribers. Other agents perform this task.

The snapshot should be refreshed often when snapshot replication is used and the data is changing on the publisher. Because the snapshot is regularly copied to subscribers, it should be current.

Note When transactional or merge replication is being used and new subscriptions are not being added, it is unnecessary to refresh the snapshot at all.

Log Reader Agent

The Log Reader Agent is used in transactional replication to extract change information from the transaction log on the publisher in order to replicate these commands into the distribution database. Each database that uses transactional replication has its own Log Reader Agent on the publisher. The Log Reader Agent is covered in detail in Chapter 27.

Distribution Agent

The Distribution Agent propagates snapshots and transactions from the distribution database to subscribers. Each publication has its own Distribution Agent. If you are using a push subscription, the Distribution Agent runs on the distributor. If you are using a pull subscription, the Distribution Agent runs on the subscriber.

Merge Agent

The Merge Agent is used in merge replication to reconcile (merge) incremental changes that have occurred since the last reconciliation. When you use merge replication, the Distribution Agent and the Snapshot Agent aren't used—the Merge Agent communicates with both the publisher and the distributor. The Merge Agent is covered in detail in Chapter 28.

Queue Reader Agent

The Queue Reader Agent is used to propagate changes made to subscribers of snapshot or transaction replication that have been configured with the queued updating option. This option allows changes to be made on the subscriber without the need to use a distributed transaction.

Monitoring Agent Activity

You can monitor any of the agents by using Enterprise Manager. To do so, follow these steps:

1. In Enterprise Manager, expand a server group, and then expand the folder for the server designated as the distributor.
2. Expand the Replication Monitor folder, and then expand the Agents folder.
3. Expand the agent type that you want to monitor.
4. In the right-hand pane, right-click the agent you want to monitor and choose Agent History from the shortcut menu that appears to view a history of the agent's activities.

Configuring Publishing and Distribution

Now that you have been introduced to basic replication concepts, let's look at how to perform the first step in configuring replication in SQL Server: setting up publishing and distribution. To carry out this task, you use the Configure Publishing

And Distribution Wizard. (Although it is possible to completely configure SQL Server replication by using stored procedures, the preferred method is to use the replication configuration wizards.) Other wizards used in the process of configuring replication (all accessed through Enterprise Manager) are listed here:

- Create Publication Wizard
- Create Pull Subscription Wizard
- Create Push Subscription Wizard
- Disable Publishing And Distribution Wizard

You use the procedures described in this section to set up publishing and distribution no matter which type of replication you want to implement. You configure a replication type after you configure publishing and distribution. Instructions for setting up specific types of replication are provided later in this chapter and in the next two chapters. To configure publishing and distribution, follow these steps:

1. In Enterprise Manager, click the server you want to configure as the distributor. Choose Wizards from the Tools menu. In the Select Wizard dialog box that appears, expand the Replication folder, and then select Configure Publishing And Distribution Wizard, as shown in Figure 26-1. Click OK.

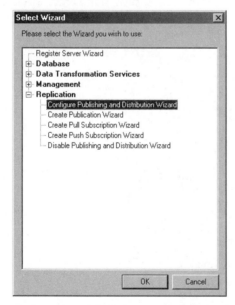

Figure 26-1. *The Select Wizard dialog box.*

2. The Configure Publishing And Distribution Wizard welcome screen appears, as shown in Figure 26-2.

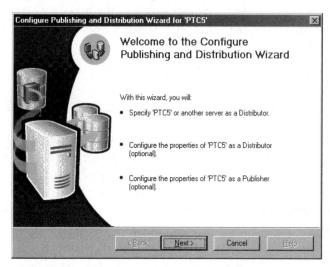

Figure 26-2. *The Configure Publishing And Distribution Wizard welcome screen.*

3. Click Next to display the Select Distributor screen, shown in Figure 26-3.

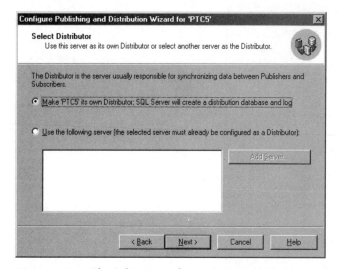

Figure 26-3. *The Select Distributor screen.*

4. In this screen, you can choose to make the server you selected in step 1 the distributor as well as the publisher or you can choose to configure only publishing and use an already configured distributor. If you choose

to set up the recently selected system as the distributor, click the first
option button. The wizard will eventually create the distribution database and log for you. If you want to use another SQL Server system as
the distributor, click the second option button. If no other SQL Server
systems are configured as distributors, only the first option will be available. You will likely want to use a dedicated system as the distributor.

Note   A publisher can have only one distributor defined on it. All publications
must use the same distributor.

5. If you choose to use another system as the distributor, you must register
   the SQL Server system and it must already be configured as a distributor. Click Add Server and, in the Registered SQL Server Properties window, select an authentication method to establish a connection to the
   SQL Server system on the distributor.

6. For our example, choose to make the system that you are configuring
   the distributor. After all, this section is about how to configure the
   distributor.

7. At this point, the wizard makes sure that the publisher has access to the
   distributor. If the account that SQL Server runs under does not have
   access, the SQL Server Agent Properties window is invoked to allow you
   to modify the agent login account. This window is shown in Figure 26-4.

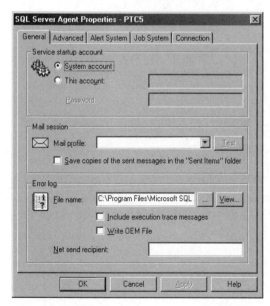

Figure 26-4. *The SQL Server Agent Properties window.*

Note   If you had configured SQL Server to use the LocalSystem account when you installed it, you will see this message. The LocalSystem account has permissions only on the local system; hence the name. If you had configured SQL Server during the installation process to use a domain account, you will not get the warning and you will not need to access the SQL Server Agent Properties window.

8. In this window, you can modify other features of SQL Server Agent. (For more information, see Chapter 31.) When you are finished modifying SQL Server Agent, click OK.

9. The Configure SQL Server Agent screen appears, as shown in Figure 26-5. This screen prompts you to configure the SQL Server Agent to start automatically. Replication is run under the command of the SQL Server Agent, so if the Agent is not running, neither will replication. Choose to have the SQL Server Agent start automatically (recommended) or choose to start it manually. Click Next to continue.

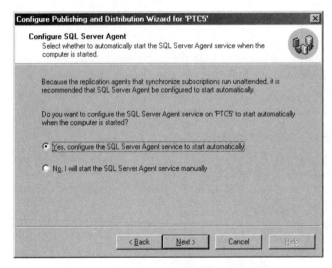

Figure 26-5. *The Configure SQL Server Agent screen.*

10. The Specify Snapshot Folder screen appears, shown in Figure 26-6. This screen allows you to set the snapshot location. This location is the directory where snapshots will reside. Choose a new location or keep the default location. Click Next to continue

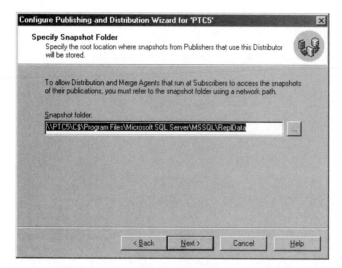

Figure 26-6. *The Specify Snapshot Folder screen.*

11. The Customize The Configuration screen appears, as shown in Figure 26-7.

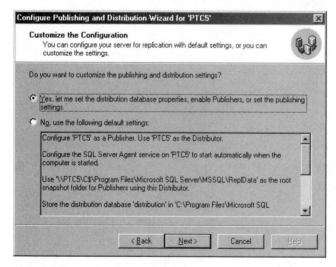

Figure 26-7. *The Customize The Configuration screen.*

12. In this screen, you can either accept the default configuration options for the distribution database (the second option) or customize the distribution database (the first option). If you accept the default settings, the process is complete, and you will proceed to a final screen. For this example, select the first option.

> **Note** The default location of the SQL Server data files might be on a disk drive with insufficient performance and space. In the next step, you will see how to relocate the distribution database to a disk drive with sufficient space and I/O performance capacity.

13. Click Next to display the Provide Distribution Database Information screen, shown in Figure 26-8. Here you can specify the database name and the locations for the distribution database and log files. You must do this if the distribution database will exceed the space available in the default location.

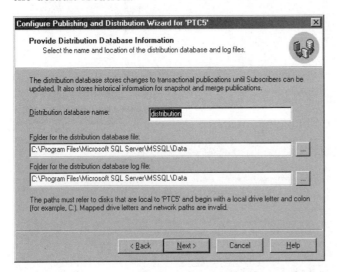

Figure 26-8. *The Provide Distribution Database Information screen.*

14. Click Next to display the Enable Publishers screen, shown in Figure 26-9. In this screen, you can choose to use a different publisher than the server selected in step 1, or you can add publishers. (Click New to establish a connection to SQL Server on the new publisher.)

15. Click Next to display the Enable Publication Databases screen, shown in Figure 26-10. Here you can enable transactional replication or merge replication for specific databases. By default, no databases on the publisher are enabled. If you skip this step, you will create a publisher and

distributor but will have no publications defined. You can then define publications by using the Create Publication Wizard, which is the preferred method.

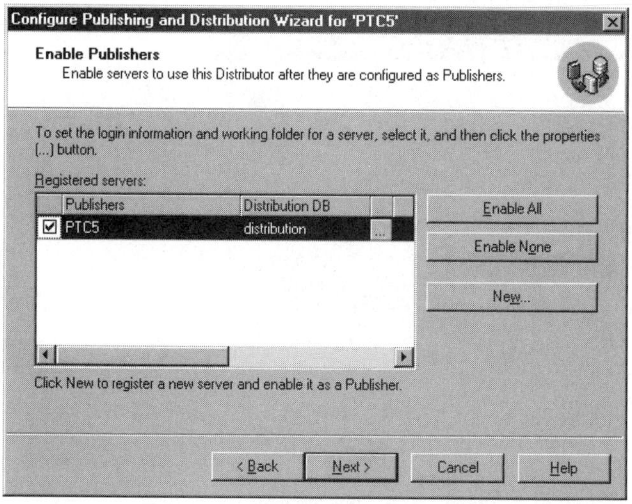

Figure 26-9. *The Enable Publishers screen.*

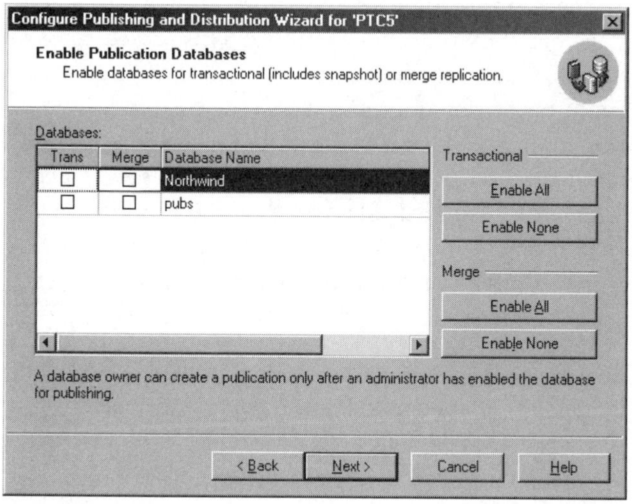

Figure 26-10. *The Enable Publication Databases screen.*

16. Click Next to display the Enable Subscribers screen, shown in Figure 26-11. In this screen, you can choose a subscriber for the publisher you selected. However, it's preferable to do this separately using the Configure Publishing And Distribution Wizard.

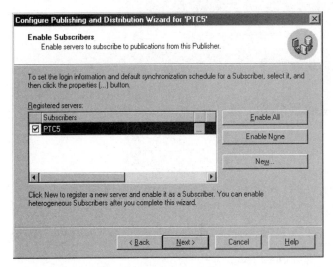

Figure 26-11. *The Enable Subscribers screen.*

17. Click Next to display the Completing The Configure Publishing And Distribution Wizard screen, shown in Figure 26-12. This screen shows a summary of your settings. Click Finish to apply the configuration you have created. This might take a few minutes. After the process is complete, you will be presented with several informational screens that tell you about the progress of the setup as well as whether you need to configure SQL Server Agent for automatic startup. For the replication agents to run, SQL Server Agent must be running. Notice that once this wizard is completed, the Replication Monitor folder appears in Enterprise Manager.

Note If you want to alter the configuration of a replicated database, click the database in Enterprise Manager, and point to Replication on the Tools menu to display a submenu containing options for managing your replication configuration.

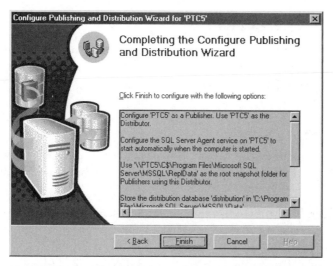

Figure 26-12. *The Completing The Configure Publishing And Distribution Wizard screen.*

Snapshot Replication

This section provides you with detailed information about the snapshot replication method. First you'll learn when you should use snapshot replication. Then you'll learn how to configure this replication type.

Uses of Snapshot Replication

Snapshot replication is highly useful in certain situations where static data is sufficient. As you have learned, with snapshot replication, a snapshot of data is taken and copied to subscribers. This data is not updated until the next snapshot is applied. If you use snapshot replication, you should not modify the data on the subscriber because it will be overwritten when the next snapshot is applied.

The types of applications that can benefit from snapshot replication include the following:

- **Price lists that are distributed to remote store locations**   Typically, updating prices once per night is quite sufficient.

- **Lookup tables that do not require frequent updates**   Lookup tables typically have fairly static data.

Other applications can benefit from snapshot replication as well. However, when updates to data need to be replicated frequently, transactional or merge replication is more useful.

Configuring Snapshot Replication

As mentioned, before you configure any type of replication, you must set up publishing and distribution, which you learned how to do earlier in this chapter. To set up snapshot replication, you first configure a publication, and then you configure subscribers.

Configuring Publications

Configuring a publication enables you to specify what data is replicated, how it is replicated, and when the replication occurs. To configure a publication, follow these steps:

1. In Enterprise Manager, click the Tools menu. Next either point to Replication and then choose Create And Manage Publications, or choose Wizards, expand the Replication folder in the Select Wizard dialog box that appears, and choose Create Publication Wizard. Performing either procedure will display the Create And Manage Publications dialog box, shown in Figure 26-13. This dialog box allows you to select a database or table containing the data you want to publish.

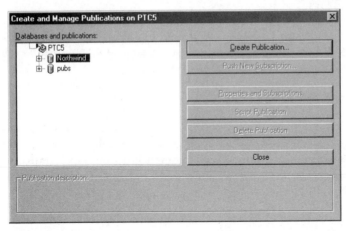

Figure 26-13. *The Create And Manage Publications dialog box.*

If publications already exist, the following buttons will be available in addition to the Create Publication button:

- **Push New Subscription** Enables you to create a new push subscription for an already existing publication. This process is described in the section "Configuring Subscriptions" later in this chapter.

- **Properties And Subscriptions** Enables you to modify both publication and subscription properties.

- **Script Publication**   Enables you to create a script that can be used to create more publications.
- **Delete Publication**   Enables you to delete an already configured publication.

2. Select the database you want to use for the publication (in Figure 26-13, Northwind is selected), and then click Create Publication to invoke the Create Publication Wizard. The Create Publication Wizard welcome screen appears, as shown in Figure 26-14.

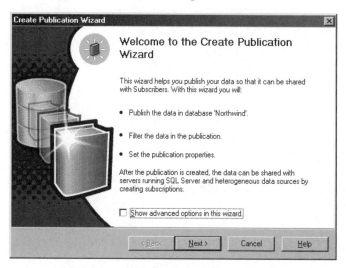

Figure 26-14. *The Create Publication Wizard welcome screen.*

3. Note the check box, Show Advanced Options In This Wizard, at the bottom of this screen. For this example, we will not select this check box. If we were to select it, an option to create immediate updating and queued updating subscriptions would be offered in the wizard. This advanced option allows subscribers to update the publication as well as the publisher. In addition, an option to allow data transformation of subscriptions would be presented.

Click Next to display the Choose Publication Database screen, as shown in Figure 26-15. This screen allows you to (again) select the database containing the data that you want to publish. The database you chose in step 2 will be selected.

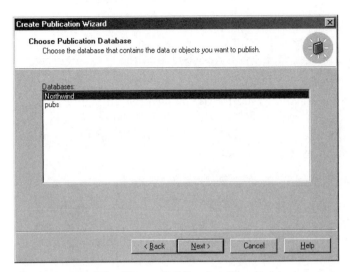

Figure 26-15. *The Choose Publication Database screen.*

4. Click Next to display the Select Publication Type screen, as shown in Figure 26-16.

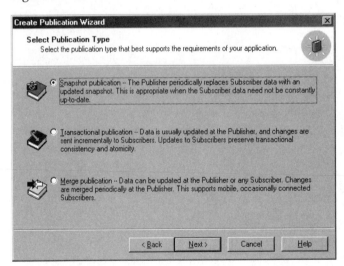

Figure 26-16. *The Select Publication Type screen.*

This screen allows you to select one of the three replication types. The options on the Select Publication Type screen are described here:

- **Snapshot Publication** Creates a snapshot publication that periodically copies a snapshot of the article to the subscriber. A snapshot publication can be created from any table.

- **Transactional Publication**   Creates a transactional replication publication that updates the subscriber with changes made to the publisher, based on transactions. Articles can be created only from tables with a primary key.

- **Merge Publication**   Creates a merge replication publication that allows two-way replication between the publisher and subscriber. Articles can be created from any tables.

5. Click Snapshot Publication, and click Next to display the Specify Subscriber Types screen, shown in Figure 26-17. This screen lets you specify whether all of the subscribers will be running SQL Server. Figure 26-17 shows the default setting selected, which specifies that all subscribers are running SQL Server 2000. If you accept this setting, you are configuring replication to use native SQL Server 2000 data types. If you have SQL Server 7 systems in the configuration, select the second check box. If you have non–SQL Server systems in the configuration, you should select the third check box, which causes replication data to be converted to character format. This conversion of complex native data types causes additional overhead.

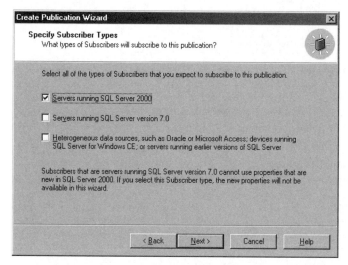

Figure 26-17. *The Specify Subscriber Types screen.*

6. Click Next to display the Specify Articles screen, shown in Figure 26-18. In this screen, you can specify the tables and other objects that will be replicated as articles. These articles will make up the publication that you are creating. In the left-hand list on this screen, you can select one or more check boxes in the Show column to display a list of objects, which can include tables, stored procedures, and views, in the right-hand

list. Then, by selecting check boxes in the right-hand list, you can individually specify any number of tables, stored procedures, and views to publish. Or you can simply select one or more check boxes in the Publish column of the left-hand list to select all items of one or more object types in the current database for publication. Remember, each table, stored procedure, or view is considered an article, and a publication is a set of articles that are logically grouped together.

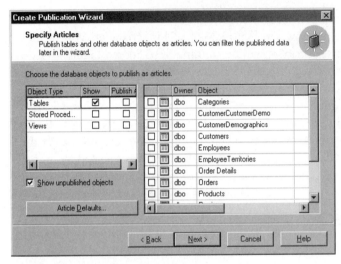

Figure 26-18. *The Specify Articles screen.*

Notice also the Article Defaults button on this screen. This button allows you to set the defaults for the various articles in your system. When you click this button, you will be asked to select the article type. Click Table Articles and then click OK. The Default Table Article Properties window is invoked, as shown in Figure 26-19. The General tab allows you to specify options such as the following:

• The article name

• The article description

• The name of the article's destination table

• The owner of the article's destination table

The Snapshot tab, which is shown in Figure 26-20, enables you to do the following:

• Truncate any existing data and specify how indexes are handled

• Specify whether clustered and nonclustered indexes are copied

- Specify whether user-defined data types are converted to base data types
- Specify whether constraints are replicated

Specify the setting you want and click OK.

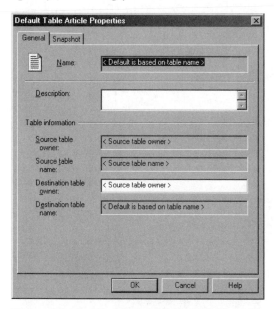

Figure 26-19. *The General tab of the Default Table Article Properties window.*

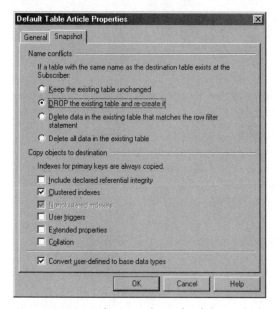

Figure 26-20. *The Snapshot tab of the Default Table Article Properties window.*

7. Make your selections in the Specify Articles screen, and then click
   Next. An analysis of the publication is made. If you are publishing the
   Northwind database, as in this example, the screen shown in Figure
   26-21 is displayed, informing you that you are attempting to replicate
   an identity column and that the IDENTITY property on the published
   column will not be transferred to the column on the subscriber's table.

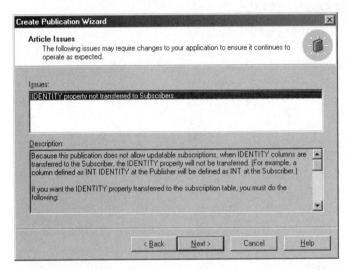

Figure 26-21. *The screen displayed when you try to replicate an identity column.*

8. After the publication analysis is completed (and after you click OK to
   return to the wizard if the informational message box appears), the
   Select Publication Name And Description screen appears, as shown in
   Figure 26-22. In this screen, you specify simply a publication name and
   a description. You can also choose to list this publication in Active Directory services.

9. Click Next to display the Customize The Properties Of The Publication
   screen, shown in Figure 26-23. In this screen, you specify whether you
   will define data filters (by clicking Yes) or use default configuration
   options (by clicking No). Clicking No and then clicking Next takes
   you to the Completing The Create Publication Wizard screen, shown
   in Figure 26-31 (near the end of this section). In this example, we'll click
   Yes so we can view the remaining screens and set additional options.

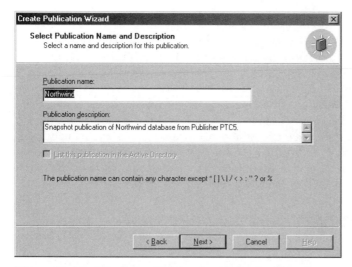

Figure 26-22. *The Select Publication Name And Description screen.*

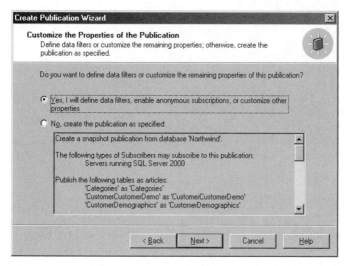

Figure 26-23. *The Customize The Properties Of The Publication screen.*

10. Click Next to display the Filter Data screen, shown in Figure 26-24. In this screen, you specify whether you want to filter the data vertically (filter columns) or horizontally (filter rows) or both. In this example, we will select both vertical filtering and horizontal filtering.

Note Filtering serves the same function whether you are using snapshot or transactional replication. However, the manner in which filtering works depends on the type of replication you use. In the next chapter, more information about the effects of filtering on transactional replication is provided. With snapshot replication, the WHERE clause used to create the snapshot performs the filtering. (Step 13 in this section describes how you specify this WHERE clause.)

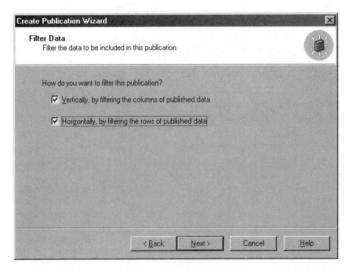

Figure 26-24. *The Filter Data screen.*

11. Click Next to display the Filter Table Columns screen, shown in Figure 26-25. This screen allows you to exclude columns from replication. First select the table from the Tables In Publication list, and then, in the Columns In Selected Table list, clear the check boxes beside the columns that you don't want to be replicated. This allows you to vertically filter the article, which will create the replicated table with fewer columns than the table on the publisher has.

Note Primary key columns cannot be filtered out. You will learn why in the next chapter.

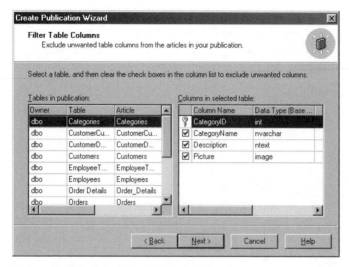

Figure 26-25. *The Filter Table Columns screen.*

12. Click Next to display the Filter Table Rows screen, shown in Figure 26-26. This screen allows you to select tables in which you want to filter the data by rows. Select a table, and click the Build [...] button to set up the filter.

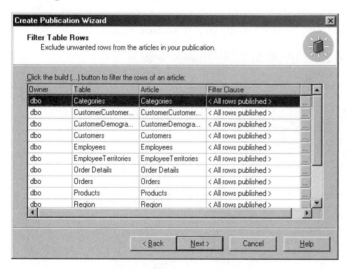

Figure 26-26. *The Filter Table Rows screen.*

13. The Specify Filter dialog box appears, as shown in Figure 26-27. This dialog box allows you to add a WHERE clause to an SQL statement that will filter the row data. When you are finished specifying which rows will be replicated, click OK to return to the wizard.

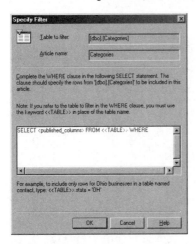

Figure 26-27. *The Specify Filter dialog box.*

14. Click Next to display the Allow Anonymous Subscriptions screen, shown in Figure 26-28. This screen allows you to specify whether anonymous subscribers or only known subscribers can access the replication data. Your choice should be based on your configuration needs.

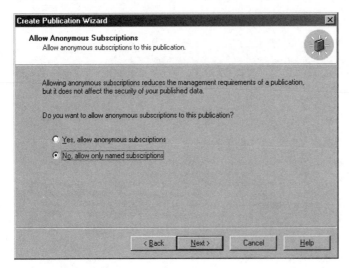

Figure 26-28. *The Allow Anonymous Subscriptions screen.*

15. Click Next to display the Set Snapshot Agent Schedule screen, shown in Figure 26-29. This screen lets you either accept the default schedule for when the Snapshot Agent runs or invoke a dialog box in which you can set a new schedule.

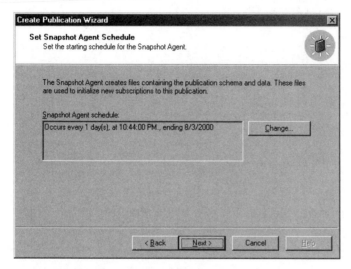

Figure 26-29. *The Set Snapshot Agent Schedule screen.*

16. Click Change to display the Edit Recurring Job Schedule dialog box, shown in Figure 26-30. This dialog box lets you specify when the snapshot job occurs. Choose the schedule that best fits your needs. The schedule shown in Figure 26-30 expires the same day that it begins. If you are configuring snapshot replication, as we are doing here, you should specify the snapshot job to run on a recurring schedule if you want the snapshot to be updated periodically. When configuring trans-actional replication, you must run the snapshot after you create a new subscription, unless the subscription is anonymous. Merge replication always applies the most recent snapshot to your subscriber. Therefore, when configuring merge replication, you can run the snapshot either just before or just after you create a new subscription. When you are finished setting the schedule, click OK.

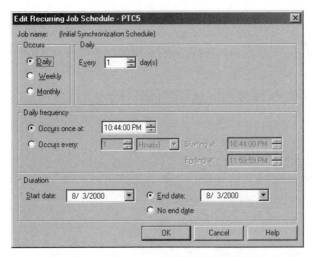

Figure 26-30. *The Edit Recurring Job Schedule dialog box.*

17. Click Next to display the Completing The Create Publication Wizard screen, shown in Figure 26-31. Here you are presented with a summary of the publication that you have specified.

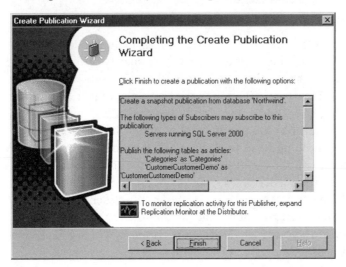

Figure 26-31. *The Completing The Create Publication Wizard screen.*

18. Once you have reviewed this summary, click Finish. You will see the progress of the wizard as the publication is created. The dialog box shown in Figure 26-32 will then appear to inform you that the creation of the publication has been completed.

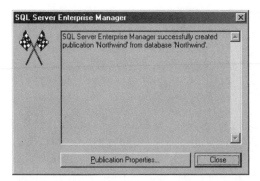

Figure 26-32. *The dialog box informing you of the completed task.*

You have now created a publication that can be distributed to subscribers. You can enable subscribers or modify the properties of this publication in the Create And Manage Publications dialog box (described earlier in this section).

Modifying the Snapshot Schedule

As conditions on your network change, you might need to modify the snapshot schedule. (Instructions for initially configuring the snapshot schedule are provided in the preceding section.) When configuring the snapshot replication schedule, you must consider several factors, which are listed here:

- **The volatility of the data** If the data is frequently changing, the snapshot should be refreshed fairly often. If the data is fairly stable, the snapshot does not need to be refreshed as often.

- **The criticality of the changes** Do the subscribing systems depend on the refreshed data? If so, the snapshot should be refreshed more frequently.

- **The speed of the system** If the network, publisher, distributor, and subscribers are extremely fast, the snapshot can be updated more frequently without causing performance problems on other components in the system.

To configure the snapshot schedule, follow these steps:

1. In Enterprise Manager, expand the server that you want to modify, expand the Replication Monitor folder, expand the Agents folder, and then click the Snapshot Agents folder.

2. In the right-hand pane, right-click the publication and choose Agent Properties from the shortcut menu that appears, as shown in Figure 26-33.

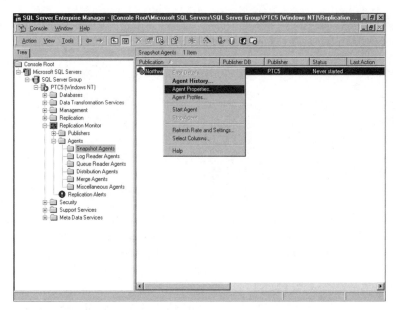

Figure 26-33. *A publication shown in Enterprise Manager.*

3. A Properties window appears, as shown in Figure 26-34. This window displays properties for the publication agent you selected.

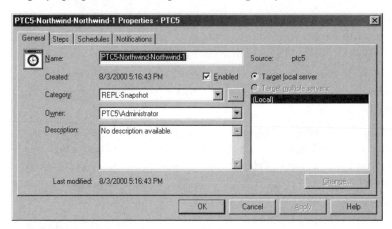

Figure 26-34. *The General tab of an agent's Properties window.*

4. Click the Schedules tab (Figure 26-35). On this tab, you can view the current publication schedule. The New Schedule button allows you to add a new schedule. The New Alert button allows you to create a new alert. The Edit button is used to modify an existing schedule. The Delete button is used to delete an existing schedule.

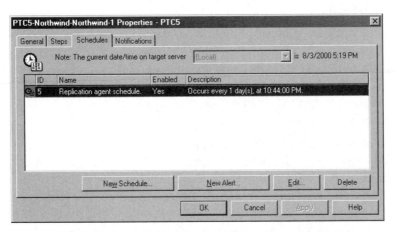

Figure 26-35. *The Schedules tab of an agent's Properties window.*

5. Click Edit to display the Edit Job Schedule dialog box, shown in Figure 26-36. This dialog box allows you to configure the Snapshot Agent to run on a schedule that fits your needs. You change a recurring schedule by first clicking Change, which invokes the Edit Recurring Job Schedule dialog box. In the Edit Job Schedule dialog box, you can configure the agent to run whenever the CPU is idle, which is a new feature in SQL Server 2000. This type of schedule can be useful in some cases, but if you select it, you will not know exactly when the agent will run. Enter the desired schedule, and click OK.

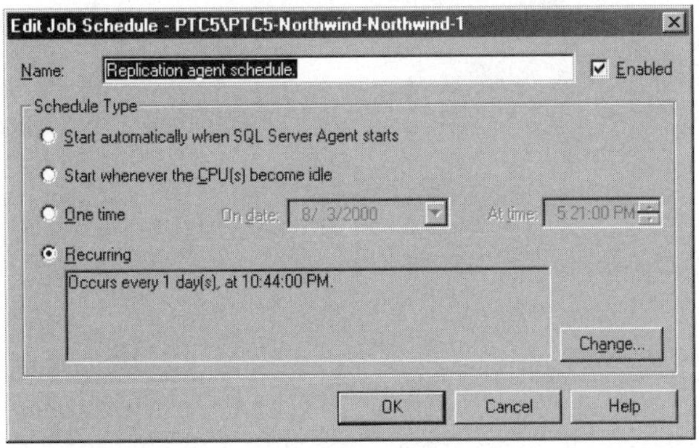

Figure 26-36. *The Edit Job Schedule dialog box.*

When you have completed these steps, the publisher will update snapshot schedule information in the distribution database. This schedule will determine how often the snapshot is created. To modify how often the snapshot is copied to the subscribers, you need to configure the Distribution Agent for that subscription.

Enabling Subscribers

Before you can configure subscribers, you must enable them in the distribution database. Enabling a subscriber allows the SQL Server system to communicate with the distribution database. Once you set up the connection between the distribution database and the subscriber, you can configure subscriptions. (This process is described in the next section, "Configuring Subscriptions.") To enable a subscriber, follow these steps:

1. In Enterprise Manager, click the Tools menu. Next either point to Replication and then choose Configure Publishing, Subscribers, And Distribution, or choose Wizards, expand the Replication folder in the Select Wizard dialog box that appears, and then select Configure Publishing And Distribution Wizard. Performing either procedure displays the Publisher And Distributor Properties window, shown in Figure 26-37.

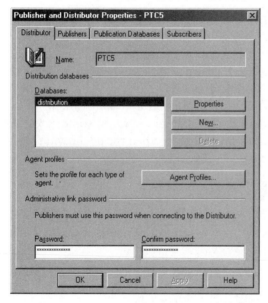

Figure 26-37. *The Publisher And Distributor Properties window.*

2. In the Publisher And Distributor Properties window, click the Subscribers tab, shown in Figure 26-38. Here you will see a list of currently defined subscribers on your network. In order for a subscription to be sent to a subscriber, the subscriber must be defined here.

   In this tab, you can select subscribers that have permission to subscribe to the publisher specified on the tab. The first time that you open the Publisher And Distributor Properties window, you will see only the publisher system listed, since you haven't yet added any subscribers.

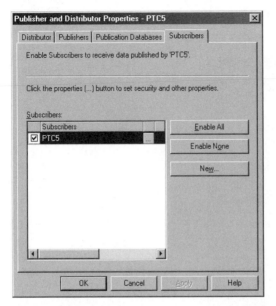

Figure 26-38. *The Subscribers tab of the Publisher And Distributor Properties window.*

3. To add a subscriber, first click New to display the Enable New Subscriber dialog box, shown in Figure 26-39. In this dialog box, you select the kind of subscriber you want to enable (SQL Server, Microsoft Access, OLE DB, ODBC, and so on). This setting determines the type of publications the new subscriber can subscribe to. Select SQL Server Database, and then click OK.

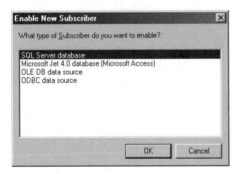

Figure 26-39. *The Enable New Subscriber dialog box.*

4. The Registered SQL Server Properties window appears, as shown in Figure 26-40. Because we chose the SQL Server database option in the previous step, the SQL Server–specific connection options are presented here. If we had chosen a different option in the Enable New Subscriber dialog box, we would be presented with a different window here. Specify

the system name and authentication method for the system that you are enabling as a subscriber.

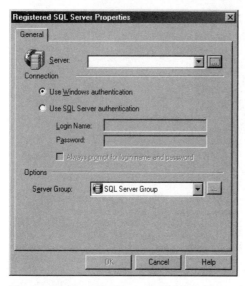

Figure 26-40. *The Registered SQL Server Properties window.*

If you want to see a list of available SQL Server systems to choose from, click the [...] button next to the Server box. This will invoke the Select Server dialog box, shown in Figure 26-41. Here you can select a server to enable as a subscriber.

Figure 26-41. *The Select Server dialog box.*

5. Once you have completed the tasks listed in step 4 and clicked OK in the Select Server dialog box and the Registered SQL Server Properties window, the Publisher And Distributor Properties window appears again, with the new subscriber appearing in the Subscribers list, as shown in

Figure 26-42. The added system can now be used as a subscriber to the specified publisher.

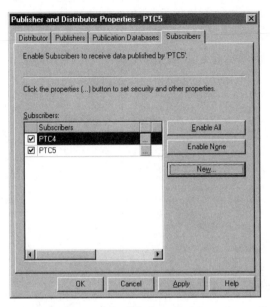

Figure 26-42. *The Publisher And Distributor Properties window, showing the new subscriber.*

Configuring Subscriptions

Now that you have configured the publisher, distributor, and publications and have enabled the subscribers, you are ready to configure the subscriptions. You can configure subscriptions from either the subscriber or the publisher. From the subscriber, you can configure a pull subscription; from the publisher, you can configure a push subscription.

Configuring Pull Subscriptions   Pull subscriptions are controlled by and configured from the subscriber. Thus, you must select the subscriber system in the Enterprise Manager before you start the Pull Subscription Wizard. Typically, subscribers that are not constantly connected to the network use pull subscriptions. For example, pull subscriptions are appropriate for the portable computers used by a mobile sales force that irregularly connects to the network and updates the subscription. To configure a pull subscription, follow these steps:

1. In Enterprise Manager, click the Tools menu. Next either point to Replication, choose Pull Subscription To, and then select Pull New Subscription in the Pull Subscription dialog box that appears, or choose Wizards, expand the Replication folder in the Select Wizard dialog box that

appears, and then select Pull Subscription Wizard. Either way, the Pull Subscription Wizard welcome screen appears, as shown in Figure 26-43. (In the figures in this section, a server called PTC5 is the selected subscriber, and a server named PTC4 is the publisher.)

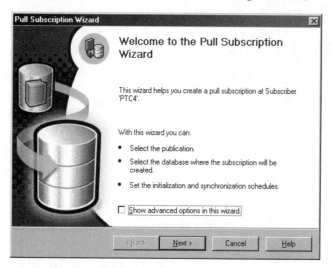

Figure 26-43. *The Pull Subscription Wizard welcome screen.*

2. Click Next to display the Look For Publications screen, shown in Figure 26-44. This screen allows you to choose the method of finding the publisher, which can be either through registered servers (the default) or by looking through the active directory. This will determine how the publishers are found and will affect the results shown in the next screen.

3. Click Next to display the Choose Publication screen, shown in Figure 26-45. This screen is used to identify the publication that will be used in the replication. Servers that are registered with your SQL Server system are listed here. Expand the desired publisher system and select the publication you want to use, as shown in Figure 26-45.

If you need to register a server, click Register Server. The Registered SQL Server Properties window appears. We used this window when we enabled a subscriber in the last section.

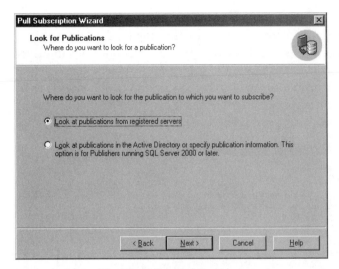

Figure 26-44. *The Look For Publications screen.*

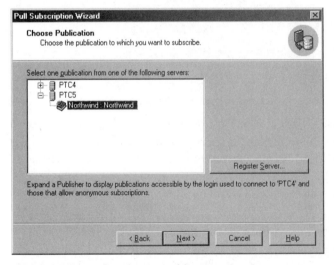

Figure 26-45. *The Choose Publication screen.*

4. Once you have selected the publication, click Next to display the Specify Synchronization Agent Login screen, shown in Figure 26-46. In this screen, you can specify how and with what login account the subscriber connects to the distributor. The default selection of Impersonate The SQL Server Agent Account is usually the best option. If the system that you are configuring has the SQL Server Agent configured to use a special login, the login should be specified here.

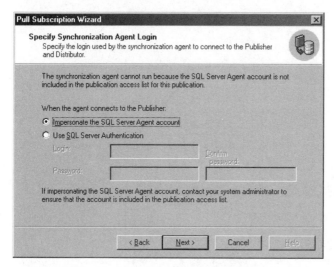

Figure 26-46. *The Specify Synchronization Agent Login screen.*

5. Click Next to display the Choose Destination Database screen, shown in Figure 26-47. In this screen, you specify which database you want the replicated articles to be placed in. Figure 26-47 shows a database called Sub selected for the subscription. If you want to create a new database, click New to open the Database Properties window.

6. If you opened the Database Properties window to create a new database, click OK to return to the Choose Destination Database screen when you are finished. Click Next to display the Initialize Subscription screen, shown in Figure 26-48. Click Yes to initialize the database schema and data at the subscriber.

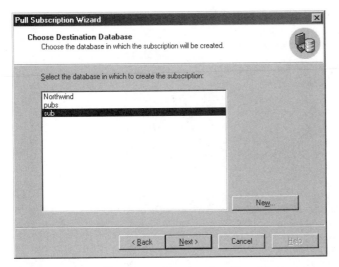

Figure 26-47. *The Choose Destination Database screen.*

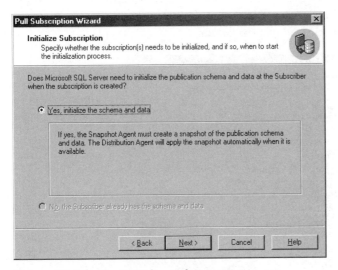

Figure 26-48. *The Initialize Subscription screen.*

7. Click Next to display the Snapshot Delivery screen, shown in Figure 26-49. This screen allows you to select where the snapshot is delivered from. It is usually sufficient to accept the default setting, which specifies that the snapshot will be selected from the default location.

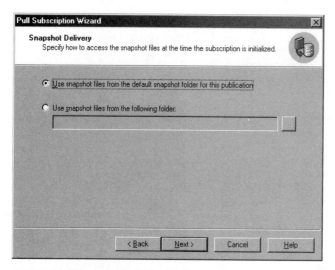

Figure 26-49. *The Snapshot Delivery screen.*

8. Click Next to display the Set Distribution Agent Schedule screen, shown in Figure 26-50. This screen enables you to select continuous updates, scheduled updates, or updates on demand.

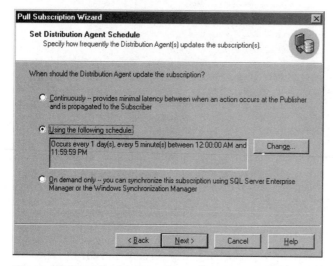

Figure 26-50. *The Set Distribution Agent Schedule screen.*

Remember that we have set up snapshot replication in this example, so the entire contents of the articles will be copied to the subscriber whenever an update occurs. Depending on how often data is changed and how important it is to keep the data synchronized, you could select any of the options. Clicking Change invokes the Edit Recurring Job Schedule dialog box described earlier in this chapter. This dialog box allows you to set up your own recurring schedule.

9. Click Next to display the Start Required Services screen, shown in Figure 26-51. You can start SQL Server Agent from this screen, if it is not running already. This screen shows whether SQL Server Agent is running on the subscriber. If SQL Server Agent is not running, you will be prompted to start it. If you want to start SQL Server Agent manually, expand the Management folder in Enterprise Manager, right-click SQL Server Agent, and use the options on the shortcut menu that appears to start and stop SQL Server Agent.

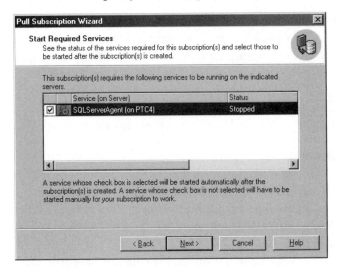

Figure 26-51. *The Start Required Services screen.*

10. If the SQL Server Agent is not currently configured to start automatically, you will see the Configure SQL Server Agent screen. Configure the agent, and click OK. If the SQL Server Agent is already configured to start automatically, you will not see this screen.

11. Click Next to display the Completing The Pull Subscription Wizard screen, shown in Figure 26-52. Click Finish to complete the tasks of setting up the subscription.

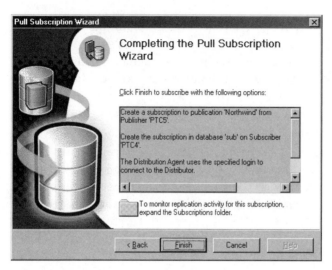

Figure 26-52. *The Completing The Pull Subscription Wizard screen.*

The articles will now be replicated on the subscriber and will be regularly updated according to the schedule you have set up. You might have to verify the schedule that the publication agents are running on before the replication can begin. Because Snapshot Agent runs on its own schedule, if you did not configure it to immediately propagate the snapshot to the distributor, the data might take some time to reach the distributor. Even though replication is working, the actual data will not reach the subscriber until the Snapshot Agent has done its job.

Configuring Push Subscriptions   A push subscription is initiated on the publisher. You configure a push subscription by using the Push Subscription Wizard. When a push subscription is used, the schedule on which the replication occurs is determined on the distributor. The push subscription is the typical subscription method for nonportable subscribers. These subscriptions are used because of the convenience of being able to manage all subscriptions from the distributor, rather than having to manage each subscription individually from the subscriber. To run the Push Subscription Wizard, follow these steps:

1. Invoke the Push Subscription Wizard by using either of two methods. To use the first method, in Enterprise Manager, point to Replication on the Tools menu, and then choose Push Subscription To Others. The Create And Manage Publications dialog box appears, as shown in Figure 26-53. Select a publication in the Databases And Publications list box, and then click Push New Subscription.

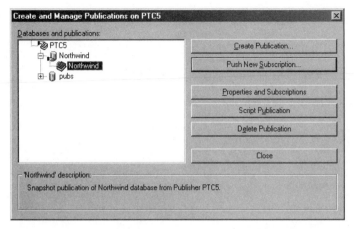

Figure 26-53. *A publication selected in the Create And Manage Publications dialog box.*

To use the second method, choose Wizards from the Tools menu, expand the Replication folder in the Select Wizards dialog box that appears, choose Push Subscription Wizard, select a publication in the Create And Manage Publications dialog box that appears, and then click Push New Subscription. Either way, the Push Subscription Wizard welcome screen appears, as shown in Figure 26-54.

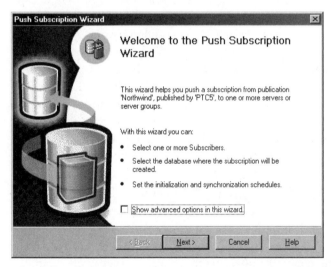

Figure 26-54. *The Push Subscription Wizard welcome screen.*

2. Click Next to display the Choose Subscribers screen, as shown in Figure 26-55. This screen is used to specify the subscribers that the publication will be pushed to. In this case, the system PTC4 is selected. These

subscribers must be enabled, as described in the section "Enabling Subscribers" earlier in this chapter.

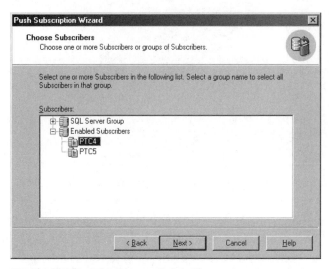

Figure 26-55. *The Choose Subscribers screen.*

3. Click Next to display the Choose Destination Database screen, shown in Figure 26-56. In this screen, you specify the database that will accept the publication on the subscriber. You can choose a database that already exists, or you can create a new database, depending on your system configuration and your needs. To use an existing database, either type the database name or click Browse and select the database from the list of existing databases that appears. To create a new database, click Browse Or Create and then click Create New in the Browse Databases dialog box that appears. You will be presented with the Database Properties window, which is used in Enterprise Manager to create a new database. After you have created the new database, you will be returned to the Choose Destination Database screen.

4. Click Next to display the Set Distribution Agent Schedule screen, shown in Figure 26-57. Here you can choose to continually update the subscription or to update it based on a schedule you specify. With snapshot replication, selecting the option to continually update the subscription doesn't make much sense. If you want to update the schedule, click Change to display the Edit Recurring Job Schedule dialog box described earlier. Here you can easily configure a recurring schedule.

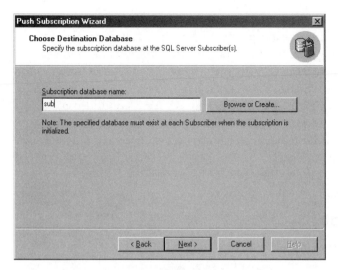

Figure 26-56. *The Choose Destination Database screen.*

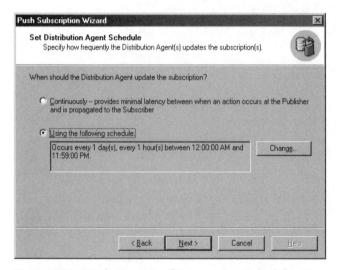

Figure 26-57. *The Set Distribution Agent Schedule screen.*

Note   The schedule that you are setting in this wizard is the schedule that is used to refresh the client from the snapshot. This schedule should be coordinated with the snapshot refresh schedule. If the snapshot has not been updated, the subscription will be updated with old snapshot data.

5. Click Next to display the Initialize Subscription screen, shown in Figure 26-58. In this screen, you specify whether the subscription needs to be initialized. The option to initialize the schema and data set on the subscriber is selected by default. If the schema already exists, the option to not initialize the schema is available. In this screen, you can also start the Snapshot Agent if it is not already started. It's a good idea to start the Snapshot Agent when you initialize the snapshot; otherwise, you must start the agent by hand. It's also important to set the schedule for the Snapshot Agent so that it corresponds to the schedules of the pull and push subscriptions, as described in the section "Modifying the Snapshot Schedule" earlier in this chapter.

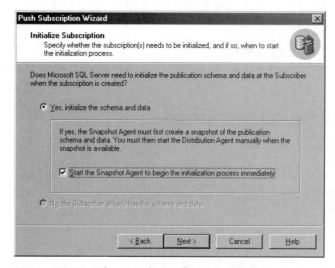

Figure 26-58. *The Initialize Subscription screen.*

6. Click Next to display the Start Required Services screen (shown in Figure 26-51), which enables you to start SQL Server Agent if it is not already started.

7. Click Next to display the Completing The Push Subscription Wizard screen, shown in Figure 26-59. Review your settings, and then click Finish to begin the process of copying the snapshot to the subscriber. You will see a dialog box describing the progress of the wizard, which is followed by a message box indicating that the operation was successfully completed. Once you have completed this wizard, the push subscription is created and will be updated on a regular basis.

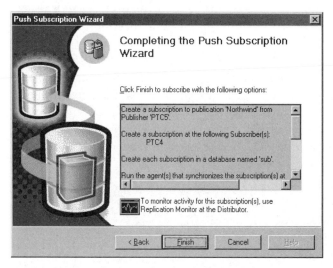

Figure 26-59. *The Completing The Push Subscription Wizard screen.*

Managing Replication

You now know how to create and configure a replicated database in a SQL Server 2000 environment. To manage this replicated environment or troubleshoot if the replication has not started, you'll use the monitoring capabilities and configuration options in Enterprise Manager.

Monitoring and Managing Replication Agents

The replication agents can be found in the Replication Monitor folder in Enterprise Manager. To access the agents, follow these steps:

1. Expand a server group, expand a server, and then expand the Replication Monitor folder.

2. If the server you expanded is a publisher, Publishers and Agents folders will appear under the Replication Monitor folder. The Publishers folder contains the publishers that belong to this server. The Agents folder contains folders for the Snapshot Agents, the Log Reader Agents, the Distribution Agents, the Merge Agents, and miscellaneous agents that are used for cleanup and historical logging.

3. Although agents do not normally need to be started or stopped, you can use Replication Monitor to do so. If your replicated system does not seem to be working after you have configured it, chances are that the

Snapshot Agent has not been started, probably because the agent is using the default schedule. (This is why during the configuration process you have the option of performing the initial snapshot immediately.) Check the status of the agents by clicking an agent folder in Enterprise Manager and viewing information about the agents in the right-hand pane. An example of this is shown in Figure 26-60. Here you can determine whether the agent has been run, and you can start it if necessary. Once you have started the agent, it will run until it has completed its job, and then it will become inactive. SQL Server Agent will then start the replication agent on its regular schedule.

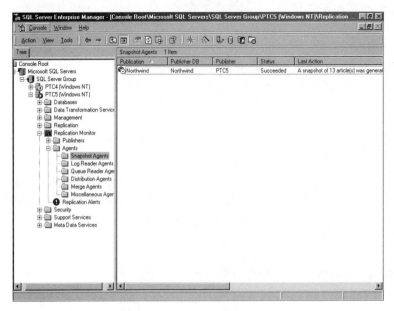

Figure 26-60. *A Snapshot Agent shown in Enterprise Manager.*

4. Right-click the agents to display a shortcut menu containing a number of options you can use to monitor and manage the agents. This menu is shown in Figure 26-61.

Figure 26-61. *The replication agent options.*

The options are described here:

- **Error Details** Lists the details of any errors that have occurred.

- **Agent History** Lists the agent's activities.

- **Agent Properties** Lets you modify the replication agent's schedule. You can also modify the database access method, the agent's tasks, and notifications. In addition, you can choose to receive e-mail messages notifying you of agent events.

- **Agent Profiles** Lets you view and modify agent parameters such as login time-outs, batch size, and query time-outs.

- **Start Agent and Stop Agent** Lets you start the agent if it is stopped or stop the agent if it is running.

- **Refresh Rate And Settings** Lets you modify how often Performance Monitor data is refreshed.

- **Select Columns** Lets you specify which columns are viewed in the results pane.

- **Help** Provides help information for this window.

Note Monitoring of the Distribution Agents will be covered in more detail in the next two chapters.

Disabling Replication

You can easily disable all or some replication operations on your system by using Enterprise Manager's replication wizards to remove certain replication components. In this section, you'll learn how to accomplish this simple task.

Removing Push Subscriptions

To remove a push subscription, use Enterprise Manager on the distributor system to invoke the Push Subscription Wizard. The Create And Manage Publications dialog box appears after you invoke the Push Subscription Wizard. In the Databases And Publications list box, select the subscription you want to delete, and then click Delete Publication. You will be prompted to verify that you want to delete the subscription. Click Yes to drop the subscription.

Removing Pull Subscriptions

To remove a pull subscription, use Enterprise Manager on the subscriber system to invoke the Pull Subscription Wizard. The Create And Manage Publications dialog box appears after you invoke the Pull Subscription Wizard. In the Databases And Publications list box, select the subscription you want to delete, and then click Delete Publication. You will be prompted to verify that you want to delete the subscription.

Removing Distribution and Publications

To drop distribution and publications, you must invoke the Disable Publishing And Distribution Wizard. In the first screen of this wizard, you specify whether you want to disable all distribution and publications or to remove just publications. If you choose the first option, all publishing, distribution, and publications will be removed. If you accept the second option (the default), only the publications will be removed. You then select the publications you want to disable. After you have made your selection, you will be presented with a verification screen, giving you one last chance to change your mind. Click Yes to remove the replication components you selected in this wizard.

Tuning for Snapshot Replication

In this section, you will learn how to configure and tune a snapshot replication system for optimal performance. The snapshot replication system is much simpler to configure and tune than are transactional and merge replication systems. With transactional and merge replication, a snapshot is initially propagated to the subscribers and then smaller amounts of replicated data are constantly applied to these systems. By contrast, a snapshot replication operation fully refreshes the database and is therefore much more straightforward. This section begins with a review of the attributes of snapshot replication, and then it presents configuration, monitoring, and tuning guidelines.

Attributes of Snapshot Replication

Because snapshot replication copies an existing database to the distributor and then to the subscriber, the performance of snapshot replication depends on the ability of certain system components to move large amounts of data. Factors that can affect the performance of snapshot replication are listed here. By properly sizing and configuring your snapshot replication system, you can reduce the effects these factors have on performance.

- **I/O performance on the publisher** Because the entire database (or parts of it) is copied from the publisher, the performance of the I/O subsystem on the publisher can be a limiting factor. The snapshot creation task is more I/O intensive than CPU intensive; thus, CPU power is not usually a factor.

- **I/O performance on the distributor**   The distributor receives large amounts of data at one time, and at some later time, it distributes that data. A slow I/O subsystem on the distributor will bog down the snapshot creation process.

- **I/O performance on the subscriber**   The distributor attempts to distribute a database or subset of a database to the subscriber all at once. If the I/O subsystem on the subscriber is inadequate, replication performance will suffer.

- **The bandwidth of the network between the publisher, distributor, and subscriber**   Because large amounts of data are being transferred, a bottleneck can easily occur on the network. Make sure that your network does not limit replication performance.

Configuring Snapshot Replication

This section provides some guidelines for configuring snapshot replication. Because snapshot replication uses the distribution database for storing only state information about the replication process, and not the replication data itself (which is done in a file), it is not typically necessary to tune SQL Server on the distributor. These guidelines should help you set up a snapshot replication system that performs optimally. The guidelines are listed here:

- Configure sufficient I/O capacity on the publisher, distributor, and subscriber

- Configure the distributor to keep the snapshot on the publisher system

- Configure the distributor and publisher on the same system

- Increase the number of BCP threads

Let's look at each of these configuration guidelines in more detail.

Configure Sufficient I/O Capacity

As mentioned in the preceding section, in snapshot replication a large amount of data is copied at one time, so a slow disk subsystem will slow down the entire process. By increasing the performance of certain I/O subsystems, you will enhance the performance of the entire replication process. On a system involved in replication, as on any SQL Server system, the transaction log should be located on its own RAID 1 volume for data protection. The data files should be located on one or more RAID 10 or RAID 5 volumes. The RAID level that you use depends on whether you are configuring the publisher, the distributor, or the subscriber.

Configuring the I/O Subsystem on the Publisher Whether you use a RAID 5 or RAID 10 volume for the data files on the publisher depends on the read/write ratio of the access to that data volume. As mentioned in Chapter 5, any disk volume that is experiencing more than 10 percent writes is not a good candidate for RAID 5 and should use RAID 10. This is because of the excessive overhead associated with RAID 5 writes. So, in determining whether you can use RAID 5, monitor the system and track the number of writes versus the number of reads. Regardless of the RAID level you choose, you should properly size the I/O subsystem, as outlined in Chapter 5 and Chapter 6.

Configuring the I/O Subsystem on the Distributor Because snapshot replication stores a file on the distributor rather than using the SQL Server database, you must make sure that the snapshot location has sufficient I/O capacity to absorb a large number of writes. Thus, the snapshot location is more suited for RAID 10 than for RAID 5. As you will see later in this section, in some cases, storing the snapshot on the publisher is more efficient.

Configuring the I/O Subsystem on the Subscriber You can enhance the performance of snapshot replication by using a RAID 10 volume rather than a RAID 5 volume for the data files on the subscriber. This is because of the large number of writes that the subscriber experiences during snapshot replication.

Note When configuring I/O subsystems for snapshot replication, you should consider the size of the snapshot publication. A snapshot replication that replicates only a few hundred rows and takes only a few seconds can easily work on any RAID level.

Select the Snapshot Location

Because snapshot replication copies the snapshot to the distributor and then later copies it to the subscriber, you can remove this extra step from the replication process. The distributor is still used, but it can be configured to store the snapshot on the publisher. This will eliminate an extra network copy operation. To configure the distributor to store the snapshot on the publisher, follow these steps:

1. On the distributor, invoke the Configure Publishing And Distribution Wizard. When the Publisher And Distributor Properties window appears, click the Publishers tab, shown in Figure 26-62.

2. Click the [...] button. This will invoke the Publisher Properties window, shown in Figure 26-63.

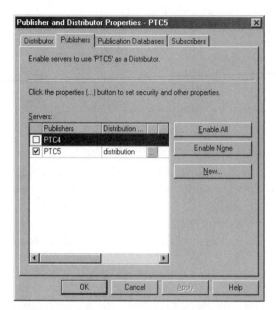

Figure 26-62. *The Publishers tab of the Publisher And Distributor Properties window.*

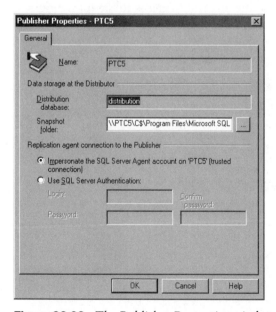

Figure 26-63. *The Publisher Properties window.*

3. In this window, you can configure the snapshot location to be on the system where the snapshot is generated. In doing so, you must make sure that this location has enough I/O capacity to handle the additional load that is generated from the snapshot.

Note When configuring the snapshot location on the distributor, you are configuring the location for all publications. If you are servicing more than one publisher system with the distributor, you should not do this.

Configure the Distributor and Publisher on the Same System

If the only type of replication you are using is snapshot replication, you can easily configure the publisher and distributor to be the same system. This will reduce network traffic because the snapshot doesn't have to be copied over the network to the distributor. However, if performance on the publisher is an issue, you should leave the snapshot on the distributor and let the distributor handle the distribution overhead.

Increase BCP Threads

You can also enhance replication performance by increasing the BCP threads that are used for the snapshot process. To do this, follow these steps:

1. In Enterprise Manager, expand the Replication Monitor folder, expand the Agents folder, and then click the Snapshot Agents folder. In the right-hand pane, right-click the desired publication and choose Agent Profiles from the shortcut menu that appears. This will invoke the Snapshot Agent Profiles dialog box, shown in Figure 26-64.

Figure 26-64. *The Snapshot Agent Profiles dialog box.*

2. Click New Profile. This will create a new profile and will invoke the Replication Agent Profile Details dialog box, in which you can modify the profile. This dialog box is shown in Figure 26-65. Here you can change the *MaxBcpThreads* parameter.

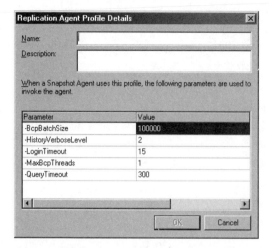

Figure 26-65. *The Replication Agent Profile Details dialog box.*

3. Once you have made your changes, name the profile and click OK. This will save the profile. Then select that profile in the Snapshot Agent Profiles dialog box.

Monitoring the Snapshot System

You monitor the snapshot system by using Microsoft Windows 2000 Performance Monitor. Within Performance Monitor are a number of objects that are added when SQL Server replication is used. In addition, a number of standard Performance Monitor objects are useful for monitoring snapshot replication. These objects include the following:

- *SQLServer:Replication Agents*   Provides the number of each type of agent that is running.

- *SQLServer:Replication Dist*   Provides information about distribution latency.

- *SQLServer:Replication Snapshot*   Provides information about snapshot replication performance.

- *PhysicalDisk*   Provides information about I/O activity. This information is highly useful because many performance problems related to snapshot replication are I/O related.

- *Processor*   Enables you to monitor the system processors.
- *System*   Provides information about the entire system.

These counters will give you a fairly good idea of how smoothly the replication process is running, but snapshot replication can occur quite quickly, so don't blink. If your system is well configured and well tuned, the snapshot process will run fairly quickly. To ensure optimal replication performance, watch for these potential problems:

- **I/O bottlenecks**   Are I/O rates too high? Look for I/O operations per second and seconds per I/O operation.
- **Network bottlenecks**   It is difficult to find a network bottleneck, but you might be able to determine if you have one by calculating the network throughput and comparing that to the snapshot replication time.

Tuning the Snapshot System

Tuning the snapshot system usually involves simply properly configuring it. The most significant problems that affect replication performance are I/O and network performance problems. You should look at the performance of your network and then determine whether your network is sufficient for your replication needs. Let's look at an example.

Suppose you have a 5-gigabyte (GB) database. If you are using a 10BaseT network, your network will have a maximum bandwidth of 10 megabits per second (Mbps), which is approximately 1 megabyte per second (MBps). Thus, a 5-GB database will take 5120 seconds, or 1.4 hours to replicate on this network. Here is the calculation: (5 GB * 1024 (MB/GB)) / 1 (MBps) = 5120 seconds, or 1.4 hours. In contrast, a 100BaseT network can perform the same replication operation in 8.3 minutes. A Gigabit Ethernet network can do this same task in 51 seconds. The network comparison is summarized in Table 26-1.

Table 26-1.   Network comparison

Network Speed	Time to Perform a Snapshot of a 5-GB Database
10BaseT	5120 seconds, or 85.3 minutes, or 1.4 hours
100BaseT	516 seconds, or 8.3 minutes
Gigabit Ethernet	51 seconds

As you can see, the size of your network really does count. By performing calculations like this, you should get a good idea of how fast the replication should be performed. If replication is taking much longer, you probably are experiencing a bottleneck somewhere else, such as I/O, memory, disk, and so on.

Summary

In this chapter, you've learned about the three types of SQL Server replication: snapshot replication, transactional replication, and merge replication. You were also introduced to the publish-and-subscribe metaphor for SQL Server replication, which first appeared in SQL Server 6. And you learned how to configure snapshot replication. As you gain experience with replication, you'll begin to see the flexibility built into SQL Server replication. In Chapters 27 and 28, you will learn more about the more complex forms of replication: transactional replication and merge replication.

Chapter 27
Transactional Replication

Chapter 26 provided an overview of Microsoft SQL Server 2000 replication, including a brief description of transactional replication. This chapter continues that discussion by providing a detailed examination of transactional replication. It explains how this replication method works, when it should be used, and how to configure, monitor, and tune transactional replication systems.

Transactional replication is probably the most popular replication method. It allows updates to be sent to subscribers fairly quickly after they are applied to publishers, and it does this without requiring high overhead on publishers.

Introduction to Transactional Replication

As indicated by its name, transactional replication is used to replicate transactions. When this replication method is used, the initial subscriber database is created by means of a snapshot, and then subsequent changes to the publisher database are replicated to the subscriber on a per-transaction basis. All database updates, insertions, and deletions are propagated in this manner.

Transactions are read from the transaction log on the publisher by the Log Reader Agent, which runs on the distributor and connects to the publisher. Those transactions are processed and put into the distribution database on the distributor. At a later time, the Distribution Agents read this information out of the distribution database and apply the transactions to the subscriber's database.

Each database that uses transactional replication has its own Log Reader Agent that runs on the distributor and monitors that database's transaction log on the publisher. Only one Log Reader Agent per database is used, regardless of the number of publications that are defined on a database.

The Log Reader Agent runs on the distributor on a schedule that is determined at the time that the publication is created. The Log Reader Agent will run either on a regularly scheduled basis or continuously, whichever you choose. When the Log Reader Agent runs, the sequence of events is as follows:

1. The Log Reader Agent reads the publication system's transaction log and creates a list of any INSERT, UPDATE, or DELETE statements, and other modifications to the data that have been marked for replication, including table drops, column definition changes, and so on.

2. The Log Reader Agent processes the data from the transaction log and performs any filtering that has been defined on the articles. This includes all horizontal and vertical filtering.

3. These modifications are batched and sent to the distribution database on the distributor. Within the distribution database there are multiple tables that keep track of replication changes and tasks. The modifications to the publisher that must be propagated to the subscribers are kept in a table called MSRepl_commands. This table holds the actual replication commands in a compressed format. The MSRepl_commands table contains one row for each insert, update, and delete for each article that has been defined. If a modification is made to a table on the publishing database that is contained in multiple articles, that change will be duplicated in the distribution database. For example, if table A is contained in three articles, an update to A will cause three rows to be created in the distribution database.

4. After each batch has been successfully sent to the distribution database, the transactions in the batch are committed. If the commit fails, an error message will be written to the agent error log.

5. Following the successful commit of the changes to the distribution database, the Log Reader Agent marks the last change included in the most recent replication operation so that changes are not repeated.

6. Once the transaction has been read from the transaction log and committed into the distribution database, the Log Reader Agent marks those rows in the transaction log as eligible to be truncated.

Every modification in the publication database will create at least one entry in the distribution database. In some cases, a modification in the publication database will cause multiple entries to be created in the distribution database. Those cases are described here:

- An insert into a table will create an insert into the distribution database for every article that the table is a member of. If a table exists in two different publications, it will be defined as two separate articles. Both articles will have a row in the distribution database for each insert, update, and delete from the publication database.

- An update or delete that affects multiple rows will create a row in the distribution database for each row affected. The SQL statement that performs an update to or a delete of multiple rows will cause the Log Reader Agent to create an individual command in the distribution database for each row that is affected. The WHERE clause in the SQL statement is converted to a WHERE clause that specifies a row in the database based on the primary key value. For example, an update that affects all the rows in a 10-row table will create 10 entries in the distribution database, each specifying the primary key values in the WHERE clause.

Uses of Transactional Replication

Transactional replication can be used when subscribers need to be kept up-to-date with the publisher. Transactional replication can be configured so that the subscriber is updated shortly after the publisher is updated. Even when the Log Reader Agent is running continuously, it reads the transaction log every few seconds instead of constantly in order to lower overhead on the publisher's transaction log.

Transactional replication can also be configured so that the subscribers can also update the database. Because of this, transactional replication is highly flexible and has many uses. These uses consist of applications such as the following:

- **Passing messages** Transactional replication can be used in order to pass messages between systems when it is important to ensure that the subscriber receives the messages. If the network goes down, the data is transferred whenever the network comes back up.

- **Keeping stores up-to-date** Many companies use transactional replication to move data between the main office and the retail stores. Whenever prices are updated at the home office, they are also updated on the systems at the retail stores.

- **Spreading the load** Transactional replication can be used to offload databases to reporting systems that can offload long-running, resource-intensive queries, thus freeing up the main servers.

There are many applications for transactional replication. Depending on your system's configuration and your application, you might find transactional replication to be quite useful.

Configuring the Transactional Replication System

Configuring transactional replication is similar to configuring snapshot replication. First you must configure the publication, and then you configure that publication to be pushed to the subscriber or to be pulled by the subscriber.

Note Before you configure any type of SQL Server replication, you must first configure publishing and distribution. See Chapter 26 for instructions.

Configuring Publications

The process of creating a transactional publication is nearly identical to the process of creating a snapshot publication. To configure a transactional publication, follow these steps:

1. In Enterprise Manager, click the Tools menu. Next either point to Replication and then choose Create And Manage Publications, or choose Wizards, expand the Replication folder in the Select Wizard dialog box that appears, and select Create Publication Wizard. Performing either procedure will display the Create And Manage Publications dialog box, shown in Figure 27-1. This dialog box allows you to select a database or table containing the data you want to publish.

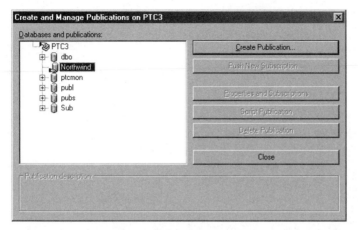

Figure 27-1. *The Create And Manage Publications dialog box.*

If publications already exist, the following buttons will be available in addition to the Create Publication button:

- **Push New Subscription** Enables you to create a new push subscription for an already existing publication. This process is described in the section "Configuring Subscriptions" later in this chapter.

- **Properties And Subscriptions** Enables you to modify both publication and subscription properties.

- **Script Publication** Enables you to create a SQL script that can be used to create more publications.

- **Delete Publication** Enables you to delete an already configured publication.

2. Select the database you want to use for the publication (in Figure 27-1, Northwind is selected), and then click Create Publication to invoke the Create Publication Wizard. The wizard's welcome screen appears, as shown in Figure 27-2. Select the Show Advanced Options In This Wizard check box.

3. Click Next to display the Choose Publication Database screen, shown in Figure 27-3. This screen allows you to (again) select the database containing the data that you want to publish. By default, the database that you chose in step 2 is selected.

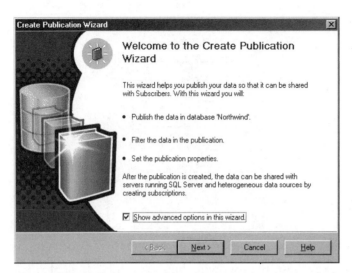

Figure 27-2. *The Create Publication Wizard welcome screen.*

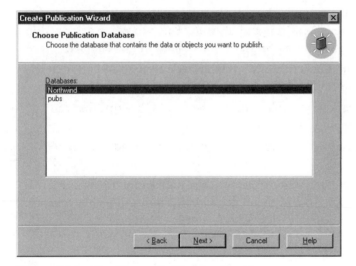

Figure 27-3. *The Choose Publication Database screen.*

Note If the system you had chosen in step 1 does not already have a distributor defined for it, you will be prompted to select a distributor in the Select Distributor screen. Remember, a publisher can only have one distributor, regardless of the number of publications. If you already have a Distributor defined, you will see the Choose Publication Database screen as described.

4. Click Next to display the Select Publication Type screen, as shown in Figure 27-4.

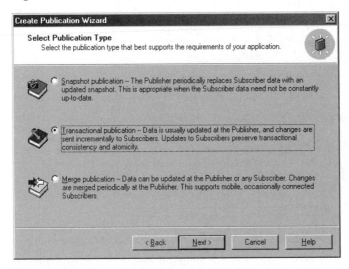

Figure 27-4. *The Select Publication Type screen.*

This screen allows you to choose one of three replication types. The options on the Select Publication Type screen are described here:

- **Snapshot Publication**   Creates a snapshot publication that periodically copies a snapshot of the article to the subscriber. A snapshot publication can be created from any table.

- **Transactional Publication**   Creates a transactional replication publication that updates the subscription with changes made to the publisher, based on transactions. Articles can be created only from tables with primary keys.

- **Merge Publication**   Creates a merge replication publication that allows two-way replication between the publisher and subscriber. Articles can be created from any tables.

5. Click Transactional Publication and click Next to display the Updatable Subscriptions screen, shown in Figure 27-5. This screen appears because we selected the Show Advanced Options In This Wizard check box, shown in Figure 27-2. (If this check box had not been selected, the Specify Subscriber Types screen would have appeared instead.)

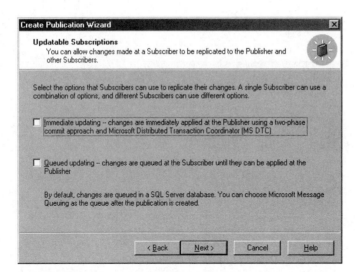

Figure 27-5. *The Updatable Subscriptions screen.*

In this screen, you specify how changes made at subscribers are replicated to publishers. The screen's check boxes are described here:

- **Immediate Updating**   Enables immediate-updating subscriptions. This means that the replication agents will use Microsoft Distributed Transaction Coordinator (MS DTC) to perform two-phase commits on the transactions that update subscribers so that changes can be made on the subscriber and immediately replicated on the publisher. (MS DTC and two-phase commits are described in Chapter 25.) The default is to not allow immediate-updating subscriptions.

- **Queued Updating**   Enables queued-updating subscriptions. This means updates on the subscriber will be queued until they can be applied to the publisher. This option allows the subscriber to update the database but does not require two-phase commits with the publisher.

Note   Immediate-updating replication is useful when having identical systems is a requirement, but be aware that the overhead involved in performing a two-phase commit is high. And if both systems are not immediately available, the transaction will not be able to commit. Immediate-updating replication should be used only when absolutely necessary.

6. Click Next to display the Transform Published Data screen, shown in Figure 27-6. The option to transform data is a new SQL Server feature. Microsoft Data Transformation Services (DTS) is used to transform the replicated data. DTS allows the following transformations to data:

- Converting data values or types
- Changing text case
- Data merging
- Data splitting

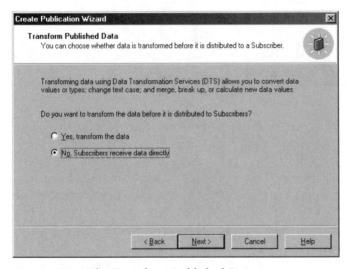

Figure 27-6. *The Transform Published Data screen.*

7. Click Next to display the Specify Subscriber Types screen, shown in Figure 27-7. This screen lets you specify whether all of the subscribers will be running SQL Server. If possible, accept the default setting, which specifies that all subscriber servers are running SQL Server 2000. If you accept this setting, you are configuring replication to use native SQL Server 2000 data types. If SQL Server 7 systems are in the replicated configuration, select the second check box. If you have non–SQL Server systems in the configuration, you should select the third check box, which causes replication data to be converted to character format. This conversion of complex native data types causes additional overhead.

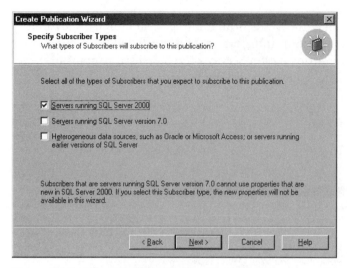

Figure 27-7. *The Specify Subscriber Types screen.*

8. Click Next to display the Specify Articles screen, shown in Figure 27-8. In this screen, you can specify the tables, stored procedures, and views that will be replicated as articles. These articles will make up the publication that you are creating. Select as many tables, stored procedures, and views as you want in the right-hand box, or select one or more check boxes in the Publish All column to select all items of one or more object types in the database. Remember, each object is considered an article, and a publication is a set of articles that are logically grouped together.

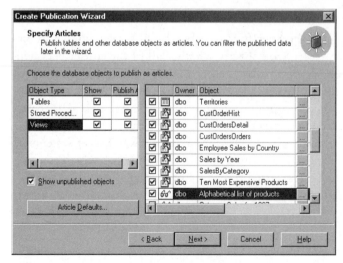

Figure 27-8. *The Specify Articles screen.*

> **Note** If stored procedures exist on the subscriber, replication can be configured to replicate the calls to the stored procedures rather than the results of the stored-procedure calls.

9. Click Next. At this point, SQL Server checks the publication, and if it finds errors, you will see a screen such as the one shown in Figure 27-9.

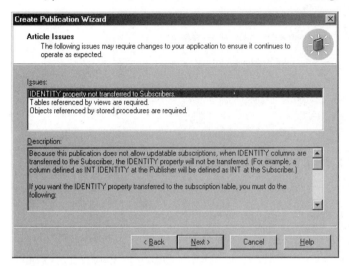

Figure 27-9. *The Article Issues screen.*

10. After the publication analysis is completed (and after you click OK to return to the wizard if the informational dialog box appears), click Next to display the Select Publication Name And Description screen, shown in Figure 27-10. In this screen, you specify a publication name and a description.

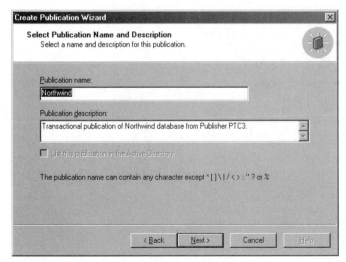

Figure 27-10. *The Select Publication Name And Description screen.*

11. Click Next to display the Customize The Properties Of The Publication screen, shown in Figure 27-11. In this screen, you specify whether you want to define data filters and customize other properties. Click Yes.

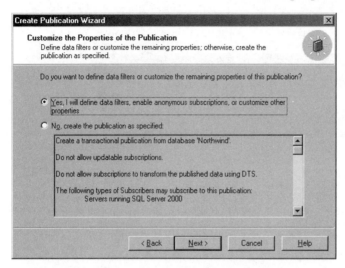

Figure 27-11. *The Customize The Properties Of The Publication screen.*

12. Click Next to display the Filter Data screen, shown in Figure 27-12. In this screen, you specify whether you want to filter the data vertically (filter columns) or horizontally (filter rows). Select both check boxes, and click Next.

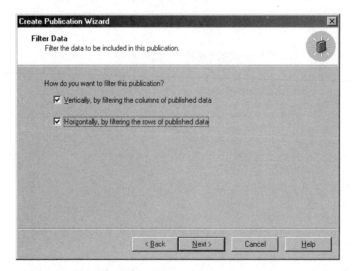

Figure 27-12. *The Filter Data screen.*

13. The Filter Table Columns screen, shown in Figure 27-13, appears. This screen allows you to exclude columns from replication. First select the table from the Tables In Publication list, and then, in the Columns In Selected Table list, clear the check boxes beside the columns that you don't want to be replicated. This allows you to vertically filter the article, which will create the replicated table with fewer columns than the table on the publisher has.

Note   Primary key columns cannot be filtered out because the primary key columns are used in transactional replication, as described earlier in this chapter.

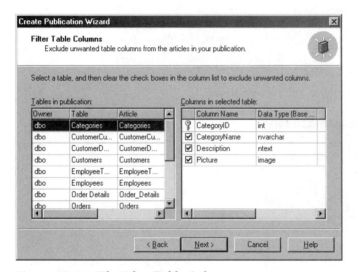

Figure 27-13. *The Filter Table Columns screen.*

14. Click Next to display the Filter Table Rows screen, shown in Figure 27-14. This screen allows you to select tables in which you want to filter the data by rows. Select a table and click the Build [...] button to set up the filter.

15. The Specify Filter dialog box appears, as shown in Figure 27-15. This dialog box allows you to add a WHERE clause to an SQL statement that will filter the row data. When you are finished specifying which rows will be replicated, click OK to return to the wizard.

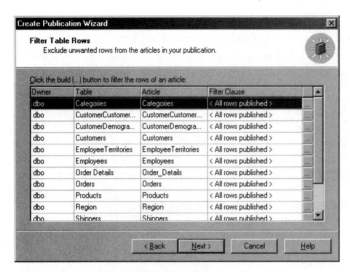

Figure 27-14. *The Filter Table Rows screen.*

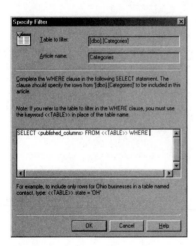

Figure 27-15. *The Specify Filter dialog box.*

16. Click Next to display the Allow Anonymous Subscriptions screen, shown in Figure 27-16. This screen allows you to specify whether anonymous subscribers or only known subscribers can access the replication data. Your choice should be based on your configuration and security needs.

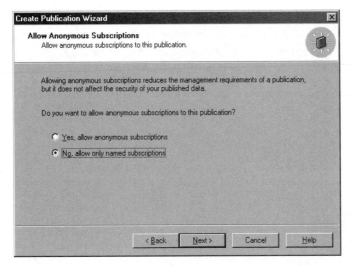

Figure 27-16. *The Allow Anonymous Subscriptions screen.*

17. Click Next to display the Set Snapshot Agent Schedule screen. For information about using this screen, see steps 15 and 16 in the subsection "Configuring Snapshot Replication" in Chapter 26. Because in transactional replication the snapshot is used only to initially create the subscriber database, you will probably not need to set a regular schedule for snapshot creation; instead you can create the snapshot manually.

18. After setting the schedule, click Next to display the Completing the Create Publication Wizard screen, review the summary of your publication, and then click Finish. A dialog box will inform you when the creation of your publication is complete.

Configuring the Log Reader Agent

Once you have created the publication, you might want to modify the behavior of the Log Reader Agent. For example, you can specify how the Log Reader Agent is invoked by selecting which mode it runs in. In continuous mode, which is the default mode, the Log Reader Agent is started when the SQL Server Agent is started. It then connects to the transaction log on the publisher and continually reads the log. In scheduled mode, the Log Reader Agent starts according to a schedule you specify, and it becomes inactive after it reads all of the replicated transactions from the transaction log. By changing the mode and other properties, you can improve performance and reduce the amount of overhead on the publisher. To configure the Log Reader Agent, follow these steps:

1. In Enterprise Manager, expand a server, expand the Replication Monitor folder, expand the Agents folder, and then click the Log Reader Agents folder.

2. In the right-hand pane of Enterprise Manager, right-click the publication. The shortcut menu shown in Figure 27-17 appears.

Figure 27-17. *The shortcut menu for a publication.*

3. Choose Agent Properties from the available options. The Log Reader Agent's Properties window appears, as shown in Figure 27-18.

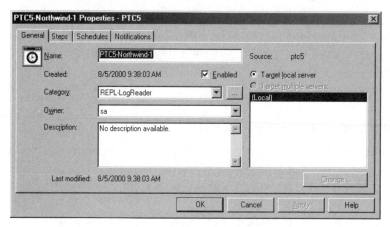

Figure 27-18. *A Log Reader Agent's Properties window.*

4. Click the Steps tab, as shown in Figure 27-19. On this tab, you will see the steps that the Log Reader Agent performs whenever it is invoked. The three steps are listed and described here:

- **Log Agent Startup Message** Logs a message into the Log Reader Agent history table (the *MSLogreader_history* table in the distribution database).

- **Run Agent** Starts the agent according to the specified schedule. When running in continuous mode, the agent will run until the system is shut down.

- **Detect Nonlogged Agent Shutdown** Puts a message into the Log Reader Agent history table in the event of an agent failure.

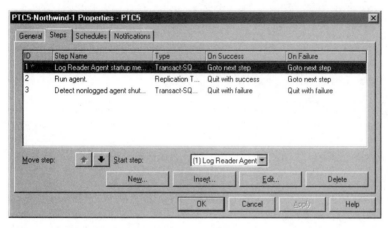

Figure 27-19. *The Steps tab of a Log Reader Agent's Properties window.*

5. Select the Run Agent step, and click Edit to display the Edit Job Step dialog box, shown in Figure 27-20. This dialog box allows you to configure how the Log Reader Agent is invoked.

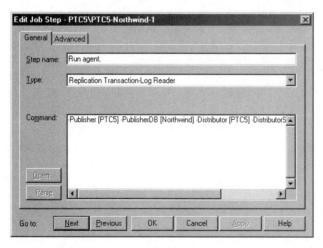

Figure 27-20. *The General tab of the Edit Job Step dialog box.*

Many options can be configured for the Log Reader Agent. The default Log Reader Agent parameters can be modified in the Command box of the Edit Job Step dialog box and in the Replication Agent Profile Details dialog box (Figure 27-22). Two of the parameters you can modify in the Edit Job Step dialog box are described here:

- *Continuous*   Specifies whether the Log Reader Agent runs in continuous mode or in scheduled mode. To specify scheduled mode, remove this parameter.

- *DistributorSecurityMode*   Specifies whether the Log Reader Agent uses SQL Server or Microsoft Windows 2000 authentication mode.

In addition, you can specify other parameters in the Edit Job Step dialog box, such as *AsynchLogging*, *Buffers*, *DefinitionFile*, distributor and publisher information, and *MessageInterval*.

More Info   An explanation of these parameters can be found in SQL Server Books Online. Look up "Log Reader Agent, starting" in the Books Online index.

6. Once you have finished modifying the Log Reader Agent's properties, click OK to save your changes.

You can modify additional options via the Log Reader Agent's profile. To modify the profile, follow these steps:

1. In the right-hand pane of Enterprise Manager, right-click the Log Reader Agent and choose Agent Profiles from the shortcut menu that appears. This will invoke the Log Reader Agent Profiles dialog box, shown in Figure 27-21.

2. Click New Profile in order to create a new profile. The current profile cannot be modified. This will invoke the Replication Agent Profile Details dialog box, shown in Figure 27-22.

3. In this dialog box, you can modify the following parameters:

- *HistoryVerboseLevel*   Specifies how much information is logged. The default level is usually sufficient, unless you are experiencing problems.

- *LoginTimeout*   Specifies the number of seconds that the Log Reader Agent will wait before timing out.

- *PollingInterval*   Specifies how often the transaction log on the publisher is polled for new transactions.

- *QueryTimeout*   Specifies how many seconds a query waits before timing out.
- *ReadBatchSize*   Specifies the number of transactions to be read out of the transaction log in one batch.

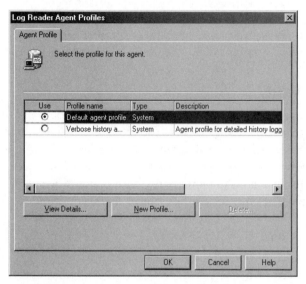

Figure 27-21. *The Log Reader Agent Profiles dialog box.*

Figure 27-22. *The Replication Agent Profile Details dialog box.*

Note As mentioned, if the Log Reader Agent is running in scheduled mode rather than continuous mode, it will be invoked by SQL Server Agent and will read all transactions from the transaction log that have been marked for replication. The Log Reader Agent will read the number of transactions or commands from the transaction log specified by the *ReadBatchSize* parameter and insert them into the distribution database. Once all of the transactions that have been marked for replication have been read, the Log Reader Agent will become inactive until it is next scheduled to run.

Configuring Subscriptions

As when you configure snapshot replication, the final step when you configure transactional replication is to set up the subscribers. You must first enable subscribers in the distribution database; this process was outlined in the section "Enabling Subscribers" in the previous chapter. Then you configure subscriptions from either the subscriber or the publisher. From the subscriber, you can configure a pull subscription; from the publisher, you can configure a push subscription.

Configuring Pull Subscriptions

Pull subscriptions are controlled by and configured from the subscriber. Thus, you must configure the pull subscription using Enterprise Manager on the subscriber system. To configure a pull subscription, follow these steps:

1. In Enterprise Manager, click the Tools menu. Next, either point to Replication, choose Pull Subscription To, and then click Pull New Subscription in the Pull Subscription To dialog box that appears; or, from the Tools menu choose Wizards, expand the Replication folder in the Select Wizard dialog box that appears, and then select Create Pull Subscription Wizard and click OK. Either way, the Pull Subscription Wizard welcome screen appears, as shown in Figure 27-23. Note the check box that lets you specify whether advanced options are shown in the wizard. For this example, we'll select the check box. This will allow data transformation to be enabled.

2. Click Next to display the Look For Publications screen shown in Figure 27-24. This screen prompts you to determine where you want to look for a publication. You have the option to select from standard Windows 2000 networking or the Active Directory service. Select the default, which specifies that you should look at publications from registered servers.

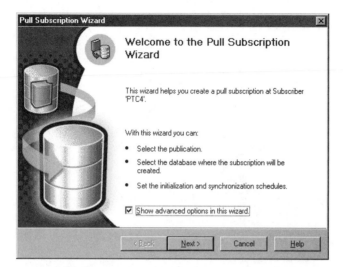

Figure 27-23. *The Pull Subscription Wizard welcome screen.*

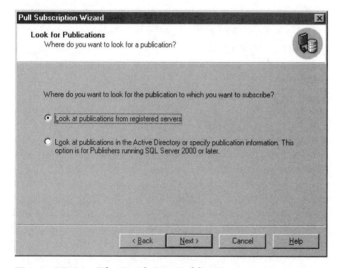

Figure 27-24. *The Look For Publications screen.*

3. Click Next to display the Choose Publication screen, shown in Figure 27-25. This screen is used to identify the publication that will be used in the replication. Servers that are registered with your SQL Server system are listed here. Select the publication that you want to replicate.

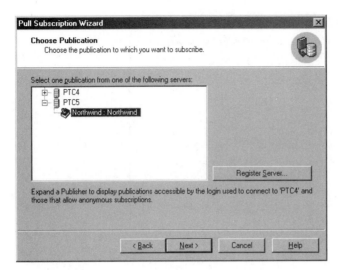

Figure 27-25. *The Choose Publication screen.*

4. Click Next to display the Specify Synchronization Agent Login screen, shown in Figure 27-26. In this screen, you specify the SQL Server login ID and password for the distributor.

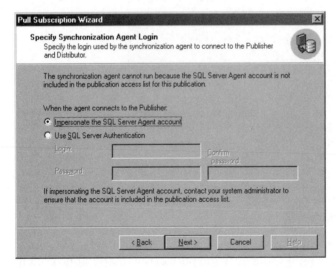

Figure 27-26. *The Specify Synchronization Agent Login screen.*

5. Click Next to display the Choose Destination Database screen, shown in Figure 27-27. In this screen, you specify which database you want the replicated articles to be placed in. If you want to create a new database, click New to open the Database Properties window.

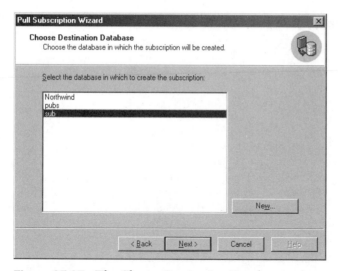

Figure 27-27. *The Choose Destination Database screen.*

6. Click Next to display the Initialize Subscription screen, shown in Figure 27-28. Click Yes to initialize the database schema and data at the subscriber. If you have previously created the schema, click No.

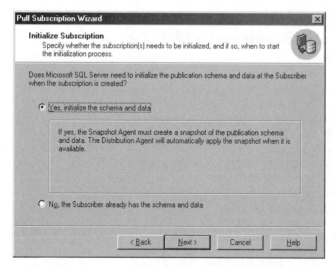

Figure 27-28. *The Initialize Subscription screen.*

7. Click Next to display the Snapshot Delivery screen, shown in Figure 27-29. Here you can specify a snapshot folder different from the default snapshot folder. If you have not modified the snapshot folder, accept the default.

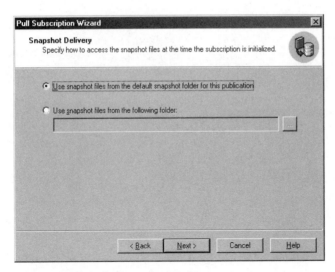

Figure 27-29. *The Snapshot Delivery screen.*

8. Click Next to display the Set Distribution Agent Schedule screen, shown in Figure 27-30. This screen enables you to select continuous updates, scheduled updates, or updates on demand. In most cases, the scheduled updates option is the preferred option.

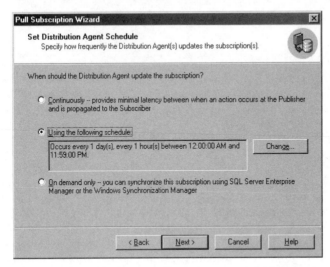

Figure 27-30. *The Set Distribution Agent Schedule screen.*

When deciding how updates will be handled on your system, remember that the more often the Distribution Agent runs, the more overhead there is on both the distributor and subscriber. Run the agent as much as necessary, but don't run it excessively.

In order to change the schedule for the Distribution Agent, click Change and modify the schedule in the Edit Recurring Job Schedule dialog box that appears.

Note If you had chosen to transform the publication, you would have been presented with the Specify DTS Package screen at this point. In order to proceed from this point you must have created a DTS package. If you do not have a package available, you must stop, create one, and then run the wizard again. For our example we are not transforming data.

9. Click Next to display the Start Required Services screen, shown in Figure 27-31. You can start the SQL Server Agent from this screen, if it is not running already. This screen shows you whether the SQL Server Agent is running on the subscriber. If the SQL Server Agent is not running, you will be prompted to start it. If you want to start the SQL Server Agent manually, expand the Management folder in Enterprise Manager, right-click on SQL Server Agent and use the options on the shortcut menu that appears to start and stop the SQL Server Agent.

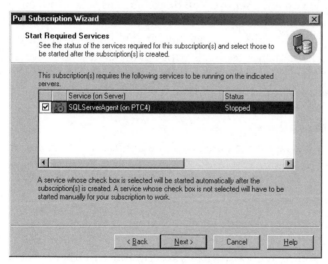

Figure 27-31. *The Start Required Services screen.*

10. Click Next to display the Completing The Pull Subscription Wizard screen, shown in Figure 27-32. Click Finish to complete the tasks of setting up the subscriber.

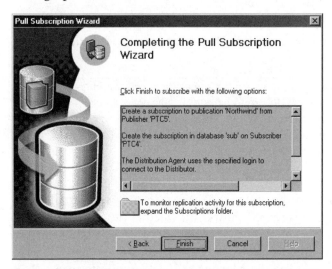

Figure 27-32. *The Completing The Pull Subscription Wizard screen.*

The articles will now be replicated on the subscriber and will be regularly updated according to the schedule you have set up. You might have to verify the schedule that the publication agents are running on before the replication can begin. Because the Snapshot Agent runs on its own schedule, if you did not configure it to immediately propagate the snapshot to the distributor, the data might take some time to reach the distributor. Even though replication is working, the actual data will not reach the subscriber until the Snapshot Agent has done its job.

Configuring Push Subscriptions

A push subscription is initiated on the publisher. You configure a push subscription by using the Push Subscription Wizard. When a push subscription is used, the schedule on which the replication occurs is determined on the distributor. To run the Push Subscription Wizard, follow these steps:

1. Invoke the Push Subscription Wizard by using either of two methods. To use the first method, in Enterprise Manager, point to Replication on the Tools menu, and then choose Push Subscription To Others. The Create And Manage Publications dialog box appears, as shown in Figure 27-33. Select a publication in the Databases And Publications list box, and then click Push New Subscription. To use the second method,

choose Wizards from the Tools menu, expand the Replication folder in the Select Wizard dialog box that appears, select Create Push Subscription Wizard, and click OK. Select a publication in the Create And Manage Publications dialog box that appears, and then click Push New Subscription.

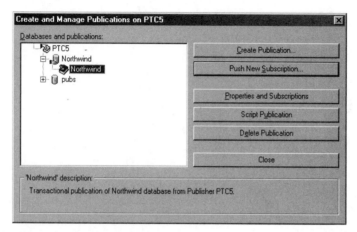

Figure 27-33. *A publication selected in the Create And Manage Publications dialog box.*

The Push Subscription Wizard welcome screen appears, as shown in Figure 27-34.

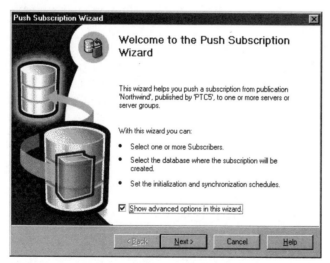

Figure 27-34. *The Push Subscription Wizard welcome screen.*

2. Click Next to display the Choose Subscribers screen, as shown in Figure 27-35. In this screen, you select the system that will be the recipient of the publication you just selected.

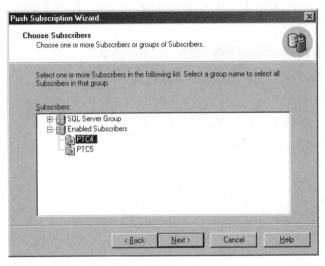

Figure 27-35. *The Choose Subscribers screen.*

3. Click Next to display the Choose Destination Database screen, shown in Figure 27-36. In this screen, you specify the database that will accept the publication on the subscriber. You can choose to use a database that already exists, or you can create a database, depending on your system configuration and your needs.

4. Click Next to display the Set Distribution Agent Location screen, shown in Figure 27-37. Here you can choose to run the distribution agent on the distributor (default and recommended) or to run it on the subscriber. For those of you familiar with transactional replication under SQL Server 7, this is a new option.

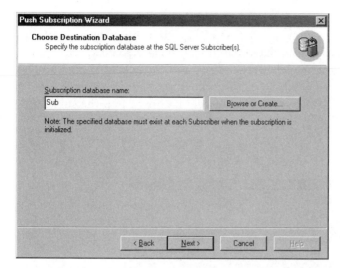

Figure 27-36. *The Choose Destination Database screen.*

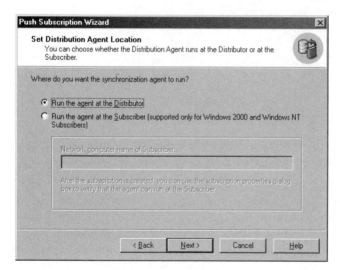

Figure 27-37. *The Set Distribution Agent Location screen.*

5. Click Next to display the Set Distribution Agent Schedule screen, shown in Figure 27-38. Here you can choose to have the subscription continually updated or to have it updated based on a schedule you specify. Click the Using The Following Schedule option, and then click Change to display the Edit Recurring Job Schedule dialog box. Here you can easily configure a recurring schedule. When deciding how often the subscription should be updated, keep in mind that continuous updates use a lot of overhead. Note that the replicate-on-demand option is not available for push subscriptions.

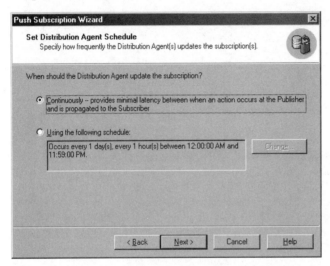

Figure 27-38. *The Set Distribution Agent Schedule screen.*

6. Click Next to display the Initialize Subscription screen, shown in Figure 27-39. In this screen, you specify whether the subscription needs to be initialized. The option to initialize the schema and data set on the subscriber is selected by default. In this screen, you can also start the Snapshot Agent if it is not already started. It's a good idea to start the Snapshot Agent when you initialize the snapshot; otherwise, you must start the agent by hand. Once the snapshot has been initialized and replication begins, you don't need to use a snapshot until the next time you create a subscription. Each time you create a subscription, create a new snapshot, and don't bother creating snapshots on a regular schedule unless you plan on resynchronizing the subscriber database using the snapshots.

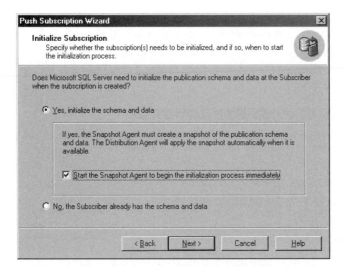

Figure 27-39. *The Initialize Subscription screen.*

7. Click Next to display the Start Required Services screen, shown in Figure 27-40, You can specify that SQL Server Agent start automatically if it is not already started.

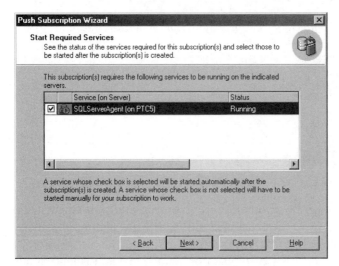

Figure 27-40. *The Start Required Services screen.*

8. Click Next to display the Completing The Push Subscription Wizard screen, shown in Figure 27-41. Review your settings and then click Finish to begin the copying of the snapshot to the subscriber. Once you have completed this wizard, the push subscription is created and will be updated on a regular basis.

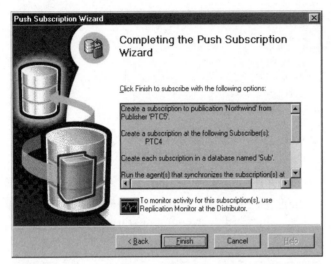

Figure 27-41. *The Completing The Push Subscription Wizard screen.*

 More Info Please refer to "Managing Replication" in Chapter 26 for information about managing and troubleshooting replication; monitoring and managing replication agents; disabling replication; and removing subscriptions, distribution, and publications.

Configuring, Monitoring, and Tuning the Distributor for Transactional Replication

In this section, you'll learn how to configure, monitor, and tune the distributor for transactional replication. As mentioned in the previous chapter, the distributor is a server containing the SQL Server database, called the distribution database, that is used as a repository of replication data. This data is held in a SQL Server database to provide several benefits, including the following:

- **Excellent performance** SQL Server provides the performance the distributor needs to acquire, hold, and then distribute data.

- **Reliability** Because SQL Server supports a high level of recoverability, a SQL Server database is ideal for replication data. Using the transaction log, SQL Server is able to recover from system failures without losing any data.

- **Ease of use** Because SQL Server replication communicates directly with the distributor via SQL Server communications protocols, setting up and configuring the distributor is easy.

Configuring the Distributor

Depending on the frequency of modifications to your database, the amount of activity in the distributor can be quite high. Because the distributor uses a SQL Server database, all modifications to the distributor must be logged in the transaction log. You should configure the distribution database and the log to be large enough to perform the work required and fast enough to perform it efficiently. While the default distribution configuration can work for smaller replication systems, it is inadequate for many systems because the SQL Server replication wizards do not place the SQL Server transaction log and data files optimally. They are usually placed on the default SQL Server volume and both transaction log and database files are placed on the same volume.

By configuring the distribution database appropriately, you can avoid costly performance problems. Here are a few guidelines for configuring the distribution database:

- Use a RAID controller on the distribution database system. Using a hardware RAID controller is more efficient than using software RAID.

- Configure the distribution database's transaction log on a RAID 1 volume. The transaction log should be isolated to allow for the higher performance that is achieved with sequential I/O operations.

- Configure the transaction log to be large enough so that it is not necessary to constantly back up the transaction log. Depending on your needs, you might be able to back up the transaction log only once a day (preferably at night).

- Configure the distribution database on a RAID 1 or RAID 10 volume. RAID 5 is not appropriate because of the high number of writes to the distribution database.

- Configure the distribution database to be large enough to hold extra replication data. If a subscriber fails, the database might have to hold several days' worth of replication data.

- Tune the distribution database as you would any other SQL Server database.

Configuring the Distributor by Using Enterprise Manager

To properly configure the distribution database as outlined in the preceding list, you need to specify where this database resides. To do this by using Enterprise Manager, first invoke the Configure Publishing And Distribution Wizard. Use this wizard to set up publishing and distribution, specifying in the Customize The Configuration screen that you want to customize the distribution settings (by clicking Yes). This option allows you to set the distribution database location manually. (It also allows you to pick a name for the database, enable publishing, and create publications as well as subscribers.)

Unfortunately, when you use the wizard, you can't set the size of the distribution database. You can increase the size of the distribution database by selecting that database's properties in Enterprise Manager and changing the size of the database or transaction log files. If you prefer specifying the location and the size of the database at one time, you can use the *sp_adddistributiondb* stored procedure.

Configuring the Distributor by Using *sp_adddistributiondb*

The system stored procedure *sp_adddistributiondb* allows you to script the creation of the distribution database. This is useful when you want to specify the size and location of the database and its transaction log. And once you have written a script that creates the distribution database, you can use it on different systems, or you can use it to re-create the distribution database in the event of a system reconfiguration.

Note Before you can create the distribution database, you must enable the distributor. You accomplish this by using the system stored procedure *sp_adddistributor*, followed by the distributor's system name.

The syntax for the *sp_adddistributiondb* stored procedure is shown in SQL Server Books Online. An example of using that stored procedure is shown here:

```
sp_adddistributor Dash
```

The following SQL statement initializes the system named Dash as a distributor.

```
sp_adddistributiondb
@database=dist,
@data_folder='C:\mssql2000\data',
@data_file='dist.mdf',
@data_file_size=10,
@log_folder='C:\mssql2000\data',
@log_file='dist.ldf',
@log_file_size=2,
@min_distretention=0,
@max_distretention=72,
@history_retention=96,
@security_mode=0,
@login='sa',
@password='',
@createmode=0
```

Monitoring the Distributor

You monitor the distributor by using Windows 2000 Performance Monitor (perfmon). Within perfmon are a number of objects that are added when SQL Server replication is used. These objects are as follows:

- *SQLServer:Replication Agents*   Provides the number of each type of agent that is running

- *SQLServer:Replication Dist.*   Provides information about distribution latency

- *SQLServer:Replication Logreader*   Provides data about Log Reader Agent activity and latency

- *SQLServer:Replication Merge*   Provides data about merge rates

- *SQLServer:Replication Snapshot*   Provides information about snapshot replication performance

By using Performance Monitor to monitor these values, you can sometimes determine whether the distributor is experiencing a performance problem. This perfmon data provides a lot of valuable information, but it does not always identify problems. For monitoring the distributor, we are most concerned with the *SQLServer:Replication Dist.* object. This object provides the following counters:

- *Dist:Delivered Cmds/sec* Monitors the number of commands per second delivered to the subscriber. This counter gives you a good idea of how much activity is occurring on the subscriber.

- *Dist:Delivered Trans/sec* Monitors the number of transactions per second delivered to the subscriber. This counter also gives you a good idea of how much activity is occurring on the subscriber.

- *Dist:Delivery Latency* Monitors the amount of time it takes for transactions to be applied to the subscriber after they are delivered to the distributor. This counter can give you some insight into how backed up the distributor is.

While these counters give you some general indication of how the distribution process is running, they are of limited usefulness when you are determining whether you need to tune the distributor because the most important aspect of tuning the distributor is tuning the SQL Server database. Thus, you should look mainly for the following problems:

- **High CPU usage** Are one or more CPUs running at high rates (greater than 75 percent of their capacity) for long periods?

- **I/O bottlenecks** Are I/O rates too high? Monitor I/O operations per second and seconds per I/O operation.

- **Response times** Are SQL Server response times too high?

Tuning the Distributor

As mentioned earlier, the distributor is the server containing the distribution database, and this database must be tuned in the same manner as any other SQL Server database. You can enhance the performance of the distributor by properly sizing it, although, as you learned in Chapter 6, sizing is not always an easy task. The distributor should have enough capacity to handle extra work. The distributor is the link between the publishers and the subscribers and should be configured so that it is not a bottleneck. Some tips for configuring and tuning the distributor are provided here:

- **Tune the I/O subsystem** Ensure that the distributor, like any other SQL Server system, has sufficient I/O capacity.

- **Use a multiprocessor system** CPU power is not usually a problem because in most cases, operations that take place on the distributor are not extremely CPU intensive. However, you should use at least two CPUs to allow concurrent operations to take place.

- **Tune the operating system** Configure the Server service to maximize throughput for network applications. This will configure the memory system to favor applications over file services. You make this setting through the Network icon in Control Panel. Also, remove any services that won't be used, such as IIS and FTP services.

- **Monitor the distributor during snapshot replication** When snapshot replication is running, including when the initial snapshot is being copied in transactional and merge replication, a large number of I/O operations will occur at one time. Because so much data is being written to the distributor, the distributor's I/O subsystem might become overloaded. If this happens, the time it takes to apply the snapshot will increase. Therefore, you should monitor the distributor during the transmission of the snapshot.

- **Tune SQL Server** Using the techniques and guidelines you've learned from this book, tune the SQL Server system.

Tuning Transactional Replication

In this section, you will learn how to configure and tune a transactional replication system for optimal performance. This section begins with a review of the attributes of transactional replication, and then it presents configuration, monitoring, and tuning guidelines.

Attributes of Transactional Replication

Transactional replication starts with the copying of a snapshot to the distributor and then to the subscriber. Once the snapshot has been copied, the Log Reader Agent, which runs on the distributor, reads the publisher's transaction log either on a continual basis or according to a regular schedule. How often the transaction log is read is determined by how you configure the Log Reader Agent. (The overhead incurred on the publisher when the transaction log is being read is the only replication-related overhead the publisher requires.)

The transactions that the Log Reader Agent reads from the transaction log on the publisher are put into the distribution database. These transactions are then eventually sent to the subscribers. Factors that can limit the performance of transactional replication include the following:

- **I/O performance on the publisher's transaction log** The transaction log on the publisher is read in order to determine what changes have been made. Because the transaction log is read as well as written to when replication is used, the sequential access to the transaction log can be disrupted. This can cause a bottleneck. To prevent this, the log must be carefully configured.

- **Performance of the distributor** Depending on how many replication operations are occurring and how many publishers are using the distributor, the distributor might experience performance problems. Earlier in this chapter, you learned how to configure and tune the distributor.

- **Performance of the subscriber** The subscriber can experience performance problems, depending on what activity is occurring on it. To prevent these problems, perform standard tuning operations on the subscriber's SQL Server database.

As you can see, several factors can limit performance. By properly sizing and configuring the systems involved, you can reduce the effects of these factors and ensure efficient performance.

Configuring Transactional Replication

Configuring a transactional replication system involves several tasks. As mentioned in the previous section, you must properly configure the transaction log on the publisher because it experiences additional overhead when replication is used. In this section, we'll look at several other guidelines that you should keep in mind when you configure your transactional replication system. These guidelines are summarized here:

- Configure sufficient I/O capacity on all the replication systems, following general guidelines for configuring I/O capacity. (You might need to configure more I/O capacity for the transaction log on the publisher than is normally required.)
- Increase the commit batch size on the distributor.
- Tune the Log Reader Agent.

Configure Sufficient I/O Capacity

By configuring sufficient I/O capacity, you can enhance the performance of the entire replication process. As on any SQL Server system, the transaction log on a system participating in replication should be located on its own RAID 1 volume for data protection. The data files should be located on one or more RAID 10 or RAID 5 volumes. Unlike snapshot replication, transactional replication requires only minor adjustments to standard I/O configurations. Those requirements are described in this section.

Configuring the I/O Subsystem on the Publisher   In general, you should follow the standard SQL Server configuration guidelines described throughout this book when you are configuring the publisher's I/O subsystem. However, you might need to configure more I/O capacity for the publisher's transaction log than is usually required. Normally, the transaction log should be configured on a RAID 1 volume. If necessary (depending on how busy your system is), you should configure it on a RAID 10 volume, using more disk drives. RAID 5 is not appropriate for the transaction log.

Configuring the I/O Subsystem on the Distributor   The distributor should be configured such that the distribution database has its transaction log on a dedicated RAID 1 disk volume. This will allow the distribution database's log to achieve maximum performance, thus improving the performance of the distributor.

Configuring the I/O Subsystem on the Subscriber   Transactional replication does not require any special I/O configuration on the subscriber. Simply follow the general sizing and configuration guidelines described throughout this book.

Configure the Commit Batch Size on the Distributor

The commit batch size on the distributor determines how many replication transactions are committed on the distributor in a single batch. If you increase the batch size, more rows will be committed at a time, thus increasing the time that the distribution tables are unavailable to other processes. (Locks are held on the tables while the distribution database is being updated.) If you decrease the batch size, fewer rows will be committed at a time, thus giving other processes a chance to access the distribution database.

If the distribution database experiences a large amount of activity that is generated by several sources (that is, by the publisher and several subscribers), try reducing the batch size. If the Log Reader Agent is running on a periodic schedule and has many transactions to insert into the distribution database at once, you might benefit from configuring a larger batch size. You might not need to change the batch size, but if you do, compare the differences between increasing and decreasing the batch size in order to determine which is better.

You can configure the commit batch size in Enterprise Manager by accessing the properties of the Distribution Agent. For more information, see the section "Monitoring and Managing Replication Agents" in this chapter.

Tune the Log Reader Agent

As mentioned, reads to the publisher's transaction log performed by the Log Reader Agent can randomize the otherwise sequential I/O operations of the log. By configuring the Log Reader Agent, you might be able to reduce its effect on the log. There are several ways to make the Log Reader Agent's operations more efficient. One way is to use a caching controller for the log drive volume. Because the Log Reader Agent reads from the log drive, a cache on a controller will allow the read to take place from the cache, rather than cause a random I/O operation to occur.

Another way to tune the Log Reader Agent is to configure it to run less frequently. The Log Reader Agent can run on a continuous basis or periodically. If your system is not experiencing a large number of updates, you might be able to run the Log Reader Agent continuously without disrupting the transaction log. If your system's transaction log is busy, you can improve performance of the publisher by configuring the Log Reader Agent to run less frequently. That way, the Log Reader Agent will not be reading from the transaction log as often, thus allowing the transaction log I/O operations to remain sequential.

Yet another way to make the Log Reader Agent more efficient in heavily used systems is to increase the read batch size. This specifies how many transactions are read from the transaction log and copied to the distributor at a time. In heavily used systems, increasing this parameter can improve performance. In addition, when you increase the polling interval, you might find it useful to increase the batch size. If you increase the read batch size on the Log Reader Agent, you should increase the commit batch size on the distributor to correspond to the new read batch size.

You can configure the Log Reader Agent by accessing its properties in Enterprise Manager. See the section "Monitoring and Managing Replication Agents" for more information.

Monitoring the Transactional Replication System

You monitor transactional replication activities, like you monitor other types of replication activities, via perfmon. Within perfmon are a number of objects that are added when SQL Server replication is used. These objects are as follows:

- *SQLServer:Replication Agents*   Provides the number of each type of agent that is running.

- *SQLServer:Replication Dist.*   Provides information about distribution latency. Long latencies can be a sign that the distributor is overloaded.

- *SQLServer:Replication Logreader*   Provides data about Log Reader Agent activity and latency. Look for long latencies. This can be an indication that a problem exists relating to the Log Reader Agent's reading of the transaction log on the publisher. Also, watch the number of delivered transactions per second. If this number is high, you might need to add more I/O capacity to the transaction log disk volumes.

By using Performance Monitor to monitor these values, you can sometimes determine if the Log Reader Agent or the distributor is experiencing a performance problem. This perfmon data provides a lot of valuable information, but it does not always identify problems.

Tuning the Transactional Replication System

The main steps in tuning the transactional replication system are to properly configure and monitor the system, as described in the preceding sections. In addition, after the system is in production and you can monitor it, you might need to modify the polling interval. The default value of 10 seconds is usually adequate. If you increase the polling frequency (by making the polling interval shorter), transactions will be replicated faster, but overhead on the transaction log will be increased. By decreasing the polling frequency (making the polling interval longer), you will reduce the overhead on the transaction log, but transactions will take longer to replicate.

In addition, if your system experiences frequent updates, you might need to increase the read batch size. As mentioned, this will let the Log Reader Agent read more transactions out of the transaction log at a time. If you increase this value and leave the polling interval at 10 seconds, more transactions will be replicated and less additional overhead will be required.

You also need to monitor the capacity of the network and increase it if necessary, just as you do if you use snapshot replication. If your system does not appear to be performing adequately—for example, if CPUs and I/O subsystems are reaching their capacity and if the replication process seems to be taking too long—you might have a network problem. Unfortunately, network problems cannot be diagnosed via perfmon. A network-monitoring product such as Microsoft Systems Management Server (SMS) should be used. Monitor the network card to see if it's reaching its capacity.

Finally, remember that the publisher, distributor, and subscribers are SQL Server systems. You should therefore tune these systems just as you would tune any other SQL Server system. Tuning guidelines for SQL Server systems are given throughout this book.

Implementing Transactional Replication

In this section, you'll learn about methods of implementing transactional replication. Transactional replication can be implemented in a one-to-many scheme or in a many-to-one scheme. Often, transactional replication is implemented over a wide area network (WAN).

One-to-Many Replication

Most implementations of transactional replication involve a one-to-many replication scheme. In this type of implementation, one table is published to one or more subscribers.

Many-to-One Replication

In a many-to-one replication scheme, one database subscribes to more than one subscription. This is not the most common replication scheme, but it is nevertheless widely used. Because transactional replication works by reading the transaction log on the publisher and applying inserts, updates, and deletes to the subscriber, it is perfectly suited for this replication scheme. The only potential drawback is the fact that the subscribing table must have a primary key defined on it. As long as your data sources do not violate this primary key, the many-to-one replication scheme will function properly.

Replication over a WAN

Replication over a WAN is not only possible, but also quite common. If you replicate data over a WAN, you should continuously monitor the distribution history and look for excessive replication times caused by network bandwidth limitations. In addition, if possible, configure replication such that only the Distribution Agent connects over the WAN. That is, configure the system such that the distributor and publisher are on the same side of the WAN.

Summary

In this chapter, you have learned the basics of transactional replication. You have learned what transactional replication is, how it works, how to monitor it, and how to tune it. By understanding how transactional replication works and what it does, you can use it and configure it effectively. In the next chapter, you will learn about merge replication.

Chapter 28
Merge Replication

Merge replication differs from transactional replication in that it is inherently multidirectional. With merge replication, publishers and subscribers can update the publication equally. Transactional replication also allows subscribers to update the publication, but the two replication types function quite differently. In this chapter, you will learn how merge replication works and how to configure, monitor, and tune merge replication.

Introduction to Merge Replication

Merge replication performs multidirectional replication between the publisher and one or more subscribers. This allows multiple systems to have updatable copies of the publication and to modify their own copies. A modification on the publisher will be replicated to the subscribers. A modification on a subscriber will be replicated to the publisher and then replicated to the other subscribers.

Unlike transactional replication, merge replication works by installing triggers on the publisher and on the subscribers. Whenever a change is made to the publication or a copy of it, the appropriate trigger is fired, which causes a replication command to be queued up to be sent to the distribution database. This command is eventually sent to the distribution database and then sent to participating systems. Because merge replication operates this way, it requires much more overhead, especially on the publisher, than does transactional replication.

As you will learn in this chapter, the key components involved in the merge replication system are the Merge Agent and the distribution database. The Merge Agent reconciles (merges) incremental changes that have occurred since the last reconciliation. When you use merge replication, no Distribution Agent is used—the Merge Agent communicates with both the publisher and the distributor. The Snapshot Agent is used only to create the initial database. The Merge Agent performs the tasks listed on the following page.

1. The Merge Agent uploads all changes from the subscriber.

2. All of the rows without a conflict (rows not modified on both the publisher and the subscriber) are uploaded immediately; those with a conflict (rows modified on both systems) are sent to the conflict resolver. The *resolver* is a module that is used to resolve conflicts in merge replication. You can configure this module to resolve conflicts based on your needs.

3. All changes are applied to the publisher.

4. The Merge Agent uploads all changes from the publisher.

5. All of the rows without a conflict are uploaded immediately; those with a conflict are sent to the conflict resolver.

6. All changes are applied to the subscriber.

This process will repeat as scheduled. With push subscriptions, the Merge Agent runs on the distributor. With pull subscriptions, the Merge Agent runs on the subscriber. Each merge publication has its own Merge Agent.

Uses of Merge Replication

Merge replication is used when multidirectional replication is needed. Merge replication has many applications. Its ability to allow subscribers to modify data increases its usefulness. Uses of merge replication include the following:

- **Interoffice data sharing** Departments handling payroll, accounts payable, and accounts receivable, for example, can have access to the same data. Users in each department can modify the data and have the changes merged on the other departments' systems.

- **Multisite data sharing** Merge replication can be used when users at multiple locations require the same data and need to make changes to that data.

- **Message passing** Merge replication can be used as a message-passing system, in which data can be modified and the changes sent back to the originating system.

Configuring the Merge Replication System

Configuring merge replication is similar to configuring snapshot and transactional replication. First you must configure the publication, and then you configure that publication to be pushed to the subscriber or to be pulled by the subscriber.

> **Note**   Before you configure any type of SQL Server replication, you must first configure publishing and distribution. See the section "Configuring Publishing and Distribution" in Chapter 26 for instructions.

Configuring Publications

Even though the process of configuring publications was described in Chapters 26 and 27, the procedures used to create a merge publication are listed here because they differ slightly from the procedures used to created the other types of publications. To configure a merge publication, follow these steps:

1. In Enterprise Manager, click the Tools menu. Next either point to Replication and then choose Create And Manage Publications, or choose Wizards, expand the Replication folder in the dialog box that appears, and choose Create Publication Wizard. Performing either procedure will display the Create And Manage Publications dialog box, shown in Figure 28-1. This dialog box allows you to select a database or table containing the data you want to publish.

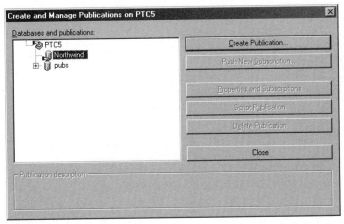

Figure 28-1. *The Create And Manage Publications dialog box.*

If publications already exist, the following buttons will be available in addition to the Create Publication button:

- **Push New Subscription** Enables you to create a new push subscription for an already existing publication. This process is described in the section "Configuring Subscriptions" later in this chapter.

- **Properties And Subscriptions** Enables you to modify both publication and subscription properties.

- **Script Publication** Enables you to create a SQL script that can be used to create more publications.

- **Delete Publication** Enables you to delete an already configured publication.

2. Select the database you want to use for the publication (in Figure 28-1, Northwind is selected), and then click Create Publication to invoke the Create Publication Wizard. The wizard's welcome screen appears, as shown in Figure 28-2. Select the Show Advanced Options In This Wizard check box.

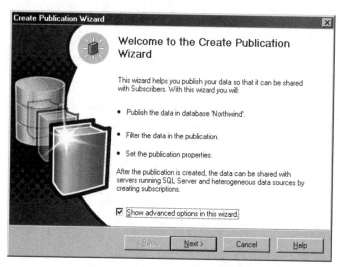

Figure 28-2. *The Create Publication Wizard welcome screen.*

3. Click Next to display the Choose Publication Database screen, shown in Figure 28-3. This screen allows you to (again) select the database containing the data you want to publish. By default, the database that you chose in step 2 is selected.

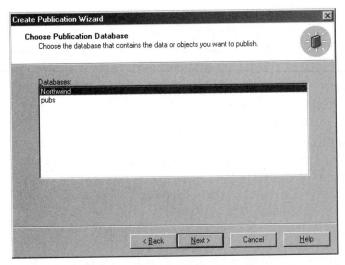

Figure 28-3. *The Choose Publication Database screen.*

4. Click Next to display the Select Publication Type screen, shown in Figure 28-4.

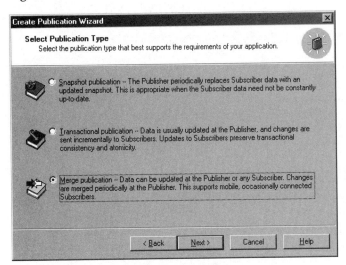

Figure 28-4. *The Select Publication Type screen.*

This screen allows you to choose one of the three replication types. The options on the Select Publication Type screen are described here:

- **Snapshot Publication**   Creates a snapshot publication that periodically copies a snapshot of the article to the subscriber. A snapshot publication can be created from any table.

- **Transactional Publication** Creates a transactional replication publication that updates the subscription with changes made to the publisher, based on transactions. Articles can be created only from tables with a primary key.

- **Merge Publication** Creates a merge replication publication that allows two-way replication between the publisher and subscriber. Articles can be created from any tables.

5. Click Merge Publication, and click Next to display the Specify Subscriber Types screen, shown in Figure 28-5. This screen lets you specify whether all of the subscribers will be running Microsoft SQL Server. If possible, accept the default setting, which specifies that all subscriber servers are running SQL Server 2000. If you accept this setting, you are configuring replication to use native SQL Server 2000 data types. If Microsoft SQL Server 7 systems are in the replicated configuration, select the second check box. If SQL Server CE devices are being used, check the third box. If you have non–SQL Server systems in the configuration, you should select the fourth check box, which causes replication data to be converted to character format. This conversion of complex native data types causes additional overhead.

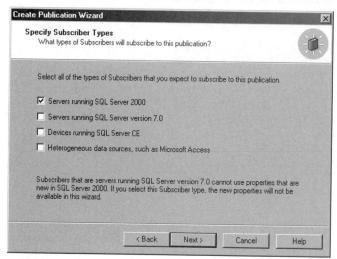

Figure 28-5. *The Specify Subscriber Types screen.*

6. Click Next to display the Specify Articles screen, shown in Figure 28-6. In this screen, you can specify the tables, stored procedures, and views that will be replicated as articles. These articles will make up the publi-

cation that you are creating. Select as many tables, stored procedures, and views as you want in the right-hand box, or select one or more check boxes in the Publish All column to select all items of one or more object types in the database. Remember, each object is considered an article, and a publication is a set of articles that are logically grouped together.

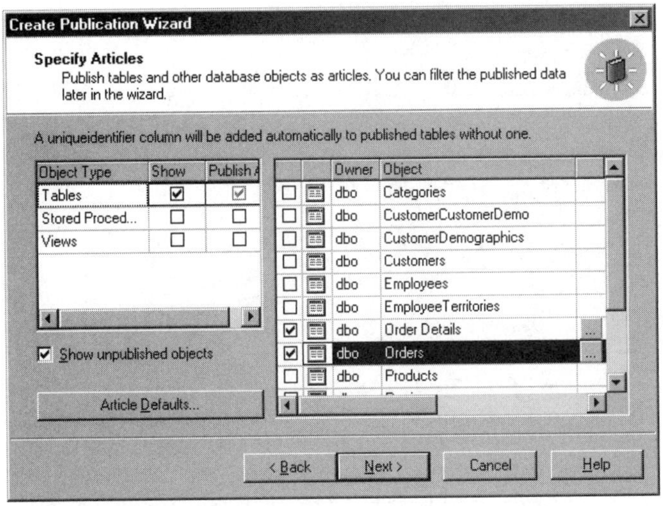

Figure 28-6. *The Specify Articles screen.*

Note If stored procedures exist on the subscriber, replication can be configured to replicate the calls to the stored procedures rather than the results of the stored-procedure calls.

7. Because we are specifying merge replication, we can define additional attributes on the articles. To configure these attributes, first click the [...] button to the right of the article definition. You will then see the Table Article Properties window, shown in Figure 28-7.

   In the tabbed pages of this window, you can configure various properties of the article. Figure 28-7 shows the General tab. Here you can specify the name of the article and the destination database owner, and you can define what constitutes a conflict. The default option specifies that modifications to a column by two sources will be treated as a conflict. You can broaden this definition by specifying that changes to a row by two sources will be treated as a conflict.

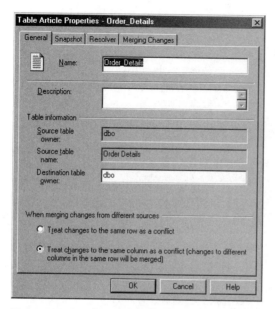

Figure 28-7. *The General tab of the Table Article Properties window.*

8. Click the Resolver tab (shown in Figure 28-8) to specify the resolver to use. If you use the default resolver, the publisher always wins a conflict with the subscriber. In addition, the first subscriber to synchronize wins a conflict between subscribers. This is normally the desired behavior. You can instead select one of a number of other resolvers, including custom resolvers that you define yourself.

9. The Merging Changes tab, shown in Figure 28-9, allows you to specify additional security for certain operations. By selecting one or more check boxes in the Check Permissions area, you specify that Merge Agent permissions to perform the specified operation or operations be checked before the operation or operations are executed. In addition, the tab contains a check box that is selected by default. This check box specifies that multiple column updates to one row be performed in one UPDATE statement operation. You should accept this default setting. Click OK when you are ready to continue.

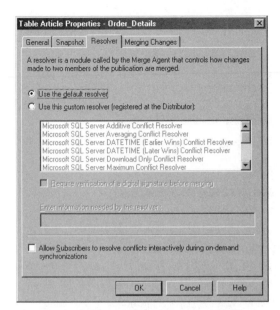

Figure 28-8. *The Resolver tab of the Table Article Properties window.*

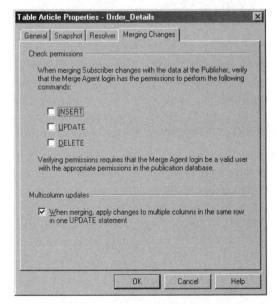

Figure 28-9. *The Merging Changes tab of the Table Article Properties window.*

10. Click Next. At this point, a check of the publication is made, and most likely, you will see a screen such as the one shown in Figure 28-10. Merge replication requires a unique identifier column. This column will automatically be added to the table for you. In addition, identity columns will be created with the NOT FOR REPLICATION option.

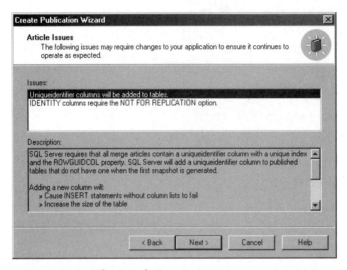

Figure 28-10. *The Article Issues screen.*

11. Click Next. The Select Publication Name And Description screen appears, as shown in Figure 28-11. In this screen, you specify simply a publication name and a description.

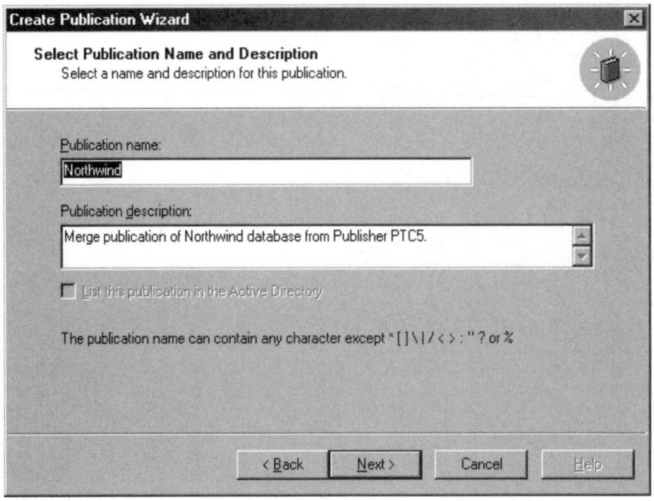

Figure 28-11. *The Select Publication Name And Description screen.*

12. Click Next to display the Customize The Properties Of The Publication
    screen, shown in Figure 28-12. In this screen, you specify whether you
    want to define data filters and customize other publication properties.
    Click No. (The options presented if you click Yes were described in the
    previous chapter.)

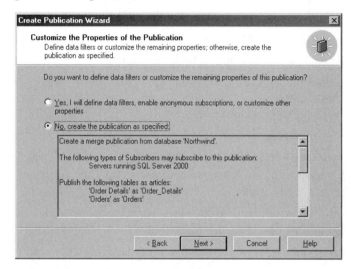

Figure 28-12. *The Customize The Properties Of The Publication screen.*

13. Click Next. The Completing The Create Publication Wizard screen ap-
    pears. Click Finish and the publication will be created for you. You will
    see the progress as the various steps are being performed. Finally you
    will see a screen that shows you the steps were completed and that pro-
    vides a summary of the operation.

If you now check the Replication Monitor folder for Merge Agents, you will find
that there are none. Because the Merge Agents are used for two-way replication,
it is necessary to have subscribers configured before replication begins. Once you
configure the subscribers, the Merge Agents will appear in the Replication Monitor folder.

Configuring Subscriptions

As when you configure snapshot and transactional replication, the final step when
you configure merge replication is to set up the subscribers. You must first enable
subscribers in the distribution database; this process was outlined in the section
"Enabling Subscribers" in Chapter 26. Then you configure subscriptions from
either the subscriber or the publisher. From the subscriber, you can configure a
pull subscription; from the publisher, you can configure a push subscription.

Configuring Pull Subscriptions

Pull subscriptions are controlled by and configured from the subscriber. Thus, you must run Enterprise Manager on the subscriber system to set up a subscription for it. We have already seen in Chapter 27, "Configuring Pull Subscriptions," how to configure a pull subscription. Because in this case steps are almost identical, we will summarize them here briefly and concentrate on differences instead.

1. Invoke the Pull Subscription Wizard.

2. The Pull Subscription Wizard welcome screen appears.

3. Click Next to display the Look for Publications screen. Choose registered servers for this example.

4. Click Next to display the Choose Publications screen, and select the publication that will be replicated.

5. Click Next to display the Specify Synchronization Agent Login screen, and specify which account the merge agent will use to go communicate with the Publisher and Distributor.

6. Click Next to display the Choose Destination Database screen, and choose the database.

7. Click Next to display the Initialize Subscription screen, and make your selections.

8. Click Next to display the Snapshot Delivery screen, and specify the snapshot location.

9. Click Next to display the Set Merge Agent Schedule screen. This screen is similar to the Set Distribution Agent Schedule screen you saw in the previous chapter. Make your selections.

10. Click Next to display the Set Subscription Priority screen, shown in Figure 28-13. Here you can set the priority of the subscription, which will be used to determine the winner in a conflict. The default setting (recommended) specifies that the priority setting on the publisher will be used for conflict resolution.

11. Click Next to display the Start Required Services screen, and start SQL Server Agent if it is not already started.

12. Click Next to display the Completing The Pull Subscription Wizard screen. Review your settings and then click Finish. Once you have completed this wizard, the push subscription is created and will be updated on a regular basis.

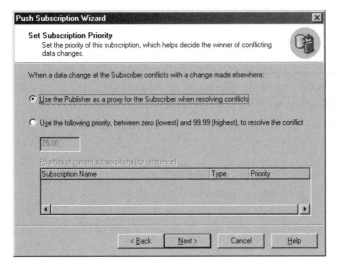

Figure 28-13. *The Set Subscription Priority screen.*

Configuring Push Subscriptions

A push subscription is initiated on the publisher. You configure a push subscription by using the Push Subscription Wizard. To run this wizard, follow these steps:

1. Invoke the Push Subscription Wizard by using either of two methods. To use the first method, in Enterprise Manager, point to Replication on the Tools menu, and then choose Push Subscriptions To Others. The Create And Manage Publications dialog box appears, as shown in Figure 28-14.

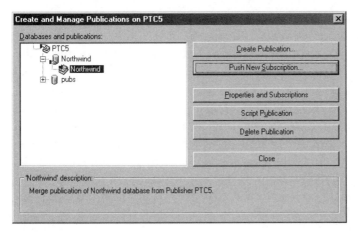

Figure 28-14. *A publication selected in the Create And Manage Publications dialog box.*

Select a publication in the Databases And Publications list box, and then click Push New Subscription. To use the second method, choose Wizards from the Tools menu, expand the Replication folder in the Select Wizard dialog box that appears, choose Create Push Subscription Wizard, select a publication in the Create And Manage Publications dialog box that appears, and then click Push New Subscription.

2. The Push Subscription Wizard welcome screen appears, as shown in Figure 28-15.

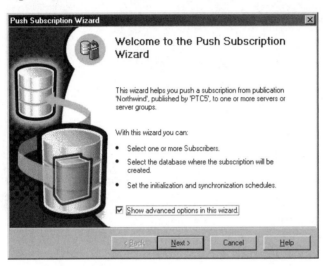

Figure 28-15. *The Push Subscription Wizard welcome screen.*

3. Click Next to display the Choose Subscribers screen, shown in Figure 28-16. In this screen, you select the system that will be the recipient of the publication you just selected. Choose from the list of enabled subscribers.

4. Click Next to display the Choose Destination Database screen, shown in Figure 28-17. In this screen, you specify the database that will accept the publication on the subscriber. You can choose to use a database that already exists, or you can create a database, depending on your system configuration and needs. To see a list of existing databases, click Browse Or Create. If you want to create a database, click Browse Or Create, click Create New, and then create the database in the Database Properties window that appears.

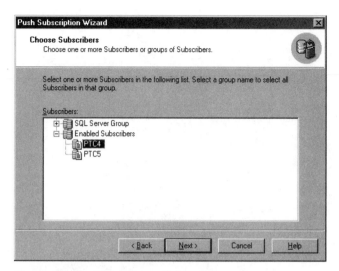

Figure 28-16. *The Choose Subscribers screen.*

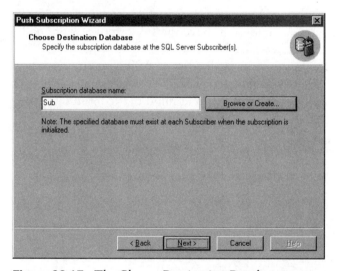

Figure 28-17. *The Choose Destination Database screen.*

5. Click Next to display the Set Merge Agent Location screen (Figure 28-18). Here you can select where the Merge Agent will run. You can accept the default setting, which specifies that the Merge Agent will run on the distributor, or you can select to run the agent on the subscriber. You should accept the default setting unless your distributor is extremely busy.

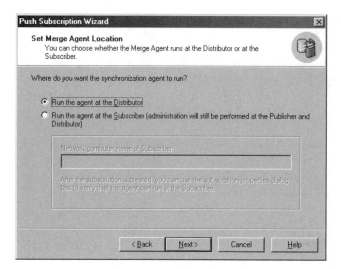

Figure 28-18. *The Set Merge Agent Location screen.*

6. Click Next to display the Set Merge Agent Schedule screen, shown in Figure 28-19. Here you can choose to have the subscription continually updated or to have it updated based on a schedule you specify. Click Change to display the Edit Recurring Job Schedule dialog box. Here you can easily configure a recurring schedule. When deciding how often the subscription should be updated, keep in mind that continuous updates use a lot of overhead.

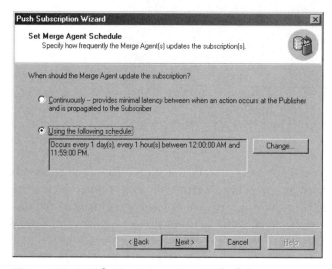

Figure 28-19. *The Set Merge Agent Schedule screen.*

7. Click Next to display the Initialize Subscription screen, shown in
   Figure 28-20. In this screen, you specify whether the subscription needs
   to be initialized. The option to initialize the schema and data set on the
   subscriber is selected by default. In this screen, you can also start the
   Snapshot Agent if it is not already started. It's a good idea to start the
   Snapshot Agent when you initialize the snapshot; otherwise, you must
   start the agent by hand. Once the snapshot has been initialized and
   replication begins, you don't need to use a snapshot until the next
   time you create a subscription. Each time you create a subscription,
   create a new snapshot, and don't bother creating snapshots on a regular schedule unless you plan on resynchronizing the subscriber database with the snapshots.

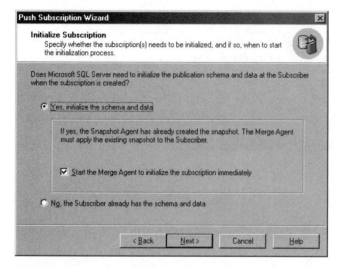

Figure 28-20. *The Initialize Subscription screen.*

8. Click Next to display the Set Subscription Priority screen, shown in
   Figure 28-21. Here you can set the priority of the subscription, which
   will be used to determine the winner in a conflict. The default setting
   (recommended) specifies that the priority setting on the publisher will
   be used for conflict resolution.

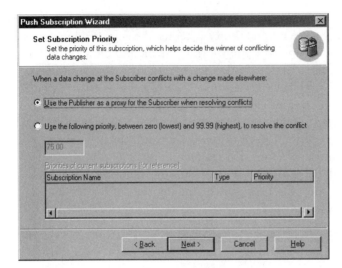

Figure 28-21. *The Set Subscription Priority screen.*

9. Click Next to display the Start Required Services screen, shown in Figure 28-22, which enables you to start SQL Server Agent if it is not already started.

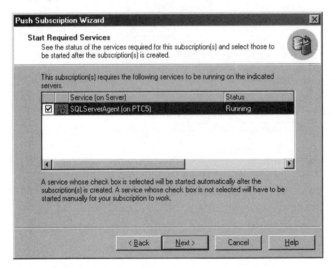

Figure 28-22. *The Start Required Services screen.*

10. Click Next to display the Completing The Push Subscription Wizard screen (Figure 28-23). Review your settings, and then click Finish to begin the copying of the snapshot to the subscriber. Once you have completed this wizard, the push subscription is created and will be updated on a regular basis.

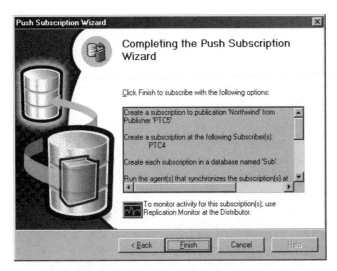

Figure 28-23. *The Completing The Push Subscription Wizard screen.*

Managing Replication

You now know how to create and configure a replicated database in a SQL Server 2000 environment. To manage this replicated environment or troubleshoot if the replication has not started, you'll use the monitoring capabilities and configuration options in Enterprise Manager.

Monitoring and Managing Replication Agents

The replication agents can be found in the Replication Monitor folder in Enterprise Manager. To access the agents, follow these steps:

1. Expand a server group, expand a server, and then expand the Replication Monitor folder.

2. If the server you expanded is a publisher, Publishers and Agents folders will appear under the Replication Monitor folder. The Publishers folder contains the publishers that belong to this server. The Agents folder contains folders for the Snapshot Agents, the Log Reader Agents, the Distribution Agents, the Merge Agents, and miscellaneous agents that are used for cleanup and historical logging.

3. Although agents do not normally need to be started or stopped, you can use Replication Monitor to do so. If your replicated system does not seem to be working after you have configured it, chances are that the Snapshot Agent has not been started, probably because the agent is using the default schedule. (This is why during the configuration process you have the option of performing the initial snapshot immediately.) Check the status of the agents by clicking an agent folder in Enterprise Manager and viewing information about the agents in the right-hand pane. An example of this is shown in Figure 28-24. Here you can determine whether the agent has been run, and you can start it if necessary. Once you have started the agent, it will run until it has completed its job, and then it will become inactive. SQL Server Agent will then start the replication agent on its regular schedule.

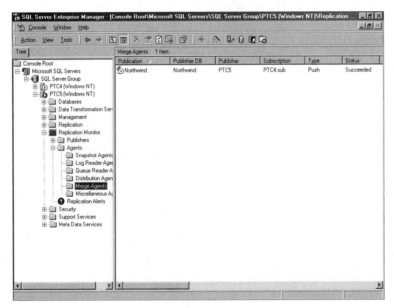

Figure 28-24. *A Merge Agent shown in Enterprise Manager.*

4. Right-click the agents to display a shortcut menu containing a number of options you can use to monitor and manage the agents. The menu that appears when you right-click a Merge Agent is shown in Figure 28-25.

The options available for a Merge Agent are described here:

- **Error Details**   Lists the details of any errors that have occurred.
- **Agent History**   Lists the agent's activities.

- **Agent Properties**   Lets you modify the replication agent's schedule. You can also modify the database access method, the agent's tasks, and notifications. For example, you can choose to receive e-mail messages notifying you of agent events.

- **Agent Profiles**   Lets you view and modify agent parameters such as login time-outs, batch size, and query time-outs.

- **Run Agent At Subscriber**   Lets you specify to run the agent on the subscriber.

- **Run Agent At Distributor**   Lets you specify to run the agent on the distributor.

- **Start Agent and Stop Agent**   Let you start the agent if it is stopped or stop the agent if it is started.

- **Refresh Rate And Settings**   Lets you modify how often Performance Monitor data is refreshed.

- **Select Columns**   Lets you specify which columns are viewed in the results pane.

- **Show Anonymous Subscriptions**   Specifies whether anonymous subscriptions are shown in this window.

- **Help**   Provides help information for this window.

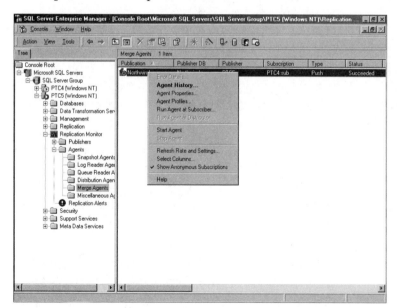

Figure 28-25. *The Merge Agent options.*

Configuring the Merge Agent

Once you have created a publication, you might want to modify the behavior of the Merge Agent. For example, you can specify how the Merge Agent is invoked by selecting which mode it runs in. In continuous mode, the Merge Agent is started when SQL Server Agent is started. In scheduled mode, which is the preferred mode, the Merge Agent starts according to a schedule and becomes inactive whenever all of the replicated transactions have been delivered. To configure the Merge Agent, follow these steps:

1. In Enterprise Manager, expand a server, expand the Replication Monitor folder, expand the Agents folder, and then click the Merge Agents folder.

2. In the right-hand pane of Enterprise Manager, right-click the publication and choose Agent Properties from the shortcut menu that appears.

3. The Merge Agent's Properties window appears, as shown in Figure 28-26.

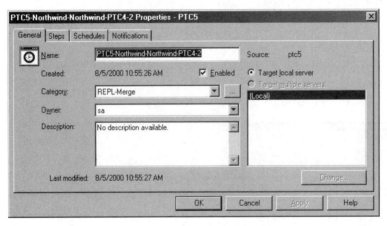

Figure 28-26. *The General tab of a Merge Agent's Properties window.*

4. Click the Steps tab, shown in Figure 28-27. On this tab, you will see the steps that the Merge Agent performs whenever it is invoked. The three steps are listed and described here:

   - **Merge Agent Startup Message** Logs a message into the Log Reader Agent history table (the *MSLogreader_history* table in the distribution database).

   - **Run Agent** Starts the agent according to the specified schedule. When running in continuous mode, the agent will run until the system is shut down.

   - **Detect Nonlogged Agent Shutdown** Puts a message into the Log Reader Agent history table in the event of an agent failure.

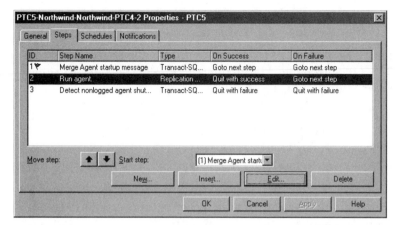

Figure 28-27. *The Steps tab of a Merge Agent's Properties window.*

5. Select the Run Agent step, and click Edit to display the Edit Job Step dialog box, shown in Figure 28-28. This dialog box allows you to configure how the Merge Agent is invoked.

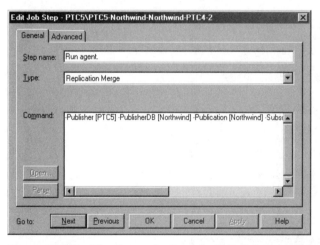

Figure 28-28. *The General tab of the Edit Job Step dialog box.*

Many options can be configured for the Merge Agent. The default Merge Agent parameters can be modified in the Command box of the Edit Job Step dialog box and in the Replication Agent Profile Details dialog box (described later in this section). Two of the parameters you can modify in the Edit Job Step dialog box are described here:

- **Continuous**   Specifies whether the Merge Agent runs in continuous mode or in scheduled mode. To specify scheduled mode, remove this parameter.

- *DistributorSecurityMode* Specifies whether the Merge Agent uses SQL Server or Windows NT authentication mode.

In addition, you can specify other options in the Edit Job Step dialog box, such as *LoginTimeout*, *PollingInterval*, *QueryTimeout*, distributor and publisher information, and *Output*.

More Info An explanation of these options can be found in SQL Server Books Online. Look up "Merge Agent, starting" in the Books Online index.

6. Once you have finished modifying the Merge Agent's properties, click OK to save your changes.

You can modify additional options via the Merge Agent's profile. To modify the profile, follow these steps:

1. In the right-hand pane of Enterprise Manager, right-click the Merge Agent, as described earlier in this section, and choose Agent Profiles from the shortcut menu that appears. This will invoke the Merge Agent Profiles dialog box, as shown in Figure 28-29.

Figure 28-29. *The Merge Agent Profiles dialog box.*

Notice that this dialog box contains many more options than does the Log Reader Agent Profiles dialog box you saw in Chapter 27. These profiles provide a range of functionality so that you can choose a profile that best suits your system's specific configuration.

2. Click New Profile to create a new profile. The current profile cannot be modified. This will invoke the Replication Agent Profile Details dialog box as shown in Figure 28-30.

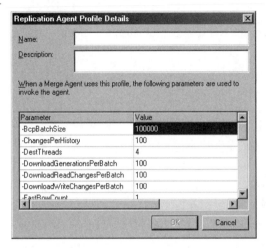

Figure 28-30. *The Replication Agent Profile Details dialog box.*

3. In this dialog box, you can modify the following parameters:

- *BcpBatchSize*   Specifies the number of rows to be sent in a bulk copy operation. This is used mainly for logging.

- *ChangesPerHistory*   Specifies the threshold above which uploading and downloading messages are logged.

- *DownloadGenerationsPerBatch*   Specifies the number of generations to be downloaded in a batch.

- *DownloadReadChangesPerBatch*   Specifies the number of changes to be read in a batch.

- *DownloadWriteChangesPerBatch*   Specifies the number of changes to be applied in a batch.

- *FastRowCount*   Specifies the type of validation to be used. The value *1* specifies a fast method, and the value *0* indicates a rowcount method.

- *HistoryVerboseLevel*   Specifies how much information is logged.

- *KeepAliveMessageInterval*   Specifies the number of seconds between heartbeat checking, a technique performed by members of the replication set to determine if other members are functioning.

- *LoginTimeout* Specifies the number of seconds that the Merge Agent will wait before timing out.
- *MaxDownloadChanges* Specifies the maximum number of downloads in a single session.
- *MaxUploadChanges* Specifies the maximum number of uploads in a single session.
- *MaxDeadlockRetries* Specifies the number of times that the agent will retry if a deadlock occurs.
- *PollingInterval* Specifies how often the transaction log on the publisher is polled for new transactions.
- *QueryTimeout* Specifies how many seconds a query waits before timing out.
- *UploadGenerationsPerBatch* Specifies the number of generations of uploads to be processed in a single batch.
- *UploadReadChangesPerBatch* Specifies the number of reads to be processed in a single batch.
- *UploadWriteChangesPerBatch* Specifies the number of writes to be processed in a single batch.
- *Validate* Specifies whether validation should be done at the end of the session.
- *ValidateInterval* Specifies how often validation should be done, if at all, when the agent is running in continuous mode.

  If the Merge Agent is running in scheduled mode rather than continuous mode, it will be invoked by SQL Server Agent, and it will process the number of changes specified by *MaxUploadChanges* and *MaxDownloadChanges* before terminating.

Disabling Replication

You can easily disable all or some replication operations on your system by using Enterprise Manager's replication wizards to remove certain replication components. In this section, you'll learn how to accomplish this simple task.

Removing Push Subscriptions

To remove a push subscription, use Enterprise Manager on the distributor system to invoke the Push Subscription Wizard. The Create And Manage Publications dialog box appears after you invoke this wizard. In the Databases And Publications list box, select the subscription you want to delete, and then click Delete Publication. You will be prompted to verify that you want to delete the subscription. Click Yes to drop the subscription.

Removing Pull Subscriptions

To remove a pull subscription, use Enterprise Manager on the subscriber system to invoke the Pull Subscription Wizard. The Create And Manage Publications dialog box appears after you invoke this wizard. In the Databases And Publications list box, select the subscription you want to delete, and then click Delete Publication. You will be prompted to verify that you want to delete the subscription.

Removing Distribution and Publications

To drop distribution and publications, you must invoke the Disable Publishing And Distribution Wizard. In the first screen of this wizard, you specify whether you want to disable all distribution and publications or to remove just publications. If you choose the first option, all publishing, distribution, and publications will be removed. If you accept the second option (the default), only the publications will be removed. You then select the publications you want to disable. After you have made your selection, you will be presented with a verification screen, giving you one last chance to change your mind. Click Yes to remove the replication components you selected in this wizard.

Monitoring and Tuning the Merge Replication System

This section explains how to monitor and tune a merge replication system for optimal performance. Additionally, this section presents some configuration guidelines for merge replication systems. This section also includes a review of the attributes of merge replication.

Attributes of Merge Replication

Merge replication is quite different from the other replication methods. Unlike transactional replication and snapshot replication, merge replication is not a one-way replication method. Modifications can be made either on the publisher or on any number of subscribers. Additionally, with transactional replication, the transaction log is read to track changes, which is an operation external to the normal operations of SQL Server, whereas with merge replication, triggers are created on the replicated tables in order to track changes to them.

Merge replication begins with the application of a snapshot, but because this operation occurs only once, you don't have to tune the snapshot replication process. The merge system creates tables on both the publisher and the distributor in order to perform the replication. In addition, a new column that holds a unique row identifier is added to every replicated table. This is used to uniquely identify each row so that the replication agent can effectively track changes.

When a row is inserted or modified, the trigger marks that row for replication. At a later time, the Merge Agent is activated, collects all marked rows, and sends them to the distributor for replication. At the same time, the Merge Agent modifies any rows in the publisher's tables that have been modified in the tables of the subscriber system or systems. In this way, two-way replication is accomplished.

Configuring Merge Replication

When you use merge replication, properly configuring the participating systems' I/O subsystems and the network is extremely important in improving replication performance, just as it is when you use other replication methods. You can also improve merge replication performance by configuring the merge batch size. By increasing the batch size, you ensure that fewer, larger batches will be used, which is more efficient. In addition, you might want to tune snapshot replication; however, because the application of the snapshot occurs only once, you can skip this step. Finally you can modify the Merge Agent; this process was described earlier in this chapter. In this section, I/O configuration and merge batch size configuration are described.

Configure Sufficient I/O Capacity

By configuring sufficient I/O capacity, you can enhance the performance of the entire replication process. As on any SQL Server system, the transaction log on a system participating in replication should be located on its own RAID 1 volume for data protection. The data files should be located on one or more RAID 10 or RAID 5 volumes. Like transactional replication, merge replication requires only minor adjustments to standard I/O configurations.

Configuring the I/O Subsystem on the Publisher   In general, you should follow the standard SQL Server configuration guidelines described throughout this book when you are configuring the publisher's I/O subsystem. Unlike transactional replication, merge replication puts no additional load on the transaction log, so follow standard tuning guidelines when you configure the I/O capacity for the log.

Configuring the I/O Subsystem on the Distributor   The distributor should be configured such that the distribution database has its transaction log on a dedicated RAID 1 disk volume. This will allow the distribution database's log to achieve maximum performance, thus improving the performance of the distributor.

Configuring the I/O Subsystem on the Subscriber   Because merge replication is multidirectional, the subscriber and publisher are similarly tuned. Simply follow the general sizing and configuration guidelines described throughout this book.

Configure the Merge Batch Size

In busy systems, you can improve merge replication performance by configuring the merge batch size. The merge batch size determines how many changed rows are copied to the distributor at a time. When the batch size is increased, fewer, larger batches are sent, which might be more efficient.

Monitoring the Merge Replication System

You monitor merge replication via Windows 2000 Performance Monitor (perfmon). Within perfmon are a number of objects that are added when SQL Server replication is used. These objects include the following:

- *SQLServer:Replication Agents*   Provides the number of each type of agent that is running.

- *SQLServer:Replication Merge*   Provides data about merge rates. This includes information about conflicts per second, uploads per second, and downloads per second. This information does not really help with tuning merge replication.

The SQL Server merge replication counters are not extremely helpful for determining performance problems. The best way to tune a merge replication system is to simply tune it as you would any SQL Server system and to pay special attention to how the network is performing. Look for bottlenecks in the places they normally occur on a network, and follow the guidelines presented in this chapter and the previous two chapters to determine whether the distributor is overloaded.

Tuning the Merge Replication System

The main steps in tuning the merge replication system are to properly configure and monitor it, as described in the preceding sections, paying particular attention to I/O and network performance. You can monitor the system via perfmon, but, as mentioned, perfmon will not provide highly useful merge replication data. Instead, you must rely on other SQL Server counters and Microsoft Windows 2000 counters to tune the system.

As mentioned in Chapter 24, you might want to modify the BCP batch size and the merge batch size if your system is doing a lot of updates. By increasing the BCP batch size, you will increase the performance of the application of the original snapshot. By increasing the merge batch size, you will ensure that more changes are copied at a time, which might be more efficient. When more changes are copied at a time, the system is affected less often, but it must handle more work during the replication operation.

In addition, you can change the polling interval. However, this is not recommended. The default polling interval is usually adequate. Before tuning the polling interval, try changing the batch sizes. If you feel that you need merge replication to run more frequently or less frequently, change the polling interval.

You also need to monitor the network and increase its capacity if necessary, just as you do if you use snapshot or transactional replication. If your system does not appear to be performing optimally—for example, if CPUs and I/O subsystems are reaching their capacity and if the replication process seems to be taking too long—you might have a network problem. Perfmon does not have a counter that will show you network problems. A network-monitoring product such as Microsoft Systems Management Server (SMS) should be used. Monitor the network card to see if it's reaching its capacity. If your network is reaching its capacity, either purchase faster network cards or add a private network for replication, backup and recovery, or both. Finally remember that the publisher, distributor, and subscribers are SQL Server systems. You should thus tune these systems just as you would tune any other SQL Server system. Tuning guidelines for SQL Server systems are given throughout this book.

Summary

This chapter completes the three-chapter series about SQL Server replication. In this chapter, you learned how merge replication works, why you might want to use merge replication, and how to properly configure, monitor, and tune merge replication. In the next chapter, you will learn what Microsoft Analysis Services is and how to use it.

Using Microsoft SQL Server Analysis Services

Microsoft SQL Server 2000 Analysis Services, formerly called OLAP Services, is a component of SQL Server 2000 designed to assist you with online analytical processing (OLAP), with which you can access and mine data in your data warehouse and data mart. In this chapter, you'll learn what the components of Analysis Services are, how to install them, and how to use them. In addition, you'll learn about the enhancements to Analysis Services found in SQL Server 2000. Because this book is intended for SQL Server administrators, not application developers, this discussion is limited to the topics of installing, configuring, and administering Analysis Services. Application development topics are not covered here.

Note The terms "data warehouse" and "data mart" are used throughout this chapter. The term "data warehouse" is defined in a number of ways. One way to think of a data warehouse is as a repository for business data that is made up of historical data as well as current data from a company's online transaction processing (OLTP) systems. A data mart is similar to a data warehouse but contains data relating to only one aspect of the company. For example, a company could have a data warehouse containing accounts payable, accounts receivable, and human resources information, and a data mart containing only accounts payable data. Both data warehouses and data marts are usually made up of data configured in a star schema or a snowflake schema, both of which are explained later in this chapter. The concepts discussed in this chapter apply to both data warehouses and data marts. Unless otherwise noted, the term "data warehouse" is used to refer to both types of databases.

Overview of Analysis Services

Analysis Services is a set of tools provided to assist you in developing and managing data used in online analytical processing. Analysis Services consists of the Analysis Service server, English Query, and other supporting components. The Analysis Service server constructs cubes of data to assist in multidimensional analysis. The term "cube" is used to describe aggregate data. This aggregate, or summary, data is used for complex analytical queries such as monthly sales re-sults and sales projections. (Cubes are described in more detail in the section "OLAP Cubes" later in this section.)

In multidimensional analysis, multiple queries look at a database from different points of view, or dimensions. Let's look at an example. Imagine a bicycle store database in which sales data for the last year is kept. One query in a multidimensional analysis operation can look at customer buying habits. Another query can look at monthly sales. Yet another query can look at sales of a particular bicycle or component. Although the data is shared by all of these queries, each query takes a different view (dimension) of the data.

Analysis Services Components

Analysis Services provides a number of tools and wizards you can use to access multidimensional data. Analysis Services consists of the following components:

- **Analysis Manager**   Provides a graphical user interface for accessing the Analysis services such as building cubes, managing security, and browsing data sources.

- **Data Warehousing Framework**   Consists of a set of components and APIs that implement SQL Server's data warehousing features.

- **Data Transformation Services (DTS)**   Assists in loading and transforming data into the data mart or data warehouse. DTS consists of an Import Wizard and an Export Wizard that allow for movement of data as well as data transformation. DTS is described in detail in Chapter 24.

- **Repository**   Contains a number of interfaces, database schema models, and predefined data transformations to fit into the Data Warehousing Framework. Because data transformations occur on a regular basis, their definitions can be stored for future reuse.

- **Data Mining**   Provide algorithms for defining and implementing multidimensional cubes.

- **English Query**   Transforms English-language questions into SQL statements that can be run against the database.

- **Extensible Markup Language (XML)**   Provides a standard formatting and data representation language. XML is a key component of application-to-application data transfer and is used for publishing data to the Internet.

As you'll see in this chapter, these components fit together like pieces in a puzzle to provide a uniform tool.

OLAP Cubes

The primary form of data representation within Analysis Services is the OLAP cube. A *cube* is a multidimensional representation of both detail and summary data. *Detail data* is specific row data, whereas *summary data* is aggregate data. Cubes are designed based on the analytical requirements set by the data itself. Each cube represents a different business entity, such as sales or inventory. Each side of the cube presents a different dimensional picture of the data. In other words, a cube consists of various planes of data, hence the term "cube of data."

Analysis Services cubes are built using one of two types of database schemas: the star schema or the snowflake schema. (Even though the topic of schemas is really a development topic, this chapter briefly describes the two types of schemas just mentioned so that you can better understand Analysis Services.) Both the star schema and the snowflake schema are composed of fact tables and dimension tables. Analysis Services aggregates the data in these tables to create the cubes. Let's look at this process in a bit more detail.

Fact Tables

A *fact table* is the table in the data warehouse that stores historical data. This historical data is the core information of the data warehouse. In our bicycle store example, this information is a record of transactions (both database transactions and sales transactions) that have occurred in the bicycle store. This record includes data such as the transaction date, transaction type, item sold, dollar amount of the transaction, customer name, and salesperson name. This record can be used as the basis for the multidimensional analysis.

As you can see, fact table data revolves around a business transaction. This transaction can be the sale of an item, a credit card transaction, a return, and so on. In essence, the fact table records some type of business event.

The fact table in a data warehouse is the largest table of the database and experiences the most activity. As you might imagine, the fact table can contain millions of records and can take up over a terabyte (or 1024 gigabytes) of space.

Dimension Tables

A *dimension table* is used to define the fields in the fact table—for example, the salesperson name, the transaction type, or the item. This process is similar to normalization, or the breaking down of data into groups for more efficient processing. While the fact table contains historical information about transactions, the dimension tables contain information that is used to derive useful material from the fact table. In other words, dimension tables are used to specify the meaning of the data contained in the fact table.

For example, a fact table containing sales records might have a dimension table containing information about sales representatives that is used to create summary data such as monthly sales per salesperson. And it might have a dimension table containing regional data that is used to create summary data such as monthly data per region.

Unlike the fact table, dimension tables are usually quite small and contain only a few rows each. A data warehouse contains usually only one or two fact tables but typically several dimension tables.

Schemas

The star schema, or flat schema, is common in data warehouses. This schema consists of a single fact table and several dimension tables. The star schema is usually represented as a fact table surrounded by dimension tables, in the shape of a star. Each dimension table corresponds to a column in the fact table. The dimension tables are used to form the basis of the analysis on the data in the fact table.

In a snowflake schema, or multidimensional schema, several dimension tables are joined before being joined to the fact table—in other words, several layers of dimension tables are created, and each layer corresponds to a column in the fact table. The star and snowflake schemas are illustrated in Figure 29-1.

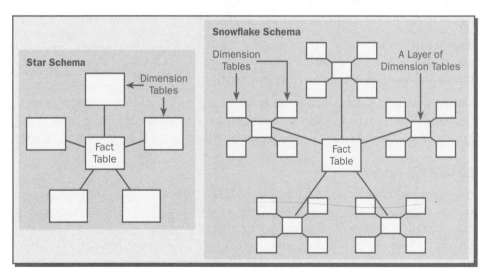

Figure 29-1. *The star and snowflake schemas.*

Data Aggregation

Analysis Services creates aggregates of columns in the fact table based on the data in the dimension tables. So, for example, dimension tables that relate to employees can be used to create summations of sales data by employee. Dimension tables related to items can be used to create summations of data based on items. Because the aggregations based on the dimension tables create different slices, or dimensions, of the data, a virtual cube of data is formed, as described earlier.

The OLAP cubes created by Analysis Services are essentially the aggregation functions that are calculated according to the star or snowflake schema. You use the Analysis Services Wizard to create these aggregations, which you use as you will to create business models and make business decisions.

Metadata

The term "metadata" is used to describe data about data. Thus, the summary and detail data that is used to describe the data in the database is considered metadata. In the example we've been using, the sales table and surrounding dimension tables represent the data. The summary information that we create (sales by salesperson, sales by item) is the metadata. The ability to create metadata (summary tables or aggregations) is the main benefit provided by Analysis Services. With Analysis Services, you can create the metadata easily and then get on with other work without having to maintain this data by hand.

Data Analysis Enhancements in SQL Server 2000

SQL Server 2000 incorporates several enhancements and new features for data analysis and data warehouses. These enhancements provide additional tools and information to aid in the data analysis process. In this section, you'll learn about some of the major enhancements.

Data-Mining Enhancements

Analysis Services includes new data-mining technology that can be used to discover data relationships in both relational databases and OLAP cubes. These relationships can be added to existing OLAP cubes to provide additional data analysis. One unique new data-mining feature is the Microsoft Decision Tree. The Decision Tree uses sophisticated classification techniques and algorithms to analyze data. The decision tree process then constructs one or more decision trees that can be used to perform predictive analysis on new data. For example, a decision tree could be constructed to analyze the credit history and buying history of potential customers at our bicycle store. This decision tree could thus be used to predict the credit worthiness of a customer.

Another new data-mining feature in Analysis Services is the use of clustering. The clustering technology used in data mining is completely different from the type of clustering described in Chapter 12. When Analysis Services performs clustering, it uses an algorithm called the nearest-neighbor algorithm to quickly group data records into clusters that have similar characteristics. Many times, these relationships are not obvious or intuitive. Thus, clustering technology can open up new avenues of data analysis.

Additionally, the SQL Server data-mining components incorporate new wizards and dialog boxes that make them easy to use. These enhancements enable the DBA to quickly perform most of the tasks involved in creating and maintaining a data mart or data warehouse.

Dimension Enhancements

SQL Server 2000 contains several enhancements to dimension tables. SQL Server now supports parent/child dimensions, relational OLAP (ROLAP) dimensions, and write-enabled dimensions.

The parent/child dimension allows the definition of hierarchies that are based on parent/child links between the members in a source table. An example of a parent/child relationship is assembling a component from parts. A single part, the parent, can have many subcomponents, the children. Using a parent/child dimension "ties" the subcomponents to the part when data analysis is performed.

A ROLAP dimension alleviates the size limitations inherent in the standard multidimensional OLAP (MOLAP) model that Analysis Services uses. The MOLAP model allows dimensions containing up to approximately 5 million members. Once the member set grows beyond this limit, a ROLAP dimension is required. The ROLAP model can grow extremely large, but the MOLAP model significantly outperforms ROLAP when querying the member set. For that reason, you should define ROLAP models only on dimensions that are extremely large.

When a write-enabled dimension is used, the members of the dimension can be updated by using Analysis Manager and client applications that support dimension write-back. SQL Server roles are used to control the client applications' write access to the dimension. SQL Server roles are explained in Chapter 34.

Security Enhancements

SQL Server 2000 also includes security enhancements that enable you to better protect the data used in the analysis of your business, which can be extremely sensitive. The enhancements include changes to the security of dimension tables, cell security features, and support for additional authentication techniques.

The dimension tables now function within the role-based security model of SQL Server. For each role defined, you can limit access to the individual dimensions, levels, and members. In addition, you can set read and read/write permissions on those resources. SQL Server 2000 supports role-based security on both FAT-based and NTFS-based systems.

SQL Server 2000 allows you to apply roles at the level of a cube's cell. Analysis Manager includes dialog boxes that allow you to control a role's access to any combination of a cube's cells. In addition, you can vary the cube's read and read/write permissions for each role.

Because it includes the Windows 2000 security model, SQL Server 2000 allows the Kerberos protocol, NT License Manager Security Support Provider, or any other provider that uses the Security Support Provider Interface (SSPI) to perform authentication when a user or an application requests access to cubes and their data. This allows you to use a consistent security model across all levels of your SQL Server installation.

English Query Enhancements

English Query has been enhanced in SQL Server 2000 to provide greater integration with the Microsoft Visual Studio 6 suite of products. This allows developers to integrate English statements rather than T-SQL statements into applications. In addition, a new graphical authoring tool is included to assist in the development of English Query statements. SQL Server 2000 also includes the SQL Project Wizard, which automatically creates the underlying database structures to support English Query, alleviating some of the complexity of setting up an English Query environment. The wizard scans the tables of a database and builds the associated SQL Server components.

Installing Analysis Services

Analysis Services is installed with SQL Server 2000 as part of the SQL Server 2000 Components. To install Analysis Services, follow the steps on the next page.

1. From the SQL Server 2000 installation menu, click SQL Server 2000 Components, and then click Install Analysis Services. The Welcome screen appears.

2. Click Next to advance to the Software License Agreement dialog box. After you read and agree to the license, click Yes.

3. The Select Components dialog box appears, as shown in Figure 29-2. In this dialog box, you choose the components of Analysis Services that you want to install. Choose all of the components by selecting the check box adjacent to each component's name. If you have already installed a particular component, you will not be able to alter its check box. To select a new installation location for Analysis Services, click Browse. Click Next when you have chosen a destination folder.

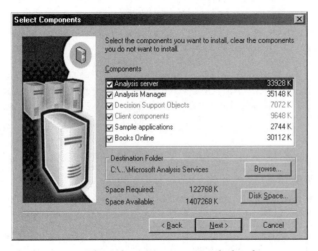

Figure 29-2. *The Select Components dialog box.*

4. The Data Folder Location dialog box appears, as shown in Figure 29-3. This dialog box looks similar to the Choose A Destination Location dialog box. However, here you choose a location for the Data folder. You can click Browse to specify a location other than the default. Click Next when you have chosen a Data folder location.

5. The Select Program Folder dialog box appears, as shown in Figure 29-4. Here you choose the folder that will house the Analysis Services option. The default setting is normally acceptable. Click Next to complete the installation.

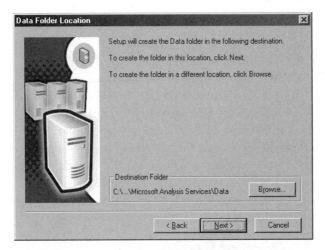

Figure 29-3. *The Data Folder Location dialog box.*

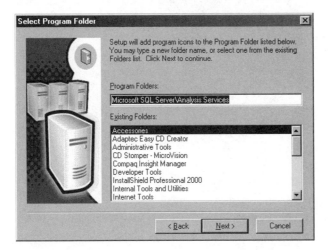

Figure 29-4. *The Select Program Folder dialog box.*

Once you have completed the Analysis Services installation, you can install English Query. The English Query option is considered to be a part of Analysis Services, but it is installed separately. You don't have to install English Query to use Analysis Services. To install English Query, follow these steps:

1. From the SQL Server 2000 Installation menu, click SQL Server 2000 Components, and then click Install English Query. The installation process will first install the Microsoft Data Access Components (MDAC) and the Microsoft Visual Studio Components. Once these

components are installed, the welcome screen appears. Click Continue to proceed.

2. The Software License Agreement dialog box appears. After you read and agree to the license, click I Agree.

3. The Microsoft English Query 2000 Setup dialog box appears, as shown in Figure 29-5. Here you choose an installation type—Complete or Run-time Only. A Complete installation installs all components, while a Run-time Only installation allows you to specify which components to install. You can also specify an installation folder, but the default is usually acceptable. Unless you are an expert in English Query, click Complete. The English Query Components will then be installed. Click OK to complete the setup.

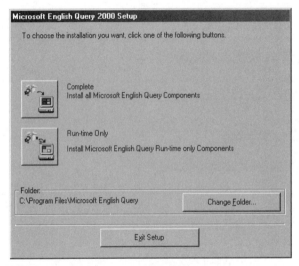

Figure 29-5. *The Microsoft English Query 2000 Setup dialog box.*

To access Analysis Services and the English Query components after you install them, click Start, point to Programs, point to Microsoft SQL Server, and then point to Analysis Services. In the Analysis Services submenu, you can choose one of the following options:

- **Analysis Manager** Invokes the primary component of Analysis Services. This component includes the wizards and utilities that enable you to use Analysis Services.

- **Books Online** Invokes the Analysis Services online documentation.

- **MDX Sample Application** Invokes a sample application that is provided with Analysis Services.

Using Analysis Services

Now that you know what Analysis Services is and how to install it, let's look at how to use the services it provides to create and manage your data warehouse. In this section, we will configure a data source, build an OLAP database on the data source, and finally build a cube on the database.

Configuring the Data Source

The first step in connecting Analysis Services to a SQL Server database is to set up an Open Database Connectivity (ODBC) system data source for the server. You accomplish this task by using the ODBC Data Sources utility located in the Administrative Tools folder. To set up a system data source, follow these steps:

1. Click Start, point to Programs, point to Administrative Tools, and then choose Data Sources (ODBC). The ODBC Data Source Administrator dialog box appears, as shown in Figure 29-6.

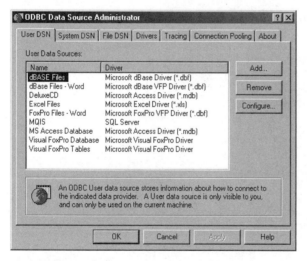

Figure 29-6. *The User DSN tab of the ODBC Data Source Administrator dialog box.*

2. Click the System DSN tab, shown in Figure 29-7. You will notice several data sources listed in the System Data Sources list box. Some of these data sources are already defined as connections to SQL Server. It is acceptable and sometimes desirable to have multiple ODBC data sources referencing the same database, depending on how the database is used. In this example, we'll create an ODBC data source that references the Northwind database.

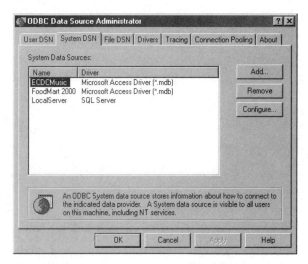

Figure 29-7. *The System DSN tab of the ODBC Data Source Administrator dialog box.*

3. Click Add. The Create New Data Source dialog box appears, as shown in Figure 29-8. In the list box, select SQL Server. Then click Finish.

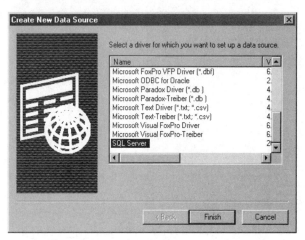

Figure 29-8. *The Create New Data Source dialog box.*

4. The Create A New Data Source To SQL Server dialog box appears, as shown in Figure 29-9. Here you must assign a name to your data source, give it a description, and specify which SQL server you want to connect to. Click Next to continue.

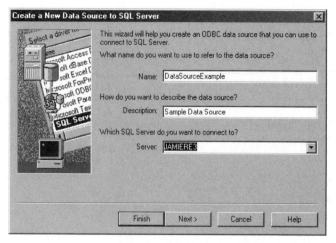

Figure 29-9. *The Create A New Data Source To SQL Server dialog box.*

5. In the next dialog box, shown in Figure 29-10, you specify the authentication mode that will be used when users connect to SQL Server. You can select Windows NT authentication or SQL Server authentication. (The user authentication modes are described in Chapter 34.) In the lower part of the dialog box, you will see a check box that is selected by default. If you do not want to log into SQL Server at this time to retrieve default information for the rest of the setup process, clear this check box. Click Next to continue.

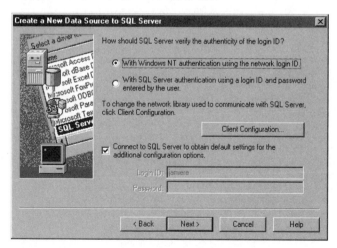

Figure 29-10. *Specifying the authentication mode.*

6. In the next dialog box, shown in Figure 29-11, you specify the database to use, the database filename, and ANSI modes. Analysis Services will allow you to select the database you will be connecting to, so providing a default database name is not necessary. However, it doesn't hurt to supply one, because other applications might use this data source name (DSN). When you are finished, click Next.

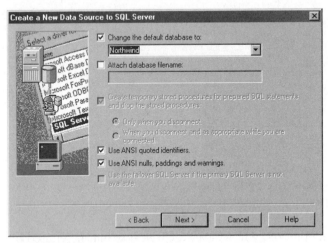

Figure 29-11. *Specifying the default database.*

7. In the next dialog box, shown in Figure 29-12, you can change the language used for SQL Server messages to a language other than English, enable translations, specify regional settings, and specify log file locations for long-running queries and driver statistics. When you are ready to continue, click Finish.

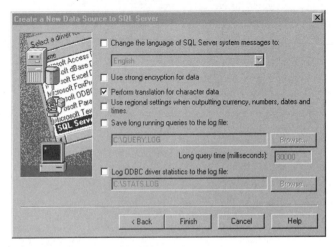

Figure 29-12. *Specifying language and other settings.*

8. The ODBC Microsoft SQL Server Setup dialog box appears, as shown in Figure 29-13. This dialog box states that a new ODBC data source will be created and lists all the options you chose for that data source.

Figure 29-13. *The ODBC Microsoft SQL Server Setup summary dialog box.*

9. You should test the data source by clicking Test Data Source. When you do this, the connection to the database will be tested. Once you have successfully tested the connection, click OK, and the DSN will be available for use.

Note   In order for you to configure and test the data source, SQL Server must be up and running.

Creating an OLAP Database

Now that you have configured and tested the ODBC data source, you're ready to create an OLAP database. Creating an OLAP database involves setting up an existing database as an OLAP database. You must be prepared to specify which tables will be used as fact tables and which will be dimension tables.

Note   In this section, we'll set up the Northwind database as an OLAP database. This database does not have all of the properties of a data mart or data warehouse, but we'll use it in this example because it comes with SQL Server, and the example can be easily reproduced.

In the OLAP database creation process, you use Analysis Manager, the Cube Wizard, the Dimension Wizard, and the Storage Design Wizard. To create the database, follow these steps:

1. Click Start, point to Programs, point to Microsoft SQL Server, point to Analysis Services, and then choose Analysis Manager. The Analysis Manager window appears, as shown in Figure 29-14.

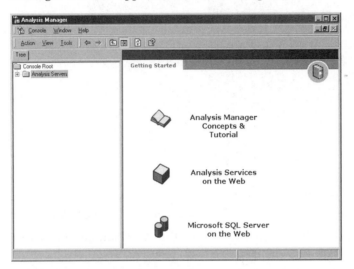

Figure 29-14. *The Analysis Manager window.*

2. Expand the Analysis Servers folder in the left pane, and then expand your server name folder. Right-click the server name and choose New Database from the shortcut menu to display the Database dialog box, shown in Figure 29-15. Name the new database and provide a brief description. In this example, we'll name the database Northwind_OLAP.

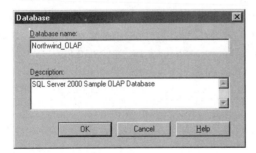

Figure 29-15. *The Database dialog box.*

Note   When you expand your server name folder, you'll see a sample database already configured in Analysis Manager. This database, named FoodMart 2000, was set up automatically if you selected the Sample Applications check box in the Select Components dialog box during Analysis Services installation.

3. Click OK to return to the Analysis Manager window. If you expand the Analysis Servers folder and expand your server name, you will see that the new database has been added. (The database is named, but it does not have a connection to the SQL Server data source—we'll take care of that shortly.) Expand the database folder (in this case, the Northwind_ OLAP folder) to reveal the Data Sources, Cubes, Shared Dimensions, Mining Models, and Database Roles folders, as shown in Figure 29-16.

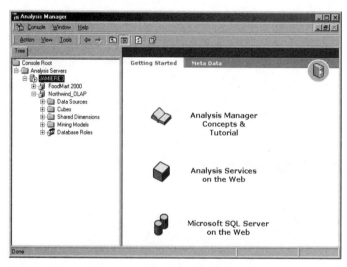

Figure 29-16. *An expanded OLAP database.*

4. Right-click the Cubes folder, point to New Cube in the shortcut menu, and then choose Wizard from the New Cube submenu. The Cube Wizard welcome screen appears, as shown in Figure 29-17. This wizard is used to select a data source, which is specified at the cube level.

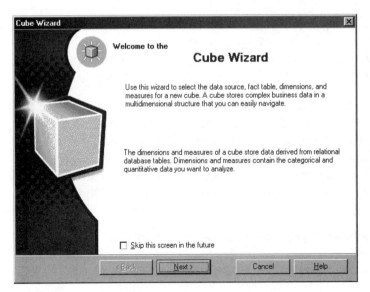

Figure 29-17. *The welcome screen of the Cube Wizard.*

5. Click Next to display the Select A Fact Table From A Data Source screen, shown in Figure 29-18. To select the SQL Server database, click New Data Source.

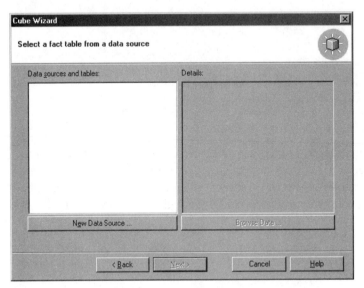

Figure 29-18. *The Select A Fact Table From A Data Source screen.*

6. The Data Link Properties window appears, as shown in Figure 29-19. On the Provider tab, you can specify a data source for the cube—however, in this case, we'll use the Connection tab to select the data source that we created earlier in this chapter.

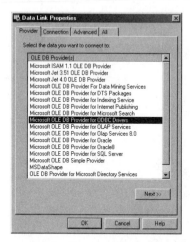

Figure 29-19. *The Provider tab of the Data Link Properties window.*

7. On the Connection tab of the Data Link Properties window (Figure 29-20), select the data source name (DataSourceExample, in this example), type the login user name and password, and enter the initial catalog to use. If you don't have an administrator password (you should have one if you are on a network), select the Blank Password check box.

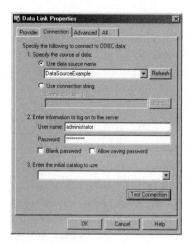

Figure 29-20. *The Connection tab of the Data Link Properties window.*

8. At this point, you should test the connection by clicking Test Connection. If the test succeeds, you will receive a "connection succeeded" message. If the test fails, you have probably entered something incorrectly. After the connection test is successful, click OK to return to the Select A Fact Table From A Data Source screen of the Cube Wizard, as shown in Figure 29-21.

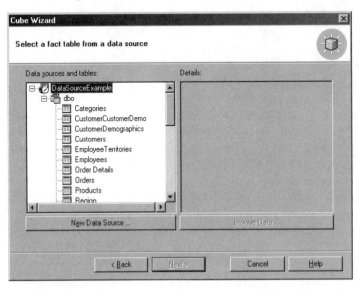

Figure 29-21. *The Select A Fact Table From A Data Source screen of the Cube Wizard, populated with data sources and tables.*

9. In the Data Sources And Tables list box of this screen, double-click a table that you want to use as the data source for your cube. In this example, we will double-click the *Orders* table. Even though the *Orders* table is not exactly a dimension table, it's similar to one. (This table is used here so that the general user can work through this example.)

10. Click Next to display the Select The Numeric Columns That Define Your Measures screen, shown in Figure 29-22. Here you can select a column or columns that define the numeric measures of the cube; these will be used for the aggregations. In this case, choose *OrderID* and *Freight* by double-clicking or by selecting each column name and clicking the right-arrow button.

11. Click Next to display the Select The Dimensions For Your Cube screen, shown in Figure 29-23. Here you select the dimension tables that will be used in this cube. In this example, we'll create a dimension table.

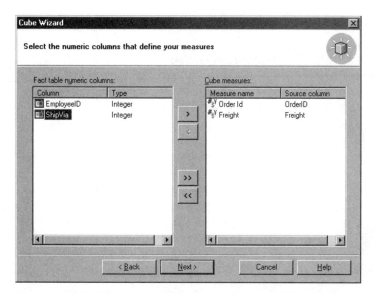

Figure 29-22. *The Select The Numeric Columns That Define Your Measures screen.*

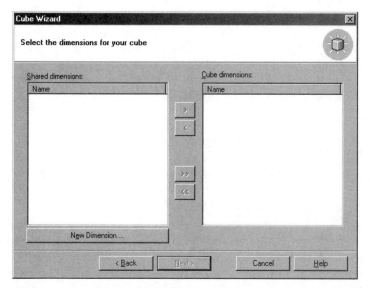

Figure 29-23. *The Select The Dimensions For Your Cube screen.*

12. Click New Dimension to display the Dimension Wizard welcome screen, shown in Figure 29-24.

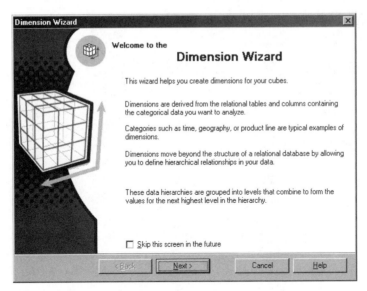

Figure 29-24. *The welcome screen of the Dimension Wizard.*

13. Click Next to continue. The Choose How You Want To Create The Dimension screen appears, as shown in Figure 29-25. In this screen, you specify how you want to create the dimension. You can choose a star schema, a snowflake schema, a parent/child relationship, a virtual dimension, or a mining model. For this example, click Star Schema.

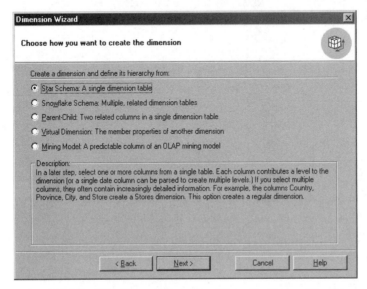

Figure 29-25. *The Choose How You Want To Create The Dimension screen.*

14. Click Next to display the Select The Dimension Table screen, shown in Figure 29-26. For this example, select the *Employees* table as the dimension table.

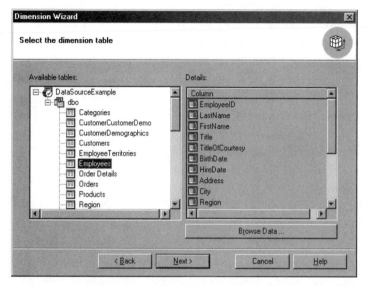

Figure 29-26. *The Select The Dimension Table screen.*

15. Click Next to display the Select The Dimension Type screen, shown in Figure 29-27. Here you can select whether to use a standard dimension or a time dimension. For this example, click Standard Dimension.

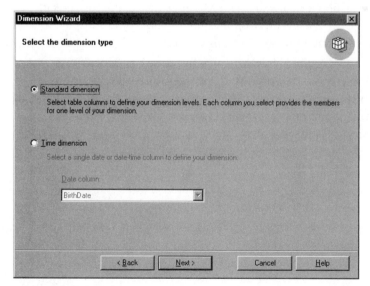

Figure 29-27. *The Select The Dimension Type screen.*

16. Click Next to display the Select The Levels For Your Dimension screen, shown in Figure 29-28. You can select several levels of aggregations in this screen, but in this simple example, we'll select only one level—Employee Id. To choose a level, select the column and click the right-arrow button, or simply double-click the column name.

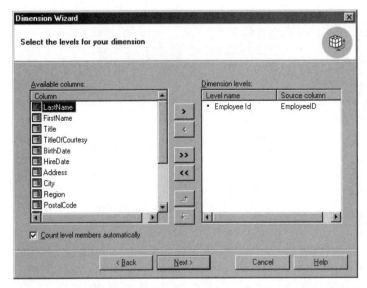

Figure 29-28. *The Select The Levels For Your Dimension screen.*

17. Click Next to display the Specify The Member Key Columns screen, shown in Figure 29-29. If you are building a cube from multiple tables, you specify the table key columns here.

18. Click Next to display the Select Advanced Options screen, shown in Figure 29-30. Here you can modify the dimension, specify the sort order used on the members, and define the storage model. If the cube you are creating is extremely large, you should specify the ROLAP storage model, as discussed previously in this chapter. If you select any of these options, the wizard will display the appropriate screens to help you make the selection. We will not discuss these screens here.

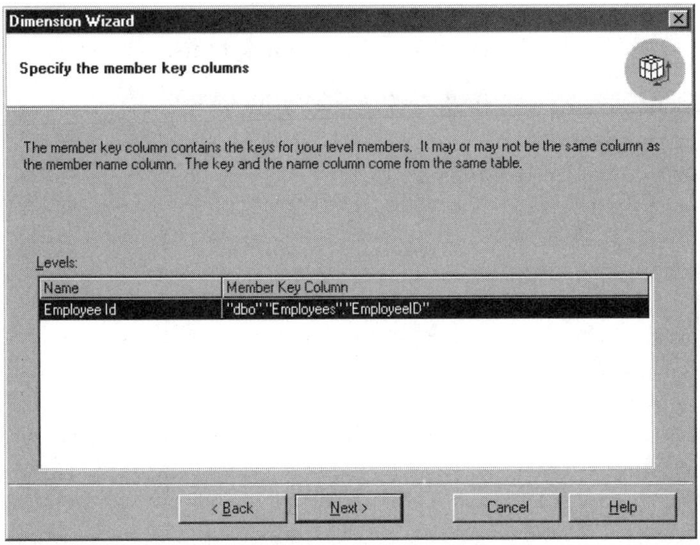

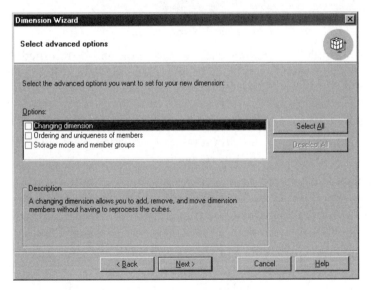

Figure 29-29. *The Specify The Member Key Columns screen.*

Figure 29-30. *The Select Advanced Options screen.*

19. Click Next to display the Finish The Dimension Wizard screen, shown in Figure 29-31. Name the dimension and then click Finish.

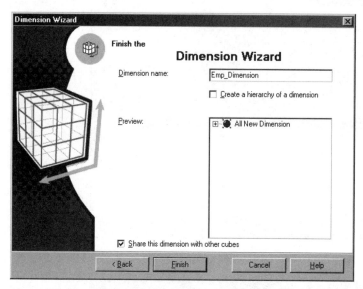

Figure 29-31. *The Finish The Dimension Wizard screen.*

20. Once you have completed the Dimension Wizard, you will be returned to the Select The Dimensions For Your Cube screen (shown earlier in Figure 29-23) of the Cube Wizard. Your new dimension appears in the Cube Dimensions list. From here, you can proceed with selecting the dimension table that is used to create the summary data on the fact table, or you can create more dimension tables by clicking New Dimension and running the Dimension Wizard again.

    To proceed, click Next. If you are asked if you want to count the rows, click yes. The Finish The Cube Wizard screen appears, as shown in Figure 29-32. All that remains to be done in this wizard is to name the cube.

21. Clicking Finish takes you to the Cube Editor window, shown in Figure 29-33. Edit the cube as necessary, and then exit the Cube Editor window by clicking the Close button. Usually, no editing is needed.

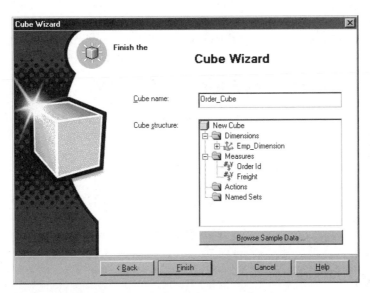

Figure 29-32. *The Finish The Cube Wizard screen.*

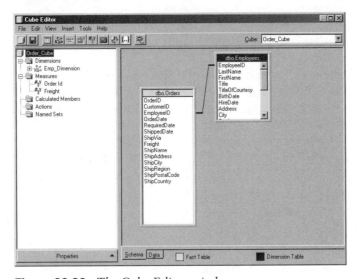

Figure 29-33. *The Cube Editor window.*

22. When you exit the Cube Editor window, you will be asked whether you want to create storage options for the cube. Click Yes. The Storage Design Wizard welcome screen appears, as shown in Figure 29-34.

Figure 29-34. *The welcome screen of the Storage Design Wizard.*

23. Click Next to display the Select The Type Of Data Storage screen, as shown in Figure 29-35. Here you specify whether you want to store your data dimensionally, relationally, or using a combination of both data types—for this example, click MOLAP to store the data within the data structures of Analysis Services. If you choose to store the data relationally (using ROLAP), the new tables will be stored in the database you are working with, in this case, Northwind database. The final option is HOLAP (Hybrid OLAP), in which the underlying data is stored relationally and the aggregation data is stored multidimensionally.

24. Click Next to display the Set Aggregation Options screen, shown in Figure 29-36, where you can specify optional ways of creating aggregates. For this example, accept the default, 100 MB, and click Start to create the aggregates.

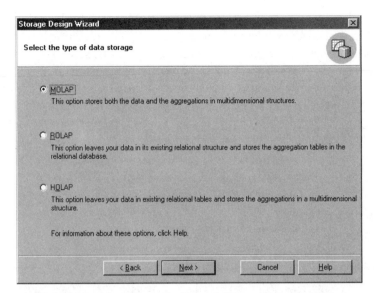

Figure 29-35. *The Select The Type Of Data Storage screen.*

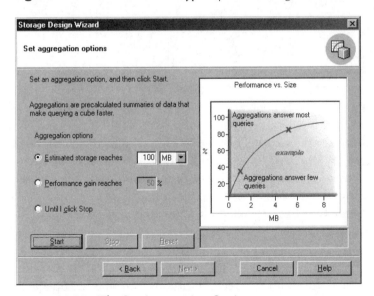

Figure 29-36. *The Set Aggregation Options screen.*

Because the table we're using in this example is such a small table, only a few seconds are needed to calculate the aggregates. The resulting aggregates are then charted, and the Set Aggregation Options screen is shown again (Figure 29-37). Note that we have not charted much in this example, so the graph is just a vertical line on the far left side of the chart.

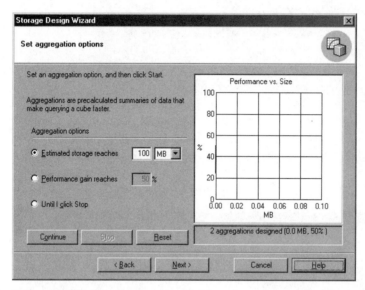

Figure 29-37. *The Set Aggregation Options screen with the aggregates charted.*

25. Click Next to display the Finish The Storage Design Wizard screen, shown in Figure 29-38. Here you specify whether to finish the Storage Design Wizard now or save your settings and wait until later. The latter option can be useful if you want to wait until after business hours, when the system load is low, to create the storage. In this example, we'll select Process Now.

26. Click Finish. The Process dialog box appears, as shown in Figure 29-39. Once the operation of creating the cube storage is complete, a message will appear at the bottom of the screen, informing you that the operation was completed successfully. Click Close to finish the process.

Figure 29-38. *The Finish The Storage Design Wizard screen.*

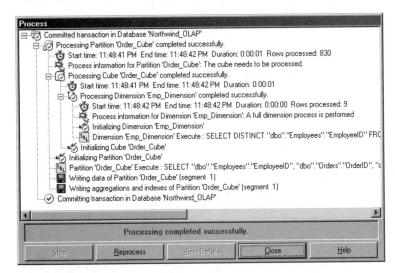

Figure 29-39. *The Process dialog box.*

Modifying an Existing OLAP Database

You modify an OLAP database through Analysis Manager in a manner similar to that in which you created the OLAP database. In this section, we'll modify the FoodMart 2000 database. The FoodMart 2000 database is provided as part of the Analysis Services installation (if you selected the Sample Applications check box during the installation). To edit a cube in the FoodMart 2000 database, follow these steps:

1. In the Analysis Manager window, expand the Analysis Servers folder, expand a server, expand the FoodMart 2000 folder, and then expand the Cubes folder, as shown in Figure 29-40.

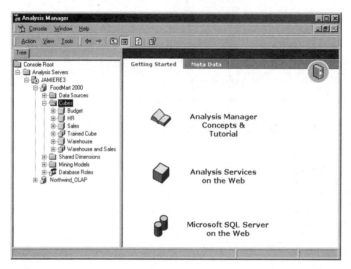

Figure 29-40. *The Analysis Manager window.*

2. Right-click the Sales folder and choose Edit from the shortcut menu. This invokes the Cube Editor window, shown in Figure 29-41. This window shows the relationships of the dimension and fact tables within the cube.

   Once you have invoked the Cube Editor window, a number of options are available to you. These options are described here:

   - **Create a new dimension.** Invoke the Dimension Manager by right-clicking either the Dimensions folder or any dimension name in the left pane. The Dimension Manager is similar to the Dimension Wizard that you saw earlier in this chapter. It is used to add new dimensions to a database or to remove existing dimensions.

- **Delete a dimension.**   Delete a dimension by right-clicking it and choosing Remove. This action will permanently remove a dimension from the database.

- **Create, delete, or rename a measure.**   Right-click the measure and choose New Measure, Delete, or Rename.

- **Create a new calculated member.**   Either right-click the Calculated Members folder or right-click a calculated member, and choose New Calculated Member.

- **Edit, delete, or rename a calculated member.**   Right-click a calculated member and then choose Edit, Delete, or Rename.

On the Schema tab of the right pane, you can right-click the headings of either dimension or fact tables and choose the following options:

- **Insert Tables**   Allows you to add tables to the database.

- **Change Alias**   Allows you to rename an existing cube property. You can define a derived cube property that is based on another cube property without changing the underlying property.

- **Browse Data**   Allows you to retrieve table data for viewing.

- **Replace**   Allows you to select a different table to replace a table that is already in the database.

- **Remove (dimension table only)**   Allows you to remove a dimension table from the database.

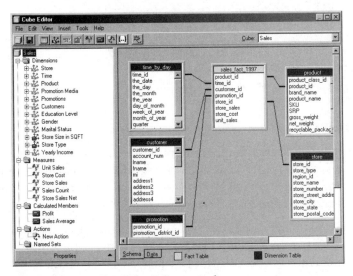

Figure 29-41. *The Cube Editor window.*

3. Choose Data from the View menu of Analysis Manager or click the Data tab to witness the true usefulness of the OLAP system. On the Data tab of the Cube Editor window, shown in Figure 29-42, you can select summary data based on criteria that you can select through a number of drop-down menus. These menus are derived from the dimensions in the cube. The Data tab is similar to the Cube Browser dialog box that we'll see in a moment.

On the Data tab, you can select different combinations of variables to achieve different views of the data. Because the summary data is already calculated, the results are instantaneous. If the summary data were not available, you would have to run individual queries. In a large data mart or data warehouse, the process of calculating the aggregates could take a long time.

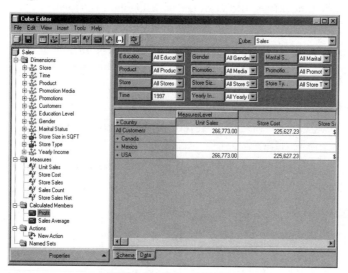

Figure 29-42. *The Data tab of the Cube Editor window.*

Processing the Data

Once you have created the cubes, a number of options are available that enable you to view and process that data. You can access many of these services by right-clicking the cube name in the left-hand pane of the Analysis Manager window. Some of these options include the following:

• **Process** Used to update the aggregates. Because the aggregates are not automatically updated when the underlying data is changed, they must be periodically updated. This process can be time consuming and should be scheduled accordingly (for nights, weekends, and so forth).

- **Design Storage**   Invokes the Storage Design Wizard. This allows you to modify the underlying storage properties of the OLAP cubes. Earlier in this chapter, you learned how to use the Storage Design Wizard.

- **Usage-Based Optimization**   Invokes the Usage Based Optimization Wizard, which helps you tune the cube by improving the aggregations based on a history of queries that have been run against them. You accomplish this by viewing the queries that have been run against the database and optimizing those queries. The Usage Based Optimization Wizard offers suggestions of ways to modify the queries or the aggregates themselves.

- **Browse Data**   Enables you to view the aggregations. Choosing the Browse Data option invokes the Cube Browser dialog box, shown in Figure 29-43 for the FoodMart 2000 database example. As you can see, this dialog box is similar to the Data tab of the Cube Editor window. In the Cube Browser dialog box, you can easily create customized results, using the stored aggregates within the cube.

- **Usage Analysis**   Invokes the Usage Analysis Wizard, which enables you to analyze queries that are sent to the cube. The Usage Analysis Wizard uses data about the queries that were run against the cube based on your criteria. This wizard is similar to the Usage Based Optimization Wizard in that it allows you to choose criteria to judge which queries take the longest time to run. The Usage Analysis Wizard, however, is used just for viewing that data.

Because Analysis Services does not automatically update the OLAP cubes and because the underlying data might change, you must update these cubes as often as you think necessary for your system. If the data is modified often and users depend on up-to-date information, you might need to update the cubes frequently. If yesterday's data is acceptable, a nightly refresh might be good enough.

You update all cubes by right-clicking the Cubes folder of the desired OLAP database folder and choosing Process All Cubes. As mentioned, if you want to update cubes individually, right-click the cube name and choose Process from the shortcut menu.

You access the SQL Server OLAP cubes through an OLE DB application, by viewing data through Analysis Manager, or by setting up a link to the OLAP database. The Cube Browser dialog box of the Analysis Manager is a useful tool for viewing data based on the cubes that you have created.

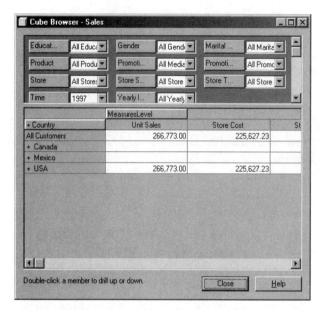

Figure 29-43. *The Cube Browser dialog box.*

However, if you have a data warehouse or data mart that is already functioning, you might find SQL Server Analysis Services difficult to merge into your existing operation because Analysis Services works by creating new data cubes that are based on your database and that are accessed via an OLE DB interface. If your current application does not use OLE DB, you might not be able to take advantage of these services.

Analysis Services can be used to perform multidimensional analysis in many types of data warehouses and data marts. From the aggregates, you can use the Cube Browser dialog box of Analysis Manager to perform multidimensional analysis. Whether you can take advantage of Analysis Services depends on how well the services it provides fit into your business.

Summary

In this chapter, you learned what Analysis Services is and how to set it up. You also learned how to create cubes and how aggregation data is maintained in a SQL Server database. The information presented in this chapter should help you determine whether Analysis Services can be of use to you. In the next chapter, you'll learn about some of the tasks and tools associated with the administration of a SQL Server installation.

Part V
Management, Tuning, Maintenance, and Troubleshooting

Chapter 30
Microsoft SQL Server Administration

Configuring your SQL servers appropriately and performing routine maintenance tasks on your databases are key to good performance. In this chapter, you'll learn about the dynamic configuration features of Microsoft SQL Server 2000, which help simplify the process of configuring the database system. And you'll learn how to use the Database Maintenance Plan Wizard to create an automated maintenance plan for your databases. Using maintenance plans is a great way to keep your databases in good health.

Automatic Configuration Features of SQL Server

SQL Server is packed with automatic features that are designed to reduce the overhead normally associated with configuring and tuning a relational database management system (RDBMS). In this section, you'll be introduced to some of these features. (Those who are familiar with Microsoft SQL Server 7 will recognize these features because they originated in SQL Server 7.) You'll learn how they work, how to use them to reduce your work as a DBA, and how to override these automatic features, if necessary.

Dynamic Memory Management

Dynamic memory management enables SQL Server to configure the amount of memory it will use for the buffer cache and for the procedure cache dynamically, based on available system memory. Because SQL Server includes dynamic memory management, the DBA does not have to manually control the size of these caches. But in certain situations, you will want to restrict the amount of memory used by SQL Server, and this is possible as well.

How Dynamic Memory Management Works

The dynamic memory management feature works by constantly monitoring the amount of physical memory available in the system. SQL Server increases or decreases the SQL Server memory pool (described in the next section) based on its needs and on the amount of available memory. This capability can be quite useful in systems where the amount of memory used is relatively stable, but it can be problematic when the amount of memory used by a system's non–SQL Server processes varies, because SQL Server will be constantly changing its memory allocation.

A computer system that is used primarily as a SQL Server database server is a good candidate for dynamic memory management. In this type of system, the amount of memory used by processes other than SQL Server is stable, so SQL Server will automatically allocate the amount of memory necessary for it to work effectively, up to the point where no more physical memory is available. Then it will maintain that amount as long as no other process requires memory. If another process does require memory, SQL Server will deallocate the amount of memory that is needed so that it is available to the other process.

A computer system that runs processes with constantly changing memory requirements and on which processes are frequently added or removed is not a good candidate for dynamic memory management. On such a system, memory usage is constantly changing, requiring SQL Server to continually allocate and deallocate memory as the other processes need it—a procedure that can be inefficient because of the extra overhead produced. This type of system might perform better if you manually allocate a fixed amount of memory for SQL Server or if you specify the minimum and maximum amounts of memory that SQL Server can allocate. You'll see how to do this later in this chapter.

Thus, whether your system will perform better using dynamic or manual memory management is determined by the volatility of the memory usage in the system. By monitoring SQL Server memory allocation, you can determine whether the amount of memory used is changing on a regular basis or remaining fairly stable. To monitor the memory usage, you can use Microsoft Windows 2000 Performance Monitor. The *Total Server Memory (KB)* counter within the *SQLServer: Memory Manager* object displays the amount of memory, in kilobytes (KB), that SQL Server is currently consuming. To find out how memory usage has changed over time, look at this counter in the chart window.

The Memory Pool

SQL Server dynamically allocates and deallocates memory in a pool. The memory pool consists of memory that is divided among the following components:

- **Buffer cache**   Holds the database data pages that have been read into memory. The buffer cache usually takes up most of the memory pool.

- **Connection memory** Used by each connection into SQL Server. Connection memory consists of data structures that keep track of each user's context and includes cursor-positioning information, query parameter values, and stored-procedure information.

- **Data structures** Consist of global information about both locks and database descriptors, including information about lock holders, about the types of locks that are held, and about various files and filegroups.

- **Log cache** Used to hold log information that will be written to the transaction log. It is also used when log information that has recently been written into the log cache is read. The log cache improves performance of log writes. The log cache is not the same as the buffer cache.

- **Procedure cache** Used to store the execution plans for Transact-SQL (T-SQL) statements and stored procedures when they are being executed.

Because memory allocation changes dynamically, if dynamic memory management is allowed, the memory pool might be constantly increasing or decreasing. Also, the five components of the memory pool can change their individual sizes dynamically. This capability is not configurable and is controlled by SQL Server. For example, if more memory is needed so that more T-SQL statements can be stored in the procedure cache, SQL Server might take some memory from the buffer cache and use it for the procedure cache.

Using Additional Memory

The amount of memory that SQL Server can access depends on the Windows operating system used. Microsoft Windows NT Server 4 supports 4 gigabytes (GB) of memory, of which 2 GB is allocated for user processes and 2 GB is reserved for system use. This 2-GB limit represents the maximum amount of memory that can be allocated for SQL Server with NT 4. But with Windows NT Server 4 Enterprise Edition, the amount of virtual memory allocated for a process is 50 percent larger—3 GB. This increase is possible because the system allocation is reduced to 1 GB. This increase in virtual memory allocated to processes allows you to increase the size of the memory pool to close to 3 GB. To enable this support in Windows NT 4 Enterprise Edition, you must add the flag */3GB* to the boot line in the Boot.ini file, which can be done through the System icon that appears in Control Panel.

For two editions of the Windows 2000 operating system, SQL Server 2000 Enterprise Edition can use the Windows 2000 Address Windowing Extensions (AWE) API to support larger address spaces. SQL Server supports close to 8 GB on Windows 2000 Advanced Server and close to 64 GB on Windows 2000 Datacenter Server. AWE is supported on only these two operating systems; it is not supported on Windows 2000 Professional. (See Chapter 2 of this book and the topic "Using AWE Memory on Windows 2000" in Books Online for more details.)

SQL Server Memory Configuration Options

The following SQL Server configuration parameters are associated with specific aspects of memory allocation. You can set these parameters by using either SQL Server Enterprise Manager or the *sp_configure* stored procedure. To view all of these parameters by using *sp_configure*, you must have the option *show advanced options* set to *1*.

- *awe enabled*   Enables SQL Server to use extended memory (the AWE memory mentioned previously). Setting this option to *1* enables it. This option is available only in SQL Server Enterprise Edition and can be set only by using *sp_configure*.

- *index create memory*   Limits the amount of memory used for sorts during index creation. The *index create memory* option is self-configuring. It should not require adjustment in most cases. However, if you experience difficulties creating indexes, you might want to try increasing the value of this option from its default value.

- *max server memory*   Sets the maximum amount of memory that SQL Server can allocate to the memory pool. Leave the default setting if you want to allow SQL Server to dynamically allocate and deallocate memory. If you want to allocate memory statically (so the amount used will not change), set this option and *min server memory* to the same value.

- *min memory per query*   Specifies the minimum amount of memory (in kilobytes) that will be allocated to execute a query.

- *min server memory*   Sets the minimum amount of memory that SQL Server can allocate to the memory pool. Leave the default value to allow dynamic memory allocation. If you want to allocate memory statically, set this option and *max server memory* to the same value.

- *set working set size*   Specifies that the memory that SQL Server has allocated cannot be swapped out, even if that memory can be more effectively used by another process. The *set working set size* option should not be used when SQL Server is allowed to allocate memory dynamically. It should be used only when *min server memory* and *max server memory* are set to the same value. In this way, SQL Server will allocate a static amount of memory as nonpageable.

Note   To take advantage of the AWE memory options, you must be running Windows 2000 Advanced Server or Windows 2000 Datacenter Server along with SQL Server 2000 Enterprise Edition.

Other Dynamic Configuration Options

Several dynamic configuration options that do not pertain to server memory are available in SQL Server. If you leave the default values of these options, SQL Server will dynamically configure them. The default values can be overridden. This is not usually necessary, but you should understand how the options work in case you do want to configure them manually.

You set configuration options by using either SQL Server Enterprise Manager (not all options can be set through Enterprise Manager) or *sp_configure*. To set an option by using *sp_configure*, open Query Analyzer or an *osql* connection in a command prompt window and run the stored procedure with its parameters, as follows:

```
sp_configure "option name", value
```

The parameter *option name* is the name of the configuration option, and *value* is the value you want to set it to. If you run this command without including the *value* parameter, SQL Server will return the current value for the specified option. To see a list of all the options and their values, run *sp_configure* with no parameters. Several options are considered to be advanced options. In order to view and configure these options by using *sp_configure*, you must first set the option *show advanced options* to *1*, as shown here:

```
sp_configure "show advanced options", 1
```

The options that are configurable through Enterprise Manager are not affected by *show advanced options*.

To set an option by using Enterprise Manager, first open the Properties window for a server in Enterprise Manager by right-clicking the server name and choosing Properties from the shortcut menu. A sample Properties window is shown in Figure 30-1.

Figure 30-1. *The General tab of a server's Properties window in Enterprise Manager.*

You can then access certain dynamic options on the window's tabbed pages. In the following sections, the non-memory-related dynamic options of SQL Server are described, and each section explains whether the option described in it can be set in Enterprise Manager, and if so, where the option can be found in the Properties window.

The *locks* Option

SQL Server dynamically configures the number of locks used in the system according to the current needs. You can set the *locks* option to indicate the maximum number of available locks, thus limiting the amount of memory SQL Server uses for locks. The default setting is *0*, which allows SQL Server to allocate and deallocate locks dynamically based on changing system requirements. SQL Server allows up to 40 percent of its total memory to be used for locks. You should leave the *locks* parameter at the default value of *0* and allow SQL Server to allocate locks as necessary. This option is an advanced option and can be set only by using *sp_configure*.

The *recovery interval* Option

The *recovery interval* value indicates the maximum number of minutes that SQL Server can spend per database to recover from a failure. (See the section "Automatic Checkpoints" later in this chapter for more details about how checkpoints work) The time SQL Server needs to recover a database depends on when the last checkpoint occurred. Therefore, the *recovery interval* value is used by SQL Server to determine dynamically when to run automatic checkpoints.

For example, each time SQL Server is shut down cleanly, checkpoints are run on all databases, and therefore, when SQL Server is restarted, recovery takes little time. But if SQL Server is forced to stop without shutting down cleanly (because of a power failure or some other type of failure), when SQL Server starts up again, it must recover each database by rolling back transactions that did not commit and rolling forward transactions that did commit but whose changes were not yet written to disk at the time of the failure. If the last checkpoint on a particular database occurs shortly before the system failure, the recovery time for that database will be shorter. If the last checkpoint occurs a long time before the system fails, the recovery time will be longer.

SQL Server determines how often to run checkpoints according to a built-in algorithm and, as mentioned, according to the *recovery interval* setting. So if you set *recovery interval* to 5, for example, SQL Server will run checkpoints on each database often enough such that the recovery of a database in case of a failure would take about 5 minutes. The default *recovery interval* value is 0, indicating automatic configuration by SQL Server. When the default setting is used, the recovery time is less than 1 minute, and a checkpoint occurs approximately every minute for active databases. In many cases, the benefit provided by frequently running checkpoints is outweighed by the performance degradation caused by running the checkpoints. Thus, over time, you should reduce the number of checkpoints performed by increasing the *recovery interval* value. The value you choose will depend on your business requirements concerning how long users can wait for the system to recover in case of a failure. Generally, a value of 5 to 15, indicating a recovery time of 5 to 15 minutes, should be used.

The *recovery interval* option is an advanced option. You can set it in Enterprise Manager by clicking the Database Settings tab of the Properties window and typing a value in the Recovery Interval (Min) box, as shown in Figure 30-2.

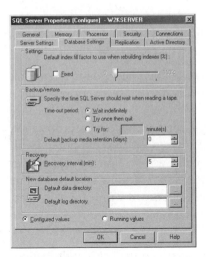

Figure 30-2. *Setting the recovery interval.*

The *user connections* Option

SQL Server dynamically configures the number of user connections allowed into SQL Server. SQL Server allows a maximum of 32,767 user connections. By setting the *user connections* option to a value other than *0*, you specify the maximum number of simultaneous user connections allowed into SQL Server. (The number of user connections allowed also depends on the limits of your applications and hardware.) User connections will still be dynamically configured, up to the maximum.

For example, if only 10 users are logged in, only 10 user connection objects are allocated. If the maximum is reached and SQL Server needs more user connections, you will get an error message stating that the maximum number of user connections has been reached.

In most cases, the default value for the *user connections* option does not need to be changed. Note that each connection does require about 40 KB of memory.

You can use SQL Server Query Analyzer and the following T-SQL statement to determine the maximum number of user connections that your system allows:

```
SELECT @@MAX_CONNECTIONS
```

The *user connections* option is an advanced option. You can set it in Enterprise Manager by clicking the Connections tab of the server's Properties window and entering a number in the Maximum Concurrent User Connections spin box, as shown in Figure 30-3.

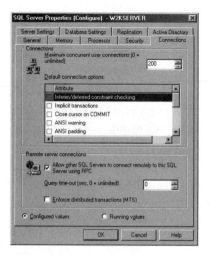

Figure 30-3. *Setting user connections.*

The *open objects* Option

The *open objects* option is an advanced option and can be set only by using *sp_configure*. Setting this option determines the maximum number of database objects—such as tables, views, stored procedures, triggers, rules, and defaults— that can be open at the same time. The default value of *0* indicates that SQL Server will dynamically adjust the number of open objects allowed on the system. You should leave the default setting. If you do change it and SQL Server needs more open objects than you have configured, you will get an error message from SQL Server stating that it has exceeded the allowed number of open objects. Also, each open object consumes some memory, so your system might need more physical memory to support the number of open objects needed.

Statistics

Column statistics are needed to achieve better query performance on your system. SQL Server is able to gather statistical information regarding the distribution of values in a table column. Query Optimizer then uses this information to determine the optimal execution plan for a query. Statistics can be gathered on two types of columns: those that are part of an index and those that are not in an index but are used in a predicate of a query (in the WHERE clause). By leaving the default SQL Server settings for a database, you allow both types of statistics to be created automatically by SQL Server. Indexed-column statistics are created when the index is created. Non-indexed-column statistics are created when they are needed for a query (on a single column only, not multiple columns, as you will see in the section "CREATE STATISTICS" later in this section). Once the statistics are aged (not used for a period of time), SQL Server will automatically drop them.

To create both non-indexed-column statistics and indexed-column statistics, SQL Server uses only a sample of the data in the table, not every row in the table. This minimizes the overhead required by the operation, but in some cases, sampling does not characterize the data well, and the statistics will not be completely accurate.

In Enterprise Manager, you can enable or disable the automatic creation of statistics for a database. To do this, first open the Properties window for a database. Click the Options tab, where you will see the Auto Create Statistics check box. (Figure 30-4 shows this check box for an example database, MyDB.) This option is selected (enabled) by default.

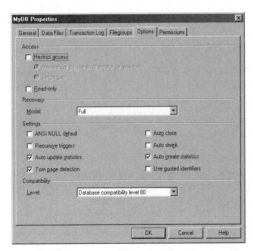

Figure 30-4. *The Properties window for the MyDB database.*

In the database's Properties window, you will also see an option called Auto Update Statistics. This option, which is also enabled by default per database, indicates that SQL Server will automatically update the statistics on table columns when necessary. These statistics need to be updated when a large number (or high percentage) of rows in the table have changed (through update, insert, or delete operations). When many changes to the data are made, the current statistics are less accurate. SQL Server will automatically determine when the statistics should be updated. If you choose to disable statistics creation by disabling this option, you must perform these tasks manually to ensure your database performs well. The following sections show you how to both create and update statistics manually.

CREATE STATISTICS

You can create statistics manually on specific columns in a table by using the T-SQL command CREATE STATISTICS. Creating statistics manually differs from automatic creation in that it allows you to combine statistics on multiple columns, which generates information such as the average number of duplicate values and distinct values for the combination of columns. The syntax of CREATE STATISTICS is as follows:

```
CREATE STATISTICS stats_name ON
    table_name ( column [ , column... ] )
  [ [WITH [ FULLSCAN | SAMPLE size PERCENT ]
  [ , NORECOMPUTE ]
```

You must provide a name for the statistic collection you are creating, a table name, and at least one column name. You can specify multiple column names in order to gather statistics on a combination of columns. Note that you cannot specify computed columns or columns assigned the *ntext*, *text*, or *image* data type as statistics columns. Either a full scan or a sampling of data can be used for statistics gathering. A full scan will take longer to complete than a sample, because it scans every row of the table, but it can be more accurate. If you use a sampling, you must specify the percent of data to be sampled. The NORECOMPUTE keyword specifies that automatic updating of these statistics be disabled, allowing statistics that no longer represent the data well to still be used.

You might want to create statistics on columns that are used together in a predicate of a query. For example, you can create statistics on the *FirstName* and *LastName* columns of the *Employees* table of the Northwind database to search for an employee name by first name and last name. The T-SQL code used to do this is as follows:

```
CREATE STATISTICS name
ON Northwind..Employees (FirstName, LastName)
WITH FULLSCAN, NORECOMPUTE
```

This statement calculates statistics for all rows in the *FirstName* and *LastName* columns, and disables automatic recomputation of the statistics.

If you want to manually create statistics for all columns in all tables of a database without having to type CREATE STATISTICS statements for each column of each table, you can use the *sp_createstats* stored procedure. This stored procedure is described in the next section.

sp_createstats

You can create statistics on all eligible columns of all user tables in a database by using the stored procedure *sp_createstats*. Statistics will be created for all columns that do not already have statistics. Each set of statistics will be on a single column only. The syntax for *sp_createstats* is as follows:

```
sp_createstats [ 'indexonly' ] [ , 'fullscan' ]
   [ , 'norecompute' ]
```

The *indexonly* parameter specifies that only columns that participate in an index will have statistics created on them. The *fullscan* parameter specifies that a full scan of all rows, rather than a random sampling, will be performed—in other words, 100 percent of the data is sampled. The *norecompute* parameter specifies that automatic statistics updating be disabled on the new statistic. The new statistic is given the name of the column on which it is created.

UPDATE STATISTICS

SQL Server automatically updates statistics by default. You can disable this option and then manually update the statistics to make them current by using the UPDATE STATISTICS command. This command allows you to update indexed-column and non-indexed-column statistics. You might want to create a script that executes UPDATE STATISTICS on your most modified tables and then run that script as a SQL Server job periodically. This will help keep statistics up-to-date and ensure better query performance. (See the section "Rebuilding Indexes" in Chapter 17 for more details about the syntax and options of UPDATE STATISTICS.) To enable or disable the automatic update status of a particular statistic, you can use the *sp_autostats* stored procedure, as explained in the next section.

sp_autostats

By using the system stored procedure *sp_autostats,* you can enable or disable the automatic updating of particular statistics. Running this procedure does not cause the statistics to be updated; rather, it determines whether or not automatic updating should occur. This stored procedure is called with one, two, or three parameters: a table name and optionally a flag and a statistic name. The flag indicates the status of automatic updating and can be set to *ON* or *OFF*. To display the current update status for all statistics in a table (indexed-column and non-indexed-column statistics), run the command with the table name specified. The following command displays the status for statistics in the *Customers* table:

```
USE Northwind
GO
sp_autostats Customers
GO
```

The output shows the name of each statistic, whether automatic updating is set to *ON* or *OFF*, and when the statistics were last updated. Do not be confused by the column heading "Index Name" above the first column of the output. It refers to all statistics, not just indexes. If you have not manually turned off updating for these statistics, they should be displayed with a status of *ON*, as this is the SQL Server default.

To disable automatic updating of all statistics in the *Customers* table in the Northwind database, use the following command:

```
USE Northwind
GO
sp_autostats Customers, 'OFF'
GO
```

You can reenable automatic statistics updating by setting the flag value to *ON*. To change the status of a particular statistic or the statistics for an index, include the statistic name or index name, respectively. For example, the following command enables automatic statistics updating for the *PK_Customers* index:

```
USE Northwind
GO
sp_autostats Customers, 'ON', 'PK_Customers'
GO
```

The status of all other statistics on the *Customers* table will be unchanged.

File Growth

With SQL Server 2000, you can configure data files to grow automatically as needed. This feature is useful because it prevents you from inadvertently letting your files run out of space. However, using this feature is not an excuse for not monitoring your database size and performing capacity-planning exercises occasionally. You should always be aware of how fast tables are growing. Then you can determine whether you need to perform regular deletions on unnecessary, possibly out-of-date data in some tables and, by doing so, slow their growth. As the amount of data in a table increases, queries take more time and performance levels decline. The topic of configuring automatic file growth when you create a database was touched on in Chapter 9—here, you will learn how to alter the growth options for an existing database. The automatic file growth option can be configured from within Enterprise Manager. To do so, follow these steps:

1. In the left pane of Enterprise Manager, expand a server and then click the Databases folder. Right-click the database that you want to modify (in this example, we'll modify the MyDB database), and choose Properties from the shortcut menu to open the database's Properties window.

2. Click the Data Files tab (Figure 30-5) to see the properties of the data files for that database. The options in the File Properties area are designed to let you control how the data file will expand. To enable automatic file growth, select the Automatically Grow File check box. If you are using automatic file growth, you should set limits so that the file cannot grow uncontrollably.

Figure 30-5. *The Data Files tab of the MyDB Properties window.*

You specify a maximum file size by using the options in the Maximum File Size area. You should click Restrict File Growth and enter a maximum size in the spin box. If instead you click Unrestricted File Growth, you might later find that your entire disk subsystem has filled up without notice, causing both performance and operational problems.

You specify how fast a file grows by using the options in the File Growth area. If you click In Megabytes, whenever the data file is filled, SQL Server will increase its size by the specified amount. If you click By Percent, SQL Server will increase the data file's size by the specified percentage of its current size.

3. Click the Transaction Log tab, shown in Figure 30-6, to set the automatic growth options for the transaction log. These options are used the same way as the corresponding options in the Data Files tab are used. For transaction log files, as for data files, you should set limits so that they do not grow uncontrollably.

Figure 30-6. *The Transaction Log tab of the MyDB database's Properties window.*

The automatic file growth feature is convenient in many cases. Just be sure that you do not accidentally let a file consume all of the disk space on your system.

Checkpoints

SQL Server performs checkpoint operations automatically. The frequency of checkpoints will be automatically calculated according to the value you specify for the SQL Server configuration option *recovery interval*. This option specifies how long, in minutes, you can wait for a database recovery in the event of a system failure. Checkpoints will occur often enough to ensure that a system recovery will never take longer than the specified number of minutes. Checkpoints also occur automatically whenever SQL Server is shut down by a SHUTDOWN statement or by Service Control Manager. You can also issue checkpoints manually by using the CHECKPOINT statement.

If you want your system to perform optimally and if you can tolerate a long recovery time, you can set *recovery interval* to a high value, such as *60*. This means that if your system fails, automatic recovery could take up to 60 minutes to complete. Checkpoints cause a large number of disk writes when they occur, and they can take away processing power from user transactions, thus slowing user response times. This is why running checkpoints less often can help improve transaction performance overall. Of course, setting this value too high could result in an excessively long downtime if a failure does occur. A common setting for *recovery interval* is between *5* and *15* (minutes).

By default, *recovery interval* is set to *0*. This setting allows SQL Server to determine the best time to perform checkpoints based on the system load. Generally, when the default setting is used, checkpoints occur about once a minute. If you notice that checkpoints are occurring this often, you might want to adjust the *recovery interval* setting. To determine whether SQL Server is performing checkpoints excessively, use the SQL Server trace flag *–T3502*. This flag causes checkpoint information to be written to the SQL Server error log. Notice that checkpoints occur per database.

Database Maintenance Plans

A *maintenance plan* is a set of tasks that SQL Server will perform on your databases automatically, according to the schedule you specify. The purpose of a maintenance plan is to automate important administrative tasks so that they will not be forgotten and to reduce the amount of manual work for the DBA. You can create a separate plan for each database, multiple plans for a single database, or a single plan for multiple databases.

The four main categories of administrative tasks that you can schedule by creating a maintenance plan are as follows:

- Optimizations
- Integrity checks
- Complete database backups
- Transaction log backups

Performing these tasks is important for maintaining a well-performing and recoverable database. Which types of optimization tasks you include in your plan will depend on the performance and usage of your database. Performing integrity checks is a good way to ensure a consistent, healthy database. And regular backups are required to ensure the recoverability of the database in case of a system failure or user error. Because these backups are so important, you should create an automated-backup strategy. We'll look at each of these categories of tasks in more detail later in this section.

To create a maintenance plan, you use the Database Maintenance Plan Wizard. In this section, you'll learn how to use this wizard, and then you'll learn how to display the jobs in a maintenance plan and how to edit a plan.

Using the Database Maintenance Plan Wizard to Create a Maintenance Plan

To run the Database Maintenance Plan Wizard, follow these steps:

1. Start the wizard from within Enterprise Manager by using one of the following techniques:

   - Choose Database Maintenance Planner from the Tools menu.

   - Click a database name in the left pane, and click New Maintenance Plan under the Maintenance heading in the right pane. If you do not see the Maintenance heading, make sure you have selected Taskpad in the View menu of Enterprise Manager. You also might have to scroll down to see the Maintenance heading.

   - Click a database name, choose Wizards from the Tools menu, expand the Management folder in the Select Wizard dialog box that appears, and then choose Database Maintenance Plan Wizard.

   - Expand a server in the left pane, expand the Management folder, right-click Database Maintenance Plans, and choose New Mainte-nance Plan from the shortcut menu.

   - Right click on the database name and select All Tasks, and choose Maintenance Plan from the menu.

   Once you open the wizard, you will see the Database Maintenance Plan Wizard welcome screen, shown in Figure 30-7.

Figure 30-7. *The welcome screen of the Database Maintenance Plan Wizard.*

2. Click Next to display the Select Databases screen, shown in Figure 30-8. Here you can select the database or databases for which you want to create this maintenance plan.

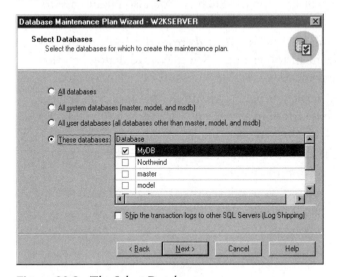

Figure 30-8. *The Select Databases screen.*

3. Click Next to display the Update Data Optimization Information screen, shown in Figure 30-9. You can choose from the following types of optimizations for the database or databases you selected in the previous step:

- **Reorganize Data And Index Pages**   This option causes all indexes on all tables in the database to be dropped and re-created, using a specified fill factor (or amount of free space on each page), which can improve the performance of updates. For read-only tables, reorganizing pages is not necessary. For tables that are inserted into or updated frequently, the free space that was originally available in your index pages starts to fill, and page splits will begin to occur. Select this option to re-create your indexes and reestablish free space for future growth, thus avoiding the delay and overhead caused by page splits.

  You can choose to re-create the indexes with the original amount of free space, or you can specify a new percent per page to leave free. If you make this percentage too high, you run the risk of causing the performance of data reads to degrade. If you select this option, you cannot select the next option, Update Statistics Used By Query Optimizer.

Tip   Dropping and re-creating indexes can take longer than using DBCC DBREINDEX, as discussed in the section "Rebuilding Indexes" in Chapter 17. You might want to create your own job to rebuild indexes instead of using this option.

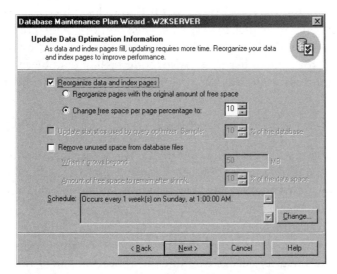

Figure 30-9. *The Update Data Optimization Information screen.*

- **Update Statistics Used By Query Optimizer**   Selecting this option will cause SQL Server to resample the distribution statistics on all indexes in the database. It uses this information to choose the optimal execution plan for queries. If you have not changed the default option for updating statistics (explained earlier in this chapter), SQL Server automatically generates statistics by sampling a small percentage of the data in the table that corresponds to each index.

The option in this screen can be used to force SQL Server to perform another sampling using a greater percentage of data (which you specify) or to determine how often SQL Server should update these statistics, instead of letting it decide. The larger the percentage of data sampled, the more accurate the statistics will be, but the longer SQL Server takes to generate them. This information can help improve performance when the data in the indexed columns has been modified greatly. You can verify the execution plan being used for your queries with SQL Query Analyzer to determine whether your indexes are being used efficiently and whether choosing this option is necessary. If you select this option, you cannot select the previous option, Reorganize Data And Index Pages.

- **Remove Unused Space From Database Files** This option is used to remove unused space; this process is also known as a file shrink. You can specify how large the amount of unused space should grow before the compression takes place and the percent of space that should remain free after compression. Once you have removed the free space, you can use DBCC SHRINKFILE to reduce the size of the file. You can make it smaller than it was when you originally created it, if desired. This will allow the disk space formerly occupied by the file to be used for some other need. Also, compressing data by removing unused space can improve performance. In read-only tables, compression is not necessary.

  You can specify a time for these tasks to be performed by clicking Change and entering a new schedule in the Edit Recurring Job Schedule dialog box that appears (Figure 30-10). These tasks should be run when the system utilization is low, such as on the weekend or at night, as they might take some time to complete and might delay user response times.

4. Click Next to display the Database Integrity Check screen, shown in Figure 30-11. In this screen, you can choose whether integrity checks will be performed. Integrity checks examine the allocation and structural integrity of tables and indexes (if the index option is chosen) by running the DBCC CHECKDB command. You can choose whether indexes should be included in the checks, whether SQL Server should attempt to repair minor problems found (selecting this option is

recommended), and whether all integrity checks should be run before backups are performed. If you select to have checks performed before a backup and a problem is found, the backup will not execute. Click Change to change the time that these tasks will be performed. Integrity checks might take several hours to run, depending on the size of your databases, so be sure to schedule them to occur when database usage is low. Checks should be run on a regular basis, perhaps weekly or monthly or before database backups.

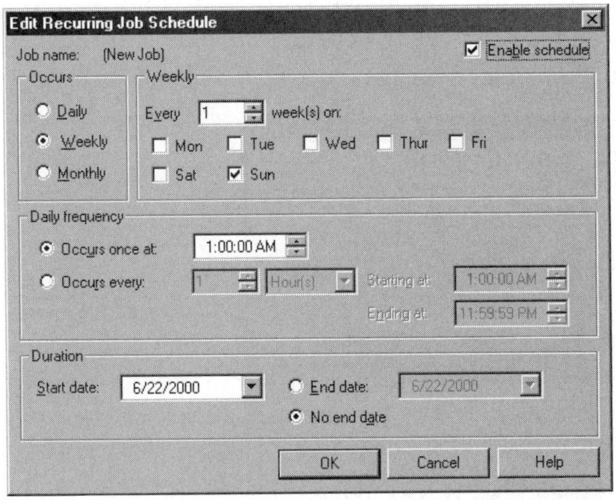

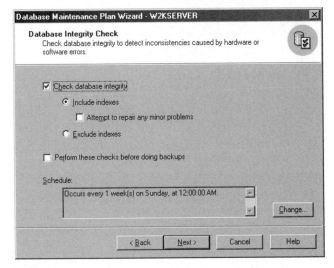

Figure 30-10. *The Edit Recurring Job Schedule dialog box.*

Figure 30-11. *The Database Integrity Check screen.*

5. Click Next to display the Specify The Database Backup Plan screen, shown in Figure 30-12. In this screen, you choose whether to create an automated-backup plan. (Creating such a plan is recommended.) To enable automatic backups, select the Back Up The Database As Part Of The Maintenance Plan check box. (See Chapter 32 for more information about performing backups.) You can instruct SQL Server to verify the integrity of the backup when it has finished. SQL Server does this by confirming that the backup is complete and that all the backup volumes are accessible. You can also indicate whether the backup should be stored on tape or disk. Click Change to change the time that the backup will be performed.

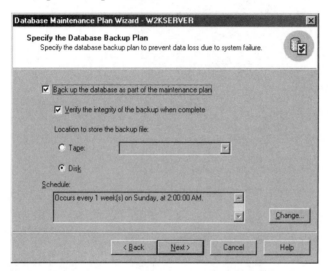

Figure 30-12. *The Specify The Database Backup Plan screen.*

6. Click Next to display the Specify Backup Disk Directory screen, shown in Figure 30-13. This screen appears only if you specified a backup to disk in the previous screen; it does not appear if you specified a backup to tape. In this screen, you can specify a location for the backup file, or you can use the default backup directory. If you have more than one database that you are backing up (such as master, model, msdb), you can choose to place the backup of each database in its own subdirectory to keep your backup files better organized. You can choose to have backup files of a certain age automatically deleted to free up disk space, and you can specify what filename extension you want to use for the backup files.

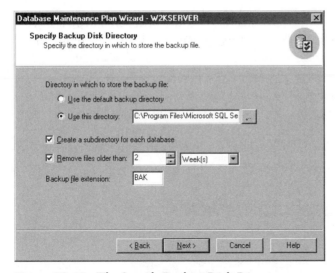

Figure 30-13. *The Specify Backup Disk Directory screen.*

7. Click Next to display the Specify The Transaction Log Backup Plan screen, as shown in Figure 30-14. This screen is similar to the Specify The Database Backup Plan screen shown in Figure 30-12, but the options on this screen are used to create a plan for backing up the transaction log. The transaction log backups should be performed between your database backups. To recover any changes since the last database backup, you use the transaction log backup. In other words, transaction log backups allow you to recover data between database backups.

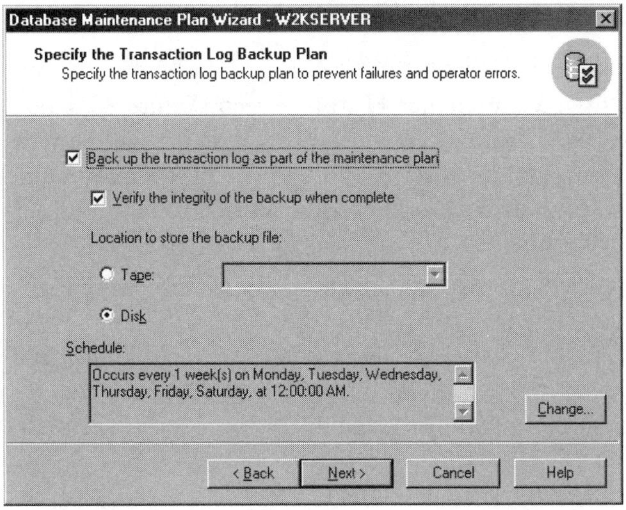

Figure 30-14. *The Specify The Transaction Log Backup Plan screen.*

If you choose to store the backups on disk, the next screen you see will be the Specify Backup Disk Directory screen, in which you supply the backup file location information.

8. Click Next to display the Reports To Generate screen, as shown in Figure 30-15. This screen gives you the option of creating a report that contains the results of the execution of the maintenance plan tasks. This report includes the details of the steps executed and any errors encountered. In this screen, you also select the location to store the report, and you can choose to delete reports older than a certain date and to e-mail the report to a specified e-mail alias.

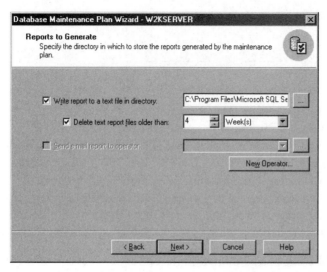

Figure 30-15. *The Reports To Generate screen.*

9. Click Next to display the Maintenance History screen (Figure 30-16). Here you can choose whether a maintenance history report will be written to a database table on the local server, and you can set a maximum size for the report. You can also have the report written to a remote server and specify the maximum size of that report.

10. Click Next to display the Completing The Database Maintenance Plan Wizard screen, shown in Figure 30-17. This screen shows a summary of your maintenance plan. The plan will have a default name, but you can specify a name by typing it into the Plan Name text box. Check the summary and backtrack if you want to change any options. If the plan looks satisfactory, click Finish.

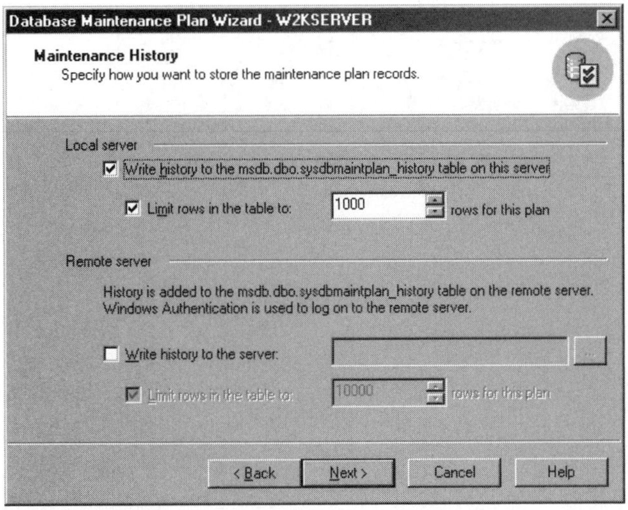

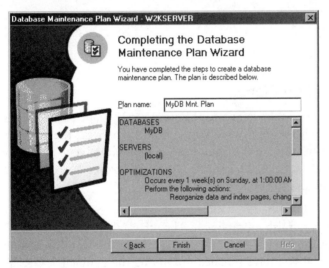

Figure 30-16. *The Maintenance History screen.*

Figure 30-17. *The Completing The Database Maintenance Plan Wizard screen.*

Displaying the Jobs in a Maintenance Plan

For our sample maintenance plan, we created a task in each of the four categories. To see a list of the jobs, or scheduled tasks, expand the Management folder in the left pane of Enterprise Manager, expand SQL Server Agent, and then click Jobs, as shown in Figure 30-18.

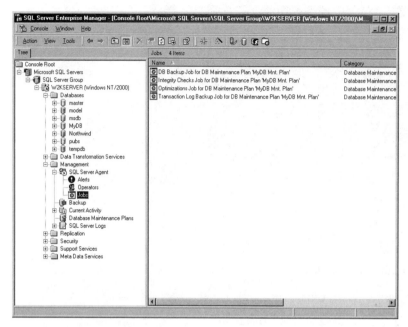

Figure 30-18. *The jobs created by our sample maintenance plan.*

Editing a Maintenance Plan

To edit a maintenance plan, in the left pane of Enterprise Manager, click the name of the database for which the plan was created, and then select the plan name under the Maintenance heading in the right pane. You might have to scroll down to see the Maintenance heading. The Database Maintenance Plan dialog box appears, as shown in Figure 30-19.

The General tab allows you specify which databases will be affected by your maintenance plan after you finish modifying it. The other tabs allow you to change the settings for the options that you configured by using the Database Maintenance Plan Wizard. When you have finished modifying the plan, click OK. Your plan will now begin running according to your schedule.

Note You must have the SQL Server Agent service started for the automatic maintenance plans to run as scheduled. See Chapter 31 for more information about SQL Server Agent.

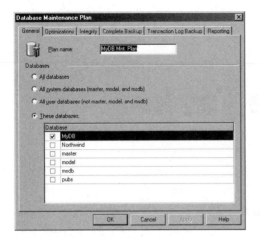

Figure 30-19. *The General tab of the Database Maintenance Plan dialog box.*

Summary

In this chapter, you've learned about the dynamic configuration features of SQL Server 2000, which help reduce the amount of database tuning that DBAs must perform. And you learned how to create a database maintenance plan to automatically run administrative tasks. Chapter 31 will show you how to use SQL Server Agent to define jobs and alerts. By creating jobs and alerts, you can further automate administrative tasks.

Chapter 31
Automating Administrative Tasks

In Chapter 30, we looked at some of the automatic configuration options and database options provided by Microsoft SQL Server 2000 that help reduce database-tuning work for the DBA. In this chapter, you'll learn how to use some additional tools provided by SQL Server that allow you to automate other administrative tasks through the SQLServerAgent service. The SQLServerAgent service's capabilities include automatically executing certain tasks periodically on the database and notifying the DBA or another specified person that a problem or an event has occurred on the server. By taking advantage of these capabilities, a DBA does not have to manually and continually monitor the database system to determine when to perform certain tasks and therefore has more time to dedicate to more difficult database issues, such as building and tuning indexes, optimizing queries, or planning for future growth.

Three primary tools are used for automating administrative tasks: jobs, alerts, and operators. In this chapter, you'll learn about the SQLServerAgent service and how to use the service to create and use jobs, alerts, and operators. You'll also find out about the SQLServerAgent error log, which you can use to track the work performed by SQLServerAgent.

The SQLServerAgent Service

The SQL Server Agent runs a service separate from SQL Server, called SQLServerAgent. The service is included with SQL Server 2000, but it must be started separately, either manually or automatically. See Chapter 8 for instructions about how to start SQLServerAgent. Once the service is started, you're ready to begin defining any jobs, alerts, and operators that you need.

Note The SQLServerAgent service was called SQL Executive in Microsoft SQL Server 6.5 and earlier. It is also used for replication, as explained in Chapters 26, 27, and 28.

Jobs

Jobs are administrative tasks that are defined once and can be run many times. You can run a job manually, or you can schedule the job to be executed by SQL Server at a specified time, on a regular schedule, or when an alert occurs. (Alerts are described in the section "Alerts" later in this chapter.) Jobs can consist of Transact-SQL (T-SQL) statements, Microsoft Windows NT or Microsoft Windows 2000 commands, executable programs, or Microsoft ActiveX scripts. Jobs are also automatically created for you when you use replication or when you create a database maintenance plan. A job can consist of a single step or many steps, and each step can be a call to a more complex set of steps—for example, a call to a stored procedure. SQL Server automatically monitors jobs for success or failure; you can set alerts to be sent out for either case.

Jobs can be run locally on a server, or if you have multiple servers on a network, you can designate one of the servers as the master server and designate the remaining servers as target servers. The master server stores the job definitions for all of the servers and acts as a job clearinghouse to coordinate all job activity. Each target server periodically connects to the master server, updates its job list if any jobs have changed, downloads any new jobs from the master server, and then disconnects to run those jobs. When a target server completes a job, it reconnects to the master server and reports its completion status.

Let's look at a situation in which you might want to create a job. Assume you have a database table that keeps a record of each transaction made in a banking environment, such as deposits, withdrawals, and money transfers. Each record has a *timestamp* column that indicates when the transaction occurred. This table will grow continuously and will need to be deleted periodically. To delete rows from this table, you could write a small stored procedure that uses the DELETE statement to delete rows that are older than two months, assuming the bank must keep records for only two months. Then you could create a job to run this stored procedure once each week on Sunday night, for example. In this way, you can ensure that the table will not grow endlessly. This saves disk space and usually improves performance as well. With less data in a table to search through when performing a query, SQL Server can finish the query faster. Now let's look at the details of how to create a job.

 Note   The SQLServerAgent service must be running in order for your jobs to function.

Creating a Job

To define a job, you can use Enterprise Manager, T-SQL scripts, the Create Job Wizard, or SQL-Distributed Management Objects (SQL-DMO). Because the SQL-DMO method is programming related, it is beyond the scope of this book. You will learn about the other three methods for creating jobs in this section.

More Info   For information about using SQL-DMO to create jobs, look up "jobs" in the Books Online index and select "Creating SQL Server Agent Jobs (SQL-DMO)" in the Topics Found dialog box.

Using Enterprise Manager

First let's create a job by using Enterprise Manager. One of the most common uses of a job is to run database backups. (This can also be accomplished using the Maintenance Plan Wizard as discussed in Chapter 30.) The following example creates a job to back up the MyDB database. It schedules the backup to run every night at 11 P.M. and records the success or failure of the backup job in the Windows NT or Windows 2000 application event log and in an output file. To create this job, which we will name *MyDB_backup_job*, follow these steps:

1. In the left pane of Enterprise Manager, expand a server folder, expand the Management folder, and then expand the SQL Server Agent folder. Right-click Jobs and choose New Job from the shortcut menu. The New Job Properties window appears, as shown in Figure 31-1.

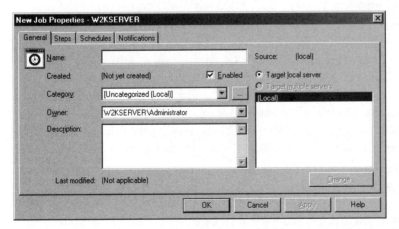

Figure 31-1. *The General tab of the New Job Properties window.*

2. On the General tab, set the following options:

- **Name** Type the name of the job—in this case, *MyDB_backup_job*—in the Name text box. The job name can have up to 128 characters. Each job on a server must have a unique name. Be sure to use a descriptive name.

- **Enabled** You use the Enabled check box to specify whether the job should be enabled or disabled. You might want to initially disable the job to test it manually to ensure it functions properly. When you have tested the job and know that it is working correctly, use this check box to enable the job so that it will run as scheduled.

- **Category** Select a category for the job—in this case, we'll use the default category, Uncategorized (Local). You can choose from the job categories that are created when you install SQL Server, or you can create your own categories. (To learn how to create a new category, see the section "Creating a New Category" later in this section.) The installed categories are Uncategorized (Local), Database Maintenance, Full Text, Web Assistant, and the 10 categories for replication. Categories are used to group related jobs. For example, you can group all jobs that are used to perform database maintenance in one category, or you can group jobs by department, such as accounting, sales, and marketing. Categories enable you to keep track of multiple jobs—you don't have to search through the entire list of jobs when you're concerned with only a portion of the jobs.

- **Owner** The owner is the user who creates the job or the user for whom the job is created. Only sysadmin roles can change who owns a job or can alter a job owned by another user. (SQL Server roles are explained in Chapter 34.) All sysadmin roles and the job owner can alter a job definition and start and stop a job. In the Owner drop-down list, always select the user who will run the job. For this example, that's the same person who is creating the job, so the correct owner is automatically selected, and you can leave the setting as it is.

- **Description** In the Description text box, you identify what tasks a job performs and the purpose of the job. You should always provide a description. A description allows other users to quickly determine the function of the job. The description can be up to 512 characters long.

- **Target Local Server** If you click this option, the job will be run on the local server only. If you have remote servers connected to this server, the option Target Multiple Servers will be available. Click it to specify remote servers on which this job should be run as well.

Figure 31-2 shows the completed General tab for our sample job.

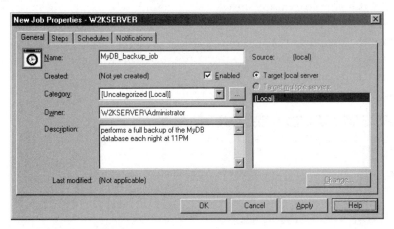

Figure 31-2. *The filled-in General tab.*

3. Click the Steps tab and click New to display the New Job Step dialog box, shown in Figure 31-3. *Job steps* are the commands or statements that define the tasks of the job. Every job must have at least one job step and can have multiple steps. On the General tab of the New Job Step dialog box, enter the following information:

- In the Step Name text box, type the step name—in this case, type *MyDB_backup*.

- In the Type drop-down list, select a type of step to be performed. For this example, select Transact-SQL Script (TSQL) because we will use T-SQL commands to perform the job. The other choices are ActiveX Script, Operating System Command, Replication Distributor, Replication Transaction-Log Reader, Replication Merge, QueueReader, and Replication Snapshot.

- Select the name of the database that this job will run on in the Database drop-down list. For this example, select the MyDB database.

- Type the commands you want to be part of the step in the Command text box. For this example, these commands are the T-SQL commands to back up the MyDB database to a backup device named MyDB_backup1. (This backup device must be created beforehand. Creating backup devices is detailed in Chapter 32. Also, ours is a simple example in which the database backup will be written to the same file each night. In practice, you should use a database maintenance plan, as described in Chapter 30, to perform the backup, as it will allow you to create a new backup device for each day.) You can also click Open to open a file if you have a prepared script that you want to enter as a job.

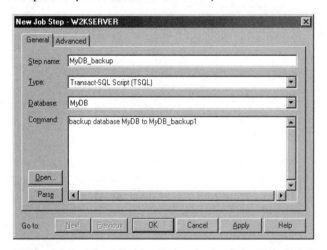

Figure 31-3. *The filled-in General tab of the New Job Step dialog box.*

4. Click Parse to check the syntax of your T-SQL steps, and then click the Advanced tab and set the options, as shown in Figure 31-4. On this tab, you can select which action to take upon success and upon failure of the job: quit the job reporting success, quit the job reporting failure, or go to the next step. You can also specify how many times the job should be retried if it does not succeed and the interval between retries. If the job consists of a T-SQL command or script, you can select an output file to which the output of the T-SQL will be reported. You can either append the output to this file each time the job is run or overwrite the output each time. Click View to view the contents of the output file. Select the Append Output To Step History check box to have the job output added to the job history table entry for this job. You can also specify the user who will run the T-SQL.

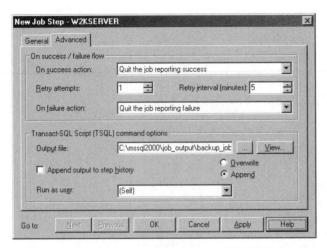

Figure 31-4. *The filled-in Advanced tab of the New Job Step dialog box.*

5. Click Apply and then click OK to return to the Steps tab of the New Job Properties window, where you can define more job steps if you want. Click New to add a new step to follow the existing selected step. To insert a new step to be performed before an existing step, select the existing step that you want the new step to precede, and then click Insert to display the New Job Step dialog box. Enter the information for the step you want to insert. To delete a step, select the step and click Delete; to edit a step, select it and click Edit. You can also move a step in the list by selecting it and clicking the up or down arrow to the right of the label Move Step. The Start Step drop-down list allows you to select which step will be the first one executed in the job. A green flag will appear next to the ID number of the step that is selected to execute first. Click Apply to apply your steps to the job. If any flow logic between multiple steps would cause a step not to execute, SQL Server will display a warning message when you click Apply and will allow you to change the flow logic.

6. To create a schedule for the job, click the Schedules tab. To find the current time on a server, select the server name in the NOTE: The Current Date/Time On Target Server drop-down list. Now click New Schedule to display the New Job Schedule dialog box, as shown in Figure 31-5. Schedules specify at what times and on which days a job should be executed. Execution can occur one time or regularly. If you want to run a job manually at random times, you do not have to set up a job schedule—you can simply run the job whenever you want to. Fill in the

schedule name, *MyDB_backup_schedule*, set the options in the Schedule Type area (in this case, select Recurring), and select the Enabled check box. (These settings are shown in Figure 31-5.) The Enabled check box has the same function here as it did in the New Job Properties window.

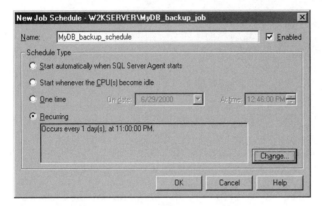

Figure 31-5. *The New Job Schedule dialog box.*

7. Because we chose a recurring schedule type, you must set the times and days when you want the job to be performed. To do so, click Change to display the Edit Recurring Job Schedule dialog box. Enter the new times and days, and click OK to return to the New Job Schedule dialog box. (Remember that we want to set up a daily backup that occurs at 11 P.M.)

8. Click OK in the New Job Schedule dialog box to accept your schedule and return to the New Job Properties window. To delete a schedule, select the schedule name and click Delete. To edit a schedule, select the schedule name and click Edit.

Note You can also create a new alert for this job. Alerts will be covered in detail later in this chapter.

9. Click the Notifications tab, shown in Figure 31-6. On this tab, you can set up a notification process so that an operator (or specified user) will be notified of the success, failure, or completion of a job. This notification can be sent by e-mail, by pager, or as a message across the network by using the NET SEND command. You can have the job status written to the Windows NT or Windows 2000 event log, and you can even automatically delete the job after it succeeds, fails, or is completed. To configure operator notification, select the E-mail Operator, Page Operator, and Net Send Operator check boxes, as appropriate, and select the

operator name in the drop-down list to the right. (See the "Operators" section later in this chapter to learn how to create operators.) Select the condition on which to perform the notification in the rightmost drop-down list. To write the results to the event log or to automatically delete the job when it is completed, select the appropriate check boxes, and then select the condition on which to perform the action in the associated drop-down lists. In this example, select the Write To Windows Application Event Log check box.

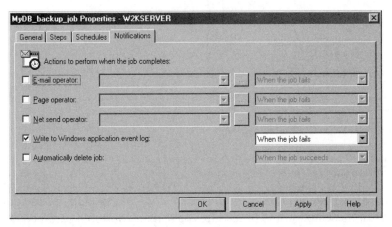

Figure 31-6. *The Notifications tab of the New Job Properties window.*

10. When you have finished setting options, click Apply to create your job, and then click OK to exit the New Job Properties window and to return to Enterprise Manager.

11. Click Jobs in the left pane of Enterprise Manager. You will see *MyDB_backup_job* included in the list of jobs in the right pane.

Creating a New Category To create a new category, expand a server in the left pane of Enterprise Manager, expand the Management folder, right-click Jobs, point to All Tasks in the shortcut menu, and then choose Manage Job Categories. The Job Categories dialog box appears, as shown in Figure 31-7, enabling you to add a new category, view existing categories and the jobs that are in them, and delete categories.

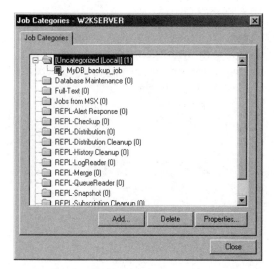

Figure 31-7. *The Job Categories dialog box.*

Using T-SQL

The T-SQL commands used to create a job, add steps to a job, and create a schedule for a job are the system stored procedures *sp_add_job*, *sp_add_jobstep*, and *sp_add_jobschedule*. These stored procedures have many optional parameters, as shown in the code presented in this section. SQL Server assigns each unspecified parameter a default value. Enterprise Manager is much simpler to use for creating jobs because its GUI guides you through the options for the job, preventing your forgetting anything. With T-SQL, you must either include values for all of the optional parameters or be certain that the default values for any omitted parameters are satisfactory values for your job. You should use Enterprise Manager instead of running these stored procedures by hand. You can then generate the T-SQL scripts that were used by Enterprise Manager to create a job by right-clicking the job name, pointing to All Tasks in the shortcut menu, and then choosing Generate SQL Script. This technique will allow you to re-create the job using the script, if you ever need to.

To run any of the stored procedures just mentioned, you must be using the msdb database because the procedures are stored there. Let's look at the parameters that are available with the stored procedures, in case you do want to use the procedures. All the stored procedures described in this chapter use the same general syntax. The *sp_add_job* stored procedure's syntax is shown here:

```
sp_add_job [@job_name =] 'job_name'
[,[@enabled =] enabled]
[,[@description =] 'description']
[,[@start_step_id =] step_id]
[,[@category_name =] 'category']
[,[@category_id =] category_id]
[,[@owner_login_name =] 'login']
[,[@notify_level_eventlog =] eventlog_level]
[,[@notify_level_email =] email_level]
[,[@notify_level_netsend =] netsend_level]
[,[@notify_level_page =] page_level]
[,[@notify_email_operator_name =] 'email_name']
[,[@notify_netsend_operator_name =] 'netsend_name']
[,[@notify_page_operator_name =] 'page_name']
[,[@delete_level =] delete_level]
[,[@originating_server =] 'server_name'
[,[@job_id =] job_id OUTPUT]
```

The syntax for *sp_add_jobstep* is shown here:

```
sp_add_jobstep [@job_id =] job_id | [@job_name =] 'job_name']
[,[@step_id =] step_id]
{,[@step_name =] 'step_name'}
[,[@subsystem =] 'subsystem']
[,[@command =] 'command']
[,[@additional_parameters =] 'parameters']
[,[@cmdexec_success_code =] code]
[,[@on_success_action =] success_action]
[,[@on_success_step_id =] success_step_id]
[,[@on_fail_action =] fail_action]
[,[@on_fail_step_id =] fail_step_id]
[,[@server =] 'server']
[,[@database_name =] 'database']
[,[@database_user_name =] 'user']
[,[@retry_attempts =] retry_attempts]
[,[@retry_interval =] retry_interval]
[,[@os_run_priority =] run_priority]
[,[@output_file_name =] 'file_name']
[,[@flags =] flags]
```

The syntax for *sp_add_jobschedule* is shown here:

```
sp_add_jobschedule [@job_id =] job_id, | [@job_name =] 'job_name',
[@name =] 'name'
[,[@enabled =] enabled]
[,[@freq_type =] freq_type]
```

(continued)

continued

```
[,[@freq_interval =] freq_interval]
[,[@freq_subday_type =] freq_subday_type]
[,[@freq_subday_interval =] freq_subday_interval]
[,[@freq_relative_interval =] freq_relative_interval]
[,[@freq_recurrence_factor =] freq_recurrence_factor]
[,[@active_start_date =] active_start_date]
[,[@active_end_date =] active_end_date]
[,[@active_start_time =] active_start_time]
[,[@active_end_time =] active_end_time]
```

More Info For a description of each parameter and its default value, look up the name of the relevant stored procedure in the Books Online index.

Note The stored procedures described here, as well as all other stored procedures related to creating and managing jobs, operators, notifications, and alerts, are stored in the msdb database. You must be using this database to run these procedures.

Using the Create Job Wizard

Enterprise Manager provides a wizard that guides you through the job creation process in a step-by-step fashion. One limitation of using the wizard is that it restricts you to creating a job that has only one job step. It does, however, allow you to supply a schedule for the job and to specify operators who will be notified of the job's status. You can add more steps to the job after you create it by modifying the job later using Enterprise Manager.

To use the Create Job Wizard to create a job, follow these steps:

1. Choose Wizards from the Enterprise Manager Tools menu, expand the Management folder in the Select Wizard dialog box that appears, and select Create Job Wizard to display the Create Job Wizard welcome screen, shown in Figure 31-8.

2. Click Next to display the Select Job Command Type screen, shown in Figure 31-9. This screen lets you specify which type of step you will create for the job. For this example, select Transact-SQL Command.

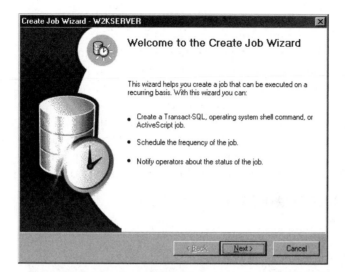

Figure 31-8. *The Create Job Wizard welcome screen.*

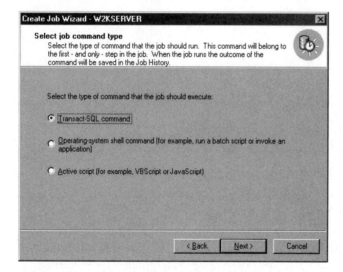

Figure 31-9. *The Select Job Command Type screen.*

3. Click Next to display the Enter Transact-SQL Statement screen (Figure 31-10). For a T-SQL command, you must select the database in which to run the command and then either type the statement or statements for the job or click Open to find and open the file that contains the T-SQL statements you want to use. Click Parse to check the syntax of the T-SQL statements you have entered. If you had selected Operating-System Shell Command or Active Script as the command type, you would be prompted to enter the commands for those types. For this example, type the T-SQL command to back up the master database to a previously created device named backup_master_dev, as shown in Figure 31-10.

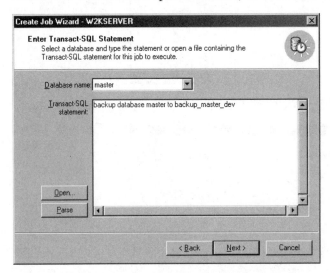

Figure 31-10. *The Enter Transact-SQL Statement screen.*

4. Click Next to display the Specify Job Schedule screen, shown in Figure 31-11. Here you can specify when the job should be run.

   The Now option specifies that the job will be run as soon as the wizard is finished. The other options are self-explanatory. For this example, select On A Recurring Basis, and then select Schedule to set the schedule. The Edit Recurring Job Schedule dialog box appears, as shown in Figure 31-12. Use the options to create the desired schedule, and click OK to accept it and to return to the Specify Job Schedule screen.

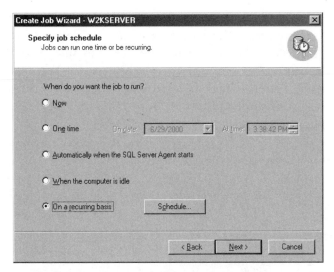

Figure 31-11. *The Specify Job Schedule screen.*

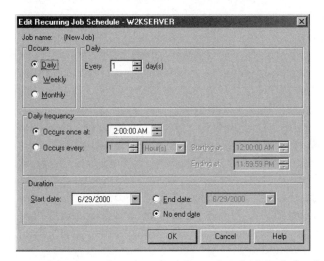

Figure 31-12. *The Edit Recurring Job Schedule dialog box.*

5. Click Next to display the Job Notifications screen, shown in Figure 31-13. In the Net Send or E-mail drop-down list or both, select an operator to be notified of the job completion status. You must have already

defined the operators for them to appear in the drop-down list. (Figure 31-13 shows no operators defined.) If you want to notify an operator that has not been defined, complete the wizard and then add an operator as described in the section "Operators" later in this chapter. You can then modify the job properties to notify that operator. You can also cancel the wizard, create the operator, and restart the wizard.

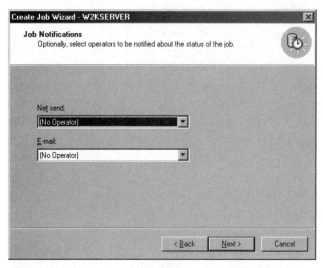

Figure 31-13. *The Job Notifications screen.*

6. Click Next to display the Completing The Create Job Wizard screen, shown in Figure 31-14. Here you can assign a name for your job by replacing the default name in the Job Name text box—in this example, our job is named *Backup_master_job*. Check the text in the Description box to be sure it reflects the options you want, and if so, click Finish to create the job. If not, click Back and make the appropriate changes. An informational message box appears if the job was created successfully. Click OK to close this message box.

After you complete the Create Job Wizard, the new job appears in the Jobs folder in Enterprise Manager.

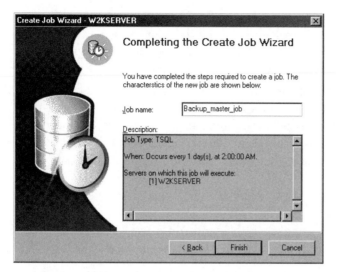

Figure 31-14. *The Completing The Create Job Wizard screen.*

Managing a Job

You can manage and edit your jobs through Enterprise Manager or by using T-SQL. Again, Enterprise Manager might be easier for you to use because you don't have to worry about the syntax and default values involved with T-SQL stored procedures and because the Enterprise Manager GUI guides you through setting the job properties.

Using Enterprise Manager

You can manually start, stop, disable, enable, edit, and create T-SQL scripts for a job by using Enterprise Manager. Instructions for each of these tasks are given here:

- To start a job, right-click the job name in the right pane of Enterprise Manager and choose Start Job from the shortcut menu.

- To stop a job that is currently running and to cancel any retries that are configured, right-click the job name and choose Stop Job from the shortcut menu.

- To disable a job so that it can be tested without allowing it to be performed at its scheduled time, or for any other reason, right-click the job name and choose Disable Job from the shortcut menu. Choose Enable Job to re-enable the job.

- To edit a job, a schedule, or any other property of a job, right-click the job name and choose Properties from the shortcut menu to display the job's Properties window, which contains the same four tabs you used to create the job. Make your modifications, click Apply, and then click OK.

- To create a T-SQL script for your job in case you want to re-create the job at any time without having to retype the statements, right-click the job name, point to All Tasks in the shortcut menu, and then choose Generate SQL Script to display the Generate SQL Script dialog box. Type a filename, choose a file format (Unicode, ANSI, or OEM text), and click OK.

Using T-SQL

You can also start, stop, enable, disable, and edit a job by using the following T-SQL stored procedures. Remember to use the msdb database when you run these procedures.

- *sp_start_job* Starts the specified job immediately. This procedure requires a job name or job ID number.

- *sp_stop_job* Stops a job that is currently running. This procedure requires a job name, job ID, or master server name.

- *sp_update_job* Allows you to enable, disable, and change the properties of a job. This procedure requires a job name or job ID number.

More Info To view the syntax of these procedures and the options that can be used with them, look up the specific stored procedure in the Books Online index.

Viewing the Job History

SQL Server maintains a history of job execution information in the *sysjobhistory* table of the msdb system database. You can view the job history information by using Enterprise Manager or T-SQL.

Using Enterprise Manager

To view the job history by using Enterprise Manager, follow these steps:

1. Right-click the job name in the right pane of Enterprise Manager and choose View Job History from the shortcut menu to display the Job History dialog box, as shown in Figure 31-15. Here you'll see a line of information describing each execution of the job, any operators notified, and errors or messages received from SQL Server.

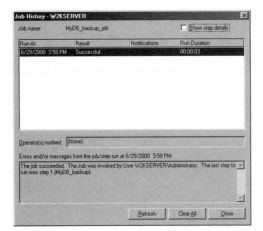

Figure 31-15. *The Job History dialog box.*

2. To view additional details about job execution status, select the Show Step Details check box in the upper right corner of the dialog box. Figure 31-16 shows the details for the MyDB backup.

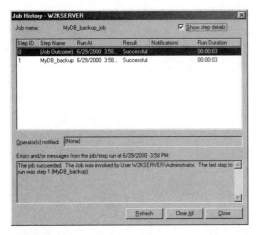

Figure 31-16. *Step details displayed in the Job History dialog box.*

3. To clear all messages, click Clear All. To refresh the screen to view the status of any new jobs that have been run since you opened the Job History dialog box, click Refresh. To close the Job History dialog box, click Close.

Using T-SQL

To view job history information about scheduled jobs by using T-SQL, run the stored procedure *sp_help_jobhistory* in the msdb database. The syntax is shown here:

```
sp_help_jobhistory [[@job_id =] job_id]
[, [@job_name =] 'job_name']
[, [@step_id =] step_id]
[, [@sql_message_id =] sql_message_id]
[, [@sql_severity =] sql_severity]
[, [@start_run_date =] start_run_date]
[, [@end_run_date =] end_run_date]
[, [@start_run_time =] start_run_time]
[, [@end_run_time =] end_run_time]
[, [@minimum_run_duration =] minimum_run_duration]
[, [@run_status =] run_status]
[, [@minimum_retries =] minimum_retries]
[, [@oldest_first =] oldest_first]
[, [@server =] 'server']
[, [@mode =] 'mode']
```

If you run this procedure with no parameters or with no *job id* or *job name* parameter, information about all scheduled jobs will be returned. The *mode* parameter specifies whether to return all history information (*FULL*) or a summary (*SUMMARY*). The default setting is *SUMMARY*.

More Info For details about all other options of this stored procedure, look up "sp_help_jobhistory" in the Books Online index.

Alerts

An *alert* is an action that occurs on a server in response to an event or to a performance condition. Alerts can notify operators, cause specified jobs to be executed, and forward events to another server. An *event* is an error or a message that is written to the Windows NT or Windows 2000 application event log (which you can view by using the Windows NT or Windows 2000 Event Viewer). A *performance condition* is a characteristic of the system's performance that can be monitored by using the Windows NT Performance Monitor or the Windows 2000 System Monitor, such as CPU utilization or the number of locks being used by SQL Server. In this chapter, we will focus on the System Monitor from Windows 2000, although the Windows NT Performance Monitor is very similar.

When an event occurs, SQLServerAgent compares the event to the list of alerts you have defined, and if an alert is defined for that event, the alert is triggered.

An alert for a performance condition is fired when a defined performance threshold is reached for a specified SQL Server object in System Monitor, such as the counter *User Connections* under the System Monitor object *General Statistics*. For example, you could set an alert to occur if the value for this counter reaches *50*. (System Monitor is described in Chapter 36.)

> **Note** The SQLServerAgent service must be running in order for your alerts to function.

Event Message Logging

Before we look at how to create an alert for an event, let's review the types of events that cause messages to be sent to the Windows NT or Windows 2000 application event log; only these events are available to be used to set alerts. Events (or errors) with a severity level of *19* through *25* are automatically reported to the Windows NT or Windows 2000 application event log and are therefore able to trigger alerts. By default, events that have a severity level less than *19* are not logged, and therefore, an alert cannot be triggered by those events. To enable those events to be logged so that an alert can be triggered, you must use *sp_altermessage*, the RAISERROR WITH LOG statement, or *xp_logevent* to change the logging status of the event or message. In this section, you'll learn how to create a user-defined event message and how to alter that message to ensure that it will be written to the application event log.

> **Note** When a SQL Server message is logged in the Windows NT or Windows 2000 application event log, it is also logged in the SQL Server log. To view the SQL Server log in Enterprise Manager, expand the Management folder for your server, and expand the SQL Server Logs folder.

Creating a User-Defined Event Message

All information for system and user-defined messages is stored in the *sysmessages* table in the master database. To create a user-defined message, use the T-SQL system stored procedure *sp_addmessage*. The syntax is shown here:

```
sp_addmessage [@msg_num =] msg_id,
[@severity=] severity,
[@msg_text=] 'msg_text'
[,[@lang =] 'language']
[,[@with_log=] 'with_log']
[,[@replace =] 'replace']
```

A user-defined messag must have a message ID value (*msg_id*) of *50001* or greater. The *severity* parameter is the severity level of the error that the message refers to, ranging from *1* through *25*, with higher numbers indicating higher severity of error. Only the system administrator can set severity levels *19* through *25*. The *msg_text* parameter is the text of the error message that will appear in the application event log when the error occurs. The *language* parameter specifies in which language the message is written, because multiple languages can be installed with SQL Server. The *with_log* parameter can be set to either *TRUE* or *FALSE*, indicating whether the message will always be logged to the Windows NT or Windows 2000 application event log. The default value is *FALSE*. Using RAISERROR WITH LOG (described in the next section) will override this setting if it is *FALSE*. The *replace* parameter indicates that the message should replace an existing message that has the same message ID number.

Members of the *public* role have permission to execute *sp_addmessage*, but to create a message with a severity level greater than *18* or to set *with_log* to *TRUE*, you must be a member of the *sysadmin* role.

Let's look at an example of using *sp_addmessage*. The following statement creates a new message that will always be logged in the event log (because *with_log* is set to *TRUE*):

```
sp_addmessage 50001, 16, "Customer ID is out of range.", @with_log = "TRUE"
GO
```

Altering the Log Settings of an Event Message

Suppose an existing message or a message you just created does not allow logging (or you did not include the *with_log* parameter), as in the following example:

```
sp_addmessage 50001, 16, "Customer ID is out of range.", @with_log = "FALSE"
GO
```

If you later want to log the message, you must change the logging state of the message. To do so, use *sp_altermessage* to set logging to always occur, as in the following example:

```
sp_altermessage 50001, WITH_LOG, "TRUE"
GO
```

Alternatively, you could use the RAISERROR statement with the WITH LOG option to return the message to your application, as well as to the application event log and the SQL Server log. For example, the following statement sends the message *50001* with a severity level of *16* and a *state* value of *1*, where *state* is a number that can be used for tracking when the error is raised in more than one place in your code:

```
RAISERROR (50001, 16, 1) WITH LOG
GO
```

More Info For more details about using RAISERROR, look up "RAISERROR" in the Books Online index and select "Using RAISERROR" in the Topics Found dialog box.

To change the logging status of a message, you can also use the extended stored procedure *xp_logevent*, which is located in the master database. When you use this procedure, the message is sent to the event log and to the SQL Server log, but not to the client application. An example of using this procedure is shown here:

```
USE master
GO
xp_logevent 50002, "Customer ID out of range", warning
GO
```

The first two parameters are required and consist of a user-defined message ID number (which, again, must be greater than 50,000) and message text that will appear in the output to the logs. The third parameter, the severity level, is optional. Severity can be one of three character strings: *informational*, *warning*, or *error*. The severity level setting determines what type of icon appears next to the message in Event Viewer, enabling you to quickly identify warnings or errors. For Windows 2000, an informational message has a blue "i" icon, a warning has a yellow "!" icon, and an error has a red "X" icon. If no severity is specified, the default value is *informational*.

Creating an Alert

Now we're ready to create an alert on an event and on a performance condition. To create an alert, you can use Enterprise Manager, T-SQL, or SQL-DMO. Again, we will look at only the Enterprise Manager and T-SQL methods because SQL-DMO is beyond the scope of this book.

Using Enterprise Manager to Create an Event Alert

In this example, we'll create an alert on a system message that already has a severity level of 24. The message will be logged by default in the event log, with no user intervention needed to change its logging status. To create the event alert, follow these steps:

1. In the left pane of Enterprise Manager, expand a server folder, expand the Management folder, and then expand the SQL Server Agent folder.

Right-click Alerts and choose New Alert from the shortcut menu. The New Alert Properties window appears, as shown in Figure 31-17. On the General tab, type the name of the alert, which can have up to 128 characters. For this example, type *IO_error_alert*. The Enabled check box allows you to enable or disable the alert. Disabling an alert will cause it to not be fired, similar to disabling a job. For this example, be sure the alert is enabled. In the Type drop-down list, select SQL Server Event Alert because we want to create an alert that will be fired when a certain event occurs. (The other alert type option is SQL Server Performance Condition Alert—an example of this type of alert will be shown in the next section.) For our example, we will create an alert that will be fired when an I/O error occurs.

Figure 31-17. *The General tab of the New Alert Properties window.*

2. In the Event Alert Definition area of the New Alert Properties window, you specify the event you want to trigger the alert by selecting either Error Number or Severity, and then specifying an error number or a severity level. If a severity level is specified, all errors with that severity level will fire the alert. For this example, select Error Number and then click the Browse (...) button to search for the number. The Manage SQL Server Messages dialog box appears, as shown in Figure 31-18.

3. To search for a specific error, you select a category in the Severity list box on the Search tab, and click Find. The errors found are listed on the Messages tab. The two check boxes at the bottom of the Search tab can be used to limit the search. The Only Include Logged Messages check box allows the search to retrieve messages that are automatically logged in the event log. The Only Include User-Defined Messages check

box limits the search to only those messages defined by users. For our example, we want to find all fatal hardware errors, so select 024 - Fatal Error: Hardware Error in the Severity list box, and then click Find. Error number 823 (with a severity level of *24*) appears on the Messages tab, as shown in Figure 31-19.

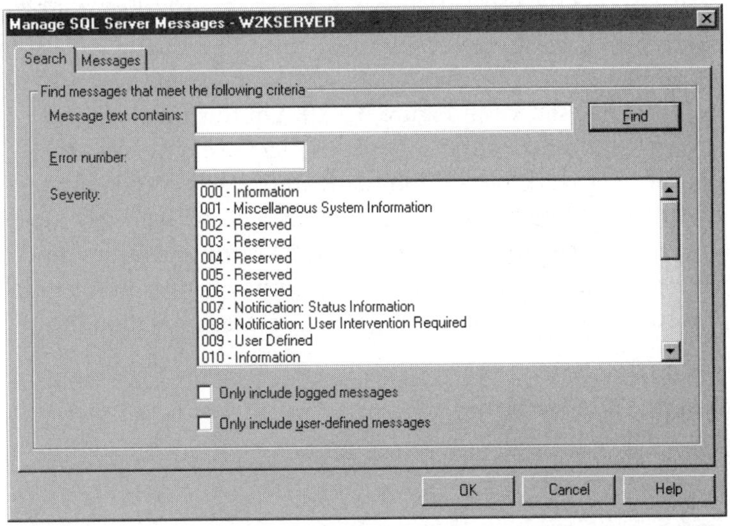

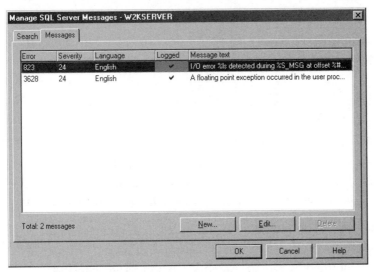

Figure 31-18. *The Search tab of the Manage SQL Server Messages dialog box.*

Figure 31-19. *The Messages tab of the Manage SQL Server Messages dialog box.*

4. Click OK to accept this message and to return to the General tab of the New Alert Properties window. The Database Name drop-down list lets you specify that the alert will fire only if the event is from the selected database. Keep the default setting of All Databases. The Error Message Contains This Text text box allows you to type a string of characters (up to 100) that restricts the errors that will fire the alert to those whose error text contains that string. If you leave this text box blank, no restriction will apply.

5. Click the Response tab, shown in Figure 31-20. On this tab, you can specify what action should be taken when this alert occurs. Select the Execute Job check box, and select a job name in the drop-down list to cause that job to be executed when the alert occurs. Clicking New Operator lets you create a new operator to notify. Existing operators appear in the Operators To Notify list. You can specify whether an operator should be notified by e-mail, pager, NET SEND, or a combination of those methods.

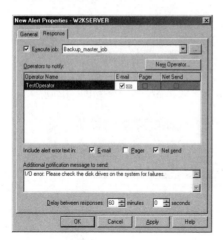

Figure 31-20. *The Response tab of the New Alert Properties window.*

If you specify an operator to be notified by e-mail and also select the Include Alert Error Text In E-mail check box, the error text will be sent to the operator in the alert message. You include the additional text in the e-mail by typing it in the Additional Notification Message To Send text box at the bottom of the tab. The maximum number of additional text characters is 512. Figure 31-20 shows an operator, TestOperator, selected to be notified by e-mail. An additional message is included.

Notice also the Delay Between Responses spin boxes. The settings in these spin boxes specify how often the operator will be notified if an alert occurs repeatedly. A setting of 60 minutes means that the operator will be notified only once during any 60-minute period.

6. To accept the alert and the response you have entered, click Apply. Then click OK to close the window.

Using Enterprise Manager to Create a Performance Condition Alert

Now we'll use Enterprise Manager to create an alert that fires when a certain performance condition occurs. Note that SQLServerAgent polls performance counters at 20-second intervals, so if a peak or a low occurs for only a few seconds between polls, it might not be detected. To create the alert, follow these steps:

1. In the left pane of Enterprise Manager, expand a server folder, expand the Management folder, and then expand the SQL Server Agent folder. Right-click Alerts and choose New Alert from the shortcut menu. The New Alert Properties window appears (Figure 31-21). Type a name for the alert in the Name text box on the General tab. (Use *user_alert* for this example.) To specify a performance condition alert, select SQL Server Performance Condition Alert in the Type drop-down list.

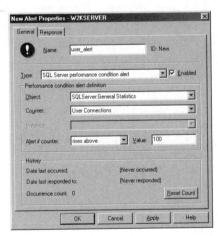

Figure 31-21. *The General tab of the New Alert Properties window.*

2. In the Performance Condition Alert Definition area, you define the performance condition that will trigger the alert. Select the SQL Server performance object that you want to use as the trigger object in the Object drop-down list, and then select the counter that you want to use in the Counter drop-down list. Set the Alert If Counter option to indicate in which situation the alert should be fired. Finally set a value for the threshold that, if crossed, will trigger the alert. Figure 31-21 shows the settings used to fire an alert when the SQL Server *User Connections* counter rises above *100*.

3. To finish creating this alert, set the options on the Response tab as described in step 5 of the preceding section, click Apply, and then click OK.

Using T-SQL to Create an Event Alert or a Performance Condition Alert

You can also use T-SQL to create your alerts, but remember that if you create alerts by using Enterprise Manager, you can later generate the T-SQL scripts for those alerts. (To do so, right-click Alerts in the SQL Server Agent folder, point to All Tasks in the shortcut menu, and then choose Generate SQL Script.) You might find using Enterprise Manager to create alerts easier because the T-SQL method requires learning and remembering many optional parameters and their defaults.

To add an alert by using T-SQL, you use the *sp_add_alert* stored procedure. You use this procedure whether you want to create an event alert or a performance condition alert. The parameter options determine which type of alert is created. The syntax of *sp_add_alert* is shown here:

```
sp_add_alert [@name =] 'name'
[, [@message_id =] message_id]
[, [@severity =] severity]
[, [@enabled =] enabled]
[, [@delay_between_responses =] delay_between_responses]
[, [@notification_message =] 'notification_message']
[, [@include_event_description_in =] include_event_description_in]
[, [@database_name =] 'database']
[, [@event_description_keyword =] 'event_description_keyword_pattern']
[, {[@job_id =] job_id | [@job_name =] 'job_name'}]
[, [@raise_snmp_trap =] raise_snmp_trap]
[, [@performance_condition =] 'performance_condition']
[, [@category_name =] 'category']
```

The stored procedures used to modify an alert, view alert information, and delete an alert are *sp_update_alert*, *sp_help_alert*, and *sp_delete_alert*, respectively. Remember, all of these stored procedures are found in the msdb database.

More Info   For more details about the procedures described in this section, look up the procedures in the Books Online index.

Operators

Operators are individuals who can receive notification from SQL Server upon the completion of a job or the occurrence of an event. An operator is a person who is responsible for the maintenance of one or more systems running SQL Server. You've learned how to define the notification message that will be sent to the operator. As mentioned, the three methods used to communicate with operators are sending e-mail messages, paging, and using the NET SEND command (which sends a network message to the operator's computer). Your system must meet several prerequisites to make each of these methods work. For e-mail and pager communication, you must install a MAPI-1–compliant e-mail client ("MAPI" stands for "Messaging API") such as Microsoft Outlook or Microsoft Exchange Client on the server, and you must create a mail profile for SQLServerAgent. For paging, you will also need to install third-party e-mail–to–pager software on the mail server, which processes inbound e-mail messages and converts them to pager messages. To use NET SEND, you must be running Windows NT or Windows 2000 as your operating system—NET SEND is not supported under Microsoft Windows 95/98.

More Info   For information about how to set up mail profiles, see your e-mail client software documentation. For information about pager–to–e-mail software, see your pager service provider or your pager documentation.

You must define each operator in SQL Server. You can create more than one operator in order to share responsibilities, as well as a fail-safe operator who will be notified when the others cannot be reached (for example, if a paging attempt fails). You can create an operator by using Enterprise Manager, T-SQL, or SQL-DMO. We will look at the Enterprise Manager and T-SQL methods in this section; the SQL-DMO method is beyond the scope of this book.

Using Enterprise Manager to Create an Operator

To create an operator by using Enterprise Manager, follow these steps:

1. In Enterprise Manager, expand a server folder, expand the Management folder, and then expand the SQL Server Agent folder. Right-click Operators and choose New Operator from the shortcut menu to display the New Operator Properties window, shown in Figure 31-22. On the General tab, type a name for the new operator, and then enter one or more of the following: that operator's e-mail address, pager address, and NET SEND address.

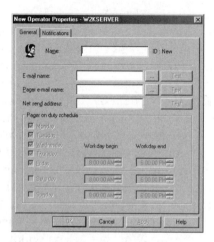

Figure 31-22. *The General tab of the New Operator Properties window.*

If you enter a pager address, you can specify when that operator can be paged in the Pager On Duty Schedule area. For example, if you had more than one operator, you could divide their duties by allowing one operator to be paged on Monday, Wednesday, Friday, and Sunday and another operator to be paged on Tuesday, Thursday, and Saturday.

2. Click the Notifications tab. If you click Alerts (in the upper right corner of the tab), a list of any existing alerts is displayed, as shown in Figure 31-23. By selecting the check boxes in the appropriate columns, you can specify which alerts will cause the operator to be notified and by which method of communication the operator will be notified.

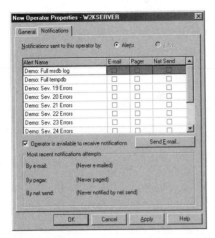

Figure 31-23. *The Notifications tab of the New Operator Properties window, showing Alerts.*

3. When creating a new operator, you will not be able to click Jobs because no jobs could have been created that would notify the new operator, since that operator did not yet exist. To prevent this new operator from receiving notifications, clear the Operator Is Available To Receive Notifications check box. Disabling this option enables you to temporarily stop notifications from being sent to an operator—for example, while the operator is on vacation. You can then re-enable notifications by deselecting the check box when the operator returns.

4. Click the Send E-mail button to create a test message to be sent to the operator listed on the General tab. (You will get an error if you did not enter an e-mail address on the General tab.) You can then send the e-mail, which describes the types of notifications that have been set up for that operator. At the bottom of the Notifications tab, you'll see information about the most recent notification attempts, by type, for that operator.

Using T-SQL to Create an Operator

The T-SQL commands used to create an operator, modify operator information, view operator information, and delete an operator are these system stored procedures, found in the msdb database: *sp_add_operator*, *sp_update_operator*, *sp_help_operator,* and *sp_delete_operator,* respectively. Again, you might find using Enterprise Manager to be the easier method. You can generate the T-SQL scripts after you have created the operators by using Enterprise Manager.

Here is the syntax for *sp_add_operator*:

```
sp_add_operator [@name =] 'name'
[, [@enabled =] enabled]
[, [@email_address =] 'email_address']
[, [@pager_address =] 'pager_address']
[, [@weekday_pager_start_time =] weekday_pager_start_time]
[, [@weekday_pager_end_time =] weekday_pager_end_time]
[, [@saturday_pager_start_time =] saturday_pager_start_time]
[, [@saturday_pager_end_time =] saturday_pager_end_time]
[, [@sunday_pager_start_time =] sunday_pager_start_time]
[, [@sunday_pager_end_time =] sunday_pager_end_time]
[, [@pager_days =] pager_days]
[, [@netsend_address =] 'netsend_address']
[, [@category_name =] 'category']
```

More Info For details about the options of the stored procedures listed in this section, look up the stored procedures by name in the Books Online index.

The SQLServerAgent Error Log

The SQLServerAgent service has its own error log that records the startup and shutdown of SQLServerAgent and any warnings, errors, and informational messages that occur related to a SQLServerAgent job or alert. To use the SQLServerAgent error log, follow these steps:

1. In Enterprise Manager, expand a server folder and expand the Management folder. Right-click SQL Server Agent and choose Display Error Log from the shortcut menu. The error log appears, as shown in Figure 31-24.

2. The Type drop-down list lets you view error messages, warning messages, informational messages, or all three (All Types). Figure 31-25 shows what the error log looks like just after SQLServerAgent is started. (Notice that All Types is selected in the Type drop-down list.)

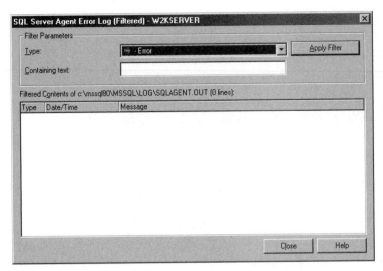

Figure 31-24. *The SQL Server Agent Error Log dialog box.*

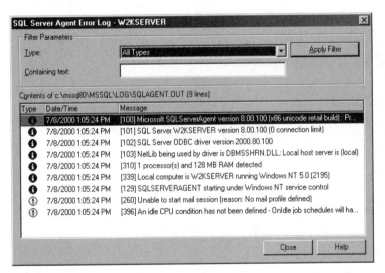

Figure 31-25. *The SQL Server Agent Error Log dialog box, showing all types of messages.*

3. Each time you start SQLServerAgent, the error log is restarted, over-writing any existing messages in the log. You can search for a message that contains a particular string by typing that string in the Containing Text text box and then pressing Enter or clicking Apply Filter. Figure 31-26 shows the error log after a search for the string "CPU."

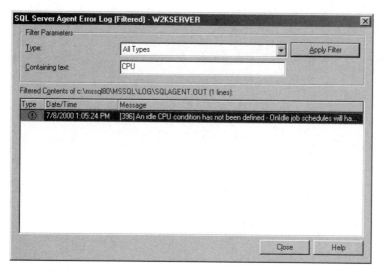

Figure 31-26. *The results of a search for a string in the error log messages.*

4. Double-click the message itself to view the SQL Server Agent Error Log Message dialog box, shown in Figure 31-27.

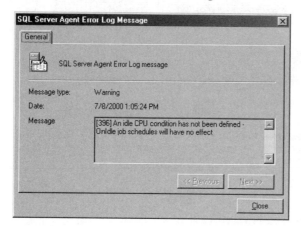

Figure 31-27. *The SQL Server Agent Error Log Message dialog box.*

If more than one message results from the search, you can use the Next and Previous buttons to switch between messages. These buttons will be unavailable if only one message is found.

The SQLServerAgent error log receives an error message if an operator is not successfully reached for some reason or if a job cannot be run. You should check this error log occasionally to determine whether any errors have occurred that need to be addressed.

Summary

In this chapter, you've learned how to use the SQLServerAgent service to automate some of your administrative tasks by defining jobs and operators, setting up notification to operators, and creating event alerts and performance condition alerts. You've learned the importance of error severity levels in creating alerts on events and how to alter the logging status of an error message to enable it to be logged in the Windows NT or Windows 2000 application event log. And you've learned how to view the SQLServerAgent error log file, which records information about SQLServerAgent and any errors and warnings that occur during alerts and jobs. In Chapter 32, we'll look at backing up SQL Server databases.

Chapter 32
Backing Up Microsoft SQL Server

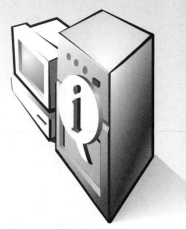

Backing up the database is one of the DBA's most important tasks. Having backup files and carefully planning for disaster recovery enable the DBA to restore the system in the event of a failure. The DBA is responsible for keeping the system up and running as much as possible and, in the event of a system failure, for restoring service as quickly as possible. Downtime can be both inconvenient and extremely expensive. Getting the database back up and running as soon as possible is essential. Technologies such as clustering and fault-tolerant disk subsystems can help, but they are no substitute for good planning and a reliable backup method.

Because the topics of backing up, restoring, and recovering the database are so important, they are covered in this book over the course of two chapters. In this chapter, you'll learn about the Microsoft SQL Server transaction log and the various methods of backing up the database. In Chapter 33, you'll learn how to restore the database, how SQL Server recovery works, and how to create and implement a disaster recovery plan.

Backup Terminology

Before we look at backup techniques, let's review some terminology. In this section, you'll learn some basic facts about backup, restore, and recovery operations.

Backup and Restore

Backup and *restore* operations are related and involve saving data from the database for later use, similar to the backup and restore operations that can be performed by the operating system. During the backup, data is copied from the database and saved in another location. The difference between an operating system backup and a database backup is that the operating system backup can save individual files, whereas the database backup saves the entire database. Usually, a database is shared by many users, whereas many operating system files belong to individual users. Thus, a database backup backs up all of the user's data at once. Because SQL Server is designed for maximum uptime, the backup process is designed to work while the database is up and running, and even while users are accessing the database.

During the restore, the backed up data is copied back to the database. (Don't confuse restore with recovery; these are two separate operations.) Unlike the backup process, the restore process cannot be done while SQL Server is up and running. In addition, a table cannot be restored separately. If one user loses some data in the database, the lost data cannot be easily restored because the restore operation will restore the entire database or a portion of it. Distinguishing a single user's data from all the data in the database can be difficult.

Recovery

Recovery involves the ability of the relational database management system (RDBMS) to survive a system failure and replay (recover) transactions. SQL Server does not immediately write changes to disk every time a change is made in the database. If it did, a large system (such as the system at a bank) would perform more slowly, because every transaction would have to wait for writes to complete before proceeding. This would cause every transaction to experience a delay.

With the delay in writing changes to disk, a system failure might leave the database in a corrupted state because some changes made to the database might not have been written to disk or changes written to disk might not have been committed. To maintain the integrity of the database, SQL Server logs all changes in a transaction log. (The transaction log is described in detail in the section "The Transaction Log" later in this chapter.) When SQL Server restarts after a system failure, it uses the transaction log to roll forward transactions that were committed but not written to disk and to roll back transactions that were not committed at the time of the failure. In this manner, data accuracy is guaranteed.

SQL Server must be prepared to handle several types of transactions during recovery, including the following:

- **Transactions that are queries only** No recovery is necessary.
- **Transactions that changed data in the database and were committed but were not written to disk** During recovery, SQL Server reads the data pages from disk, reapplies the changes, and then rewrites the pages to disk.

- **Transactions that changed data in the database, were committed, and were written to disk**   During recovery, SQL Server determines that the changes were written to disk. No other intervention is required.

- **Transactions that changed data in the database and were not committed**   During recovery, SQL Server uses the transaction log to undo any changes that were made to data pages and restores the database to the state it was in before the transactions started.

When SQL Server restarts from a system failure, the recovery mechanism starts automatically. The recovery mechanism uses the transaction log to determine which transactions need to be recovered and which do not. Many of the transactions will not need recovery, but SQL Server must read the transaction log to determine which transactions do require recovery. SQL Server starts reading the transaction log at the point where the last checkpoint occurred. (Checkpoints are covered later in this chapter.)

Note   Because the transaction log is crucial for the recovery of transactions in the event of a failure, it should always reside on a RAID 1 (mirrored) volume. (RAID is explained in Chapter 5.)

In the event of a system failure that requires the database to be restored from backup files (such as the loss of a disk drive), the transaction log and transaction log backups are used to restore the database to the state it was in at the point of failure. Thus, restore and recovery operations usually work together. In the event of a power failure, only recovery might be necessary.

Note   A transaction that is rolled back by SQL Server is identical to a transaction that ends with the ROLLBACK command. The transaction is nullified, and all the data is restored to its original state.

When a transaction is rolled forward, the changes made to the database but not written to disk are replayed, so the data files are returned to the state they were in at the time of failure. In other words, rolling forward transactions brings the database back to the state it was in at the point of failure, minus all uncommitted transactions, by redoing the committed transactions.

System Failure

You might be wondering whether backups are really necessary if you use technologies such as Microsoft Cluster Services and RAID fault tolerance. The answer is a resounding "yes." Your system can fail in a number of ways, and those methods of fault tolerance and fault recovery will help keep your system functioning properly through only some of them. In this section, we'll explore some of the potential causes of failure and ways to survive those failures.

Some system failures can be mild; others can be devastating. To understand why backups are so important, you need to know about the three main categories of failures: hardware failures, software failures, and human error.

Hardware Failures

Hardware failures are probably the most common type of failure you will encounter. Although these failures are becoming less frequent as computer hardware becomes more reliable, components will still wear out over time. Typical hardware failures include the following:

- **CPU, memory, or bus failure**   These failures usually result in a system crash. After you replace the faulty component and restart the system, SQL Server automatically performs a database recovery. The database itself is intact, so it does not need to be restored—SQL Server needs simply to replay the lost transactions.

- **Disk failure**   If you're using RAID fault tolerance, this failure type will probably not affect the state of the database at all. You must simply repair the RAID array. If you are not using RAID fault tolerance or if an entire RAID array fails, your only alternative is to restore the database from the backup and use the transaction log backups to recover the database.

- **Catastrophic system failure or permanent loss of server**   If the entire system is destroyed in a fire or some other disaster, you might have to start over from scratch. The hardware will need to be reassembled, the database restored from the backup, and the database recovered by means of the data and transaction log backups.

Software Failures

Software failures are rare, and your system probably will never experience them. However, a software failure is usually more disastrous than a hardware failure because software has built-in features that minimize the effect of hardware failures, and without these protective features, the system is vulnerable to disaster if a hardware failure occurs. The transaction log is an example of a software feature designed to help systems recover from hardware failures. Typical software failures include the following:

- **Operating system failure**   If a failure of this type occurs in the I/O subsystem, data on disk can be corrupted. If no database corruption occurs, only recovery is necessary. If database corruption occurs, your only option is to restore the database from a backup.

- **RDBMS failure**   SQL Server itself can fail. If this type of failure causes corruption to occur, the database must be restored from a backup and recovered. If no corruption occurs, only the automatic recovery is needed to return the system to the state it was in at the point of failure.

- **Application failure**   Applications can fail, which can cause data corruption. Like an RDBMS failure, if this type of failure causes corruption to occur, the database must be restored from a backup. If no corruption occurs, no restore is necessary; the automatic recovery will return the system to the state it was in at the point of failure. You might also need to obtain a patch from your application vendor to prevent this type of failure from recurring.

Note   Companies often try beta versions of SQL Server. Beta versions of software are designed for evaluation and testing only and should not be used in a production environment. Sometimes, beta versions contain software bugs and include features that have not been fully tested. You should use the production release of Microsoft SQL Server 2000, which has been fully tested and is ready for production use.

Human Error

The third main category of failure is human error. Human errors can occur at any time and without notice. They can be mild or severe. Unfortunately, these types of errors can go unnoticed for days or even weeks, which can make recovery more difficult. By establishing a good relationship (including good communication) with your users, you can help make recovery from user errors easier and faster. Users should not be afraid to come to you immediately to report a mistake. The earlier you find out about an error, the better. The following failures can be caused by human error:

- **Database server loss**   Human errors that can cause the server to fail include accidentally shutting off the power or shutting down the server without first shutting down SQL Server. Recovery is automatic when SQL Server is restarted, but it might take some time. Because the database is intact on disk, a restore is not necessary.

- **Data loss**   This type of loss can be caused by someone's accidentally deleting a data file, for example, thus causing loss of the database. Restore and recovery operations must be performed to return the database to its prefailure state.

- **Table loss or corrupted data**   If a table is dropped by mistake or its data is somehow incorrectly changed, you can use backup and recovery to return the table to its original state. Recovery from this type of failure can be quite complex because a single table or a small set of data that is lost cannot simply be recovered from a backup. An example of restoring data after this type of failure is shown in Chapter 33.

SQL Server Logging

To understand how backup and restore operations work in conjunction with database recovery, you must first understand how SQL Server logging works. This section provides an overview of SQL Server logging and checkpoints and shows you how to back up the transaction log.

The Transaction Log

The *transaction log* is used to record all transactions and the modifications that those transactions make to the database. This record makes recovery possible. When a transaction is committed, the commit operation is not completed until the commit record for that transaction has been written to the transaction log. Because changes to the database are not necessarily written to disk immediately, this log is the only means whereby transactions can be recovered in the event of a system failure.

Note   If a data file is damaged and must be restored from backup, all of the transactions that have occurred on that data file must be replayed to recover the database to the state it was in just before the failure. Because the transaction log is critical for this process and has limited space, transaction log backups must be performed. You must save all of the transaction log data that has been generated since the last backup in order to recover the database. If you are interested in restoring only to the last backup, you can skip transaction log backup, but the current transaction log will not be able to recover the transactions that have occurred since that backup.

The Lazywriter Thread

Changes made to a database are first made to data inside the SQL Server cache. Cache data is changed first mainly to improve performance, because waiting for I/O operations is quite time consuming. These changes are eventually written to disk, but this process occurs in the background and is unknown to the user. Because modified pages are stored in the cache, a significant amount of time might elapse before these pages (called *dirty pages*) are written to disk by the SQL Server thread responsible for doing so. This thread is called the *lazywriter thread*.

The lazywriter thread uses a least recently used (LRU) page list, meaning that the data that has been used least recently is at the beginning of the list to be written to disk and that the data that has just been used is at the end of the list and is least likely to be written to disk. A page that is constantly being modified (and thus moving repeatedly to the end of the list) might never be written to disk by the lazywriter thread. This can increase the recovery time because many log records might have to be read in order to apply all the changes to that data. For example, on a large system with more than 1 gigabyte (GB) of RAM and many changes to the database, the recovery can take several hours.

In addition to the lazywriter thread, the *checkpoint thread* writes dirty pages to disk. (We'll look at the checkpoint thread in detail later in this section.)

Sequential Logging

Because the transaction log is a history of transactions, the I/O operations to the transaction log are mainly writes and are generally sequential in nature. In the event of a transaction rollback, the transaction log will be read, and the sequential nature of the I/O operations will be disrupted. Because rollbacks are fairly rare (since system crashes are rare and users do not undo transactions often), the I/O pattern in the transaction log is fairly stable. You can greatly enhance I/O performance by placing the transaction log on its own disk drive or RAID array, as explained in Chapters 4 and 5. You should protect the transaction log with RAID because the transaction log is so important to database recovery.

Transaction Log Size

Depending on the number of changes to your database, the transaction log can grow to be quite large. Because the transaction log consists of one or more files whose size is finite, the log will eventually be filled and therefore must be truncated periodically. The log is automatically truncated at the completion of a log backup, as we'll see later in this chapter.

> **Note** You can truncate a database's log without backing up the log by setting the database option *trunc. log on chkpt* to *TRUE* for that database. However, after doing so, you will not be able to back up the transaction log. Using this setting will make the database unrecoverable and is therefore not recommended.

Recovery Using the Transaction Log

In the event of a system failure in which data files are not damaged, the current transaction log is used to recover the database because only those transactions that have not yet been written to disk must be recovered. The number of pages that must be recovered depends on the number of dirty pages in the database, which, in turn, is governed by the checkpoint interval. A checkpoint writes dirty pages to disk to reduce the time needed to perform a recovery. Checkpoints and the checkpoint interval are described in detail in the section "Checkpoints" later in this chapter.

Transaction Log Properties

The transaction log has come a long way since Microsoft SQL Server 6.5. The SQL Server 2000 transaction log has the same characteristics as the Microsoft SQL Server 7 transaction log. These characteristics include the following:

- The SQL Server transaction log is not treated in the same manner as a data file. Transactions are not written to and read from the transaction log in 8-kilobyte (KB) pages as they are for data files. The transaction log can now write in chunks of whatever size it needs—the information no longer follows the format of data pages. Thus, if the logwriter thread needs to write only a small amount, it does not have to write 8 KB of data. If the system is experiencing frequent updates, the logwriter thread can write using a large block size (16 KB, 32 KB, and so on).

- The transaction log can be configured to automatically grow as needed. This feature allows more space to be added as required, but you should use it with caution to prevent the transaction log from growing uncontrollably and consuming the entire disk drive.

- The transaction log can now be implemented across several files. These files can be configured to grow automatically as well. The transaction log files are not striped; they are used one after another. (Data striping is explained in Chapter 5.)

- The transaction log can be shipped to other systems in order to be replayed on a standby system. This is known as log shipping and is described in more detail in the next chapter.

Nonlogged Operations

Now that you are familiar with the rules of logging and recovery, you are ready to learn about the exceptions to those rules. As mentioned, normally, all transactions and the changes they produce are recorded in the transaction log. However, you can perform certain operations that are not recorded in the log. These operations are called *nonlogged* operations. By performing a bulk operation (which uses a large amount of transaction log resources) as a nonlogged operation, you improve the performance of the operation.

Because nonlogged operations are not recorded in the transaction log, you must redo them if a recovery is necessary. Therefore, you should carefully consider the effects of enabling nonlogged operations before you do so. The operations that can be performed as nonlogged operations are as follows:

- SELECT INTO
- BULK COPY and Bulk Copy Program (BCP)
- CREATE INDEX
- Certain text operations

Later in this section, we'll look at the operations in the preceding list in a bit more detail.

In order to enable nonlogged bulk operations on a database, you must set the database to run in BULK_LOGGED recovery mode. The other recovery options are FULL and SIMPLE. Set these options by using the ALTER DATABASE command, as shown here for the Northwind database:

```
ALTER DATABASE Northwind
SET RECOVERY BULK_LOGGED

ALTER DATABASE Northwind
SET RECOVERY FULL

ALTER DATABASE Northwind
SET RECOVERY SIMPLE
```

When BULKED_LOGGED recovery mode is used, the bulk operations described in the sections that follow will not be logged (with certain exceptions, which are explained in the next few sections), and all other operations are logged. If FULL recovery mode is chosen, all operations are logged. And when SIMPLE recovery mode is implemented, data can be recovered only to the last backup.

> **Note** Because the recovery mode defines your system's level of tolerance of failure, BULK_LOGGED recovery mode should be used with caution. If you use this mode, the performance of nonlogged bulk operations will improve, but in the event of a failure, recovery time will be increased.

SELECT INTO

The SELECT INTO statement is used to create a new table in the database. Because the SELECT INTO statement cannot be used to select data into an existing object, it cannot be used for updating data, only for creating data. This creation process can often be easily repeated; thus, SELECT INTO statement operations are quite suitable for being performed as nonlogged operations.

BULK COPY and BCP

In order for BULK COPY and BCP operations to be performed as nonlogged operations, several requirements must be met. These requirements are as follows:

- The database option *select into/bulkcopy* must be set to *TRUE*.
- The target table cannot have any indexes unless they are empty when the bulk copy starts.
- The target table cannot be replicated, because transactional replication uses entries in the transaction log for its replication.
- The TABLOCK hint must be specified in order to force a table lock.

These restrictions will allow the bulk copy operations both to save space in the transaction log and to run faster. However, in the event that the database needs to be restored from a backup, these nonlogged operations must be redone.

CREATE INDEX

CREATE INDEX statement operations are also suitable for being performed as nonlogged operations because indexes can be re-created as needed. Re-creating indexes is not difficult. However, if the tables are large, the process can be quite time consuming and resource intensive.

Text Operations

Text operations that can be performed as nonlogged operations include WRITETEXT and UPDATETEXT. To enable these operations to run without being logged, you simply use the BULK_LOGGED recovery option, as described earlier.

Checkpoints

A *checkpoint* is an operation that is used to synchronize the physical data files with the database cache to reduce the necessary recovery time in the event of a system failure. The amount of time needed to recover the database is determined by the amount of time since the last checkpoint and by the number of dirty pages in the buffer cache. Thus, decreasing the checkpoint interval will reduce the recovery time, but at a cost: the checkpoint process incurs a lot of overhead.

Checkpoints occur whenever a CHECKPOINT statement is issued, whenever SQL Server is shut down by means of a SHUTDOWN statement, whenever SQL Server is shut down by means of the Service Control Manager, and whenever SQL Server automatically issues a checkpoint.

Checkpoint Operations

The checkpoint process performs a number of operations, including the following:

- **Writes out all dirty data pages that were dirty at the beginning of the checkpoint**   All pages that contain changed data and have not yet been written to disk are now written to disk.

- **Writes a list of outstanding transactions to the transaction log**   This gives SQL Server data about the transactions that were in progress when the checkpoint was occurring. If a failure occurs, the recovery process uses this data to recover these transactions.

- **Writes all dirty log pages to disk**   This ensures that the log buffer is flushed to disk.

- **Stores checkpoint log records in the database**   This preserves a record of the checkpoint outside the transaction log, which is needed because the log might be backed up and truncated.

Checkpoint Interval Configuration

The checkpoint interval is defined by the SQL Server configuration option *recovery interval*. This parameter is set for the entire SQL Server system, not for each database, but checkpoints occur per database. This parameter specifies the number of minutes that SQL Server should take to recover each database in the event of a system failure. The default value *0* instructs SQL Server to determine the checkpoint interval for you—usually less than 1 minute. For systems that have a large amount of memory and a lot of insert and update activity, the default setting might cause an excessive number of checkpoints to occur. In that case, you might want to set the parameter to a higher value. If your users can tolerate a longer recovery in the event of a system failure (30 minutes, for example), transaction performance on your system will improve. You should set this parameter according to your company's ability to handle the downtime and the frequency of failures.

The checkpoint interval is also based on the number of records in the transaction log. It is not based on the system time or the size of the log. The more records in the transaction log, the shorter the checkpoint interval. As more changes are made, more records will be inserted into the transaction log, and consequently, SQL Server will configure the checkpoint interval to write those changes to disk more often. If few or no changes are made to the database, the transaction log will contain only a few records, and the checkpoint interval will be long.

You can change the *recovery interval* parameter in two ways: by using Enterprise Manager or by using Transact-SQL (T-SQL). To set *recovery interval* from Enterprise Manager, in the left-hand pane, right-click the name of the server for which you want to set this parameter and choose Properties from the shortcut menu to display the SQL Server Properties window. Click the Database Settings tab, shown in Figure 32-1, and specify the desired recovery interval, in minutes, in the Recovery Interval spin box.

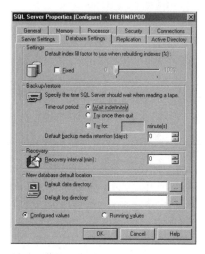

Figure 32-1. *The SQL Server Properties window.*

To set *recovery interval* by using T-SQL, use the *sp_configure* stored procedure, as shown here:

```
sp_configure "recovery interval", 1
GO
```

You will see the following output:

```
DBCC execution completed. If DBCC printed error messages,
contact your system administrator.
Configuration option changed. Run the RECONFIGURE statement
to install.
```

The change will not be implemented unless you run the RECONFIGURE command. If you are sure of your change, enter the following T-SQL statement:

```
RECONFIGURE
GO
```

The RECONFIGURE command signals SQL Server to accept the configuration changes. SQL Server does not need to be restarted in order for changes to the *recovery interval* parameter to take effect.

To ensure that the setting you have made is actually in effect, use the following T-SQL statement:

```
sp_configure "recovery interval"
GO
```

The output looks like this:

```
name                    minimum maximum config_value run_value
---------------------   ------- ------- ------------ ---------
recovery interval (min) 0       32767   1            1
```

Notice that the *recovery interval* parameter has indeed been set.

Caution   The *recovery interval* parameter is an advanced option, and you should change it only after careful planning. Increasing the *recovery interval* setting will increase the time necessary to perform a database recovery.

Backup Methods

There are several methods of backing up a database: full, differential, transaction log, filegroup, and data file. Each has its own modes of operation and features. A *full backup* consists of backing up all of the data in the database, the filegroup, or the data file. A *differential backup* involves backing up only the data that has changed since the last backup. A *transaction log backup* is used to back up and truncate the transaction log. (As we've seen, backing up the transaction log is a crucial DBA task because transaction log data is used in conjunction with database backups.) *Filegroup* and *data file backups* are used to back up a particular filegroup or data file in the database.

All SQL Server backups are performed for a specific database. To completely back up your system, you should back up all databases in the system and their transaction logs. Don't forget to back up the master database as well. And remember, without good backups, you might not be able to restore your data in the event of a failure.

Full Backups

As mentioned, a full backup involves backing up an entire database. All of the filegroups and data files that are part of this database are backed up. If you have multiple databases, you should back up all of them. A full backup is probably the most common technique for backing up small- to medium-size databases. Depending on how large the databases are, this process can be quite time consuming, so if time is an issue, you might consider performing differential backups or filegroup backups, as described next. Once you start a backup, you cannot pause it—the backup will continue until the entire database is backed up. Performing a full database backup is described in the section "Performing a Backup" later in this chapter.

Differential Backups

Differential backups enable you to back up only the information that has changed since the last backup. Because they back up only part of the data, differential backups are faster and take less space than full backups. However, differential backups are more difficult and time consuming to restore than full backups. Restoring a differential backup requires the restoration of the last full backup and all differential backups that have occurred since the last full backup.

Transaction Log Backups

Transaction log backups enable you to back up the transaction log. These backups are important for database recovery, as explained earlier in this chapter.

Filegroup Backups

A filegroup backup involves backing up all of the data files associated with a single file in a database. This process is similar to a full backup in that it backs up all of the data in the data files regardless of when the data was last backed up. You can use a filegroup backup to back up a filegroup that is associated with a particular department or workgroup, depending on how your system is configured. If your system is divided into individual departments accessing their own filegroups, you can back up each department's data according to a different schedule.

Data File Backups

Data file backups enable you to back up a single file in a filegroup. This backup type works in conjunction with SQL Server 2000's capability to restore a single data file separately. A data file backup can be useful if you don't have enough time each night to back up an entire filegroup, because it allows you to rotate data files for backup. In the event of a disk failure in which a data file is lost or corrupted, you can restore only that data file. The greater the amount of time that has passed since that data file was backed up, however, the longer the recovery process will take.

Performing a Backup

You can perform backups by using Enterprise Manager, T-SQL commands, or the Create Database Backup Wizard. The Create Database Backup Wizard method is the easiest in many cases, but Enterprise Manager is also easy to use. On the other hand, T-SQL commands can be put into SQL scripts that can be replayed over and over again. You should use the method that best suits your needs.

The backup operations themselves can be directed to either a physical device or a logical device. A *physical device* is an item such as a tape drive or a disk drive. Physical devices are assigned names by the operating system, and you must use these names to access the devices. Because these preassigned names can be hard to remember, you might want to create an alias, or user-defined name, for a physical device. Such an alias is called a *logical device*. This logical device exists only within SQL Server and can be used only for SQL Server backups, so it is also referred to as a *logical backup device*. If you want to back up data to a logical device, you must create the device beforehand. Before we look at the various methods of performing a backup, let's look at how to create a logical backup device. We'll use a logical backup device for the examples in this section. (See your system administrator for details about adding physical devices to the system.)

Creating Logical Backup Devices

You can create logical backup devices by using either Enterprise Manager or T-SQL. We'll look at both techniques in this section. The use of multiple backup devices can improve performance. (Backup performance tips are given in the section "Improving Backups" later in this chapter.)

Creating Backup Devices by Using Enterprise Manager

To create a backup device by using Enterprise Manager, follow these steps:

1. In the left pane of Enterprise Manager, expand the SQL Server Group folder, expand a server folder, and then expand the Management folder.

2. Right-click Backup and choose New Backup Device from the shortcut menu to display the Backup Device Properties window, shown in Figure 32-2.

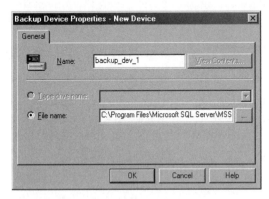

Figure 32-2. *The Backup Device Properties window.*

3. Simply type a descriptive name for the backup device in the Name text box. The File Name text box is filled automatically. To change the file-name path, either type a new path in the File Name text box or click the Browse [...] button to open the Backup Device Location dialog box. In this example, the backup device name is backup_dev_1. If you are adding a tape device, click View Contents to view any backup sets that are currently on the tape device.

Once you have finished these steps, the device is ready for use. You'll learn how to use backup devices later in this section, when you learn how to create a backup. Notice that if you do not have any tape devices connected to your system, the Tape Drive Name option will be unavailable.

Creating Backup Devices by Using T-SQL

To create a backup device by using T-SQL, use the stored procedure *sp_addumpdevice*. The syntax of *sp_addumpdevice* is shown here:

```
sp_addumpdevice device_type, logical_name, physical_name
```

The *device_type* parameter can be *disk* for a disk drive, *tape* for a tape drive, or *pipe* for connecting third-party software to the backup system. The *logical_name* parameter is the name you assign to the device; this name is used to reference the device in BACKUP and RESTORE statements. The *physical_name* parameter is the system-assigned name of the device or file.

For example, to create a logical device named Backup_dev_2 that is a disk file, use the following syntax:

```
sp_addumpdevice 'disk', 'Backup_dev_2',
'C:\MSSQL2K\BACKUP\Backup_dev_2.BAK'
```

Creating a Remote Backup Device

In order to back up your database to a remote system, you must first create the backup device by using the system stored procedure *sp_addumpdevice*. You cannot create a backup device on a remote server by using Enterprise Manager. In order to specify a remote system, you must specify the entire Universal Naming Convention (UNC) name as the physical name, as shown in this example:

```
sp_addumpdevice 'disk', 'netbackup1',
'\\ptc4\c$\backup\netbackup1.bck'
```

Once you have created this backup device, you can back up data to it by using either Enterprise Manager or T-SQL commands.

Note   To back up data to a remote system, you must have installed SQL Server to run under an account other than "LocalSystem." The "LocalSystem" account does not have privileges to access remote systems, and the backup will fail.

Backing Up Data over Multiple Networks

You can also perform a backup over multiple network interface cards. By backing up data to multiple devices over several LAN segments, you can overcome network bandwidth problems that might limit performance. If you are backing up data to several computer systems, simply specify the system names. If you are backing up data to one system via two LAN segments, you can specify the IP address in the UNC address, as shown here:

```
sp_addumpdevice 'disk', 'netbackup1',
'\\100.100.100.1\c$\backup\netbackup1.bck'
sp_addumpdevice 'disk', 'netbackup2',
'\\100.100.200.1\c$\backup\netbackup2.bck'
```

Once you have created these backup devices, you can back up data to them by using either Enterprise Manager or T-SQL commands.

Backing Up Using Enterprise Manager

Once you create one or more backup devices, you're ready to perform a backup. We'll look at the Enterprise Manager method first. To avoid repetition, the transaction log and database backup methods are presented together where possible, with the specific options for each identified and the differences between them noted.

Performing the Backup

To perform a backup by using Enterprise Manager, follow these steps:

1. Invoke the SQL Server Backup utility by using one of the following techniques:

    - Expand a server folder in the left pane of Enterprise Manager, and then expand the Management folder. Right-click Backup and choose Backup A Database from the shortcut menu.

    - Expand a server folder in the left pane of Enterprise Manager, right-click Database, point to All Tasks in the shortcut menu, and then choose Backup Database.

    - Expand a server folder in the left pane of Enterprise Manager, and then click the Databases folder. In the right pane, right-click a database, point to All Tasks in the shortcut menu, and then choose Backup Database.

    The SQL Server Backup dialog box appears, as shown in Figure 32-3.

Figure 32-3. *The General tab of the SQL Server Backup dialog box.*

2. In the Database drop-down list in the top section of this dialog box, select the database that you want to back up. (If you used the third tech-

nique in step 1, the database name will already be selected.) The backup name is based on the database name and is automatically generated for you, although you can override the automatic name by typing a backup name in the Name text box. You can also type a backup description in the Description text box. The description might be important when you are trying to restore the database. For example, if you are creating this backup immediately before dropping a table, a note about that in the description of the backup will be valuable. If you are backing up prior to loading some new data, include that information in your description.

3. In the Backup area of this dialog box, you must specify the type of backup to perform. The options that are available will vary depending on which database you select. For example, by default the Northwind database has the Truncate Log On Checkpoint option set. With this option set, the Transaction Log and File And Filegroup options are not available to the backup program. The backup options are described here:

- **Database - Complete**   Performs a complete database backup; this will back up all of the data in the database.

- **Database - Differential**   Performs a differential database backup; this will back up all data that has changed since the last backup.

- **Transaction Log**   Performs a transaction log backup; this will also truncate the log.

- **File And Filegroup**   Backs up single filegroups or files; you can specify the filegroup or file to back up.

Only one of these backup types can be selected. To perform a complete database backup and a transaction log backup, you must run the backup program twice.

4. In the Destination area, you must specify whether the backup is to tape or to disk. You can add more logical or physical backup devices by clicking Add. The Select Backup Destination dialog box appears, as shown in Figure 32-4. In this dialog box, you can specify a filename or select the backup devices from the Backup Device drop-down list. Click OK to return to the General tab of the SQL Server Backup dialog box. In the example in Figure 32-3, two devices are listed in the Backup To list. To remove a device, select the device and click Remove. Click Contents to view the contents of a device.

Figure 32-4. *The Select Backup Destination dialog box.*

If a backup device has been used previously, the following information about the backup is available:

- **Name** The name that was chosen by the person who ran the backup
- **Server** The name of the server that the backup was performed on
- **Database** The name of the database that the backup was performed on
- **Type** The type of backup (Complete, Differential, Transaction Log, Filegroup, or File)
- **Date** The date and time that the backup was performed
- **Expiration** The expiration date that was specified for the backup
- **Size** The total size of the backup set
- **Description** The description of the backup

Remember, multiple backups can be (and frequently are) performed to the same backup device.

5. In the Overwrite area of the SQL Server Backup dialog box, you can choose to overwrite the medium (such as a tape or a disk) or append to it. A disk device is typically appended to. But if you are using tapes and you are alternating them, you need to remove the previous information. Although you could overwrite that information by clicking Overwrite Existing Media in this dialog box, you should instead get into the habit of erasing the information before you perform a backup. Taking this precaution helps ensure that you will not accidentally overwrite a tape or a disk device.

6. In the Schedule area, you can choose to schedule the backup for a later time. Scheduling backups can be especially useful for transaction log backups that must occur on a regular basis to prevent the transaction log from filling up. If you want to schedule the backup, select the Schedule check box, and then click the Browse button to display the Edit Schedule dialog box, shown in Figure 32-5.

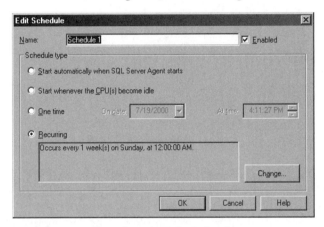

Figure 32-5. *The Edit Schedule dialog box.*

7. Provide a name for the schedule in the Name text box. Naming the schedules allows you to create multiple schedules—a schedule for each of your backups, perhaps.

   In the Schedule Type section, you can specify whether the backup will start automatically when SQL Server Agent starts, whether to delay the backup until the CPUs become available, and whether the backup will run once or will recur. If you choose to run the backup once, you use the On Date popup calendar to select the date the backup is performed and the At Time spin box to select the time.

   To set the schedule for a recurring backup, click Recurring and then click Change. The Edit Recurring Job Schedule dialog box appears, as shown in Figure 32-6.

   This dialog box gives you tremendous scheduling flexibility. Within the Daily, Weekly, and Monthly options, you can schedule the frequency and duration of the job.

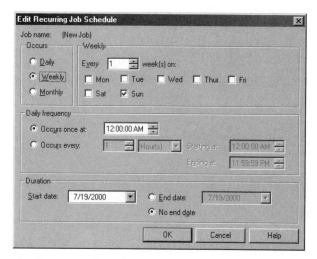

Figure 32-6. *The Edit Recurring Job Schedule dialog box.*

8. Click OK to return to the Edit Schedule dialog box, click OK again to return to the SQL Server Backup dialog box, and then click the Options tab, shown in Figure 32-7. In this tab, you can specify whether the backup media should be verified on backup completion, and you can indicate whether and how the media should be labeled. The options on this tab are described here:

- **Verify Backup Upon Completion**   Causes the backup media to be verified as readable. Only media integrity is verified; the process does not verify that the data was backed up.

- **Eject Tape After Backup (tape devices only)**   Ejects the tape from the tape device after the backup is complete. This option is useful when multiple applications or users are accessing the tape devices. This option can save your tape from being overwritten by someone else.

- **Remove Inactive Entries From Transaction Log (transaction log backups only)**   Truncates the transaction log after the backup.

- **Check Media Set Name And Backup Set Expiration**   Specifies that the media be checked and not overwritten unless the expiration date has been reached.

- **Backup Set Will Expire (tape devices only)**   Allows you to set the media expiration date.

- **Initialize And Label Media (tape devices only)**   Allows you to specify a label for the media.

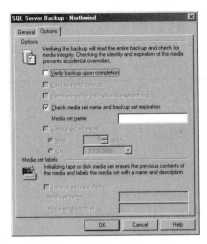

Figure 32-7. *The Options tab of the SQL Server Backup dialog box.*

9. When you finish setting the options, click OK to begin running the backup you configured.

Managing the Backup

To view, delete, or modify backup jobs that have been scheduled, follow these steps:

1. In the left pane of Enterprise Manager, expand a server folder, expand the Management folder, expand the SQL Server Agent folder, and click Jobs. The scheduled jobs are listed in the right pane of Enterprise Manager, as shown in Figure 32-8.

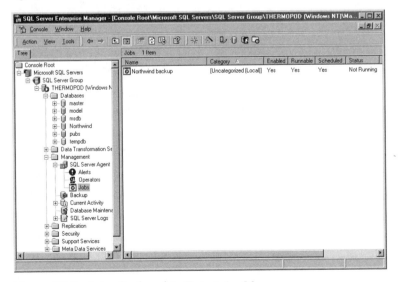

Figure 32-8. *Jobs displayed in Enterprise Manager.*

2. To delete a job, simply right-click the job name and choose Delete from the shortcut menu.

3. To view or modify a job, right-click the job name and choose Properties from the shortcut menu to display the job's Properties window. Make your modifications, click Apply, and then click OK.

Backing Up Using T-SQL Commands

Using T-SQL to back up a database can be a little more difficult than using Enterprise Manager at first, but if you're the type of DBA who prefers to automate operations in scripts, this technique should be more to your liking. The T-SQL BACKUP command also offers a few more options than does the backup program in Enterprise Manager. In this section, we'll look at the syntax and the options of the BACKUP command. There are actually two T-SQL backup commands; which one you use depends on the type of backup you're performing. These commands are listed here:

- **BACKUP DATABASE**   Used for backing up either the entire database or a file or filegroup
- **BACKUP LOG**   Used for backing up the transaction log

Because these two commands provide most of the same options, we'll look at them together.

Performing the Backup

The syntax of the BACKUP statement for a full database backup is shown here:

```
BACKUP DATABASE database_name
TO backup_device
[ WITH options ]
```

This statement requires only the name of the database and the name of the backup device. (Examples of BACKUP statements can be found in the sidebar "Using BACKUP" later in this chapter.)

The syntax of the statement for a file or filegroup backup is shown here:

```
BACKUP DATABASE database_name
file_name or filegroup_name [,...n]
TO backup_device
[ WITH options ]
```

This statement requires only the name of the database, the filename or filegroup name, and the backup device name. Multiple filenames or filegroup names can be included, separated by commas.

The syntax of the statement for a transaction log backup is shown here:

```
BACKUP LOG database_name
{
[ WITH { NO_LOG | TRUNCATE_ONLY )]
}
|
{
TO backup_device
}
[ WITH options ]
```

This statement requires a database name, and either the WITH NO_LOG or WITH TRUNCATE_ONLY option or a backup device name. You can then add any options you want. The NO_LOG and TRUNCATE ONLY options are synonyms, and both truncate the log without making a backup copy of it.

> **Caution**   If you use either of these options in your BACKUP LOG statement, in the event of a failure, you will not be able to recover the database to the state it was in at the point of failure because no log records will be saved. These options are not recommended; use them at your own risk.

In all three of these backup commands, *database_name* is the name of the database that the backup will be performed on. The *backup_device* parameter is either a logical backup device name or the name of a physical device. If a physical device is specified, the device name must be preceded by *DISK =*, *TAPE ?*, or *PIPE ?*, depending on the type of device. You can specify either one device or a comma-delimited set of devices, as shown in the following two examples:

```
Backup_dev_1, Backup_dev_2, Backup_dev_3

TAPE = '\\.\Tape0', TAPE = '\\.\Tape1', TAPE = '\\.\Tape2'
```

Options

Table 32-1 lists the options available with the BACKUP command. If an option is available to only the database backup or only the log backup, the exception is noted.

Table 32-1. The BACKUP command options

Option	Description
BLOCKSIZE	This option specifies the physical block size in bytes.
DESCRIPTION	This option specifies the text description of the backup set. It is useful for locating the correct backup set from which to restore.
DIFFERENTIAL	This option specifies a differential backup. It is available with only a full database backup.
EXPIREDATE = *date* | RETAINDAYS = *days*	The EXPIREDATE option specifies the date on which the backup set expires (and can be overwritten). RETAINDAYS specifies the number of days before the backup set expires.
PASSWORD = *password*	The PASSWORD option allows you to specify a password for the backup. This provides greater security for the backup itself.
FORMAT | NOFORMAT	The FORMAT option specifies that the media header should be rewritten, thus invalidating the original data on the media. NOFORMAT specifies that the media header should not be rewritten.
INIT | NOINIT	The INIT option specifies that the backup set be located in the first file on the media and preserves the media header but over-writes all data on the media—in other words, INIT overwrites whatever is on the tape. The NOINIT option specifies that the backup set be appended to the media. If you are reusing tapes, you will need to use this option.
MEDIADESCRIPTION = *text*	The description of the media set is set by this text field.
MEDIANAME = *media_name*	This option specifies the name of the media.
MEDIAPASSWORD = *password*	This option allows you to specify a password for the media set.
NAME = *backup_set_name*	This option allows you to set the name of the backup set.
NOSKIP | SKIP	The NOSKIP option specifies that the expiration dates of the backup sets on the media be checked before they are overwritten. The SKIP option disables expiration date checking.
NO_TRUNCATE	This option specifies that the transaction log not be truncated after the backup. It is available with only log backups.
NOUNLOAD | UNLOAD	The NOUNLOAD option specifies that the media not be unloaded (for example, that a tape not be ejected) after the backup is completed. The UNLOAD option specifies that the media be unloaded after the backup is completed.
RESTART	This option instructs SQL Server to restart a backup that was interrupted.
STATS [= *percentage*]	This option displays a message after the specified percentage of the backup is completed. It is useful if you like to view the progress of operations.

Be sure you specify whether the backup should be appended to the media or the media should be overwritten, as described earlier; the option you choose can affect the amount of data that can fit on a tape. If you are backing up data to a previously used tape device and do not either erase the tape or specify that it should be overwritten, you might soon find yourself out of space on the tape. In append mode, the backup program will use only the space available at the end of the tape.

Real World   Using BACKUP

In this section, we'll look at a couple of examples of using the BACKUP T-SQL command.

The following statement will back up the data files for the Example database:

```
BACKUP DATABASE Example
TO Backup_Dev_1, Backup_Dev_2
WITH
DESCRIPTION = "DB backup of example",
STATS = 5
GO
```

The backup devices are Backup_Dev_1 and Backup_Dev_2, and a status message will be displayed each time 5 percent of the backup is completed. Notice that a description of the backup is provided in the preceding example.

If you are testing this example on a small database, such as Northwind, you won't see the statistics showing 5 percent increments. Instead, you might see increments such as 7 percent, 16 percent, and so forth. This discrepancy occurs because the backup program is reading and writing more than 5 percent of the entire backup at a time. With larger data sets, the increments written will each be smaller than 5 percent, so the messages will appear as expected.

The following statement will back up the transaction log for the Example database:

```
BACKUP LOG Example
TO Backup_Dev_3, Backup_Dev_4
WITH
DESCRIPTION = "DB backup of example",
STATS = 25
GO
```

The backup devices are Backup_Dev_3 and Backup_Dev_4, and status messages will be displayed at 25 percent intervals. The resulting output displays the percentage of the operation that is completed, as well as the outcome of the backup. You will be informed how many pages were backed up, how long the backup took, and how fast the backup was performed (in megabytes per second).

Managing the Backup

Because the T-SQL command BACKUP does not run under Enterprise Manager and thus does not run under the SQL Server Agent, you cannot schedule a job from within the BACKUP command. You can, however, schedule a T-SQL BACKUP command by using the SQL Server scheduling features. Once the job has been scheduled, it can be managed in exactly the same way the Enterprise Manager backup is managed.

Backing Up Using the Create Database Backup Wizard

Let's turn now to the third method of performing backups: using the Create Database Backup Wizard.

Performing the Backup

To perform a backup using the Create Database Backup Wizard, follow these steps:

1. In Enterprise Manager, click the database you want to back up, and then choose Wizards from the Tools menu to display the Select Wizard dialog box. Expand the Management folder in the Select Wizard dialog box, select Backup Wizard, and then click OK. The Create Database Backup Wizard welcome screen appears, as shown in Figure 32-9.

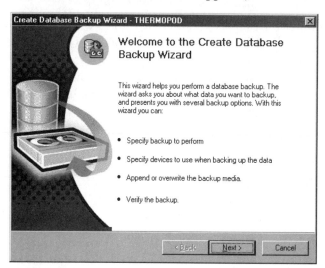

Figure 32-9. *The Create Database Backup Wizard welcome screen.*

2. Click Next to display the Select Database To Backup screen, shown in Figure 32-10. In this screen, you specify the database that will be backed up—Figure 32-10 shows the Northwind database selected.

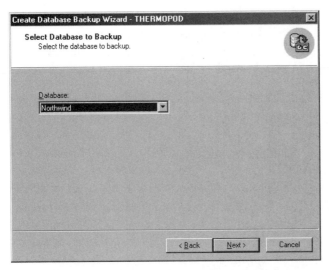

Figure 32-10. *The Select Database To Backup screen.*

3. Click Next to display the Type Name And Description For Backup screen, shown in Figure 32-11. Here you provide a name and a description for the backup set by typing the desired name in the Name text box and the desired description in the Description text box. A good description can be helpful later if you have many backups.

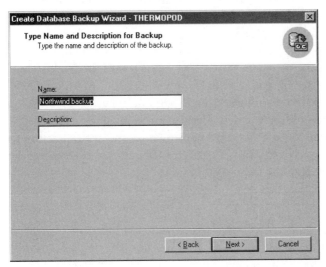

Figure 32-11. *The Type Name And Description For Backup screen.*

4. Click Next to display the Select Type Of Backup screen, shown in Figure 32-12. Here you select the type of backup you want to perform—a full backup, a differential backup, or a transaction log backup. Figure 32-12 shows a full backup selected.

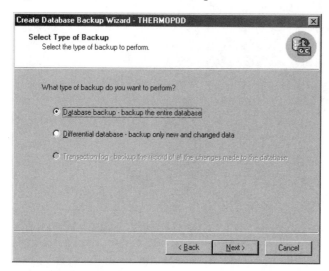

Figure 32-12. *The Select Type Of Backup screen.*

5. Click Next to display the Select Backup Destination And Action screen, shown in Figure 32-13. In the Select Backup Device area, specify whether you want to back up data to tape, file, or a particular backup device, and, if necessary, specify the filename or device name in the appropriate box. In the Properties area, specify whether the backup media should be overwritten or appended to, whether the tape should be ejected after the backup (if you are using tape), and whether the integrity of the backup should be verified. Verifying the integrity of the backup is a good idea because a bad tape can cause the entire backup to be useless. SQL Server verifies the integrity of the backup by reading the tape and verifying that all of the data is readable.

Note Unfortunately, the Create Database Backup Wizard allows you to select only one backup device, which can drastically affect the performance of your backup, as you'll see in the section "Improving Backups" later in this chapter. For this reason, the Enterprise Manager backup method might be preferable to using the Create Database Backup Wizard.

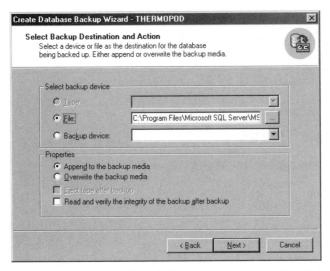

Figure 32-13. *The Select Backup Destination And Action screen.*

6. Click Next to display the Backup Verification And Scheduling screen, shown in Figure 32-14. Here you have the options of specifying that the media labels should be checked and setting expiration dates, as described in the section "Backing Up Using Enterprise Manager." You can also schedule backups to be run at a later time by using the Edit Schedule dialog box, also described earlier (shown in Figure 32-5).

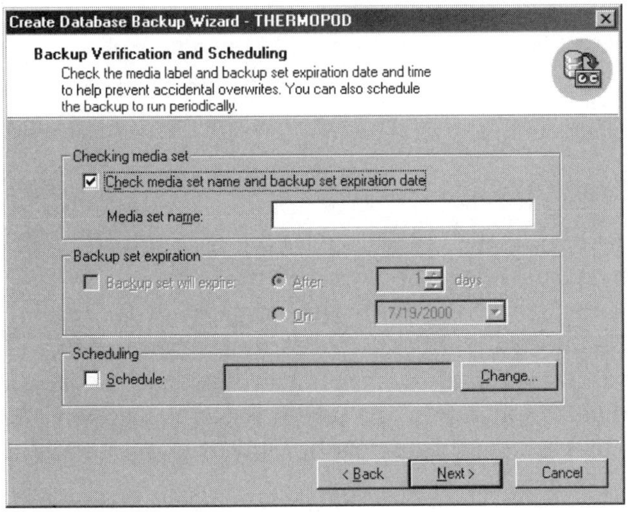

Figure 32-14. *The Backup Verification And Scheduling screen.*

7. Click Next to display the Completing The Create Database Backup Wizard screen, shown in Figure 32-15. Verify the information in the text box, and click Finish to launch the backup.

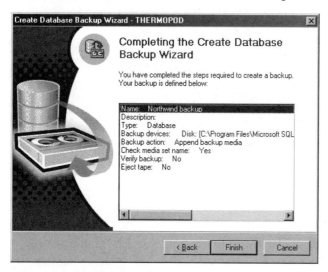

Figure 32-15. *The Completing The Create Database Backup Wizard screen.*

Managing the Backup

You can only perform a backup or create a scheduled backup job by using the Create Database Backup Wizard. If you create a job, you must use Enterprise Manager or T-SQL commands to manage that job. Managing jobs is described briefly in the section "Backing Up Using Enterprise Manager" earlier in this chapter.

Keeping Track of Backups

When you perform a backup, whether it is through Enterprise Manager, T-SQL, or the Create Database Backup Wizard, a record of the backup is saved. This record is stored as a row within the *backupfile* table in the msdb database. During database recovery, this information is used to determine when the last backup was performed on that database. Other information, such as the backup set ID and the names of files that were backed up, is also saved. It is therefore important that the system databases be backed up periodically as well so that this information can be recovered if necessary.

Scheduling Backups

Scheduling backups is a highly subjective task. Numerous factors are involved in designing the backup schedule. Because system performance is degraded during backups, backups might be limited to off-hours. You also might have only a small window of time in which to complete the backup. In this section, we'll review a few tips that can help you in setting up a backup schedule. Keep in mind that even though backups affect the performance of the system, they are crucial operations that must be done in order to protect the system from data loss.

Backup Scheduling Tips

The following tips can help you determine the ideal backup schedule for your system:

- **Plan full backups for off-hours.**   If your company does not run in a 24-by-7 environment (24 hours a day, 7 days a week), off-hours are the best time to perform backups.

- **Schedule a full backup over several days.**   If your database is large and you cannot perform a full backup in the allotted time, divide the backup operation into sections. You can perform a file or filegroup backup on one piece of the database at a time. Over a period of several days, you can back up all of the data.

- **Use differential backups.**   If you cannot afford the time to perform a full backup every night, you can perform differential backups during the week and a full backup over the weekend.

- **Customize your backup plan.**   Every system is different, and every company is different. Design the backup schedule that best fits your needs.

Real World Planning Backups

Here are a few sample backup plans that might help you develop your own backup schedule:

- **Small system in an 8-by-5 environment** This type of system will usually allow for full backups every evening. The transaction log might need to be backed up only once per day, depending on the size of the transaction log and the number of transactions performed.

- **Medium-sized system in a 24-by-7 environment** A medium-sized system that is running in a 24-by-7 environment does not allow a lot of downtime for backups. However, if you have a system of this size, you might be able to perform full backups on the weekends. The following table shows what a backup schedule for a medium-sized company might look like:

Mon	Differential database backup
Tue	Differential database backup
Wed	Differential database backup
Thu	Differential database backup
Fri	Differential database backup
Sat	Differential database backup
Sun	Full database backup
All days	Transaction log backups as necessary

- **Large system in a 24-by-7 environment** Extremely large systems might not allow a full backup to be done in just one day. A compromise would be to split the full backup over several days, as shown in the following table. (In this sample schedule, the full backup is performed over Saturday and Sunday.)

Mon	Differential database backup
Tue	Differential database backup
Wed	Differential database backup
Thu	Differential database backup
Fri	Differential database backup
Sat	Full filegroup backup
Sun	Full filegroup backup
All days	Transaction log backups as necessary

This information is intended to give you an idea of how to schedule backups. Because every system and its requirements are different, only you can decide how best to schedule your backups.

Improving Backups

You can improve both the performance and the execution of backups by using a few simple techniques. In this section, you'll find tips for enhancing performance and for improving your backups in other ways.

Enhancing Backup Performance

Enhancing backup performance is an important topic because the faster the backup runs, the shorter the time SQL Server's performance is degraded by the backup. Using the following techniques will help improve backup performance and in some cases can help improve restore performance as well. (Database restoration is explained in Chapter 33.)

- **Use multiple backup devices.**   Having multiple backup devices enables SQL Server to perform some of the backup operations in parallel. SQL Server accomplishes this by striping the backup among several devices. To do this, SQL Server creates a number of threads based on the number of data files and the number of backup devices. Backup performance is also improved by additional threads that are used in writing to these devices. Performing operations in parallel reduces the amount of time that these operations take, especially on a multiple-processor system. This technique will improve both backup and recovery performance.

- **Use multiple data files in the database.**   By using several smaller data files in the database rather than one large one, you will enable SQL Server to perform more of the backup in parallel. This technique will improve both backup and recovery performance.

- **Use multiple LAN segments to perform the backup.**   By splitting the backup over multiple LAN segments, you can increase the network bandwidth available for the backup. Two LAN segments provide twice the bandwidth of one segment, three segments provide three times the bandwidth, and so on.

- **Stage the backup.**   To improve backup performance, you can perform the backup as a disk backup and then copy the disk backup files to tape. This method improves performance because a disk is faster than tape, and it allows you to keep the last few backups available on disk. This technique will improve restore performance for only the backup files left on disk.

- **Use differential backups.** Differential backups will improve the performance of each backup, but if you use them, a restoration of the entire database will take much longer, as you'll see in Chapter 33. If backup times are unacceptable, this method might provide the best solution for your system. If you need to restore data only rarely, the risk might be acceptable.

Miscellaneous Tips

The following tips for performing backups might or might not apply in your environment:

- **Store backups off-site.** If you store your backups off-site, the backups might survive a disaster such as a fire or flood. The backup data is much more important than the computer system itself.

- **Verify the backup.** A backup might not always be good. Tapes can go bad, especially if you use the same tapes over and over again. By verifying the backup (at least occasionally), you will at least know that the tape is good.

- **Don't reuse the same backup medium every day.** If you reuse the same backup medium every day, you might not be able to recover data that is deleted several days before you try to recover it. Rotate the backup tapes so that you can restore at least several days' worth of information.

- **Keep records.** You should document how the backup works and how to rebuild the system if necessary. Remember, you might not always be there to rebuild the system yourself.

- **Back up system tables.** Remember to periodically back up system databases such as master and msdb.

These tips are designed to help you develop your own backup strategy. Every system is different and every company's needs are different. Again, you must develop the strategy that is right for you.

Summary

In this chapter, you've learned how SQL Server logging works and how to use checkpoints to reduce the amount of time needed to recover a database. You've also learned the fundamentals of performing SQL Server backups and the differences between full and differential backups and between database and transaction log backups. And you've learned how to schedule backups and improve your backups. Chapter 33 continues our examination of backing up, restoring, and recovering the database. In that chapter, you'll learn how to restore the database and how to plan for disaster recovery.

Chapter 33
Restoring and Recovering the Database

In Chapter 32, you learned the importance of backing up your system and how to perform those backups. This chapter continues our examination of database protection and builds upon the explanations presented in the previous chapter. You'll learn how to restore the database, how to plan for a disaster recovery, and you'll learn more about how database recovery works. As you'll see, the type of backup performed affects how recovery occurs. In addition to learning about restoring and recovering the database, you will be introduced to the concept of *log shipping*. Log shipping is new in Microsoft SQL Server 2000 and allows you to create a standby copy of your database on another server by using the original server's transaction log.

Note Some DBAs refer to the process of restoring and then recovering the database as "recovering the database." However, these procedures are quite distinct. Chapter 32 explains the differences between restoring the database from backup and the SQL Server recovery process. In any case, bringing the database back to the state it was in at the point of failure is the main goal when backup, restore, and recovery operations are performed.

Restore Methods

As mentioned, the type of backup performed affects the nature of the restore operation. In this section, you'll learn how to perform a restore from a full backup, from a differential backup, and from transaction log backups.

Restoring from a Full Backup

Restoring from a full backup is a fairly straightforward process: you simply restore the backup files by using either SQL Server Enterprise Manager or Transact-SQL (T-SQL) commands. Instructions for restoring data by using these two methods are given later in this chapter. If you're planning on restoring from differential backups after you restore from a full backup, be sure you back up the current transaction log, as described in the section "Restoring from the Transaction Log Backups" later in this chapter, and specify the NORECOVERY option when you perform the restore.

> **Note**   An important feature of the restore operation is the RECOVERY option. The RECOVERY option instructs SQL Server to attempt to recover the database by using the online transaction log after the restore is complete. If you're planning on using differential backup files or transaction log backup files, be sure you specify the NORECOVERY option.

Restoring from a Differential Backup

To restore from a differential backup, you must first restore from a full backup and then restore all of the differential backups that have been created since the last full backup. Remember, a differential backup is used to back up information that has changed since the last full or differential backup. Be sure you use the NORECOVERY option unless you are restoring the most recent backup file, for which you will use the RECOVERY option. If you are restoring from the transaction logs in addition to the differential backup, you must also back up the current log and apply all of the changed log files, as described in the next section.

Restoring from the Transaction Log Backups

To perform a recovery in which the database is returned to the state it was in just before the point of failure, you must first restore the data files from the latest full backup and then restore the changes that have been made to the database since that backup. You restore these changes by restoring all of the transaction log backups that have occurred since the failure.

To ensure that you do not lose any of the newest transactions when you restore the logs, you must first save the current log. If you forget to save the current log, you will lose the most recent changes recorded in the log because the restore operations will overwrite the transaction log.

To use transaction logs to restore the database to the state it was in just prior to failure, follow these general steps, building upon the techniques you learned in Chapter 32:

1. Back up the currently active transaction log, using the NO_TRUNCATE option.

2. Restore the latest full backup.

3. Restore any differential backups to return the database to the state it was in when the latest backup was performed.

4. Restore all transaction log backups created since the last differential backup to replay any transactions that have occurred since that last backup.

5. Restore the transaction log backup you created in step 1 to return the database to the state it was in just prior to the failure.

Restoring a Database in BULK_LOGGED Recovery Mode

If you are running your database in BULK_LOGGED recovery mode, you must redo any minimally logged operations if a restore is necessary. These operations include SELECT...INTO, BULK COPY, BCP, and some CREATE INDEX operations, in addition to the text operations that were mentioned in the previous chapter. If this places an undue burden on you, you should not be running your database in BULK_LOGGED recovery mode.

Performing a Database Restore

As mentioned, you can perform a restore operation by using either Enterprise Manager or T-SQL commands—both techniques produce the same results. Unlike for backup operations, for restore operations, SQL Server does not provide a wizard.

Using Enterprise Manager to Perform a Restore

To perform a restore operation by using Enterprise Manager, follow these steps:

1. In Enterprise Manager, right-click the name of the database you want to restore, point to All Tasks in the shortcut menu, and then choose Restore Database to display the Restore Database dialog box, shown in Figure 33-1.

Figure 33-1. *The General tab of the Restore Database dialog box.*

2. At the top of the General tab is the Restore As Database drop-down list, which enables you to specify what database the backup will be restored as. Figure 33-1 shows the Example database selected.

You are not required to restore a database directly—in fact, at times, you will definitely need to restore a database using a different database name. For instance, suppose a user accidentally deletes a table. If you were to restore the entire database, you would replace all data with the earlier data. Instead, you can restore the data to a database with a different name, extract the deleted table, and insert the table into the live database.

3. Next specify the type of restore operation: Database, Filegroups Or Files, or From Device. The Database option lets you specify the database to restore. The Filegroups Or Files option lets you specify filegroups or files to restore. The From Device option lets you specify the device to restore from, and the contents of the device will then determine the type of restore. Figure 33-1 shows the Database option selected.

4. The Parameters area enables you to set options such as whether the backups of other databases should be shown (for restoring from another database's backup), which backup should be restored first (if multiple backup sets are available), and whether a point-in-time restore should be performed. A *point-in-time restore* enables you to restore data to the state it was in at a particular instant. For instance, if you accidentally deleted a table at 12:01, you could use a point-in-time restore to restore the database to the state it was in at 12:00, just before the deletion. Because you have the list of all of the backups available, you can

choose the one that you want to use. You are not required to restore the most recent backup.

In the Restore Database dialog box, you can also select a backup set and then view its properties by clicking Properties. A sample Backup Set Properties window is shown in Figure 33-2.

Figure 33-2. *The Backup Set Properties window.*

5. Click OK to return to the General tab of the Restore Database dialog box, and click Filegroups Or Files to display a slightly different view, shown in Figure 33-3. All of the file and filegroup backups set up for the Example database are displayed in Figure 33-3. To view the properties for the file and filegroup backups, select a backup and click Properties.

Figure 33-3. *The General tab of the Restore Database dialog box, after Filegroups Or Files is clicked.*

6. Now select From Device, as shown in Figure 33-4. As mentioned, you use this option when you want to select a particular backup device to restore from. If you specify this option, you must manually select the backup set and then specify whether SQL Server should perform a complete restore, a differential restore, a transaction log restore, or a file or filegroup restore. You can also have SQL Server read the backup set information and store it with other backup history information in the msdb database. Then the information about that backup is available in case you want to perform a database restore.

Figure 33-4. *The General tab of the Restore Database dialog box, after From Device is clicked.*

7. Click the Options tab of the Restore Database dialog box, shown in Figure 33-5. At the top of this tab, you will see three check boxes. The Eject Tapes After Restoring Each Backup check box can be used to guarantee that the tape won't remain in the tape drive and be overwritten. Selecting the Prompt Before Restoring Each Backup option gives you the opportunity to change your mind about performing the backup. And selecting the Force Restore Over Existing Database check box lets you overwrite the existing database with the database restore. On this tab, you can also restore the database under a new data filename, which can be useful if you want to save the original database.

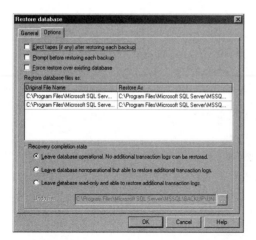

Figure 33-5. *The Options tab of the Restore Database dialog box.*

The remaining options on this tab let you specify in what state the database should be left after the recovery is completed, as follows:

- **Leave Database Operational. No Additional Transaction Logs Can Be Restored.**   This option allows no further recovery of differential restores or transaction log restores. This option essentially sets the RECOVERY flag on the restore. You cannot restore transaction log backups if this option is set.

- **Leave Database Nonoperational But Able To Restore Additional Transaction Logs.**   This option sets the NORECOVERY flag on the restore. With this flag set, you can apply further differential backup restores and transaction log restores. While this restore is under way, the database is nonoperational, meaning that users cannot access the database until you finish the entire restore.

- **Leave Database Read-Only And Able To Restore Additional Transaction Logs.**   This option will also set the NORECOVERY flag on the restore, and you can perform differential backup restores and transaction log restores. Unlike the previous option, this option allows users to have read-only access to the database while you are performing the restore operation.

8. When you have finished setting the options, click OK to begin the restore operation. You will be kept informed of the restore operation's progress via a message box that contains a status bar, as shown in Figure 33-6. When the operation is completed, you will see a status box informing you of the success or failure of the restore.

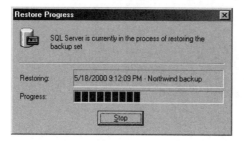

Figure 33-6. *The Restore Progress message box.*

Note A SQL Server backup device can hold the output of many backup operations. The converse is also true: a single backup can be split among several devices. The contents of the group of backup devices that collectively form one backup are called a *backup set*. Thus, a backup device (tape, disk file, and so on) can hold parts of many backup sets for different databases or many backup sets for the same database.

Using T-SQL to Perform a Restore

The RESTORE T-SQL command is similar to the BACKUP command (covered in Chapter 32). Like the BACKUP command, RESTORE can be relatively difficult to use at first, but some DBAs prefer to put their administrative procedures into SQL scripts so that they can be run over and over again. And like the BACKUP command, the RESTORE command provides a few more options than using Enterprise Manager does.

In this section, we'll look at the syntax of the RESTORE command and the various options this command provides. The RESTORE command has two forms, shown here:

- **RESTORE DATABASE** Restores either the entire database or a file or filegroup
- **RESTORE LOG** Restores the transaction log

As you can see, which command you use depends on the type of restore operation you are performing. Because these commands have most of the same options, we'll look at all the options for both types of restores (database and log) in a single list later in this section.

The RESTORE Statement

The syntax for the RESTORE statement when a full database restore is performed is shown here:

```
RESTORE DATABASE database_name
[ FROM backup_device ]
[ WITH options ]
```

This statement requires only the database name and the location of the backup.

The syntax for the statement when a file or filegroup restore is performed is shown here:

```
RESTORE DATABASE database_name
[FILE = file_name ]
[FILEGROUP = filegroup_name ]
[ FROM backup_device ]
[ WITH options ]
```

This statement requires only the database name, the filename or filegroup name, and the location of the backup.

The syntax for the statement when a transaction log restore is performed is shown here:

```
RESTORE LOG database_name
[ FROM backup_device ]
[ WITH options ]
```

With any of these commands, *database_name* is the name of the database that the restore will be performed on. The *backup_device* parameter is either a logical backup device name or the name of a physical device. If you want to specify a physical device, you must qualify it with a device type—that is, the name of the device must be preceded by *DISK* =, *TAPE* =, or *PIPE* =. You can specify one or more devices. (You separate multiple device names by using commas.)

> **Note** If you don't specify the FROM clause, a restore will not take place, but a recovery will still be performed (unless you specify the NORECOVERY option). This technique can be used to set a database to recovery mode without restoring any additional data. For example, you can perform several differential restore operations and then run the RESTORE statement without the FROM clause to set the database to recovery mode, thus launching the recovery process.

Options

Table 33-1 lists the options available for use with the RESTORE command. As you will see, these options provide a great deal of flexibility in performing the restore operation. (One of the options listed is available for only transaction log restores; this limitation is noted.)

Table 33-1. The RESTORE command options

Option	Description
RESTRICTED_USER	Sets the security of the newly restored database so that members of only the *db_owner*, *dbcreater*, and *sysadmin* roles can access it.
FILE = *file_number*	Identifies the backup set to be used if more than one set exists on a medium. For example, setting this value to 2 will cause the second backup set on the medium to be used.
PASSWORD = *password*	Specifies the password for the save set.
MEDIANAME = *media_name*	Specifies the name of the medium.
MEDIAPASSWORD = *password*	Specifies the password that was assigned to the media set.
MOVE '*logical_file_name*' TO '*OS_file_name*'	Changes the location of the restored file, for example, *MOVE 'Northwind' TO 'D:\data\Northwind.mdf'*. You can use this option if you are restoring to a new disk because the old disk is unusable.
NORECOVERY | RECOVERY | STANDBY = *undo_file*	NORECOVERY specifies that transactions will not be rolled back or rolled forward after the restore. Using this option is necessary if you will be restoring other backups (differential or transaction log). RECOVERY, the default option, specifies that the recovery operation will be performed and any uncommitted changes will be rolled back. STANDBY specifies that an undo file will be created in case the recovery needs to be undone.

Table 33-1. *continued*

Option	Description
KEEP_REPLICATION	Specifies that replication settings be preserved when the database that is being restored is a publisher.
NOUNLOAD	UNLOAD	NOUNLOAD specifies that the medium not be unloaded after the restore is completed (for example, that the backup tape not be rewound and ejected). UNLOAD, the default, specifies that the medium be unloaded after the restore is completed.
REPLACE	Indicates that SQL Server will restore data files even if those files currently exist. The existing data files will be deleted and written over. If you do not specify REPLACE, SQL Server checks to see whether the database you specified already exists. If it does exist, the restore operation fails. This safety feature helps you avoid unintentionally restoring over a live database.
RESTART	Specifies that SQL Server should restart a restore operation that was interrupted.
STATS [= *percentage*]	Displays a message after the specified percentage of the restore operation is completed. This option is useful if you want to watch the progress of operations.
PARTIAL	Specifies that a partial restore be done.
STOPAT = *date_time* (log restore only)	Specifies that the database should be recovered to the state it was in on the date specified by *date_time*.
STOPATMARK = '*mark*'	Specifies that the restore operation proceed until the specified mark is reached.
STOPBEFOREMARK = '*mark*'	Specifies that the restore operation proceed until just before the specified mark is reached.

Note Named transactions are a new feature in SQL Server 2000. These named transactions, which are created with the command BEGIN TRANSACTION ... WITH MARK *mark_name* option, allow you to use the STOPATMARK and STOPBEFOREMARK features of the RESTORE command.

Real World   Using RESTORE

This sidebar shows a few examples of using the RESTORE T-SQL command.

This statement restores the data files for the Example database:

```
RESTORE DATABASE Example
FROM Backup_Dev_1, Backup_Dev_2
WITH
NORECOVERY,
STATS = 5
GO
```

This statement restores the transaction log for the Example database:

```
RESTORE LOG Example
FROM Backup_Dev_3, Backup_Dev_4
WITH
NORECOVERY,
STATS = 5,
UNLOAD
GO
```

The output will display the percentage of the operation that is completed, as well as the outcome of the restore. You'll be informed of how many pages were restored up, how long the restore took, and how fast the restore was performed (in megabytes per second).

You can now recover this database by using the following command:

```
RESTORE LOG Example
WITH RECOVERY
GO
```

You will again see statistics regarding the restore operation.

Planning for Disaster Recovery

To increase your system's uptime, it's not enough simply to cluster your servers (as explained in Chapter 12) or use RAID (as described in Chapter 5)—you must also plan for recovery before disaster strikes. Knowing how to perform good backups and restores of your database when you need to is vital, but you must also be prepared to rebuild your system from scratch if necessary. Being ready involves documenting and planning. In addition, you might find the use of the new SQL Server 2000 feature *log shipping* to provide sufficient recoverability. This feature allows transaction logs from the primary system to be applied to standby systems.

As a DBA, you should develop a plan for providing maximum uptime. This plan should include the following components:

- Documenting the current configuration
- Creating a fault-tolerant environment
- Preparing for immediate recovery
- Documenting the database recovery plan

All of these steps involve planning, creating documentation, or both. Often the recovery plan is not documented, and only the developer of the plan is able to execute it—this can be disastrous if that person is unavailable.

Note Be sure you document your disaster recovery plan and designate a person to execute the plan if you are unavailable when disaster strikes.

Documenting the Current Configuration

If the steps involved in creating your current configuration are not well documented, problems can arise if the system needs to be reconstructed or even if new hardware is added to the system. Documenting the current configuration enables you to more quickly rebuild, reinstall, and reconfigure the system. Be sure you include the following information:

- **Hardware configuration**   Include the type and the amount of hardware, the RAID configuration, and other configuration details.
- **Software products installed**   Include complete information about all software that is installed on the server.

Creating a Fault-Tolerant Environment

As we saw in Chapter 5, the use of fault-tolerant RAID volumes can greatly reduce the chance of system failure. Disk drives are mechanical components and, as such, are subject to wear and tear. By using a fault-tolerant volume, you might be able to spare yourself the trouble of having to reinstall the operating system and SQL Server and to rebuild the database from backups, which can be a time-consuming and costly process (costly in terms of both labor and lost revenues caused by the system outage).

If one of your fault-tolerant disk drives fails, replace it as soon as possible. Eventually, another disk might fail, and some RAID levels can survive the loss of only one disk. Be prepared with spares, and be ready to use them.

Preparing for Immediate Recovery

Be ready to recover the database if necessary. Backups should be stored off-site to safeguard them against disasters such as fires or floods, but you should also keep a copy of the latest backups close at hand because you might not be able to retrieve off-site backups quickly. The use of a backup staging area is a popular way of keeping the latest backups on-site as well as improving backup and restore performance. A backup staging area is located on your network and consists of disks that store the latest database and transaction log backups. In case a restore is needed, you will not need to use tapes or retrieve them from off-site storage—the restore can begin immediately. This technique is useful if you need to perform a restore immediately, but it can be quite costly because you must devote hardware resources to storing the backups. You must evaluate your budget and your needs to determine whether a backup staging area is feasible for you.

Documenting the Database Recovery Plan

Because you might not be present when database recovery is necessary, you should carefully document the database recovery plan and share this information with others so that they can recover the system if necessary. The database recovery plan document can also be a helpful reminder if it's been a long time since your last database restore. In any event, keeping a written copy of the database recovery plan will make the restoration process run more smoothly.

Log Shipping

The Log Shipping feature of SQL Server 2000 allows for a standby system to be created and kept up to date by applying recent transaction logs to the standby system. The standby system is kept in a permanent recovery mode, continually having transactions logs applied to it. Even though this system is in recovery mode, read-only queries are allowed, thus enabling you to use the standby database for offloading reporting tasks.

In the event of a catastrophic failure on the primary server, the standby server can quickly and easily be converted into the new primary server. This feature has been used in the field by many people with SQL Server 7, but is now officially supported by Microsoft and usability features have been added. These features include the ability to setup and maintain the standby systems via the Database Maintenance Plan Wizard and the SQL Server Agent.

Summary

This chapter completes our examination of database backup, restore, and recovery operations. In this chapter and the last chapter, you've learned how to effectively back up and restore a system and how SQL Server recovery works. You've seen how to perform these operations by using both Enterprise Manager and T-SQL commands. This chapter focused on restore operations and on preparing a disaster recovery plan, a critical job. Remember, the security of the system is a major responsibility of the DBA.

Chapter 34

User and Security Management

In this chapter, you'll learn how to manage users and security in a Microsoft SQL Server 2000 environment. Along with backup and recovery planning, sizing, and space management, security management is one of the most common jobs of the DBA. It is also one of the most important tasks that the DBA must perform. If the security of the system is breached, data could be lost or corrupted.

This chapter covers a number of topics related to user and security management. You'll learn how to create and manage user logins and about the modes of authentication; in addition, you'll learn about SQL Server user IDs. A *user login* is used to authenticate access to SQL Server. The user login can be authenticated through Microsoft Windows NT or Microsoft Windows 2000 or through SQL Server. A *user ID* is used to assign a user permissions to access specific objects within the individual databases. User IDs are associated with user logins and might or might not consist of the same name, as you'll see later in this chapter. You'll also learn about the types of permissions that can be assigned in SQL Server and how to use them. And you'll learn how to use roles to more easily manage users. Finally you will learn about an important feature in SQL Server 2000 called security account delegation. By the end of this chapter, you'll have the knowledge necessary to manage user logins and security.

Creating and Administering User Logins

Let's begin our examination of user and security management by looking at user logins. In this section, we'll first look at why logins are important and at the authentication methods that can be used to maintain logins. We'll then look at three methods for creating logins: using SQL Server Enterprise Manager, using Transact-SQL (T-SQL), and using the Create Login Wizard. And finally, we'll see how to use Enterprise Manager and T-SQL to create new user accounts.

Why Create User Logins?

User logins enable you to protect your data from being intentionally and unintentionally modified by unauthorized users. With user logins, SQL Server is able to identify individual authorized users. Each user login is assigned a unique name and password. Each user should be assigned his or her own SQL Server login account. Without user logins, all connections to SQL Server would use the same identifier, which means that you could not create different levels of security based on who is accessing the database.

With user logins, you can create multiple levels of security by granting different login accounts different permissions to access objects and to perform functions. You can also encrypt certain database objects, such as stored procedures and views, to hide their definitions from unauthorized users. And with user logins, you can allow only some users to insert and update information in certain database tables, and grant read-only access to the tables to the general user community.

To see how data access can be limited with user logins, let's return to the example, first presented in Chapter 18, of using a view to restrict access to sensitive data. Suppose you have an *Employee* table that contains information about employees, including each employee's name, phone number, office number, grade level, salary, bonus, and so on. To prevent certain users from accessing the confidential data in the table, you would first create a view that contains only nonsensitive information, such as employee names, phone numbers, and office numbers. Then, by implementing user logins, you can restrict access to the underlying table while allowing all users to access the view. However, if you did not take advantage of user logins, any user could access either the view or the table, thus defeating the purpose of using the view.

Authentication Modes

Two authentication modes are available for accessing SQL Server: Microsoft Windows Authentication and Mixed Mode Authentication. With Windows Authentication, the operating system is responsible for authenticating the user. SQL Server then uses this operating system authentication to determine which user permissions to apply. With Mixed Mode Authentication, both Windows NT/2000 and SQL Server are responsible for authenticating the user. To access SQL Server, you always have to first log on to a Windows NT/2000 account, so when choosing an authentication mode, you must decide simply whether you want to use SQL Server Authentication in addition to Windows Authentication. Let's look at each of these authentication modes in more detail. Later in this section, you'll learn how to implement these modes.

Windows Authentication

As mentioned, with Windows Authentication, SQL Server relies on Windows NT/ 2000 to provide the login security. When a user logs on to Windows NT/2000, the user's account identity is validated. SQL Server verifies that the user was validated by Windows NT/2000 and allows access based on that authentication. SQL Server integrates its login security process with the Windows login security process to provide these services. Network security attributes are validated through a sophisticated encryption process provided by Windows NT/2000. Because the SQL Server and Windows login security processes are integrated when this mode is used, once you are authenticated by the operating system, no further authentication methods are required for you to access SQL Server. The only password you need to supply in order to log on to SQL Server is your Windows NT/ 2000 password.

Windows Authentication is considered a better security method than Mixed Mode Authentication because of the additional security features it provides. These features include secure validation and encryption of passwords, auditing, password expiration, minimum password length, and automated account lockout after a certain number of unsuccessful logon attempts.

Mixed Mode Authentication

With Mixed Mode Authentication, users can access SQL Server by using either Windows Authentication or SQL Server Authentication. When Mixed Mode Authentication is used, if a connection is made from an insecure system, SQL Server authenticates the login by verifying whether a SQL Server login account has been set up for the user requesting access. SQL Server performs this account authentication by comparing the name and password provided by the user attempting to connect to SQL Server with login account information stored in the database. If a login account has not been set up for the user or if the user does not provide the correct name and password, SQL Server access is denied.

Windows Authentication mode is not available when you are running SQL Server on Windows 95/98, so you must use SQL Server Authentication (by using Mixed Mode Authentication) on those platforms. In addition, Web applications require SQL Server Authentication (through Microsoft Internet Information

Server) because users of these applications will most likely not be within the same domain as the server and thus they can't rely on Windows security. Other applications that require database access might require SQL Server Authentication as well: some application developers prefer to use SQL Server security for their applications because it simplifies the security of their applications. When applications use SQL Server security (within a trusted network), application developers do not have to provide security authentication within the application itself, which simplifies their job.

Setting Up the Authentication Mode

To set up the authentication mode, follow these steps:

1. Open the Enterprise Manager window. In the left-hand pane, right-click the name of the server that hosts the database for which you want to set the authentication mode, and choose Properties from the shortcut menu to display the SQL Server Properties window. Click the Security tab, shown in Figure 34-1.

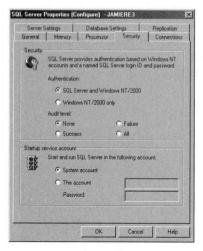

Figure 34-1. *The Security tab of the SQL Server Properties window.*

2. On this tab, you can choose both the security method and the startup service account. In the Security area, specify whether Windows NT/ 2000 and SQL Server (Mixed Mode) Authentication should be used or whether just Windows NT/2000 Authentication should be used. You can also specify the login audit level. This setting determines what, if any, type of login auditing is performed. The audit level you choose will depend on your security requirements. The following four levels are available:

- **None**   Performs no login auditing. This is the default setting.
- **Success**   Logs all successful login attempts.
- **Failure**   Logs all failed login attempts.
- **All**   Logs all login attempts.

Note   The auditing level is a database property. As such, the same auditing level will apply to all logins.

3. In the Startup Service Account area, specify which Windows NT account should be used when the SQL Server service is started up. You can either use the built-in local system account or specify an account, such as Administrator, and a password. Click OK to accept your settings.

Logins vs. Users

In the next couple of sections, you'll learn how to create logins and users. But before you start this process, you need to understand what logins and users are. This section provides brief definitions of these two terms.

As we've seen, a Windows NT/2000 user account might be needed to connect to the database. SQL Server Authentication might also be involved. Whether you are using Windows NT/2000 Authentication or Mixed Mode Authentication, the account that you use to connect to SQL Server is known as the SQL Server *login*. In addition to the SQL Server login, each database has a set of user pseudo-accounts assigned to it. These pseudoaccounts provide aliases to SQL Server login accounts. For example, in the Northwind database, you might have a user named manager that is associated with the SQL Server *guest* login, and the pubs database might have a user named manager that is associated with the SQL Server *sa* login account. By default, a SQL Server login account does not have a database user ID associated with it; thus, it has no permissions.

Creating SQL Server Logins

You can perform most SQL Server administrative tasks by using one of several methods, and the task of creating user logins is no exception. As mentioned earlier, you can create a login in one of three ways: using Enterprise Manager, using T-SQL, or using the Create Login Wizard. In this section, you'll learn how to create SQL Server logins by using each of these methods.

Using Enterprise Manager to Create SQL Server Logins

To create SQL Server logins by using Enterprise Manager, follow these steps:

1. In the left-hand pane of the Enterprise Manager window, expand the server group, expand the server, and then expand the Security folder. Right-click Logins, and choose New Login from the shortcut menu to display the SQL Server Login Properties window, shown in Figure 34-2. On the General tab, enter a SQL Server login name in the Name text box. If you are using Windows Authentication, this name must be a valid Windows NT or Windows 2000 account name. Next specify the Windows NT or Windows 2000 domain in the Domain text box. In the Default area, specify the default database and language that the user will use. In the Authentication area, specify whether a Windows NT or Windows 2000 account will be used or whether SQL Server Authentication will be used. If you choose SQL Server Authentication, Mixed Mode Authentication will be used.

Figure 34-2. *The General tab of the SQL Server Login Properties window.*

2. Click the Server Roles tab, shown in Figure 34-3. On this tab, you can specify which server roles the new login will be able to choose by selecting roles from the list of roles available to the user. Clicking Properties allows you to view and modify the role that you selected. (Roles are explained in the section "Administering Database Roles" later in this chapter.)

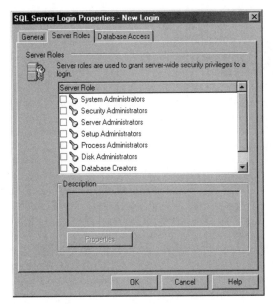

Figure 34-3. *The Server Roles tab of the SQL Server Login Properties window.*

3. Click the Database Access tab, shown in Figure 34-4. This tab lets you specify which databases the user has permission to access. (Database permissions are covered in the section "Administering Database Permissions" later in this chapter.) You can select multiple databases and the roles that are available to those databases. Clicking Properties allows you to view and manage the database role properties.

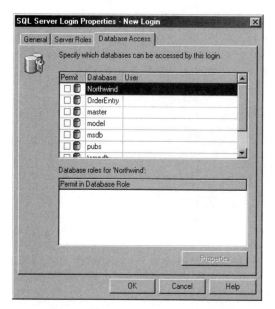

Figure 34-4. *The Database Access tab of the SQL Server Login Properties window.*

4. When you have finished specifying options, save the login by clicking OK. To see the new login listed with the other logins, click the Logins folder in Enterprise Manager. The logins will be listed in the right-hand pane.

Using T-SQL to Create Logins

To create logins by using T-SQL, you use the *sp_addlogin* stored procedure or the *sp_grantlogin* stored procedure. The *sp_addlogin* stored procedure can add only a SQL Server–authenticated user to a SQL Server database. The *sp_grantlogin* stored procedure can add a Windows NT/2000–authenticated user.

The *sp_addlogin* stored procedure has the following syntax:

```
sp_addlogin [ @loginame = ] 'login'
        [ , [ @passwd = ] 'password' ]
        [ , [ @defdb = ] 'database' ]
        [ , [ @deflanguage = ] 'language' ]
        [ , [ @sid = ] 'sid' ]
        [ , [ @encryptopt = ] 'encryption_option' ]
```

The optional parameters are as follows:

- *password*   Specifies the SQL Server login password. The default is *NULL*.
- *database*   Specifies the default database of the login. The default is master.
- *language*   Specifies the default language of the login. The default is the current SQL Server language setting.
- *sid*   Specifies the security identifier, which is a unique number. If you do not specify a value, one will be generated for you. The *sid* parameter is not generally used by users, but administrators use *sid* in a number of situations. When the DBA performs troubleshooting tasks, *sid* might be needed to determine which login is being checked. The *sid* parameter is the internal identifier for the login.
- *encryption_option*   Specifies whether the password will be encrypted in the system tables. The default value is *NULL*, which means that the password will be encrypted. The password will not be encrypted if you specify *skip_encryption*. If you specify *skip_encryption_old*, the password that was encrypted already by an earlier version of SQL Server will not be encrypted again. This setting should be changed from the default only if you want to avoid encrypting the password in the system tables.

A simple example of adding a login is shown here:

```
EXEC sp_addlogin 'PatB'
```

Remember to use the EXEC keyword before the stored-procedure name.

A more complex example of adding a login is shown here:

```
sp_addlogin 'SharonR', 'mypassword', 'Northwind', 'us_english'
```

This command creates a user named SharonR with the password "mypassword." The default database is Northwind, and the default language is U.S. English. In general, you should let SQL Server create a security identifier for you instead of creating your own.

The *sp_grantlogin* stored procedure has the following syntax:

```
sp_grantlogin 'login_name'
```

An example of using the *sp_grantlogin* stored procedure is shown here:

```
EXEC sp_grantlogin 'MOUNTAIN_DEW\DickB'
```

"DickB" is the Windows NT or Windows 2000 account name. "MOUNTAIN_DEW" is the system name.

After you add these logins, you can view them in Enterprise Manager. To do so, click the Logins folder in the left pane.

Using the Create Login Wizard

To create a SQL Server login by using the Create Login Wizard, follow these steps:

1. In Enterprise Manager, expand a server group, and click a server name. From the Tools menu, choose Wizards. In the Select Wizard dialog box that appears, expand the Database folder, click Create Login Wizard (shown in Figure 34-5), and then click OK. The Create Login Wizard welcome screen appears, as shown in Figure 34-6.

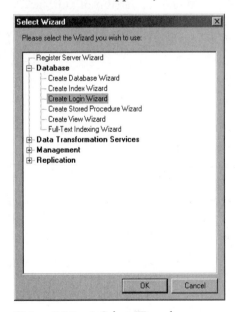

Figure 34-5. *A Select Wizard screen.*

Figure 34-6. *The Create Login Wizard welcome screen.*

2. Click Next to display the Select Authentication Mode For This Login screen, as shown in Figure 34-7. In this screen, you can specify whether Windows Authentication or SQL Server (Mixed Mode) Authentication should be used.

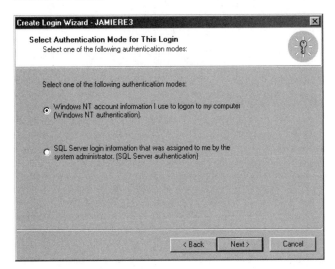

Figure 34-7. *The Select Authentication Mode For This Login screen.*

3. Click Next to display the Authentication With Windows NT screen or Authentication With SQL Server screen, depending on the authentication mode you selected in step 2. Figure 34-8 shows the latter screen. In this screen, you specify the login ID and password. If you had selected Windows NT Authentication, you would be prompted to enter a domain name and user account name for the authentication.

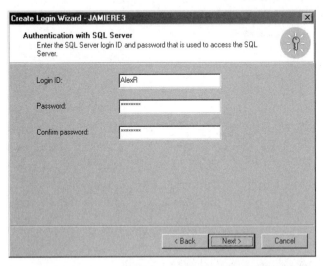

Figure 34-8. *The Authentication With SQL Server screen.*

4. Click Next to display the Grant Access To Security Roles screen, as shown in Figure 34-9. In this screen, you can select the database roles to be assigned to this login.

Create Login Wizard - JAMIERE3

Grant Access to Security Roles
Select the security roles for this login account, if any.

Server roles:

Server role
☐ System Administrators
☐ Security Administrators
☐ Server Administrators
☐ Setup Administrators
☐ Process Administrators
☐ Disk Administrators
☐ Database Creators

< Back   Next >   Cancel

Figure 34-9. *The Grant Access To Security Roles screen.*

5. Click Next to display the Grant Access To Databases screen, shown in
Figure 34-10. In this screen, you can select the databases to which this
login will have access.

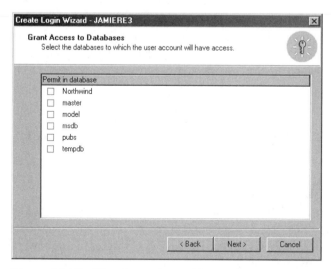

Figure 34-10. *The Grant Access To Databases screen.*

6. Click Next to display the Completing The Create Login Wizard screen,
shown in Figure 34-11, where you can examine the summary information in the text box. Click Back to make any changes, and click Finish
to create the login.

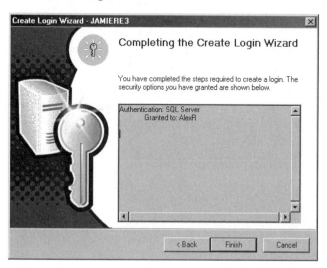

Figure 34-11. *The Completing The Create Login Wizard screen.*

Creating SQL Server Users

You can create SQL Server users by using Enterprise Manager or T-SQL. (SQL Server does not include a wizard to help you with this process.) In this section, you'll learn how to use both these methods to create SQL Server users. Remember, a SQL Server user is defined for a particular database and permissions are assigned for that database to a specific user login. The SQL Server user ID can be thought of as analogous to the SQL Server login, but it is not required to have the same name as the login.

Note To create a SQL Server user, you must already have defined the SQL Server login for that user because the user name is a reference to a SQL Server login.

Using Enterprise Manager to Create Users

Unlike SQL Server logins, which are created from within the Security folder of Enterprise Manager, SQL Server users are created from within the specific database folder in the left-hand pane of Enterprise Manager. To create users by using Enterprise Manager, follow these steps:

1. Right-click the database in which the user is to be created, point to New in the shortcut menu, and then choose Database User to display the Database User Properties window, shown in Figure 34-12. Enter a valid SQL Server login name in the Login Name drop-down list, and type a new user name in the User Name text box. Then specify the database roles that you want the new user to be a member of by selecting the appropriate check boxes in the Database Role Membership list box. As you'll see later in this chapter, by assigning permissions to these roles, you can apply the permissions to the user.

2. Click Properties to display the Database Role Properties window, as shown in Figure 34-13. In this window, you can modify a database role you have selected. This task is explained in the section "Administering Database Roles" later in this chapter.

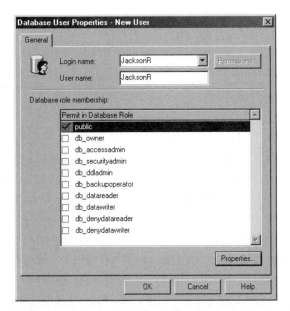

Figure 34-12. *The Database User Properties window.*

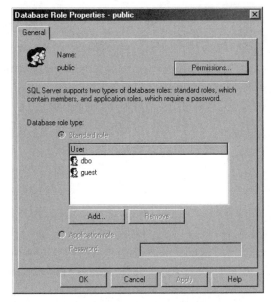

Figure 34-13. *The Database Role Properties window.*

3. When you are finished setting options, click OK twice to create the
   database user.

Using T-SQL to Create Users

To use T-SQL to create database users, you run the *sp_adduser* stored procedure. This stored procedure can be run from ISQL or OSQL and has the following syntax:

```
sp_adduser[ @loginame = ] 'login'
    [ , [ @name_in_db = ] 'user' ]
    [ , [ @grpname = ] 'group' ]
```

The *login* parameter is the SQL Server login account name and must be provided. The *user* variable is the new user name, and *group* is the group or role that the new user will belong to. If a *user* value is not specified, it will be the same as the *login* parameter.

The following command creates a new database user with the name JackR and the Windows NT or Windows 2000 account FORT_WORTH\DB_User:

```
sp_adduser 'FORT_WORTH\DB_User', 'JackR'
```

"FORT_WORTH" is the system or domain name. "DB_User" is the Windows NT or Windows 2000 account name.

Administering Database Permissions

Permissions are used to control access to database objects and to specify which users can perform certain database actions. You can set both server and database permissions. *Server permissions* are used to allow DBAs to perform database administration tasks. *Database permissions* are used to allow or disallow access to database objects and statements. In this section, we'll look at the types of permissions and how to allocate them.

Server Permissions

As just mentioned, server permissions are assigned to DBAs and allow them to perform administrative tasks. These permissions are defined on the fixed server roles. User logins can be assigned the fixed server roles, but these roles cannot be modified. (Server roles are explained in the section "Using Fixed Server Roles" later in this chapter.) Server permissions include SHUTDOWN, CREATE DATA-BASE, BACKUP DATABASE, and CHECKPOINT permissions. Server permissions are used only for authorizing DBAs to perform administrative tasks and do not need to be modified or granted to individual users.

Database Object Permissions

Database object permissions are a class of permissions that are granted to allow access to database objects. Object permissions are necessary to access a table or view by using SQL statements such as SELECT, INSERT, UPDATE, and DELETE. An object permission is also needed to use the EXECUTE statement to run a stored procedure. You can use Enterprise Manager or T-SQL commands to assign object permissions.

Using Enterprise Manager to Assign Object Permissions

To use Enterprise Manager to grant database object permissions to a user, follow these steps:

1. Expand a server group, expand a server, expand the database you want to assign permissions for, and click the Users folder. The users are then listed in the right pane. Right-click a user name, and choose Properties from the shortcut menu to display the Database User Properties window, shown in Figure 34-14.

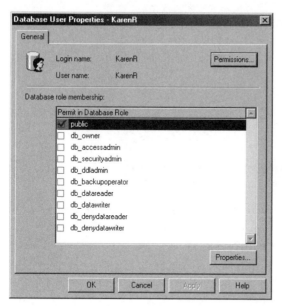

Figure 34-14. *The Database User Properties window.*

2. Click the Permissions button to display the Database User Properties window, shown in Figure 34-15. (To display this tab, you can also right-click the user name, point to All Tasks in the shortcut menu, and then choose Manage Permissions.) On this tab, you manage the permissions assigned to this user. To assign permissions to this user to access objects within the database, select the appropriate check boxes in the SELECT, INSERT, UPDATE, DELETE, EXEC, and DRI columns of the list box. ("DRI" stands for "declarative referential integrity.") The objects are listed in the Object column. You can use the option buttons at the top of the window to view all objects or just those that this user already has permissions to access.

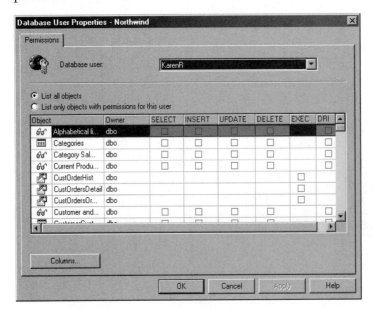

Figure 34-15. *The Permissions tab of the Database User Properties window.*

Using T-SQL to Assign Object Permissions

To use T-SQL to assign object permissions to a user, you run the GRANT statement. The GRANT statement has the following syntax:

```
GRANT { ALL | permission }
    [ column ON {table | view} ] |
    [ ON table(column) ] |
    [ ON view(column) ] |
    [ ON { stored_procedure | extended_procedure } ] ]
```

```
TO security_account
    [ WITH GRANT OPTION ]
    [ AS { group | role } ]
```

The *security_account* parameter must be one of the following account types:

- SQL Server user
- SQL Server role
- Windows NT or Windows 2000 user
- Windows NT or Windows 2000 group

Using the GRANT OPTION keyword allows the user or users specified in the statement to grant the specified permission to other users. This can be useful when you grant permissions to other DBAs. However, the GRANT option should be used with care.

The AS option specifies whose authority the GRANT statement is run under. To run the GRANT statement, a user or role must have been specifically granted authority to do so.

Here is an example of using the GRANT statement:

```
GRANT SELECT, INSERT, UPDATE
ON      Customers
TO      MaryW
WITH    GRANT OPTION
AS      Accounting
```

The *AS Accounting* option is used because the *Accounting* role has permissions to grant permissions on the *Customers* table. The GRANT OPTION keyword allows MaryW to grant these permissions to other users.

More Info   To view a list of permissions that can be specified in the GRANT statement, look up "GRANT, described (GRANT)" in the Books Online index.

Using T-SQL to Revoke Object Permissions

You can use the T-SQL REVOKE command to revoke a user's object permissions. The REVOKE statement has the following syntax:

```
REVOKE [ GRANT OPTION FOR ]
    { ALL [ PRIVILEGES ] | permission }
        [ column ON {table | view} ] |
        [ ON table(column) ] |
        [ ON view(column) ] |
        [ ON { stored_procedure | extended_procedure } ]
```

```
{ TO | FROM } security_account
      [ CASCADE ]
      [ AS { group | role } ]
```

The *security_account* parameter must be one of the following account types:

- SQL Server user
- SQL Server role
- Windows NT or Windows 2000 user
- Windows NT or Windows 2000 group

The GRANT OPTION FOR option allows you to revoke permissions you previously granted by using the GRANT OPTION keyword, as well as revoke the permission. The AS option specifies whose authority the REVOKE statement is run under.

Here is an example of using the REVOKE statement:

```
REVOKE ALL
ON     Customers
FROM   MaryW
```

The REVOKE ALL statement will remove all permissions the user MaryW has on the *Customers* table.

More Info To view a list of permissions that can be specified in the REVOKE statement, look up "REVOKE, described (REVOKE)" in the Books Online index.

Database Statement Permissions

In addition to assigning database object permissions, you can assign statement permissions. Object permissions enable users to access existing objects within the database, whereas statement permissions authorize them to create database objects, including databases and tables. The statement permissions are listed here:

- **BACKUP DATABASE** Allows the user to execute the BACKUP DATABASE command
- **BACKUP LOG** Allows the user to execute the BACKUP LOG command
- **CREATE DATABASE** Allows the user to create new databases
- **CREATE DEFAULT** Allows the user to create default values that can be bound to columns

- **CREATE PROCEDURE**   Allows the user to create stored procedures
- **CREATE RULE**   Allows the user to create rules
- **CREATE TABLE**   Allows the user to create new tables
- **CREATE VIEW**   Allows the user to create new views

You can assign statement permissions by using either Enterprise Manager or T-SQL.

Using Enterprise Manager to Assign Statement Permissions

To use Enterprise Manager to grant database statement permissions to a user, follow these steps:

1. Expand a server group, expand a server, and then expand the Databases folder. Right-click the name of the database you want to assign permissions for, and choose Properties from the shortcut menu to display the database's Properties window, shown in Figure 34-16.

Figure 34-16. *A database's Properties window.*

2. Click the Permissions tab, shown in Figure 34-17. Here you can assign statement permissions to the users and roles that have access to this database. The columns containing check boxes define the statement permissions that can be assigned, and the User/Role column lists the users and roles that have access to this database.

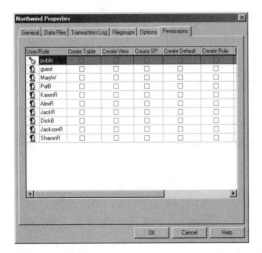

Figure 34-17. *The Permissions tab of a database's Properties window.*

Using T-SQL to Assign Statement Permissions

To assign statement permissions to a user by using T-SQL, you use the GRANT statement. The GRANT statement has the following syntax:

```
GRANT { ALL | statement }
TO    security_account
```

The statement permissions that can be assigned to a user are CREATE DATA-BASE, CREATE DEFAULT, CREATE PROCEDURE, CREATE RULE, CREATE TABLE, CREATE VIEW, DROP TABLE, DROP VIEW, BACKUP DATABASE, and BACKUP LOG, as described earlier. For example, to add the CREATE DATA-BASE and CREATE TABLE statement permissions to the user account JackR, use the following command:

```
GRANT CREATE DATABASE, CREATE TABLE
TO    'JackR'
```

As you can see, adding statement permissions to a user account is not a complex process.

Using T-SQL to Revoke Statement Permissions

You can use the T-SQL statement REVOKE to remove statement permissions from a user account. The REVOKE statement has the following syntax:

```
REVOKE { ALL | statement }
FROM    security_account
```

For example, to remove just the CREATE DATABASE statement permissions from the user account JackR, use the following command:

```
REVOKE CREATE DATABASE
FROM   'JackR'
```

As you can see, removing statement permissions from a user account is also not a complex process.

Administering Database Roles

You can simplify the task of managing many permissions to many users by using database roles. Database roles are designed to allow groups of users to receive the same database permissions without your having to assign these permissions individually. Rather than assigning individual permissions to individual users, you can create a role that represents the permissions used by a group of users and then assign it to the group.

Typically, roles are set up for particular workgroups, job classes, or job tasks. In this manner, new users can be members of one or more database roles based on the jobs they will be performing. For example, roles might be defined for job classes such as accounts payable, accounts receivable, engineering, and human resources. When a user joins one of these departments or groups, he or she is simply assigned as a member of the role created for that group. A user can be a member of one or more roles, but the user is not required to be a member of any roles. In addition to being assigned as a member of a database role, a user can be assigned individual permissions.

Creating and Modifying Roles

You accomplish the tasks of creating and modifying database roles by using the same tools that you use to perform most tasks related to database administration: Enterprise Manager or T-SQL commands. (SQL Server does not provide a wizard for these tasks.) Whichever method you use, you must accomplish the following tasks when you implement a role:

- Create the database role.
- Assign permissions to the role.
- Assign users to the role.

When viewing a role, you will be able to see both the permissions assigned to the role and the users assigned to the role.

Using Enterprise Manager to Administer Roles

To create database roles by using Enterprise Manager, follow these steps:

1. Expand a server group, expand a server, and then expand the Databases folder. Right-click the database you want to create the role in (we will use Northwind for this example), point to New in the shortcut menu, and then choose Database Role. Alternatively, you can expand the database, right-click Roles, and choose New Database Role from the shortcut menu. Either way, the Database Role Properties window appears, as shown in Figure 34-18.

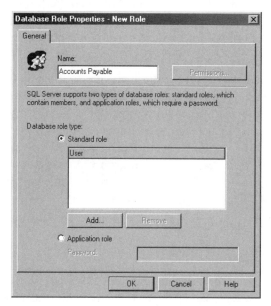

Figure 34-18. *The Database Role Properties window.*

2. Assign a descriptive name to the role by typing the name in the Name text box—choose a name that will help you remember the function of the role. Figure 34-18 shows the name *Accounts Payable* chosen for a role.

3. To assign users to the role, click Add. A list of user accounts that have access to the database appears, as shown in Figure 34-19. Select the users you want to assign to this role. To cancel a selection, simply click the appropriate user name again. When you have finished modifying

the membership of the role, click OK and the role will be created. You will be returned to the Enterprise Manager window.

Figure 34-19. *The Add Role Members dialog box.*

4. To assign permissions to the role, first open the Database Role Properties window by expanding the Roles folder, right-clicking the role name, and choosing Properties from the shortcut menu. Then click Permissions to display the Database Role Properties - Northwind window, as shown in Figure 34-20.

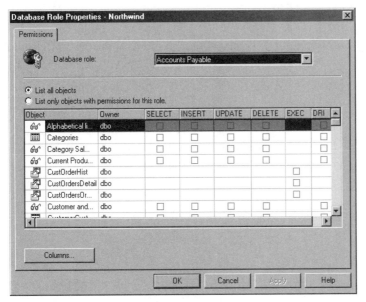

Figure 34-20. *The Database Role Properties - Northwind window.*

In this window, you can assign various permissions to this role for the objects within the database containing the role. To do so, select the appropriate check boxes in the list box. The database objects are listed in the Object column. You can use the option buttons at the top of the window to view all objects or just those for which this role already has permissions. Once you assign this role to a user, the user will receive all of the permissions that have been assigned to the role.

Once you create a role, you can modify it in the Database Role Properties window. To modify a role, follow the steps used to add permissions to a role. You can add and delete users and permissions in the Database Role Properties window.

Using T-SQL to Administer Roles

You can also create roles by using the *sp_addrole* stored procedure. The *sp_addrole* stored procedure has the following syntax:

```
sp_addrole [ @rolename = ] 'role'
      [ , [ @ownername = ] 'owner' ]
```

For example, to add a role named *readonly* to the Northwind database, use the following T-SQL command:

```
USE Northwind
GO
sp_addrole 'readonly' , 'dbo'
GO
```

The *USE Northwind* command will select Northwind as your current database. If you do not specify a database, the role will be created in your default database.

This stored procedure will only create the role. To add permissions to the role, use the GRANT statement, which was described earlier. To remove permissions from the role, use the REVOKE statement, also described earlier.

For example, to add the SELECT permission on the *Employees*, *Customers*, and *Orders* tables to the *readonly* role, use the following GRANT statement:

```
USE Northwind
GO
GRANT SELECT
ON      Employees
TO      readonly
GO
```

```
GRANT SELECT
ON    Customers
TO    readonly
GO
```

To add users to the role, use the *sp_addrolemember* stored procedure. The *sp_addrolemember* stored procedure has the following syntax:

```
sp_addrolemember 'role', 'security_account'
```

The following command adds a user to the *readonly* role:

```
USE Northwind
GO
sp_addrolemember 'readonly' , 'Guest'
GO
```

Using Fixed Server Roles

A number of predefined roles that apply at the server level are created when SQL Server is installed. These fixed server roles are used to grant permissions to DBAs and can contain both server permissions and object and statement permissions. These roles are listed here:

- *bulkadmin*   Can perform bulk inserts
- *dbcreator*   Can create and alter databases
- *diskadmin*   Can manage disk files
- *processadmin*   Can manage SQL Server processes
- *securityadmin*   Can manage logins and create database permissions
- *serveradmin*   Can set any server options and can shut down the database
- *setupadmin*   Can manage linked servers and startup procedures
- *sysadmin*   Can perform any server activity

By assigning user accounts to fixed server roles, you enable users to perform the administrative tasks that those roles have permissions for. Depending on your needs, this setup might be preferable to having all DBAs use the same administrative account. Like database roles, fixed server roles are much easier to maintain than individual permissions, but fixed server roles cannot be modified. You can assign a user to a fixed server role by following the steps listed on the next page.

1. In Enterprise Manager, expand a server group, expand a server, expand the Security folder, and then click Server Roles. Right-click the fixed server role you want to add the user to and choose Properties from the shortcut menu. This invokes the Server Role Properties window, shown in Figure 34-21.

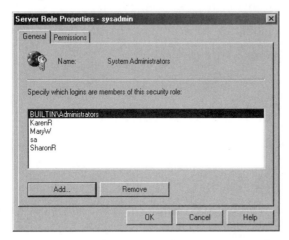

Figure 34-21. *The Server Role Properties window.*

2. To add a user account to the role, first click Add. This invokes the Add Members dialog box, shown in Figure 34-22, in which you select new role members.

Figure 34-22. *The Add Members dialog box.*

3. After you have selected the users that you want to add to the fixed server role, click OK. This will return you to the Server Role Properties window. Click OK to add the user to the security role.

Security Account Delegation

SQL Server 2000 builds on the Windows 2000 security features by using the Kerberos security model. (Information about the Kerberos security model can be found in Chapter 2.) SQL Server 2000 uses the Kerberos protocol to support mutual authentication between the client and the server. This allows the security credentials of a client to be passed between computers so that the client can connect to multiple servers; when a new server is accessed, the server can proceed by using the credentials of the impersonated client. This credential sharing is known as security account delegation.

Let's look at an example of security account delegation. Suppose a client connects to ServerA as NTDOMAIN\AlexR, and ServerA connects to ServerB. ServerB then knows that the connection security identity is NTDOMAIN\AlexR. This alleviates the need for the client to log in to ServerB.

If you want to use security account delegation, all servers that you are connecting to must be running Windows 2000 with Kerberos support enabled, and you must be using Active Directory services. The following options must be set in Active Directory services for delegation to work:

- **Account Is Sensitive And Cannot Be Delegated**   This option must not be selected for the user requesting delegation.
- **Account Is Trusted For Delegation**   This option must be selected for the service account of SQL Server 2000.
- **Computer Is Trusted For Delegation**   This option must be selected for the server running an instance of SQL Server 2000.

Configuring SQL Server

Prior to using security account delegation, you must configure SQL Server 2000 to accept the delegations. Delegation enforces mutual authentication. To use security account delegation, SQL Server 2000 must have a Service Principal Name

(SPN) assigned by the Windows 2000 account domain administrator. The SPN must be assigned to the service account of the SQL server on that computer. The SPN is necessary to prove that SQL Server is verified on the particular server and at the particular socket address by the Windows 2000 account domain administrator. You can have your domain administrator establish an SPN for SQL Server by using the Setspn utility, which is accessible through the Windows 2000 Resource Kit.

To create an SPN for SQL Server, you run the following command:

```
setspn -A MSSQLSvc/Host:port serviceaccount
```

Here is an example of using this command:

```
setspn -A MSSQLSvc/MyServer.MyDomain.MyCompany.com sqlaccount
```

More Info   For more information about the Setspn utility, see the Windows 2000 documentation.

You must also be using TCP/IP to use security account delegation. You cannot use named pipes because the SPN targets a particular TCP/IP socket. If you are using multiple ports, you must have an SPN for each port.

You can enable delegation by using the LocalSystem account. SQL Server will self-register at service startup and automatically register the SPN. This option is easier than enabling delegation by using a domain user account. However, when SQL Server shuts down, the SPNs will be unregistered for the LocalSystem account. To enable delegation to run under the LocalSystem account, run the following command in the Setspn utility:

```
setspn -A MSSQLSvc/Host:port serviceaccount
```

Note   If you change a service account in SQL Server 2000, you must delete any previous SPNs that were defined and create new ones.

Summary

In this chapter, you've learned about SQL Server user and security management. You've seen how both database logins and database user accounts are used to allow access to the database, and you've learned how to create and manage logins and database users. You've also learned how database roles can make user management easier by allowing a set of permissions to be assigned to a group of users and by allowing those permissions to be modified in a single location. And you've learned about a special group of roles called fixed server roles, which are used to assign administrative permissions to users and DBAs. Finally we looked at a security enhancement included in SQL Server 2000 that enables security accounts to be securely passed between servers in a Windows 2000 environment. In Chapter 35, you'll learn about SQL stored procedures and optimizing your queries.

Chapter 35

Using SQL Query Analyzer and SQL Profiler

In this chapter, we'll continue our examination of stored procedures, which we began in Chapter 21. This chapter will show you how to analyze stored procedures and other Transact-SQL (T-SQL) statements by using SQL Query Analyzer and SQL Profiler. From this analysis, you'll be able to determine whether the T-SQL statements are efficient. An efficient SQL Server query uses the appropriate sequence of operations and the appropriate indexes to reduce the number of rows processed and to minimize the number of I/O operations.

Using Query Analyzer, you can view the execution plan that the SQL Server query optimizer has chosen for a T-SQL statement. The query optimizer is an internal module that attempts to find the best execution plan for each T-SQL statement. The query optimizer analyzes each T-SQL statement, looks at a number of possible execution plans, and calculates the estimated cost of each plan, in terms of resources needed and processing time. The least expensive plan is chosen. The cost of each plan is determined based on the available statistics that the system collects about the data, which might not be current. Because you might know more about your database and your data than the query optimizer, you might be able to determine a better plan than the query optimizer can. By using the information that Query Analyzer provides, you can determine whether the query optimizer's plan for a statement is efficient, and if you determine it is not, you can then try to optimize the statement by modifying it or by using an SQL hint. In this chapter, you'll learn how to optimize T-SQL statements in addition to learning how to use Query Analyzer.

Using Profiler, you can analyze activity within your SQL Server system in order to determine which SQL statements and stored procedures are using excessive system resources. Once you know which SQL statements are using excessive resources, you can concentrate your tuning efforts on those statements and stored procedures first. In addition to showing you how to use Profiler, this chapter will show you how to most effectively use the information that Profiler provides.

Using SQL Query Analyzer

The Query Analyzer tool, supplied with Microsoft SQL Server 2000, has replaced Interactive SQL for Windows (ISQL/W) as an SQL GUI, however you may have noticed that the Query Analyzer shows up as isqlw.exe in the task manager. You can use Query Analyzer to process T-SQL statements and view the results of those statements. Query Analyzer can also be used as a debugging tool to evaluate the execution plan that is generated by the query optimizer for your T-SQL statement.

Running T-SQL Statements

Running T-SQL statements and displaying the results of those statements are the most basic capabilities of Query Analyzer. To use Query Analyzer to run a T-SQL statement, follow these steps:

1. Click Start, point to Programs, point to Microsoft SQL Server, and then choose Query Analyzer. The Connect To SQL Server dialog box appears, as shown in Figure 35-1. You use this dialog box to make a connection to a SQL Server system.

Figure 35-1. *The Connect To SQL Server dialog box.*

2. Enter the server name in the SQL Server combo box. This can be the name of a local server or a remote server. Figure 35-1 shows a period (.) in the box. Entering a period indicates that you want to connect to the local server. The check box immediately below the SQL Server box lets you specify whether you want to start the server if it is not already running. In the Connect Using area, choose the authentication method you want to use to connect to SQL Server. If you choose to use Microsoft Windows NT Authentication, you don't have to specify a user name or password because the Microsoft Windows 2000 account will be used to authenticate access to SQL Server. If you choose to use

SQL Server Authentication, you must then specify a SQL Server user name and password in order to access SQL Server.

3. Click OK to connect to the specified SQL server and to start Query Analyzer. When the Query Analyzer window first appears, only the Query pane and the navigation panes are visible, but this will change once you start submitting T-SQL statements. Maximize the Query pane to fill the entire right-hand side of the Query Analyzer window, as shown in Figure 35-2. In the drop-down list on the toolbar, select the database you want to run queries against. Figure 35-2 shows the master database selected. For our example, click the down arrow and choose Northwind.

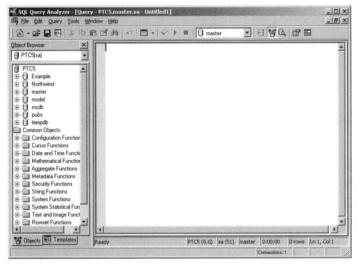

Figure 35-2. *The Query Analyzer window.*

4. After selecting a database, type a T-SQL statement in the right-hand pane—in this case, *SELECT * FROM Customers*. You now have several options. You can check the syntax of the T-SQL statement by clicking the Parse Query button on the toolbar (the blue check mark), or you can run the statement by clicking the Execute Query button (the green triangle pointing to the right). You can stop a query's execution by clicking the Cancel Executing Query button (the square). Figure 35-3 shows a completed query against the *Customers* table in the Northwind database.

Once you have submitted a T-SQL statement, Query Analyzer creates a pane that lets you scroll vertically and horizontally to view the results, as shown in Figure 35-3. Query Analyzer can also be used to help you tune your T-SQL statements, as we'll see in the section "Optimizing T-SQL Statements" later in this chapter.

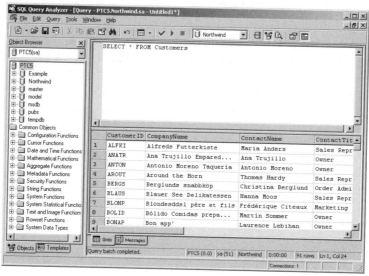

Figure 35-3. *A completed Query Analyzer query.*

Viewing Execution Plans and Modifying T-SQL Statements

As mentioned, you can also use Query Analyzer to display the execution plan that the query optimizer chooses for a T-SQL statement. This feature can help you determine whether your T-SQL statement is efficient and what execution path and data access paths have been chosen. You can then make changes to the T-SQL statement and the database schema and see whether performance improves. To use Query Analyzer to view the estimated execution plan of a T-SQL statement, follow these steps:

1. In the Query Analyzer window, type a T-SQL statement for Query Analyzer to evaluate, as described earlier, and then click the Display Estimated Execution Plan button (the button to the right of the database selection drop-down list) or press Ctrl+L. The Estimated Execution Plan pane is displayed, as shown in Figure 35-4. In this pane, the query is graphically depicted, and the cost of each operation is shown. The data access method is also shown here. In the pane shown in Figure 35-4, the index name *Customers.PK_Customers* appears, which means that the clustered index *Customers.PK_Customers* is used to access the data.

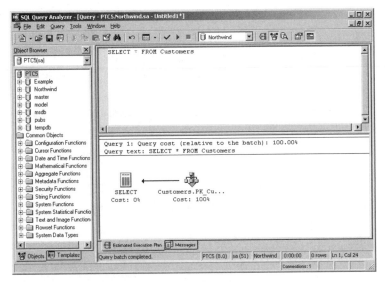

Figure 35-4. *The Estimated Execution Plan.*

2. The Estimated Execution Plan pane provides access to additional data about the operations shown in it. To view this additional data for any operation, hold the mouse pointer over the operation's icon. A pop-up window containing additional data appears, as shown in Figure 35-5.

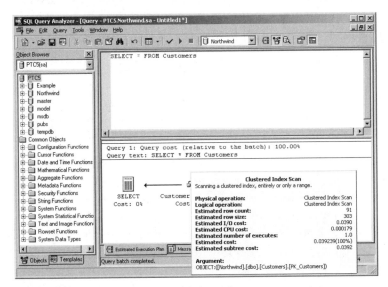

Figure 35-5. *Viewing additional data about an operation.*

This pop-up window contains the following information:

- **Physical Operation/Logical Operation**   The operations performed by the query, such as index scans, joins, aggregations, and so on. If the physical operator is displayed in red, the query optimizer has issued a warning, and you should fix your T-SQL statement.

- **Estimated Row Count**   The number of rows that the query optimizer estimates will be retrieved by the operation.

- **Estimated Row Size**   The estimated size of the rows being retrieved in bytes.

- **Estimated I/OCost/Estimated CPU Cost**   The estimated I/O resources and CPU time that will be used by this operation. A lower value means a more efficient T-SQL statement.

- **Estimated Number Of Executes**   The estimated number of times that this operation will be executed during the execution of the T-SQL statement.

- **Estimated Cost**   The cost of the operation as estimated by the query optimizer. This cost is shown as a percentage of the total cost of the T-SQL statement.

- **Estimated Subtree Cost**   The estimated cost of executing the preceding parts and this particular part of the T-SQL statement. If there are several subtrees, this option allows you to see the costs of executing each subtree.

- **Argument**   The parameters used by the T-SQL statement.

> **Note**   The *execution plan* describes how the query optimizer will execute a T-SQL statement. This plan shows the types of operations that will be used and the order in which they will be performed. The *data access method* describes how the database objects (tables, indexes, and so on) will be accessed. These two are related—the data access method is sometimes considered part of the execution plan, but it can also be considered separately.

Next we'll look at some more complex examples of using Query Analyzer. These examples also demonstrate how inefficient T-SQL statements can affect performance, both by slowing response times and by using system resources that could have been used by other processes. We'll first look at an example of using Query Analyzer to view and modify the execution plan for a T-SQL statement. As mentioned, by modifying your T-SQL statements, you might be able to achieve better performance for them. In many cases, you can create a more efficient, functionally equivalent T-SQL statement. Then we'll look at progressively more complex estimated execution plans for several types of T-SQL statements.

The examples in the remainder of this section use the *Orders* table from the Northwind database. Let's review the organization of this table. When we look at the examples, this information will help you determine whether the query optimizer is choosing the appropriate execution plan. The *Orders* table has a clustered index named *PK_Orders* on the *OrderID* column and has eight other indexes, as shown in the Manage Indexes dialog box in Figure 35-6. (To access this dialog box by using Enterprise Manager, expand a server group, expand a server, expand Databases, expand the Northwind database, and click the Tables folder. Right-click the *Orders* table in the right-hand pane, point to All Tasks in the short-cut menu, and then choose Manage Indexes. Or simply choose Manage Indexes from the Query Analyzer Tools menu, and choose the Orders table from the drop-down menu.)

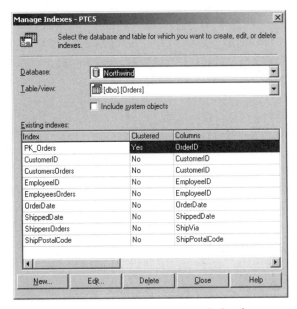

Figure 35-6. *The Manage Indexes dialog box.*

Viewing the Plan for and Modifying a SELECT Statement

In this section, we'll look at a query that requests information about orders that have been placed by an employee whose employee ID is *4*. The query is shown here:

```
SELECT OrderID, CustomerID, EmployeeID, OrderDate
FROM Orders
WHERE EmployeeID = 4
```

In this employee's organization, each employee handles a small portion of the total orders, so you might expect SQL Server to use the *EmployeeID* index when processing the query. Instead, Query Analyzer informs you that the access method SQL Server will use is the *PK_Orders* clustered index, as shown in Figure 35-7.

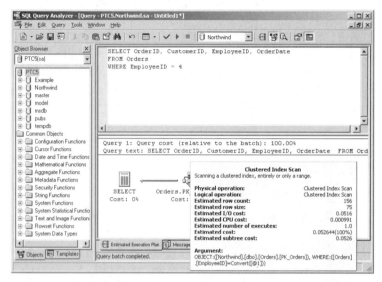

Figure 35-7. *The Estimated Execution Plan pane, which shows that the* PK_Orders *clustered index will be used.*

To direct the query optimizer to use the *EmployeeID* index instead, you can use a hint with the SELECT statement, as shown in the following code. (Hints are discussed in the section "Using Hints" later in this chapter.)

```
SELECT OrderID, CustomerID, EmployeeID, OrderDate
FROM Orders WITH (INDEX(EmployeeID))
WHERE EmployeeID = 5
```

Note In Microsoft SQL Server 7, the preferred index hint was INDEX=*index_name*. With SQL Server 2000, the index hint INDEX(*index_name*) is preferred.

By providing this extra information in the command, you instruct the query optimizer to use the execution plan that you want, rather than the one that the query optimizer has chosen for you. The adjusted Estimated Execution Plan pane is shown in Figure 35-8. As you can see from the data access method displayed, the *EmployeeID* index will be used as the input to a bookmark lookup, which will then retrieve the data from the database. (A bookmark lookup searches for an internal identifier for a row of data.)

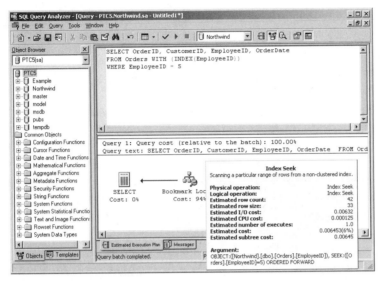

Figure 35-8. *The adjusted Estimated Execution Plan pane.*

The query optimizer is an efficient tool and constantly updates statistics to enable it to choose the best execution plan. But because you understand your organization and your data, in some cases, you might be better equipped than the query optimizer to choose the best execution plan.

Caution When you use a hint to override the query optimizer, you do so at your own risk. Although there is little or no danger of data loss or corruption, you can adversely affect your system's performance.

Viewing the Plan for a Join Operation

Performing a join operation involves many more processes than does performing a select operation, as you will see in the Estimated Execution Plan pane shown later in this section. A join operation involves several table accesses followed by the combining of the retrieved data. (Joins are discussed in Chapter 14.) An example of a statement specifying a join operation is shown here:

```
SELECT OrderID, CustomerID, Employees.EmployeeID, FirstName,
    LastName, OrderDate
FROM Orders JOIN Employees ON Orders.EmployeeID = Employees.EmployeeID
```

The preceding statement includes the SQL-92 JOIN operator. Using this operator is the recommended way to perform joins in SQL Server 2000. The following statement uses the more traditional join syntax, which SQL Server still supports:

```
SELECT OrderID, CustomerID, Employees.EmployeeID, FirstName,
    LastName, OrderDate
FROM Orders, Employees
WHERE Orders.EmployeeID = Employees.EmployeeID
```

Either of these T-SQL statements joins the *Orders* and *Employees* tables on the *EmployeeID* column. The resulting estimated execution plan is shown in Figure 35-9.

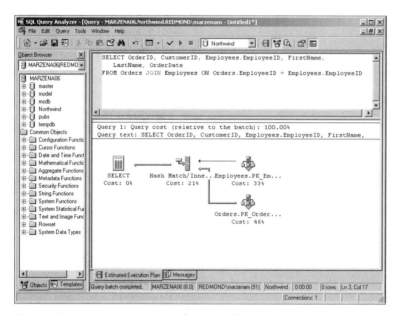

Figure 35-9. *A join operation shown in the Estimated Execution Plan pane.*

In this pane, you can see which of the two subtrees has a greater cost. You can also see the type of join operation planned. SQL Server supports several join operations, including hash joins, nested loops joins, and merge joins. With a complex join operation, the execution plan can be quite complicated. (Query Analyzer will adjust the size of the Estimated Execution Plan pane to accommodate the number of branches needed.) Because your goal is to reduce the amount of CPU time as well as the number of I/O operations, you should try to determine whether a better execution plan can be used. In some cases, you can use a hint to specify that you want to use a particular index, thus reducing both CPU and I/O activity. You can also use hints with table joins. For the query shown in Figure 35-9, because the join is the only operation specified in the FROM clause, the execution plan shown is probably the best.

Viewing the Plan for an Aggregate Operation

The T-SQL statement shown here performs not only a join operation but also an aggregate operation:

```
SET QUOTED_IDENTIFIER ON
GO
SELECT CustomerID, SUM("Order Details".UnitPrice)
FROM Orders JOIN "Order Details" ON Orders.OrderID = "Order Details".OrderID
GROUP BY CustomerID
```

> **Note**   Because the table name *Order Details* contains a keyword and a space, the option SET QUOTED_IDENTIFIER ON must be used. This allows the table name *Order Details* to be specified in double quotes. For more information about this option, look up "SET QUOTED_IDENTIFIER" in the Books Online index.

The Estimated Execution Plan pane for this complex operation is shown in Figure 35-10.

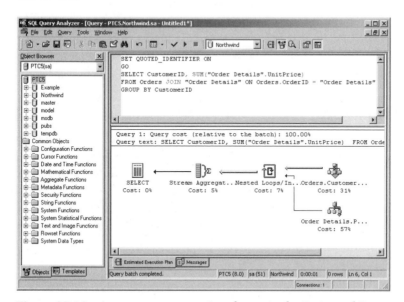

Figure 35-10. *An aggregate operation shown in the Estimated Execution Plan pane.*

Viewing the Plan for a Stored Procedure

To view the execution plan of a stored procedure, you simply invoke that stored procedure from Query Analyzer. Query Analyzer will display the estimated execution plan for the stored procedure you are calling. Figure 35-11 shows the plan for *sp_who*. (Notice that the execution plan for this commonly used stored procedure is quite complex.) You can view the execution plan for a stored procedure without having to know which T-SQL statements make up the stored procedure.

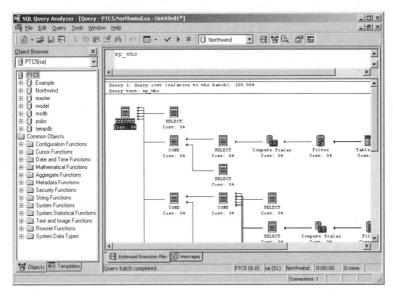

Figure 35-11. *A stored procedure shown in the Estimated Execution Plan pane.*

Using Object Browser

Object Browser is an enhancement to Query Analyzer included in SQL Server 2000. When you start up Query Analyzer, you will see Object Browser in the left-hand side of the window. Object Browser is split into two sections, the database objects section and the common objects section. In the database objects section, you can browse objects such as tables and views. In the common objects section, you can conveniently access system objects and functions. You should explore

Object Browser to find out what information it provides and then determine what you can use.

Database Objects

The top portion of Object Browser contains the database objects. You can immediately see the default databases and any databases that you have created, shown under the SQL Server system that they belong to. In order to see what information is available within Object Browser, simply expand objects. Let's expand the Northwind database and then expand User Tables. Now you can see the tables available within the Northwind database. This is shown in Figure 35-12.

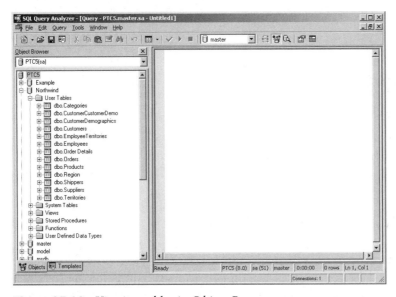

Figure 35-12. *Viewing tables in Object Browser.*

You can next expand a user-defined table and then expand folders containing information about columns, indexes, constraints, dependencies, and triggers. Figure 35-13 shows the *Orders* table expanded. Or you can expand the appropriate folders to view information about system tables, views, stored procedures, functions, and user-defined data types.

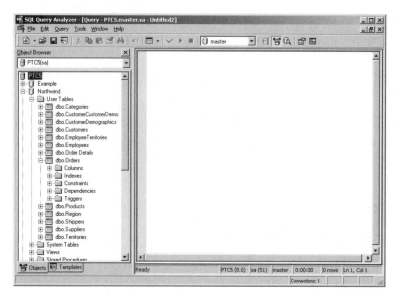

Figure 35-13. *Expanding a table in Object Browser.*

Having database object information available within Query Analyzer is quite convenient because it allows you to create SQL statements and stored procedures without having to look up object information outside Query Analyzer. Not only can you view information in Object Browser, but you can also edit objects, drag and drop objects, and even script object creation and object modification. These features add functionality to an already useful tool.

Common Objects

In the lower part of Object Browser is a folder named Common Objects (shown in Figure 35-14). Within this folder are folders containing information about objects such as configuration functions, cursor functions, date and time functions, and mathematical functions. You can thus quickly access a function without having to look up its syntax.

If you expand a folder in this area, you will be presented with configuration functions, as shown in Figure 35-14. You can drag these functions to the Query pane, or, by placing the mouse pointer over the function, you can see a brief description. This is convenient for ad-hoc query processing.

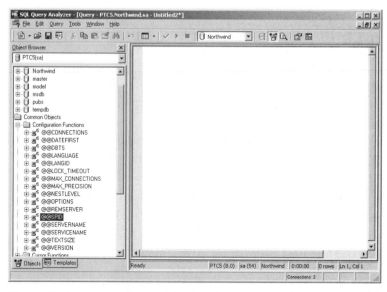

Figure 35-14. *Expanding a folder in the common objects part of Object Browser.*

In addition to accessing the global variables, you can access many other useful shortcuts to functions such as mathematical and string functions. By continuing to expand objects, you can get information about the parameters required by these functions, for example. Figure 35-15 shows the Parameters folder of a mathematical function expanded.

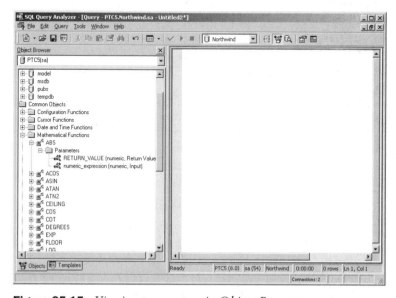

Figure 35-15. *Viewing parameters in Object Browser.*

Using SQL Profiler

In addition to using Query Analyzer to find inefficient T-SQL statements, you can use the SQL Profiler utility. Profiler can view all T-SQL statements that are running on the system and graphically display information about them. It also provides sorting and filtering options you can use to locate the T-SQL statements that are using the most CPU and I/O resources. With this information, you can determine which T-SQL statements to concentrate on when you tune the statements. T-SQL statements that are invoked through an application can be viewed in Profiler; you don't have to access the application source code.

The Profiler utility in SQL Server 2000 is similar to the Profiler utility included in SQL Server 7, but it contains a few enhancements. One useful enhancement is the introduction of the trace template, which can be used to create trace files. (A trace must still be created before you can use it to trace SQL Server activities.) With SQL Server 7, traces had to be created by hand.

To invoke the Profiler utility and run a trace, follow these steps:

1. Click Start, point to Programs, point to Microsoft SQL Server, and then choose Profiler. When the Profiler window first appears, it will be empty. No panes are opened within Profiler, and nothing is being profiled in SQL Server.

2. To start profiling, you must choose an existing trace template or create a new trace template to run. (The startup process is described in step 4.) SQL Profiler provides a number of trace templates to choose from. Using these trace templates can save you time because you don't have to set up the trace from scratch. To examine the list of trace templates, click the File menu, point to Open, and choose Trace Templates to display the Open dialog box, shown in Figure 35-16.

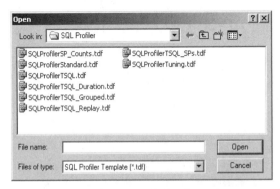

Figure 35-16. *The Open dialog box showing available trace templates.*

The trace templates that come with SQL Server are described here:

- **SQLServerProfilerSP_Counts.tdf** Counts the number of stored procedures that have been run. The results are grouped by the stored-procedure name and include the number of times the procedure was executed.

- **SQLServerProfilerStandard.tdf** Collects general information about connections, stored procedures executed, and SQL batches in the order that they were executed.

- **SQLServerProfilerTSQL.tdf** Collects all the T-SQL statements in the order in which they were submitted to SQL Server by the user community. The trace contains simply the T-SQL statements and the times they were issued.

- **SQLServerProfilerTSQL_Duration.tdf** Displays the T-SQL statements that have been issued as well as the time (in milliseconds) those T-SQL statements required to execute.

- **SQLServerProfilerTSQL_Grouped.tdf** Collects data similar to that collected by the SQLServerProfilerTSQL trace, but groups the statements by the users that submitted them.

- **SQLServerProfilerTSQL_Replay.tdf** Provides detailed information about the T-SQL statements that have been issued. This trace provides data that can be used to replay T-SQL statements in Query Analyzer.

- **SQLServerProfilerTSQL_SPs.tdf** Displays the specified stored procedure as well as the T-SQL commands within that stored procedure. The results are displayed in the order that they were executed.

- **SQLServerProfilerProfilerTuning.tdf** Collects data about stored-procedure and SQL batch execution.

These trace templates can be quite useful. For example, the trace template SQLServerProfilerTSQL_Duration can help you determine which T-SQL statements are taking the most time to execute. This information gives you a place to start when you want to optimize a query. The statement might be running slowly because it has a lot of work to do, or it might be running slowly because it is inefficient. As you will see in the next step, you must use a predefined template for every trace.

3. To start a trace, click File, point to New, and then choose Trace. The Connect To SQL Server dialog box appears, as shown in Figure 35-17. In this dialog box, select a SQL Server system to trace, and then click OK.

Figure 35-17. *The Connect To SQL Server dialog box.*

4. The Trace Properties window appears, as shown in Figure 35-18. On the General tab, you can name the trace and choose a trace template to start from. For this example, select the SQLServerProfilerTSQLDuration trace template. On the lower part of the tab, you can specify whether you want to capture the trace to a file or to a SQL Server table. If neither of these options is chosen, the trace will be sent only to your screen. In addition, you can specify a time for the trace to finish. This can be quite useful for long-running traces.

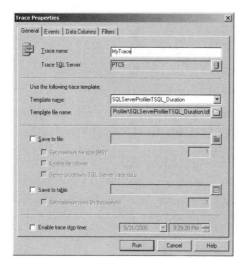

Figure 35-18. *The General tab of the Trace Properties window.*

5. Next click the Events tab, shown in Figure 35-19. This tab allows you to select one or more events that the trace will capture. A number of categories of events and specific events can be traced. Event classes listed in the Available Event Classes list box include Cursors, Errors And Warnings, Locks, Objects, Scans, SQL Operators, Stored Procedures, Transactions, and TSQL.

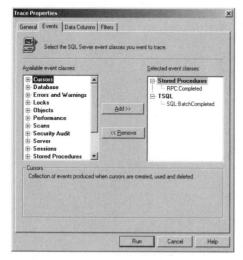

Figure 35-19. *The Events tab of the Trace Properties window.*

6. After you select events you want to trace, click the Data Columns tab, shown in Figure 35-20. On this tab, specify what data will be collected during the trace. This data can include end time, object ID, and so on.

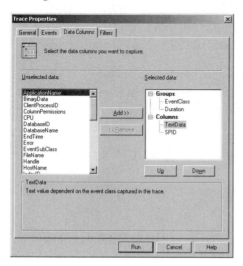

Figure 35-20. *The Data Columns tab of the Trace Properties window.*

7. Click the Filters tab, shown in Figure 35-21. On this tab, you can specify whether you want Profiler to include or exclude specific events. For example, you should exclude tracing Profiler itself. (This is the default setting.) By excluding SQL Server processes, you will make the Profiler window less cluttered and easier to read.

Figure 35-21. *The Filters tab of the Trace Properties window.*

8. When you are finished setting options, click Run to start the trace. If you have made any modifications to the trace template, it is recommended that you save this modified trace template under a different name using the Save As option under the File menu. Once the trace is started, events appear in the Profiler window as they happen. With the trace template we chose in this example, the events are sorted by duration (in milliseconds). Figure 35-22 shows the Profiler window displaying the results of a trace.

Caution Profiler can use significant system resources in a busy environment. The more events you trace, the more overhead will be used.

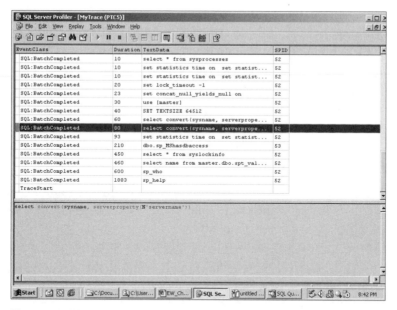

Figure 35-22. *A running trace.*

Optimizing T-SQL Statements

In the previous sections, you learned how to view the T-SQL statements running in the system by using Profiler and how to determine the execution plan and data access method by using Query Analyzer. You also were presented with a simple example of modifying a T-SQL statement in order to improve its performance. Armed with these tools, you now can modify many types of T-SQL statements to make them perform better. In this section, you'll learn about several ways that T-SQL statements can be optimized to provide better performance or to use fewer system resources.

Optimizing the Execution Plan

Modifying the execution plan can be difficult, and creating a better execution plan than the query optimizer creates can be even more difficult. The operations most likely to benefit from changes in the execution plan are JOIN, GROUP BY,

ORDER BY, and UNION. You can easily modify these operations by trying various hints and viewing the results, as described in the section "Using Hints" later in this chapter. By changing the hint and viewing the output of Query Analyzer, you might find that you have achieved a more efficient operation.

Unfortunately, no magic formula exists for tuning T-SQL statements for better performance. Because each database is unique and each application is different, modifications must be made on a case-by-case basis.

Choosing a Data Access Method

As mentioned earlier in this chapter, data access methods are essentially the objects SQL Server uses in retrieving data from the database. By analyzing your database and the data it contains, you might be able to optimize the data access method, with the goal of reducing the number of I/O operations.

Modifications to the data access method, like modifications to the execution plan, must be made on a case-by-case basis. The following guidelines will help you choose the data access method that performs best:

- **Use the best index.**   Using the best index for an operation is necessary to achieve the best performance possible. The best index for a particular operation is the one that finds the data fastest and uses the fewest I/O operations. You can determine the best index either by using your intimate knowledge of your database and its data or by using Query Analyzer. Query Analyzer lets you try various scenarios to determine which index will retrieve the least number of rows. (Remember that Query Analyzer simply estimates the number of rows that will be returned; to determine the exact number of rows, you must use Profiler.)

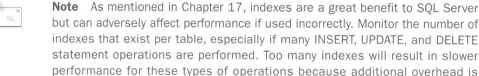

Note   As mentioned in Chapter 17, indexes are a great benefit to SQL Server but can adversely affect performance if used incorrectly. Monitor the number of indexes that exist per table, especially if many INSERT, UPDATE, and DELETE statement operations are performed. Too many indexes will result in slower performance for these types of operations because additional overhead is needed to modify the indexes.

- **Use covering indexes.**   As mentioned in Chapter 17, the use of covering indexes might help you eliminate an I/O operation in the data retrieval process. Instead of having to access the underlying table, you might be able to retrieve the needed data from the index itself.

- **Reduce the number of rows returned.**   Determine whether all the data that is returned from queries is actually needed. Modify your T-SQL statements so that they access only the data that is necessary. Do not retrieve rows that will be discarded later. Reducing the number of rows retrieved from the database can be achieved by increasing the selectivity of the query.

Using Hints

You can change the data access method and the execution plan by modifying the T-SQL statement itself, but if you are not careful, this technique can change the functionality of the T-SQL statement. A safer method of optimizing T-SQL statements is using hints. Hints let you specify which operations you want the query optimizer to perform and which objects you want it to use. In this section, you'll learn about the various SQL Server hints and how to use them.

Join Hints

Join hints are used to specify which types of join operations the query optimizer should perform. (If no type is specified in a query, the query optimizer selects one.) With SQL Server, you can perform nested loops joins, hash joins, merge joins, and remote joins. You specify a method of joining by using the following hints:

- **LOOP**   Specifies a nested loops join. In a nested loops join, for each row in the outer table, every row in the inner table is checked to see whether the values of specified fields are equal.

- **HASH**   Specifies a hash join. In a hash join, one table is reorganized as a hash table. The other table is scanned one row at a time, and the hash function is used to search for equalities.

- **MERGE**   Specifies a sort merge join. In a sort merge join, each table is sorted, and then one row at a time from each table is compared with the corresponding row in descending order.

- **REMOTE**   Specifies a remote join. A remote join is a join in which at least one participating table is remote.

Let's look at an example of using a join hint. We'll use the example from the "Viewing the Plan for a Join Operation" section earlier in this chapter, and we'll specify a hash join, as follows:

```
SELECT OrderID, CustomerID, Employees.EmployeeID, FirstName,
    LastName, OrderDate
FROM Orders, Employees
WHERE Orders.EmployeeID = Employees.EmployeeID
OPTION (HASH JOIN)
```

Note Join hints are mutually exclusive—only one can be used at a time.

If you choose to use the SQL-92 syntax for joins, you can specify the type of join by using a hint also. Using the SQL-92 syntax, you could rewrite the preceding query as follows:

```
SELECT OrderID, CustomerID, Employees.EmployeeID, FirstName,
    LastName, OrderDate
FROM Orders INNER HASH JOIN Employees
ON (Orders.EmployeeID = Employees.EmployeeID)
```

The topic of join hints is an advanced topic, and there are no rules of thumb concerning when to use join hints. There are many reasons for choosing a particular join operation, such as predicates, the size of each table in the join, and how many tables are being joined. The best way to determine whether changing the join operation will provide better performance is to try each type in Query Analyzer and see which offers the lowest cost. However, the query optimizer will usually choose the best join operation for you.

Query Hints

Query hints are used to specify how particular query operations should be performed. Query hints are split into three categories: GROUP BY, UNION, and miscellaneous.

GROUP BY Hints The following hints specify how GROUP BY or COMPUTE operations should be performed:

- **HASH GROUP BY** Specifies that a hashing function be used to perform the GROUP BY operation

- **ORDER GROUP BY**   Specifies that a sorting operation be used to perform the GROUP BY operation

Using the GROUP BY example we looked at in the "Viewing the Plan for an Aggregate Operation" section earlier in this chapter, we can specify how a HASH GROUP BY operation should be performed by using a hint, as follows:

```
SELECT CustomerID, SUM(OrderDetails.UnitPrice)
    FROM Orders, OrderDetails
HASH GROUP BY CustomerID
OPTION (HASH GROUP)
```

Note   GROUP BY hints are mutually exclusive—only one can be used at a time.

UNION Hints   The following hints are used to specify how UNION operations should be performed:

- **MERGE UNION**   A MERGE operation is used to perform the UNION operation.
- **HASH UNION**   A hashing function is used to perform the UNION operation.
- **CONCAT UNION**   A concatenation function is used to perform the UNION operation.

Here is an example of using a CONCAT UNION hint:

```
SELECT OrderID, CustomerID, EmployeeID, OrderDate
    FROM orders
    WHERE CustomerID = 'TOMSP'
UNION
SELECT OrderID, CustomerID, EmployeeID, OrderDate
    FROM orders
    WHERE EmployeeID = '4'
OPTION (CONCAT UNION)
```

Note   UNION hints are mutually exclusive.

Unfortunately, there is no secret formula that you can use to determine which UNION operation will perform better in your situation. Again, the best route is to use Query Analyzer to try various UNION hints and to see which offers the best cost. Usually, the SQL Server query optimizer will determine the best strategy for UNION operations.

Miscellaneous Hints   The following hints can be used to perform various query operations:

- **FORCE ORDER**   Forces tables to be accessed in the order in which the tables appear in the query. By default, SQL Server can reorder the table accesses.

- **ROBUST PLAN**   Forces the query optimizer to be prepared for the maximum potential row size. Here is an example of using this hint:

```
SELECT OrderID, CustomerID, Employees.EmployeeID, FirstName,
    LastName, OrderDate
FROM Orders, Employees
WHERE Orders.EmployeeID = Employees.EmployeeID
OPTION (ROBUST PLAN)
```

Table Hints

Table hints are used to control the way in which tables are accessed. Two table hints are described here:

- **FAST *n***   Replaces FASTFIRSTROWS, which is retained for backward compatibility. Using this hint instructs SQL Server to optimize the retrieval of the first *n* rows of data.

- **INDEX = *index_name***   Forces the query optimizer to use the specified index when possible. One of the first examples in this chapter demonstrated how to use an INDEX hint. This example is repeated here:

```
SELECT OrderID, CustomerID, EmployeeID, OrderDate
    FROM orders WITH (INDEX = EmployeeID)
    WHERE EmployeeID = 5
    OPTION (FAST 10)
```

The WITH qualifier is optional.

The INDEX = *EmployeeID* hint specifies that the *EmployeeID* index be used. If you specify *FAST 10*, SQL Server will optimize the retrieval of the first 10 rows (if possible) and then return the rest of the rows.

Summary

In this chapter, you've learned how to use Query Analyzer to determine the execution plan and data access methods that are best for your query. In addition, you've learned how to use Profiler to view the T-SQL statements that are active in your system and how to run traces to determine whether some of these T-SQL statements might be causing performance problems. And you've discovered how to optimize the execution plan and data access methods based on your database and your data. Finally you've learned how to use hints to specify a particular execution plan or data access method to be used. In Chapter 36, this theme will be developed further; you'll learn about performance problems and how to solve them.

Chapter 36
Solving Common Performance Problems

Throughout this book, you've learned about tools you can use and parameters you can adjust to help you find and solve certain performance problems. For example, in the preceding chapter, you learned how to identify problems with your SQL statements and stored procedures and how to tune those statements and procedures for optimal performance. This chapter is designed to help you easily find the information you need to solve various types of performance problems. It reviews some of the topics related to performance that were covered in other chapters, provides references to earlier chapters in which performance issues were examined, and presents some additional information about performance monitoring and system tuning.

We'll start by briefly reviewing the definition of "bottleneck." Then we'll look at how to use Microsoft Windows 2000 System Monitor (called Performance Monitor in Microsoft Windows NT) and Microsoft SQL Server Enterprise Manager to determine whether a performance problem exists. Next we'll look at how to solve a number of common performance problems, which occur at several levels, including the application level, the SQL Server level, operating system level, and the hardware level. The rules of thumb used for system capacity planning that were described in Chapter 6 are reviewed in this chapter because you can use them to analyze an existing system to determine whether you need additional hardware to improve performance. Finally we'll review several SQL Server configuration parameters, described in previous chapters, that you can adjust to change the way your system performs.

By the end of this chapter, you should be able to identify a performance bottleneck and determine its cause. You can't always solve performance problems, but most are solvable if you have the time and resources to deal with them.

What Is a Bottleneck?

The term "bottleneck" is commonly used in discussions about software and hardware performance issues and refers to a performance-limiting condition caused by a component or set of components. For example, an I/O subsystem with insufficient capacity can cause a significant bottleneck—it can slow down the entire system. (We'll look at this scenario in detail in the section "I/O Subsystem" later in this chapter.)

Almost any component that is active in the system has the potential to cause a bottleneck. A bottleneck can be caused by a single component, such as one disk drive; a set of components, such as the I/O subsystem; or a combination of different components. For example, let's say you detect a bottleneck caused by the I/O subsystem and solve the problem by adding more disks to support the number of I/O operations occurring on the system (a hardware solution), by optimizing inefficient queries so that fewer I/O operations occur (a software solution), or by doing both. Once the I/O problem has been solved, you might find that you have a CPU-related bottleneck and need to increase the CPU speed or the number of CPUs.

Discovering the Problem

To determine whether your system is experiencing problems, you can first make some general observations about system performance. For example, find out whether users are experiencing slower-than-expected response times when they perform database queries and modifications. This is a common symptom of a performance problem or a bottleneck. You might notice, for example, that when a certain query is run, all the other operations being performed on the system run more slowly than they usually do. You would therefore focus on optimizing the query that is causing the problem, or you could try running it at a time when fewer users are accessing the system.

Another way to determine whether a problem exists is to periodically test and monitor the system. You can use several tools to do so, including Windows 2000 System Monitor and SQL Server Enterprise Manager. In this section, you'll learn how to use these two tools to examine the health of your system. You'll also be introduced to the *sp_who* stored procedure, which you can use to monitor active SQL Server processes.

Note Refer to Chapter 35 if you need instructions for using SQL Profiler and SQL Query Analyzer to detect performance problems that relate to your SQL statements.

System Monitor

Windows 2000 System Monitor provides not only Windows 2000 counters but also SQL Server counters. These counters monitor system characteristics, such as the percent of CPU utilization or the SQL Server cache hit ratio, which help you determine what is happening in your system. (Information about specific performance counters is provided throughout this chapter.) You can watch the monitoring in real time, or you can log the data to a file and look at the data later.

To use System Monitor to monitor your system, follow these steps:

1. Click Start, point to Programs, point to Administrative Tools, and then choose Performance to display the system monitor window.

2. Specify whether you want to view the counter data in chart, report, or histogram form or to view data previously saved to a log file by clicking the appropriate button on the toolbar. Figure 36-1 shows a chart view in System Monitor. If you choose to view a log file, a dialog box appears in which you choose the file to open.

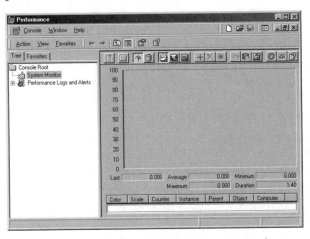

Figure 36-1. *Windows 2000 Performance window.*

3. To add a counter to be viewed in the Performance window, click the plus sign button on the toolbar. The Add Counters dialog box appears, as shown in Figure 36-2. Click Use Local Computer Counters to view counters for the local system, or click Select Counters From Computer and select the name of a remote computer from the drop-down list beneath the option button to view counters for that computer.

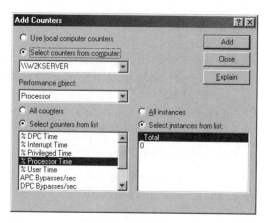

Figure 36-2. *The Add Counters dialog box.*

4. Select a System Monitor object from the Performance Object drop-down list. These objects represent system components. The counters for the object you select are then shown in the list box in the bottom left corner of the dialog box. If you want to observe all the object's counters, click All Counters. If you want to monitor only certain counters, click Select Counters From List, and select the counters from the list. For certain counters, more than one instance exists; these instances are shown in the list box in the bottom right corner of the dialog box. Click Select Instances From List if you want to select one or more particular instances to view, or click All Instances to view them all.

5. Click Add. The counter or counters you selected are added to the Performance window. (If you selected multiple instances of a counter, they are all added.) You can then continue to add counters. Click Close when you are ready to return to the Performance window. You will now be able to see the performance data provided by the counters. Figure 36-3 shows a chart view displaying the results returned by three counters: *Context Switches/Sec, Total Server Memory (KB),* and *% Processor Time.*

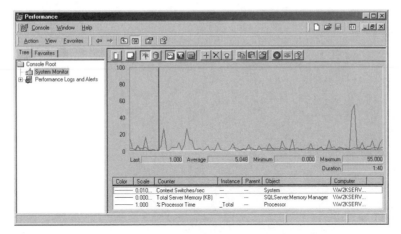

Figure 36-3. *System Monitor in action.*

To save performance data to a log file, follow these procedures:

1. Expand Performance Logs And Alerts in the left pane of the Performance window. Right-click Counter Logs and choose New Log Settings from the shortcut menu. The New Log Settings dialog box appears. Here you type the name of your log settings, as shown in Figure 36-4. Click OK to continue.

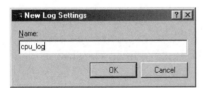

Figure 36-4. *The New Log Settings dialog box.*

2. The window named after your new log file appears. In the General tab, click Add. In the Add Counters dialog box that appears, select the counters that you want to be logged, as described in steps 3 through 5 in the preceding description of how to use System Monitor to monitor your system. The General tab also lets you change the log file name and specify how often performance data is sampled.

3. Click the Log Files tab to set additional properties of the log file. Figure 36-5 shows the settings for a file that will have a date added to the end of its name and that will be created as a binary file.

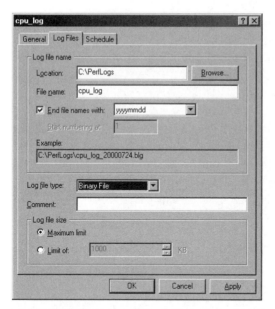

Figure 36-5. *The Log Files tab of a new log file's window.*

4. Click the Schedule tab. In this tab, you assign a start time and a stop time for the log file. You can also choose to start a new log or run a command when the current log file closes.

5. Click OK to close the window and to save your log file information. If you chose to start the log immediately, it will start when you click OK. An entry for the log file will appear in the Performance window, as shown in Figure 36-6.

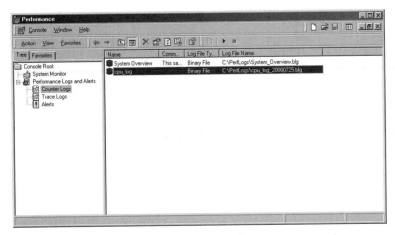

Figure 36-6. *The Performance window, showing an entry for a new counter log.*

You should use System Monitor on a regular basis to check the state of your system. Monitoring on a daily or weekly basis is a good idea because it lets you get to know your system, which enables you to recognize out-of-the-ordinary events. Saving the performance data in a log file for later inspection is also recommended—the data in the log file will come in handy when you want to compare performance data logged before a change is made to the system to the data logged after a change is made to determine whether the change was a good one. You can also use the logs to find out how user and system activity changes from one day to another. For example, you might notice that during the last few days of the month, user activity is much higher than at other times. You'll want to ensure that your system is capable of handling the load at those times of peak usage.

Enterprise Manager

In addition to using Enterprise Manager to automate day-to-day administrative functions, you can use it to assist with monitoring SQL Server processes and locks. (See Chapter 19 for information about locking.) For example, you can gather data about which processes are using locks and about which objects are being locked— an object in this case being a table, a database, or a temporary table. To view this information, follow the steps beginning on the next page.

1. In the Enterprise Manager window, expand Microsoft SQL Server, expand SQL Server Group, expand the server, expand the Management folder, and expand Current Activity, shown in Figure 36-7. The Current Activity folder contains three folders: Process Info, Locks / Process ID, and Locks / Object.

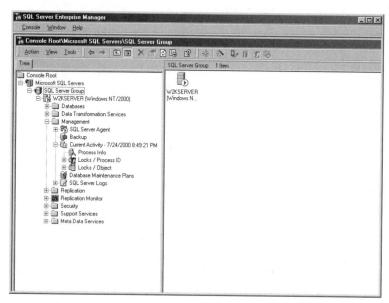

Figure 36-7. *The expanded Current Activity folder in Enterprise Manager.*

2. Click Process Info to view the names of users who are currently connected to SQL Server; the process IDs of those users; the status of the user processes (running, sleeping, or background); the database each user is connected to; the commands and application each user is running; the wait time (the time a user spends waiting for a resource to become available); the CPU, physical I/O, and memory usage of each process; and the blocking status of each process (whether the process is blocking others or is being blocked by others). To see all of the information, you will have to scroll to the right. Figure 36-8 shows some of this information.

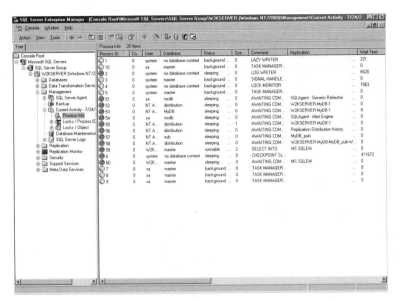

Figure 36-8. *The Process Info information in Enterprise Manager.*

3. Click Locks / Process ID to view in the right pane the list of system process identification numbers (SPIDs) of the currently active processes, shown in Figure 36-9. Double-click a SPID in the right pane to view the Process Details dialog box, shown in Figure 36-10. This dialog box shows the last T-SQL command the selected process ran.

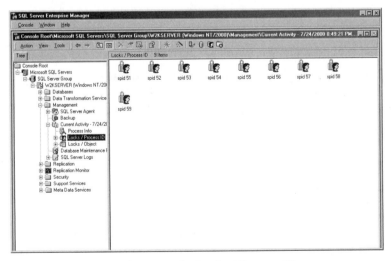

Figure 36-9. *SPIDs shown in the Locks / Process ID pane.*

Figure 36-10. *The Process Details dialog box.*

4. Expand the Locks / Process ID folder to view the current SPIDs in the left pane, shown in Figure 36-11.

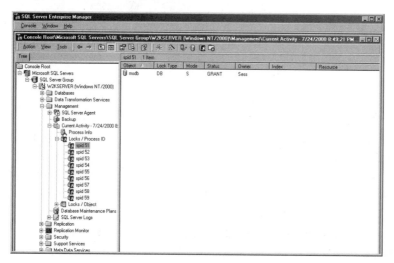

Figure 36-11. *The expanded Locks / Process ID folder.*

5. Click a SPID in the left pane to view the lock information for that process in the right pane, also shown in Figure 36-11. This information includes the lock type, the lock mode, the status of the lock, and the lock owner. The lock type can be one of the following:

- **RID** Row lock
- **KEY** Row lock within an index
- **PAG** Data or index page lock
- **EXT** Extent lock
- **TAB** Table lock, which includes all data and index pages for the locked table
- **DB** Database lock

The lock mode can be one of the following:

- **S** Shared lock
- **X** Exclusive lock
- **U** Update lock
- **BU** Bulk update lock
- **IS** Intent shared
- **IX** Intent exclusive
- **SIX** Shared with intent exclusive
- **Sch-S** Schema lock for compiling queries
- **Sch-M** Schema lock for DDL operations

The status of a lock can be one of the following:

- **GRANT** Means that the lock has been granted to the selected process
- **WAIT** Means that the process is blocked by another process and is waiting for a lock
- **CNVT** Means that the lock is being converted to another type of lock

6. Expand the Locks / Object folder to view a list of objects that are locked, as shown in Figure 36-12. Objects that can be locked include tables, temporary tables, databases, and so on.

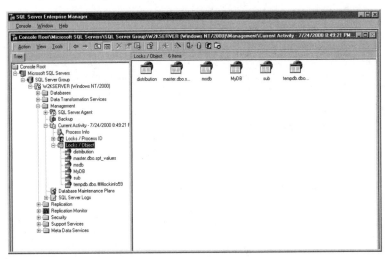

Figure 36-12. *The expanded Locks / Object folder.*

7. Click the name of a locked database or table to view its locking information in the right pane, as shown in Figure 36-13. The information shown is the same as that shown when a SPID in the Locks / Process ID folder is clicked, just from a different perspective.

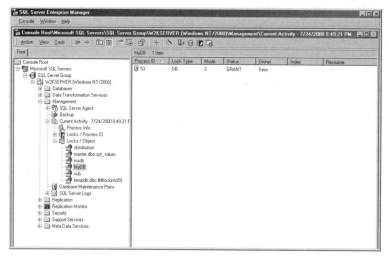

Figure 36-13. *Viewing lock information for an object.*

The *sp_who* Stored Procedure

You can also view information about active processes by running the following command in Query Analyzer or at an OSQL prompt:

```
sp_who active
GO
```

Sample results from running this command in Query Analyzer are shown in Figure 36-14. If a process is being blocked, the "blk" column will show the SPID of the process that is blocking it.

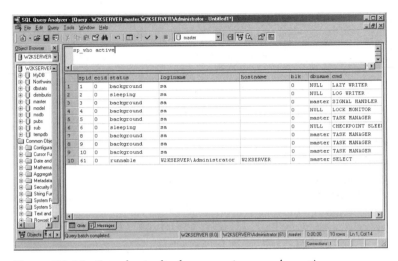

Figure 36-14. *Sample results from running* sp_who active.

When users complain that their transactions are slow, you can run this command to find blocks. Many times, you will find that most of the blocked processes are being blocked by one process, and once you find what process that is, you can determine why it is holding locks for so long.

You should occasionally monitor locking to determine whether any processes are holding a lock for a long period of time and whether processes are being blocked often (they have a WAIT status) because of exclusive locks or table locks held by other processes. But usually, you will get complaints from users about slow response times if blocking is a problem. If blocking is occurring too often or for long periods of time, you might want to determine which processes are holding the exclusive locks or table locks that might be the cause of the blocking and to monitor the SQL statements those processes are running. Then try to optimize those statements, if possible, so that they release the locks sooner or do not hold exclusive table locks. In general, when a process has to wait to obtain a lock, the process takes more time to finish. Therefore, reducing locking contention can improve transaction response times.

More Info For more details about viewing lock information, look up "displayinglocks," in Books Online and select "Displaying Locking Information" in the Topics Found dialog box.

Common Performance Bottlenecks

Now that you know how to use performance-monitoring tools such as System Monitor, Enterprise Manager, Query Analyzer, and Profiler, you are ready to tackle performance bottlenecks. In this section, we'll look at some of the most common performance bottlenecks and at various solutions to them. Many of these bottlenecks are closely related, and one bottleneck can disguise itself as another. You must look for both hardware-caused and software-caused bottlenecks—many performance problems stem from a combination of bottlenecks. Hardware components that can cause bottlenecks include the CPU, memory, and the I/O subsystem; software that can cause bottlenecks includes SQL Server applications and SQL statements. We'll examine each of these types of problems in more detail in the following sections.

CPU

One common performance problem is simply a lack of horsepower. The processing power of the system is determined by the number, type, and speed of the CPUs in the system. If your system doesn't have enough CPU power, it will not be able to process transactions fast enough to satisfy users. To use System Monitor to determine the percentage of CPU utilization, check the *%Processor Time* counter of the *Processor* object. (If you have a multiple-processor system, select all CPU instances.) If your CPUs are running at 75 percent or higher for long periods (75 percent is the desired maximum, according to the rules set out in Chapter 6), your system is likely experiencing a CPU bottleneck. If you consistently see CPU utilization as low as 60 percent, you might still benefit from adding faster CPUs or more CPUs to the system.

Be sure to monitor the other characteristics of the system before making the decision to upgrade your CPUs. If your SQL statements are highly inefficient, for example, your system might be doing much more processing than is necessary, and optimizing the statements can help lower the CPU utilization. Or suppose the cache hit ratio for the SQL Server data cache is below 90 percent. You might need to add memory to the data cache (either by increasing the *max server memory* parameter or by adding physical memory to the system). This will allow more data to be cached and therefore fewer physical disk I/O operations, leading to lower CPU utilization since less processing time will be spent dealing with I/O requests. You can sometimes get better performance out of your system by simply adding processors, especially if you are starting with a single-processor system. However, not all applications scale across multiple-processor systems. SQL Server scales well, but not all of the SQL statements that you might run will scale. A process will run on only one CPU at a time, and a single CPU is certainly sufficient for a single SQL statement. For the performance to improve by using multiple processors, your SQL Server system must be running many SQL statements concurrently—multiple statements can be running simultaneously on different CPUs, so the multiple CPUs can concurrently process the statements.

In general, you can almost always improve performance by using more and faster CPUs. However, in some cases, you must increase the memory and I/O capacity when you add faster CPUs to prevent moving the bottleneck to another location. For example, if you originally had a CPU bottleneck and you solved that problem by adding a CPU, you might find that your system is able to perform more work, resulting in more disk I/O. A disk I/O bottleneck could then occur. Also, be sure to check the Level 2 (L2) cache size of any new CPUs that you decide to add. The larger the CPU cache, the better the performance will be, especially in a multiple-processor system.

If you do decide you need more processing power, you can either add CPUs or replace your existing CPUs with faster ones. For example, if your system has two CPUs but can be expanded to contain four, try adding two more CPUs of the same type or switching to four new, faster CPUs. If your system already holds the maximum number of CPUs and you need more processing power, try getting faster CPUs to replace them. For example, let's say you have four CPUs that each run at a speed of 200 MHz. You could replace them with four CPUs that each run at a speed of, say, 500 MHz. Faster CPUs will allow processing to be completed more quickly.

Memory

The amount of memory available to SQL Server is one of the most critical factors in SQL Server performance. The relation of memory to the I/O subsystem is also an important factor. For example, in I/O-intensive systems, the more memory SQL Server can use for caching data, the fewer physical I/O operations must be performed. This is because the data is retrieved from the data cache instead of from the disk. SQL Server uses a complex caching system to speed up system performance: it accesses as much data as possible from memory and as little data as possible from disks, which provide slower performance. The more data SQL Server can access from memory, the better your system performance will be. Memory accesses are much faster than physical disk accesses.

In some cases, an insufficient amount of memory can result in an apparent disk bottleneck because more physical disk I/O is caused by the system's inability to cache effectively. To see how much of the system memory SQL Server is using, use System Monitor to check the *Total Server Memory (KB)* counter of the *SQL Server: Memory Manager* object. If SQL Server is not using the amount of memory you expect it to, you might need to adjust the memory configuration parameters described in the section "SQL Server Configuration Settings" later in this chapter.

To determine whether SQL Server has a sufficient amount of cache, use System Monitor to check the *Buffer Cache Hit Ratio* counter of the *SQL Server: Buffer Manager* object. The general rule is that SQL Server should have a 90 percent or higher cache hit rate, if possible. Add more memory to the cache if the hit rate is lower than 90 percent. Note that some systems never achieve a 90 percent cache hit rate because of the nature of the application being used. This might be the case if data pages are rarely reused and the system continually flushes out old data pages in the cache to bring in new ones.

> **Note**   Microsoft SQL Server 2000 dynamically allocates memory for the buffer cache based on available system memory and the memory parameter settings. Some external processes, such as printing processes and other applications, can cause SQL Server to free up much of its memory for their use. Monitor the system memory carefully, and isolate SQL Server on its own system, if possible. See Chapter 30 and the section "SQL Server Configuration Settings" later in this chapter for details about using the memory parameters.

I/O Subsystem

Bottlenecks occurring in the I/O subsystem are the most common hardware-related problems database systems experience. Poorly configured I/O subsystems are second only to poorly written SQL statements as the top cause of performance problems. Fortunately, problems with the I/O subsystem are also some of the easiest performance problems to fix. In many cases, the addition of disk drives will completely eliminate the performance bottleneck.

The I/O subsystem problem stems from the fact that the number of I/O operations a disk drive can perform is limited—for example, a drive might be able to handle no more than 85 random I/O operations per second. If disk drives are overloaded, the I/O operations to those disk drives are queued and SQL Server experiences long I/O latencies. These long I/O latencies can cause locks to be held longer or threads to sit idle while waiting for a resource. The net result is that the performance of the entire system suffers, which, in turn, results in angry users who complain that their transactions take too long to be completed.

In most cases, I/O subsystem performance problems occur because the I/O subsystem has not been properly sized for the load that it is experiencing. The topic of sizing was covered in detail in Chapters 5 and 6, but let's review it briefly here.

Sizing is necessary because, as mentioned, the number of I/O operations per second a single disk drive can perform is limited. When a disk drive performs mostly sequential I/O operations, as it does for the transaction log, it might achieve over 150 I/O operations per second without becoming overloaded. (As mentioned, overloading results in long latencies.) When the disk performs random I/O operations, on the other hand, as is common for data files, it might have a capacity of only 85 I/O operations per second. If the demand for I/O is higher, increasingly long latencies will occur.

To determine whether you are overdriving your disk drives, monitor the counters provided by the System Monitor objects *PhysicalDisk* and *LogicalDisk*. These counters, some of which are described in more detail later in this section, collect data about physical and logical disk I/O activity, such as the number of reads and writes per second that occur on a disk. These counters are enabled when you install the operating system, but you should know how to enable and disable them. These counters use system resources, such as CPU time, when they gather statistics, so you should enable them only when you want to monitor the system I/O. To enable or disable these counters, you enable or disable the Windows NT/2000 command DISKPERF.

To see if DISKPERF is enabled, run the following command at a command prompt:

```
diskperf
```

If DISKPERF is enabled, you will see this message: "Physical Disk Performance counters on this system are currently set to start at boot." If DISKPERF is disabled, you will see this message: "Both Logical and Physical Disk Performance counters on this system are now set to never start."

To enable DISKPERF if it is disabled, type the following command at a command prompt:

```
diskperf -Y
```

To disable DISKPERF, run this command:

```
diskperf -N
```

You must restart the computer for the changes to DISKPERF to take effect. Type the following command to see more options for DISKPERF:

```
diskperf ?
```

Of particular importance are the counters *Disk Writes/Sec*, *Disk Reads/Sec*, *Avg. Disk Queue Length*, *Avg. Disk Sec/Write*, and *Avg. Disk Sec/Read*. These counters can be invaluable in helping you determine whether you are overdriving the disk subsystem. Both the *PhysicalDisk* object and the *LogicalDisk* object provide these counters. To view details about the information these counters provide, click Explain in the Add Counters dialog box when you are adding the counter in System Monitor.

Let's look at an example of using these counters. Suppose you believe your system is experiencing an I/O bottleneck. You would check the *Avg. Disk Sec/Transfer*, *Avg. Disk Sec/Read*, and *Avg. Disk Sec/Write* counters of the *PhysicalDisk* object because they monitor disk latency (the amount of time the disk requires to perform a read or write), and increased latency is a sign that you are overdriving your disk drives or disk array. The general rule is that a normal reading for these counters is between 1 and 15 milliseconds (between 0.001 and 0.015 seconds), but you should not be concerned if latencies are as long as 20 milliseconds (0.020 seconds) at times of peak usage. If you are seeing values higher than 20 milliseconds, your system is definitely experiencing an I/O subsystem performance problem.

You would also look at *Disk Writes/Sec* and *Disk Reads/Sec*. Let's say these counters show that a disk performs 20 writes and 20 reads per second, for a total of 40 I/O operations, and the disk's capacity is 85 I/O operations per second. If, at the same time, the disk's latency is long, the disk drive might be faulty. Now let's say that the disk is performing 100 I/O operations per second and that the latencies are around 20 milliseconds or more. In this case, you need to add drives to improve performance.

To determine how many I/O operations your system is performing if you are using a RAID array, divide the number of I/O operations per second that you see in System Monitor by the number of drives in the array and factor in the RAID overhead. The following table lists the number of physical I/O operations that are generated for reads and writes when RAID technology is used.

Table 36-1. Number of physical I/Os performed for a read and a write per RAID level

RAID Level	Read	Write
0	1	1
1 or 10	1	2
5	1	4

In general, the best way to correct an I/O subsystem bottleneck is simply to add more disk drives. But remember to look at other possible causes of the I/O bottleneck, such as a low cache hit rate and transactions that perform more I/O operations than are necessary. (As mentioned, in most cases, a cache hit rate below 90 percent is too low.) If you do find an I/O bottleneck, review the directions in Chapter 6 for determining the number of disk drives needed for your system.

Faulty Components

Occasionally, your system might experience performance problems because of faulty components. If the faulty component has not failed completely but is degrading, the problem could be difficult to debug. Because these problems and their solutions take so many different forms and are so complex, this book does not cover them in detail. Instead, we'll look at a few basic tips for identifying faulty-component problems:

- **Compare disk drives and arrays.** When you view statistics in System Monitor, compare like components. If you notice, for example, that two disks are performing about the same number of I/O operations but are displaying different latencies, the slower disk drive might be experiencing a problem.

- **Watch the lights.** Network hubs usually have collision lights. If you notice that a particular network segment is experiencing an unusually high number of collisions, you might have a faulty component, possibly the network card or the network cable.

- **Get to know your system.** The more time you spend observing your system, the better you will understand its quirks. You will begin to recognize when the system is not performing normally.

- **Use System Monitor.** This is a good way to monitor the behavior of the system on a regular basis.

- **Read the logs.** Make a habit of regularly checking the SQL Server and the Windows 2000 Event Viewer system and application logs. Review these logs every day to catch problems before they get out of hand. This can't be emphasized enough.

Application

Another system component that commonly causes performance problems is the SQL Server applications. These problems can originate in the application code or in the SQL statements that the application is running. This section provides tips and guidelines for solving performance problems related to SQL Server applications.

Optimize Execution Plans

As you saw in Chapter 35, it's important to choose the best execution plan and data access method for a query. Unfortunately, there is no secret formula for determining the best plan. SQL Server automatically chooses the execution plan that Query Optimizer calculates is the best. You can use various types of hints in your queries, including query hints, table hints, and join hints. As you become familiar with these hints, you might be able to analytically determine the best plan for a query. Usually, you will need to look at various plans before you find an acceptable one.

Use Indexes Judiciously

As you saw in Chapters 17 and 35, the correct use of indexes is critical to good performance. Finding the desired data by using an index might require only 10 to 20 I/O operations, whereas finding the desired data via a table scan could require thousands or millions of I/O operations. However, indexes should be used with caution. Remember that when you modify data in a table by using an INSERT, UPDATE, or DELETE statement, the index or indexes associated with that data will be automatically updated to reflect the changed data, which produces I/O operations in addition to those produced by the table modification. Be careful to not create too many indexes; if you do, the performance of data modification operations will be affected by the overhead needed to maintain the indexes.

Use Stored Procedures

As you saw in Chapter 21, stored procedures are used to run prepackaged and precompiled SQL statements on the server. Calling stored procedures from your applications instead of calling individual SQL statements can help performance both by improving the reusability of SQL statements on the server and by greatly reducing network traffic. The amount of data sent between clients and servers can be reduced because a stored procedure resides on the server and because you can program processing and filtering of the data within the stored procedure, rather than within the application.

SQL Server Configuration Settings

SQL Server 2000 is virtually self-tuning, but you can still alter the way your system operates and performs by modifying the settings of certain configuration parameters. In this section, you'll learn how to configure these options and how they affect the operation of your system. You will most likely not need to change these parameters, but knowing what they are and what they do gives you the opportunity to decide whether to modify them. You can configure these parameters by using either Enterprise Manager or the T-SQL *sp_configure* stored procedure.

To use Enterprise Manager, right-click the name of the server you want to configure and choose Properties from the shortcut menu to display the SQL Server Properties window. This window contains nine tabs, and each tab contains options you can configure. These tabs and their options are explained in the following sections.

When using *sp_configure* to configure these options, you must remember that certain options are classified as advanced options. (The following sections indicate which options are advanced.) You must set the *show advanced options* option to *1* (enabled) to change an advanced option by using *sp_configure*. The option is set to *0* (disabled) by default. (You don't need to worry about this option when you use Enterprise Manager to set advanced options.) To enable *show advanced options*, use the following statement:

```
sp_configure "show advanced options", 1
GO
```

In general, to set any option by using *sp_configure*, use the following syntax:

```
sp_configure "option name", value
```

The *affinity mask* Option

The *affinity mask* option is used to specify which CPUs SQL Server threads can run on in a multiple-processor environment. The default value of *0* specifies that the Windows 2000 scheduling algorithms determine the thread affinity. A nonzero value sets a bitmap defining the CPUs that SQL Server can run on. A decimal value of *1* (or a binary bit mask value of *00000001*) indicates that only CPU 1 can be used, *2* (or *00000010*) indicates that only CPU 2 can be used, *3* (or *00000011*) indicates that CPU 1 and CPU 2 can be used, and so on.

This option is an advanced option, meaning that you must set *show advanced options* to *1* to configure the option by using *sp_configure*. You can configure *affinity mask* by using Enterprise Manager as well. To do so, click the Processor tab in the SQL Server Properties window, and, in the Processor Control area, select the check box next to each CPU that you want SQL Server to use. Click Apply and then click OK to save the change. You must also stop and restart SQL Server for this change to take effect.

On a dedicated SQL Server system, you should set the *affinity mask* option to allow SQL Server to use all of the CPUs. On a system that is not dedicated to SQL Server (and thus contains other processes that need CPU time), you might want to try setting *affinity mask* so that SQL Server uses all but one of the CPUs.

The *lightweight pooling* Option

The *lightweight pooling* option is used to configure SQL Server to use lightweight threads, or fibers. The use of fibers can reduce context switches by allowing SQL Server (rather than the Windows NT or Windows 2000 scheduler) to handle scheduling. If your application is running on a multiple-processor system and you are seeing a large number of context switches, you might want to try setting the *lightweight pooling* parameter to *1*, which enables lightweight pooling, and then monitoring the number of context switches again to verify that they have been reduced. The default value is *0*, which disables the use of fibers.

The *lightweight pooling* option is an advanced option that you can set by using *sp_configure* when *show advanced options* is set to *1*. You can also configure *lightweight pooling* by using Enterprise Manager. Click the Processor tab in the SQL Server Properties window, and, in the Processor Control area, select the Use Windows NT Fibers check box to enable the option, or clear the box to disable the option. Click Apply, click OK, and then stop and restart SQL Server to allow the option to take effect.

The *max server memory* Option

SQL Server dynamically allocates memory. To specify the maximum amount of memory, in megabytes, that SQL Server will allocate to the buffer pool, you can set the *max server memory* option. Because SQL Server will take some time to release memory, if you have other applications that periodically need memory, the *max server memory* option can be set so that SQL Server leaves some memory free for the other applications. The default value is *2147483647*, which means that SQL Server will acquire as much memory as it can from the system while dynamically deallocating and allocating memory as other applications need it and release it. This is the recommended setting for a dedicated SQL Server system. If you are going to change this setting, calculate the maximum memory you can give to SQL Server by subtracting the memory needed for Windows 2000 plus the memory needed for any non–SQL Server uses from the total physical memory.

This is an advanced option—you must set *show advanced options* to *1* to configure this option by using *sp_configure*. To set the option by using Enterprise Manager, click the Memory tab in the SQL Server Properties window, and adjust the Maximum (MB) slider. Next click Dynamically Configure SQL Server Memory. This option takes effect immediately, without requiring you to stop and restart SQL Server. (If you click Use A Fixed Memory Size, you can set a fixed amount of memory. SQL Server will allocate memory up to that amount and not release memory after the fixed amount has been allocated.)

The *min server* memory Option

The *min server memory* option is used to specify the minimum amount of memory, in megabytes, that is to be allocated to the SQL Server buffer pool. Setting this parameter is useful in systems in which SQL Server might reserve too much memory for other applications. For example, in an environment in which the server is used for print and file services as well as for database services, SQL Server might relinquish too much memory to these other applications. This slows user response times.

The default value of *min server memory* is *0*, which allows SQL Server to dynamically allocate and deallocate memory. This is the recommended setting, but you might need to change it if your server is not dedicated to SQL Server.

This option is an advanced option—you must set *show advanced options* to *1* to configure this option by using *sp_configure*. You can also configure this option by using Enterprise Manager. Click the Memory tab in the SQL Server Properties window, adjust the Minimum (MB) slider, and click Dynamically Configure SQL Server Memory. This option takes effect immediately, without requiring you to stop and restart SQL Server.

The *recovery interval* Option

You can use the *recovery interval* option to define the maximum amount of time, in minutes, it will take for the system to recover in the event of a failure. SQL Server uses this setting and a special built-in algorithm to determine how often to perform automatic checkpoints so that recovery will take only the specified number of minutes. SQL Server determines how long the interval between checkpoints should be according to how much work is happening in the system. If a lot of work is being performed, checkpoints will be issued more frequently than if the system is not doing much work. The less work being performed, the less time SQL Server needs to recover from a crash. Also, the longer the recovery interval, the longer the interval between checkpoints will be.

Increasing the recovery interval will improve performance by reducing the number of checkpoints. (Checkpoints cause a large number of writes to disk, which might slow down user transactions for a few seconds.) However, it will also increase the amount of time SQL Server requires for recovery. The default value is *0*, which specifies that SQL Server will determine the interval for you—about a 1-minute recovery time. Increase the *recovery interval* option at your own risk. A value of *5* to *15* (minutes) is not unusual, but depends entirely on whether you can risk waiting 5 to 15 minutes for your database to recover in case of a system crash. In general, you might want to increase *recovery interval* to reduce the frequency of checkpoints and their high number of writes, thereby allowing users more freedom to perform the I/O for their transactions without interruption.

This is an advanced option—you must set *show advanced options* to *1* to configure this option by using *sp_configure*. To set this option by using Enterprise Manager, click the Database Settings tab in the SQL Server Properties window, and enter a value in the Recovery Interval (Min) spin box. A change to this option takes effect immediately, without requiring you to stop and restart SQL Server.

Summary

In this chapter, you've learned about some of the performance problems you might encounter as a DBA. You've seen how System Monitor and Enterprise Manager can be used to monitor the system and help locate performance bottlenecks. You've also learned how to detect and solve common system performance problems.

This book has taken you through the hows, whats, and whys of administering SQL Server 2000. You should now be able to effectively manage and configure your SQL Server system and perform day-to-day administrative tasks easily and efficiently. The authors hope that you have enjoyed reading this book as much as they enjoyed writing it.

Part VI
Appendixes

Appendix A
Microsoft SQL Server Configuration Parameters

This appendix provides descriptions of the Microsoft SQL Server configuration parameters. It also explains how you set these parameters.

Parameters

You set SQL Server configuration parameters in one of two ways: by selecting database properties in SQL Server Enterprise Manager or by using the system stored procedure *sp_configure*. The Enterprise Manager method of setting parameters is described later in this appendix. To use the *sp_configure* stored procedure, you run the following command:

```
sp_configure 'parameter_name', value
```

For example, you can set the *max worker threads* configuration parameter to *200* by using the following command:

```
sp_configure 'max worker threads', 200
Go
```

The SQL Server configuration parameters are briefly described in the following sections. Complete descriptions of these parameters can be found in SQL Server Books Online

affinity mask

The *affinity mask* parameter is a bitmap variable that specifies the CPUs that SQL Server is allowed to run on. The default value of *0* lets the Microsoft Windows NT/2000 scheduler determine which CPUs SQL Server will run on. Because the variable is a bitmap, the binary representation of the value determines which CPUs will be used. The first few binary values are shown on the next page.

```
0=0000
1=0001
2=0010
3=0011
4=0100
```

For example, if you use a four-processor system, you can set *affinity mask* to *15 (1111)* to allow SQL Server to run on all CPUs.

allow updates

The *allow updates* parameter allows users with the appropriate privileges to update system tables directly. When *allow updates* is set to *0* (the default), the system tables can be updated only by using the system stored procedures.

awe enabled

The *awe enabled* parameter allows the use of the Address Windowing Extensions (AWE) option in Microsoft Windows 2000. When *awe enabled* is set to *1*, the use of memory above 4 gigabytes (GB) is allowed.

C2 audit mode

The *C2 audit mode* parameter enables C2 security mode auditing. This security auditing logs specific events in SQL Server in order to achieve the C2 security level.

cost threshold for parallelism

The *cost threshold for parallelism* parameter specifies a cost to be used in determining whether parallelism is used for queries. If the cost of the query in serial mode exceeds the value of *cost threshold for parallelism*, the query will be parallelized. The default value is *5*.

cursor threshold

The *cursor threshold* parameter specifies the number of rows in the cursor set that must be exceeded before the cursor keysets are created asynchronously. If the number of rows is less than the value of *cursor threshold*, the keysets will be created synchronously. The default value of *–1* specifies that all cursor keysets will be created synchronously.

default full-text language

The *default full-text language* parameter specifies the ID of the default language used by SQL Server full-text indexing. The default of *1033* is the ID of U.S. English.

default language

The *default language* parameter specifies the ID of the default language used by SQL Server. The default of *0* is the ID of U.S. English.

fill factor

The *fill factor* parameter specifies how densely SQL Server will pack index pages when they are created. A value of *1* specifies that pages be mostly empty; a value of *100* causes index pages to be completely packed. The default value of *0* specifies that leaf pages be fully packed but that nonleaf pages should have some space left available.

index create memory

The *index create memory* parameter specifies the amount of memory used for index creation sorts. The default value of *0* specifies that SQL Server will determine this value.

lightweight pooling

The *lightweight pooling* parameter, which is set to *TRUE (1)* or *FALSE (0)*, specifies whether SQL Server will use Windows NT/2000 fiber mode scheduling to reduce context switching. Context switches incur a lot of system overhead and will be reduced if SQL Server is allowed to do its own scheduling. The default value is *0*, which specifies that fiber mode scheduling not be used.

locks

The *locks* parameter specifies the maximum number of locks that can be allocated. The default value of *0* allows SQL Server to dynamically allocate and deallocate locks. You can monitor the number of locks in your system by using Windows NT or Windows 2000 Performance Monitor; if you see a lot of allocation and deallocation, you might want to statically allocate locks. In most cases, however, the default value of *0* should be used.

max degree of parallelism

The *max degree of parallelism* parameter specifies the maximum number of threads that can be allocated for use in a parallel execution. The default value of *0* specifies that all CPUs in the system can be used, making the number of threads equal to the number of CPUs in the system. A value of *1* disables parallel execution. Because parallelism can help improve performance of I/O-bound queries, you might find that better performance can be achieved if you set a higher value for *max degree of parallelism*. The maximum value is *32*.

max server memory

The *max server memory* parameter is used to specify the maximum amount of memory that can be dynamically allocated by SQL Server. You use this parameter in conjunction with *min server memory*. The amount of memory allocated by SQL Server will be between the value set for *min server memory* and *max server memory*. If you want to reserve additional space for processes other than SQL Server, you can use this parameter. The default value of *0* specifies that SQL Server automatically allocate memory.

max text repl size

The *max text repl size* parameter specifies the maximum number of bytes of text and image data that can be added to a replicated column in a single SQL statement.

max worker threads

You use the *max worker threads* parameter to specify the maximum number of Windows threads that SQL Server can use. This parameter can be adjusted in order to allow more threads for processing within SQL Server. If SQL Server uses too many threads, however, the operating system will become overloaded.

media retention

The *media retention* parameter specifies the number of days that a backup medium is retained. SQL Server will not overwrite a backup medium until this time has passed.

min memory per query

The *min memory per query* parameter specifies the minimum amount of memory that will be allocated for a query. The default value is *1024*, but you can choose a value from a large range of values between 512 bytes and 2 GB. Setting this parameter such that memory is allocated when the query begins can help the performance of large sorts and hashing operations.

min server memory

The *min server memory* parameter is used in conjunction with *max server memory* to manually set the minimum amount and maximum amount of memory that SQL Server will use. The default value of *0* specifies that SQL Server automatically allocate memory.

nested triggers

The *nested triggers* parameter specifies whether a trigger can initiate another trigger. The default value of *1* specifies that this be allowed.

network packet size

With the *network packet size* parameter, you can specify the size of incoming and outgoing SQL Server data packets. The default value of *4096* specifies a packet size of 4 KB. If many of your result sets are large, you might want to increase this value.

open objects

The *open objects* parameter specifies the maximum number of objects that can be opened at one time in the SQL Server database. The default number of open objects is *500* with a maximum of 2 billion.

priority boost

A value of *1* for the *priority boost* parameter specifies that SQL Server run at a higher Windows NT/2000 scheduling priority than it normally would. The default value of *0* disables *priority boost*. Setting this parameter to *1* can improve SQL Server performance but can keep other processes from getting sufficient CPU time. Only if SQL Server is the only program running on the Windows NT system should you set this value. Changing this value can cause problems if you are not careful. Change this parameter at your own risk.

query governor cost limit

The *query governor cost limit* parameter specifies the maximum amount of time, in seconds, that a query can run. Before a query is executed, the query optimizer estimates how long the query will run. When set, this option prevents large queries from running.

query wait

When sufficient memory for a query to run is not available, SQL Server will queue the query until the resources are available. By default, the wait time is 25 times the estimated cost of the query. By setting the *query wait* parameter, you can set the time-out value.

recovery interval

The *recovery interval* parameter is quite important. The setting of the *recovery interval* parameter determines how often checkpoints occur by specifying the maximum amount of time that SQL Server can take to recover the database in the event of a system failure. The default value of 0 lets SQL Server determine this value automatically.

remote access

The *remote access* parameter is a Yes/No parameter that specifies whether logins from remote SQL Server systems are allowed. The default value of 1 allows remote logins.

remote login timeout

The *remote login timeout* parameter specifies how long, in seconds, a remote login waits before timing out. The default value is 5.

remote proc trans

When you set the *remote proc trans* parameter to 1, remote transactions running under Microsoft Distributed Transaction Coordinator (MS DTC) support ACID properties of the transactions.

remote query timeout

The *remote query timeout* parameter specifies how many seconds must elapse before a remote query times out. The default value of 0 specifies that queries do not time out.

scan for startup procs

The *scan for startup procs* parameter is a Yes/No parameter that specifies whether SQL Server will automatically scan for automatic execution of stored procedures. The default value of 0 specifies that SQL Server will not scan for these stored procedures, and thus they will never be executed.

set working set size

The *set working set size* parameter works in conjunction with *min server memory* and *max server memory*. When set, the *set working set size* parameter specifies that SQL Server memory not be paged out, even when SQL Server is idle. If you are allowing SQL Server to allocate memory dynamically, do not set this parameter to *1*. The default value of *0* disables *set working set size*.

show advanced options

When *show advanced options* is set to *1*, you can use the *sp_configure* stored procedure to display the advanced parameters.

two digit year cutoff

The *two digit year cutoff* parameter specifies how Y2K behavior works in SQL Server. For dates that are two digits in length, a value less than this number indicates a 20xx date, and a value greater than this setting specifies a 19xx date. For example, if *two digit year cutoff* were set to *2049* (the default), a date of *51* would be interpreted as 1951 and a date of 48 would be interpreted as 2048.

user connections

Use the *user connections* parameter to specify the maximum number of users that can be connected into SQL Server. By default, SQL Server will dynamically adjust the number of allowed user connections, but this dynamic operation causes additional overhead. This parameter allows you to statically set the number of allowed user connections.

user options

The *user options* parameter is used to specify global defaults for all users.

Parameter Specifications

Some of the parameters just described are advanced parameters, and others are standard parameters. Some parameters take effect immediately, and others require you to restart SQL Server before they take effect. The following table lists the SQL Server parameters and specifies each parameter's classification and requirements for taking effect.

Table A-1. SQL Server parameters

Parameter	Advanced Option	Restart Required
affinity mask	Yes	Yes
allow updates	No	No
awe enabled	Yes	Yes
C2 audit mode	Yes	Yes
cost threshold for parallelism	Yes	No
cursor threshold	Yes	No
default full-text language	Yes	No
default language	No	No
fill factor	Yes	Yes
index create memory	Yes	No
lightweight pooling	Yes	Yes
locks	Yes	Yes
max degree of parallelism	Yes	No
max server memory	Yes	No
max text repl size	No	No
max worker threads	Yes	Yes
media retention	Yes	Yes
min memory per query	Yes	No
min server memory	Yes	No
nested triggers	No	No
network packet size	Yes	No
open objects	Yes	Yes
priority boost	Yes	Yes
query governor cost limit	Yes	No
query wait	Yes	No
recovery interval	Yes	No
remote access	No	Yes
remote login timeout	No	No
remote proc trans	No	No
remote query timeout	No	No
scan for startup procs	Yes	Yes
set working set size	Yes	Yes
show advanced options	No	No
two digit year cutoff	No	No
user connections	Yes	Yes
user options	No	No

Changing Parameters by Using Enterprise Manager

You can modify the settings of many of the SQL Server parameters by using Enterprise Manager. To use Enterprise Manager to modify parameter settings, you first need to open the SQL Server Properties window. To do so, you right-click a server name in the Enterprise Manager window and choose Properties from the shortcut menu. Each of the following sections describes the options available on one of the tabs in the SQL Server Properties window.

General

The initial tab that you will see is the General tab, as shown in Figure A-1. The General tab does not change any underlying configuration parameters as the other tabs do. However, you can set several autostart parameters and startup parameters on this tab. (Click Startup Parameters to change the settings for the startup parameters.)

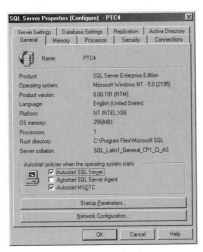

Figure A-1. *The General tab of the SQL Server Properties window.*

Memory

The Memory tab is shown in Figure A-2. On this tab, you can choose whether SQL Server should allocate memory dynamically or should use a fixed amount of memory. To make a setting, click the appropriate option button and move the appropriate sliders. On the Memory tab, you can also set the minimum amount of memory SQL Server will use to execute a query.

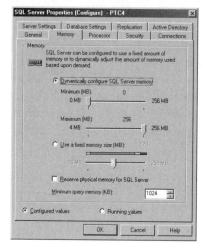

Figure A-2. *The Memory tab of the SQL Server Properties window.*

The configuration parameters that are set on the Memory tab are:

- *min server memory*
- *max server memory*
- *min memory per query*

Processor

The Processor tab is shown in Figure A-3. On this tab, you can select the CPUs that are available for SQL Server to use. You can set the number of worker threads, and you can boost SQL Server's priority and specify that Windows fibers should be used by selecting the appropriate check boxes. Finally you can specify how SQL Server parallelizes queries.

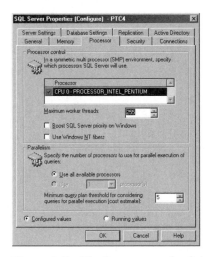

Figure A-3. *The Processor tab of the SQL Server Properties window.*

The parameters that are set on the Processor tab are:

- *affinity mask*
- *max worker threads*
- *priority boost*
- *lightweight pooling*
- *max degree of parallelism*
- *cost threshold for parallelism*

Security

The Security tab is shown in Figure A-4. You cannot set any tuning parameters on this tab. Instead, you can set the authentication method, the audit level, and the startup and run Windows accounts.

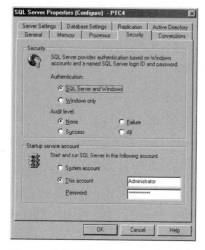

Figure A-4. *The Security tab of the SQL Server Properties window.*

Connections

The Connections tab is shown in Figure A-5. This tab provides a number of options related to user connections. Here you can set the maximum number of user connections allowed and the level of constraints checking. In the Remote Server Connections area, you can choose whether RPC connections should be allowed and whether distributed transactions should be enforced, and you can set the query time-out.

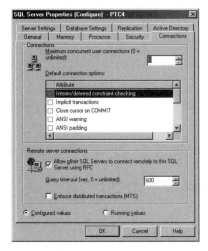

Figure A-5. *The Connections tab of the SQL Server Properties window.*

The parameters that are set on the Connections tab are:

- *user connections*
- *user options*
- *remote access*
- *remote query timeout*
- *remote proc trans*

Server Settings

The Server Settings tab is shown in Figure A-6. This tab gives you the option of setting general server parameters. Here the default language for the user can be set. You can also set options to allow catalog modification, to allow triggers to fire triggers, and to enable the use of the query governor. You can also set the SQL mail profile and year 2000 support.

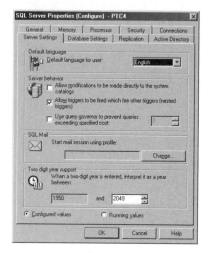

Figure A-6. *The Server Settings tab of the SQL Server Properties window.*

The parameters that are set on the Server Settings tab are used to set the following parameters:

- *default language*
- *allow updates*
- *nested triggers*
- *query governor cost limit*
- *two digit year cutoff*

Database Settings

The Database Settings tab is shown in Figure A-7. This tab gives you the option of setting the database fill factor as well as backup parameters and the recovery interval. In addition the default file location can be specified here. This location will be used for creation of new databases, when not specified in the create database command.

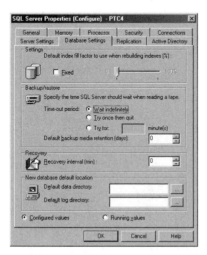

Figure A-7. *The Database Settings tab of the SQL Server Properties window.*

The parameters that are set on the Database Settings tab are:

- *fill factor*
- *media retention*
- *recovery interval*

Replication

The Replication tab is shown in Figure A-8. The Replication tab is used to view and set replication publishing and distribution options. Here you can also add the current system to the replication monitoring group. This allows your system to be grouped with other systems when replication is monitored.

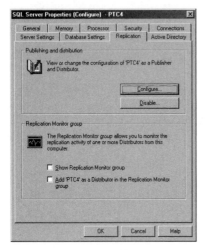

Figure A-8. *The Replication tab of the SQL Server Properties window.*

Active Directory

The Active Directory tab—shown in Figure A-9—is used to modify Active Directory entries. You can add the current system to Active Directory, refresh its status in Active Directory, or delete this system from Active Directory.

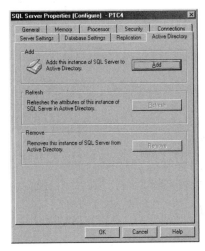

Figure A-9. *The Active Directory tab of the SQL Server Properties window.*

Appendix B
Microsoft SQL Server Monitoring

Microsoft SQL Server provides objects and counters that a performance monitor uses to monitor processes in SQL Server systems. Objects represent Microsoft Windows and SQL Server resources, and each object contains one or more counters, which monitor various aspects of the object. This appendix lists each object and its counters. The entry for each counter includes a brief description of the data returned by the counter, and some counter entries contain additional information.

SQL Server: Access Methods

This object provides counters that monitor various object access methods and properties. These counters are as follows:

- *Extent Deallocations/sec*   Number of extents released per second by SQL Server.
- *Extents Allocated/sec*   Number of extents allocated per second by SQL Server.
- *Forwarded Records/sec*   Number of records retrieved per second through forward record pointers.
- *FreeSpace Page Fetches/sec*   Number of pages returned per second by free space scans.
- *FreeSpace Scans/sec*   Number of scans performed per second to find free space for record insertion.
- *Full Scans/sec*   Number of full table or index scans per second. If this counter shows a value greater than *1* or *2*, you should analyze your queries and see if table scans are really necessary or if the queries can be optimized.

- *Index Searches/sec*   Number of times an index lookup is done per second. This could be a single record lookup or the start of an index range scan.

- *Mixed Page Allocations/sec*   Number of pages allocated per second that are used to store the first eight pages allocated to an extent or index.

- *Page Deallocations/sec*   Number of pages deallocated per second.

- *Page Splits/sec*   Number of page splits per second that happen as the result of an index page's overflowing.

- *Pages Allocated/sec*   Number of pages allocated per second for index or data storage.

- *Probe Scans/sec*   Number of scans performed per second to directly look up rows in base tables or indexes.

- *Range Scans/sec*   Number of range scans through indexes per second.

- *Scan Point Revalidations/sec*   Number of times per second that the scan point had to be revalidated before the scan could be continued.

- *Skipped Ghosted Records/sec*   Number of ghosted records that were skipped per second during a scan.

- *Table Lock Escalations/sec*   Number of times per second that a table lock was escalated.

- *Workfiles Created/sec*   Number of workfiles (used in query execution) that were created per second.

- *Worktables Created/sec*   Number of worktables (used in GROUP BY, ORDER BY, and UNION operators) that were created per second.

- *Worktables From Cache Ratio*   Percent of worktables that were created when the initial pages were available in the worktable cache.

SQL Server: Backup Device

This object defines a single counter, which reports the performance of backup devices. Each instance of the object has its own counter.

- *Device Throughput Bytes/sec*   Number of bytes per second being transferred to a backup device during a backup operation. This is useful for monitoring both the throughput and distribution of I/O operations involving the backup device.

SQL Server: Buffer Manager

This object contains a number of counters related to the SQL Server buffer cache. These counters include the following:

Note   In the following list, "AWE" refers to the Address Windowing Extensions. AWE is used to support SQL Server's use of physical memory above 4 gigabytes (GB). SQL Server makes special system calls in order to use this much memory.

- *AWE Lookup Maps/sec*   Number of AWE map calls made per second for pages in the buffer pool. Because AWE uses a window of memory where the actual pages are held, mappings of that window must be done. This counter represents the number of times per second those maps are called.

- *AWE Stolen Maps/sec*   Number of AWE map calls made per second for pages stolen from the buffer pool.

- *AWE Unmap Calls/sec*   Number of AWE unmap calls made per second. At each call, one or more buffers can be unmapped.

- *AWE Unmap Pages/sec*   Number of AWE pages unmapped per second.

- *AWE Write Maps/sec*   Number of AWE map calls per second that map to a dirty buffer and that cause writing data to disk.

- *Buffer Cache Hit Ratio*   Percentage of pages that were found in memory, thus not requiring a physical I/O operation. This is your indicator of how well the SQL Server buffer cache is performing.

- *Checkpoint Pages/sec*   Number of pages written to disk by the checkpoint process. The checkpoint process causes all dirty pages to be flushed to disk. This process will reduce the recovery time and is controlled by the *recovery interval* configuration parameter. If this counter consistently shows a high value, your system might be experiencing checkpoints too frequently. You should configure the frequency of checkpoints based on your needs. Frequent checkpoints guarantee faster recovery time; less frequent checkpoints offer better performance. In addition, this counter monitors the number of pages written to disk on behalf of other operations that require all dirty pages to be flushed.

- *Database Pages*   Number of pages that currently make up the SQL Server cache. Because the SQL Server buffer cache is dynamic, this counter is one way to determine how big the cache is. You can monitor this counter to see how the size of the cache constantly changes. If the cache size changes significantly a number of times during the day, you might want to fix the cache size by using the *min server memory* and *max server memory* parameters. This is due to the fact that dynamic memory allocation and deallocation uses significant system resources such as CPU and I/O.

- *Free List Stalls/sec*   Number of requests per second that had to wait for a page to be freed before they could continue.

- *Free Pages*   Number of pages on all of the free lists. A *free list* is a linked list of available pages. This is the number of free (unused, but allocated) buffers available in the buffer cache. Don't worry if the number reported by this counter seems low. Remember that SQL Server dynamically creates buffers when they are needed.

- *Lazy Writes/sec*   Number of buffers per second written by the lazy writer. The lazy writer frees up dirty buffers by using the LRU (least recently used) algorithm.

- *Page Life Expectancy*   Estimated number of seconds a page will stay in the buffer pool before it is written out (if not referenced).

- *Page Lookups/sec*   Number of requests to find a page in the buffer pool made per second.

- *Page Reads/sec*   Number of physical database page reads issued per second.

- *Page Writes/sec*   Number of physical database page writes issued per second.

- *Procedure Cache Pages*   Number of pages used for the procedure cache. The procedure cache stores compiled queries.

- *Readahead Pages/sec*   Number of pages per second that SQL Server reads in anticipation of a user request. SQL Server anticipates requests based on previous requests.

- *Reserved Pages*   Number of reserved pages in the buffer cache.

- *Stolen Pages*   Number of pages that have been stolen from the buffer cache to satisfy a memory request.

- *Target Pages*   Optimal number of pages (according to SQL Server) in the buffer pool.

- *Total Pages*   Total number of pages in the buffer pool.

SQL Server: Cache Manager

This object is used to view Cache Manager statistics. Each of the counters can monitor the following instances of the object: *Adhoc SQL Plans, Misc. Normalized Trees, Prepared SQL Plans, Procedure Plans, Replication Procedure Plans,* and *Trigger Plans.* The counters are as follows:

- *Cache Hit Ratio*   Ratio between cache hits and misses. This counter is quite useful if you want to determine how effective the SQL Server cache is for your system. If the number that the counter returns is low, you might want to add more memory.

- *Cache Object Counts*   Number of cache objects in the cache.

- *Cache Pages*   Number of 8-kilobyte (KB) pages used by cache objects.

- *Cache Use Counts/sec*   Number of times per second each type of cache object has been used.

SQL Server: Databases

This object contains a set of counters that monitor each database in the system. The object instance chosen represents the database that you can monitor. Databases that can be monitored include the master, model, msdb, and tempdb databases, as well as the Northwind database, the pubs database, and all of your user-created databases. The counters are as follows:

- *Active Transactions*   Number of active transactions in the database.

- *Backup/Restore Throughput/sec*   Throughput of active backup and restore operations per second.

- *Bulk Copy Rows/sec*   Number of rows per second currently being copied via a bulk copy operation.

- *Bulk Copy Throughput/sec*   Number of kilobytes per second currently being copied via a bulk copy operation.

- *Data File(s) Size (KB)*   Total size, in kilobytes, of all of the data files in the database.

- *DBCC Logical Scan Bytes/sec*   Logical read scan rate for DBCC commands.

- *Log Bytes Flushed/sec*   Number of log bytes that are flushed per second.

- *Log Cache Hit Ratio*   Percentage of log reads that were satisfied from the log cache.
- *Log Cache Reads/sec*   Number of log cache reads per second.
- *Log File(s) Size (KB)*   Total size of the log file or files, in kilobytes.
- *Log File(s) Used Size (KB)*   Total amount of space currently used in the log file or files.
- *Log Flush Wait Time*   Total wait time for log flushes, in milliseconds.
- *Log Flush Waits/sec*   Number of log flush waits per second.
- *Log Flushes/sec*   Number of log flushes per second.
- *Log Growths*   Number of log growths, or the number of times the log has extended itself.
- *Log Shrinks*   Number of log shrinks, or the number of times the log has shrunk itself.
- *Log Truncations*   Number of times the log for this database has been truncated.
- *Percent Log Used*   Percentage of the log that is being used.
- *Repl. Pending Xacts*   Number of pending replication transactions in this database.
- *Repl. Trans. Rate*   Number of replication transactions per second.
- *Shrink Data Movement Bytes/sec*   Rate that data is being moved by an *autoshrink* operation or by a DBCC command.
- *Transactions/sec*   Number of transactions per second for this database. This counter shows you how much activity is occurring in your system. The higher the value, the more activity that is occurring.

SQL Server: General Statistics

This object's counters provide you with some general information about SQL Server user connections. These counters are as follows:

- *Logins/sec*   Number of logins per second.
- *Logouts/sec*   Number of logouts per second.
- *User Connections*   Number of users currently connected. This counter is useful because it lets you see exactly how many users are connected.

SQL Server: Latches

This object is used to show SQL Server latch statistics. Latches are internal locking mechanisms used by SQL Server. This object provides information on these internal latches and includes these counters:

- *Average Latch Wait Time (ms)*   Average amount of time, in milliseconds, that a SQL Server thread has to wait for a latch. If this number is high, your system could be experiencing severe contention problems.

- *Latch Waits/sec*   Number of waits for latches per second. If this number is high, your system is experiencing a high amount of contention for resources.

- *Total Latch Wait Time (ms)*   Total amount of time, in milliseconds, that latch requests had to wait in the last second.

SQL Server: Locks

This object contains a number of counters that keep track of lock activity. Each counter monitors activities related to the following SQL Server lock types: database locks, extent locks, key locks, page locks, RID locks (row locks), and table locks. These counters show you the types of locks that are being used in your system and how often these locks are used. The counters are as follows:

- *Average Wait Time (ms)*   Average time, in milliseconds, that a thread is waiting for the specified type of lock.

- *Lock Requests/sec*   Number of requests per second for the specified type of lock.

- *Lock Timeouts/sec*   Number of times per second that a lock could not be obtained by spinning. The setting of the SQL Server configuration parameter *spin counter* governs the number of times that a thread spins before timing out and sleeping.

- *Lock Wait Time (ms)*   Total wait time for locks, in milliseconds, for the last second.

- *Lock Waits/sec*   Number of times a lock request caused a thread to wait in the last second.

- *Number of Deadlocks/sec*   Number of lock requests per second that resulted in a deadlock.

SQL Server: Memory Manager

This object provides information about SQL Server memory other than the buffer cache. This object's counters are as follows:

- *Connection Memory (KB)* Amount of memory, in kilobytes, that is used for maintaining connections.

- *Granted Workspace Memory (KB)* Total amount of memory, in kilobytes, that has been granted to processes for sort and index creation operations.

- *Lock Blocks* Number of lock blocks in use on the server.

- *Lock Blocks Allocated* Total number of allocated lock blocks.

- *Lock Memory (KB)* Total amount of memory, in kilobytes, that is allocated to locks.

- *Lock Owner Blocks* Number of lock owner blocks that are currently in use on the server.

- *Lock Owner Blocks Allocated* Number of lock owner blocks that have been allocated on the server.

- *Maximum Workspace Memory (KB)* Total amount of memory that has been allocated to executing processes. This memory can be used for hash, sort, and index creation operations.

- *Memory Grants Outstanding* Number of current processes that have acquired a workspace memory grant.

- *Memory Grants Pending* Number of processes waiting for a workspace memory grant.

- *Optimizer Memory (KB)* Amount of memory, in kilobytes, that the server is using for query optimization.

- *SQL Cache Memory (KB)* Total amount of memory, in kilobytes, that the server is using for the dynamic SQL cache.

- *Target Server Memory (KB)* Total amount of dynamic memory, in kilobytes, that the server can consume.

- *Total Server Memory (KB)* Total amount of dynamic memory, in kilobytes, that the server is currently consuming. SQL Server dynamically allocates and deallocates memory based on how much memory is available in the system. This counter offers you a view of the memory that is currently being used. If large swings in memory usage occur over the course of a day, or when special events occur, you might want to fix the amount of memory that SQL Server is using by setting the *min server memory* and *max server memory* parameters. For example, if every day another application runs that consumes large amounts of memory, such as OLAP services, you may want to reserve memory, rather than making SQL Server go through the resource-intensive task of releasing memory.

SQL Server: Replication Agents

This object provides one counter:

- *Running*   Number of replication agents that are running

SQL Server: Replication Dist.

This object is used to view information about distributors and subscribers. The following counters are available:

- *Dist: Delivered Cmds/sec*   Number of commands per second delivered to the subscriber
- *Dist: Delivered Trans/sec*   Number of transactions per second delivered to the subscriber
- *Dist: Delivery Latency*   Amount of time from when transactions are delivered to the distributor to when they are applied to the subscriber

SQL Server: Replication Logreader

This object is used to view information about distributors and publishers. The following counters are available:

- *Logreader: Delivered Cmds/sec*   Number of Log Reader Agent commands per second delivered to the distributor
- *Logreader: Delivered Trans/sec*   Number of Log Reader Agent transactions per second delivered to the distributor
- *Logreader: Delivery Latency*   Amount of time from when transactions are applied to the publisher to when they are delivered to the distributor

SQL Server: Replication Merge

This object pertains to the merge replication process. It provides the following counters:

- *Conflicts/sec*   Number of conflicts per second occurring during the merge process. Normally, this value should be *0*.
- *Downloaded Changes/sec*   Number of rows per second merged from the publisher to the subscriber.
- *Uploaded Changes/sec*   Number of rows per second merged from the subscriber to the publisher.

SQL Server: Replication Snapshot

This object pertains to the snapshot replication process. It provides the following counters:

- *Snapshot: Delivered Cmds/sec*   Number of commands per second delivered to the Distributor
- *Snapshot: Delivered Trans/sec*   Number of transactions per second delivered to the distributor

SQL Server: SQL Statistics

This object offers useful statistics about SQL statements that have been run. Its counters are as follows:

- *Auto-Param Attempts/sec*   Number of auto-parameterization attempts per second. Auto-parameterization occurs when the optimizer has a cached execution plan of a SQL statement that is similar, but not the same as the one being optimized. The optimizer will attempt to reuse the already optimized plan.
- *Batch Requests/sec*   Number of T-SQL batch requests per second that have been received by the server.
- *Failed Auto-Params/sec*   Number of auto-parameterization attempts that have failed per second.
- *Safe Auto-Params/sec*   Number of safe auto-parameterizations per second.

- *SQL Compilations/sec*   Number of times per second that SQL compilations have occurred. This counter includes recompiles.

- *SQL Re-Compilations/sec*   Number of times per second that SQL recompilations have occurred.

- *Unsafe Auto-Params/sec*   Number of unsafe auto-parameterizations per second.

SQL Server: User Settable

The *SQL Server: User Settable* object contains a set of counters that you can define. You can set these counters from within any SQL statement by calling the system stored procedures *sp_user_counter1* through *sp_user_counter10* followed by an integer value to set the counter with. You can read these counters through Performance Monitor by viewing the following counter:

- *Query*   Represents the user-settable value. This counter has 10 instances associated with it: *User counter 1* through *User counter 10*. The value displayed is the value that your program or SQL statement has set.

Appendix C
DBCC Commands

Within Microsoft SQL Server is a set of commands designed to assess and correct consistency problems in the SQL Server database. When you run one of these commands, you use the string DBCC as a prefix. In fact, "DBCC" stands for "database consistency checker." Although DBCC commands were originally designed to be used as consistency-checking tools, the scope of the DBCC commands has expanded over the years.

This appendix lists the DBCC commands and provides a brief description for each one, allowing you to quickly find the command that you need. This appendix does not show all of the options for each DBCC command. You'll find complete instructions for running these commands in SQL Server Books Online.

- **CHECKALLOC**   Checks the allocation and use of all of the pages in the specified database. CHECKALLOC is a subset of CHECKDB.
- **CHECKCATALOG**   Checks for consistency within the system tables for the specified database.
- **CHECKCONSTRAINTS**   Checks the integrity of a single constraint or of all constraints on a table.
- **CHECKDB**   Checks the allocation (of rows, pages, and extents) and structural integrity of all the objects in the specified database. This command catches and repairs problems with the database allocation and tables. In fact, DBCC CHECKDB validates the integrity of everything within the database. Expect it to take some time to run.
- **CHECKFILEGROUP**   Checks the allocation and structural integrity of objects in a specific filegroup in the database. You can use this command rather than DBCC CHECKDB if you suspect that only a filegroup has been corrupted, which can occur because of a hardware failure.
- **CHECKIDENT**   Checks and, if necessary, corrects the current identity value for the specified table.

- **CHECKTABLE** Checks the integrity of the *data*, *index*, *text*, *ntext*, and *image* pages for the specified table. This command is useful for checking a table you suspect might be corrupted.

- **CLEANTABLE** Reclaims space that was formerly used for variable-length *varchar* data as well as *text* data.

- **CONCURRENCYVIOLATION** For SQL Server Standard Edition and Personal Edition, reports when more than five concurrent SQL batches are being executed on the server.

- **DBREINDEX** Was used to reindex a table's indexes. This command is no longer supported in SQL Server 2000. With Microsoft SQL Server 2000, use the DROP EXISTING clause with the CREATE INDEX command to accomplish this task.

- **DBREPAIR** Was used to drop a damaged database. This command is not supported in SQL Server 2000. You should use the DROP DATA-BASE command instead.

- *dllname* **(FREE)** Unloads the specified extended stored procedure DLL from memory.

- **DROPCLEANBUFFERS** Removes all clean buffers from the buffer pool.

- **FREEPROCCACHE** Removes all elements from the procedure cache.

- **HELP** Returns the syntax of a specific DBCC statement, thus allowing you to quickly use that command without having to refer to SQL Server Books Online. Do not include the DBCC keyword when you specify the statement name.

- **INDEXDEFRAG** Defragments clustered and secondary indexes for the specified table.

- **INPUTBUFFER** Displays the last statement sent by the user associated with the specified system process ID (SPID) to SQL Server.

- **MEMUSAGE** Provided a detailed report about memory usage. This command is no longer supported.

- **NEWALLOC** Provided the same functionality as DBCC CHECKALLOC does. This command is no longer supported.

- **OPENTRAN** Displays information about the oldest active transaction in the database. This is useful for finding stalled or long-running transactions.

- **OUTPUTBUFFER** Displays the output data sent by SQL Server to the user associated with the specified SPID.

- **PINTABLE**   Marks the table to be pinned. A pinned table does not re-linquish itself from the cache. In other words, it is permanently placed in the cache and does not get ejected. This is useful for small tables that are infrequently used but that require immediate access. You should ensure the pinned table does not use enough memory to adversely affect other SQL Server processing.

- **PROCCACHE**   Displays information about the SQL Server procedure cache. This information can be valuable in assessing the effectiveness of the procedure cache and SQL statements.

- **ROWLOCK**   Was used in Microsoft SQL Server 6.5 in order to enable row locking. This is automatic in SQL Server 2000.

- **SHOWCONTIG**   Displays information about the fragmentation of the data and indexes of the specified table. A heavily fragmented index should be rebuilt. A heavily fragmented table should be exported and imported back into the database.

- **SHOW_STATISTICS**   Displays statistics for the specified target on the specified table. These are the statistics that are used by the query optimizer.

- **SHRINKDATABASE**   Shrinks the size of the files associated with the specified database. The recommended method of performing this task is using the *autoshrink* feature of *sp_dboption*.

- **SHRINKFILE**   Shrinks the size of the specified file. This file can be a data file or a log file.

- **SQLPERF**   Provides information about the transaction log space usage in all databases. Using this command to track log space usage is helpful for capacity planning and sizing.

- **TEXTALL**   Was used to check the consistency of tables that contain *text*, *ntext*, and *image* columns. In SQL Server 2000, DBCC CHECKDB and CKECKTABLE perform this task. However, DBCC CHECKDB is the recommended replacement for DBCC TEXTALL.

- **TEXTALLOC**   Was used to check the consistency of tables that contain *text*, *ntext*, and *image* columns. In SQL Server 2000, DBCC CHECKDB and CHECKTABLE perform this task. However, DBCC CHECKTABLE is the recommended replacement for DBCC TEXTALLOC. DBCC TEXTALL previously ran DBCC TEXTALLOC.

- **TRACEOFF**   Disables the specified SQL Server trace flag or flags.

- **TRACEON**   Enables the specified SQL Server trace flag or flags.

- **TRACESTATUS** Displays the status of the specified trace flag or flags.
- **UNPINTABLE** Marks a previously pinned table to be unpinned. The table is subsequently treated in the cache as any other object.
- **UPDATEUSAGE** Reports and corrects inaccuracies in the *sysindexes* table. These inaccuracies might cause *sp_spaceused* to return incorrect data.
- **USEROPTIONS** Returns the status of the SET statement operations that are currently set for the current connection. This works for only the current connection.

Glossary

A

Active Server Pages (ASP) page A Web page that creates HTML pages dynamically on the server. ASP pages are commonly used to access Microsoft SQL Server from the World Wide Web.

ad hoc A term used to describe a spontaneous query. Typically, an ad hoc query is not optimized and is typed into Query Analyzer, ISQL, or OSQL, not used through an application.

agent A program that runs independently within Microsoft Windows NT or Windows 2000 to perform a service. An agent usually has a particular task, such as scheduling operations or performing replication tasks. The equivalent in the UNIX world is a daemon.

aggregate function A function that performs an operation on a set of values and returns a single value. The SQL Server aggregate functions are AVG, COUNT, DISTINCT, GROUP BY, HAVING, MAX, MIN, STDEV, STDEVP, SUM, VAR, and VARP.

API *See* application programming interface (API).

AppleTalk The Apple networking protocol.

application The code that communicates with the user. A database application typically also communicates with the RDBMS.

application programming interface (API) The standard and documented interface that programs are coded to. By coding to an API, developers can create programs that use external functions, such as SQL Server access functions.

article A table or subset of data that is selected to be replicated.

ASP *See* Active Server Pages (ASP) page.

Asynchronous Transfer Mode (ATM) A network hardware protocol.

B

backup A copy of the contents of a SQL Server database to be used in the event of a system failure. The backup can be copied back into the database in order to return the database to the state it was in when the backup was performed.

bandwidth The throughput capacity of a device or system. This term is typically associated with a network device or computer bus.

batch processing system A system distinguished by scheduled loading and processing of data in groups. These long-running jobs are done off line, with little or no user intervention.

BCP *See* Bulk Copy Program.

bit The smallest unit of data. A bit is either on (1) or off (0).

block *See* page.

bottleneck A performance-limiting component. The term comes from an analogy to a bottle containing liquid: the narrowing of the neck slows the flow of liquid.

branch node An intermediate node in an index. Branch nodes are between the root node and the leaf nodes.

buffer cache *See* cache.

bulk copy A generic term relating to the act of copying large amounts of data to or from a SQL Server database. Typically, the BULK INSERT T-SQL statement is used to perform a bulk copy.

Bulk Copy Program (BCP) A program provided with SQL Server that is used for loading data from text files into the database.

BULK INSERT A T-SQL command used to copy large amounts of data from a data file into a SQL Server table from within SQL Server.

bulk load The act of loading the database by using bulk insert operations. This can be accomplished by using either the BULK INSERT T-SQL statement or the BCP utility.

byte A sequence of 8 binary bits. A byte is the basic unit of data used in computers. It is made up of bits (ones and zeros) that represent numbers, characters, and so forth.

C

cache The RAM used to hold frequently accessed data in order to improve performance. SQL Server contains its own cache made up of Windows memory used to hold commonly accessed pages. This is referred to as the SQL Server buffer cache or page cache. CPU chips contain their own on-board caches, and some I/O controllers also contain caches.

capacity planning The activity of planning for the increased utilization of the system and, by doing so, anticipating capacity that must be added. This task is performed in order to maintain the level of service expected by the user community while the load on the system is increasing.

capacity-planning measurement A collection of performance statistics (counters) used to determine the resource consumption of a workload in order to plan for additional hardware resources. This type of measurement is of a longer duration than a performance measurement (usually hours or even a day).

Cartesian product The result of a join that does not have a WHERE clause. The size of the resulting data set is the number of rows in the first table multiplied by the number of rows in the second table. A Cartesian product is not usually an intentional result of a query.

central processing unit (CPU) The brains of the computer; that is, the chip that processes data.

checkpoint An operation performed to synchronize the data files with the current contents of the database memory cache in order to reduce the recovery time needed in the event of a system failure. The checkpoint process traverses the list of dirty pages and flushes them to disk.

client/server model The programming model in which the user interface portion of the program resides in an executable program on a user's PC and accesses data in a database on a server. The application logic is divided between the client (PC) and the server.

cluster *See* clustered index; Microsoft Cluster Services (MSCS).

clustered index A combination of an index and a table. The index is stored as a B-tree, and the data is stored in the leaf nodes of the index.

collision A condition that occurs when two controllers attempt to use the network at the same time. Each controller detects the collision and usually waits a random amount of time before trying again. In a heavily utilized network, collisions can cause a performance bottleneck. This term is usually associated with Ethernet networks.

column A collection of corresponding fields in all rows of data in a table. Each column has a data type associated with it. All the columns in a row make up a database record.

COMMIT The SQL statement that finalizes an SQL transaction. Until the COMMIT statement is issued, the transaction can be undone by the issuing of the ROLLBACK statement.

Component Object Model (COM) COM technologies are a set of APIs and tools developed by Microsoft. These applications run under the control of Microsoft Transaction Services (MTS) on the server system and under the control of Distributed COM (DCOM) on client systems. Developers create COM clients by using platforms such as Microsoft Visual Basic and Microsoft Visual C++. Applications can also be made up of newer technologies such as ASP pages and Internet Server API (ISAPI).

Component Services The component services is a set of products based on the Component Object Model (COM) and Distributed COM (DCOM), Microsoft Transaction Server, Microsoft Internet Information Server, and Microsoft Message Queue Server from Windows NT 4. With Windows 2000 the COM and DCOM models have evolved to the next level, COM+. The COM+ applications and other system services make up the Windows 2000 Component Services.

composite index An index that is created on a combination of two or more columns.

configuration parameter A variable that allows you to change the behavior of SQL Server. These parameters are used to tune the SQL Server engine. Configuration parameters affect things such as SQL Server memory allocation, thread counts, and the number of user connections allowed.

constraint A restriction placed on a table to guarantee integrity.

CPU *See* central processing unit (CPU).

cube A multidimensional representation of both detail and summary data. Cubes are typically used in OLAP.

D

database A repository of data. This can be anything from a small list of names to a record of the entire population of the world.

database administrator (DBA) The person or persons responsible for maintaining the database. The DBA's role can vary depending on a company's needs.

database consistency checker (DBCC) A utility for finding and correcting problems in the consistency of the database.

database management system (DBMS) The programs, files, processes, and memory that make up the database. SQL Server is a relational DBMS (RDBMS).

database role A role that helps in the assignment of permissions to users. Rather than assigning individual permissions to individual users, you can create a role that represents the permissions granted to a set of users. When this method is used, only the roles need be assigned to the users.

data definition language (DDL) SQL statements that are used in the definition or declaration of database objects. DDLs include statements such as CREATE DATABASE and DROP DATABASE.

data file The physical operating system file that holds the data associated with a filegroup and, in turn, the database. Under SQL Server, this can be an NTFS file or a Windows NT/2000 raw device.

data integrity *See* integrity.

data manipulation language (DML) SQL statements that are used to insert data into the database or to update, delete, or retrieve database data.

data mart A decision support system created from company OLTP data. A data mart differs from a data warehouse in that the former contains data that is typically used by one business segment, such as accounts receivable or accounts payable, whereas the latter can contain all a company's data.

Data Transformation Services (DTS) The SQL Server tool for transforming data between systems.

data warehouse A decision support system created from OLTP data. A data warehouse is usually quite large, sometimes containing terabytes of data.

DBA *See* database administrator (DBA).

DBCC *See* database consistency checker (DBCC).

DB-LIB The abbreviation of DB-Library; a SQL Server connectivity protocol.

DBMS *See* database management system (DBMS).

DDL *See* data definition language (DDL).

decision support system (DSS) A database system that is used to aid in business decisions based on data in the database. These decisions can be based on sales trends, product sales, and so forth.

differential backup A mode of backup that saves only the data that has changed since the previous backup. When you use this mode, you can back up the database faster than you could using a full backup, but a database restore usually takes longer when a differential backup is used.

dirty page A page in the SQL Server cache that has been modified but has not been written to disk.

disk In this book, the term identifies a fixed disk drive. A fixed disk drive is a magnetic medium that is used to store data. A disk provides persistent storage: data remains on the disk even after power is turned off or fails.

distributor The intermediary component in SQL Server replication. A distributor takes replication data from a publisher and presents it to a subscriber.

DML *See* data manipulation language (DML).

domain A Windows 2000 or Windows NT network group. Systems in a domain use the same user list and passwords.

DSS *See* decision support system (DSS).

DTS *See* Data Transformation Services (DTS).

E

encryption The process of encoding data or stored procedures for security reasons.

enterprise A term for a system that services the entire company.

Enterprise Manager The main utility used to administer the SQL Server RDBMS.

equijoin A join that uses an equality operator in the WHERE clause of the SQL statement performing the join.

Ethernet A popular network hardware protocol.

execution plan The method that the parsed SQL Server statement uses to perform operations on the database.

F

fault tolerance The ability of a subsystem to continue functioning after a component has failed. This is accomplished via the use of redundant components. Fault tolerance is typically associated with the I/O subsystem and RAID controllers, but other subsystems, such as power supplies, can be fault tolerant.

fiber or **fiber optics** A network hardware protocol.

Fibre Channel A new I/O protocol that operates using either copper wire or fiber-optic connection hardware.

field *See* column.

filegroup A group of files that is used as a repository for SQL Server objects. A filegroup can be made up of one or more data files. When SQL Server objects are created, they can be assigned to a specific filegroup.

filegroup backup A form of backup, introduced in SQL Server 7, that enables you to back up and restore a single filegroup, rather than the entire database. This allows for the entire database backup to be performed over several days.

foreign key A field in a table that is also a primary key in another table.

FOREIGN KEY constraint A requirement that a foreign key be a valid primary key in the database. This type of constraint is typically used to verify that referenced data is available.

full backup A backup that saves all data in a database.

full table scan A select operation in which all rows in the table are read in order to find the desired data. A full table scan is not usually desired, because it involves a large amount of I/O overhead.

G

gigabyte (GB) A unit of data equal to 2^{30} (1,073,741,824) bytes or 1024 megabytes.

graphical user interface (GUI) An application interface that is graphical in nature in order to simplify the use of the application. A GUI can be used to show data in an easy-to-understand format.

GROUP BY An SQL clause used to divide a table into groups of data. These groups can consist of column names or results in computed columns.

GUI *See* graphical user interface (GUI).

H

HBA *See* host bus adapter (HBA).

hint An optional clause you can make to an SQL statement to give the query optimizer information about how you would like the execution plan to be constructed.

host bus adapter (HBA) A computer adapter used to communicate with an I/O bus.

hub A passive network device that is used to connect the network cards from multiple systems. A hub is an electrical device that has no application logic; thus, hubs are extremely fast.

I

index An auxiliary data structure used to speed access to data within the database.

index scan An operation that occurs when a group of index entries have to be read in order to find the desired data. Such a scan is typically used when a composite index is accessed and not all the columns that make up the index are supplied in the WHERE clause of the query.

input/output (I/O) The movement of data from one computer component to another. The term can be used to describe access to the disk subsystem or other data transfer components.

integrity The accuracy and completeness of data in the database. When data integrity is preserved, only valid data (data consistent with the business model) exists in the database.

Internet Server API (ISAPI) A set of function calls that are designed to provide Internet application developers with a method of extending the functionality of IIS.

Internetwork Packet Exchange/ Sequenced Packet Exchange (IPX/ SPX) A network protocol used in Novell networks.

I/O *See* input/output.

I/O capacity The amount of work that can be supported by the I/O subsystem. The I/O capacity is constrained by either the number of I/O operations (if random seeks are the limiting factor) or throughput (if seeks are sequential).

IPX/SPX *See* Internetwork Packet Exchange/Sequenced Packet Exchange (IPX/SPX).

ISQL An application supplied by Microsoft that allows access into the SQL Server RDBMS. ISQL uses the DB-LIB protocol; OSQL uses the ODBC protocol.

J

JBOD An acronym for "just a bunch of disks"; a non-RAID disk configuration.

join An operation that combines data from two or more tables by taking advantage of the relationship between the tables.

K

key The column or set of columns that is used to define the access point into an index. If a composite index is made up of two columns, those two columns make up the index key.

kilobyte (KB) A unit of data equal to 2^{10} (1024) bytes.

L

latency The term used to describe the time a process spends waiting for an operation to be completed. Most often, the term is used to describe the time a thread waits for an I/O operation to be completed.

lazywriter The thread that takes dirty blocks from the SQL Server cache and writes them to disk. It is called the lazywriter because it is a background process that operates according to its own schedule and that has its own priorities.

leaf node The lowest node in an index. The leaf node contains either pointers to the row data or the data itself (in the case of a clustered index).

level 1 (L1) cache The memory built into a CPU chip that is used for holding data and instructions to speed access from the CPU. This cache usually stores 16 KB or 32 KB of data.

level 2 (L2) cache The memory that is either built into or external to a CPU chip and that is used as an overflow for the level 1 cache.

lock An object that is used to allow only one thread to access a resource at a time. Locking is quite important, especially in an SMP system, because many threads might be trying to access resources simultaneously.

log *See* transaction log.

logical disk drive A virtual disk drive that appears to the operating system as a physical disk drive but that, in reality, is made up of two or more disk drives in a RAID system.

logwriter The SQL Server thread that is responsible for reading the log buffer and writing the contents out to the transaction log.

M

medium (plural: media) An object to which data is written. Both physical disk drives and tapes are media.

megabyte (MB) A unit of data equal to 2^{20} (1,048,576) bytes or 1024 kilobytes.

memory A term used to describe random access memory (RAM) that is allocated and used by the operating system and SQL Server. The term "memory" in this book refers to main memory. The main use of SQL Server memory is as a database cache. Memory is not durable; its contents are lost upon loss of power.

merge replication A replication scheme that has been designed for multi-directional replication. With merge replication it is possible to update data on both publishers and subscribers without the use of MS DTC.

Microsoft Cluster Services (MSCS) A SQL Server add-in program that allows a SQL Server system to operate in standby mode for the primary server. In the event that the primary server fails, the secondary server takes over.

Microsoft Distributed Transaction Coordinator (MS DTC) The Microsoft SQL Server component that coordinates transactions between systems by performing two-phase commits.

Microsoft Transaction Server (MTS) A framework for developing three-tiered distributed applications.

mirroring A fault tolerance technique in which a duplicate of a component is created, thus providing a redundant copy that can be used in the event that the original fails. Mirroring is usually associated with I/O subsystems. Both RAID 1 and RAID 10 use mirroring.

MSCS *See* Microsoft Cluster Services (MSCS).

MS DTC *See* Microsoft Distributed Transaction Coordinator (MS DTC).

MTS *See* Microsoft Transaction Server (MTS).

N

named pipes A SQL Server net-library. Named pipes is required for SQL Server/Windows NT installations. Named pipes is a secure net-library and supports several underlying network protocols, such as IPX/SPX, NetBEUI, and TCP/IP.

network packet A unit of data, including control information, that is transferred across the network as a whole. A SQL Server request might fit into one network packet, or multiple network packets might be required.

NWLINK The SQL Server network library that supports Novell's IPX/SPX network protocol.

O

ODBC *See* Open Database Connectivity (ODBC).

OLAP *See* online analytical processing (OLAP).

OLAP Services *See* SQL Server Analysis Services (OLTP).

OLTP *See* online transaction processing.

online analytical processing (OLAP) The manipulation of data for analytical purposes. OLAP is usually associated with data marts or data warehouses.

online transaction processing (OLTP) A system of database processing in which many users access various data in real time. Because users are waiting for processing to be completed, response time is critical for OLTP systems.

Open Database Connectivity (ODBC) A Microsoft-designed database connectivity API that can be used to communicate from applications to a multitude of different RDBMS's.

Optimizer *See* SQL Server query optimizer.

ORDER BY A clause that specifies the sort order of columns returned as the result of a SELECT operation.

OSQL An application supplied by Microsoft that allows access into the SQL Server RDBMS. OSQL uses the ODBC protocol; ISQL uses the DB-LIB protocol.

outer join An operation that returns all rows from at least one of the tables or views mentioned in a FROM clause, as long as those rows meet any WHERE or HAVING search conditions.

P

packet *See* network packet.

page The fundamental unit of data storage in SQL Server. A page is the smallest unit of data that is written to or read from disk or memory. The page size for Microsoft SQL Server 2000 is 8 KB; it was 8 KB for Microsoft SQL Server 7 and 2 KB for Microsoft SQL Server 6.5.

page lock *See* lock.

paging A process that occurs when the operating system and SQL Server use more memory than is physically available and which involves the temporary copying of data to disk. When paging occurs, the performance of the system is severely degraded. Another term for paging is "swapping."

parity The extra data (or pseudodata) that is used to validate or correct the base data. Typically, "parity" refers to a bit that is used to force the underlying data bits to be either even or odd. By checking the data in order to determine if the data is even or odd, the system can validate that it is correct. RAID 5 uses parity to protect its data.

parse A process performed by SQL Server to break down an SQL statement into its fundamental components before passing it to the query optimizer.

partitioning The process of dividing a table or database into separate components in order to create smaller and more easily managed data sets.

peak utilization period The time a computer is most used during a measurement of utilization or a working day.

performance counter An object that reflects resource usage.

performance measurement A collection of performance statistics (called performance counters) that is used to monitor and tune a computer system. This type of measurement lasts a short time (usually seconds or minutes, but sometimes hours) in order to capture system performance anomalies and correct them.

Performance Monitor A utility that is included with the Windows NT and Microsoft Windows 2000 operating systems that allows you to look at various performance counters within the operating system and SQL Server.

physical memory The chips that are used for memory within the system.

predictive analysis The use of mathematics in order to predict the outcome of a specific change to the system. Predictive analysis can be used to predict the effect of adding users or resources to the system.

primary key A column or combination of columns whose values uniquely identify each row in the table. The column or columns are used to enforce the data integrity of the table.

procedure cache The part of SQL Server memory used for caching stored procedures and parsed SQL statements. The procedure cache is used to improve SQL Server performance.

processor The central processing unit (CPU); the brains of the computer. A standard computer system consists of one or more CPUs, main memory, and disk storage.

Profiler *See* SQL Profiler.

publication A group of articles that is replicated from a publisher.

publisher The SQL Server system that is replicating its data to other systems. The recipient of the replication data is called a subscriber.

pull subscription A form of replication in which the replication is initiated by the subscriber.

push subscription A form of replication in which the replication is initiated by the publisher or distributor.

Q

query An SQL SELECT statement that is used to retrieve data from the database. In this book, "query" refers to a read-only operation.

Query Analyzer *See* SQL Query Analyzer.

Query Optimizer *See* SQL Server query optimizer.

queue The list of processes, or threads, that are awaiting processing.

queuing The act of waiting in line for processing. Queuing occurs in SQL Server, in the operating system, and in hardware.

R

RAID (redundant array of independent disks) A disk array that is used to form one large logical disk drive. Data is partitioned, or distributed, across the physical disk drives. RAID controllers can be configured in various ways. Each type of RAID configuration offers different fault tolerance and performance characteristics.

RAID level The identifier that is used to specify which RAID configuration is being used.

RAID 0 The RAID level that provides data striping. This is the most economical and the fastest RAID level, but it provides no tolerance for disk failures.

RAID 1 The RAID level commonly known as mirroring. RAID 1 volumes consist of two identical disk drives.

RAID 5 The RAID level known as distributed parity RAID. This RAID level creates a parity for each stripe. It is economical and provides fault tolerance.

RAID 10 The RAID level that combines both disk mirroring and disk striping. RAID 10 is sometimes referred to as RAID 0+1 or RAID 1/0.

random access memory (RAM) Nonpersistent storage that is used for data processing. RAM is faster than a disk, but all data is lost when the power is turned off or fails.

raw device A method of accessing a disk drive through a raw interface; that is, by bypassing the file system.

RDBMS *See* relational database management system (RDBMS).

record A single row in the database.

recovery An operation in which SQL Server is restarted after a system failure; the transaction log is used to roll forward all committed transactions and roll back all uncommitted transactions in order to bring the database to the state it was in at the point of failure.

recovery interval The amount of time SQL Server needs to recover from a system failure.

referential integrity *See* integrity.

relational database management system (RDBMS) A database system that stores data according to the relational data model. Data is arranged in a hierarchy that reflects on the relations between objects. SQL Server is one example of an RDBMS.

replication A feature of SQL Server that allows you to enable the automatic creation of copies of SQL Server objects or subsets of objects on a system and the propagation of the objects to other systems. Replication comes in three forms: snapshot, transactional, and merge.

response time The length of time between the submission of a request for data (the execution of a transaction) by a user and the returning of that data to the user. Often, the response time is used to judge the performance of the system.

restore An operation in which a SQL Server backup file is copied back into the SQL Server database. This operation takes the database back to the state it was in when the backup was created.

roles *See* database role.

ROLLBACK The SQL Server statement used to undo a transaction. Prior to committing a transaction, you can issue a ROLLBACK statement that will undo all the activity performed by that transaction.

root node The top node in an index.

rotational latency The amount of time a disk drive requires to rotate to the position at which the requested data resides.

router A network device that passes data from one subnet to another according to the network addresses.

row A single record in the database. A row, or record, of data represents one entry in the database. This entry consists of multiple pieces of data known as columns, or fields.

row lock *See* lock.

S

SAN *See* Storage Area Network (SAN).

schema A collection of objects associated with a database. Schema objects include tables, indexes, views, and so on.

SCSI *See* Small Computer System Interface (SCSI).

seek time The amount of time disk heads require to move to a track where desired data resides.

selectivity The ability of an index to identify objects. An index with few unique values is said to have poor selectivity. A unique index has excellent selectivity.

self-join A join of a table with itself.

service level agreement (SLA) A contract between the provider of computer or database services and the user of those services. This agreement specifies the minimal level of service that is guaranteed, usually by specifying maximum response times for certain transactions.

sizing The task of determining the proper amount of hardware (CPUs, memory, disks, and so forth) for a computer system. A system needs to be sized before it is designed and built. After the system has been in production, capacity planning is performed to plan for future growth.

SLA *See* service level agreement (SLA).

Small Computer System Interface (SCSI) An I/O interface that is highly popular in today's computer systems. SCSI disks are disks that use the SCSI interface.

SMP *See* symmetric multiprocessor (SMP) system.

SMS *See* Systems Management Server (SMS).

snapshot replication A form of replication in which the entire publication is periodically copied from the publisher to the subscriber.

snowflake schema A schema involving dimension tables that are joined with other dimension tables before being joined with the fact table. Several layers of dimension tables can be created before the dimension tables are joined to the fact table. If you were to diagram this arrangement, you would see that the shape of the diagram resembles the shape of a snowflake.

SPID *See* system process ID (SPID).

split seek A feature of RAID 1 and RAID 10, in which both disks in a mirror can simultaneously seek for data.

SQL *See* Structured Query Language (SQL).

SQL Profiler A SQL Server utility that is used to monitor server performance and activity. SQL Profiler is quite useful for tracking events within SQL Server.

SQL Query Analyzer SQL Query Analyzer has replaced ISQL/W as the tool for ad hoc SQL Server access. In the Query Analyzer window, you can type an SQL statement and view the results of the statement in order to debug it. Query Analyzer also displays the execution plan of an SQL statement, allowing you to tune the statement.

SQL Server Microsoft's RDBMS product.

SQL Server Agent A program that performs background tasks, such as scheduling SQL Server jobs and notifying the appropriate persons of problems within SQL Server. The SQL Server Agent Scheduler is used for the execution of other agents, such as the replication agents. SQL Server Agent was known as SQLExecutive in SQL Server 6.5.

SQL Server Analysis Services A SQL Server 2000 add-in program designed to assist you with online analytical processing (OLAP); you can use it to access data in your data warehouses and data marts. In SQL Server 7, this tool was called OLAP Services.

SQL Server query optimizer An internal component of SQL Server that analyzes SQL Server statistics and object statistics to determine the optimal execution plan for a query. Users do not access the query optimizer; instead, the parser passes parsed SQL statements to the query optimizer.

staging table A temporary table in which to insert data so that it can then be extracted or transformed and copied into permanent tables. Using staging tables is a common way of transforming data within a database.

star schema A single fact table surrounded by dimension tables. The dimension tables are used to form the basis of the analysis of the data in the fact table. Each of the dimension tables is joined to a column in the fact table. If you imagine a fact table surrounded by dimension tables, you can see how the structure resembles the shape of a star. A star schema is quite common for data warehouses.

steady state The average utilization factor of a computer for either a measurement period or a working day.

Storage Area Network (SAN) An I/O subsystem in which multiple computer systems can share a RAID subsystem.

stored procedure One or more T-SQL statements compiled into a single execution plan. This compiled plan is stored in the SQL Server database.

striping The spreading of data, in equal chunks, among two or more disk drives. With RAID controllers, data is distributed in equal pieces among all the drives in the logical volume.

Structured Query Language (SQL) A language commonly used with relational databases. Both the American National Standards Institute (ANSI) and the International Organization for Standardization (ISO) define standards for SQL. Most modern DBMS products support the Entry Level of SQL-92, the latest SQL standard (published in 1992).

subscriber The recipient of SQL Server replication data.

swapping *See* paging.

switch A network device in which one connector is electronically connected to another via a path determined by network addresses. This differs from a hub, in which all connectors see all traffic, and from a router, in which packets are modified.

symmetric multiprocessor (SMP) system A system with multiple CPUs that all share memory and that function equivalently. Typically, each CPU in an SMP system has cache memory but no main memory associated with it.

system administrator The person or persons responsible for maintaining a company's computer hardware and operating system. The system administrator's role can vary depending on how a company is organized.

system process ID (SPID) A unique integer (*smallint*) assigned to each user connection when the connection is made. The assignment is not permanent.

Systems Management Server (SMS) Microsoft's enterprise management platform.

T

table lock *See* lock.

table scan An operation in which all rows in the table are read before the desired data is found. Scanning an entire table is not usually a desired way of performing a query.

TCP/IP *See* Transmission Control Protocol/Internet Protocol (TCP/IP).

terabyte (TB) A unit of data equal to 2^{40} (1,099,511,627,776) bytes or 1024 gigabytes.

thread A feature of the Windows NT and Windows 2000 operating systems that allows application logic to be separated into several concurrent execution paths. All threads are part of the same process and share memory.

throughput The transmission capacity of a data conduit such as a network or CPU bus. The term is used to describe how much data can pass through the conduit in a particular time.

token ring A popular network hardware protocol developed by IBM.

transaction A set of SQL statements that ends with either a COMMIT or a ROLLBACK statement. The term "transaction" is usually used to describe statements that modify data, and the term "query" is usually used to describe SELECT (read-only) statements.

transactional replication A form of replication that operates by duplicating on the subscriber each transaction that has run on the publisher.

transaction log A file in the database that is used to record all modifications to the database. Information about the transactions that perform modifications is also kept in the transaction log. The transaction log stores enough information to undo a transaction (in case a rollback is needed) or to redo a transaction (in case the transaction needs to be rolled forward).

Transact-SQL (T-SQL) The procedural SQL language that is used by SQL Server. Transact-SQL is a superset of SQL.

Transmission Control Protocol/Internet Protocol (TCP/IP) A popular network protocol.

trigger A special type of stored procedure that fires, or runs, automatically whenever a predefined event occurs. This event can be the execution of an

UPDATE, INSERT, or DELETE statement on a table.

truncate An operation that removes all rows from an object without deleting the object itself. You can truncate a table by using the TRUNCATE TABLE command. The transaction log can also be truncated.

two-phase commit A protocol used to coordinate a transaction between two independent systems by guaranteeing an all-or-nothing approach to the commit. The two-phase commit splits the commit operation into two parts. The first part is the prepare phase; the second part is the commit phase. These phases are initiated by a COMMIT command from the application.

U

UNION An SQL statement used to combine the results of two or more queries into a single result set consisting of all the rows that are returned from all the queries in the UNION statement.

unique A term used to describe a value of which no duplicate exists. You can create either a constraint or a unique index to enable SQL Server to enforce uniqueness.

Universal Naming Convention (UNC) name A full Windows NT/2000 name of a resource on the network. The UNC name conforms to this syntax: *servername**sharename*. Here *servername* is the name of the network server, and *sharename* is the name of the

shared resource. The UNC name also usually includes the directory path, as follows: *servername**sharename**directoryname**filename*.

UPDATE The SQL statement used to modify a record in the database.

V

view An auxiliary data structure that is used to create a virtual table. This virtual table is defined by an SQL statement that makes the table appear as either a subset or superset of the underlying objects.

VINES The Banyan network protocol.

virtual memory A memory management scheme that allows Windows NT/ 2000 to access more memory than is actually present in the system through the use of paging and swapping. At any time, only a portion of the virtual memory is actually in physical memory.

W

WHERE A clause in an SQL statement that you use to define the conditions for the data that you want to retrieve.

wizard A user-friendly tool provided by Microsoft in order to make system administration tasks and configuration tasks easier.

working set The amount of memory that is currently being used by a process.

Index

Page numbers in italics refer to figures, tables, or code listings.

X

Y

Marcilina S. (Frohock) Garcia, a senior consultant at Performance Tuning Corporation, specializes in database performance benchmarks, SQL Server performance and database design, and system configuration. Mrs. Garcia formerly worked at Compaq Computer Corporation in Houston, Texas, as a database performance engineer. She has co-authored two previous SQL Server books for Microsoft Press: *Microsoft SQL Server 7.0 Administrator's Companion* and *Microsoft SQL Server 7.0 Performance Tuning Technical Reference*.

Jamie Reding is a Performance Engineer with the SQL Server team at Microsoft Corporation. He is responsible for developing and maintaining the Transaction Processing Council (TPC) benchmark kits and analyzing SQL Server system performance. Prior to Microsoft, Mr. Reding worked at the Compaq Computer Corporation in the capacity of database performance engineer. Mr. Reding has been participating in performance benchmarks and systems analysis since 1984. In addition to his work at Microsoft and Compaq, Mr. Reding spent 11 years with the IBM Corporation. He has previously co-authored a SQL Server book for Microsoft Press entitled *Microsoft SQL Server 7.0 Performance Tuning Technical Reference.*

Edward Whalen is president of Performance Tuning Corporation, a consulting company specializing in database performance, administration, and backup/recovery solutions. Prior to founding Performance Tuning, Mr. Whalen worked at Compaq Computer Corporation as an operating system developer and a database performance engineer. He has extensive experience in database system design and tuning for optimal performance and has worked on numerous benchmarks and performance tuning projects for Oracle and SQL Server. Mr. Whalen has co-authored two previous SQL Server books for Microsoft Press: *Microsoft SQL Server 7.0 Administrator's Companion* and *Microsoft SQL Server 7.0 Performance Tuning Technical Reference;* and has written two books on the Oracle RDBMS: *Oracle Performance Tuning and Optimization* and *Teach Yourself Oracle8 in 21 Days*.

Steve Adrien DeLuca is currently Lead Program Manager in the Distributed Management Division at Microsoft Corporation. He is now developing operations management and performance solutions for the enterprise server clients. Prior to working at Microsoft, Mr. DeLuca worked as an architect engineer at Oracle Corporation, where he co-invented and developed the Oracle System Sizer. In addition to his work at Microsoft and Oracle, Mr. DeLuca has worked as a performance engineer specializing in sizing and capacity planning for such organizations as DEC, Tandem, Apple, and the U.S. Air Force. Mr. DeLuca has been participating in performance benchmarks, developing performance tools, writing books, and lecturing around the world since 1980. He currently holds 13 patents, plus patents that are pending for inventions pertaining to performance and capacity planning.

The manuscript for this book was prepared and galleyed using Microsoft Word 2000. Pages were composed by Microsoft Press using Adobe PageMaker 6.52 for Windows, with text in Sabon and display type in ITC Franklin Gothic. Composed pages were delivered to the printer as electronic prepress files.

Manuscript Editor:	Elizabeth Cate
Principal Compositor:	Barb Runyan
Principal Copy Editor:	Cheryl Penner
Principal Electronic Artist:	Michael Kloepfer
Indexer:	Richard Shrout
Cover Designer:	Girvin | Strategic Branding & Design
Cover Illustration:	Tom Draper Design
Interior Graphic Designer:	James D. Kramer

MICROSOFT LICENSE AGREEMENT

Book Companion CD

IMPORTANT—READ CAREFULLY: This Microsoft End-User License Agreement ("EULA") is a legal agreement between you (either an individual or an entity) and Microsoft Corporation for the Microsoft product identified above, which includes computer software and may include associated media, printed materials, and "online" or electronic documentation ("SOFTWARE PROD-UCT"). Any component included within the SOFTWARE PRODUCT that is accompanied by a separate End-User License Agreement shall be governed by such agreement and not the terms set forth below. By installing, copying, or otherwise using the SOFTWARE PRODUCT, you agree to be bound by the terms of this EULA. If you do not agree to the terms of this EULA, you are not authorized to install, copy, or otherwise use the SOFTWARE PRODUCT; you may, however, return the SOFTWARE PROD-UCT, along with all printed materials and other items that form a part of the Microsoft product that includes the SOFTWARE PRODUCT, to the place you obtained them for a full refund.

SOFTWARE PRODUCT LICENSE

The SOFTWARE PRODUCT is protected by United States copyright laws and international copyright treaties, as well as other intellectual property laws and treaties. The SOFTWARE PRODUCT is licensed, not sold.

1. **GRANT OF LICENSE.** This EULA grants you the following rights:

   a. **Software Product.** You may install and use one copy of the SOFTWARE PRODUCT on a single computer. The primary user of the computer on which the SOFTWARE PRODUCT is installed may make a second copy for his or her exclusive use on a portable computer.

   b. **Storage/Network Use.** You may also store or install a copy of the SOFTWARE PRODUCT on a storage device, such as a network server, used only to install or run the SOFTWARE PRODUCT on your other computers over an internal network; however, you must acquire and dedicate a license for each separate computer on which the SOFTWARE PRODUCT is installed or run from the storage device. A license for the SOFTWARE PRODUCT may not be shared or used concurrently on different computers.

   c. **License Pak.** If you have acquired this EULA in a Microsoft License Pak, you may make the number of additional copies of the computer software portion of the SOFTWARE PRODUCT authorized on the printed copy of this EULA, and you may use each copy in the manner specified above. You are also entitled to make a corresponding number of secondary copies for portable computer use as specified above.

   d. **Sample Code.** Solely with respect to portions, if any, of the SOFTWARE PRODUCT that are identified within the SOFT-WARE PRODUCT as sample code (the "SAMPLE CODE"):

      i. **Use and Modification.** Microsoft grants you the right to use and modify the source code version of the SAMPLE CODE, *provided* you comply with subsection (d)(iii) below. You may not distribute the SAMPLE CODE, or any modified version of the SAMPLE CODE, in source code form.

      ii. **Redistributable Files.** Provided you comply with subsection (d)(iii) below, Microsoft grants you a nonexclusive, royalty-free right to reproduce and distribute the object code version of the SAMPLE CODE and of any modified SAMPLE CODE, other than SAMPLE CODE, or any modified version thereof, designated as not redistributable in the Readme file that forms a part of the SOFTWARE PRODUCT (the "Non-Redistributable Sample Code"). All SAMPLE CODE other than the Non-Redistributable Sample Code is collectively referred to as the "REDISTRIBUTABLES."

      iii. **Redistribution Requirements.** If you redistribute the REDISTRIBUTABLES, you agree to: (i) distribute the REDISTRIBUTABLES in object code form only in conjunction with and as a part of your software application product; (ii) not use Microsoft's name, logo, or trademarks to market your software application product; (iii) include a valid copyright notice on your software application product; (iv) indemnify, hold harmless, and defend Microsoft from and against any claims or lawsuits, including attorney's fees, that arise or result from the use or distribution of your software application product; and (v) not permit further distribution of the REDISTRIBUTABLES by your end user. Contact Microsoft for the applicable royalties due and other licensing terms for all other uses and/or distribution of the REDISTRIBUTABLES.

2. **DESCRIPTION OF OTHER RIGHTS AND LIMITATIONS.**

   - **Limitations on Reverse Engineering, Decompilation, and Disassembly.** You may not reverse engineer, decompile, or disassemble the SOFTWARE PRODUCT, except and only to the extent that such activity is expressly permitted by applicable law notwithstanding this limitation.

   - **Separation of Components.** The SOFTWARE PRODUCT is licensed as a single product. Its component parts may not be separated for use on more than one computer.

   - **Rental.** You may not rent, lease, or lend the SOFTWARE PRODUCT.

   - **Support Services.** Microsoft may, but is not obligated to, provide you with support services related to the SOFTWARE PRODUCT ("Support Services"). Use of Support Services is governed by the Microsoft policies and programs described in the user manual, in "online" documentation, and/or in other Microsoft-provided materials. Any supplemental software code provided to you as part of the Support Services shall be considered part of the SOFTWARE PRODUCT and subject to the terms and conditions of this EULA. With respect to technical information you provide to Microsoft as part of the Support Services, Microsoft may use such information for its business purposes, including for product support and development. Microsoft will not utilize such technical information in a form that personally identifies you.

- **Software Transfer.** You may permanently transfer all of your rights under this EULA, provided you retain no copies, you transfer all of the SOFTWARE PRODUCT (including all component parts, the media and printed materials, any upgrades, this EULA, and, if applicable, the Certificate of Authenticity), **and** the recipient agrees to the terms of this EULA.

- **Termination.** Without prejudice to any other rights, Microsoft may terminate this EULA if you fail to comply with the terms and conditions of this EULA. In such event, you must destroy all copies of the SOFTWARE PRODUCT and all of its component parts.

3. **COPYRIGHT.** All title and copyrights in and to the SOFTWARE PRODUCT (including but not limited to any images, photographs, animations, video, audio, music, text, SAMPLE CODE, REDISTRIBUTABLES, and "applets" incorporated into the SOFTWARE PRODUCT) and any copies of the SOFTWARE PRODUCT are owned by Microsoft or its suppliers. The SOFTWARE PRODUCT is protected by copyright laws and international treaty provisions. Therefore, you must treat the SOFTWARE PRODUCT like any other copyrighted material **except** that you may install the SOFTWARE PRODUCT on a single computer provided you keep the original solely for backup or archival purposes. You may not copy the printed materials accompanying the SOFTWARE PRODUCT.

4. **U.S. GOVERNMENT RESTRICTED RIGHTS.** The SOFTWARE PRODUCT and documentation are provided with RESTRICTED RIGHTS. Use, duplication, or disclosure by the Government is subject to restrictions as set forth in subparagraph (c)(1)(ii) of the Rights in Technical Data and Computer Software clause at DFARS 252.227-7013 or subparagraphs (c)(1) and (2) of the Commercial Computer Software—Restricted Rights at 48 CFR 52.227-19, as applicable. Manufacturer is Microsoft Corporation/One Microsoft Way/Redmond, WA 98052-6399.

5. **EXPORT RESTRICTIONS.** You agree that you will not export or re-export the SOFTWARE PRODUCT, any part thereof, or any process or service that is the direct product of the SOFTWARE PRODUCT (the foregoing collectively referred to as the "Restricted Components"), to any country, person, entity, or end user subject to U.S. export restrictions. You specifically agree not to export or re-export any of the Restricted Components (i) to any country to which the U.S. has embargoed or restricted the export of goods or services, which currently include, but are not necessarily limited to, Cuba, Iran, Iraq, Libya, North Korea, Sudan, and Syria, or to any national of any such country, wherever located, who intends to transmit or transport the Restricted Components back to such country; (ii) to any end user who you know or have reason to know will utilize the Restricted Components in the design, development, or production of nuclear, chemical, or biological weapons; or (iii) to any end user who has been prohibited from participating in U.S. export transactions by any federal agency of the U.S. government. You warrant and represent that neither the BXA nor any other U.S. federal agency has suspended, revoked, or denied your export privileges.

DISCLAIMER OF WARRANTY

NO WARRANTIES OR CONDITIONS. MICROSOFT EXPRESSLY DISCLAIMS ANY WARRANTY OR CONDITION FOR THE SOFTWARE PRODUCT. THE SOFTWARE PRODUCT AND ANY RELATED DOCUMENTATION ARE PROVIDED "AS IS" WITHOUT WARRANTY OR CONDITION OF ANY KIND, EITHER EXPRESS OR IMPLIED, INCLUDING, WITHOUT LIMITATION, THE IMPLIED WARRANTIES OF MERCHANTABILITY, FITNESS FOR A PARTICULAR PURPOSE, OR NONINFRINGEMENT. THE ENTIRE RISK ARISING OUT OF USE OR PERFORMANCE OF THE SOFTWARE PRODUCT REMAINS WITH YOU.

LIMITATION OF LIABILITY. TO THE MAXIMUM EXTENT PERMITTED BY APPLICABLE LAW, IN NO EVENT SHALL MICROSOFT OR ITS SUPPLIERS BE LIABLE FOR ANY SPECIAL, INCIDENTAL, INDIRECT, OR CONSEQUENTIAL DAMAGES WHATSOEVER (INCLUDING, WITHOUT LIMITATION, DAMAGES FOR LOSS OF BUSINESS PROFITS, BUSINESS INTERRUPTION, LOSS OF BUSINESS INFORMATION, OR ANY OTHER PECUNIARY LOSS) ARISING OUT OF THE USE OF OR INABILITY TO USE THE SOFTWARE PRODUCT OR THE PROVISION OF OR FAILURE TO PROVIDE SUPPORT SERVICES, EVEN IF MICROSOFT HAS BEEN ADVISED OF THE POSSIBILITY OF SUCH DAMAGES. IN ANY CASE, MICROSOFT'S ENTIRE LIABILITY UNDER ANY PROVISION OF THIS EULA SHALL BE LIMITED TO THE GREATER OF THE AMOUNT ACTUALLY PAID BY YOU FOR THE SOFTWARE PRODUCT OR US$5.00; PROVIDED, HOWEVER, IF YOU HAVE ENTERED INTO A MICROSOFT SUPPORT SERVICES AGREEMENT, MICROSOFT'S ENTIRE LIABILITY REGARDING SUPPORT SERVICES SHALL BE GOVERNED BY THE TERMS OF THAT AGREEMENT. BECAUSE SOME STATES AND JURISDICTIONS DO NOT ALLOW THE EXCLUSION OR LIMITATION OF LIABILITY, THE ABOVE LIMITATION MAY NOT APPLY TO YOU.

MISCELLANEOUS

This EULA is governed by the laws of the State of Washington USA, except and only to the extent that applicable law mandates governing law of a different jurisdiction.

Should you have any questions concerning this EULA, or if you desire to contact Microsoft for any reason, please contact the Microsoft subsidiary serving your country, or write: Microsoft Sales Information Center/One Microsoft Way/Redmond, WA 98052-6399.

For information about Microsoft Press®
products, visit our Web site at
mspress.microsoft.com